Sociology

Introductory Readings

Revised Edition

Sociology
Introductory Readings

Revised Edition

Edited by Anthony Giddens

Polity

First published in 2001 by Polity Press in association with
Blackwell Publishers Ltd

Reprinted 2004, 2005

First edition published in 1997 by Polity Press

Polity Press
65 Bridge Street
Cambridge CB2 1UR, UK

Polity Press
350 Main Street
Malden, MA 02148, USA

ISBN 0-7456-2439-1
ISBN 0-7456-2440-5 (pbk)

A catalogue record for this book is available from the British Library.

Typeset in Galliard on 10/12.5pt by Graphicraft Ltd, Hong Kong
Printed in Great Britain by TJI Digital, Padstow, Cornwall
This book is printed on acid-free paper.

Contents

Editor's Note

An ellipsis in square brackets has been used whenever material from the original has been omitted. Where a paragraph or more has been omitted, a line space appears above and below [. . .].

Part 1 What is Sociology?

Sociology is an engrossing subject because it concerns our own lives as human beings. All humans are social – we could not develop as children, or exist as adults, without having social ties to others. Society is thus the very condition of human existence. At the same time, as the opening reading in the book emphasizes, we all actively shape the society in which we live. As sociologists, we seek to understand both how, as individuals, all of us are influenced by the wider society, and at the same time how we actively structure that society in our own actions. More than most other intellectual endeavours, sociology presumes the use of disciplined imagination. Imagination, because the sociologist must distance her- or himself from the here and now in order to grasp how societies have changed in the past and what potential transformations lie in store; discipline, because the creative ability of the imagination has to be restrained by conceptual and empirical rigour.

C. Wright Mills's discussion of the sociological imagination (Reading 2) has long been the classic discussion of these issues. We cannot understand ourselves as individuals, Mills emphasizes, unless we grasp the involvement of our own biography with the historical development of social institutions. On the other hand, we cannot comprehend the nature of those institutions unless we understand how they are organized in and through individual action. It is the business of sociology to analyse the social orders which constrain our behaviour, but at the same time to acknowledge that we actively make our own history.

These ideas are echoed by Zygmunt Bauman (Reading 3). The focus of his discussion, however, is the similarities and differences between sociology and common-sense understandings of social life. Sociology, he agrees with Mills, teaches us to see our own individual experiences in relation to wider social systems, as well as to broad patterns of social change. As such, it is a distinctive way of thinking about the social world. Studying human social activity, Bauman says, is different from analysing objects or events in the natural world. We are all in some sense knowledgeable and skilful in respect of our participation in day-to-day social activity. Sociological knowledge builds upon the practical forms of knowing by means of which we organize our everyday lives. Sociological concepts, however, need to be more clearly formulated and precise than those of ordinary language.

Sociological investigation ranges over much broader arenas, in time as well as in space, than the immediate settings of interaction with which we are most familiar in the daily round. Moreover, sociologists focus attention upon unintended and unanticipated consequences of human activity, whereas in ordinary activities we concern ourselves mainly with the intentions and emotions of other people. As Mills also stresses, sociological thought must take an imaginative leap beyond the familiar, and the sociologist must be prepared to look behind the routine activities in which much of our mundane life is enmeshed.

1 The Scope of Sociology

Anthony Giddens

Sociology is a subject with a curiously mixed reputation. On the one hand, it is associated by many people with the fomenting of rebellion, a stimulus to revolt. Even though they may have only a vague notion of what topics are studied in sociology, they somehow associate sociology with subversion, with the shrill demands of unkempt student militants. On the other hand, quite a different view of the subject is often entertained – perhaps more commonly than the first – by individuals who have had some direct acquaintance with it in schools and universities. This is that in fact it is rather a dull and uninstructive enterprise, which far from propelling its students towards the barricades is more likely to bore them to death with platitudes. Sociology, in this guise, assumes the dry mantle of a science, but not one that proves as enlightening as the natural sciences upon which its practitioners wish to model it.

I think that those who have taken the second reaction to sociology have a good deal of right on their side. Sociology has been conceived of by many of its proponents – even the bulk of them – in such a way that commonplace assertions are disguised in a pseudo-scientific language. The conception that sociology belongs to the natural sciences, and hence should slavishly try to copy their procedures and objectives, is a mistaken one. Its lay critics, in some considerable degree at least, are quite correct to be sceptical of the attainments of sociology thus presented.

My intention in this [discussion] will be to associate sociology with the first type of view rather than the second. By this I do not mean to connect sociology with a sort of irrational lashing-out at all that most of the population hold to be good and proper ways of behaviour. But I do want to defend the view that sociology, understood in the manner in which I shall describe it, necessarily has a subversive quality. Its subversive or critical character, however [. . .], does not carry with it (or should not do so) the implication that it is an intellectually disreputable enterprise. On the contrary, it is exactly because sociology deals with problems of such pressing interest to us all (or should do so), problems which are the objects of major controversies and conflicts in society itself, that it has this character. However kempt or otherwise student radicals, or any other radicals, may be, there do exist broad connections between the impulses that stir them to action and a sociological awareness. This is not [. . .] because sociologists directly preach revolt; it is because the study of sociology, appropriately understood, [. . .] demonstrates how fundamental are the social questions that have to be faced in today's world. Everyone is to some extent aware of these questions, but the study of sociology helps bring them into much sharper focus. Sociology cannot remain a purely academic subject, if 'academic' means a disinterested and remote scholarly pursuit, followed solely within the enclosed walls of the university.

Sociology is not a subject that comes neatly gift-wrapped, making no demands except that its contents be unpacked. Like all the social sciences – under which label one can also include, among other disciplines, anthropology, economics and history – sociology is an inherently controversial endeavour. That is to say, it is characterized by continuing disputes about its very nature. But this is not a weakness, although it has seemed such to many of those who call themselves professional 'sociologists', and also to many others on the outside, who are distressed that there are numerous vying conceptions of how the subject-matter of sociology should be approached or analysed. Those who are upset by the persistent character of sociological debates, and a frequent lack of consensus about how to resolve them, usually feel that this is a sign of the immaturity of the subject. They want sociology to be like a natural science, and to generate a similar apparatus of universal laws to those which they see natural science as having discovered and validated. But [. . .] it is a mistake to suppose that sociology should be modelled too closely on the natural sciences, or to imagine that a natural science of society is either feasible or desirable. To say this, I should emphasize, does not mean that the methods and objectives of the natural sciences are wholly irrelevant to the study of human social behaviour. Sociology deals with a factually observable subject-matter, depends upon empirical research, and involves attempts to formulate theories and generalizations that will make sense of facts. But human beings are not the same as material objects in nature; studying our own behaviour is necessarily entirely different in some very important ways from studying natural phenomena.

The development of sociology, and its current concerns, have to be grasped in the context of changes that have created the modern world. We live in an age of massive social transformation. In the space of only something like two centuries a sweeping set of social changes, which have hastened rather than lessened their pace today, have occurred. These changes, emanating originally from Western Europe, are now global in their impact. They have all but totally dissolved the forms of social organization in which humankind had lived for thousands of years of its previous history. Their core is to be found in what some have described as the 'two great revolutions' of eighteenth- and nineteenth-century Europe. The

first is the French revolution of 1789, both a specific set of events and a symbol of political transformations in our era. For the 1789 revolution was quite different from rebellions of previous times. Peasants had sometimes rebelled against their feudal masters, for example, but generally in an attempt to remove specific individuals from power, or to secure reductions in prices or taxes. In the French revolution (to which we can bracket, with some reservations, the anti-colonial revolution in North America in 1776) for the first time in history there took place the overall dissolution of a social order by a movement guided by purely secular ideals – universal liberty and equality. If the ideals of the revolutionaries have scarcely been fully realized even now, they created a climate of political change that has proved one of the dynamic forces of contemporary history. There are few states in the world today that are not proclaimed by their rulers to be 'democracies', whatever their actual political complexion may be. This is something altogether novel in human history. It is true that there have been other republics, most especially those of Classical Greece and Rome. But these were themselves rare instances; and in each case those who formed the 'citizens' were a minority of the population, the majority of whom were slaves or others without the prerogatives of the select groups of citizenry.

The second 'great revolution' was the so-called 'industrial revolution', usually traced to Britain in the late eighteenth century, and spreading in the nineteenth century throughout Western Europe and the United States. The industrial revolution is sometimes presented merely as a set of technical innovations: especially the harnessing of steam power to manufacturing production and the introduction of novel forms of machinery activated by such sources of power. But these technical inventions were only part of a very much broader set of social and economic changes. The most important of these was the migration of the mass of the labour force from the land into the constantly expanding sectors of industrial work, a process which also eventually led to the widespread mechanization of agrarian production. This same process promoted an expansion of cities upon a scale again previously unwitnessed in history. [. . .]

Sociology came into being as those caught up in the initial series of changes brought about by the 'two great revolutions' in Europe sought to understand the conditions of their emergence, and their likely consequences. Of course, no field of study can be exactly pinpointed in terms of its origins. We can quite readily trace direct continuities from writers in the middle of the eighteenth century through to later periods of social thought. The climate of ideas involved in the formation of sociology in some part, in fact, helped *give rise* to the twin processes of revolution.

How should 'sociology' be defined? Let me begin with a banality. Sociology is concerned with the study of human societies. Now the notion of society can be formulated in only a very general way. For under the general category of 'societies' we want to include not only the industrialized countries, but large agrarian imperial states (such as the Roman Empire, or traditional China), and, at the other end of the scale, small tribal communities that may comprise only a tiny number of individuals.

A society is a cluster, or system, of *institutionalized* modes of conduct. To speak of 'institutionalized' forms of social conduct is to refer to modes of belief and behaviour that occur and recur – or, as the terminology of modern social theory would have it, are socially *reproduced* – across long spans of time and space. Language is an excellent example of such a form of institutionalized activity, or institution, since it is so fundamental to social life. All of us speak languages which none of us, as individuals, created, although we all use language creatively. But many other aspects of social life may be institutionalized: that is, become commonly adopted practices which persist in recognizably similar form across the generations. Hence we can speak of economic institutions, political institutions and so on. Such a use of the concept 'institution', it should be pointed out, differs from the way in which the term is often employed in ordinary

language, as a loose synonym for 'group' or 'collectivity' – as when, say, a prison or hospital is referred to as an 'institution'.

These considerations help to indicate how 'society' should be understood, but we cannot leave matters there. As an object of study, 'society' is shared by sociology and the other social sciences. The distinctive feature of sociology lies in its overriding concern with those forms of society that have emerged in the wake of the 'two great revolutions'. Such forms of society include those that are industrially advanced – the economically developed countries of the West, Japan and Eastern Europe – but also in the twentieth century a range of other societies stretched across the world. [. . .]

In the light of these remarks, a definition can be offered of the subject as follows. *Sociology is a social science, having as its main focus the study of the social institutions brought into being by the industrial transformations of the past two or three centuries.* It is important to stress that there are no precisely defined divisions between sociology and other fields of intellectual endeavour in the social sciences. Neither is it desirable that there should be. Some questions of social theory, to do with how human behaviour and institutions should be conceptualized, are the shared concern of the social sciences as a whole. The different 'areas' of human behaviour that are covered by the various social sciences form an intellectual division of labour which can be justified in only a very general way. Anthropology, for example, is concerned [. . .] with the 'simpler' societies: tribal societies, chiefdoms and agrarian states. But either these have been dissolved altogether by the profound social changes that have swept through the world, or they are in the process of becoming incorporated within modern industrial states. The subject-matter of economics, to take another instance, is the production and distribution of material goods. However, economic institutions are plainly always connected with other institutions in social systems, which both influence and are influenced by them. Finally, history, as the study of the continual distancing of past and present, is the source material of the whole of the social sciences.

[. . .] Although this type of standpoint has been very pervasive in sociology, it is one I reject. To speak of sociology, and of other subjects like anthropology or economics, as 'social sciences' is to stress that they involve the systematic study of an empirical subject-matter. The terminology is not confusing so long as we see that sociology and other social sciences differ from the natural sciences in two essential respects.

1   We *cannot* approach society, or 'social facts', as we do objects or events in the natural world, because societies only exist in so far as they are created and re-created in our own actions as human beings. In social theory, we cannot treat human activities as though they were determined by causes in the same way as natural events are. We have to grasp what I would call the *double involvement* of individuals and institutions: we create society at the same time as we are created by it. [. . .]

2   It follows from this that the practical implications of sociology are not directly parallel to the technological uses of science, and cannot be.

2 The Sociological Imagination and the Promise of Sociology

C. Wright Mills

The sociological imagination enables its possessor to understand the larger historical scene in terms of its meaning for the inner life and the external career of a variety of individuals. It enables [the sociologist] to take into account how individuals, in the welter of their daily experience, often become falsely conscious of their social positions. Within that welter, the framework of modern society is sought, and within that framework the psychologies of a variety of men and women are formulated. By such means the personal uneasiness of individuals is focused upon explicit troubles and the indifference of publics is transformed into involvement with public issues.

The first fruit of this imagination – and the first lesson of the social science that embodies it – is the idea that the individual can understand his[1] own experience and gauge his own fate only by locating himself within his period, that he can know his own chances in life only by becoming aware of those of all individuals in his circumstances. In many ways it is a terrible lesson; in many ways a magnificent one. We do not know the limits of man's capacities for supreme effort or willing degradation, for agony or glee, for pleasurable brutality or the sweetness of reason. But in our time we have come to know that the limits of 'human nature' are frighteningly broad. We have come to know that every individual lives, from one generation to the next, in some society; that he lives out a biography, and that he lives it out within some historical sequence. By the fact of his living he contributes, however minutely, to the shaping of this society and to the course of its history, even as he is made by society and by its historical push and shove.

The sociological imagination enables us to grasp history and biography and the relations between the two within society. That is its task and its promise. [. . .]

No social study that does not come back to the problems of biography, of history and of their intersections within a society has completed its intellectual journey. Whatever the specific problems of the classic social analysts, however limited or however broad the features of social reality they have examined, those who have been imaginatively aware of the promise of their work have consistently asked three sorts of questions:

1 What is the structure of this particular society as a whole? What are its essential components and how are they related to one another? How does it differ from other varieties of social order? Within it, what is the meaning of any particular feature for its continuance and for its change?
2 Where does this society stand in human history? What are the mechanics by which it is changing? What is its place within and its meaning for the development of humanity as a whole? How does any particular feature we are examining affect, and how is it affected by, the historical period in which it moves?

And this period – what are its essential features? How does it differ from other periods? What are its characteristic ways of history-making?

3   What varieties of men and women now prevail in this society and in this period? And what varieties are coming to prevail? In what ways are they selected and formed, liberated and repressed, made sensitive and blunted? What kinds of 'human nature' are revealed in the conduct and character we observe in this society in this period? And what is the meaning for 'human nature' of each and every feature of the society we are examining?

Whether the point of interest is a great power state or a minor literary mood, a family, a prison, a creed – these are the kinds of questions the best social analysts have asked. They are the intellectual pivots of classic studies of man in society – and they are the questions inevitably raised by any mind possessing the sociological imagination. For that imagination is the capacity to shift from one perspective to another – from the political to the psychological; from examination of a single family to comparative assessment of the national budgets of the world; from the theological school to the military establishment; from considerations of an oil industry to studies of contemporary poetry. It is the capacity to range from the most impersonal and remote transformations to the most intimate features of the human self – and to see the relations between the two. Back of its use there is always the urge to know the social and historical meaning of the individual in the society and in the period in which he has his quality and his being [. . .]

Perhaps the most fruitful distinction with which the sociological imagination works is between 'the personal troubles of milieu' and 'the public issues of social structure'. This distinction is an essential tool of the sociological imagination and a feature of all classic work in social science [. . .]

In these terms, consider unemployment. When, in a city of 100,000, only one man is unemployed, that is his personal trouble, and for its relief we properly look to the character of the man, his skills and his immediate opportunities. But when, in a nation of 50 million employees, 15 million men are unemployed, that is an issue, and we may not hope to find its solution within the range of opportunities open to any one individual. The very structure of opportunities has collapsed. Both the correct statement of the problem and the range of possible solutions require us to consider the economic and political institutions of the society, and not merely the personal situation and character of a scatter of individuals.

Consider war. The personal problem of war, when it occurs, may be how to survive it or how to die in it with honour; how to make money out of it; how to climb into the higher safety of the military apparatus; or how to contribute to the war's termination. In short, according to one's values, to find a set of milieux and within it to survive the war or make one's death in it meaningful. But the structural issues of war have to do with its causes; with what types of men it throws up into command; with its effects upon economic and political, family and religious institutions, with the unorganized irresponsibility of a world of nation states.

Consider marriage. Inside a marriage a man and a woman may experience personal troubles, but when the divorce rate during the first four years of marriage is 250 out of every 1,000 attempts, this is an indication of a structural issue having to do with the institutions of marriage and the family and other institutions that bear upon them.

Or consider the metropolis – the horrible, beautiful, ugly, magnificent sprawl of the great city. For many upper-class people, the personal solution to 'the problem of the city' is to have an apartment with a private garage under it in the heart of the city and, forty miles out, a house by Henry Hill, garden by Garrett Eckbo, on a hundred acres of private land. In these two controlled environments – with a small staff at each end and a private helicopter connection – most people could solve many of the problems of personal milieux caused by the facts of the city. But all this, however splendid, does not solve the public issues that the structural fact of the city poses. What should be done with this wonderful monstrosity? Break it all up into scattered units, combining residence and work? Refurbish it as it stands? Or, after evacuation, dynamite it and build new cities according to new plans in new places? What should those plans be? And who is to decide and to accomplish whatever choice is made? These are structural issues; to confront them and to solve them requires us to consider political and economic issues that affect innumerable milieux.

In so far as an economy is so arranged that slumps occur, the problem of unemployment becomes incapable of personal solution. In so far as war is inherent in the nation-state system and in the uneven industrialization of the world, the ordinary individual in his restricted milieu will be powerless – with or without psychiatric aid – to solve the troubles this system or lack of system imposes upon him. In so far as the family as an institution turns women into darling little slaves and men into their chief providers and unweaned dependants, the problem of a satisfactory marriage remains incapable of purely private solution. In so far as the overdeveloped megalopolis and the overdeveloped automobile are built-in features of the overdeveloped society, the issues of urban living will not be solved by personal ingenuity and private wealth.

What we experience in various and specific milieux, I have noted, is often caused by structural changes. Accordingly, to understand the changes of many personal milieux we are required to look beyond them. And the number and variety of such structural changes increase as the institutions within which we live become more embracing and more intricately connected with one another. To be aware of the idea of social structure and to use it with sensibility is to be capable of tracing such linkages among a great variety of milieux. To be able to do that is to possess the sociological imagination.

NOTE

1 Mills uses language that would now be regarded as sexist. Virtually all authors in the field of sociology today recognize that words like 'he' and 'his', when used to mean human beings as a whole, are an expression of gender power – and that such usage should be avoided [ed.].

3 Thinking Sociologically

Zygmunt Bauman

The central question of sociology, one could say, is: in what sense does it matter that in whatever they do or may do people are dependent on other people; in what sense does it matter that they live always (and cannot but live) in the company of, in communication with, in an exchange with, in competition with, in co-operation with other human beings? It is this kind of question (and not a separate collection of people or events selected for the purpose of study, nor some set of human actions neglected by other lines of investigation) that constitutes the particular area of sociological discussion and defines sociology as a relatively autonomous branch of human and social sciences. Sociology, we may conclude, is first and foremost a *way of thinking* about the human world; in principle one can also think about the same world in different ways.

Among these other ways from which the sociological way of thinking is set apart, a special place is occupied by so-called *common sense*. Perhaps more than other branches of scholarship, sociology finds its relation with common sense (that rich yet disorganized, non-systematic, often inarticulate and ineffable knowledge we use to conduct our daily business of life) fraught with problems decisive for its standing and practice.

Indeed, few sciences are concerned with spelling out their relationship to common sense; most do not even notice that common sense exists, let alone that it presents a problem. Most sciences settle for defining themselves in terms of boundaries that separate them from or bridges that connect them with other sciences – respectable, systematic lines of enquiry like themselves. They

do not feel they share enough ground with common sense to bother with drawing boundaries or building bridges. Their indifference is, one must admit, well justified. Common sense has next to nothing to say of the matters of which physics, or chemistry, or astronomy, or geology speak (and whatever it has to say on such matters comes courtesy of those sciences themselves, in so far as they manage to make their recondite findings graspable and intelligible for lay people). The subjects dealt with by physics or astronomy hardly ever appear within the sight of ordinary men and women: inside, so to speak, your and my daily experience. And so we, the non-experts, the ordinary people, cannot form opinions about such matters unless aided – indeed, instructed – by the scientists. The objects explored by sciences like the ones we have mentioned appear only under very special circumstances, to which lay people have no access: on the screen of a multi-million-dollar accelerator, in the lens of a gigantic telescope, at the bottom of a thousand-feet-deep shaft. Only the scientists can see them and experiment with them; these objects and events are a monopolistic possession of the given branch of science (or even of its selected practitioners), a property not shared with anybody who is not a member of the profession. Being the sole owners of the experience which provides the raw material for their study, the scientists are in full control over the way the material is processed, analysed, interpreted. Products of such processing would have to withstand the critical scrutiny of other scientists – but their scrutiny only. They will not have to compete with public opinion, common sense or any other form in which non-specialist views may appear, for the simple reason that there is no public opinion and no commonsensical point of view in the matters they study and pronounce upon.

With sociology it is quite different. In sociological study there are no equivalents of giant accelerators or radio telescopes. All experience which provides raw material for sociological findings – the stuff of which sociological knowledge is made – is the experience of ordinary people in ordinary, daily life; an experience accessible in principle, though not always in practice, to everybody; [. . .] experience that, before it came under the magnifying glass of a sociologist, had already been lived by someone else – a non-sociologist, a person not trained in the use of sociological language and seeing things from a sociological point of view. All of us live in the company of other people, after all, and interact with each other. All of us have learned only too well that what we get depends on what other people do. All of us have gone more than once through the agonizing experience of a communication breakdown with friends and strangers. Anything sociology talks about was already there in our lives. And it must have been; otherwise we should be unable to conduct our business of life. To live in the company of other people we need a lot of knowledge; and common sense is the name of that knowledge.

Deeply immersed in our daily routines, though, we hardly ever pause to think about the meaning of what we have gone through; even less often have we the opportunity to compare our private experience with the fate of others, to see the *social* in the *individual*, the *general* in the *particular*; this is precisely what sociologists can do for us. We would expect them to show us how our individual *biographies* intertwine with the *history* we share with fellow human beings. And yet whether or not the sociologists get that far, they have no other point to start from than the daily experience of life they share with you and me – from that raw knowledge that saturates the daily life of each one of us. For this reason

alone the sociologists, however hard they might have tried to follow the example of the physicists and the biologists and stand aside from the object of their study (that is, look at your and my life experience as an object 'out there', as a detached and impartial observer would do), cannot break off completely from their insider's knowledge of the experience they try to comprehend. However hard they might try, sociologists are bound to remain on both sides of the experience they strive to interpret, inside and outside at the same time. (Note how often the sociologists use the personal pronoun 'we' when they report their findings and formulate their general propositions. That 'we' stands for an 'object' that includes those who study and those whom they study. Can you imagine a physicist using 'we' of themselves and the molecules? Or astronomers using 'we' to generalize about themselves and the stars?)

There is more still to the special relationship between sociology and common sense. The phenomena observed and theorized upon by modern physicists or astronomers come in an innocent and pristine form, unprocessed, free from labels, ready-made definitions and prior interpretations (that is, except such interpretations as had been given them in advance by the physicists who set the experiments that made them appear). They wait for the physicist or the astronomer to name them, to set them among other phenomena and combine them into an orderly whole: in short, to give them *meaning*. But there are few, if any, sociological equivalents of such clean and unused phenomena which have never been given meaning before. Those human actions and interactions that sociologists explore had all been given names and theorized about, in however diffuse, poorly articulated form, by the actors themselves. Before sociologists started looking at them, they were objects of commonsensical knowledge. Families, organizations, kinship networks, neighbourhoods, cities and villages, nations and churches and any other groupings held together by regular human interaction have already been given meaning and significance by the actors, so that the actors consciously address them in their actions as bearers of such meanings. Lay actors and professional sociologists would have to use the same names, the same language when speaking of them. Each term sociologists may use will already have been heavily burdened with meanings it was given by the commonsensical knowledge of 'ordinary' people like you and me.

For the reason explained above, sociology is much too intimately related to common sense to afford that lofty equanimity with which sciences like chemistry or geology can treat it. You and I are allowed to speak of human interdependence and human interaction, and to speak with authority. Don't we all practise them and experience them? Sociological discourse is wide open: no standing invitation to everybody to join, but no clearly marked borders or effective border guards either. With poorly defined borders whose security is not guaranteed in advance (unlike sciences that explore objects inaccessible to lay experience), the sovereignty of sociology over social knowledge, its right to make authoritative pronouncements on the subject, may always be contested. This is why drawing a boundary between sociological knowledge proper and the common sense that is always full of sociological ideas is such an important matter for the identity of sociology as a cohesive body of knowledge; and why sociologists pay this matter more attention than other scientists.

We can think of at least four quite seminal differences between the ways in which sociology and common sense – your and my 'raw' knowledge of the business of life – treat the topic they share: human experience.

To start with, sociology (unlike common sense) makes an effort to subordinate itself to the rigorous rules of *responsible speech*, which is assumed to be an attribute of science (as distinct from other, reputedly more relaxed and less vigilantly self-controlled, forms of knowledge). This means that the sociologists are expected to take great care to distinguish – in a fashion clear and visible to anybody – between the statements corroborated by available evidence and such propositions as can only claim the status of a provisional,

untested guess. Sociologists would refrain from misrepresenting ideas that are grounded solely in their beliefs (even the most ardent and emotionally intense beliefs) as tested findings carrying the widely respected authority of science. The rules of responsible speech demand that one's 'workshop' – the whole procedure that has led to the final conclusions and is claimed to guarantee their credibility – be wide open to an unlimited public scrutiny; a standing invitation ought to be extended to everyone to reproduce the test and, be this the case, prove the findings wrong. Responsible speech must also relate to other statements made on its topic; it cannot simply dismiss or pass by in silence other views that have been voiced, however sharply they are opposed to it and hence inconvenient. It is hoped that once the rules of responsible speech are honestly and meticulously observed, the trustworthiness, reliability and eventually also the practical usefulness of the ensuing propositions will be greatly enhanced, even if not fully guaranteed. Our shared faith in the credibility of beliefs countersigned by science is to a great extent grounded in the hope that the scientists will indeed follow the rules of responsible speech, and that the scientific profession as a whole will see to it that every single member of the profession does so on every occasion. As to the scientists themselves, they point to the virtues of responsible speech as an argument in favour of the superiority of the knowledge they offer.

The second difference is related to the *size of the field* from which the material for judgement is drawn. For most of us, as non-professionals, such a field is confined to our own life-world: things we do, people we meet, purposes we set for our own pursuits and guess other people set for theirs. Rarely, if at all, do we make an effort to lift ourselves above the level of our daily concerns to broaden the horizon of experience, as this would require time and resources most of us can ill afford or do not feel like spending on such effort. And yet, given the tremendous variety of life-conditions, each experience based solely on an individual life-world is necessarily partial and most likely one-sided. Such shortcomings can be rectified only if one brings together and sets against each other experiences drawn from a multitude of life-worlds. Only then will the incompleteness of individual experience be revealed, as will be the complex network of dependencies and interconnections in which it is entangled – a network which reaches far beyond the realm which could be scanned from the vantage point of a singular biography. The overall result of such a broadening of horizons will be the discovery of the intimate link between individual biography and wide social processes the individual may be unaware of and surely unable to control. It is for this reason that the sociologists' pursuit of a perspective wider than the one offered by an individual life-world makes a great difference – not just a quantitative difference (more data, more facts, statistics instead of single cases), but a difference in the quality and the uses of knowledge. For people like you or me, who pursue our respective aims in life and struggle for more control over our plight, sociological knowledge has something to offer that common sense cannot.

The third difference between sociology and common sense pertains to the way in which each one goes about *making sense* of human reality; how each one goes about explaining to its own satisfaction why this rather than that happened or is the case. I imagine that you (much as myself) know from your own experience that you are the 'author' of your actions; you know that what you do (though not necessarily the results of your actions) is an effect of your intention, hope or purpose. You normally do as you do in order to achieve a state of affairs you desire, whether you wish to possess an object, to receive an accolade from your teachers or to put an end to your friends' teasing. Quite naturally, the way you think of your action serves you as a model for making sense of all other actions. You explain such actions to yourself by imputing to others intentions you know from your own experience. This is, to be sure, the only way we can make sense of the human world around us as long as we draw our tools of explanation solely from

within our respective life-worlds. We tend to perceive everything that happens in the world at large as an outcome of somebody's intentional action. We look for the persons responsible for what has happened and, once we have found them, we believe our enquiry has been completed. We assume somebody's goodwill lies behind every event we like and somebody's ill intentions behind every event we dislike. We would find it difficult to accept that a situation was not an effect of intentional action of an identifiable 'somebody'; and we would not lightly give up our conviction that any unwelcome condition could be remedied if only someone, somewhere, wished to take the right action. Those who more than anyone else interpret the world for us – politicians, journalists, commercial advertisers – tune in to this tendency of ours and speak of the 'needs of the state' or 'demands of the economy', as if the state or the economy were made to the measure of individual persons like ourselves and could have needs or make demands. On the other hand, they portray the complex problems of nations, states and economic systems (deeply seated in the very structures of such figurations) as the effects of the thoughts and deeds of a few individuals one can name, put in front of a camera and interview. Sociology stands in opposition to such a personalized world-view. [. . .] When thinking sociologically, one attempts to make sense of the human condition through analysing the manifold webs of human interdependency – that toughest of realities which explains both our motives and the effects of their activation.

Finally, let us recall that the power of common sense over the way we understand the world and ourselves (the immunity of common sense to questioning, its capacity for self-confirmation) depends on the apparently self-evident character of its precepts. This in turn rests on the routine, monotonous nature of daily life, which informs our common sense while being simultaneously informed by it. As long as we go through the routine and habitualized motions which fill most of our daily business, we do not need much self-scrutiny and self-analysis. When repeated often enough, things tend to become familiar, and familiar things are self-explanatory; they present no problems and arouse no curiosity. In a way, they remain invisible. Questions are not asked, as people are satisfied that 'things are as they are', 'people are as they are', and there is precious little one can do about it. Familiarity is the staunchest enemy of inquisitiveness and criticism – and thus also of innovation and the courage to change. In an encounter with that familiar world ruled by habits and reciprocally reasserting beliefs, sociology acts as a meddlesome and often irritating stranger. It disturbs the comfortingly quiet way of life by asking questions no one among the 'locals' remembers being asked, let alone answered. Such questions make evident things into puzzles: they *defamiliarize* the familiar. Suddenly, the daily way of life must come under scrutiny. It now appears to be just one of the possible ways, not the one and only, not the 'natural', way of life. [. . .]

One could say that the main service the art of thinking sociologically may render to each and every one of us is to make us more *sensitive*; it may sharpen up our senses, open our eyes wider so that we can explore human conditions which thus far had remained all but invisible. Once we understand better how the apparently natural, inevitable, eternal aspects of our lives have been brought into being through the exercise of human power and human resources, we will find it hard to accept once more that they are immune and impenetrable to human action – our own action included. Sociological thinking is, one may say, a power in its own right, an *anti-fixating* power. It renders flexible again the world hitherto oppressive in its apparent fixity; it shows it as a world which could be different from what it is now. It can be argued that the art of sociological thinking tends to widen the scope, the daring and the practical effectiveness of your and my *freedom*. Once the art has been learned and mastered, the individual may well become just a bit less manipulable, more resilient to oppression and regulation from outside, more likely to resist being fixed by forces that claim to be irresistible.

To think sociologically means to understand a little more fully the people around us, their cravings and dreams, their worries and their misery. We may then better appreciate the human individuals in them and perhaps even have more respect for their rights to do what we ourselves are doing and to cherish doing it: their rights to choose and practise the way of life they prefer, to select their life-projects, to define themselves and – last but not least – vehemently defend their dignity. We may realize that in doing all those things other people come across the same kind of obstacles as we do and know the bitterness of frustration as well as we do. Eventually, sociological thinking may well promote solidarity between us, a solidarity grounded in mutual understanding and respect, solidarity in our joint resistance to suffering and shared condemnation of the cruelty that causes it. If this effect is achieved, the cause of freedom will be strengthened by being elevated to the rank of a *common* cause.

Thinking sociologically may also help us to understand other forms of life, inaccessible to our direct experience and all too often entering the commonsensical knowledge only as stereotypes – one-sided, tendentious caricatures of the way people different from ourselves (distant people, or people kept at a distance by our distaste or suspicion) live. An insight into the inner logic and meaning of the forms of life other than our own may well prompt us to think again about the alleged toughness of the boundary that has been drawn between ourselves and others, between 'us' and 'them'. Above all, it may prompt us to doubt that boundary's natural, preordained character. This new understanding may well make our communication with the 'other' easier than before, and more likely to lead to mutual agreement. It may replace fear and antagonism with tolerance. This would also contribute to our freedom, as there are no guarantees of my freedom stronger than the freedom of all, and that means also of such people as may have chosen to use their freedom to embark on a life different from my own. Only under such conditions may our own freedom to choose be exercised.

Part 2 Culture and Society

Rosamond Billington and her colleagues provide in Reading 4 a useful discussion of the concept of culture – one of the most important notions in sociology. The idea of culture, they point out, has been used in different ways in varying traditions of sociology and anthropology. These varying usages, however, share something in common. The core definition of 'culture' refers to ways of life that are shared in common by the members of a group.

'Culture' refers to learned patterns of behaviour, which human beings acquire through social experience or direct teaching. But some core aspects of what we are as human beings are not learned: they are determined by nature, not culture. The modern science of genetics, discussed in Reading 5, gives us a means of analysing the natural components of human behaviour. Scientists are currently in the process of mapping the whole genetic structure of human beings. In so doing, they are helping us unravel the complex relations between the cultural and the natural roots. For instance, it is often claimed that 'racial' differences between human groups – marked principally by skin colour – bring with them a wide range of other biological differences. Genetic studies show that this is not the case – genetically speaking there are no distinct 'races'.

Use of the internet is still heavily weighted towards the developed societies. However, the internet is spreading rapidly to less developed regions of the world, as is discussed in Reading 6. In countries with authoritarian governments the authorities fear the growth of the internet because it makes information freely available to those who wish to seek it. Yet the progress of the internet seems more or less unstoppable, whatever governments may say or do. Newspapers or other printed materials that are banned by the authorities can normally easily be found on the internet. The main factor limiting the spread of the internet is not really government hostility but cost. The internet is likely to reach poorer countries on a much more extensive basis now that wireless technologies are available. As carried by mobile phones, for example, the internet does not need expensive computer equipment or wiring to work.

4 Defining 'Culture'

Rosamund Billington, Sheelagh Strawbridge,
Lenore Greensides and Annette Fitzsimons

Definitions

There are at least two everyday, commonsense meanings of culture. The first is the 'best' achievements and products in art, literature and music. The second is the artificial growth or development of microscopic organisms or species of plants, a meaning deriving from a much older usage of the verb 'to cultivate': meaning to husband, and originally referring to agricultural techniques. Both these meanings are relevant to what is discussed [below]. More immediately we need to remember that although sociology is concerned with commonsense meanings, it must also look beyond them for theories, explanations and interpretations. Durkheim saw the study of 'collective representations' and their symbolic meaning as central to a sociological understanding of the social. In a very different tradition, Max Weber saw sociology as one of the 'cultural sciences', concerned with values and meaning, developing concepts and interpretations relevant to the society in which they take shape. A basic proposition of modern sociology is that concepts, ideas, words and other symbolic systems arise out of the society or group in which they operate. [. . .] the development and use of the concept 'culture' relates to the beliefs and values people have about societies, social change and the ideal society they seek [. . .]

The complex of social and economic changes we call industrialisation in Britain, Western Europe and North America brought with them a range of theories and concepts through which people tried to explain the structural changes which were occurring, based on the belief that it was possible to study society 'scientifically'. From these theories the related disciplines of sociology and anthropology developed, both utilising the concept of culture in a variety of ways. By looking at some of these in detail we hope to clarify some of the issues, assumptions and problems involved in the definition and study of culture.

Anthropologists and culture

An important change in Western ideas in the nineteenth century was the notion of the 'evolution' of species in the natural world. Among other things, this theory established human beings as part of the animal world. The pseudo-science of physical anthropology attempted to investigate some of the differences between the 'races' of humankind at the same time that 'armchair' anthropologists were studying their cultures. Since then, studies by ethologists of primates and other 'higher' animal groups have emphasised the complex group activities of animals. Scientists, including psychologists, have utilised animal studies as a basis for research on some aspects of human behaviour. In popular thought people commonly explain human behaviour and arrangements as an aspect of their 'animal nature' but sociologists and modern anthropologists reject such reductionist explanations. They begin from the premise that only humankind possesses culture, in the sense of the classical definition by the nineteenth-century anthropologist Tylor: 'that complex whole which includes knowledge, belief, art, morals, law, custom and any other capabilities and habits acquired by man [*sic*] as a member of society'.[1]

Like sociologists today, anthropologists (who owe a considerable intellectual debt to Durkheim) have attempted to explain societies in their own terms, that is, not simply as the sum total of the activities of individuals or deriving from the biological properties of human beings, but as unique social entities. To distinguish society from the biological or organic, the American anthropologist Kroeber, for example, talked about culture as the superorganic, stressing that there was nothing about the varied cultures of the world which was biologically inherited. He made the important point that culture is learned and transmitted through groups and individuals in societies.[2] Other writers and anthropologists have stressed the importance of humankind's ability to symbolise and to communicate through symbols, in the development of culture. Culture is 'species specific': although other species can communicate, only humans can communicate through symbols, language being the most important symbol system. These ideas are part of the nature/nurture debate, in which sociologists and anthropologists agree on the importance of the social and cultural as determinants of human action. Through the use of symbols humans bestow value and meaning on objects, relationships and ideas, and studies by modern anthropologists have shown us the tremendous range of these.

Many early anthropologists and ethnologists were concerned to list cultural 'traits', that is to analyse abstracted items of culture, such as religious beliefs or kinship arrangements, or items of 'material' culture, often finding similarities in these items in different societies [. . .] Their findings were used as evidence for constructing evolutionary typologies and theories of societies or institutions such as kinship and religion. Partly in reaction against such theories and their wrenching of cultural items out of context (and their assumption that social evolution occurred in a similar way to biological evolution) later anthropologists stressed the importance of studying 'primitive' cultures as systematic wholes, to understand the significance, function and meaning for the cultures themselves of particular beliefs,

customs and practices. Such a holistic approach to the study of other cultures usually adopted the structural–functionalist assumptions of Durkheim which have important implications for the study of culture, a point to which we shall return.

We have used the concept of 'culture' almost interchangeably with society, but in sociology and anthropology important distinctions between the two have been made. [. . .] because of the all-embracing nature of culture as defined by Tylor above, British social anthropologists have tended to concentrate on social structure – social institutions. Study of aspects of culture, for example, belief systems – has been in terms of the functioning of these for the institutional system. American anthropologists have concentrated more on culture *per se*. [. . .]

What becomes clear, when we look at classical works of British and American anthropology, is that given humans' innate capacity to develop culture as well as the biological limitations on such development, we cannot fully understand social activities unless we understand the place of beliefs, values and customs – culture – in these activities [. . .] This is shown in the discussion of culture by the American anthropologist Clyde Kluckhohn. He adds to previous definitions of culture, saying that it consists of different components, it is dynamic, structured and the means by which individuals adjust to social life and learn 'creative expression'. Kluckhohn argues that cultures do not merely have content but also structure. They are cultural systems in that they are not random but have organised patterns, independent of particular individuals. Cultures are 'designs for living', formed through historical processes. Social scientists need to study both the explicit culture, which can be directly observed and is largely consciously understood by participants, and the implicit culture, which Kluckhohn calls 'an abstraction of the second order' [. . .]

Kluckhohn writes in the Durkheimian tradition, stressing the shared and normative nature of culture and its functions for integrating the individual into the group. He emphasises that although some aspects of culture are relevant only to particular groups – generational, sex, work, class – all aspects are interrelated and form a whole, although culture is not necessarily perfectly integrated. In particular, he points out that individuals in Western societies, because of the cultural stress on individualism and freewill, are not always willing to conform to cultural patterns. Two points are implied in this argument. One is that in general culture serves an overall integrative function in society and the second is that there is a functional if complex relationship between culture and social structure, an analysis similar to that of the sociologist, Talcott Parsons.

More recently Clifford Geertz has stressed the creativity of culture and the agency of human action in negotiating and manipulating culture, using an 'action frame of reference' derived from the sociology of Max Weber and Talcott Parsons. Geertz has also emphasised the particularity of cultures and the necessity for 'thick description', that is, an interpretative approach:

the concept of culture . . . is essentially a semiotic one. Believing, with Max Weber, that man is an animal suspended in webs of significance he himself has spun, I take culture to be those webs, and the analysis of it . . . not an experimental science in search of law but an interpretative one in search of meaning [. . .]

Functions of culture

Parsons's structural–functionalism has been one of the most influential theoretical approaches in sociology until quite recently. Despite his attempt to synthesise ideas from a variety of nineteenth- and twentieth-century social theorists most of his work is in a direct line from Durkheim in his stress on the nature and necessity of social integration. Parsons's theory (or theories) is complex and changed over time, but what is relevant here is the priority given in his most influential work to what he called the cultural system in the overall integration of society and the integration and socialisation of individuals into society. For Parsons, 'social action' by individuals, which results in what anthropologists call social institu-

tions, involves choices based on values and norms which are specified within the cultural system. Put simply, people behave as they are expected to in a given situation because they have internalised the norms and values – the culture – of society (Durkheim termed this 'morality'). This ensures the stability both of the individual and society: the social action of individuals is functional for the maintenance of the social system.

[. . .]

Culture and industrial society

Sociologists and anthropologists are not alone in developing theories and ideas about culture. Raymond Williams has attempted to show how modern notions of culture in Britain arose out of the nineteenth-century changes and processes indicated by the 'keywords', industry, democracy, class, and art.[3] Williams is pointing essentially to what sociologists have called social differentiation, the increasing specialisation of functions in society. In the nineteenth century he argues, the concept of culture 'as an abstraction and an absolute' emerged 'as a recognition of the practical separation of certain moral and intellectual activities' from the rest of society, and as an attempt to create ultimate values at which to aim and by which to judge other social and economic activities'.[4] Williams stresses that this new concept of culture was not simply a response to industrialisation but a search for 'new kinds of personal and social relationship' – just the concern of social theorists like Saint-Simon, Comte, Durkheim, Spencer and Marx. Similar 'cultural consequences of modernization' were felt in America too [. . .] If we accept that an essential part of the 'spirit of the age' was the idea of human progress, then the various theories of culture are part of the attempt to regulate and channel progress. In the United States this attempt was couched in terms of the need to develop a national culture commensurate with democracy and freedom of the individual and one which was the equal of European culture [. . .]

The idea that humankind should seek perfection was not new, but European, British and American writers in the late eighteenth and early nineteenth centuries connected this search with the new possibilities and problems of industrialism. In this context, the concept of culture was equated with the idea of civilisation. Underlying this equation, as we have seen, was some notion that societies evolved from less civilised forms and Western industrialised societies were closer to the top of this evolutionary scale – a notion stated quite explicitly by early writers on primitive societies. But writers like Coleridge, Mill and Arnold also began to distinguish culture (with particular emphasis on the arts and philosophy) from the more general terms civilisation and progress. Doubting (like Durkheim and other sociologists) that the prevailing philosophy and practice of Utilitarianism was adequate to deal with morals and standards, they specified conditions necessary for a culture to develop which would provide the ultimate source of judgement and values Coleridge wanted to integrate the cultivation of feelings and experience with scientific progress, but also speculated on the desirability of a specific 'class' of people, endowed by the state, who would be responsible for the general 'cultivation' of society. J. S. Mill's 'humanitarian' liberal Utilitarianism recognised that cultivation of 'feelings' should be part of the total culture and stressed the importance of a much-improved national system of education, which would elevate the level of knowledge and information for all classes in society. He also argued that such a culture must allow for free development of individuality so that each individual could contribute better to the collective culture, based on the individual worth of each person. [. . .]

Nineteenth-century sociological theorists sought to understand social processes because they were anxious and often pessimistic about the nature of the new industrial society and what would replace traditional sources of stability. We can see this same concern, in a slightly different form, in the discussion of culture. The theoretical search for mechanisms of social integration was paralleled by the search for the 'harmonious development' of human intellectual and cultural perfection. For Matthew Arnold, whose ideas were widely applied to Britain and America, this development of 'culture' was the only alternative to 'anarchy', by which he meant lack of standards of morality, intellect and judgement. He defined culture as 'the study of perfection' in general, criticising those 'philistines' who believed that the ultimate value was wealth, success and technological efficiency. Like Mill, Arnold thought a truly liberal educational system important in the process of ensuring the development of culture, but like de Tocqueville he distrusted the power which democracy might give to the 'raw and rough' working classes. He emphasised the importance of harmony in this search for perfection and the need for the state to coordinate, control and guarantee that the influence of the 'best' people should predominate. He was clearly arguing for culture as the means of ensuring a consensus of values and an élite or class to safeguard this consensus: 'without order there can be no society, and without society there can be no human perfection'.

Culture as a way of life

It is useful to note some important similarities between the theories we have examined. Most of the [. . .] theories have a more or less explicit view of culture as the creation of a consensus over values and standards. [. . .] In addition, since culture is seen to represent ultimate values, the best of which humanity is capable, all the theories have some notion, however vague, that the determination and dissemination of 'culture' must be associated with a particular class or élite. Finally, we must note that a fairly clear distinction is emerging in these theories, between the notion of 'society' and 'culture', and that culture is something which overarches, reflects and ultimately has its own effect on the social.

[. . .]

NOTES

1   E. B. Tylor, 'Culture Defines' (1891), in L. A. Coser and B. Rosenberg (eds), *Sociological Theory* (London: Macmillan, 1964), p. 18.

2   A. L. Kroeber, 'The Supererogic' (1952), ibid.

3   R. Williams, *Culture and Society, 1780–1950* (London: Chatto and Windus, 1958; Harmondsworth: Penguin, 1963).

4   Ibid. (1963), p. 17.

5 The Proper Study of Humankind

The Economist

Until the late 1980s, the most useful tools that could be deployed by people who were interested in human origins were the trowel and the cleaning brush. Fossil-hunters had done wonders uncovering specimens of early humanity that told a story of an African genesis, followed by the spread to Eurasia of a species called *Homo erectus*. But the emergence of modern man, *Homo sapiens*, was a mystery. Some researchers argued that modern people evolved in one place and then, like *Homo erectus*, spread out, though they did not agree about where and when this happened. Others believed that the whole *erectus* population gradually and simultaneously evolved into *sapiens*.

That argument was settled by genetics. The late Allan Wilson, a researcher at the University of California at Berkeley, managed to show the truth about human evolution without picking up a single trowel. He studied the pattern of DNA in people now alive, and produced a human family tree showing that the species emerged in Africa about 200,000 years ago and first left the continent to begin its worldwide spread 100,000 years ago.

The work of Wilson, and of Luca Cavalli-Sforza, at Stanford University, who began looking at human genetic variation in the 1950s, has touched off a whole new field, and one that has extensive ramifications. It has revealed some surprisingly fine detail about human history. It challenges the assumption that there are significant genetic differences between human races and, indeed, the idea that 'race' has any useful biological meaning at all. And it holds out the promise of identifying just what it is that makes humans human in the first place.

The fruit of the tree of knowledge

Wilson's work relied on a type of DNA found not in the cell nucleus, but in its mitochondria. These structures, which convert sugar and oxygen into carbon dioxide, water and the energy that runs the cell, are the descendants of bacteria that took up residence in eukaryotic cells about 2 billion years ago. One consequence of their origins is that they carry their own genes. And since (in people, at least) individuals receive all their mitochondria from their mothers, it is easy to trace mitochondrial DNA back through the generations without having to worry about the mixing of genes from mother and father that goes on in the rest of the DNA.

Wilson's map worked by constructing a tree out of the mutations that have accumulated, one at a time, in mitochondrial DNA since *Homo sapiens* emerged as a distinct species. Place this tree on a map of the world, and the result looks to be a very plausible synopsis of human history. But it is now possible to do more than that, and to draw some interesting, and perhaps unexpected, conclusions.

For example Mark Sejelstad, of Harvard University, has compared variations in mitochondrial DNA with variations on the Y-chromosome (which carries the genetic 'switch' for maleness, and is thus passed only from fathers to sons). Traditional views of human behaviour often involve tales of wide-ranging and adventurous males

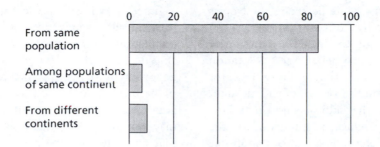

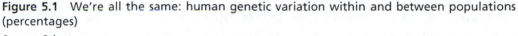

Figure 5.1 We're all the same: human genetic variation within and between populations (percentages)

Source: Science

and stay-at-home, hearth-loving females. But the genes tell a different story. In both Africa and Europe, individual variations in the DNA of Y-chromosomes are much more localised than variations in the DNA of mitochondria. That suggests that it is the men who are the stay-at-homes, and the women who wander. In fact, a detailed analysis of the variation involved suggests that the average woman migrates eight times as far before she reproduces as does the average man. There are exceptions: the Y-chromosomes of Muslims in western China resemble those of the Middle-Eastern conquerors who brought Islam to that part of the world. But these serve only to prove the rule. General, peaceful, small-scale migration is a female rather than a male phenomenon.

Genetics can, however, confirm traditions as well. The legends of the Lemba, a southern-African people, claim they are descended from the Jews, a Middle-Eastern people. An analysis of Lemba Y-chromosomes supports this idea; around 50 per cent of those chromosomes carry genetic markers that are common amongst Jewish men, but absent in the Lemba's neighbours in Africa.

Despite the existence of such genetic markers for particular groups, though, the genes carry a wider, paradoxical, lesson about 'racial' differences – which is that, in the main, there aren't any. The doyen of this work is Dr Cavalli-Sforza. Over the years he has examined a wide range of genes

in a wide range of populations. These populations do differ genetically, but the pattern of differences in well-known genes such as those for blood groups and the HLA proteins of the immune system rarely conform to the conventional racial picture.

In fact, it is remarkable how homogenous humanity is. Around 85 per cent of the genetic variability measured by Dr Cavalli-Sforza is variation between individuals within a given group. Another 6 per cent is variation between groups within a single continent, and 9 per cent is variation between continents (see figure 5.1). And compared with chimpanzees, humans are, indeed, a single race. One group of 55 chimps in West Africa shows more genetic diversity than the whole of humanity.

Geographically linked genetic variations exist, of course. But these tend to be in characteristics connected with resisting the environment, fending off local diseases, or the luck of the draw when a particular group of people started to expand rapidly.

The most obvious example of the first is skin colour. Dark skin, which is caused by a lot of melanin, protects against cancer-causing damage by ultraviolet light, which is strongest in the tropics. Light-skinned people have poorly functional versions of the gene for a protein called melanocortin-stimulating-hormone-receptor (MSHR), and can thrive only in places with weak sunshine. That is why white people in the tropics tend to suffer so badly from skin cancer.

Various versions of the MSHR gene result in various skin colours. The exact coloration depends on how much the resulting receptor protein, which sits on the surface of the melanin-producing cells of the skin telling them how much melanin to produce, is stimulated by the hormone. (These variations are also responsible for differences in hair colour.) But variations in MSHR are independent of variations in any other known gene, which suggests that skin colour is a poor indicator of any underlying 'racial' division of humanity.

Another 'racially' linked gene – that for sickle-cell anaemia – is also there for an evolutionary reason, though in this case its frequency is due to disease, rather than sunlight. It is found in black-skinned people, in particular those who live (or whose ancestors lived) in West Africa.

This is because West Africa is a hot-bed of malaria, and the sickle-cell gene (a mutation of one of the genes for haemoglobin, the red protein that carries oxygen in the blood) protects against malaria. One copy of the gene confers immunity to the disease without causing anaemia. Two copies, one from each parent, usually result in the anaemia. But the consequences of malaria are so bad that the sickle-cell mutation is preserved by natural selection in West Africa.

Take away this selective pressure, however, and the gene starts to disappear. Black Americans, although they carry it more frequently than their non-black compatriots, nevertheless carry it less frequently than West Africans do.

The third explanation for racial genes, chance, applies when a new group grows rapidly from small beginnings without interbreeding with the outside world. Chance differences between the founders of the group and the population from which it derived are thus preserved. This seems to be the origin of such 'racial' markers as the diseases peculiar to Ashkenazi Jews. The genetic evidence suggests that the Ashkenazim descend from a population of around 10,000 people who lived in Poland at the beginning of the 16th century.

Indeed, Wilson's work suggests that *Homo sapiens* itself is the result of a founder effect. The population from which it evolved was probably no more than 10,000 individuals. It is this happy circumstance that makes possible the idea of predicting someone's medical history using a biochip, and means that pharmacogenomics may not result in patient populations so small that few drugs will be cost-effective to develop. Eric Lander has calculated that the small initial human population means that few human genes are likely to have more than three or four significant polymorphic varieties. Even if the number of human genes is near the top end of estimates, that means all common polymorphisms should fit comfortably on a chip, and that enough people should have each of them to make tailored drugs worthwhile.

The nature of the beast

None of this, however, gets to what most people probably regard as the guts of the issue of what genes have to tell humanity about itself: genetic determinism and behaviour. Arguments about genetic influences on behaviour go back almost to the beginning of genetics. But knowing the human genome may be the first real step to resolving them.

There are two interesting questions about genetics and human behaviour, but they are often muddled up. The first is to what extent there is indeed a genetic human nature – that is, slightly paraphrased, why do people behave differently from chimpanzees? The second is how much the differences between the behaviours of individual people are a consequence of differences in their genes.

Answering the first question will involve chewing up the DNA of one or more chimpanzees in one of the world's big sequencing laboratories, and comparing the result with human DNA. This will surely be done within the next few years. But there are already some preliminary results.

People, for instance, have a slightly different form of a molecule called sialic acid from that found in chimpanzees and other apes. It lacks an oxygen atom, because the human gene which codes for the enzyme that makes sialic acid lacks 92 bases that are found in the ape genes.

That may sound almost pathetically trivial. But the presence or absence of an oxygen atom can have a big effect on a molecule's chemistry. And sialic acid, which is found on the surface membrane of almost every cell in the body, is involved in the reception of several of the messenger molecules that control cell behaviour. Even small changes in its chemistry could therefore have significant effects.

No one is saying that sialic acid is chiefly responsible for the differences between people and apes. But the discovery shows both the potential and the pitfalls of searching for meaningful genetic distinctions between species. For the sialic-acid difference is, at least, in the coding region of the gene. Many researchers, however, suspect that the critical differences between chimps and men lie not in the genes themselves but in the regions of DNA lying next to them, which regulate the genes' expression. These differences will probably be more difficult to interpret than differences in the coding regions.

Answering the second question – whether the different ways people behave are determined by their genes – will be even harder. It will involve collecting a massive amount of data of a sort that has been controversial enough when directed towards the unargued good of curing disease.

It is certain that some of the differences between people's behaviour are influenced by genes. Studies that compare close relatives (most frequently identical twins) brought up separately (which eliminates the effect of a shared environment) with less-closely related individuals (e.g. non-identical twins) and unrelated individuals, show this beyond doubt. The more closely related people are, the more similarly they behave. The interesting question is which genes are affecting which behaviours. This has proved a surprisingly intractable problem. But there are a few straws in the wind.

The least interesting straws are those where clearly pathological behaviour has been tied to particular versions of particular genes, but even these can reveal something. Several members of a Dutch family brought to prominence by the work of Han Brunner of the University of Nijmegen, for instance, have defective versions of the gene for an enzyme called monoamine oxidase. This enzyme degrades a signalling molecule called serotonin, which is found in the brain and is known to be involved in setting emotional moods. The family members in question have a tendency to extreme and sudden violence – arson, rape and so on – and the inference is that these episodes are brought about by too much serotonin in the brain.

A more interesting straw is the case of IGF2R. Here the rare form of the gene is associated with a trait, high intelligence, that is usually regarded as desirable. This was discovered by Robert Plomin of King's College, London. He and his colleagues found that the rare form existed far more frequently in a group of American children with IQ scores of around 160 than it did in the population as a whole. IGF2R is the receptor for a molecule that is active in the hippocampus, a part of the brain that plays a crucial role in learning and memory.

There are a few other examples. Work by Dean Hammer, of America's National Cancer Institute, suggests that a particular form of one of the receptors for dopamine (another signalling molecule in the brain) is associated with 'risk-seeking' behaviour. Both this and one form of the molecule that transports dopamine back into cells after use seem to be associated with hyperactivity (or fidgeting, as it used to be known) in children. And different types of serotonin transporter are associated with different, though non-pathological, levels of neuroticism.

This handful of examples might seem surprisingly small. But it does tell a story of its own, for it suggests that the individual effects of particular forms of particular genes on the spectrum of everyday behaviours is quite small. Few studies done so far have involved more than 200 subjects and that, statistically, is only enough to detect a gene that has a 5 per cent effect on a measurable trait. Dr Plomin is currently running studies with 2,000 subjects, enough to recognise 1 per cent effects. He hopes to publish the first results later this year.

Since expression-profiling suggests that some 30,000 genes are involved in constructing and running the brain, the fact that single differences in particular genes should have tiny effects might be expected, just as the search for the genes involved in polygenic diseases has proved harder than many predicted. This gives hope to those who fear that genomics will trigger off a new bout of eugenics; or, conversely, it may encourage discrimination based merely on the possession of particular genes.

But there is also another possibility. The elucidation of the mechanisms by which genes act may show what most evolutionary biologists would predict: that a lot of genetic action is responsive to the environment, and that the dichotomy between nature and nurture is, in a sense, a false one. Children with a particular form of IGF2R are, indeed, more likely to be clever than their peers. But so are children brought up in stimulating environments and sent to good schools. The latter are just as deterministic as the former, and the neural pathways they lay down in the brain are just as real.

6 The Internet in the Middle East and North Africa: A Cautious Start

Human Rights Watch

The Middle East and North Africa is one of the most under-represented areas of the world in terms of per capita Internet connectivity. In a region where nearly every government censors or punishes speech critical of the authorities, there can be little doubt that Internet growth has been slowed by the fear among those in power that democratizing Internet access will undermine state control over information. Saudi authorities stated bluntly during 1998 that the continuing delays in opening the Internet to public access were due to the search for a system by which authorities could block the flow of 'undesirable' information.

But after a slow start, the spread of the Internet in the region has accelerated over the last four years. Pro-Internet forces within governments and in the business, academic, and research communities, wishing to keep current and globally competitive, have pushed for easier access to online data and communications.

As of May 1999, every country in the region except Iraq and Libya had some form of international connectivity. Members in all of these countries except Syria could connect to the Internet in some fashion via local Internet Service Providers (ISPs).

At that time, there were an estimated 880,000 persons 'online' in the Middle East, including Israel but excluding North Africa, according to Nua, a Dublin-based information technology firm [. . .] In at least fourteen countries (Morocco, Algeria, Tunisia, Egypt, Israel, the Palestinian self-rule areas, Lebanon, Jordan, Kuwait, Bahrain, Qatar, Iran, Oman, and the United Arab Emirates) cybercafés afforded the public access to the Internet for an hourly fee.

The Arab press avidly follows Internet news, and conferences on the information revolution have become commonplace in the region. For example, Syria – which has yet to allow Internet access to the public – hosted the 'Second Al-Shaam International Conference on Information Technology' in Damascus in April 1999. Another indication of Internet growth is the publication in 1998 of a commercial yellow-pages, the *Middle East Internet Directory: A Comprehensive Guide to Middle East Web Sites* [. . .]

The following examples demonstrate how the Internet is empowering citizens and nongovernmental forces, and eroding government-imposed controls on the flow of information:

- Through e-mail and web sites, human rights organizations in Egypt, the Palestinian territories, and elsewhere disseminate information far more effectively than ever before, despite their modest resources and limited access to the local media.
- Arabic, English, and French newspapers that have been censored in Egypt, Algeria and Jordan have posted their banned stories online, where local and international readers can view them. Stories that newspapers declined to publish, due to political pressure or other factors,

have circulated widely on the Internet. When private dailies in Algeria went on strike in October 1998 to protest pressure from state-run printing presses, they published bulletins daily on the Web to mobilize support for their cause. Internet-based organizations like the Digital Freedom Network [. . .] have been making censored materials available online. During 1998, the DFN posted articles that had been banned by authorities in Egypt, Mauritania, Tunisia, and Turkey.

- Citizens of Arab countries have debated and conversed with Israelis in 'chat rooms' and other online forums at a time when it is difficult or impossible for them to have face-to-face contact, telephone conversations, and postal correspondence, due to travel restrictions and the absence of phone or mail links between most Arab countries and Israel.
- Moroccans can find copious information posted on the Web by the Polisario Front and others who challenge the official Moroccan line on the Western Sahara [. . .] Such information is either nonexistent or one-sided in the local news media, bookshops, and libraries.
- Algerians can visit numerous web sites mounted by Islamist groups that are banned and have no legal publications inside Algeria, including the Front Islamique du Salut [. . .]
- An Arab Gay and Lesbian web site [. . .] caters to people who, in many Arab countries, have few places to go to obtain information pertaining to their sexual orientation.
- The World Wide Web, with its online newspapers and radio and TV webcasting, has dramatically enhanced the diversity of news available to people in the Middle East. (So have the immensely popular Arabic-language satellite television stations.) The change is especially marked for those living in countries where foreign newspapers are either unavailable, expensive, or out-of-date when they arrive.

Most countries that have allowed Internet access have tolerated freer expression online than is permitted in the local news media. Kuwait, Morocco, Algeria, Egypt, Jordan, and Lebanon have all permitted relatively unfettered online speech for the thousands of users in each country, even as they enforce press laws against print periodicals that publish 'objectionable' material.

The extent of Internet connectivity in a country is determined by many factors in addition to government policies toward freedom of information and expression. These include the affordability to the public of computer equipment and of Internet and phone connections, and the state of a country's telecommunications infrastructure, including such attributes as the number of telephone lines per capita and the international connection's bandwidth.

In most countries of the world that have known rapid Internet growth, the public sector has played a role by, among other things, building 'backbone' telecommunications networks, providing initial funding, regulations, and standards, and by encouraging private investment and computer literacy. Thus, governments that favor development of the Internet must adopt affirmative policies, and not simply refrain from censorship and restricting access. Few governments in the Middle East and North Africa have embraced such an approach. The reasons include competing demands for scarce state resources, fear of losing control over information, and a desire to protect monopoly profits of state telecommunications companies. Chakib Lahrichi, president of the independent Internet Association in Morocco, stated that while the Moroccan government had no explicit policy of censoring or restricting access to the Internet, its growth had been stunted by unfair advantages enjoyed by the state-controlled telecommunications company Itissalat al-Maghrib in its competition with private service providers, along with the government's failure to educate the public about the Internet.

The local prices of computer equipment or services also deter Internet use in many countries of the region. Those prices may reflect government attitudes toward popularizing Internet use, insofar as those prices are set, taxed or subsidized by the government. Throughout the region, Internet and telephone costs are more expensive than they are, for example, in the United States. They are even more costly when prevailing median income levels are taken into consideration.

Another factor inhibiting Internet growth in the region is the continuing dominance of English-language materials. Although the volume of material in Arabic is growing and the Arabic software available for browsing the Web is improving, users who do not speak English remain at a disadvantage in their ability to access online resources. French speakers, such as many North Africans, have access to significantly more materials than do monolingual Arabic speakers.

Some social forces have voiced hostility to the Internet or to its availability to the public at large. Legislators in Kuwait, Israel and elsewhere have denounced the Internet as a threat to local culture, morals, or religious sensibilities. In Iran, the clerical monthly *Sobh* called for a ban on the Internet.

Governments and their supporters have sounded these themes to justify a go-slow, paternalistic approach to allowing public access to the Internet. For example, the spokesman of the Syrian Computer Society, which is chaired by the son of President Hafez al-Asad, was quoted as saying, 'Our problem is . . . we are a traditional society and we have to know if there is something that cannot fit with our society. We have to make it safe.'

Similar arguments have been made by Saudis. Saleh Abdulrahman al-'Adhel, the head of the King Abdul-Aziz City for Science and Technology (KACST), reportedly stated that the Internet presents 'an important service in relaying and distributing information but also has a negative side that conflicts with our faith and our Arab Muslim traditions.' The chair of the Saudi technology company Silkinet, explaining delays in allowing local Internet access, stated, 'Efforts are ongoing to provide the best of modern technology, while ensuring that this does not conflict with the traditions and culture of the region.'

While sites of Western origin still dominate the Internet, many advocates of Islam and Islamism have embraced the Internet as a means of projecting their message. Of all the region's political opposition forces, Islamists are among the most active online, thanks partly to a large number of computer-literate activists living in Europe and North America. At an international meeting in July 1998 in Cairo, Islamic organizations and personalities vowed to use the new information technologies to enhance the image of Islam. The Islamic Society of North America scheduled for May 1999 a conference devoted to using the Internet 'as a tool for effective presentation of knowledge on Islam.' In Iran, an official announced in June 1998 that the complete works of the late Ayatollah Ruhollah Khomeini would soon be available online in various languages. A computer institute in the city of Qom was preparing 2,000 Islamic instructional documents for presentation on the Web. The institute's director, Sheikh Ali Korani, defended the Internet thus: 'Many things have . . . a double nature and the Internet is one of them,' he explained. 'You can use it in different ways. The main thing is to use it for the good. And at present our clergy have not said that it is forbidden.'

No Middle East or North African government, not even the wariest, today wishes to be seen as anti-Internet. Syrian and Saudi officials assured their citizenry that the public would soon have access to the Internet, even as they invoked social conservatism to justify a gradual approach. The official *Tishrin* daily of January 27, 1997 reported that Internet subscriptions would be open to the Syrian public in six months, according to a dispatch the same day from United Press International. Twenty-eight months later, press reports from Syria continued to forecast that public Internet access would soon be available. In Saudi Arabia, *al-Jazira* newspaper reported on May 12, 1997 that King Fahd had agreed in principle to allow public access. It was not until January 1999 that local ISPs were allowed to serve ordinary citizens – almost five years after state institutions were first linked to the Internet. The long wait was necessary to 'finalize the technology needed to bar access to information which is contrary to our Islamic values and dangerous to our security,' explained the head of a group studying the issue at Riyadh's chamber of commerce and industry.

Regulators around the world argue that curbs on freedom of expression on the Internet are needed to protect children from harmful content, preserve religious values, safeguard local cultures, protect national security, thwart terrorists, and silence racists. In the Middle East and North Africa, few officials will admit that blocking unwelcome political information is among their objectives in imposing controls on the Internet. In the Persian Gulf countries, note scholars Grey E. Burkhart and Seymour E. Goodman, pornography is 'almost always first mentioned' when it comes to what the Internet 'may do to national, cultural and religious values.' Among other topics raised were 'proselytizing by other religions and the availability of un-Islamic information (such as how to commit suicide), the potential effects on women's roles in society, [and] dilution of local cultural norms.' These concerns, they write, surfaced 'in the press and in our interviews with government, business, academic, religious and private individuals.'

Saudi Arabia has gone furthest in defining the scope of what kind of data it wished to keep off the Internet: its Council of Ministers issued a decree requiring service providers to refrain from 'carrying out any activities violating the social, cultural, political, media, economic, and religious values of the Kingdom of Saudi Arabia.'

U.A.E. officials told Human Rights Watch that keeping out pornography was the only objective of the U.A.E.'s Internet censorship regime. Officials of other countries and corporate representatives of ISPs in the region have spoken more generally of protecting cultural values. For example, a representative of Teleyemen, Yemen's monopoly ISP, told Human Rights that the Teleyemen was under 'a general requirement' to 'limit access to information which is considered to be undesirable in terms of causing offence against social, religious, or cultural standards.' Like the U.A.E. and Saudi Arabia, Yemen filters what

users can access through the use of a proxy server and 'censorware.' A proxy server is a device that is interposed between users and the Internet; in response to user requests and according to the criteria it is programmed to follow, the proxy examines material requested by a user and either delivers it or blocks its delivery.

Pro-active approaches by governments

Governments have responded to the advent of the Internet pro-actively as well as by censorship and regulation. Every Middle East government has launched one or more web sites to get its voice heard amidst the din of alternative information sources in cyberspace. Saudi Arabia, Bahrain, Egypt, Iran, Israel, Kuwait, Morocco, Oman, Tunisia and the Palestinian Authority are among those that webcast state radio and/or television. Saudi Arabia has invested heavily in getting its message out, through an Internet presence (see, for example, the official site [. . .] and also through ownership by pro-government Saudis of influential Europe-based Arab newspapers, magazines, and broadcast media. One apparent impetus has been a wish to counter small London-based Saudi dissident groups, such as the Committee for the Defense of Legitimate Rights [. . .] and the Movement for Islamic Reform in Arabia [. . .] which had achieved a high profile through adroit use of fax machines and the Internet.

The government of Tunisia maintains several sites containing official information and links to pro-government media [. . .] Its public relations efforts were aided by a pro-Tunisian businessman in Paris who launched a web site that had an appearance likely to fool viewers into thinking they had accessed an Amnesty International web site about Tunisia. The site offered only favorable information about Tunisia's human rights record and nothing related to the findings of *Amnesty International.*

Numerous articles in the regional press have urged a more active 'Arab' presence on the Internet. An article in the official Damascus daily *Tishrin,* deploring the fact that Web-based resources dealing with the Arab–Israeli conflict were dominated by materials of Israeli origin, called for 'check[ing] all that is placed on the Internet on Syria and confront[ing] it by giving explanations or correcting distorted information.' The Syrian Arab News Agency launched a web site in 1998 to propagate official news and viewpoints at a time when local Internet access was unavailable to the Syrian public.

In a few countries, national and local governments are using the Internet to make it easier for citizens to consult official information and communicate with authorities. Several of Jordan's government ministries, as well as the General Intelligence Services, maintain their own sites and invite e-mail correspondence. Morocco, Egypt, and the Palestinian Authority have taken steps in this direction. However, few Arab governments have embarked on a systematic effort to put online information that would enhance informed political participation by their publics – materials such as legal and regulatory codes, draft legislation, official reports and statistics, transcripts of press conferences and parliamentary debates, court rulings, and economic data used to define budget allocations.

Part 3 A Changing World

Is globalization the same as Americanization? Most sociologists would answer 'no' to this question – American economic and cultural influence is apparent in many aspects of globalization, but globalization is being propelled forward by many other factors too. George Ritzer in Reading 7 offers an analysis on how one aspect of American global culture operates – the 'McDonaldization' of society. Everybody knows McDonald's: there are branches of McDonald's not only in different areas of London and New York but in Beijing, Moscow, Sydney, Mexico City and a diversity of other areas around the world. This success is not by chance. McDonald's has a systematic approach to the sale and production of fast foods that has been copied by many other corporations too.

In his contribution, Reading 8, Peter Drucker discusses the impact of the information revolution – the impact of computers and data processing on social and economic life. The internet, he argues, is likely radically to transform modern economies to as great a degree as the industrial revolution did two centuries ago. E-business will have no regard to geography any more. Every company, no matter how small, will become transnational in the sense that it has to compete in a marketplace where information is available to consumers about all of its competitors. The 'information revolution', Drucker suggests, may not be the best way of describing what is happening. The key change is towards a greater role for knowledge in economic production; the computer is merely the technological trigger for this transition.

Globalization, David Held and his colleagues made clear in Reading 9, is essentially about growing interdependence in world society. Our lives become increasingly influenced by events that might happen many thousands of miles away from us. The growth of modern communications has had an important impact upon globalizing processes. Electronic forms of communication, especially television and the internet, have made instantaneous communication across the world possible. As a result, information flows much more quickly than was ever the case previously. This affects economic life directly. The trading of information and money become crucial to the contemporary world economy.

The globalization of the world economy has seen the rise of major new companies coming to prominence on a global basis. The large corporations that used to dominate the world economy (such as General Motors, the US car manufacturer) have been to a large extent displaced by companies that specialize in areas of computers, information or finance. The biggest company in the world, Bill Gates's Microsoft, is no more than twenty years old.

7 The McDonaldization of Society

The Changing Character of Contemporary Social Life

George Ritzer

Ray Kroc, the genius behind the franchising of McDonald's restaurants, was a man with big ideas and grand ambitions. But even Kroc could not have anticipated the astounding impact of his creation. McDonald's is one of the most influential developments in twentieth-century America. Its reverberations extend far beyond the confines of the United States and the fast-food business. It has influenced a wide range of undertakings, indeed the way of life, of a significant portion of the world. And that impact is likely to expand at an accelerating rate.

However, this is *not* [a discussion of] McDonald's, or even the fast-food business. [. . .] Rather, McDonald's serves here as the major example, the 'paradigm,' of a wide-ranging process I call *McDonaldization*, that is,

> *the process by which the principles of the fast-food restaurant are coming to dominate more and more sectors of American society as well as of the rest of the world.*

As you will see, McDonaldization affects not only the restaurant business, but also education, work, health care, travel, leisure, dieting, politics, the family, and virtually every other aspect of society. McDonaldization has shown every sign of being an inexorable process by sweeping through seemingly impervious institutions and parts of the world.

McDonald's success is apparent: in 1993 its total sales reached $23.6 billion with profits of almost $1.1 billion. The average U.S. outlet has total sales of approximately $1.6 million in a year. Many entrepreneurs envy such sales and profits and seek to emulate McDonald's success. McDonald's, which first began franchising in 1955, opened its 12,000th outlet on March 22, 1991. By the end of 1993, McDonald's had almost 14,000 restaurants worldwide.

The impact of McDonaldization, which McDonald's has played a central role in spawning, has been manifested in many ways:

- The McDonald's model has been adopted not only by other budget-minded hamburger franchises such as Burger King and Wendy's, but also by a wide array of other low-priced fast-food businesses. Subway, begun in 1965 and now with nearly 10,000 outlets, is considered the fastest-growing of these businesses, which include Pizza Hut, Sbarro's, Taco Bell, Popeye's, and Charley Chan's. Sales in so-called 'quick service' restaurants in the United States rose to $81 billion by the end of 1993, almost a third of total sales for the entire food-service industry. In 1994, for the first time, sales in fast-food restaurants exceeded those in traditional full-service restaurants, and the gap between them is projected to grow.

- The McDonald's model has also been extended to 'casual dining,' that is, more 'upscale,' higher-priced restaurants with fuller menus. For example, Outback Steakhouse and Sizzler sell steaks, Fuddrucker's offers 'gourmet' burgers, Chi-Chi's and Chili's sell Mexican food, The Olive Garden proffers Italian food, and Red Lobster purveys . . . you guessed it.
- McDonald's is making increasing inroads around the world. In 1991, for the first time, McDonald's opened more restaurants abroad than in the United States. [. . .] McDonald's expects to build twice as many restaurants each year overseas than it does in the United States. By the end of 1993, over one-third of McDonald's restaurants were overseas; at the beginning of 1995, about half of McDonald's profits came from its overseas operations. McDonald's has even recently opened a restaurant in Mecca, Saudi Arabia.
- Other nations have developed their own variants of this American institution. The large number of fast-food croissanteries in Paris, a city whose love for fine cuisine might lead you to think it would prove immune to fast food, exemplifies this trend. India has a chain of fast-food restaurants, Nirula's, which sells mutton burgers (about 80 per cent of Indians are Hindus, who eat no beef) as well as local Indian cuisine. Perhaps the most unlikely spot for an indigenous fast food restaurant, war-ravaged Beirut of 1984, witnessed the opening of Juicy Burger, with a rainbow instead of golden arches and J.B. the Clown for Ronald McDonald. Its owners hoped that it would become the 'McDonald's of the Arab world.'
- Other countries with their own McDonaldized institutions have begun to export them to the United States. For example, the Body Shop is an ecologically sensitive British cosmetics chain with 893 shops [. . .] 120 of which were in the United States, with 40 more scheduled to open. [. . .] Furthermore, American firms are now opening copies of this British chain, such as The Limited, Inc.'s, Bath and Body Works.
- As indicated by the example of the Body Shop, other types of business are increasingly adapting the principles of the fast-food business to their needs. Said the vice chairman of Toys Я Us, 'We want to be thought of as a sort of McDonald's of toys.' The founder of Kidsports Fun and Fitness Club echoed this desire: 'I want to be the McDonald's of the kids' fun and fitness business.' Other chains with similar ambitions include Jiffy-Lube, AAMCO Transmissions, Midas Muffler & Brake Shops, Hair Plus, H & R Block, Pearle Vision Centers, Kampgrounds of America (KOA), Kinder Care (dubbed 'Kentucky Fried Children'), Jenny Craig, Home Depot, Barnes & Noble, Petstuff, and Wal-Mart (the nation's largest retailer with about 2,500 stores and almost $55 billion in sales.)
- Almost 10 per cent of America's stores are franchises, which currently account for 40 per cent of the nation's retail sales. It is estimated that by the turn of the century, about 25 per cent of the stores in the United States will be chains, by then accounting for a whopping two-thirds of retail business. About 80 per cent of McDonald's restaurants are franchises.

McDonald's as 'Americana'

McDonald's and its many clones have become ubiquitous and immediately recognizable symbols throughout the United States as well as much of the rest of the world. For example, when plans were afoot to raze Ray Kroc's first McDonald's restaurant, hundreds of letters poured into McDonald's headquarters, including the following:

Please don't tear it down! . . . Your company's name is a household word, not only in the United States of America, but all over the world. To destroy this major artifact of contemporary culture would, indeed, destroy part of the faith the people of the world have in your company.

In the end, the restaurant was not only saved, but turned into a museum! A McDonald's executive explained the move: 'McDonald's . . . is really a part of Americana.' Similarly, when Pizza Hut opened in Moscow in 1990, a Russian student said, 'It's a piece of America.' Reflecting on the growth of fast-food restaurants in Brazil, the president of Pepsico (of which Pizza Hut is part) of Brazil said that his nation 'is experiencing a passion for things American.'

McDonald's truly has come to occupy a central place in popular culture. It can be a big event when a new McDonald's opens in a small town. Said one Maryland high-school student at such an event, 'Nothing this exciting ever happens in Dale City.' Newspapers avidly cover developments in the fast-food business. Fast-food restaurants also play symbolic roles on television programs and in the movies. A skit on the television show *Saturday Night Live* satirized specialty chains by detailing the hardships of a franchise that sells nothing but Scotch tape. In the movie *Coming to America,* Eddie Murphy plays an African prince whose introduction to America includes a job at 'McDowell's,' a thinly disguised McDonald's. Michael Douglas, in *Falling Down,* vents his rage against the modern world in a fast-food restaurant dominated by mindless rules designed to frustrate customers. *Moscow on the Hudson* has Robin Williams, newly arrived from Russia, obtain a job at McDonald's. H. G. Wells, a central character in the movie *Time After Time,* finds himself transported to the modern world of a McDonald's, where he tries to order the tea he was accustomed to drinking in Victorian England. In *Sleeper,* Woody Allen awakens in the future only to encounter a McDonald's. Finally, *Tin Men* ends with the heroes driving off into a future represented by a huge golden arch looming in the distance.

Many people identify strongly with McDonald's; in fact to some it has become a sacred institution. At the opening of the McDonald's in Moscow, one journalist described the franchise as the 'ultimate icon of Americana,' while a worker spoke of it 'as if it were the Cathedral in Chartres . . . a place to experience 'celestial joy.'' Kowinski argues that shopping malls, which almost always encompass fast-food restaurants, are the modern 'cathedrals of consumption' to which people go to practice their 'consumer religion.' Similarly, a visit to another central element of McDonaldized society, Walt Disney World, has been described as 'the middle-class hajj, the compulsory visit to the sunbaked holy city.'

McDonald's has achieved its exalted position because virtually all Americans, and many others, have passed through its golden arches on innumerable occasions. Furthermore, most of us have been bombarded by commercials extolling McDonald's virtues, commercials that are tailored to different audiences. Some play to young children watching Saturday-morning cartoons. Others solicit young adults watching prime-time programs. Still others coax grandparents to take their grandchildren to McDonald's. In addition, these commercials change as the chain introduces new foods (such as breakfast burritos), creates new contests, and ties its products to things such as new motion pictures. These ever-present commercials, combined with the fact that people cannot drive very far without having a McDonald's pop into view, have served to embed McDonald's deep in popular consciousness. A poll of school-age children showed that 96 per cent of them could identify Ronald McDonald, second only to Santa Claus in name recognition.

Over the years, McDonald's has appealed to people in many ways. The restaurants themselves are depicted as spick-and-span, the food is said to be fresh and nutritious, the employees are shown to be young and eager, the managers appear gentle and caring, and the dining experience itself seems fun-filled. People are even led to believe that they contribute, at least indirectly, to charities such as the Ronald McDonald Houses for sick children.

The long arm of McDonaldization

McDonald's has strived to continually extend its reach within American society and beyond. As the company's chairman said, 'Our goal: to totally dominate the quick service restaurant industry worldwide. . . . I want McDonald's to be more than a leader. I want McDonald's to dominate.'

McDonald's began as a phenomenon of suburbs and medium sized towns, but in recent years it has moved into big cities and smaller towns, in the United States and beyond, that supposedly could not support such a restaurant. You can now find fast-food outlets in New York's Times Square as well as on the Champs Elysées in Paris. Soon after it opened in 1992, the McDonald's in Moscow sold almost 30,000 hamburgers a day and employed a staff of 1,200 young people working two to a cash register. McDonald's plans to open many more restaurants in the former Soviet Union and in the vast new territory in Eastern Europe that has now been laid bare to the invasion of fast-food restaurants. In early 1992, Beijing witnessed the opening of the world's largest McDonald's, with 700 seats, 29 cash registers, and nearly 1,000 employees. On its first day of business, it set a new one-day record for McDonald's by serving about 40,000 customers.

Small satellite, express, or remote outlets, opened in areas that cannot support full-scale fast-food restaurants, are expanding rapidly. They have begun to appear in small store fronts in large cities and in nontraditional settings such as department stores, service stations, and even schools. These satellites typically offer only limited menus and may rely on larger outlets for food storage and preparation. McDonald's is considering opening express outlets in museums, office buildings, and corporate cafeterias.

No longer content to dominate the strips that surround many college campuses, fast-food restaurants have moved onto many of those campuses. The first fast-food restaurant opened at the University of Cincinnati in 1973. Today, college cafeterias often look like shopping-mall food courts. In conjunction with a variety of 'branded partners' (for example, Pizza Hut and Subway), Marriott now supplies food to almost 500 colleges and universities. The apparent approval of college administrations puts fast-food restaurants in a position to further influence the younger generation.

More recently, another expansion has occurred: People no longer need to leave the highway to obtain fast food quickly and easily. Fast food is now available at convenient rest stops along the highway. After 'refueling,' we can proceed with our trip, which is likely to end in another community that has about the same density and mix of fast-food restaurants as the locale we left behind. Fast food is also increasingly available in service stations, hotels, railway stations, airports, and even on the trays for in-flight meals. The following advertisement appeared in the *Washington Post* and the *New York Times* a few years ago: 'Where else at 35,000 feet can you get a McDonald's meal like this for your kids? Only on United's Orlando flights.' Now, McDonald's so-called 'Friendly Skies Meals' are generally available to children on Delta flights. Similarly, in December 1994, Delta began to offer Blimpie sandwiches on its North American flights, and Continental now offers Subway sandwiches. How much longer before McDonaldized meals will be available on all flights everywhere by every carrier? In fact, on an increasing number of flights, prepackaged 'snacks' have already replaced hot main courses.

[. . .]

The dimensions of McDonaldization

Why has the McDonald's model proven so irresistible? Four alluring dimensions lie at the heart of the success of this model and, more generally, of McDonaldization. In short, McDonald's has succeeded because it offers consumers, workers, and managers efficiency, calculability, predictability, and control.

First, McDonald's offers *efficiency*, or the optimum method for getting from one point to another. For consumers, this means that McDonald's offers the best available way to get from being hungry to being full. [. . .] Other institutions, fashioned on the McDonald's model, offer similar efficiency in losing weight, lubricating cars, getting new glasses or contacts, or completing income-tax forms. In a society where both parents are likely to work, or where there may be only a single parent, efficiently satisfying the hunger and many other needs of people is very attractive. In a society where people rush, usually by car, from one spot to another, the efficiency of a fast-food meal, perhaps even without leaving their cars by wending their way along the drive-through lane, often proves impossible to resist. The fast-food model offers people, or at least appears to offer them, an efficient method for satisfying many needs.

Like their customers, workers in McDonaldized systems function efficiently. They are trained to work this way by managers, who watch over them closely to make sure they do. Organizational rules and regulations also help ensure highly efficient work.

Second, McDonald's offers *calculability*, or an emphasis on the quantitative aspects of products sold (portion size, cost) and service offered (the time it takes to get the product). Quantity has become equivalent quality; a lot of something, or the quick delivery of it, means it must be good. As two observers of contemporary American culture put it, 'As a culture, we tend to believe deeply that in general "bigger is better."' Thus, people order the *Quarter Pounder,* the *Big* Mac, the *large* fries. More recently, there is the lure of the 'double this' (for instance, Burger King's 'Double Whopper With Cheese') and the 'triple that.' People can quantify these things and feel that they are getting a lot of food for what appears to be a nominal sum of money. This calculation does not take into account an important point: the extraordinary profitability of fast-food outlets and other chains, which indicates that the owners, not the consumers, get the best deal.

People also tend to calculate how much time it will take to drive to McDonald's, be served the food, eat it, and return home; then, they compare that interval to the time required to prepare food at home They often conclude, rightly or wrongly, that a trip to the fast-food restaurant will take less time than eating at home. This sort of calculation particularly supports home-delivery franchises such as Domino's, as well as other chains that emphasize time saving. A notable example of time saving in another sort of chain is Lens Crafters, which promises people, 'Glasses fast, glasses in one hour.'

Some McDonaldized institutions combine the emphases on time and money. Domino's promises pizza delivery in half an hour, or the pizza is free. Pizza Hut will serve a personal pan pizza in five minutes, or it, too, will be free.

Workers at McDonaldized systems also tend to emphasize the quantitative rather than the qualitative aspects of their work. Since the quality of the work is allowed to vary little, workers focus on such things as how quickly tasks can be accomplished. In a situation analogous to that of the customer, workers are expected to do a lot of work, very quickly, for low pay.

Third, McDonald's offers *predictability*, the assurance that their products and services will be the same over time and in all locales. The Egg McMuffin in New York will be, for all intents and purposes, identical to those in Chicago and Los Angeles. Also, those eaten next week or next year will be identical to those eaten today. There is great comfort in knowing that McDonald's offers no surprises. People know that the next Egg McMuffin they eat will taste about the same as the others they have eaten; it will not be awful, but it will not be exceptionally delicious, either. The success of the McDonald's model suggests that many people have come to prefer a world in which there are few surprises.

The workers in McDonaldized systems also behave in predictable ways. They follow corporate rules as well as the dictates of their managers. In many cases, not only what they do, but also what they say, is highly predictable. McDonaldized organizations often have scripts that employees are supposed to memorize and follow whenever the occasion arises. This scripted behavior helps create highly predictable interactions between workers and customers. While customers do not follow scripts, they tend to develop simple recipes for dealing with the employees of McDonaldized systems. As Robin Leidner argues,

McDonald's pioneered the routinization of interactive service work and remains an exemplar of extreme standardization. Innovation is not discouraged . . . at least among managers and franchisees. Ironically, though, 'the object is to look for new, innovative ways to create an experience that is exactly the same no matter what McDonald's you walk into, no matter where it is in the world.'

Fourth, *control*, specially through the *substitution of nonhuman for human technology*, is exerted over the people who enter the world of McDonald's. A *human technology* (a screwdriver, for example) is controlled by people; a *nonhuman technology* (the assembly line, for instance) controls people. The people who eat in fast-food restaurants are controlled, albeit (usually) subtly. Lines, limited menus, few options, and uncomfortable seats all lead diners to do what management wishes them to do – eat quickly and leave. Further, the drive-through (in some cases walk-through) window leads diners to leave before they eat. In the Domino's model customers never come in the first place.

The people who work in McDonaldized organizations are also controlled to a high degree, usually more blatantly and directly than customers. They are trained to do a limited number of things in precisely the way they are told to do them. The technologies used and the way the organization is set up reinforce this control. Managers and inspectors make sure that workers toe the line.

McDonald's also controls employees by threatening to use, and ultimately using, nonhuman technology to replace human workers. No matter how well they are programmed and controlled, workers can foul up the system's operation. A slow worker can make the preparation and delivery of a Big Mac inefficient. A worker who refuses to follow the rules might leave the pickles or special sauce off a hamburger, thereby making for unpredictability. And a distracted worker can put too few fries in the box, making an order of large fries seem skimpy. For these and other reasons, McDonald's has felt compelled to steadily replace human beings with nonhuman technologies, such as the soft-drink dispenser that shuts itself off when the glass is full, the french-fry machine that rings and lifts itself out of the oil when the fries are crisp, the preprogrammed cash register that eliminates the need for the cashier to calculate prices and amounts, and, perhaps at some future time, the robot capable of making hamburgers. This technology increases the corporation's control over workers. Thus, McDonald's can assure customers that their employees and service will be consistent.

[. . .]

8 Beyond the Information Revolution

Peter F. Drucker

The truly revolutionary impact of the Information Revolution is just beginning to be felt. But it is not 'information' that fuels this impact. It is not 'artificial intelligence.' It is not the effect of computers and data processing on decision-making, policymaking, or strategy. It is something that practically no one foresaw or, indeed, even talked about ten or fifteen years ago: *e-commerce* – that is, the explosive emergence of the Internet as a major, perhaps eventually *the* major, world-wide distribution channel for goods, for services, and, surprisingly, for managerial and professional jobs. This is profoundly changing economies, markets, and industry structures; products and services and their flow; consumer segmentation, consumer values, and consumer behavior; jobs and labor markets. But the impact may be even greater on societies and politics and, above all, on the way we see the world and ourselves in it.

At the same time, new and unexpected industries will no doubt emerge, and fast. One is already here: biotechnology. And another: fish farming. Within the next fifty years fish farming may change us from hunters and gatherers on the seas into 'marine pastoralists' – just as a similar innovation some 10,000 years ago changed our ancestors from hunters and gatherers on the land into agriculturists and pastoralists.

It is likely that other new technologies will appear suddenly, leading to major new industries. What they may be is impossible even to guess at. But it is highly probable – indeed, nearly certain – that they will emerge, and fairly soon. And it is nearly certain that few of them – and few industries based on them – will come out of

computer and information technology. Like biotechnology and fish farming, each will emerge from its own unique and unexpected technology.

Of course, these are only predictions. But they are made on the assumption that the Information Revolution will evolve as several earlier technology-based 'revolutions' have evolved over the past 500 years, since Gutenberg's printing revolution, around 1455. In particular the assumption is that the Information Revolution will be like the Industrial Revolution of the late eighteenth and early nineteenth centuries. And that is indeed exactly how the Information Revolution has been during its first fifty years.

[. . .]

The meaning of e-commerce

E-commerce is to the Information Revolution what the railroad was to the Industrial Revolution – a totally new, totally unprecedented, totally unexpected development. And like the railroad 170 years ago, e-commerce is creating a new and distinct boom, rapidly changing the economy, society, and politics.

One example: A mid-sized company in America's industrial Midwest, founded in the 1920s and now run by the grandchildren of the founder, used to have some 60 per cent of the market in inexpensive dinnerware for fast-food eateries, school and office cafeterias, and hospitals within a hundred-mile radius of its factory. China is heavy and breaks easily, so cheap china is traditionally sold within a small area. Almost overnight this company lost more than half of its market. One of its customers, a hospital cafeteria where someone went 'surfing' on the Internet, discovered a European manufacturer that offered china of apparently better quality at a lower price and shipped cheaply by air. Within a few months the main customers in the area shifted to the European supplier. Few of them, it seems, realize – let alone care – that the stuff comes from Europe.

In the new mental geography created by the railroad, humanity mastered distance. In the mental geography of e-commerce, distance has been eliminated. There is only one economy and only one market.

One consequence of this is that every business must become globally competitive, even if it manufactures or sells only within a local or regional market. The competition is not local anymore – in fact, it knows no boundaries. Every company has to become transnational in the way it is run. Yet the traditional multinational may well become obsolete. It manufactures and distributes in a number of distinct geographies, in which it is a *local* company. But in e-commerce there are neither local companies nor distinct geographies. Where to manufacture, where to sell, and how to sell will remain important business decisions. But in another twenty years they may no longer determine what a company does, how it does it, and where it does it.

At the same time, it is not yet clear what kinds of goods and services will be bought and sold through e-commerce and what kinds will turn out to be unsuitable for it. This has been true whenever a new distribution channel has arisen. Why, for instance, did the railroad change both the mental and the economic geography of the West, whereas the steamboat – with its equal impact on world trade and passenger traffic – did neither? Why was there no 'steamboat boom'?

Equally unclear has been the impact of more recent changes in distribution channels – in the shift, for instance, from the local grocery store to the supermarket, from the individual supermarket to the supermarket chain, and from the supermarket chain to Wal-Mart and other discount chains. It is already clear that the shift to e-commerce will be just as eclectic and unexpected.

Here are a few examples. Twenty-five years ago it was generally believed that within a few decades the printed word would be dispatched electronically to individual subscribers' computer screens. Subscribers would then either read text on their computer screens or download it and print it out. This was the assumption that underlay the CD-ROM. Thus any number of newspapers and magazines, by no means only in the United States, established themselves online; few, so far, have become gold mines. But anyone who twenty years ago predicted the business of Amazon.com and barnesandnoble.com – that is, that books would be sold on the Internet but delivered in their heavy, printed form – would have been laughed off the podium. Yet Amazon.com and barnesandnoble.com are in exactly that business, and they are in it worldwide. [. . .]

Another example: Ten years ago one of the world's leading automobile companies made a thorough study of the expected impact on automobile sales of the then emerging Internet. It concluded that the Internet would become a major distribution channel for used cars, but that customers would still want to see new cars, to touch them, to test-drive them. In actuality, at least so far, most used cars are still being bought not over the Internet but in a dealer's lot. However, as many as half of all new cars sold (excluding luxury cars) may now actually be 'bought' over the Internet. Dealers only deliver cars that customers have chosen well before they enter the dealership.

[. . .]

The knowledge worker

[In the new economy] I am convinced that a drastic change in the social mind-set is required – just as leadership in the industrial economy after the railroad required the drastic change from 'tradesman' to 'technologist' or 'engineer.'

What we call the Information Revolution is actually a Knowledge Revolution. What has made it possible to routinize processes is not machinery; the computer is only the trigger. Software is the reorganization of traditional work, based on centuries of experience, through the application of knowledge and especially of systematic, logical analysis. The key is not electronics; it is cognitive science. This means that the key to maintaining leadership in the economy and the technology that are about to emerge is likely to be the social position of knowledge professionals and social acceptance of their values. For them to remain traditional 'employees' and be treated as such would be tantamount to England's treating its technologists as tradesmen – and likely to have similar consequences.

Today, however, we are trying to straddle the fence – to maintain the traditional mind-set, in which capital is the key resource and the financier is the boss, while bribing knowledge workers to be content to remain employees by giving them bonuses and stock options. But this, if it can work at all, can work only as long as the emerging industries enjoy a stock-market boom, as the Internet companies have been doing. The next major industries are likely to behave far more like traditional industries – that is, to grow slowly, painfully, laboriously.

The early industries of the Industrial Revolution – cotton textiles, iron, the railroads – were boom industries that created millionaires overnight, like Balzac's venture bankers and like Dickens's ironmaster, who in a few years grew from a lowly domestic servant into a 'captain of industry.' The industries that emerged after 1830 also created millionaires. But they took twenty years to do so, and it was twenty years of hard work, of struggle, of disappointments and failures, of thrift. This is likely to be true of the industries that will emerge from now on. It is already true of biotechnology.

Bribing the knowledge workers on whom these industries depend will therefore simply not work. The key knowledge workers in these businesses will surely continue to expect to share financially in the fruits of their labor. But the financial fruits are likely to take much longer to ripen, if they ripen at all. And then, probably within ten years or so, running a business with (short-term) 'shareholder value' as its first – if not its only – goal and justification will have become counterproductive. Increasingly, performance in these new knowledge-based industries will come to depend on running the institution so as to attract, hold, and motivate knowledge workers. When this can no longer be done by satisfying knowledge workers' greed, as we are now trying to do, it will have to be done by satisfying their values, and by giving them social recognition and social power. It will have to be done by turning them from subordinates into fellow executives, and from employees, however well paid, into partners.

9 Globalization

David Held, Anthony McGrew,
David Goldblatt and Jonathan Perraton

What is globalization?

[. . .]

While everybody talks about globalization few
people have a clear understanding of it. The 'big
idea' of the late twentieth century is in danger
of turning into the cliché of our times. Can we
give it precise meaning and content, or should
globalization be consigned to the dustbin of
history?

[. . .]

[Globalization is made up] of links across the
world's major regions and across many domains
of activity. It is not a single process, but involves
four distinct types of change:

* It stretches social, political and economic
  activities across political frontiers, regions and
  continents.
* It intensifies our dependence on each other,
  as flows of trade, investment, finance, migration and culture increase.
* It speeds up the world. New systems of transport and communication mean that ideas,
  goods, information, capital, and people move
  more quickly.
* It means that distant events have a deeper
  impact on our lives. Even the most local
  developments may come to have enormous
  global consequences. The boundaries between
  domestic matters and global affairs can become
  increasingly blurred.

In short, globalization is about the connections
between different regions of the world – from
the cultural to the criminal, the financial to the
environmental – and the ways in which they
change and increase over time.

[. . .] globalization, in this sense, has been going
on for centuries. But [. . .] globalization today is
genuinely different both in scale and in nature. It
does not signal the end of the nation-state or the
death of politics. But it does mean that politics is
no longer, and can no longer be, based simply
on nation-states. We cannot predict the future or
know what the final outcome of globalization will
be. But we can now define the central challenge
of the global age – rethinking our values, institutions and identities so that politics can remain an
effective vehicle for human aspirations and needs.

First, we need to understand what is distinctive
about globalization today. We can only do this
by studying the forms which it has taken throughout history in all areas of activity – the environment, the economy, politics and culture. And the
thread which ties these things together is people,
and so it is with the movements of people that
we must start.

[. . .]

The fate of national cultures

[. . .] the globalization of culture has a long
history. The great world religions showed how
ideas and beliefs can cross the continents and
transform societies. No less important were the
great pre-modern empires which, in the absence

of direct military and political control, held their domains together through a common culture of the ruling classes. For long periods of human history, there have only been these global cultures and a vast array of fragmented local cultures. Little stood between the court and the village until the invention of nation-states in the eighteenth century created a powerful new cultural identity that lay between these two extremes.

[. . .]

[However,] the sheer scale, intensity, speed and volume of global cultural communications today is unsurpassed. The accelerating diffusion of radio, television, the Internet, satellite and digital technologies has made instant communication possible. Many national controls over information have become ineffective. Through radio, film, television and the Internet, people everywhere are exposed to the values of other cultures as never before. Nothing, not even the fact that we all speak different languages, can stop the flow of ideas and cultures. The English language is becoming so dominant that it provides a linguistic infrastructure as powerful as any technological system for transmitting ideas and cultures.

Beyond its scale, what is striking about today's cultural globalization is that it is driven by companies, not countries. Corporations have replaced states and theocracies as the central producers and distributors of cultural globalization. Private international institutions are not new but their mass impact is. News agencies and publishing houses in previous eras had a much more limited impact on local and national cultures than the consumer goods and cultural products of global corporations today.

Though the vast majority of these cultural products come from the USA, this is not a simple case of 'cultural imperialism'. One of the surprising features of our global age is how robust national and local cultures have proved to be. National institutions remain central to public life while national audiences constantly reinterpret foreign products in novel ways.

These new communication technologies threaten states which pursue rigid closed-door policies on information and culture. For example, China sought to restrict access to the Internet but found this extremely difficult to achieve. In addition, it is likely that the conduct of economic life everywhere will be transformed by the new technologies. The central question is the future impact of cultural flows on our sense of personal identity and national identity. Two competing forces are in evidence: the growth of multicultural politics almost everywhere and, in part as a reaction to this, the assertion of fundamentalist identities (religious, nationalist and ethnic). While the balance between these two forces remains highly uncertain, it is clear that only a more open, cosmopolitan outlook can ultimately accommodate itself to a more global era.

[. . .]

The global economy

[. . .] when most people think about globalization, they think of economics. So what is happening to trade, production and finance? How do they relate to each other – and how are they changing our world?

Trade

The world has never been more open to trade than it is today. The dismantling of trade barriers has allowed global markets to emerge for many goods and services. The major trading blocs created in Europe, North America and Asia–Pacific are not regional fortresses but remain open to competition from the rest of the world.

[. . .]

Production

Global exports may be more important than ever, but transnational production is now worth even more. To sell to another country, increasingly you have to move there; this is the main way to sell goods and services abroad. The multinational corporation has taken economic interdependence to new levels.

Today, 53,000 multinational corporations, with 450,000 foreign subsidiaries, sell $9.5 trillion of goods and services across the globe every year. Multinational corporations account for at least 20 per cent of world production and 70 per cent of world trade. A quarter to a third of world trade is intra-firm trade between branches of multinationals.

[...]

How powerful are multinational corporations today? They have developed transnational networks which allow them to take advantage of differences in national cost conditions and regulations. Domestic economies are also suffering because multinational companies are becoming genuinely more multinational as they find it increasingly difficult to win competitive advantage from their home base alone. In the past, even large multinational corporations like Sony retained many national characteristics. Technological advantages were largely realised in their country of origin and were shared among various national stakeholders. This is less and less possible due to the significant growth of transnational corporate alliances, mergers and acquisitions, such as Chrysler-Daimler, and the tendency of multinationals to invest in foreign innovation clusters.

[...]

Finance

Alongside multinationals the power of global finance has been most central to economic globalization.

World financial flows are so large that the numbers are overwhelming. $1.5 trillion is traded every day on the foreign exchange markets – as a few thousand traders seem to determine the economic fate of nations. Most countries today are incorporated into global financial markets, but the nature of their access to these markets is highly uneven.

When foreign exchange markets turn over 60 times the value of world trade, this is not just a staggering increase; it is a different type of activity altogether. The instantaneous transactions of the 24 hour global markets are largely speculative, where once most market activity financed trade and long term investment.

[...]

Governing globalization

Contemporary globalization represents the beginning of a new epoch in human affairs. In transforming societies and world order it is having as profound an impact as the industrial revolution and the global empires of the nineteenth century.

We have seen that globalization is transforming our world, but in complex, multifaceted and uneven ways. Although globalization has a long history, it is today genuinely different both in scale and in form from what has gone before.

Every new epoch creates new winners and losers. This one will be no different. Globalization to date has already both widened the gap between the richest and poorest countries, and further increased divisions within, and across, societies. It has inevitably become increasingly contested and politicised.

National governments – sandwiched between global forces and local demands – are having to reconsider their roles and functions. But to say simply that states have lost power distorts what is happening – as does any suggestion that nothing much has changed. The real picture is much more complex. States today are at least as powerful, if not more so, than their predecessors on many fundamental measures of power – from the capacity to raise taxes to the ability to hurl force at enemies. But the demands on states have grown very rapidly as well. They must often work together to pursue the public good – to prevent recession or to protect the environment.

[...]

The challenge of globalization today is ultimately political. Just as the industrial revolution created new types of class politics, globalization demands that we re-form our existing territorially defined democratic institutions and practices so that politics can continue to address human aspirations and needs.

This means rethinking politics. We need to take our established ideas about political equality, social justice, and liberty and refashion these into a coherent political project robust enough for a world where power is exercised on a transnational scale, and where risks are shared by peoples across the world. And we need to think about what institutions will allow us to tackle these global problems whilst responding to the aspirations of the people they are meant to serve.

[. . .]

Globalization is not bringing about the death of politics. It is reilluminating and reinvigorating the contemporary political terrain.

Part 4

Social Interaction and Everyday Life

Erving Goffman was the pre-eminent analyst of day-to-day social interaction – above all of interaction in circumstances of 'co-presence': face-to-face social engagements between individuals present in a single physical setting. Investigating co-present interaction, Goffman points out, is distinct from the study of social groups or collectivities as such (Reading 10). The analysis of interaction in situations of co-presence can be understood as a series of *encounters* into which individuals enter in the course of their daily activities. An encounter is a unit of focused interaction, in which a number of individuals directly address each other in some way. Unfocused interaction, by contrast, refers to those forms of mutual communication which occur simply because people are in the same setting – a room, a hallway, a street – as one another.

Civil inattention, discussed by Goffman in Reading 11, is an important feature of unfocused interaction between strangers. When people pass one another in the street, or experience the multitude of fleeting social contacts which make up much of city life, they acknowledge each other in subtle, yet socially very important ways. Civil inattention, Goffman argues, is a fundamental part of orderly life in public social environments. The manipulation of the gaze – how indi-

viduals look at others, and for how long – he shows to be an essential, and again extraordinarily complex, feature of everyday social interaction.

In Reading 12, Christian Heath discusses the importance of embarrassment in social interaction. Embarrassment is the emotion which results when aspects of our encounters with others go wrong – especially when an impression an individual is seeking to sustain about his or her identity comes into question. Embarrassment is essentially a form of shame about the self. Heath looks at how doctors and patients collaborate to minimize embarrassment or shame during intimate medical examinations. Someone who undresses in front of a doctor might readily feel embarrassed, but the doctor and patient tend to work at minimizing this intrusive emotion.

Much social interaction consists of routines and everyday rituals. Repetition and habit form a key part of established relationships, as they do of many other contexts of social life. In Reading 13 Michael Young investigates why habitual actions figure so prominently in our day-to-day activities. As in so many areas of sociology, what appears 'obvious', the significance of the 'force of habit', turns out when subjected to scrutiny to be puzzling.

10 Social Interaction and Everyday Life

Erving Goffman

The study of every unit of social organization must eventually lead to an analysis of the interaction of its elements. The analytical distinction between units of organization and processes of interaction is, therefore, not destined to divide up our work for us. A division of labour seems more likely to come from distinguishing among types of units, among types of elements, or among types of processes.

Sociologists have traditionally studied face-to-face interaction as part of the area of 'collective behaviour'; the units of social organization involved are those that can form by virtue of a breakdown in ordinary social intercourse: crowds, mobs, panics, riots. The other aspect of the problem of face-to-face interaction – the units of organization in which orderly and uneventful face-to-face interaction occurs – has been neglected until recently, although there is some early work on classroom interaction, topics of conversation, committee meetings and public assemblies.

Instead of dividing face-to-face interaction into the eventful and the routine, I propose a different division – into *unfocused interaction* and *focused interaction*. Unfocused interaction consists of those interpersonal communications that result solely by virtue of persons being in one another's presence, as when two strangers across the room from each other check up on each other's clothing, posture and general manner, while each modifies his own demeanour because he himself is under observation. Focused interaction occurs when people effectively agree to sustain for a time a single focus of cognitive and visual attention, as in a conversation, a board game or a joint task

sustained by a close face-to-face circle of contributors. Those sustaining together a single focus of attention will, of course, engage one another in unfocused interaction too. They will not do so in their capacity as participants in the focused activity, however, and persons present who are not in the focused activity will equally participate in this unfocused interaction.

[. . .] I call the natural unit of social organization in which focused interaction occurs a *focused gathering*, or an *encounter*, or a *situated activity system*. I assume that instances of this natural unit have enough in common to make it worthwhile to study them as a type [. . .]

Focused gatherings and groups do share some properties and even some that are requisites. If persons are to come together into a focused gathering and stay for a time, then certain 'system problems' will have to be solved: the participants will have to submit to rules of recruitment, to limits on overt hostility and to some division of labour. Such requisites are also found in social groups. Now if social groups and focused gatherings both exhibit the same set of properties, what is the use of distinguishing between these two units of social organization? And would not this distinction become especially unnecessary when all the members of the group are the only participants in the gathering?

Paradoxically, the easier it is to find similarities between these two units, the more mischief may be caused by not distinguishing between them. Let us address the problem, then: what is the difference between a group and a focused gathering?

A social group may be defined as a special type of social organization. Its elements are individuals: they perceive the organization as a distinct collective unit, a social entity, apart from the particular relationships the participants may have to one another; they perceive themselves as members who belong, identifying with the organization and receiving moral support from doing so; they sustain a sense of hostility to outgroups. A symbolization of the reality of the group and one's relation to it is also involved.

Small groups, according to this conception of groups, are distinguished by what their size makes possible (although not necessary), such as extensive personal knowledge of one another by the members, wide consensus and reliance on informal role differentiation. Small groups themselves – let me temporarily call them 'little groups' to distinguish them from all the other phenomena studied under the title of small-group research – differ in the degree to which they are formally or informally organized; long-standing or short-lived; multi-bonded or segmental; relatively independent, as in the case of some families and gangs, or pinned within a well-bounded organizational structure, as in the case of army platoons or office cliques.

Social groups, whether big or little, possess some general organizational properties. These properties include regulation of entering and leaving; capacity for collective action; division of labour, including leadership roles; socialization function, whether primary or adult; a means of satisfying personal ends; and latent and manifest social function in the environing society. These same properties, however, are also found in many other forms of social organization, such as a social relationship binding two persons, a network of relationships interlocking a set of friends, a complex organization or a set of businessmen or gamesters who abide by ground rules while openly concerned only with defeating the designs of their co-participants. It is possible, of course, to call any social relationship between two individuals a two-person group, but I think this is unwise. A group that is just beginning or dying may have only two members, but I feel that the conceptual framework with which this ill-manned group is to be studied ought to differ from the framework used in studying the many-sidedness of the social relationship between these two individuals. And to call any two individuals a 'two-person group' solely because there is a social relationship between them is to slight what is characteristic of groups and to fail to explore what is uniquely characteristic of relationships. [. . .]

Given these definitions, differences between groups and encounters become apparent. Some of the properties that are important to focused gatherings or encounters, taken as a class, seem much less important to little groups, taken as a class. Examples of such properties include embarrassment, maintenance of poise, capacity for non-distractive verbal communication, adherence to a code regarding giving up and taking over the speaker role and allocation of spatial position. Furthermore, a crucial attribute of focused gatherings – the participants' maintenance of continuous engrossment in the official focus of activity – is not a property of social groups in general, for most groups, unlike encounters, continue to exist apart from the occasions when members are physically together. A coming-together can be merely a phase of group life; a falling-away, on the other hand, is the end of a particular encounter, even when the same pattern of interaction and the same participants appear at a future meeting. Finally, there are many gatherings – for example, a set of strangers playing poker in a casino – where an extremely full array of interaction processes occurs with only the slightest development of a sense of group. All these qualifications can be made even though data for the study of little groups and for the study of focused gatherings are likely to be drawn from the same social occasion. In the same way, these qualifications can be made even though any social group can be partly described in terms of the character of the gatherings its members maintain together, just as any gathering can be described in terms of the overlapping group affiliations of its participants.

In the life of many little groups, occasions regularly arise when all the members and only the members come together and jointly sustain a situated activity system or encounter: they hold a meeting, play a game, discuss a movie, or take a cigarette break together. To call these gatherings 'meetings of the group' can easily entrap one into thinking that one is studying the group directly. Actually, these are meetings of persons who are members of a group and, even though the meeting may have been called because of issues faced by the group, the initial data concern participants in a meeting, not members of a group.

It is true that on such occasions there is likely to be a correspondence between the realm of group life and the realm of face-to-face interaction processes. For example, leadership of a little group may be expressed during gatherings of members by the question of who is chairman, or who talks the most, or who is most frequently addressed. It is also likely that the leadership demonstrated in the gathering will both influence, and be influenced by, the leadership in the group. But group leadership is not made up exclusively of an 'averaging' of positions assumed during various gatherings. In fact, the group may face circumstances in which its leader is careful to let others take leadership during a meeting, his capacity to lead the group resting upon the tactful way in which he plays a minor role during gatherings of group members. The group leader can do this because 'taking the chair' is intrinsically a possibility of gatherings, not groups.

Similarly, the factions that occur in a little group may coincide with the coalitions formed during gatherings of group members. We know, however, that such 'open' expression of structural cleavage can be seen as dangerous to the group and destructive of the opportunity of accomplishing business during the gathering, so that this congruence will often specifically be avoided. Coalitions during the gathering will then cross-cut factions in the group.

Further, even when all the members of a group are the only participants in a gathering, and the gathering has been called in order to transact business pertaining to the group, we will inevitably find that the persons present are also members of other social groups and that each of these groups can claim only a subset – moreover, a different subset – of those present. Some of the positions in the gathering are likely to be allocated on the basis of these divisive group affiliations. Of course, other positions in the gathering are likely to be allocated on the basis of factors other than group affiliation, for example, recognized experience, command of language, priority of appearance in the meeting-place or age.

Finally, while the morale of the group and the solidarity of its members may increase with an increasing number of meetings, there are strong groups that rarely have focused gatherings containing all their members and weak groups that have many.

There are issues apart from those that arise because of the difference between being a member of a group and being a participant in a gathering. Some of the properties that clearly belong both to groups and to gatherings turn out upon close examination to mean two different ranges of things, in part because of a difference in level of abstraction employed in the two cases. For example, one form of leadership that can be extremely important in gatherings is the maintenance of communication ground rules, i.e. 'order'; this aspect of leadership does not seem to have the same importance in group analysis, however. Similarly, tension management is a requirement in both groups and gatherings, but what is managed in each case seems different. Tension in encounters arises when the official focus of attention is threatened by distractions of various kinds; this state of uneasiness is managed by tactful acts, such as the open expression in a usable way of what is distracting attention. There will be circumstances, then, when tactfully expressed ranklings may ease interaction in a gathering while destroying the group to which the participants happen to belong.

The preceding arguments are meant to suggest that a frequent empirical congruence between the structure of a group and the structure of a gathering of its members does not imply any invariant analytical relation between the two realms. The concepts tailored to the study of groups and those tailored to the study of encounters may be analytically related, but these relations are by no means self-evident.

I want to say, finally, that distinguishing between little groups and focused gatherings allows one not only to see that a gathering may itself generate a fleeting little group but also to examine the relation between this group and long-standing groups from which the participants in the encounter may derive.

When all and only the members of a little group come together in a gathering, the effect of the gathering, depending on the outcome of its activity, will be to strengthen or weaken somewhat the little group. The potentiality of the encounter for generating its own group seems to be expended in what it does for and to the long-standing group. Often, there seems to be no chance for the fleeting circle of solidarity to develop much solidity of its own, for it fits too well in a pattern already established. However, when individuals come into a gathering who are not also members of the same little group, and especially if they are strangers possessing no prior relationships to one another, then the group formation that is fostered by the encounter will stand out as a contrast to all other groups of which the encounter's participants are members. It is under these circumstances – when the participants in a gathering have not been together in a group before and are not likely to be so again – that the locally generated group seems to cast its strongest shadow. It is under these circumstances, too, that the fates of these two units of organization seem most closely tied together, the effectiveness of the gathering rather directly affecting the solidarity of the group.

Paradoxically, then, if a gathering, on its own, is to generate a group and have group-formation mark the gathering as a memorable event, then a stranger or two may have to be invited – and this is sometimes carefully done on sociable occasions. These persons anchor the group-formation that occurs, preventing it from drifting back into the relationships and groups that existed previously among the participants.

11 The Structure of Face Engagements

Erving Goffman

Civil inattention

When persons are mutually present and not involved together in conversation or other focused interaction, it is possible for one person to stare openly and fixedly at others, gleaning what he can about them while frankly expressing on his face his response to what he sees – for example, the 'hate stare' that a Southern white sometimes gratuitously gives to Negroes walking past him. It is also possible for one person to treat others as if they were not there at all, as objects not worthy of a glance, let alone close scrutiny. Moreover, it is possible for the individual, by his staring or his 'not seeing', to alter his own appearance hardly at all in consequence of the presence of the others. Here we have 'non-person' treatment [. . .]

Currently, in our society, this kind of treatment is to be contrasted with the kind generally felt to be more proper in most situations, which will here be called 'civil inattention'. What seems to be involved is that one gives to another enough visual notice to demonstrate that one appreciates that the other is present (and that one admits openly to having seen him), while at the next moment withdrawing one's attention from him so as to express that he does not constitute a target of special curiosity or design.

In performing this courtesy the eyes of the looker may pass over the eyes of the other, but no 'recognition' is typically allowed. Where the courtesy is performed between two persons passing on the street, civil inattention may take the special form of eyeing the other up to approx-imately eight feet, during which time sides of the street are apportioned by gesture, and then casting the eyes down as the other passes – a kind of dimming of lights. In any case, we have here what is perhaps the slightest of interpersonal rituals, yet one that constantly regulates the social intercourse of persons in our society.

By according civil inattention, the individual implies that he has no reason to suspect the intentions of the others present and no reason to fear the others, be hostile to them or wish to avoid them. (At the same time, in extending this courtesy he automatically opens himself up to a like treatment from others present.) This demonstrates that he has nothing to fear or avoid in being seen and being seen seeing, and that he is not ashamed of himself or of the place and company in which he finds himself. It will therefore be necessary for him to have a certain 'directness' of eye expression. As one student suggests, the individual's gaze ought not to be guarded or averted or absent or defensively dramatic, as if 'something were going on'. Indeed, the exhibition of such deflected eye expressions may be taken as a symptom of some kind of mental disturbance.[1]

Civil inattention is so delicate an adjustment that we may expect constant evasion of the rules regarding it. Dark glasses, for example, allow the wearer to stare at another person without that other being sure that he is being stared at. One person can look at another out of the corner of his eyes. The fan and parasol once served as similar aids in stealing glances, and in polite Western society the decline in use of these instruments in the last fifty years has lessened the elasticity of communication arrangements. It should be added, too, that the closer the onlookers are to the individual who interests them, the more exposed his position (and theirs), and the more obligation they will feel to ensure him civil inattention. The further they are from him, the more licence they will feel to stare at him a little. [. . .]

In addition to these evasions of rules we also may expect frequent infractions of them. Here, of course, social class subculture and ethnic subculture introduce differences in patterns, and differences, too, in the age at which patterns are first employed.

The morale of a group in regard to this minimal courtesy of civil inattention – a courtesy that tends to treat those present merely as participants in the gathering and not in terms of other social characteristics – is tested whenever someone of very divergent social status or very divergent physical appearance is present. English middle-class society, for example, prides itself in giving famous and infamous persons the privilege of being civilly disattended in public, as when the royal children manage to walk through a park with few persons turning around to stare. And in our own American society, currently, we know that one of the great trials of the physically handicapped is that in public places they will be openly stared at, thereby having their privacy invaded, while, at the same time, the invasion exposes their undesirable attributes.

The act of staring is a thing which one does not ordinarily do to another human being; it seems to put the object stared at in a class apart. One does not talk to a monkey in a zoo, or to a freak in a sideshow – one only stares.

An injury, as a characteristic and inseparable part of the body, may be felt to be a personal matter which the man would like to keep private. However, the fact of its visibility makes it known to anyone whom the injured man meets, including the stranger. A visible injury differs from most other personal matters in that anyone can deal with it regardless of the wish of the injured person; anyone can stare at the injury or ask questions about it, and in both cases communicate to and impose upon the injured person his feelings and evaluations. His action is then felt as an intrusion into privacy. It is the visibility of the injury which makes intrusion into privacy so easy. The men are likely to feel that they have to meet again and again people who will question and stare, and to feel powerless because they cannot change the general state of affairs.[2]

Perhaps the clearest illustration both of civil inattention and of the infraction of this ruling occurs when a person takes advantage of another's not looking to look at him, and then finds that the object of his gaze has suddenly turned and caught the illicit looker looking. The individual caught out may then shift his gaze, often with embarrassment and a little shame, or he may carefully act as if he had merely been seen in the moment of observation that is permissible; in either case we see evidence of the propriety that should have been maintained.

To behave properly and to have the *right* to civil inattention are related: propriety on the individual's part tends to ensure his being accorded civil inattention; extreme impropriety on his part is likely to result in his being stared at or studiously not seen. Improper conduct, however, does not automatically release others from the obligation of extending civil inattention to the offender, although it often weakens it. In any case, civil inattention may be extended in the face of offensiveness simply as an act of tactfulness, to keep an orderly appearance in the situation in spite of what is happening.

Ordinarily, in middle-class society, failure to extend civil inattention to others is not negatively sanctioned in a direct and open fashion, except in the social training of servants and children, the latter especially in connection with according civil inattention to the physically handicapped and deformed. For examples of such direct sanctions among adults one must turn to despotic societies where glancing at the emperor or his agents may be a punishable offence, or to the rather refined rules prevailing in some of our Southern states concerning how much of a look a coloured male can give to a white female, over how much distance, before it is interpreted as a punishable sexual advance.

Given the pain of being stared at, it is understandable that staring itself is widely used as a means of negative sanction, socially controlling all kinds of improper public conduct. Indeed, it often constitutes the first warning an individual receives that he is 'out of line' and the last warning that it is necessary to give him. In fact, in the case of those whose appearance tests to the limit the capacity of a gathering to proffer civil inattention, staring itself may become a sanction against staring. The autobiography of an ex-dwarf provides an illustration:

There were the thick-skinned ones, who stared like hill people come down to see a traveling show. There were the paper-peekers, the furtive kind who would withdraw blushing if you caught them at it. There were the pitying ones, whose tongue clickings could almost be heard after they had passed you. But even worse, there were the chatterers, whose every remark might as well have been 'How do you do, poor boy?' They said it with their eyes and their manners and their tone of voice.

I had a standard defense – a cold stare. Thus anesthetized against my fellow man, I could contend with the basic problem – getting in and out of the subway alive.[3]

The structure of face engagements

When two persons are mutually present and hence engaged together in some degree of unfocused interaction, the mutual proffering of civil inattention – a significant form of unfocused interaction – is not the only way they can relate to one another. They can proceed from there to engage one another in focused interaction, the unit of which I shall refer to as a *face engagement* or an *encounter*. Face engagements comprise all those instances of two or more participants in a situation joining each other openly in maintaining a single focus of cognitive and visual attention – what is sensed as a single *mutual activity*, entailing preferential communication rights. As a simple example – and one of the most common – when persons are present together in the same situation they may engage each other in a talk. This accreditation for mutual activity is one of the broadest of all statuses. Even persons of extremely disparate social positions can find themselves in circumstances where it is fitting to impute it to one another. Ordinarily the status does not have a 'latent phase' but obliges the incumbents to be engaged at that very moment in exercising their status.

Mutual activities and the face engagements in which they are embedded comprise instances of small talk, commensalism, lovemaking, gaming, formal discussion and personal servicing (treating, selling, waitressing and so forth). In some cases, as with sociable chats, the coming together does not seem to have a ready instrumental rationale. In other cases, as when a teacher pauses at a pupil's desk to help him for a moment with a problem he is involved in, and will be involved in after she moves on, the encounter is clearly a setting for a mutual instrumental activity, and this joint work is merely a phase of what is primarily an individual task. It should be noted that while many face engagements seem to be made up largely of the exchange of verbal statements, so that conversational encounters can in fact be used as the model, there are still other kinds of encounters where no word is spoken. This becomes very apparent, of course, in the study of engagements among children who have not yet mastered talk, and where, incidentally, it is not possible to see the gradual transformation of a mere physical contacting of another into an act that establishes the social relationship of jointly accrediting a face-to-face encounter. Among adults, too, however, non-verbal encounters can be observed: the significant acts exchanged can be gestures or even, as in board and card games, moves. Also, there are certain close comings-together over work tasks which give rise to a single focus of visual and cognitive attention and to intimately co-ordinated contributions, the order and kind of contribution being determined by shared appreciation of what the task-at-the-moment requires as the next act. Here, while no word of direction or sociability may be spoken, it will be understood that lack of attention or co-ordinated response constitutes a breach in the mutual commitment of the participants.

Where there are only two participants in a situation, an encounter, if there is to be one, will *exhaust* the situation, giving us a *fully focused gathering*. With more than two participants, there may be persons officially present in the situation who are officially excluded from the encounter and not themselves so engaged. These unengaged participants change the gathering into a *partly focused* one. If more than three persons are present, there may be more than one encounter carried on in the same situation – a *multi-focused* gathering. I will use the term *participation unit* to refer both to encounters and to unengaged participants; the term *bystander* will be used to refer to any individual present who is not a ratified member of the particular encounter in question, whether or not he is currently a member of some other encounter.

In our society, face engagements seem to share a complex of properties so that this class of social unit can be defined analytically, as well as by example.

An encounter is initiated by someone making an opening move, typically by means of a special expression of the eyes but sometimes by a statement or a special tone of voice at the beginning of a statement. The engagement proper begins when this overture is acknowledged by the other, who signals back with his eyes, voice or stance that he has placed himself at the disposal of the other for purposes of a mutual eye-to-eye activity – even if only to ask the initiator to postpone his request for an audience.

There is a tendency for the initial move and the responding 'clearance' sign to be exchanged almost simultaneously, with all participants employing both signs, perhaps in order to prevent an initiator from placing himself in a position of being denied by others. Glances, in particular, make possible this effective simultaneity. In fact, when eyes are joined, the initiator's first glance can be sufficiently tentative and ambiguous to allow him to act as if no initiation has been intended, if it appears that his overture is not desired.

Eye-to-eye looks, then, play a special role in the communication life of the community, ritually establishing an avowed openness to verbal statements and a rightfully heightened mutual relevance of acts. In Simmel's words:

Of the special sense-organs, the eye has a uniquely sociological function. The union and interaction of individuals is based upon mutual glances. This is perhaps the most direct and purest reciprocity which exists anywhere. This highest psychic reaction, however, in which the glances of eye to eye unite men, crystallizes into no objective structure; the unity which momentarily arises between two persons is present in the occasion and is dissolved in the function. So tenacious and subtle is this union that it can only be maintained by the shortest and straightest line between the eyes, and the smallest deviation from it, the slightest glance aside, completely destroys the unique character of this union. No objective trace of this relationship is left behind, as is universally found, directly or indirectly, in all other types of associations between men, as, for example, in interchange of words. The interaction of eye and eye dies in the moment in which directness of the function is lost. But the totality of social relations of human beings, their self-assertion and self-abnegation, their intimacies and estrangements, would be changed in unpredictable ways if there occurred no glance of eye to eye. This mutual glance between persons, in distinction from the simple sight or observation of the other, signifies a wholly new and unique union between them.[4]

It is understandable, then, that an individual who feels he has cause to be alienated from those around him will express this through some 'abnormality of the gaze', especially averting of the eyes. And it is understandable, too, that an individual who wants to control others' access to him and the information he receives may avoid looking toward the person who is seeking him out. A waitress, for example, may prevent a waiting customer from 'catching her eye' to prevent his initiating an order. Similarly, if a pedestrian wants to ensure a particular allocation of the street relative to a fellow pedestrian, or if a motorist wants to ensure priority of his line of proposed action over that of a fellow motorist or a pedestrian, one strategy is to avoid meeting the other's eyes and thus avoid co-operative claims. And where the initiator is in a social position requiring him to give the other the formal right to initiate all encounters, hostile and teasing possibilities may occur, of which Melville's *White-Jacket* gives us an example:

But sometimes the captain feels out of sorts, or in ill-humour, or is pleased to be somewhat capricious, or has a fancy to show a touch of his omnipotent supremacy; or, peradventure, it has so happened that the first lieutenant has, in some way, piqued or offended him, and he is not unwilling to show a slight specimen of his dominion over him, even before the eyes of all hands; at all events, only by some one of these suppositions can the singular circumstance be accounted for, that frequently Captain Claret would pertinaciously promenade up and down the poop, purposely averting his eye from the first lieutenant, who would stand below in the most awkward suspense, waiting the first wink from his superior's eye.

'Now I have him!' he must have said to himself, as the captain would turn toward him in his walk; 'now's my time!' and up would go his hand to his cap; but, alas! the captain was off again; and the men at the guns would cast sly winks at each other as the embarrassed lieutenant would bite his lips with suppressed vexation.

Upon some occasions this scene would be repeated several times, till at last Captain Claret, thinking that in the eyes of all hands his dignity must by this time be pretty well bolstered, would stalk towards his subordinate, looking him full in the eyes; whereupon up goes his hand to the cap front, and the captain, nodding his acceptance of the report, descends from his perch to the quarter-deck.[5]

As these various examples suggest, mutual glances ordinarily must be withheld if an encounter is to be avoided, for eye contact opens one up for face engagement. I would like to add, finally, that there is a relationship between the use of eye-to-eye glances as a means of communicating a request for initiation of an encounter, and other communication practices. The more clearly individuals are obliged to refrain from staring directly at others, the more effectively will they be able to attach special significance to a stare, in this case, a request for an encounter. The rule of civil inattention thus makes possible, and 'fits' with, the clearance function given to looks into others' eyes. The rule similarly makes possible the giving of a special function to 'prolonged' holding of a stranger's glance, as when unacquainted persons who had arranged to meet each other manage to discover one another in this way.

NOTES

1   R. K. White, B. A. Wright and T. Dembo, 'Studies in Adjustment to Visible Injuries: Evaluation of Curiosity by the Injured', *Journal of Abnormal and Social Psychology*, 43 (1948), p. 22.
2   Ibid., pp. 16–17.
3   H. Viscardi Jr, *A Man's Stature* (New York: John Day, 1952), p. 70.
4   From Simmel's *Soziologie*, cited in R. E. Park and E. W. Burgess, *Introduction to the Science of Sociology*, 2nd edn (Chicago: University of Chicago Press, 1924), p. 358.
5   H. Melville, *White-Jacket* (New York: Grove Press, n.d.), p. 276.

12 Embarrassment and Interactional Organization

Christian Heath

Embarrassment has received relatively little attention within the behavioural sciences. Unlike other forms of emotion, it is said to be a purely human experience, a social phenomenon, and as such less subject to physiological and psychological explanation than the less ephemeral forms of feeling. Sociology, on the other hand, has paid relatively little attention to the emotions, considering feelings either inaccessible to or unworthy of analytic scrutiny [. . .] [However,] embarrassment lies at the heart of the social organization of day-to-day conduct. It provides a personal constraint on the behaviour of the individual in society and a public response to actions and activities considered problematic or untoward. Embarrassment and its potential play an important part in sustaining the individual's commitment to social organization, values and convention. It permeates everyday life and our dealings with others. It informs ordinary conduct and bounds the individual's behaviour, in areas of social life that formal and institutionalized constraints do not reach. And as with so many areas of ordinary conduct, it is Erving Goffman who directs analytic attention towards the significance of embarrassment to social life and thereby throws into relief the situational and interactional nature of the emotions.

Goffman suggests that participants in interaction have a moral obligation to sustain their own and each other's claims to relevant identities and that embarrassment emerges 'if expressive facts threaten or discredit the assumptions a participant has projected about his identity'. Goffman argues that embarrassment involves an individual losing composure, and its characteristic signs such as 'blushing, fumbling and vacillating movement' undermine a person's ability to participate in the topic or business of the encounter; embarrassment threatens the line of activity in which the participants are involved. He concludes that face-to-face interaction requires 'just those capacities that embarrassment may destroy' and provides us with a framework with which to consider how persons ordinarily avoid and dispel such difficulties. [. . .]

I wish to draw on Goffman's pioneering work to explore the interactional organization of embarrassment. Unlike previous work on embarrassment and the expression of other forms of emotion, the observations are based upon the analysis of actual instances of the phenomenon drawn from naturally occurring interaction. [. . .]

The data employed in this [study] are drawn from a substantial collection of video-recordings of naturally occurring medical consultations, collected as part of a research project concerned with visual and vocal behaviour between the doctor and patient. [. . .] Current work on the project is concerned with the interaction between the doctor and patient during the physical examination and it was in this rather delicate area of social life that we became interested in embarrassment and emotion and its relation to ordinary conduct. [. . .]

The video-recordings were reviewed to unearth instances which revealed one or other of the participants exhibiting the characteristic signs of embarrassment, in particular a loss of composure and an inability to participate, if only momentarily, within the encounter. In fact such occasions

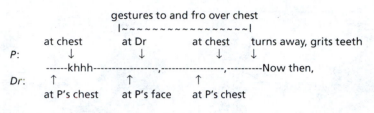

Figure 12.1 Fragment 1, transcript 2 (simplified)

prove relatively rare and one is led, like Goffman, to consider the ways in which embarrassment is avoided. More importantly, however, in locating actual instances of embarrassment embodying the characteristics described by Goffman and others, it transpires in more detailed analysis that rather than 'flooding out', the individual's behaviour is systematically organized with respect to the surrounding configuration of action and activity. Repeatedly unearthing an interactional systematics to embarrassment undermined our confidence in the way in which the phenomenon had been characterized and conceived by Goffman and others.

A moment of embarrassment

[. . .] Actual outbursts of embarrassment during the medical examination are relatively rare. If they do occur, however, they tend to happen as the participants prepare for the examination rather than as the doctor actually inspects the patient's body. It is of course following the doctor's request to examine the patient that undressing takes place, not infrequently in front of the doctor; and it is here that the patient reveals his or her body to the doctor for the first time – at least during the current consultation.

The following fragment is drawn from the juncture between the request to examine the patient and the actual inspection of the body. In this case the examination has been delayed whilst the doctor answers the telephone. The patient waits, undressed to her bra, for the examination to begin. We enter the consultation as the doctor finishes the telephone conversation and turns to the patient. [. . .] Of particular importance here are the length of the silences captured in tenths of a second and the rows of 'h's, which represent inbreaths if preceded by an asterisk (*hhh); outbreaths if not.

Fragment 1 Transcript 1 (simplified)

Dr: Slip your gear off an let's have a look.

.

[intervening phone conversation]

.

Dr: *[completes call and turns to patient]*
P: *hhh hhhhhh kh (0.2) *hhhh keh kh hm (0.8)
P: khh (2.3)
Dr: Now then, let's have a listen

The actual episode of embarrassment begins towards the end of the silence following the patient's coughing and breathlessness. As the doctor turns towards her, the patient becomes momentarily flustered and appears to lose control of her behaviour. A more detailed transcript including visual as well as vocal elements will be helpful. Unlike the previous transcript, the action is laid out across the page. The gaps are represented by dashes, each dash equivalent to 0.1 of a second. The visual behaviour of the patient is transcribed above the line used to capture the silence and vocalization, the doctor's below. The gaze of the participant is captured immediately above or below this line and a series of signs, ~~~, represents one party turning towards the other, dashes, ----, represent turning away. A continuous line or dash represents one participant looking at the other.

On finishing the phone conversation the doctor turns towards the patient and the patient reorientates towards the doctor. The moment her

(a)   (b)

Figure 12.2   Fragment 1

gaze arrives the patient turns from the doctor to her partially naked chest. There she begins to gesture rapidly, passing her open hand back and forth over the surface of her chest. Whilst gesturing she blinks and shakes her head. After a moment or so the doctor looks up from the chest and the patient follows, turning once more towards the doctor's face. By the time her gaze arrives, the doctor has returned his gaze to the chest. Finding the doctor looking at the chest the patient turns to the object of his gaze and once again begins to gesture, waving her open hand rapidly back and forth over the naked chest. Again the gesture is accompanied by the patient blinking and looking here and there. Less than a second passes and she turns away from her chest to one side, lowering her eyelids and gritting her teeth. The episode subsides as the doctor follows the patient and turns to one side, a second or so later the participants rearrange their seating positions as they begin the examination.

Figure 12.2 – (a) showing immediately before the episode begins, and (b) during its course – may help provide a sense of the action. This brief episode embodies many of the characteristic signs of embarrassment. The patient's apparently haphazard movements, the flustered gestures, the shifting gaze and blinking eyes coupled with the head movements and, towards the end of the episode, the lowered eyelids and gritting of the teeth, capture behaviour described by both Goffman and other scholars who have addressed this form of emotional expression. For example,

Goffman speaks of 'blushing, fumbling, stuttering, tremors of the hand, hesitancy and vacillating movement' as signs of embarrassment and continues by describing the associated physiological elements such as the acceleration of the heart beat and its effects on the circulation and skin colour. In the case at hand, the patient appears momentarily to lose composure and to become 'mentally confused'; she 'floods out' and undermines her ability to participate in the business at hand, the preparation for the physical examination.

In this as in other examples of embarrassment, the person's behaviour appears bizarre and idiosyncratic, unrelated to the interaction and business at hand, a moment in which the participant is overcome by a flood of emotion and unable to retain control of his or her actions. Yet however extraordinary the behaviour of the patient might appear, the moment of her emotion and its expression is systematically related to the actions of her co-participant. For example, the patient's embarrassment does not arise 'anywhere' within the developing course of the consultation but is co-ordinated with the local environment of activity. As the doctor finishes the telephone conversation and turns to the patient she too turns towards the doctor. As her gaze arrives, the patient finds the doctor looking at her chest rather than her face. She immediately turns to the object of his attention and begins to gesture. A moment or so later the doctor looks up and the patient ceases her gesture and returns her gaze to the face of the doctor, only to find him once more looking at her chest. Her embarrassment re-emerges as she once again begins to gesture and looks intermittently at the object in question.

It is the doctor's glance which gives rise to the patient's emotion, and his glance which rekindles her difficulties for a second time. The glance is 'physically' equivalent to many of the looks the doctor gives the patient during the medical examination, yet at this moment within the proceedings it fires the patient's embarrassment. The source of the difficulties arises from the state of involvement during this phase of the consultation; the juncture between the request to examine the patient and the actual inspection of the body. It is one of the few occasions during the encounter where there is no jointly co-ordinated activity in which the participants are involved; no common focus of attention. It is a sort of 'no man's land' in the interaction, a phase which frequently entails a fragmentation of involvement in which the doctor and patient attend to their distinct but related concerns in preparing for the examination. In such circumstances a glance at the body of another can gain a significance it might not otherwise have. Unlike glances exchanged between persons during the production of an activity, either talk or the examination itself, the doctor's looking does not form part of a legitimate stretch of activity to which the participants are mutually committed. Rather, the doctor's glance lies alone, divorced from the business of the consultation and, in this way, can be interpreted as 'looking at' the other, momentarily bringing the patient's chest to the forefront of mutual attention.

Thus it is not simply the temporal structure of a look which transforms glance into stare, but rather its relationship to the local configuration of activity. [. . .] In the case at hand the doctor's glance brings the patient's chest to the forefront of mutual attention and initiates a stretch of activity – the patient's brief episode of emotion. Whatever feelings the patient or anyone else associates with the revelation of particular parts of her or his body, it is a specific action, the looking, that renders the object embarrassable.

On finding the doctor looking at her chest, the patient produces her flustered gesture and the associated movements of the eyes and head. Though seemingly chaotic, the patient's gesture, like other movements which occur in face-to-face interaction, may be carefully designed with respect to the local circumstances and the action(s) it is performing. It will be recalled that in both its stages the patient's gesture consists of an open hand which is waved successively over the chest, the object of the doctor's attention. In both stages the gesture criss-crosses the line of regard of the doctor and in consequence intermittently conceals the chest from his view. Thus by gesturing over the chest the patient hides her chest if only partially from the doctor's view. As he withdraws his gaze she abandons the gesture. On finding the doctor once more looking at her chest, she conceals her chest from his wandering eye. The gesture therefore serves to interrupt the other's looking and perhaps encourages him to abandon his interest in her partially naked body.

If the sole concern of the gestures were to conceal the chest from the gaze of the doctor then one might expect the patient simply to place her hand on its surface or in some other way conceal the source of her embarrassment. The patient's gestures, however, may be concerned not solely with concealing the object from the doctor's view, but also with managing other demands and constraints within the local interactional environment. The moment of embarrassment occurs as the doctor finishes a telephone conversation and is about to begin the examination of the patient. Consequently, as the doctor finishes the call the patient reorientates towards the doctor and presents her chest for inspection. It is at this moment that the patient finds the doctor looking at the chest rather than moving forward to the patient to examine it. Simultaneously the patient is placed under two competing interactional demands; on the one hand, presenting the chest for examination, on the other, concealing it from the gaze of the doctor. The flustered gesture, the open hand successively passing to and fro over the surface of the chest, embody these simultaneous constraints on her behaviour; she attempts to present the chest and remain available for the examination whilst concealing the focus of her embarrassment from the unwanted attention of the doctor. In consequence, it is hardly surprising that the patient's actions appear flustered and disorganized as she attempts to settle the sequential constraints of the appropriate next activity with the implications of the doctor's gaze.

The shape of the gestures and the patient's apparent lack of commitment to concealing the chest fully may also be related to the potential consequences of such action. However strong the patient's inclination to conceal the chest from the gaze of the doctor, such an action would have significant retrospective implications and might lead to further embarrassment and difficulties. Were the patient to conceal her chest fully, it would cast aspersion on the actions of the doctor, suggesting that his glance was untoward and problematic. It would imply that the doctor's looking lay outside any warranted medical practice and suggest that less professional motives underlay the actions of the doctor. Fully concealing the chest would be tantamount to refusing to be examined for reasons which arose in the course of the doctor's behaviour, and both patient and doctor might be called to account. In such circumstances we can understand why the patient might avoid wholesale commitment to a course of action which would generate a definition of the other and his or her actions which could well undermine the very foundation of the consultation.

A characteristic of shame and embarrassment described in both literature and the sciences is of the sufferer 'not knowing where to look' and shielding the eyes from the gaze of the onlooker(s). Darwin captures a flavour of these difficulties in his classic treatise on the expressions of emotion in man and animals.

The habit, so general with everyone who feels ashamed, of turning away, or lowering the eyes, or restlessly moving them from side to side, probably follows from each glance directed towards those present, bringing home the conviction that he is intently regarded; and he endeavours, by not looking at those present, and especially not at their eyes, momentarily to escape from this painful conviction.[1]

In fragment 1, as with many instances of embarrassment, the patient is overcome with difficulties as to where to look. She begins by turning from the doctor to her chest, quickly returning her gaze to the doctor and then once again glancing at her chest. Finally she turns to one side and lowers her eyelids as if in shame. [. . .] with rapid changes in the direction of her gaze, the patient successively blinks and very slightly shakes her head. As Darwin suggests, the individual who suffers embarrassment and shame becomes restless, looking hither and thither or lowering the eyes. The patient during this brief episode appears quite simply not to know where to look or rest her eyes. She appears to be simultaneously drawn and repelled by the gaze of the doctor.

The behaviour of the patient arises in part through the power of a look to affect another. The patient is [. . .] drawn by the gaze of the doctor to return his look, if only to check whether he is continuing to stare at the chest. Yet, were the patient to return the gaze, then the doctor might well be encouraged to look the patient in the eye; the moment of mutual gaze giving rise to a shared recognition of the doctor's preceding behaviour and an intimacy between the participants which might well generate further difficulty. Embarrassment thrives on one person seeing another see the first, and so on; the reflexive recognition kindling further the fires of discomfort.

Yet if the patient is reluctant to face the doctor she is also troubled by looking at the object of her embarrassment. No sooner does she turn from the doctor to the chest than she looks up, then, turning once again to her chest, she rapidly looks away. Looking at her chest provides little relief from her embarrassment. It is of course first noticing the object of the doctor's attention which gives rise to the initial gesture, and finding the doctor 'continuing' to look which leads to further activity across the chest. It is as if looking at the chest and sharing the focus of the doctor's curiosity generate the embarrassment and encourage it to continue; the patient's difficulty arising as she sees herself and her body in the light of another seeing her. Again, there is something in the mutual recognition of the body which fires the embarrassment. The interactional constraints which give rise to the embarrassment and feature in its organization derive from the power of the look, in particular the sequential significance of a person's gaze in environments in which persons are co-present yet not fully engaged in the mutual production of an activity.

NOTE

1 C. Darwin, *The Expression of Emotions in Men and Animals* (London: Julian Freidman, 1979), p. 330 (first published 1872).

13 Time, Habit and Repetition in Day-to-Day Life

Michael Young

Why do people repeat themselves so much? Why do they do more or less the same thing every year at Christmas, or on their own birthdays, or every day as they go about their daily rounds, getting out of bed in the morning, washing, dressing, getting breakfast, reading the paper, opening the mail, walking to the garage or the station, talking to colleagues, telephoning the same people day after day, writing letters which are much like letters written on other days, stopping themselves going into the pub with a twinge of regret, as on other days? It cannot all be due to their biological clocks. People do not settle down to their Christmas dinner by measuring the day's length to the nearest few minutes: they are not birds compelled to fly to the dinner table (or into the oven) at just that precise moment.

Some additional force must be responsible for the regularity of Christmas, although it is one day in Western Europe and another in Eastern Europe, and for its absence in large parts of the world; and for keeping most people head-down at their daily tasks when it is not Christmas. I am in other words looking for a 'sociological clock' which is as powerful and omnipresent a synchronizer as the biological clock. I propose that this force is the force of habit and its extension, custom – the tendency we all have, in greater or lesser measure, to do again what we have done before. Habit is as intrinsic to the cyclic (including some of its irregularities) as conscious memory is to the linear. Habit and memory are each means of preserving the past to do service in the present, but in the main for different though complementary ends: the first to ensure continuity, and the second to open the way for change. [. . .]

Habits are always being created anew. As the Chinese proverb says, 'a habit begins the first time'. Habits are generated and locked into place by recurrences so that they become automatic, rather than deliberate. In his *Principles of Psychology* William James gives habit a central place as 'the enormous flywheel of society, its most precious conservative agent': 'any sequence of mental actions which has been frequently repeated tends to perpetuate itself; so that we find ourselves automatically prompted to *think*, *feel* or *do* what we have been before accustomed to think, feel or do, under like circumstances, without any consciously formed *purpose*, or anticipation of results.[1] For James habit was even more than second nature. He agreed with the Duke of Wellington:

'Habit a second nature! Habit is ten times nature', the Duke of Wellington is said to have exclaimed . . . 'There is a story, which is credible enough, though it may not be true, of a practical joker, who, seeing a discharged veteran carrying home his dinner, suddenly called out "Attention!", whereupon the man instantly brought his hands down, and lost his mutton and potatoes in the gutter. The drill has been thorough, and its effects had become embodied in the man's nervous structure.'[2]

This story also illustrates James's statement that 'in habit the only command is to start'. After that the actions are automatic. 'Second nature' is one term for it, despite the duke. Another popular term, in a society fancying airplanes for transport, is the phrase 'to go on automatic'.

There are degrees of automation. When it is complete, there is no need for thinking at all; there may not even be any conscious recognition of the situation that produces the habitual behaviour. No proposition is more self-evident than that people take a great deal as self-evident. I just act, without having to reason why. Without thinking about it, I scratch my head, or wink, or open my mouth when I am puzzled, and at a particular corner on my ordinary route to work I go through the routine motions with my arms and feet, all without being aware of it, unless on one occasion I put my foot hard on the accelerator instead of the brake or do something else eccentric, in which case I may remember it for life (if there is any left); and I do not do these things because I am so very notably absent-minded compared to others but because on such matters everyone is absent-minded. We are all to a considerable extent like A. J. Cook, the miners' leader in the British General Strike of 1926: 'Before he gets up he has no idea what he is going to say; when he's on his feet he has no idea what he is saying; and when he sits down he has no idea what he has just said.'[3] [. . .]

Habits are not usually chosen with any deliberation; they just grow, wild flowers rather than cultivated ones. They would not do this so readily and constantly without a series of overlapping advantages which assure that their growth will not be stopped. I will mention four of them. The first advantage is that habit increases the skill with which actions can be performed. The multiplication table is tiresome to learn but, once it has become habitual, reproducing it is very accurate and very quick. Reading and writing are difficult to acquire in the first place but, once acquired, both can be very efficient. To master the piano is very difficult indeed for the beginner, whose convulsive movements of the body and mangling of the keyboard make it seem impossible that any euphony will ever be achieved; but a few years later the hands may caper over the notes as though to the manner born, and all as the result of unflagging repetition. In such cases an act of will (even if abetted by the cajoling of parents or teachers) can inaugurate a habit which the will does not thereafter have to be engaged in guiding.

The second advantage is that a habit diminishes fatigue. Driving a car, or thinking about existentialism, or speaking a foreign language, or saying our prayers, is tiring the first time it is done, and if a person does not persevere because it is tiring it will always remain so. But persevere, and before too long the same person will be rattling off talk about existentialism while watching a football match or the television, or even driving a car while shouting at his children in the back to be quiet, in the hope that quietness will become as much a habit for them as shouting is for him. If fatigue could not be reduced by such means – or (to put it another way) effort invested now with an immense rate of return in reduced effort in the future – a life of any complexity could be insupportable. [. . .]

The third advantage is still more significant: a habit not only economizes on the effort put into the humdrum and the foreseen but also spares attention for the unforeseen. A capacity for attention is held in permanent reserve, ready to be mobilized to deal with the unexpected – the truck which appears from nowhere directly in front of one's own car, or the shout for help, or the summons to appear before the boss. Habit, by allowing predictable events or features of an event to be managed with hardly any effort, enables people to concentrate most of their attention on the unpredictable. Habit is necessary to allow this concentration. Without it, people would not be able to cope with the changes in their environments which cannot be reduced to rule; they would be without the adaptability which has enabled them to survive countless threats to their existence. Habits are one of our chief tools for survival.

The fourth advantage – the economizing of memory – in a sense encompasses all the other advantages. If Mr Murgatroyd on any morning arrived at work to find he had left his habits behind him, and had only his memory to guide him, he might as well get back into his car and go home. The same is true for the whole workforce. Without their usual collection of habits they would be looking at each other almost as if for the first time, in bewilderment, like a regiment lost in a forest, or an assembly of people with severe Alzheimer's disease for whom there was nothing in life except today, wondering what on earth to do with themselves while Mr M ransacked his memory about the organization of the factory and telephoned the head office for orders. Even if the head office were not stricken by the same disability – and if only one person was left with the capacity for habit he or she would soon rule the corporation, and perhaps the world – it would be a task indeed to translate their orders for axles into routines for everyone in the factory in time to get any made that day. Starting from scratch with only their conscious recollections to guide them, it would be miraculous if he and the other managers decided what exactly should be done, and by whom, in time for anyone else to do any work before the bell for the end of the shift. Without habit, every day would be more than fully absorbed in puzzling about what to do, with none of it available for anything else, until they all decided to give it up and stay at home for good – unless home too was similarly overtaken. It would be too much to have to rely on memory to reinvent the wheel, or the axle, even every year, let alone every day.

The head office might decide to send down for an inspection not another production manager but a psychiatrist. All of us know that some people are like the indecisive imaginary Mr M, who now does not know whether to put on sandals or boots when he arrives in his office, if he can find where it is. James was severe on such a condition:

The more of the details of our daily life we can hand over to the effortless custody of automatism, the more our higher powers of mind will be set free for their own proper work. There is no more miserable human being than one in whom nothing is habitual but indecision, and for whom the lighting of every cigar, the drinking of every cup, the time of rising and going to bed every day, and the beginning of every bit of work, are subjects of express volitional deliberation. Full half the time of such a man goes to the deciding, or regretting, of matters which ought to be so ingrained in him as practically not to exist for his consciousness at all. If there be such daily duties not yet ingrained in any one of my readers, let him begin this very hour to set the matter right.[4]

[...] Mr Murgatroyd and his men have something which is in many circumstances better than memory. They do not have to make room in their consciousness for the past. They do not have to recall what they did; instead they can be guided by the habit of what they did do. Jerome Bruner said about selectivity:

Selectivity is the rule and a nervous system, in Lord Adrian's phrase, is as much an editorial hierarchy as it is a system for carrying signals. We have learned too that the 'arts' of sensing and knowing consist in honoring our highly limited capacity for taking in and processing information. We honor that capacity by learning the methods of compacting vast ranges of experience in economical symbols – concepts, language, metaphor, myth, formulae. The price of failing at this art is either to be trapped in a confined world of experience or to be the victim of an overload of information.[5]

He might have added habits after formulae. A habit is a memory unconsciously edited for action.

NOTES

1   W. James, *The Principles of Psychology* (New York: Dover, 1950), vol. 1, pp. 112, 121.
2   T. H. Huxley, *Lessons in Elementary Physiology* (London: Macmillan, 1866), quoted in James, *Principles of Psychology*, vol. 1.
3   A. Marwick, *Britain in the Century of Total War* (London: Bodley Head, 1968).
4   James, *Principles of Psychology*, vol. 1, p. 122.
5   J. S. Bruner, *On Knowing: Essays for the Left Hand* (Cambridge, Mass.: Harvard University Press, 1979), pp. 6–7.

Part 5 Gender and Sexuality

In all known societies men have pretended to be dominant over women. What explains this more or less universal difference of power and influence? Some attribute the differences between the sexes to biological causes. Prominent among these are the 'sociobiologess' – scholars who study the biological roots of social life. According to them, the leading role played by men is the result of many years of evolution. The majority of sociologists, however, tend to be sceptical of such explanations. They see differences between the sexes as primarily the result of culture and society. Jane Pilcher in Reading 14 discusses various different approaches that have been developed in sociology to interpret variations in gender relations. The concept of 'patriarchy' has been one of the most influential concepts that sociologists have used in developing such accounts. It refers to the systematic practices whereby women tend to be kept in subordinate positions. For instance, the idea that women should confine their lives mainly to the domestic sphere obviously means that they tend to have little power in public life. The fact that things are changing now in many countries, with women becoming more and more successful in different areas of life, tends to reaffirm the conclusion that imbalances of power between the sexes were primarily based upon social rather than biological foundations.

Gillian Dunne's research indicates that the inequalities often found in relationships between men and women are not found to the same degree in same-sex relationships between women (Reading 15). The lesbian women who featured in her study almost universally agreed that their current relationships were more equal than those they may have had before with men. In most heterosexual relationships, for example, the man tends to have greater earning power than the woman, and tends to take most of the economic decisions. In lesbian relationships issues tend to be discussed on a more equal basis. The reason is that there is no substantial difference in the roles played between the partners as there is in most male–female relationships.

In Reading 16, Jeffrey Weeks summarizes some important aspects of the development of attitudes towards sexuality and sexual behaviour. These attitudes, he suggests, have been affected by the ways in which sexual behaviour is discussed and debated. 'Sexology' – the supposedly scientific study of sexual activity – has had a practical impact upon what sexual behaviour means for us. 'Sexuality' as such hasn't always existed: it is in part a 'social construction', an invention of those who set out to study sex in a scientific way.

To be 'male' or 'female' seems to be something fixed for life. And for most of us it is. Some individuals, however, are so unhappy with their sexual identities that they actively change them. Precisely because it is so unusual, the experience of such people tells us a great deal about the nature of gender differences. Paul Hewitt was born as a woman,

Martine. Describing his decision to live as a man, in Reading 17, Hewitt shows just how wide the gulf between men's and women's lives is.

For most of history men have dominated public positions, in politics, economic life and other areas. Mostly, they still do. Yet in Western countries far more women are in paid work than ever before and have to some degree eroded pre-existing forms of male dominance. How far will such a process proceed? Some suggest that men at some point will become the 'weaker sex'. As Reading 18, 'The Male Dodo: Are Men Necessary?' indicates, in some respects they already are. For instance, men have a lower life expectancy than women and a higher proportion suffer from major diseases. Girls are starting to do better at school than boys and rates of employment of women are overtaking those of men.

14 Explaining Gender and Gender Inequalities

Jane Pilcher

[...]

Why are there gender inequalities? How are they sustained? Can gender inequality be eradicated? There are a number of theories (sociological and otherwise) which claim to answer these questions. In [this article] I briefly summarise some of the main theories of gender inequality, pointing out their strengths and weaknesses [...] Then, I focus on the arguments of two sociologists, Sylvia Walby and Bob Connell, each of whom has proposed a broad-ranging explanation of gender inequality which attempts to overcome the weaknesses of earlier theories.

Biological theories

'Common-sense' explanations of gender inequalities centre around biology as a cause of inequalities between women and men. Such 'everyday' theories of gender inequalities have their 'scientific' equivalent in explanations put forward by natural scientists and by socio-biologists. These scientists vary as to which aspect of human biology (for example, hormones, genetics, chromosomes, size and/or 'wiring' of the brain) 'naturally' determines gender inequality. Goldberg, for example, argues that the 'neuro-endocrine system' (the interaction of the nervous system with the hormone system) is the biological basis of male dominance. Biologically based theories suggest that it is physiological, natural factors which cause and sustain universal inequalities between women and men, making it practically impossible to achieve a fully equal society. One of the main criticisms of biologically based theories is that they often use data on animal behaviour, which are then applied to human behaviour. Moreover, such theories often ignore historical, anthropological and sociological evidence on human behaviour, in particular evidence which points to variability in women and men's behaviour, status and roles over time and place. A related weakness is a tendency toward ethnocentrism. In other words, a tendency to assume that the gender relations of the white, middle class in western industrialised society are normal and typical of human behaviour. Despite such weaknesses, versions of biological theory continue to have huge popular currency. Connell[1] argues that this is because biological theories are mirrors: they reflect back what is familiar, call it 'science', and thereby justify what many people already believe. Although biologically based theories offer unsatisfactory explanations of gender inequality, their concern with the physicality of human life is increasingly accepted as valid. Sociologists like Connell have started to re-evaluate the role of the body in gender relations, although [...] 'body matters' have often featured in feminist analyses.

Socialisation theories

Functionalist-influenced socialisation theories stress social factors, rather than biological factors, in the explanation of gender inequalities. In this perspective, there are two sex roles, the female and the male, each with different 'scripts' attached to them. Females and males learn the appropriate scripts via socialisation, particularly in infancy and early childhood. Children are taught to conform to their feminine or masculine role as appropriate, through meeting the expectations or norms attached to that role, and are encouraged to do so via the application of positive ('What a big, strong boy you are!') and negative ('Little girls shouldn't play football') sanctions. In this theory, there are gender inequalities because women and men are socialised into different roles. Some versions of this perspective suggest that gender inequality can be reduced or even eradicated if the social scripts learnt via socialisation are changed, through mechanisms like non-sexist child rearing. Socialisation theories offer a plausible explanation of how individuals learn to be masculine or feminine. However, such theories neglect important issues including, where do the norms and values attached to masculine and feminine scripts come from and whose interests do they represent? Socialisation theories overemphasise voluntary conformity to the 'norm' at the expense of structural and institutional factors which constrain masculine and feminine behaviour. Moreover, the two sex roles identified by this perspective are based on biological differences between males and females, which are regarded as unproblematic. Connell argues that because socialisation theory implicitly depends upon biology for its starting point, it is a theoretical approach which has a non-social conception of the basic cause of inequality between women and men.

Feminist theories

In comparison to socialisation theories, feminist theories of gender relations can offer a more sociological conception of the differences between women and men and often place greater stress on structural and institutional factors. There are a number of feminist theories, drawing on a range of intellectual traditions and focusing on different aspects of gender relations in their explanation of gender inequality. Since the 1970s, it has become common practice to divide feminist theories into

categories ('Marxist feminism' and 'radical feminism', for example), in order to highlight the contrasts between them. However, during the 1990s, several feminist writers argued that such categories are no longer useful. Such rigid demarcations are said to be artificial and to fail to do justice to the sophistication, scope and complexity of contemporary feminist theories, which are often multiple and overlapping both in their approaches and in their substantive focus. Clearly, the 'labelling approach' is problematic, not least because a label may be inconsistently applied to a theorist, or may not match an author's own preferred description of her work. However, both historically and currently within feminist theorising, individual authors have either labelled themselves or, at the least, have aligned themselves with a particular feminist perspective, rather than with others. For this reason, I believe it necessary to review the main feminist perspectives, using the labels commonly applied, and to convey a sense of what makes each a relatively distinctive grouping. Nevertheless, the reader needs to recognise that, in addition to the problems noted above, the application of labels can operate to *falsely unify* (for example, not all 'radical feminist' analyses are identical in method or focus) and to *falsely dichotomise* (those writing from a 'black feminist' perspective can simultaneously be 'radical feminist' in their analyses) what is in reality a complex, intertwined and continuously developing body of feminist theory.

In some analyses (often labelled as 'Marxist feminism'), gender inequalities are argued to arise from the workings of the capitalist economic system: it requires, and benefits from, women's unpaid labour in the home. The subordination of women to men in society (or patriarchy), therefore, tends to be regarded as a by-product of capital's subordination of labour. Class inequality is the central feature of society and it is this which determines gender inequality. It is implicit in this perspective that gender inequality will only be eradicated once class has ceased to be a fundamental social division. [. . .] In general, Marxist-influenced accounts of gender relations have been criticised for overemphasising class relations and capitalism and for downplaying gender as an independent social division.

In another grouping of feminist theoretical perspectives, the importance of gender is very much emphasised. Maynard suggests that 'radical feminist' analyses are so called because of a shared concern 'to formulate new ways of theorising women's relationship to men'. In such perspectives, the subordination of women by men (patriarchy) is regarded as the primary and fundamental social division. A key theme in radical feminist accounts of gender inequality is the control of women's bodies by men, for example through sexuality, reproduction, motherhood and male violence in the form of rape. Arising from their concern with the role of the body in gender relations, some versions of radical feminist theories have been criticised for implying that there are essential and unchanging, biological differences between all women and all men. However, this criticism is not valid for radical feminist analyses as a whole.

A further grouping of feminist perspectives gives theoretical priority to two systems – capitalism and patriarchy – in explanation of the subordination of women. Often referred to as 'dual systems theory', this perspective in many ways represents a synthesis of Marxist and radical feminist accounts of gender relations. The work of Delphy and Leonard serves as an example of this approach. They write, 'Radical feminism and marxism have often been presented as antithetical to one another, but we believe not only that men are the primary beneficiaries of the subordination of women in western societies, but also that a marxist approach is the one which best helps us to understand why and how men oppress women'. Indeed, the dual systems approach can be seen to have emerged out of the critiques levelled at Marxist theories, which may overemphasise class and capitalism, and the critiques levelled at radical feminist theories, which may overemphasise biological sex and/or patriarchy. In some versions of dual systems theory, capitalism and patriarchy are understood as interdependent, mutually accommodating systems of oppression, whereby both systems structure and benefit from women's subordination. In dual systems theories, it is implied that both systems of oppression would have to be challenged if gender inequality is to be eradicated. Although avoiding some of the disadvantages of Marxist feminist and radical feminist theories, critics of dual systems theory point to, amongst other weaknesses, a lack of clarity about the precise nature of the relationship between patriarchy and capitalism, or gender and class.

Another grouping of feminist perspectives are less concerned with how to adequately theorise the connections between capitalism and patriarchy than with addressing the implicit ethnocentrism and racism of all the theories examined so far. In black feminist critiques [...] it is argued that analyses of gender which fail to fully examine and theorise racism are flawed and incomplete. The main argument is that most theories of gender implicitly use the experiences of white, middle-class housewives to develop their explanation of gender inequality. Black feminist critiques have been at the forefront of questioning the category 'women', through emphasising the diversity in experiences that this concept serves to conceal. For critics of 'white feminism', women's subordination can only be eliminated if the system of racism is challenged, alongside patriarchy and capitalism. Early black feminist critiques were criticised for using 'black' and 'white' as unifying categories and thereby revealing their own universalist tendencies. However, this is not a valid criticism of more recent analyses, as the use of the label 'black' by authors in the latest collection of writings by black British feminists shows.

The critique put forward by black feminists can be linked to a broader set of concerns about a tendency toward universalism in theories of gender relations, concerns which have been voiced most strongly by postmodernists. Postmodernists focus on complexity, fragmentation and disorganisation as the condition of society in the late twentieth century. They argue that this condition of society means that it is no longer possible – if it ever was – to speak of categories such as 'women' or 'men' or to use large-scale theories (or 'grand narratives') such as patriarchy and class theory. As noted earlier, postmodernists also contend that women and men are too divided (by age, class, ethnicity and racism, for example) for the concepts of 'women' and of 'men' to be useful. Postmodernist analyses rightly emphasise diversity and difference within gender relations, and their questioning of the plausibility of 'grand narratives' has some value. However, critics suggest that the perspective goes too far in denying that there is shared gender oppression, systematically structured, that exists across time and space.

In the light of such criticisms, proposals have been made to analyse gender relations from a 'postmodernist feminist' perspective. N. Fraser and L. Nicholson argue that postmodern feminists must not abandon large theories like patriarchy or large concepts like 'women', because the problems they are attempting to grapple with are large problems, with a long history.[2] However, a postmodern feminist analysis of gender relations must have a number of features. It must be explicitly historical, it must be non-universalist and sensitive to cultural contexts, and it must replace singular notions of feminine and masculine identity with plural notions – of femininities and masculinities made up of complexities of class, sexuality, ethnicity and age. The idea that there can be such a thing as 'postmodern feminism' is contested by some writers, with Evans arguing that it represents a contradiction in terms. In other words, feminism is an example of a 'grand narrative', the relevance of which postmodernism fundamentally questions. Whether or not a 'postmodern feminism' is possible, the approach to gender theorising outlined by Fraser and Nicholson has found increasing support, albeit in a variety of different formulations. Maynard is not alone in advocating what might be called 'post-postmodernist' gender theory, which 'encourages a focus on the specifics of social relations, rather than on homogeneous social systems' [. . .]

Areas of weakness

Having outlined some of the main theories of gender inequality, we can now identify several problematical issues or areas of weakness within gender theorising which have become the focus of much debate. The first issue is the relationship between gender and other social inequalities, particularly class and 'race'. As we have seen, most attempts to theorise gender have either completely neglected class and/or racism, or have inadequately theorised the precise nature of the relationships between the two/three systems of oppression. A second problematical issue concerns structure and agency. Most of the theories stress the role of structured, systemic gender oppression, based either on biology, or capitalism and/or patriarchy/racism. However, this stress on structure means that the individual women and men necessarily involved in gender relations are invisible. Their agency, as oppressors and oppressed, their resistance, struggle and defiance, is often lost. Furthermore, because of the concern to theorise the structural and systemic qualities of gender relations, it becomes difficult to explain how change occurs over time. A third problematical issue is the relationship between the body and gender. In most of the theories we have reviewed so far, the bodies of women and men do not even feature. Where they do, in biological theories and in some versions of radical feminist theories, there is a tendency towards determinism. The fourth issue I want to identify arises from postmodernist-influenced critiques, which have led to calls for theories to be explicitly historical, sensitive to cultural contexts, and to analyse femininities and masculinities as made up of class, sexuality, ethnicity and age. As we have seen, most of the theories are insensitive to historical change, to cultural variation and to the diversity of 'women' and 'men'. With these four issues in mind, we can now turn to the theories proposed by Sylvia Walby,[3] since in many respects [her] work attempts to overcome the weaknesses of earlier gender theorising.

Walby's theory of patriarchy

[. . .] Walby's explanation of why gender inequalities exist and how they are sustained centres around the concept of patriarchy. For Walby, patriarchy is a system of social structures and practices in which men dominate, oppress and exploit women. Walby identifies six structures of patriarchy (household production, paid work, the state, male violence, sexuality, culture) which together are argued to capture the depth, pervasiveness and interconnectedness of women's subordination. Her theory of patriarchy also allows for change over historical time. Walby argues that, in Britain during the twentieth century, patriarchy changed from the 'private' form to the 'public' form. Private patriarchy is based around the family and the household and involves individual men exploiting the labour of individual women. Women are largely confined to the household sphere and have limited participation in public life. In public patriarchy, women are not excluded from public life but face inequality and discrimination within it, for example, in paid work. For Walby, the feminist movement was a key factor in bringing about the change from private to public patriarchy, via the struggle for the vote, for access to education and to the professions, to have legal rights of property ownership, rights in marriage and divorce, and so on. However, patriarchy itself was and is not defeated. Walby says that it has merely changed its form so that now, as she puts it, rather than being restricted to the household, women have 'the whole of society in which to roam and be exploited'.[4]

Does Walby's theory successfully address the four issues in gender theorising identified earlier? First, the issue of the relationship between gender and other forms of inequalities. Walby's work is claimed by herself and others to belong to the dual systems branch of explanations of gender relations. In other words, she argues that to understand gender inequalities it is necessary to recognise patriarchy and capitalism. Unlike earlier dual systems theorists, though, Walby thinks the relationship between the two systems is often one of tension and conflict, with capitalism and patriarchy competing with each other to exploit women. Walby does recognise racism as a third system of oppression, saying that it 'intersects' with the other systems, but it does not feature prominently in her analysis. Walby has been criticised for her treatment of the relationship between gender and other forms of social inequality. Some others, for example, argue that Walby's theory portrays the three systems as, to a large extent, separate and independent of one another. The implication is that class and race are merely extra layers of oppression faced by some women. For Anthias and Yuval-Davies, this does not adequately account for the fully fused nature of the relationships between patriarchy, capitalism and racism, nor for the way that class and 'race' make for a qualitatively different kind of gender inequality.

Walby's theory can also be assessed in terms of whether it gives proper recognition to human agency. Walby claims to be working with a Giddens-type understanding of the relationship between structure and agency, where each is mutually constitutive of the other. Her definition of patriarchy specifies systems, structures and practices (or agency). She also cites practice or agency as a key factor in bringing about the change from private to public patriarchy, when she emphasises the important role played by feminists in securing the advancement of women into the public world. Despite these strengths, however, Walby has been criticised for her overarching tendencies towards structural analysis and for neglecting real people [. . .] Therefore, although Walby claims to work with an integrated conception of structure and agency in her theory of patriarchy, critics suggest that, in fact, structures are emphasised more than agency.

One major area of weakness in Walby's theory is that it underemphasises the importance of the body in gender relations. Moreover, because of weaknesses in her theory around the relationship between gender and other forms of social inequality and the relationship between structure and agency, Walby also largely fails to meet the criteria of 'post-postmodernist' theories of gender. Although her theory is sensitive to historical contexts, it is less successful in exploring cultural variation and the diversity of experiences between women (and men). Although Walby's theory improves on earlier theories, these criticisms suggest that her work is not without its own weaknesses.

Connell's social theory of gender

Rather than explaining why there are gender inequalities, Connell's main concern is to explain how they are sustained. For Connell, the relationship between the body and gender is a crucial issue for any theory of gender. He argues that gender is the end-product of ongoing interpretations of and definitions placed upon the reproductive and sexual capacities of the human body. Masculinities and femininities can be understood as the effects of these interpretations and definitions: on bodies, on personalities and on a society's culture and institutions. Gender is therefore an ongoing creation of human agency, which at an institutional and structural level also acts to constrain individual agency.

For Connell, empirical research has revealed labour, power and cathexis (concerned with emotional relationships, including sexuality) to be the major structures of gender relations, or the major ways in which the agency or practice of women and men is constrained. The three structures constantly interweave with each other creating the 'gender order', or the structure of gender relations in a particular society. Whether at the individual, institutional or 'gender order' level, masculinities and femininities are organised around a single fact: the dominance of men over women. The justifying ideology for this organisation of gender relations is the 'gender hierarchy', involving the ranking of masculinities and femininities. At the top of this hierarchy is 'hegemonic masculinity', the culturally dominant ideal of masculinity centred around authority, physical toughness and strength, heterosexuality and paid work. This is an ideal of masculinity that few actual men live up to, but from which most gain advantage: Connell calls this next level 'complicit masculinity'. Next in the hierarchy are 'subordinated masculinities', the most important of which is homosexual masculinity. More generally, this form of masculinity includes a range of masculine behaviour which does not fully match up to the macho ideals of hegemonic masculinity. At the bottom of the gender hierarchy are femininities. Although these may take a variety of forms, for example 'emphasised' (or compliant) femininity and 'resistant' (for example, feminist) femininity, femininity is always subordinated to masculinity.

In Connell's theory, gender relations are far from being a fixed or a 'sure thing'. They are an ongoing process, the outcome of human practice or agency, and they are subject to resistance as well as conformity, contestation as well as acceptance. All this means that gender relations are open to disruption and change, and hegemonic masculinity is subject to challenge. Connell argues that, in the contemporary industrialised world, hegemonic masculinity is indeed becoming less hegemonic and that, consequently, there are 'crisis tendencies' in the gender order. For example, in family relationships, Connell says that state policies have inevitably disrupted the legitimacy of men's domination over women (via laws on divorce, domestic violence and rape within marriage, independent pensions and taxation for married women, for example). Connell also identifies a tendency towards a crisis of sexuality, where under pressure from women's more assertive sexuality and from gay sexuality, hegemonic masculine heterosexuality becomes less hegemonic. A further example of a tendency toward crisis is the joining together of women and men in groupings which challenge the current gender order, including women's liberation movements, gay liberation, working-class feminism and anti-sexist politics amongst heterosexual men. Connell concludes that it is through individuals and groups, collectively and on a mass scale, 'prising open' the crisis tendencies in the gender order that gender inequality, along with other forms of inequality, can be eradicated.

Does Connell's theory successfully address the four issues in gender theorising identified earlier? First, the issue of the relationship between gender and other social inequalities. When describing the gender structure of labour, Connell does say that gender divisions are a fundamental and essential feature of capitalism, but in general his theory has been criticised for not paying full attention to 'race' or ethnicity. However, in Connell's more recent book, he does address this weakness. In *Masculinities*, he says that gender is 'unavoidably involved' with 'race' and class, as well as with nationality or position in the world order and that to fully understand gender, we must constantly go beyond gender. Second, the issue of structure and agency. This is an area of strength within Connell's theory. He is very much concerned to show the ways in which people constitute social institutions and structures and the ways in which social institutions and structures constitute people. Issues of power, conflict, resistance and change are central to his theory, as is a concern with identifying the constraints of gender as a structure and recognising that this is an ongoing creation of human practice or agency. Another area of strength within Connell's theory is the centrality of the body to his arguments about what gender is and how gender inequalities are sustained. Finally, Connell's theory does meet some criteria of 'post-postmodernist' theories of gender because it is historical, sensitive to cultural difference and to variations in masculinities and femininities. However, Connell's tendency to under-explain the precise relationship between gender and other forms of social inequality, especially 'race', remains a weakness here.

Clearly, theorising gender relations is a very difficult task. Each of the theoretical approaches reviewed here has some value, but none represents a completely comprehensive theory. Arguably, though, the theory proposed by Connell, with its emphasis on the body, agency and structure, the diversity of gender and the possibility of change, represents the most developed general sociological explanation of why there are gender inequalities, how they are sustained and how they might be eradicated. More so than Walby, who stresses the partial nature of 'gender transformations', Connell seems cautiously optimistic about the potential for further change in the gender order and the ways it can be brought about.

NOTES

1 R. W. Connell, *Gender and Power: Society, the Person and Sexual Politics* (Cambridge: Polity, 1987).
2 N. Fraser and L. Nicholson, 'Social Criticism without Philosophy: An Encounter between Feminism and Post-modernism', in A. Ross (ed.), *The Politics of Post-modernism* (Edinburgh: Edinburgh University Press, 1989).
3 S. Walby, *Theorizing Patriarchy* (Oxford: Blackwell Publishers, 1990).
4 Ibid., p. 201.

15 Lesbians at Home: Why Can't a Man be More Like a Woman?

Gillian A. Dunne

[. . .]

When respondents [in Dunne's research study] were asked if they could identify ways in which their relationships with women differed from heterosexual ones, the overwhelming response, volunteered in 53 cases, was that relationships with women were 'more equal'. The degree of certainty expressed was usually related to the amount of experience they had had of relationships with men, with those who had been married appearing the most confident in their assessment. What was actually meant by this was not immediately evident. However, as we will see in their commentaries, it is clear that respondents were sensitive to circumstances which supported relations of domination – between women and men, and among women. This was manifested through their adherence to an egalitarian perspective as an ideal or a political principle, which appeared to be constructed around notions of individual autonomy. Lesbian relationships, in contrast to their understandings of heterosexual relationships, were viewed as having the potential for realising these objectives. We now briefly illustrate the main differentiating features they perceived between lesbian and heterosexual relationships, which together led them to this conclusion.

There were two main aspects of heterosexual relationships which were understood by respondents to pre-empt an egalitarian outcome. The first, and most obvious, was related to their belief that women and men do not share 'equality of conditions'. In other words, there exist structural inequalities between them. For example, men's access to greater economic power was seen to support and reinforce their ability to dominate their partners. Ursula explains:

I just see that there is very little equality in heterosexual relationships – in like the definition of a man and a woman, the man is the one with the power. There is no definition of who takes the lead or the power in a lesbian relationship . . . It is in 99 per cent of the cases the man that will earn more money, he will make all the decisions – well, most of the decisions . . .

A second important differentiating feature was related to the gendered assumption guiding the actual operation of heterosexual relationships. [. . .] those who had experienced relationships with men usually identified 'heterosexual role play' as a major medium of constraint on self-determination. This role play was perceived as a taken for granted practice whereby gender inequalities were intentionally or (most importantly) *unintentionally* translated into everyday action, expectations and outcomes.

When looking back on their relationships with men, heterosexual role play was understood by many respondents to have subtly controlled their behaviour. Valerie, a divorced woman who had recently 'come out', explains:

Well [lesbian relationships] are just so much more relaxed, there's no obligation to fulfil a role, you make your own. You make your own position comfortable that fits round you, whereas I mean in most heterosexual relationships, there's no way that people can ignore the set roles, the set expectations, and it's restricting.

Sheila contrasts her lesbian relationship with her previous marriage, and highlights the consequences of adhering to heterosexual role play for decision making:

I feel more equal, I don't feel that I could leave all the decisions up to [my lover] or need to. Whereas with [my husband] I did, and I think in many ways I was happy to leave the decisions up to him because that was what I saw as his role . . . [Relationships with women are] very much more fulfilling in that I feel like a person in my own right rather than an accessory. And I think I felt very much as an accessory when I was married.

Roxanne describes some consequences of this 'role play' for women's and men's approaches to domestic tasks:

I have never found that I am toeing the line with men . . . But I had been having to fight battles of role play. Like doing the dishes and just taking on those sorts of roles naturally. In my experience, if there are dishes there waiting to be done, it will occur to a woman to do it, but it won't occur to a man. So you would always be the one saying, 'Wash up.' I just couldn't cope with that side of things. Sounds a bit crazy, but it will just be too much for me. It will be the little niggly things, which would become big, and then it gets out of hand . . . And they don't arise now. . . .

Women taking the bulk of responsibility for trying to break down gender boundaries and for constructing more egalitarian conditions in their relationships with men has been commented upon in research. For example, Statham's study of 'non-sexist' couples found that it was her female respondents who had to remind their husbands to do their share in the home. Gordon's study of feminist mothers in Finland echoes these problems.[1] She makes an interesting point about the role of same-sex reference groups: her respondents' more egalitarian male partners compared themselves favourably with other men but their contributions often fell short of their partner's ideal. My respondents often spoke of the energy and disappointment involved in their attempts to expand gender roles in their relationships with men. For these women, being in a relationship with a woman with a similar agenda and view of the world was a major reason for their enthusiasm about lesbian relationships.

A central reason for respondents' sensitivity to heterosexual role play was their experience of entering relationships which simply lacked roles based on reciprocal gender expectations. The absence of scripts based on gender difference has been mentioned in other research on lesbian couples [. . .] Yvonne sums up the feelings of many of my respondents:

Like I say before, it is more equal. There aren't any stereotypical images like in a man/woman relationship, it's something that is so dependent on the two different people. You just form the relationship that is between yourselves, if you know what I mean. There is nothing that [tells you] – this is what you should do, or this is what you shouldn't do and stuff. It's something that just clicks and every relationship is formed, and it is totally different from another one, 'cos it's just how the two people in the relationship make it. There is nothing there at the beginning to influence thoughts on how things should be done.

Importantly, the absence of prescribed roles based on notions of gender difference was seem as emancipating, because this situation expanded choices and enabled greater creativity in the negotiation process between women. This is explained by Harriet:

One of the things that struck me in my first lesbian relationship was the fact that there weren't any role models. I couldn't go and see a film on how to live. It meant that I was really free to do it the way I wanted to. I was uncluttered by images of how I should be doing it. I could more easily choose what I did want, in a way, without having to go against any thing . . . If I had got married to [my boyfriend] there would have been loads of stuff telling me how I should have been behaving. [*Why do you think this is a positive situation?*] It may be easier to fit into prescribed roles, because they are there without you having to think and you can fall into them. I think they must oppress both people actually, because it is much better if you can have the confidence to do everything in a relationship.

The lack of taken for granted guidelines for conducting relationships presented those involved with a 'problem to be solved'. It seems that women negotiating lesbian relationships have to engage in an unusual amount of creativity, and this requires reflection upon and evaluation of what constitutes interpersonal relationships. The flexibility offered in lesbian relationships was understood to provide a context within which women could more easily operate on egalitarian ideals. This is not to say that respondents were unaware of the inequalities between women and the potential this had for creating power imbalances in the relationship. Daniella discusses this:

Well, I mean I don't have any sort of romantic or idealized notions about relationships with women. I think they are really hard. But I also think that there's obviously going to be power differences, and power imbalances, but I think there's a far greater chance of working them out.

An important reason for the belief that power imbalances could be 'worked out' between women was that there was no clear overriding power dynamic shaping the relationship. This is discussed by Elspeth:

I think there are lots of power factors. She sometimes had power because she was older, I sometimes because I was younger. She sometimes had power because she had money, I because I was an academic. There were lots of power factors, none of which were overriding . . . Fluctuating power but no wild fluctuations, with a middle line of equality.

In describing their relationships as 'more equal', respondents were talking about a range of features which were often constructed as the converse of their understandings of the operation of heterosexual relationships. They believed that within lesbian relationships they could exercise greater self-determination and experience relative freedom from domination.

The definition of power is a contested area in sociology. Rather than entering into these sociological debates, my intention here is to consider my respondents' understandings of the different forms which they perceived power to take. The important point to make here is that these women were often conscious of potential power imbalances generated in interpersonal relationships. I therefore wish to place a focus on the ways that this awareness informed their approaches to relationships.

[. . .] Respondents [. . .] were usually conscious of both the positive and negative effects of power. First, they were aware of the enabling aspects of power; ways that, for instance, access to economic power expanded their ability to be self-determining, to make choices over the conditions of their lives and in particular their relationships. Second, they were aware of a range of negative ways in which power operated as a constraint upon themselves and others. They saw power expressed through structures of inequality. In terms of interpersonal relationships (heterosexual and lesbian), they associated, for example, excessive economic imbalances with providing a dependency context which allowed the higher earning partner to exercise, intentionally or unintentionally, greater control over the conditions of that relationship.

Their recognition of the operation of power, however, extended beyond structural sources to include various 'belief systems' shaping everyday practices. One major source of this awareness was perhaps generated by their experience of simply being lesbians and having to face the contradiction between broader social definitions of them as sexual 'deviants' and 'unnatural', and their own positive experience of their sexuality. A main component of the often lengthy process of 'coming out' is coming to terms with this contradiction. To view one's sexuality positively requires the recognition that dominant beliefs can be fundamentally wrong, and for many respondents this insight was viewed as empowering. Gillian explains how coming to terms with her sexuality encouraged a more critical perspective:

[My sexuality] has been very empowering and it shook me out of my middle-class marriage slot into just thinking about the ways things worked and into thinking about power structures and conditioning. It just made me think, and I don't think you can be a real person without this. Certainly society is out to stick people into little boxes and that means keeping them heterosexual . . . Keeping the myths and brutalising men in such a way as to make them 'men'. It gives you a sort of understanding . . . of what is going on. But you have to be on the wrong end of the power structure . . . So, yes, if you are a lesbian you notice the power structure against you and you have more understanding in an experiential way.

Another aspect of being positioned outside 'institutionalized heterosexuality' was that they felt they became more aware of how power worked negatively (their value judgement) through taken for granted ideas about the ways that women and men should interact with each other. Eva discusses this:

I think there's definitely a difference . . . I've had very equal relationships with women. When I see some of the relationships that straight female friends have had with men! But mostly, a lot of the time they don't see anything wrong with it, because it is what everyone around them is doing . . . [They are] accepting what to me appear to be horrendous imbalances . . . One friend goes home, a nine hour day at work and, the usual thing, prepares the meal and looks after the house and everything, and he just sits there and tells all his friends what a slob she is, and all this kind of thing. But how, how, how . . . can we try to, to point this out to people, to other women?

The inequalities that emerge though enacting heterosexual roles were often seen to be obscured from the view of participants (themselves included), because of the power of dominant ideologies which tend to naturalize and justify them.

[. . .]

From respondents' discussions of their interpersonal relationships, it was apparent that their egalitarian position extended to include a general uneasiness about being in a situation of dominance over a partner. Déidre illustrates this:

One thing I am, I'd say, I am one for equality. I don't believe anybody should dominate anyone in a relationship. The reason I like relationships with women is because the equality is there. You help each other. You know, one doesn't tell the other more, 'cos I don't like being dominated.

This situation may be reinforced by the empathy derived from a lesbian's ability to place herself in the position of her partner, which is illustrated by Catherine in this next extract:

I think there must be [a difference between lesbian and heterosexual relationships] because as a woman I would hate to be treated the way a man might treat a woman – this domineering thing. And I would never dream of doing to somebody what I would hate to have done to myself.

Lesbians' sensitivity to the operation of power may provide a more conscious awareness of its abuse by self and others and [. . .] may lead to the development of 'damage limitation' strategies.

All these factors may inform the negotiation process between women and, because a more balanced outcome is likely to be in both their interests, their more flexible relationships make it easier to achieve. Consequently, it is perfectly reasonable to assume that lesbians' home lives are more equal than the heterosexual norm.

NOTE

1 T. Gordon, *Feminist Mothers* (London: Macmillan, 1990).

16 What do We Mean When We Talk About the Body and Sexuality?

Jeffrey Weeks

What is the relationship between the body as a collection of organs, feelings, needs, impulses, biological possibilities and limits, on the one hand, and our sexual desires, behaviours and identities, on the other? What is it about these topics that make them so culturally significant and morally and politically fraught? These, and others like them, have become key questions in recent sociological and historical debates. In attempting to respond to them I will argue that though the biological body is the site for, and sets the limits on, what is sexually possible, sexuality is more than simply about the body. [. . .] I am going to suggest that the most important organ in humans is that between the ears. Sexuality is as much about our beliefs, ideologies and imaginations as it is about the physical body.

The subject of sex

Although there is a strong case for arguing that issues relating to bodies and sexual behaviour have been at the heart of Western preoccupations for a very long time, until the nineteenth century they were largely the concern of religion and moral philosophy. Since then they have largely been the concern of specialists, whether in medicine, the professions, or amongst moral reformers. Since the late nineteenth century the subject has even produced its own discipline, sexology, drawing on psychology, biology and anthropology as well as history and sociology. This has been enormously influential in establishing the terms of the debate about sexual behaviour. Yet sexuality is clearly a critical social and political issue as well as an individual concern, and it therefore deserves a sustained historical and sociological investigation and analysis.

Sexology has been an important factor in codifying the way we think of the body and sexuality. In his famous study *Psychopathia Sexualis* (first translated into English in 1892), Richard von Krafft-Ebing, the pioneering sexologist of the late nineteenth century, described sex as a 'natural instinct' which 'with all-conquering force and might demands fulfilment'. What can we deduce from this? First, there is the emphasis on sex as an 'instinct', expressing the fundamental needs of the body. This reflects a post-Darwinian preoccupation in the late nineteenth century to explain all human phenomena in terms of identifiable, inbuilt, biological forces. Today we are more likely to talk about the importance of hormones and genes in shaping our behaviour, but the assumption that biology is at the root of all things persists, and nowhere more strongly than in relation to sexuality. We talk all the time about the 'sex instinct' or 'impulse', and see it as the most natural thing about us. But is it? There is now a great deal of writing which suggests, on the contrary, that sexuality is in fact a 'social construction', a historical invention, which of course draws on the possibilities of the body, but whose meanings and the weight we attribute to them are shaped in concrete social situations. [. . .]

Havelock Ellis: pioneer sexologist

Take the second part of the Krafft-Ebing quote: sex is an 'all-conquering force', demanding fulfilment. Here we can see at work the central metaphor which guides our thoughts about sexuality. Sex is seen as a volcanic energy, engulfing the body, as urgent and incessant in pressing on our conscious selves. 'Few people', Krafft-Ebing wrote, 'are conscious of the deep influence exerted by sexual life upon the sentiment, thought and action of man in his social relations to others.' I don't think we could make such a confident statement of ignorance today. We now take for granted, in part because of the sexologists, that sexuality is indeed at the centre of our existence.

The following quotation from the English sexologist, Havelock Ellis, who was very influential in the first third of this century, illustrates the ways in which sexuality has been seen as offering a special insight into the nature of the self: 'Sex penetrates the whole person; a man's sexual constitution is a part of his general constitution. There

is considerable truth in the dictum: "a man is what his sex is".'[1]

Not only is sex seen here as an all-conquering force, but it is also apparently an essential element in a person's bodily make-up ('constitution'), the determinant of our personalities and identities – at least, if we take the language at its surface value, if we are men. This poses the question of *why* we see sexuality in this way. What is it about sexuality that makes us so convinced that it is at the heart of our being? Is it equally true for men and women?

This leads us to the third point that we can draw from the original Krafft-Ebing quotation. The language of sexuality appears to be overwhelmingly male. The metaphors used to describe sexuality as a relentless force seem to be derived from assumptions about male sexual experience. Havelock Ellis appears to be going beyond the conventional use of the male pronoun to denote universal experience. Even his use of metaphors ('penetrates') suggest a sublimely unconscious devotion to male models of sexuality. On one level this may seem an unfair criticism, given that the sexologists did attempt to recognize the legitimacy of female sexual experience. In fact, sexologists often followed a long tradition which saw women as '*the* sex', as if their bodies were so suffused with sexuality that there was no need even to conceptualize it. But it is difficult to avoid the sense that the dominant model of sexuality in their writings, and perhaps also in our social consciousness, is the male one. Men were the active sexual agents; women, despite or because of their highly sexualized bodies, were seen as merely responsive, 'kissed into life', in Havelock Ellis's significant phrase, by the man.

I am not attempting to suggest that definitions such as Krafft-Ebing's are the only ones, or even the dominant ones today. I have chosen this starting point to illustrate the major theme of this [discussion] – that our concept of sexuality has a history. The development of the language we use is one valuable index of that: it is in constant evolution. The term 'sex', for example, originally meant 'the results of the division of humanity into male or female *sections*'. It referred, of course, to the differences between men and women, but also to how they were related. [. . .] This relationship was significantly different from the one our culture now understands as given – that men and women are fundamentally different. In the past two centuries or so, 'sex' has taken on a more precise meaning: it refers to the anatomical differences between men and women, to sharply differentiated bodies, and to what divides us rather than unites us.

Such changes are not accidental. They indicate a complicated history in which sexual difference (whether we are male or female, heterosexual or homosexual) and sexual activity have come to be seen as of prime social importance. Can we therefore, with justice, describe sexual behaviour as either 'natural' or 'un-natural' in any unproblematical sense? I believe not.

[. . .] Our sexual definitions, conventions, beliefs, identities and behaviours have not simply evolved, as if propelled by an incoming tide. They have been shaped within defined power relationships. The most obvious one has already been signalled in the quotation from Krafft-Ebing: the relations between men and women, in which female sexuality has been historically defined in relationship to the male. But sexuality has been a peculiarly sensitive marker of other power relations. Church and state have shown a continuous interest in how we behave or think. We can see the intervention over the past two centuries or so of medicine, psychology, social work, schools and the like, all seeking to spell out the appropriate ways for us to regulate our bodily activities. Racial and class differences have further complicated the picture. But alongside these have appeared other forces, above all feminism and the sex reform movements of various types, which have resisted the prescriptions and definitions. The sexual codes and identities we take for granted as inevitable, and indeed 'natural', have often been forged in this complex process of definition and self-definition that have made modern sexuality central to the way power operates in modern society.

NOTE

1   H. Ellis, *The Psychology of Sex* (London: William Heinemann, 1946), p. 3.

17 A Self-Made Man

Paul Hewitt with Jane Warren

There were three of them. They were sitting behind me on the top deck of the bus, each of them playing the fool.

The double-decker lurched round a corner. Rain splattered down on the windows and Reading town centre became obscured behind the rivulets of grime and steamed-up glass.

The gang stood up *en masse*. I could hear the tinny wailing of their Walkmans and the squeaking of their leather coats. I tensed up, sensing trouble brewing. Then one of them slunk past my seat, half-way down on the right-hand side, and deliberately dragged his duffel bag over my head. I felt riled, but hid it.

Troublemaker two turned round to face me as he sauntered past with number three. In taunting mock apology he drawled in black man's language: 'Don't worry about it, man! They're animals.'

Something unfamiliar snapped inside me. 'Well, you're with them, so what does that make you?' I goaded, my eyes alive with menace. Then I baulked at my own defiance and began to tremble, the implications of my comment causing my heart to pump fight-or-flight messages around my tiny frame.

Then he got angry.

A huge fist in my face completely obscured my vision. For a moment I thought Mike Tyson had been let out early. Although my challenger was only 16 or 17 years old, he towered over me, and his knuckles were making intimate contact with my nose. His friends had paused on the stairs and all eyes were on me. I kept absolutely still, well aware that I had bitten off much, much more than I could chew. My palms were sweating.

'Just 'cos you got a nice suit, you think you're it', my aggressor hissed. His voice was hard now. I wisely resisted the urge to say, 'At least I haven't got a stupid haircut.'

The bus slowed to a halt. The fist quivered, then dropped away impassively. The boy spat on the floor before stepping on to the pavement with his mates. As the bus pulled away we made eye contact through the dirty window.

It took several minutes for my pulse to return to its normal rate. One day my big mouth is going to get me into serious trouble.

It was only three years ago that the 'look' through the window would have signalled something quite different: possible sexual interest. Three years ago I was a woman, Martine, and the bully could have been eyeing me up as a possible female conquest. For twenty-six years I had been used to having an advantage over these boys – but my power then was sensual, not physical. I would have slunk past their seats and attracted *their* attention. I would have heard a wolf-whistle, not a threat. I would have been the object of flirtation, not aggression.

Now, robbed of my power, I suddenly felt weak.

I certainly never expected that one day I would pose a threat as a rival male to young men on buses. Sometimes I feel a stranger here, thrust without social training into the tribal world of the male. For while I continue to see things through the same old eyes, society is reacting to me from a fresh perspective. I dress as a man now. I have facial hair. I no longer have a waist. And, yes, I can be bullied by gangs on buses.

I stand poised at the gates of manhood and the boys are beckoning me in. Beyond lies a whole world of macho ideals. He who dares wins.

Although I felt intimidated, the gang couldn't dampen my spirits – my artificial penis is in the post as I write.

I was born perfectly female, the ideal biological specimen in fact. I could appreciate my body, although I knew it not to be mine. Others loved my body far more than I ever did. When I wore a skirt I looked slinky and attractive and male attention was aplenty. And yet I have traded my feminine self for a substandard male body which will never function properly. Because of this, people find it hard to understand my motivation. But to remain as a woman would have been to deny myself my dreams and my peace of mind.

I was a man looking out through female eyes, but I played my role well. Most people, except the very perceptive ones, only ever saw me as a woman. Blending in was part of survival, or so I thought.

I will never be Arnold Schwarzenegger, yet now I feel as fully male as he. I have to accept that I will always be five feet two inches, yet inside I feel six feet tall. I have wanted to step out of my female skin all my life; there is nothing left for me there.

I am a victim of a medical condition invisible to the human eye. Women prefer to be held. I don't. I prefer to hold, and I feel a huge sense of protectiveness towards my twin sister. For a year I patiently played a waiting game for hormones to take effect. I used to liken myself to the man in the iron mask, looking out on the world through two narrow slits. He was a prisoner in a lonely tower, I was a prisoner in my own body. How could I communicate trapped in a body which certainly wasn't mine?

The truth about my real self has caught up with me with such pace that it has taken my breath away. Gasping for air in all the confusion, I have found a quiet spot in which to rest to gather my strength for the succession of operations that are to follow.

My decision to embark on a programme of gender reassignment was an act of pure survival. There have been times when I have felt suicidal, but I am too proud to quit. [. . .] I was born half an hour in advance of my twin sister Karen at Battle Hospital, Reading. The midwife cooed, 'Two beautiful baby girls.' Although that's what she clearly saw during her brief examination of infant genitalia, her instant assessment could not have been less accurate.

As I begin writing this diary, my outward appearance has markedly changed. Not in an overnight transformation, but in a steady sequence of social signals. Now I wear my hair cut short and manly with a slight quiff for a fringe. I am dressed in an open-necked shirt from Top Man which buttons left to right. I wear a signet ring and a single slim gold earring. There are cotton ties in my wardrobe today, three of them. They are my prized possessions, collectively symbolizing everything I have missed out on during these past twenty-six years. All three came from Top Man, a bargain at under £10 each. These slender but significant social markers are worn with a strong mix of pride and injustice. And, yes, I use the men's toilets.

Four weeks from now I will change my name by Statutory Declaration, marking for me the beginning of a new life as a man.

My new name will be Paul Hewitt, yet I was born a woman. My sister will have a twin brother. My parents a son.

I have a dream. I want to be a real man. Am I to be confined inside this foreign body with breasts forever? A female android, I mechanically sashay about, while, inside, the man stomps around this soft white body like a headless chicken shouting: 'Let me out, you bastards!'

I am 26 years old. I have an honours degree in biochemistry. I am also a female-to-male transsexual. A man born imprisoned in a female body. I suffer from a recognized medical condition called gender identity disorder. My decision to embark on a programme of gender reassignment comes down to a choice between life and death; it's an act of pure survival because my female body has always felt alien. It is not that I *want* to be male. I *am* male and, like all transsexuals, I experience an overwhelming urge to bring the gender of my body into line with the gender of my mind.

This has little to do with sex. It is not a sexual preference but an ineradicable conviction about my emotional and psychological identity. I have reached a crossing-point in my life where I have been stripped of everything. Everything except the courage to face the truth, and the courage to act upon the information I have now learned about myself.

I am not a freak. One in 15,000 people is transsexual, and sufferers are united by their total conviction that they have been born into the wrong body. Only 25 per cent of all gender reassignment patients are biological women who believe they are truly female. One hundred female-to-males like me undergo treatment every year.

The emotional pain of what I am facing is intense. It has forced me to draw on reserves of courage I never knew I had, but can it really be called courage, when I have no option? I may currently have breasts, but I ignore them. I feel as much a man as Sly Stallone – though rather more articulate. I burned my bras ten months ago and have not looked back since. Each stage I have progressed through has been symbolized by a door that has locked behind me, and since I no longer hold the keys for these doors my only way is forwards. I still can't believe this has all happened to me. The strength of my own convictions frightens me.

Now I bind up my ample 34D breasts in an elaborate chest-binding device every day and hide them beneath a suit or casual male clothes. It has

taken months of experimentation and practice to create a binding device sufficient to allow me to face the world with confidence and without fear of discovery. Eight elasticated metres of the widest crêpe bandage I could find, wound from my underarms down to my stomach, flattening the breasts which I view with contempt. When they appeared late on in puberty, how could I possibly have foreseen that I would grow to hate them so much?

For so long my real self, Paul, has lain dormant and oppressed, forced into the indignity of dressing as a woman, obliged to stick to the rules, and manipulated as one of society's obedient wooden puppets. But now I am discovering reserves of power. I will be that obedient puppet no more and the world had better watch out. Fathers, lock up your daughters.

Initially, my male self wasn't as confident or expressive as it is now. When I first started crossdressing a year and a half ago, the part of me which was Paul was happy to make a part-time appearance. Social conditioning was so deeply entrenched that, like a dog, he used to be happy with the titbits he was passed under the table. But now Paul insists on eating at the table with the rest of you. I feel as if I am being reborn, witnessing my own evolution. In two months' time, when I have lived as a man for one year, I will begin a lifetime course of fortnightly high-dosage testosterone injections. After a year of drug therapy, I plan to have a double mastectomy.

Most women get suicidal at the thought of losing a breast. To me, my enthusiasm and conviction that this is right are profound evidence of my transsexualism. It will be the final staging-post of my bid for maleness. This will be the day I will finally be liberated from my biological chains.

18 The Male Dodo: Are Men Necessary?

The Economist

Imagine a white, middle-class, Western couple about to pick the sex of their next child (this choice will soon no longer be a fantasy). If they are rational and thorough people, never in 1,000 years would they choose a boy. Not only is ours more and more a woman's world; by the second quarter of the twenty-first century, when a child born now will be mature, it will be time to wonder if men have a future. In many areas of life they will be marginal, in others an expensive nuisance.

If that sounds wild or overdone, consider the more glaring weaknesses in the so-called stronger sex. Start with medical ones. Boys are more often born with inherited diseases. Because they do not have a spare x-chromosome, whereas girls do, boys with a faulty gene have no back-up. The effects of this deficiency can range from colour-blindness to haemophilia.

Boys tend to have more troubled childhoods, too. More than twice as many boys as girls are autistic – meaning they so totally fail to develop normal social abilities that they cannot function independently. They are eight times as likely as girls to be hyperactive – uncontrollably jumpy and energetic. Dyslexia and stuttering are nearly five times as common among men. As most parents of both will tell you, bringing up a boy can be considerably more fraught and risky than bringing up a girl.

It is not much better at the other end of life. Until early this century, American men tended to live as long as or longer than women. Since then a gap has opened up, and it is getting steadily wider each year. Men now die on average fully seven years before women born in the same year. More strikingly, male mortality is rising in relation to female mortality in every age group.

One of the main reasons for this is that men get more of most diseases than women. Before the age of 65 men are more than twice as likely to die from heart disease as women; they are also more likely to suffer strokes, ulcers and liver failure. Half of all men get cancer, compared with only one-third of women. Smoking, which until recently was largely a male pastime, accounts for

some of this difference, but not all. According to Andrew Kimbrell (*The Masculine Mystique*; Ballantine), the death rate from cancer has risen by 21 per cent in men in 30 years, while it has stayed the same for women.

For these depressing medical facts, there is a one-word explanation: testosterone. The male steroid hormone weakens the body's resistance to infectious diseases and cancer; it also seems to cause the body to age more rapidly. Eunuchs usually live much longer than other men. To the conspiracy-minded, testosterone might even look like part of an evolutionary plot on behalf of females.

Next, consider boys' educational weaknesses. Evidence is growing that on many counts girls are cleverer than boys. In 1995 the top five places – and fourteen of the top twenty – in a league table of British schools ranked by exam results were all-girl schools. In 1979 roughly equal numbers of girls and boys got five or more passes at O-level, the girls doing very marginally better. Since then the performance gap has widened. Girls now are clearly likelier than boys to get five passes.

Similar findings come from America. Boys there are half as likely again to be held back a grade in school at age 13; twice as likely to be in special education and twice as likely to drop out of high school altogether. Girls are more likely than boys to go to university, still more likely to graduate, and even more likely to do a master's degree.

Testosterone's peak

After school, our putative couple's hypothetical son would then embark on another risk-fraught period of life as the output of testosterone reached a peak. Talk of violence and, more often than not, you are talking about young men. About 80 per cent of murder victims are men, as are 90 per cent of murderers. Most of these are in their twenties and the cause of most murders is hot-blooded, testosterone-induced arguments over status and love. Well aware of the connection between gender and crime, some American feminists have even proposed a male poll tax to help pay for police and prisons.

Licking wounds and drowning sorrows, young men get hooked on drugs or alcohol about twice as often as women. But that leads to more violence. More than 80 per cent of drunken drivers and those arrested for drug offences are men. The sex ratio of prisoners in United States jails is more than ten men to each woman, and men get longer sentences for similar offences. The great majority of AIDS victims in America (though not in Africa) are men. Men attempting suicide are four times as likely as women to succeed.

Should a man survive his burst of testosterone – most do – and reach the age of 30, the chances are increasing that he will find himself without steady work. The number of American men in full-time employment is falling by about 1 m a year. The number of employed women is rising at almost the same rate. If employment trends continue as now, by the end of the century, if not before, the United States will be employing more women than men.

Britain is not far behind. On Tyneside, once a byword for heavy industries employing skilled men in secure jobs while their wives stayed at home, the reversal is now so acute that a locally born playwright, Alan Plater, has written a play about it. *Shooting the Legend* is set in a colliery's social-welfare club run by unemployed men whose wives work. It is no joke. Roughly, for every new (commonly female) job in banking or airline reservation that has been created in the region since 1980, another in ship-building or heavy engineering has been lost.

One reason for this is a change in the nature of work. As each year goes by, job openings in agriculture, manual labour, metal-banging and machine-handling decline, while work in retailing, word-processing, services and health care – all traditionally female jobs – opens up. At its simplest, as computers replace tractors, brain is replacing brawn. Now that they are more and more educated, women will be almost certain to start claiming their rewards. (Conspiratorialists will recall the original idea for the modern computer was due to a woman, Ada Lovelace.)

Should some lucky male, having run this gauntlet, survive long enough to turn to sex with a woman, he will find he has entered a war zone where the enemy has many things, including law, on her side. Among many animal species males are the seducing sex; females the sex that decides whether to be seduced. Interestingly, this is less true for species where males nourish females or foster offspring – virtues females will seduce for. But a widespread pattern is that females flirt, men pounce. Among humans, this preserve is laced with rules, written or unwritten, and full of risks.

Think, to take a tricky but salient example, of date rape. According to Andrea Dworkin, an American feminist, the big difference between seduction and rape is that 'in seduction, the rapist bothers to buy a bottle of wine'. Many evolutionary biologists would agree. To them any animal seduction is an asymmetric act of more or less forcible persuasion by a very keen seller of sperm, which comes cheap, to a discriminating buyer of impregnation, which involves huge investments of time and energy. The more asymmetric the investment, the harder the male tries. In human beings a few minutes' work by a man can be leveraged into nine months of female gestation. Whether the eager male is a rapist, an over-persistent seducer or just a husband is to the thoroughgoing feminist and to the evolutionary biologist of secondary interest.

Despite the nursery rhyme about Jack Sprat and his wife, another disreputable thing men do is to eat both more meat and more fat than women. The habit goes back to the Pleistocene era, when modern human beings emerged in Africa and began to spread to the rest of the world, replacing earlier forms of the species. Among modern hunter-gatherer peoples men catch most of the meat and women gather most of the plant food. Although men share meat with women, they tend to be more carnivorous.

Red meat comes these days with all the wrong cultural labels. Eating it is increasingly treated as cruel, environmentally damaging and unhealthy. Vegetarianism is on the rise, but particularly among women. Encouraged by this trend, many governments are spending large sums of money in health campaigns devoted to the demonization of red meat.

Mummy, what are men for?

Men are not, for all that, utter weaklings. Suppose that, under-educated, diseased, sclerotic and unemployed, the hypothetical son of our putative couple has made it to middle-age some time in the 2030s. Just as he is thinking about putting his feet on the chair and cracking a can to watch football, the beer stales and the game pales. Unaccountably he finds himself asking, 'What is it all about? What has it all been for?' But this familiar midlife twinge has a new, nasty twist. He is struck with existential doubt not just about himself, but about his gender as a whole. And the bond of male solidarity makes the question no easier to face: what are men for?

Biologically, the purpose of sex is still poorly understood. There are animals and plants that get by without one. Dandelions, for example, produce baby dandelions by themselves. Whiptail lizards in the Arizona desert practise virgin birth, though they perform a pseudo-copulation to get themselves in the mood. There is a whole class of animals, the bdelloid rotifers, that, as far as scientists estimate, have not produced a male individual for around 30 m years, and they do not just survive, they thrive.

The puzzle is less why sex (and so males) arose, but why it (and they) survive. Suppose, for a moment, sex is already present. You would think it ought to die out, and here is why. Note that, by convention, biologists call even asexual creatures that reproduce themselves female. Imagine now a population of asexual females, which pass on all their genes to the next generation; and a population of sexual ones, which mix their genes with males through copulation or some other form of sexual transmission. (This pairing of sexed and unsexed populations is not as bizarre as it sounds: snails of either sort exist side by side in

New Zealand.) Suppose each female has two offspring. The asexual ones will pass their genes on to two offspring, each of which will bear two more, and so on. If the sexual females have on average a male and female offspring, only one will reproduce. In other words, the asexual gene pool should grow while the sexual one should soon die out.

But, luckily for men, it survives. There seems to be a point to sexual reproduction that counterbalances this evolutionary pressure towards femininity. That point may be summed up by saying that, once a generation, sex remixes the genes of two individuals. This spins the numbers on the genetic combination lock that seals each cell, which foils parasitic burglars such as worms, bacteria and viruses. As the main exponent of this theory, William Hamilton of Oxford University, puts it: 'Sexual species are committed to a free and fair exchange of biotechnology for the exclusion of parasites.' The reason why a defence is needed is that parasites are always trying to unlock cells using the previous generation's commonest combination.

It may sound like small comfort to a doubt-struck man to learn that he is, in effect, the female sex's health-insurance policy. But having, so to speak, invented males, our female ur-ancestors then used them for other purposes. Most strikingly, many animal species use males as genetic sieves, to sift out the good genes and discard the bad. They do this by equipping males with all sorts of encumbrances and then setting them to work in competition, either beating each other up or risking their lives against predators and parasites.

The end result, as in a deadly jousting tournament, is a lot of dead males and one or two survivors in clear possession of superior genes: thus has the species been 'sieved' for the better. Peacocks' tails and nightingales' songs are two examples of the accoutrements to these virility tests designed to get most males killed through exhaustion, disease and violence purely so that females can tell which males have the best genes.

A bull elephant seal may look to some like a male chauvinist pig – all force and no child care – but it is actually the victim of evolutionary manipulation by the female sex: to the extent that the bull seal is designed at all, it is meant to die of disease or violence trying, and usually failing, to win one chance of fathering lots of children.

The hormone testosterone, in sum, is the supreme female 'invention'. Not only does testosterone make males do dangerous things, such as fight each other or take absurd risks. It also weakens the immune system. Males, we know, are more likely to get diseases. But now we can see the biological reason why. The higher they push their testosterone levels to win fights and seduce females, the greater the risk of disease they run. The biochemical connection is direct.

Men's secret

Despite everything said so far, there is hope for men. For one thing stands in the way of a world without beer, hamburgers, pot bellies and patriarchy. Men's fate hangs by a slender thread, perhaps, but thread it is, and one of a scientifically compelling kind: for the moment, sperm is needed. If women did decide to switch to virgin birth by the simple procedure of fusing the genetic nuclei of two eggs instead of sperm and an egg, it would not actually work. At least it would not work in our species, or for any other higher mammal, though it might work, for example, in a platypus, a kangaroo or a bird.

The experiment has been done in mice. Scientists produced an embryo with a nucleus made from two sperm nuclei; and another embryo with a nucleus made from two egg nuclei. There was a remarkable difference. The all-sperm embryo developed a large and healthy placenta but a slightly deformed and rather small foetus. The all-egg embryo developed a good, healthy foetus but a small and ill-formed placenta: without a good placenta, the foetus soon died.

In other words, the placenta is largely the product of genes inherited from the father – indeed it is full of paternal genes that almost viciously set about exploiting the mother's body, not trusting the maternal genes to do so selfish a job – and without a placenta the foetus could not develop. So given the present horizons of bio-engineering, sperm remains necessary for successful fertilization and embryo growth.

But men should not sigh with relief. For a different worry looms: sperm is, or may be, disappearing. Out of the wondrous modern chemical industry flow products that appear to mimic the effects of female hormones and to reduce the sperm counts of men. (Immediately, that is a problem for both sexes; on a longer, more evolutionary scale, it is a deathknell for men.) If you believe the figures, which some scientists hotly contest, the average number of sperm in the average man's semen is falling so steadily that it 'portends the collapse of traditional means of procreation by the middle of the next century', according to one expert in the field. If that is true, it is serious. Most men spend a lot of time thinking, if that is the word, about 'traditional means of procreation'. The speed of decline is disputed. But studies done in Denmark, France and Britain all point in the same direction: fewer sperm per ejaculation each year.

What to blame for falling sperm-counts is hard to pin down. The problem is not that most chemicals are innocent but that so many are guilty. Now scientists have started looking, they are finding scores of chemicals, natural and synthetic, that mimic the effect of female hormones. When given to male rainbow trout, they cause them to start making female proteins called vitellogenins. Put a shoal of male trout downstream from a sewage farm using those chemicals and the fish are likely to start to feminize.

Just about any of the common chemicals used in making plastics seems to encourage the production of oestrogen, the female hormone. Pregnant rats fed on low doses of them give birth to male offspring with small testicles and low sperm counts. Nonylphenol, the most potent of the chemicals, first came to light in a (woman's) laboratory in Boston when some plastic tubes were traced as the source of a mysterious substance that made breast-cancer cells grow in a glass jar.

The case against men

So is Jack Lang, France's former culture minister and a fine nose for fashion, right when he claimed – in the title of his recent book – 'Tomorrow belongs to women'? Recall, a moment, how men let the species down. They are more prone to disease, more dumb at school and more troubled at home than girls. They are more violent, die earlier, and in many walks of life are becoming less and less needed at work. Biologically, males are useful chiefly as a 'genetic sieve' for the safer transmission of the genes of the reproducing female. Male sperm, in addition, seems important to the production of the embryo-protecting placenta. But, in the longer run, there are evolutionary question-marks over the need for men to perform the first of those functions and over their capacity to perform the second.

A world of tamed, feminized or vanished men would be a world with less meat, which would reduce pressure on rain forests. It would be a world with less crime, where even the slums of Rio de Janeiro would be safe at night. Pornography would largely disappear. So would rape, classically understood. Children, true, would be brought up in fatherless homes, but the evidence suggests that it is mainly boys who turn bad in such circumstances, not girls.

Nor, as a vision of things to come, need a world without men hold out such terrible fears. Civilization owes much to men. But creating cultures and technologies is one thing, preserving them another. A sex adapted to the one is not obviously adapted to the other. In the grand sweep of things, the human race may before long have completed its evolution from a warring collection of romantic, male-dominated tribes to a peaceable, cool-headed sisterhood devoted to shopping and household management – those most feminine of arts known nowadays as economics.

Part 6

Sociology of the Body: Health, Illness and Ageing

In Reading 19 Stephen Hunt and Nikki Lightly discuss the rise of 'alternative medicine' in contemporary societies. Treatments like acupuncture, aromatherapy and body massage have become increasingly popular. Such treatments do not stem from scientific investigation as orthodox medicine does. Moreover the level of professional training for many practitioners of alternative medicine is often quite limited. The rise of alternative medicines is at least to some degree to do with people's perception of the limits of orthodox health care. But they have also become popular because more and more people are giving attention to the relation between health and lifestyle. Many alternative medicines are more about the prevention of illness than its cure.

AIDS is an apparently new illness which is causing many deaths around the world. The onset of AIDS is believed to be linked to a virus, the Human Immunodeficiency Virus. Many millions of people in the world are known to be HIV-positive. AIDS is producing havoc in some African countries, where as many as one-third of the population of some cities are believed to be HIV positive. In her contribution, Reading 20, Sarah Nettleton relates the fear of AIDS to other forms of risk. The author argues that providing information about levels of risk is not enough. We have to recognise that how people respond to risk is heavily influenced by customs, habits and forms of social power.

Jeremy Rifkin, in Reading 21, discusses the social impact of genetic engineering – the capability to intervene in human genetic development. The more we achieve the capability of modifying our genes, the more we create new powers that can be used for human betterment, but which also raise a range of social problems. Companies involved in developing bio-technology are seeking to patent discoveries and exploit them primarily for financial gain. Yet surely, Rifkin argues, our genetic resources are just as much part of our public and collective life as is the natural environment. We urgently need to find ways of protecting this common genetic inheritance.

Exercise, slimming and controlled eating are linked not only to the desire to 'look good', but to attempts to follow a healthy lifestyle. A look back to two centuries ago provides graphic evidence of the level to which illness and the prospect of an early death haunted the lives of individuals in eighteenth-century society (Reading 22). Infectious diseases were rampant and the ordinary person suffered from a range of chronic complaints which many of us in modern social conditions would find intolerable.

Some of the great breakthroughs in the improvement of health care were made in the area of preventive medicine, particularly as a result of improvements in methods of hygiene. Other changes, however, have depended more upon the emergence of organized systems of health care.

19 A Sociology of 'Fringe' Medicine: A Healthy Alternative?

Stephen Hunt and Nikki Lightly

Health care today seems to have reached an important crossroads. At a time when orthodox medical services in Western societies have expanded and medical science has advanced in many areas, the number of healing methods, practitioners and people interested in what is frequently referred to as 'alternative medicine' has continued to grow. Indeed, the expansion of such 'alternatives' has been so great that a whole commercial industry has emerged around them. Increasingly, the populations of advanced industrial societies appear to be becoming health 'consumers', who want more and more information and new *choices* in health care. Moreover, it seems that many people are increasingly open to the idea of balancing the use of orthodox medicine with choices in complementary medicine; in short, taking resources from what *both* have to offer.

In considering the recent expansion of alternative medicines, a number of key questions emerge. Precisely what do we mean by 'alternatives'? How widespread is their use? How do we explain their increasing popularity? Are there particular types of people who use alternative medicines?

A starting point in our discussion might be to outline those alternatives that are enjoying the strongest growth; this will provide insights into their popularity. Ursula Sharma has described the ten most popular practices in descending order in box 19.1 (Look these up in a dictionary to discover their definitions.)

> **Box 19.1   'Alternative' medicines**
>
> (1)   Herbalism
> (2)   Osteopathy
> (3)   Homeopathy
> (4)   Acupuncture
> (5)   Chiropractic
> (6)   Spiritual healing
> (7)   Hypnotherapy
> (8)   Reflexology
> (9)   Naturopathy
> (10) Aromatherapy
>
> *Source*: U. Sharma, *Complementary Medicine Today* (Routledge, 1992)

Definitions of alternative medicines

Having identified the most popular forms, we must now decide: what exactly is meant by 'alternative'? Such a definition is not easily achieved. The first problem is that the term 'alternative', applied to medicine or therapies, tends to be interchangeable with others, such as 'complementary' or 'holistic' – each of which has its own precise meaning (see box 19.2). The definition offered by the World Health Organisation is all forms of health care that 'usually lie outside the official health sector'. However, this is a very broad

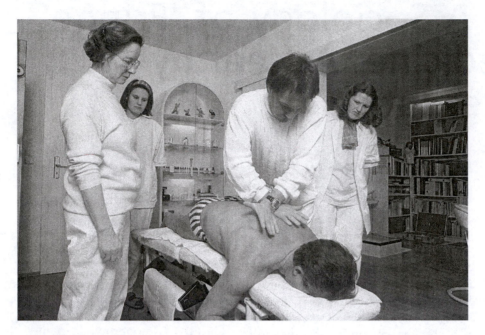

Alternative treatments: chiropractic

Alternative treatments: qi gong

definition. Another approach is to suggest that some alternatives, such as osteopathy, chiropractic and homeopathy, require a high degree of *professional training*. The second category, therefore, tends to *lack* such training; these would include everything else such as faith healing or herbalism.

The problem is that these categories are rather blurred. It might help to distinguish between them according to their orientation, emphasis and what they attempt to achieve. We can *first* identify those therapies concerned with *touch* and *relaxation*, such as reflexology. *Second*, we can categorise '*manipulation techniques*', such as chiropractic and osteopathy. A *third* category includes treatments which concentrate upon *energetic balances* in the body, such as acupuncture. *Fourth* are those forms based upon biochemistry, such as herbal medicine. *Finally*, there exists a whole host of therapies concerned with *integrating* various aspects of the mind and body or integrative methods which would include *yoga* and *Ayurveda*. While these are useful classifications, they still fail to do justice to the variety and scope of the vast range of medicines and therapies on offer.

Alternative treatments: herbalism

Box 19.2   Clarifying concepts

Alternative medicine denotes medical practices that are *different* from accepted forms. People use alternative health practices *instead* of orthodox medicine. Alternative does not guarantee that methods will be holistic. For example, someone may consult an acupuncturist or chiropractor as an alternative to receiving drug therapy or surgery. Alternative medicine may be used to address particular conditions or to transform health and lifestyle practices.

Holistic medicine embodies a particular *attitude* to health: the patient's health is regarded as integral to the human organism – an entity that is dynamic and constantly changing. The practice is concerned with an understanding of the different functional aspects of the client: physical, emotional, psychological, social and spiritual. Holistic health is not only a medical criterion but also a cultural concept and the way in which it is defined varies over time and place.

Complementary medicine implies an approach to health that recognises the potential relationship between various health-care choices and can include many orthodox and non-orthodox healing arts. It marks a shift from seeing alternatives as *separate* from modern orthodox medicine to recognising that they can enhance and support orthodox treatment.

Orthodox medicine covers the understanding and treatment of the human body and health which is widely accepted in Western societies. The medical profession claims its system of medical practices to be superior, legitimated by scientific methods in diagnosis and cure.

Source: Adapted from K. Olsen, *The Encyclopedia of Alternative Health Care* (Piatkus, 1989)

Labelling alternatives

In *defining* what alternative medicines are, it is also necessary to discuss the role of scientific medicine in *labelling* such forms of medicine as 'alternatives'. As sociological theorists of social deviance such as Jock Young have shown us, the application of the label 'deviant' may largely result from the capacity of those in positions of power to *apply* the label. This is an important point as far as alternative medicines are concerned. The definition of alternative medicines, such as that of the World Health Organisation quoted above, shows a considerable *deference* to the legitimacy of scientific medicine.

In fact, it is only the power and dominance of the medical model which gives it the authority to label these practices as 'alternative' or out of the 'norm'. Indeed, people are so strongly socialised these days towards having faith in the dominance of *biomedicine* that the 'alternative' treatments are automatically considered to be on the fringe of respected medical practice ('fringe' medicine being another term used to describe non-orthodox methods). In fact, before the Medical Registration Act of 1858, the two kinds of medicine were far less distinguishable from each other and were probably afforded a roughly *equal* measure of common legitimacy. The population at the time was likely to have relied mainly on folk remedies. The modern role of science within medicine has led many to perceive the results of its drugs and surgery as nothing less than miraculous.

Interest groups and professional power

Since the rise of alternative medicines and techniques has been, to some extent at least, a result of the perceived *deficiencies* of orthodox medicine, it is perhaps not surprising that powerful professional interests have often led the medical profession to be critical of the alternative forms. In recent years articles have appeared in medical and scientific journals which deride alternative medicine as 'the flight from science' (*British Medical Journal*) or conclude that 'alternative medicine is no alternative' (*The Lancet*).

'People get lulled into a false sense of security because many of these things are labelled "natural",' said Dr Yank D. Coble MD, an expert at the University of Florida. 'But many of these herbs or vitamin supplements can impair the absorption of medicines – and that is dangerous.' (*National Enquirer*, 7 April 1998)

Despite the considerable reservations that scientific medicine has about its unorthodox rivals, some of the alternative treatments are being slowly brought under the professional umbrella. However, they are only being offered the stamp of authenticity when they have been brought firmly under the power of the medical model. To demonstrate this, Mike Saks uses the example of the incorporation of *acupuncture*.[1] The medical profession shunned the procedure when it first became popular in the 1960s. This was largely due to its perceived 'quackish' nature and its 'unscientific' theories, based upon the Chinese philosophy of Yin and Yang. Nevertheless, in the face of growing popularity doctors began to come up with *scientific explanations* for its success and practitioners of acupuncture within the mainstream health service began to emerge. However, the dominance of the scientific view of the medical profession will certainly mean that some 'effective' alternatives will almost certainly never gain mainstream respectability.

Explaining the growth of alternatives

There are no straightforward answers as to why alternative medicines and therapies have become so popular. There are, however, probably five broad interrelated, reasons that might be considered.

1   *People find it hard to accept that orthodox medicine sometimes fails and so resort to an alternative.* This explanation is important because it suggests that it is possible to see the popularity of alternative medicine, paradoxically, as arising primarily out of frustration with

Box 19.3   Alternative and complementary therapy survey (*Daily Telegraph*, 1996)

- 96% of the British population have tried an alternative therapy at least once.
- Of those who have tried an alternative therapy at least once 25% were male and 75% were female.
- 50% of those trying an alternative at least once were between 45 and 64 years old.

Frequency of use

Once a week	28%
Once a month	26%
More than twice a year	27%
Once a year	3%
Other	16%

Most popular types of alternative therapies
(Some people used more than one kind)

Homeopathy	53%
Osteopathy	31%
Herbalism	22%
Aromatherapy	22%
Nutritional therapy	21%
Chiropractic	16%
Reflexology	13%

Complaints treated
(Some people used alternative therapy for more than one complaint)

Musculo-skeletal	60%
Respiratory	11%
Circulatory	12%
Digestive	17%
Skin disorder	8%
Uro-genital disorder	5%
Psychological	8%
Allergy	10%
Other	13%

Reason for use of alternative therapy
(Some respondents gave more than one answer)

Orthodox medicine was not helping	52%
Of benefit before	37%
Worried about side effects of orthodox medicine	25%
Wanted a second opinion	37%
Scientific evidence of benefit	10%

Effect of alternative therapy

Very helpful	77%
Quite helpful	17%
No difference	4%
Quite harmful	1%
Very harmful	1%

conventional medicine, despite its successes. This does not mean that people have lost faith in orthodox medicine; rather the opposite: they have a fundamental faith in what it can achieve, but their *expectations* have soared. In other words, people are impatient with the rate of scientific advance and, therefore, seek alternatives. Given the choice, however, orthodox medicine is still preferred by most.

2 *People are increasingly critical of the harmful effects of the orthodox services.* An early survey measuring the expansion of the alternatives (*Which?* magazine, 1981) revealed that two-thirds of those who had received alternative medical treatment during the previous

5 years said that they had earlier resorted to orthodox health care but that they did not like it or it was not helping. In line with numerous studies since, the survey showed that what people disliked most was the unpleasant side effects of medical drugs and also the 'interventionist' nature of much Western medical practice, with its preference for surgical operations.

3 *There is a growing dissatisfaction in people of all ages with what is available in the orthodox medical sphere.* This entails a criticism of modern medicine and existing health provision. There is a great deal of documented evidence in respect of the alleged failings of the orthodox

services, including its financial restrictions, the long waiting lists for treatment and, above all, its failure to cure chronic disease. Many of these factors have also to be considered against a background of economic recession over the last two or three decades where various forms of private and alternative health care, alongside self-help initiatives, have been positively encouraged by the state.

A related point is that the appeal of many alternative therapies lies in their ability to address or shift the traditional power imbalance in the doctor–client relationship. Many 'alternatives' allow much more input from the patients, thus empowering them in diagnoses and searches for cures. It is increasingly clear that the growing common interest in and appreciation of alternatives inform us that people are finding something new and positive in this approach. In short, people feel that they are listened to and treated as *individuals* (the rise of individualism), which is a major departure from the approach of orthodox medicine.

4 *Some people have religious or philosophical arguments against certain Western medical practices.* This point is more important than it might at first sound. The popularity of some forms of alternatives lies in their recognising the significance of the emotional, *psychological* and even spiritual dimensions of the patient. Modern medicine still holds strongly to the restrictions of the mind–body divide, which plays down the connection between psychiatric and emotional problems on the one hand and physical ailments on the other. In other words, many alternatives focus upon the dimensions of healing and health related to the psychological and spiritual needs of the patient. *Postmodernists* often support this attack on conventional Western approaches to science.

5 *There is a growing proportion of the population which simply needs to be different and experiment.* Many alternative medicines and therapies grew in popularity in the so-called counter-culture which developed in Western societies from the 1960s. The counter-culture

movement challenged many of the orthodoxies of the day, whether they were political, moral or medical. This led to experimentation with 'alternatives'. At the same time, the movement put considerable emphasis upon the idea of human potential – in short, an active concern with developing the mind, body and spirit. In recent years, many of these themes have furnished the beliefs of a new expression of religiosity, the New Age movement.[2] Much New Age philosophy marries Eastern and Western approaches to health and medicine. Alternative medicine is part of a *cultural current* which embraces New Age therapies, holistic health, the wholefood movement, the quest for the 'natural' in therapy, childbirth, food and so on.

Who uses alternatives?

Another way of finding out *why* alternatives are on the rise is to examine the social groups and individuals who have taken up these approaches.

Social class

At one time it was assumed that 'non-scientific' forms of medicine and healing were the preserve of the uneducated, lower social classes or the marginalised ethnic minorities. The key explanation offered here was that these groups had not been adequately socialised into the cultural mainstream and its overwhelming acceptance of orthodox medical practice.[3] Another explanation was, as we have seen, that there was a connection between 'alternative' medicine and countercultures. This tended to give the impression that subscribers were rather quirky or wacky.

Today, certain forms of alternative medicine have become a great deal more 'respectable'. The upsurge of alternative healing strategies over the last two decades has made it clear that they were increasingly attractive to *wealthier* social groups, in particular, the *middle classes* and those with higher levels of education. This does not mean to say that patients treated by the alternative methods do not come from all social classes. However, in Britain there are more 'alternative' patients from socio-economic grades A and B (professional, managerial, technical, business, academic etc.) than from other social groups.

There are several reasons for this. The most important are, first, as is the case with other aspects of the welfare state and the orthodox health provision, it is the *middle classes* who are more educated about what is available and who take the opportunity to use the full range of treatments. Second, very few of the alternatives are available *free of charge*. This may explain why, as Fulder points out,[4] spiritual healing and herbalism (and to some extent hypnotherapy) are more popular with the less well-off since they are often free.

Age, gender and ethnicity

Besides the significance of social class, other social variables, such as age, gender and ethnicity, should be considered when examining who uses the alternatives and what forms are preferred. As far as age is concerned, Fulder and Monro's survey indicates that patients tend to be predominantly young to middle-aged.[5] There were few infants or elderly patients. The elderly are probably less willing to experiment with complementary medicine and have less money to pay for it. On the other hand, the very young are likely to be healthier than most and to suffer from acute (emergency, life-threatening) conditions rather than the chronic (long-term) diseases which are the targets of alternative approaches.

Most surveys in Britain, as in other countries, show that a slightly larger number of *females* than males use non-orthodox medicine. For example, a MORI poll in 1998 showed that 71 per cent of men, compared to 67 per cent of women, had never used alternative medicine. This may simply reflect the fact that women are also more likely than men to consult *orthodox* practices. But it may also suggest some female alienation from male-dominated mainstream medicine. Second, it is well known that women are more likely than

men to experience certain chronic conditions. There is also different gender preference as far as different *types* of alternatives are concerned; females prefer such forms as herbalism and homeopathy, while males prefer massage and osteopathy. These again may reflect the prevailing medical complaints suffered by males and females but, to some extent at least, they also result from socially constructed gender roles.

The MORI poll of 1998 showed that blacks (29 per cent) in Britain were slightly less likely than whites (31 per cent) to use the most popular forms of alternative practices. The poll showed that non-whites were also more likely to use homeopathy and spiritual healing methods – most of which are derived from contrasting cultural traditions and belief systems. It follows that each ethnic group has its preferences. Many ethnic groups vary considerably in the emphasis they put upon orthodox or alternative forms, or use them to complement each other.

Conclusion: how much of an alternative?

The use of, and support for, complementary approaches is growing in Britain. According to MORI in 1992 one in seven British people were receiving such treatment and three-quarters wanted to see such methods established and offered freely as part of the NHS. Its popularity is also growing elsewhere. But is it really an 'alternative'?

So far, we have considered alternative medicine and orthodox medicine as if they have very little in common. But Crawford critically argues that alternatives are not really alternatives at all, in that they still put the emphasis in health care upon the *individual*.[6] Such a view of health, like orthodox approaches, places the major burden of change on the individual and ignores vital *social* constraints, such as poor environmental conditions, social class background and ethnic factors. The nature of *society* is thus rendered unproblematic.

Fulder argues that alternative medicine has the advantage of being holistic, that is, it frequently

A Chinese pharmacy in Soho, London

puts an emphasis upon self-healing through dealing with the mind, body and spirit. In this way it could provide a sound underpinning for improving health in society. However, he also asks whether these alternative practitioners are *really* prepared to take sole responsibility for their patients' well-being without relying on the security of the socially legitimated and mainstream doctors and hospitals.

The contemporary Western view of health carries a strong confirmation of a distinctive 'goal'. Health is something to be realised and enhanced as a continuous process. This itself reflects the hegemony (dominance) of orthodox medicine. Crawford sees alternative medicines and techniques as not so much a *rejection* of rationalised medicine as an *extension* of it. This is because they largely remain embedded in moralities and approaches which see *individual* behaviour, attitudes and emotions, rather than the causes and effects of social environments, as the essential 'symptoms' which need to be addressed. For Crawford and others a *real* revolution in health care would address the *primary* social and economic

sources of many illnesses. In the meantime, as stresses on orthodox health systems continue to grow and as identity, lifestyle and consumption continue to be strongly linked, we can expect alternative health care to thrive. Will you try it?

NOTES

1 M. Saks (ed.), *Alternative Medicine in Britain* (Oxford: Clarendon Press, 1992).
2 P. Heelas, *The New Age Movement* (Oxford: Basil Blackwell, 1992).
3 E. Friedson, *Professions of Medicine* (New York: Dodd Mead, 1970).
4 S. Fulder, *The Handbook of Complementary Medicine* (Oxford: Oxford University Press, 1992).
5 S. Fulder and R. Munro, 'Complementary Medicine in the UK', *The Lancet*, 2 (1985), pp. 242–5.
6 M. Crawford, 'You are Dangerous to your Health', *International Journal of Health Services*, 7/7 (1977).

20 The Sociology of Health and Illness

Sarah Nettleton

[. . .]

Threats to social order are mirrored in ideas about bodily order – if society is endangered, so too is the body within. Mary Douglas in her treatise on *purity* and *danger* discusses the symbolic and ritual ways in which the world is classified. 'Dirt' and 'pollution' are all those things that are 'matter out of place'; that is, they transcend socially accepted boundaries or classifications, for example, bathroom equipment in the dining room or shoes on the kitchen table. Thus by definition 'dirt' is that which cannot be classified or is not on the right side of a socially accepted boundary. Anything that does transcend boundaries is polluting and carries a considerable symbolic load:

The whole universe is harnessed to men's [sic] attempts to force one another into good citizenship. Thus we find that certain moral values are upheld and certain social rules defined by beliefs in dangerous contagion . . . as we examine pollution beliefs we find that the kinds of contacts which are thought dangerous also carry a symbolic load . . . some pollutions are used as analogies for expressing a general view of social order.[1]

Contemporary anxieties about global threats or pollutions from which no society is immune are reflected by the immunity, or lack of it, of the body. As Turner observes,

The body has once more become apocalyptic given the threat of chemical warfare, the destruction of the natural habitat, the epidemic of HIV and AIDS, the greying/declining populations of northern Europe and the apparent inability of national governments to control medical technology and medical costs.[2]

It is perhaps HIV and AIDS which more than any other disease display analogies between pollution beliefs and social order. They constitute a threat to individuals, and the reactions of social groups suggest that, for some, they are perceived as a threat to social order.

Risks and lifestyles: the example of AIDS

Perhaps more than any other condition this century, Acquired Immune Deficiency Syndrome (AIDS) has generated the most extreme and extensive responses. Since the first case was reported in the USA at the Centre for Disease Control in 1981 the amount of literature produced on the subject has been phenomenal. New journals specifically devoted to AIDS have sprung up, immunologists and virologists have reported their findings in medical journals, epidemiologists have attempted to pattern the incidence of AIDS and to identify the characteristics of those who become infected by Human Immunodeficiency Virus (HIV). Social scientists have attempted to understand the behaviours, practices and cultures of hitherto relatively neglected social groups, especially gay men, prostitutes and IVDUs. The media have incessantly reported, misreported and moralized on the subject. Given all this furore we might well ask: what is this thing called AIDS? Why all the commotion?

What is AIDS?

It is not possible to give an unequivocal answer to this question. What counts as AIDS and knowledge pertaining to it have invariably changed over the last decade and will undoubtedly continue to do so.[3] Nevertheless, and somewhat crudely, AIDS is currently taken to refer to a defected cell-mediated immunity as a result of infection by HIV. In particular HIV penetrates cells within the body which are essential to maintain our immunity. As these cells, known as CD4 cells, are depleted, the virus becomes prevalent and immunity to diseases is reduced. Diseases characteristic of AIDS include Kaposi's Sarcoma (KS) and a type of pneumonia, Pneumocystis carinii pneumonia. Some authors prefer to substitute the term 'HIV disease' for AIDS because, as they point out, the clinical definitions of AIDS fail to describe the range of health problems which occur once a person has been infected.[4] It is believed that the main ways in which HIV is transmitted are via blood, semen, cervical and vaginal secretions. Whilst the virus has been isolated in saliva and tears, it has not been transmitted through these mediums.

In 1992 the WHO *estimated* that some 2.5 million cases of AIDS and around 13 million instances of HIV had occurred globally. Although statistics in this area are highly problematic, they do give a crude indication of patterns of prevalence. As at the end of 1992, the WHO reported 611,589 *documented* cases of AIDS across the globe since 1979. Of these, 51.2 per cent were from the Americas, 34.5 per cent from Africa, 13.2 per cent from Europe, 0.66 per cent from Oceania and 0.42 per cent from Asia. In the UK, by the end of 1992, 6,510 cases had been reported since 1979. This represented a rate of about 2.0 cases per 100,000 of the population in 1991. This figure compared to rates of 16.3 for the USA, 8.7 for Spain, 7.1 for France, 6.6 for Switzerland, 6.2 for Italy, 2.4 for Germany, 1.5 for Sweden, 1.4 for Greece and 1.3 for Norway in the same year.

AIDS and the risk society

In some respects AIDS has similar characteristics to the non-calculable risks of the sort discussed by Giddens and Beck. Sontag observes this tendency:

To the death of oceans and lakes and forests, the unchecked growth of populations in the poor parts of the world, nuclear accidents like Chernobyl, the puncturing and depletion of the ozone layer . . . to all these, now add AIDS . . . The taste for worst-case scenarios reflects the need to master fear of what is felt to be uncontrollable.[5]

The epidemic of AIDS is matched by an epidemic of fear and panic. Strong refers to this as an 'epidemic psychology', that is, societies become caught up in an emotional maelstrom which seems, for a time at least, to get out of control.[6] The appearance of a new kind of disease, which may be transmitted through the most intimate of human contacts, strikes at the heart of individual and social interactions, and thereby reveals the fragility of social order. It is this perceived threat to social order that generates such fervent moralizing. Such moralizing can also be understood in terms of boundaries. As we have learned from Douglas, points of contact and pollution (such as being infected by a virus), involve the crossing of a body boundary and will therefore carry a symbolic load. Body boundaries, in turn, Douglas argues, are found to be represented metaphorically as social boundaries. If the body is under threat from a dangerous 'other', so is society.

The threat of AIDS: a menacing 'other'

Kroker and Kroker, writing in the USA, draw parallels between the fear of AIDS and a generalized fear of the breakdown of immunological systems.[7] For example, they note that there is a striking resemblance between the medical rhetoric surrounding AIDS and military rhetoric. Indeed, the prevailing metaphors within the AIDS discourse have a military ring to them; they are of 'invasion', 'pollution' and 'alien takeover'.[8] The source of the HIV virus always lies elsewhere; either in different countries or in 'different', and often presumed to be 'deviant', social groups.

There are many stories about the origins of AIDS, but the dominant one is summarized by Sontag as follows:

AIDS is thought to have started in the 'dark continent', then spread to Haiti, then to the United States and to Europe, then . . . It is understood as a tropical disease: another manifestation from the so called Third World.[9]

The idea that AIDS originated in and is now widespread in Africa fits neatly with Western conceptions of a wasting continent where poverty, illness and famine are rife.[10] From her detailed analysis of scientific literature on AIDS Patton observes:

When the West found itself beset by a deadly little virus of unknown origin, it sought the source elsewhere: nothing of this sort, it was argued, could have arisen in the germ-free West. So the best research minds of the Western world set off on a fantastic voyage in search of the source of AIDS. They went to Haiti and Zaire because the first non-Euro-American cases were diagnosed in people from these countries . . . [T]here was no scientific reason to believe that these Haitian and Zairian nationals had 'acquired' this theoretical virus in their native countries rather than in the countries (US and Belgium) where they were currently residing.[11]

This rationale which is implicit in scientific thinking is also reinforced by the media's reporting of 'African AIDS' and is common amongst lay people.[12] The idea that countries need to be insulated from HIV is illustrated by debates about the screening of immigrants. In an attempt to strengthen its 'immunity' from AIDS the USA excludes immigrants who are found to be seropositive. However, most other countries, and indeed the WHO, have denounced this discriminatory practice.

The 'otherness' associated with AIDS relates not only to geographical boundaries but also to social identities. AIDS is regarded as a 'disease' of lifestyles which are characteristic of certain social groups. In fact, the syndrome which was first found most often in gay men was called GRID – Gay Related Immune Deficiency. Before the identification of the virus some scientists thought that lifestyle variables might actually be the *cause* of AIDS. For example, it was suggested that immune overload could have been brought about by 'fast lane' gay lifestyles and certain sexual practices.[13] Although these theories have since been discredited, they are still prevalent in the public mind and have been taken up by the media, who use loaded terms such as 'gay plague' and 'gay bug'. Of course, these terms also tend to be reinforced by epidemiological categories which are created because of the higher prevalence of AIDS among gay men, bisexual men, and IVDUs. These people in turn become labelled as 'risk groups'.

'Risk groups' and 'risk behaviours'

The concept of 'risk groups' leads to the idea that individuals within these groups are inherently more at risk from AIDS and are more likely to infect the general population and so should be treated differently. Consequently the boundaries between those 'at risk' and the 'general population' are created. As Patton notes:

The categories of science, especially the conjuncture of epidemiology and virology, have placed a barely invisible *cordon sanitaire* around minority communities, 'deviant' individuals, and around the entire continent of Africa. We no longer need camps or border passes, although several countries have used them in an effort to prevent the spread of HIV. The ideologies encoded in AIDS research have laid a more sublime foundation for selecting groups of people for detention and destruction. The mechanism for this is, ironically, an education strategy which separates the 'general public' from 'communities'.[14]

The distinction between the 'general public' and 'risk groups' is of course an inappropriate one in relation to HIV. You or I have as much risk of being infected with the virus as a gay man who injects drugs and lives in Edinburgh (a city which has a relatively high incidence of HIV) if we partake in 'unsafe' practices. This is because it is certain activities or risk behaviours, such as unprotected anal or vaginal intercourse, and injecting with unsterilized needles that have been used by a person who is already infected with HIV, that increase the likelihood of AIDS, and not the social group with which we identify. Thus it is risk practices or risk behaviours that increase the likelihood of contracting HIV, not risk groups. The notion of 'risk groups' therefore serves to reinforce the idea of difference – that the source of infection lies within those people whose identity and lifestyle fit with the epidemiological data. People who do not identify with a 'risk group' may not feel that the avoidance of risk behaviours is relevant to them. This has clear implications for health promotion.

A further problem with the idea that it is groups of people at greater risk of HIV rather than unsafe practices which raise the likelihood of contracting the infection is that it may serve to reinforce moralizing and in particular the notion that AIDS is a retribution for a particular lifestyle. Within the media reporting of AIDS, if a prostitute, gay or bisexual man or an IVDU contracts HIV, he or she is often classified as 'guilty', whereas haemophiliacs, the recipients of blood transfusions and babies infected in the mother's womb are portrayed as 'innocent'.[15] In the moral and often in the medical discourse the blame for AIDS is put on lifestyles. AIDS has been used by the Moral Right as a justification for their diatribes against homosexuality and the decline of family values.

The desire to promote 'traditional lifestyles' placed the Thatcher Government of the 1980s in a compromised position. On the one hand they were obliged to provide education to counter the spread of HIV and yet, on the other hand, they were pursuing homophobic policies that would invariably be counterproductive to these ends. For example, the now famous 'Section 28' of the 1988 Local Government Act banned 'the promotion of homosexuality' and any talk about 'pretended family relationships' in local authority schools.[16] Another example of this conflict of interests was the way in which Thatcher intervened to stop a national survey into sexual behaviour to gather crucial evidence for the development

of an effective AIDS policy. However, the research was subsequently carried out, funded by non-governmental sources, and has now been published.

Given there are no medical solutions, and given that AIDS is transmitted as a result of social practices, research to throw light on such activities is essential. However, it appears that the Moral Right would prefer it if the extent of such practices was kept in the dark. Despite this, during the last decade sociologists of health and illness have provided data and insight into the 'patterns of social organization and the lifestyles of cultural sub-groups that have previously gone unnoticed or unremarked upon'. Studies have explored in detail the social context of behaviours and practices that increase the risk of HIV among gay and bisexual men, among young women and among prostitutes and IVDUs.

Perceptions of risk and responses to AIDS

It seems that people's perceptions of risk and their ideas about how the AIDS epidemic should be curtailed are closely related. Whilst between 90 and 100 per cent of the population understand that HIV can be transmitted by unprotected sexual intercourse and the exchange of contaminated needles, everyday situations such as the use of a carrier's razor, transmission via public toilets and being in hospital close to people with HIV, are still identified as 'risk situations' by a significant minority of people. This is important because it helps us to understand the persistence of repressive attitudes because risk over-estimation is a significant predictor of support for coercive policies.

A number of studies have attempted to map out lay perceptions and responses to AIDS. Pollack identified five subgroups which ranged between two extreme groups (each containing approximately 15 per cent of all respondents) – the 'coercive group' and the 'libertarian group'. The former comprised older middle-class and manual workers who did not feel personally exposed to

AIDS and had not changed their behaviours. They rated highest in terms of the over-estimation of risk in daily life and they feared that AIDS would have significant social and economic consequences. These views were used to justify their preferences for coercive measures such as compulsory HIV testing and quarantining.

At the opposite extreme the libertarian group were young (under thirty-five), highly educated single students or professionals. They often knew people who were infected or they had been tested themselves, and many reported that they had changed their behaviours. This group rejected all forms of state intervention to curtail the spread of the virus other than the provision of information and education.

An extensive study which used both focus groups and telephone interviews throughout the USA came up with similar findings to those reported above. Herek and Glunt constructed a typology founded upon two axes – pragmatism/moralism and coercion/compassion – in which these four grouped responses could be located.[17] The largest group (54 per cent of whites and 45 per cent of blacks) had views classified as 'compassionate secularism'; that is, they endorsed non-moralistic pragmatic policies such as the distribution of condoms and sterile needles. The 'compassionate moralists' were also concerned about AIDS sufferers but rejected education about safe sex and the distribution of condoms on moral grounds. Encouragingly, relatively few people (7 per cent of whites and 5 per cent of blacks) were 'punitive moralists'; that is, those who supported coercive measures and rejected non-moralistic pragmatic policies. The final group, labelled 'indiscriminate action', were those people who held a range of seemingly incompatible perceptions which, the authors suggest, may reflect an underlying ambivalence towards AIDS.

Whilst there appears to be a strong relation between knowledge about AIDS and social perceptions about it, there does not appear to be a significant relation between knowledge of transmission and reported 'safe' behaviours. Given our earlier discussion of the social embeddedness of

behaviour, this is perhaps not surprising. Behaviours associated with transmission are shaped by significant social and cultural concerns other than health. Advice about 'safe' behaviours often fails to take this into account. For example, advice about 'safe sex' directed towards young heterosexual women fails to take into account the nature of power inherent in sexual encounters. Furthermore, the term 'safe sex', which in its origins in gay culture was a type of activity positively chosen, has come to be defined narrowly in heterosexist terms, as meaning condom use rather than a range of sexual practices which might not require penile penetration. As Holland et al. point out:

The definition of safe sex in terms of effective condom use reinforces, through practice, the central place of male erection and orgasm in sexual encounters. To plan to protect oneself with a condom presupposes something to put it on. Condoms should not be seen as a neutral and rational response to HIV prevention, but as a compromise with existing patriarchal ideology and practices.[18]

Thus we can see that, given the complexity of social interactions which are mediated by social context, the discontinuity between beliefs and behaviour is hardly surprising.

[. . .]

NOTES

1   M. Douglas, *Purity and Danger: An Analysis of the Concepts of Pollution and Taboo* (London: Routledge and Kegan Paul, 1966), p. 3.
2   B. S. Turner, 'Recent Developments in the Theory of the Body', in M. Featherstone, M. Hepworth and B. S. Turner (eds), *The Body: Social Processes and Cultural Theory* (London: Sage, 1991), p. 24.
3   The definition for the identification of AIDS was developed in 1982 – before the 'discovery' of HIV. This was revised in 1987 to include HIV serological test results. From

January 1993 the Centre for Disease Control and Prevention revised the definition once again. It has been suggested that this new definition could result in a significant increase in the number of reported cases of AIDS (R. Chaisson et al., 'Impact of the 1993 Revision of the AIDS in the Clinical Setting', *AIDS*, 7 (1993), pp. 857–62.

4   J. Strang and G. Stimpson, *AIDS and Drug Misuse: The Challenge for Policy and Practice in the 1990s* (London: Routledge, 1990).

5   S. Sontag, *AIDS and its Metaphors* (Harmondsworth: Penguin, 1988), pp. 86–7.

6   P. Strong, 'Epidemic Psychology: A Model', *Sociology of Health and Illness*, 2/3 (1990), pp. 249–59.

7   A. Kroker and M. Kroker, *Body Invaders: Sexuality and the Postmodern Condition* (London: Macmillan, 1988).

8   Sontag, *AIDS*.

9   Ibid., pp. 51–2.

10 P. Treichler, 'AIDS and HIV Infection in the Third World: A First World Chronicle', in B. Kruger and P. Mariani (eds), *Discussions in Contemporary Culture: Remaking History*, 4 (1989), pp. 43–5; C. Patton, *Inventing AIDS* (London: Routledge, 1990), pp. 77–97.

11 Patton, *Inventing AIDS*, p. 83.

12 J. Kitzinger and D. Miller, ' "African AIDS": The Media and Audience Beliefs', in P. Aggleton, P. Davis and G. Hart (eds), *AIDS: Rights, Risk and Reason* (London: Falmer Press, 1992).

13 C. J. N. Lacey and M. A. Waugh, 'Cellular Immunity in Male Homosexuals', *Lancet*, 2 (1983); S. Hsia et al., 'Unregulated Production of a Virus and/or Sperm Specific Anti-idiotypic Antibodies as a Cause of AIDS', *The Lancet*, 2 (1984), pp. 212–14.

14 Patton, *Inventing AIDS*, p. 99.

15 K. Wellings, 'Perceptions of Risk: Media Treatment of AIDS' in P. Aggleton and H. Homans (eds), *Social Aspects of AIDS* (London: Falmer Press); G. Paicheler, 'Society Facing AIDS' *Current Sociology*, 40/3 (1992), pp. 11–23.

16 J. Weeks, 'AIDS and the Regulation of Sexuality', in V. Berridge and P. Strong (eds), *AIDS and Contemporary History* (Cambridge: Cambridge University Press, 1993).

17 G. M. Herek and E. K. Glunt, 'AIDS-related Attitudes in the United States: A Preliminary Conceptualization', *Journal of Sex Research*, 28/1 (1991), pp. 99–123.

21 Patenting Life

Jeremy Rifkin

Genes are the 'green gold' of the biotech century. The economic and political forces that control the genetic resources of the planet will exercise tremendous power over the future world economy, just as in the industrial age access to and control over fossil fuels and valuable metals helped determine control over world markets. In the years ahead, the planet's shrinking gene pool is going to become a source of increasing monetary value. Multinational corporations and governments are already scouting the continents in search of the new 'green gold,' hoping to locate microbes, plants, animals, and humans with rare genetic traits that might have future market potential. Once having located the desired traits, biotech companies are modifying them and then seeking patent protection for their new 'inventions.' Patenting life is the second strand of the new operational matrix of the Biotech Century.

A battle of historic proportions has emerged between the high-technology nations of the North and the poor developing nations of the South over the ownership of the planet's genetic treasures. The struggle for control of genetic resources has dominated the political agenda at the United Nations Food and Agriculture Organization's meetings for more than a decade. Some third world leaders argue that multinational corporations and Northern Hemisphere nations are attempting to seize the biological commons, most of which is found in the biologically rich tropical regions of the Southern Hemisphere. The Southern Hemisphere nations contend that genetic resources are part of their national heritage, just as oil is for the Middle East, and they should be compensated for their use. The multinational corporations and Northern Hemisphere nations maintain that genes increase in market value only when manipulated and recombined using sophisticated gene splicing techniques, and therefore they have no obligation to compensate countries from which the genes are taken. Two examples, one from agriculture, the other from the pharmaceutical field, illustrate the vast potential as well as the bitter struggle that surrounds the enclosure of the genetic commons.

Years ago, scientists discovered a rare perennial strain of maize growing in a mountain forest of south central Mexico. Only a few thousand stalks of the perennial strain existed, in three tiny patches, and they were about to be bulldozed by farmers and loggers. The newly discovered strain was found to be resistant to leaf fungus, which had devastated the U.S. corn crop in 1970, costing farmers over $2 billion. The commercial value of the strain could total several billion dollars a year, according to geneticists and seed company experts.

The rosy periwinkle, found in the tropical rain forest of Madagascar, offers another graphic example of the potential profits that lie in store with the enclosure of the genetic commons. Several years ago, researchers discovered that the rare periwinkle plant contained a unique genetic trait that could be used as a pharmaceutical to treat certain kinds of cancer. Eli Lilly, the pharmaceutical company that developed the drug, is making significant profits – $160 million in sales in 1993 alone – while Madagascar has not received so much as a penny of compensation for the expropriation of one of its natural resources.

Governments around the world have already set up gene storage facilities to preserve rare strains of plants whose genetic traits may prove commercially useful in the future. The U.S. National Seed Storage Laboratory at Fort Collins, Colorado, contains more than 400,000 seeds from all over the world. Many nations are also beginning to establish additional gene banks to store rare microorganisms and frozen animal embryos. In the years ahead, the commercial value of many of these rare strains of plants and breeds of animals will increase dramatically as the world market relies on genetic technologies to produce materials and products.

Enclosing the last frontier

The worldwide race to patent the gene pool of the planet is the culmination of a five-hundred-year odyssey to commercially enclose and privatize all of the great ecosystems that make up the Earth's biosphere. The history of 'enclosures' is critical to understanding the potential long-term consequences of current efforts to enclose the world's gene pool.

The commodification of the global commons began in Tudor England in the 1500s with the enactment of the great 'enclosure acts.' The laws were designed to privatize the feudal commons, transforming the land from a shared trust to private real estate that could be bought and sold as individual units of property in the commercial marketplace. The catastrophic change in people's relationship to the land touched off a series of economic and social reforms that would remake society and reshape humanity's relationship to the natural world for the whole of the modern era.

Much of the economic life of medieval Europe centered around the village commons. Although feudal landlords owned the commons, they leased it to peasant farmers under various tenancy arrangements. In return for their right to cultivate the land, tenant farmers had to turn over a percentage of their harvest to their landlord or devote a comparable amount of time to working the landlord's fields. With the introduction of a moneyed economy in the late medieval period, peasant farmers were increasingly required to pay rent or taxes in return for the right to farm the land.

Medieval European agriculture was communally organized. Peasants pooled their individual holdings into open fields that were jointly cultivated. Common pastures were used to graze their animals. Life was spare, demanding, and unpredictable.

The village commons existed for more than six hundred years along the base of the feudal pyramid, under the watchful presence of the landlords, monarch, and pope. Then, beginning in the 1500s, new and powerful political and economic forces were unleashed, first in Tudor England, and later on the continent, which undermined and ultimately destroyed the communitarianism of village life that had bound humans to one another and the land for centuries.

'Enclosing' means 'surrounding a piece of land with hedges, ditches, or other barriers to the free passage of men and animals.' Enclosure placed the land under private control, severing any right the community formerly had to use it. The enclosure movement was carried out by several means, including acts of Parliament, the agreement of all members of the village commune, and license by the king.

Some historians have called the enclosure movement 'the revolution of the rich against the poor.' Between the sixteenth and nineteenth centuries, a series of political and legal acts were initiated in countries throughout Europe that enclosed publicly held land. In the process, millions of peasants were dislodged from their ancestral homes and forced to migrate into the new towns and cities where, if they were fortunate, they might secure subsistence employment.

Enclosure introduced a new concept of human relationships into European civilization that changed the basis of economic security and the perception of social life. Land was no longer something people belonged to, but rather a commodity people possessed. Land was reduced to a quantitative status and measured by its exchange value. So, too, with people. Relationships were reorganized. Neighbors became employees or contractors. Reciprocity was replaced with hourly wages. People sold their time and labor where they used to share their toil. Human beings began to view each other and everything around them in financial terms. Virtually everyone and everything became negotiable and could be purchased at an appropriate price. Max Weber [. . .] called this great restructuring of relationships the 'disenchantment of the world' – life, land, existence, reduced to abstract quantifiable standards of measurement. The European enclosure movement set the stage for the modern age.

The enclosure of the European landmass and the conversion of the feudal commons to privately held real estate began a process of privatization of the land commons around the world. Today, virtually every square foot of landmass on the planet – with the exception of Antarctica which, by international agreement, has been partially preserved as a non-exploitable shared commons – is either under private commercial ownership or government control.

The enclosure of the Earth's landmass has been followed, in rapid succession, by the commercial enclosure of parts of the oceanic commons, the atmospheric commons, and, more recently, the electromagnetic spectrum commons. Today large swaths of the ocean – near coastal waters – are commercially leased, as is the air which has been converted into commercial air corridors, and the electromagnetic frequencies which governments lease to private companies for radio, telephone, television, and computer transmission.

Now, the most intimate commons of all is being enclosed and reduced to private commercial property that can be bought and sold on the global market. The international effort to convert the genetic blueprints of millions of years of evolution to privately held intellectual property represents both the completion of a half-millennium of commercial history and the closing of the last remaining frontier of the natural world.

The enclosure and privatization of the planet's genetic commons began in 1971 when an Indian microbiologist, Ananda Chakrabarty, at the time an employee of the General Electric Company (G.E.), applied to the U.S. Patents and Trademark Office (PTO) for a patent on a genetically engineered microorganism designed to consume oil spills on the oceans. The PTO rejected the patent request, arguing that living things are not patentable under U.S. patent law. To underscore its contention, the PTO pointed out that in the few cases where patents had been extended to life forms – for asexually reproducing plants – it had taken a legislative act of Congress to create a special exception.

Chakrabarty and G.E. appealed the PTO decision to the Court of Customs and Patent Appeals, where, to the surprise of many observers, they won by a narrow three-to-two decision. The majority on the court argued that 'the fact that microorganisms . . . are alive [is] without legal significance.' The justices went on to say that the patented microorganism was 'more akin to inanimate chemical compositions such as reactants, reagents, and catalysts, than [it was] to horses and honeybees or raspberries and roses.' Clearly, had the first patent request been for a genetically engineered mouse or chimpanzee, it is highly unlikely, given the justices' remarks that the microbe appeared to be closer to a chemical than a horse, that a patent would ever have been granted.

After additional judicial wrangling, the landmark case was appealed, once again, by the Patent Office, this time to the U.S. Supreme Court. The PTO was joined in the case by the People's Business Commission – shortly thereafter renamed The Foundation on Economic Trends – which provided the main amicus curiae brief. The brief, written by Ted Howard, claimed that the case before the court went directly to the heart of the question of the intrinsic value and meaning of life. If the patent were upheld by the court, Howard argued, then 'manufactured life – high and low – will have been categorized as less than life, as nothing but common chemicals.' The People's Business Commission predicted that a favorable court decision would open the door to the patenting of all forms of life in the future.

In 1980, by a slim margin of five to four, the justices ruled in favor of Chakrabarty, granting a patent on the first genetically engineered life form. Speaking for the majority, Chief Justice Warren Burger argued that 'the relevant distinction was not between living and inanimate things,' but whether or not Chakrabarty's microbe was a 'human-made invention.' Speaking for the minority, the late Justice William Brennan countered that 'it is the role of Congress, not this court, to broaden or narrow the reach of patent laws.' Brennan cautioned that in the case of patenting life, Congressional guidance is even more important since 'the composition sought to be patented uniquely implicated matters of public concern.' All of the justices believed that their decision was a narrowly construed one. Justice Burger, referring to 'the gruesome parade of horribles' outlined in the People's Business Commission amicus, made clear his conviction that the decision rendered by the court was an orthodox interpretation of existing patent law and not meant to open up the larger social issues surrounding the genetic engineering of life. These concerns, said the justices, should be left to Congress.

The court's action laid the all-important legal groundwork for the privatization and commodification of the genetic commons. In the aftermath of that historic decision, bioengineering technology shed its pristine academic garb and bounded into the marketplace, where it was heralded by many analysts as a scientific godsend, the long-awaited replacement for a dying industrial order. Nelson Sneider, an investment analyst for E. F. Hutton, a firm that had nurtured much of the initial interest in the emerging biotech-

nical field, said at the time, 'We are sitting at the edge of a technological breakthrough that could be as important as . . . [the] discovery of fire.'[1] So anxious was Wall Street to begin financing the biotechnical revolution that when the first privately held genetic engineering firm offered its stock to public investors, it set off a buying stampede within the investment community. On October 14, 1980, just months after the Supreme Court cleared the way for the commercial exploitation of life, Genentech offered over one million shares of stock at $35 per share. In the first twenty minutes of trading, the stock climbed to $89 a share. By the time the trading bell had rung in late afternoon, the fledgling biotechnology firm had raised $36 million and was valued at $532 million. The astounding thing was that Genentech had yet to introduce a single product into the marketplace.

Corporate America understood the profound implications of the court decision. Genentech gushed, 'The court has assured the country's technology future.' Chemical, pharmaceutical, agribusiness, and biotech start-up companies everywhere sped up their research and development work, mindful that the granting of patent protection meant the possibility of harnessing the genetic commons for vast commercial gain in the years ahead. Some observers, however, were not so enthused. Ethicist Leon Kass asked,

What is the principled limit to this beginning extension of the domain of private ownership and dominion over living nature . . . ? The principle used in Chakrabarty says that there is nothing in the nature of a being, not even in the human patentor himself, that makes him immune to being patented.[2]

Here, for the first time, was a judiciary claiming that, for purposes of commerce, there is no longer any need to make distinctions between living beings and inanimate objects. Henceforth, a genetically engineered organism was to be regarded as an invention in the same way as computers or other machines are considered inventions. If Chakrabarty's microbe could be patented, why not any other form of life that has been, in any way, genetically engineered? What might it mean for subsequent generations to grow up in a world where they come to think of all of life as mere invention – where the boundaries between the sacred and the profane, and between intrinsic and utility value, have all but disappeared, reducing life itself to an objectified status, devoid of any unique or essential quality that might differentiate it from the strictly mechanical?

NOTES

1 Sue Mayer, 'Environmental Threats of Transgenic Technology,' in Peter Wheale and Ruth McNally (eds), *Animal Engineering: Of Pigs, Oncomice, and Men* (London: Pluto Press, 1995), p. 128.

2 Steven E. Lindow, 'Methods of Preventing Frost Injury Caused by Epiphytic Ice-Nucleation-Active Bacteria,' *Plant Disease* (March 1983), pp. 327–33; p. 332.

22 Sickness and Health in Pre-Modern England

Roy Porter and Dorothy Porter

In the eighteenth century in particular, deadly fevers – contemporaries called them 'spotted', 'miliary', 'hectic', 'malignant', etc. – struck down hundreds of thousands, young and old alike, while the so-called 'new' diseases gained ground – some crippling, such as rickets; some fatal, such as tuberculosis. Today's minor nuisance, like flu, was yesterday's killer. 'The Hooping Cough is yet with us', wrote George Crabbe in 1829, '& many children die of it.' And all this against a background of endemic maladies, such as malaria and infantile diarrhoea, and a Pandora's box of other infections (dysentery, scarlatina, measles, etc.) that commonly proved fatal, above all to infants, to say nothing of 101 other pains, eruptions, swellings, ulcers, scrofula and wasting conditions, not least the agonizing stone and the proverbial gout, which threatened livings and livelihoods, and all too often life itself.

Resistance to infection was evidently weak. This is hardly surprising. Precipitate demographic rise under the Tudors, followed by climatic reverses and economic crises under the Stuarts, had swollen the ranks of the malnourished poor. New and virulent strains of disease possibly emerged. England's good communications network and high job and geographical mobility – it was a land of 'movers' rather than 'stayers' – proved favourable to disease spread: the market society meant free trade in maladies. Few settlements were far enough off the beaten track to escape epidemic visitations travelling along the trade routes (out-of-the-way places could, however, have impressively high life expectancies). And yet the regionality of what was still largely a rural society

also meant that disease spread erratically and patchily, with the consequence that there was always a large reservoir of susceptibles, not yet immune, especially among the young, ready sacrificial victims to smallpox or scarlet fever.

Above all, pre-modern medicine had few effective weapons against the infections from which people died like flies. Once smallpox, enteric fever or pneumonia struck, doctors fought a losing battle. In the generation after 1720, the population of England and Wales actually *declined*, primarily because of the ravagers of epidemic disease.

Our understanding of the biology of man in history has vastly improved. As yet, however, little attention has been paid to what this ceaseless Darwinian war between disease and populations meant to the individual, considering disease neither as a black block on a histogram nor just as a trope about the human condition betwixt womb and tomb, but as experienced torment and terror. Every soul lived in the shadow of death; indeed, being in the land of the living was itself the survivor's privilege, for so many of one's peers – one's brothers and sisters – had already fallen by the wayside, having died at birth, in infancy or childhood. Life's fine thread was ever precarious, and every statistic hides a personal tragedy. The historical record abounds with sad tales of those who ate a hearty breakfast in the pink of health, only to be dead of apoplexy or convulsions, plague or, later, cholera, before the week was out. Elizabeth Iremonger told her friend Miss Heber the sad tale of her nephew's wife, Eleanor Iremonger, whose delivery of a boy was followed a week later by a 'fever that baffled all art and, on the ninth morning, she sunk finally to this World!'

'Many dyed sudden deaths lately', lamented the late Stuart Nonconformist minister, Oliver Heywood, ever alert to the workings of Providence:

1, Nathan Crosly buried Octob 25 1674, 2, Timothy Wadsworth, dyed Octob 23 suddenly in his chair without sickness, 3, Edw Brooks wife dyed under the cow as she was milking, 4, a woman at great Horton wel, had a tooth drawn, cryed oh my head laid her hand on, dyed immediately, 5, one Richard Hodgsons wife at Bradford on munday Nov. 2, dyed on tuesday the day after, &c.[1]

Over a century later, the Somerset parson, William Holland, marked the bitter fate of a father buried on the day his child was christened. Amid the bumper harvest of the Great Reaper recorded in the *Gentleman's Magazine* obituary columns, many expired when apparently in the prime of health – cut off by mad-dog bites, by sudden strokes or through travelling accidents ('I shall begin to think from my frequent overturns', quipped Elizabeth Montagu, 'a bone-setter a necessary part of my equipage for country visiting'). Accidents are not unique to modern technology and urbanism. A Norwich newspaper noted in 1790 how:

On Thursday last (March) a fine boy, about five years of age, fell thro' the seat of the necessary belonging to Mr. Mapes, in the Hay-market, the reservoir to which is not less than 40 feet deep; in this shocking situation he remained from a quarter past ten till three o'clock in the afternoon, before he was discovered by his cries. A person immediately went down to his relief, and when he had raised him halfway up, the bucket in which the child was, striking against a timber that had not been perceived, he was again precipitated to the bottom head forward.[2]

This child survived; so did others, for instance James Clegg, the Derbyshire minister-cum-doctor, who reported 'a very merciful deliverance when mounting [his] mare'. Many, however, fared worse, such as Thomas Day, leading light of the Lunar Society, who died after being thrown from a half-broken-in horse. Visitations came out of the blue, and some deaths were particularly cruel. A Mrs Fitzgerald went to the theatre, and laughed so much she laughed herself to death. Or take the exemplary exit of the Revd Mr M'Kill, pastor of Bankend in Scotland, so 'remarkable' that it 'made an impression upon the minds of his parishioners':

He mounted the pulpit in good health, lectured as usual, and it being the last sabbath of the year, chose for his text these words. 'we spend our years as a tale that is told'. He was representing, in a very pathetic manner, the fleeting nature of human life, and of all earthly things, when, on a sudden, he dropped down in the pulpit and expired instantly.

'He looks much better than you would imagine', Lady Jane Coke assured a friend about her husband's convalescence on 26 February 1750: 'sleeps well, and I think I may assure you that he is better to-day than he has been for some time, so that I hope the worst is over.' She tempted fate: before sunset, he was dead.

Disease was matched by other dangers, even oncoming thunderstorms. 'William Church', writes the pious Isabella Tindal, 'was speaking to my son John at the time, and saying "The Lord cometh in his chariot, in the clouds to gather his people to himself" [. . .] he was struck by the lightning [. . .] and fell down dead.' Falls, drownings, fires, firearm explosions, mishaps with tools, knives and poisons, and traffic accidents were perpetual hazards, not least because without ambulance and casualty services, trauma or blood loss readily proved fatal before effectual medical aid was forthcoming. William III, of course, died after his horse stumbled on a mole-hill (Jacobites toasted the little gentleman in velvet), and the third Cambridge Professor of History met his end tumbling off his horse while drunk. The Revd Ralph Josselin recorded scores of such mishaps or, as he saw them, 'Providences':

I heard that Major Cletheroe, September 21, coming homewards at Redgewell his Horse, stumbled and fell downe upon him and brake his bowells, he was taken up and spake but he dyed about 4 or 5 hours later, Lord in how many dangerous falls and stumbles hast thou preserved mee. . . .[3]

Most ironically of all, William Stout, the Lancaster Quaker who distrusted doctors and championed self-care, received his first blow in years – a broken leg – when he was run down by the local surgeon's horse.

Some mortifications of the flesh had their black comedy: 'Up, and to the office', wrote Pepys, '(having a mighty pain in my forefinger of my left hand, from a strain that it received last night in struggling avec la femme que je mentioned yesterday).'[4] Yet serious injuries and often death followed from apparent trifles. Erasmus Darwin's son, Charles, a promising medical student, died of septicaemia following a trivial dissecting-room cut. Unable to take life's pains, multitudes of English people took their lives instead. More philosophical minds reflected on their chances. 'The present is a fleeting moment', mused Gibbon, just turned fifty,

the past is no more; and our prospect of futurity is dark and doubtful. This day may *possibly* be my last: but the laws of probability, so true in general, so fallacious in particular, still allow me about fifteen years; and I shall soon enter into the period, which, as the most agreeable of his long life, was selected by the judgement and experience of the sage Fontenelle.

He never did: probability, or, perhaps, Providence, was unkind, and the historian of the Roman Empire declined and fell shortly afterwards through post-operative sepsis following surgery on a hydrocele as big as a football.

Yet Gibbon was lucky: all six of his siblings died in infancy. Samuel Pepys was one of eleven children born to his parents. Only one brother and sister survived into adulthood. A single measles epidemic massacred nine members of Cotton Mather's fifteen-strong household in early eighteenth-century colonial Boston. Half a century later, Dr Johnson's friend, Hester Thrale, produced twelve children: seven of them did not reach their teens. Out of William Godwin's twelve brothers and sisters, only half survived to adult

life. His contemporary, William Holland, had four children die within a fortnight of scarlet fever. Francis Place's résumé of the brief lives of his own children conveys the appalling arbitrariness of existence:

1. Ann – born 1792. Died aged 2 years of the small pox
2. Elizabeth – April 1794. Died in Chile – Mrs Adams
3. Annie – 27 Jan 1796 – . . . Mrs Miers
4. Francis – 22 June 1798
5. Jane – died an infant
6. Henry – d........d [dates of birth and death unknown]
7. Mary – 6 Jany. 1804
8. Frederick Wm. – 14 Oct 1805
9. Jane – 29 Oct 1807
10. Alfred – died an infant
11. John – 1 Jany 1811
12. Thomas – 4 Augst. 1812. Died at Calcutta 16 Sept 1847. Widow and 5 children
13. Caroline – 29 July 1814. Died 1830
14. William } Twins 6 Feb. 1817 { died – 1829
    Henry }   { died an infant

The radical tailor himself outlived almost all his offspring.

Thus English people during the 'long eighteenth century' were overshadowed by the facts and fears of sickness and by death itself. He had only three complaints, Byron bantered to his friend, Henry Drury, in 1811:

viz. a Gonorrhea, a Tertian fever, & the Hemorrhoides, all of which I literally had at once, though [the surgeon] assured me the morbid action of only one of these distempers could act at a time, which was a great comfort, though they relieved one another as regularly as Sentinels.[5]

When John Locke's father wrote to him in 1659, assuring him of his 'health and quiet', the son – then training to be a doctor – responded that this was 'a blessing this tumbling world is very spareing of'. For sickness was all too often the unwelcome, omnipresent guest, and households doubled as hospitals. A letter from Lady Caroline Fox to her sister, the Countess of Kildare, sending for medicines, reads like a dispatch from the front:

...as yet there is no amendment in my dearest child [Stephen]; he will be better for some hours almost a whole day sometimes then be as bad as ever again. I wonder I keep my spirits so well as I do, but my trust in Providence is great. My poor Charles was restored to me when there were no hopes left, and I will hope for the same blessing again with regard to my dear Ste. Louisa is perhaps set out by this time; seeing her will be a pleasure to me, but I fear she will find a melancholy house ... Poor William has had a little fever, but was well again when I heard of him. [...]

'Every body is ill', exclaimed Keats to his brother in 1820. This was neither a metaphysical paradox nor a piece of poetic licence, but merely an update on his friends and family.

Not surprisingly, therefore, health was on everybody's mind and filled their conversations. Sickness challenges the stomach (the two are not unconnected) for pride of place in Parson Woodforde's diaries. 'I was very nervous today. My Cow a great deal better this morning', he chronicled on 17 January 1796. The next day:

Poor Mr Bodham much altered for the worse. It is thought that he cannot long survive, fallen away amazingly, takes but very, very little notice of anything. Laudanum and Bark his chief Medicine. Dr. Lubbock & Dr. Donne from Norwich have both been there lately, and they say that he is out of the reach of any Medicine, he might live some little time, but is beyond recovery.

Some things improved. The day after, his cow-doctor visited her and pronounced 'her to be [...] out of all danger'.

Thus, in the world we have lost, sickness was a constant menace. 'One's very body', suggested Tobias Smollett – himself, of course, a doctor as well as a novelist – should be seen as a 'hospital'. Just as prudence dictated that every man should be his own lawyer, so every man should be his own physician, for he, if anyone, was expert in his own 'case' (contemporary idiom for both 'body' and 'corpse'). So it is hardly surprising that the everyday lives of ordinary people in earlier centuries reverberate with their own ailments, and those of their kith and kin.

NOTES

1 J. H. Turner (ed.), *The Rev. Oliver Heywood, 1630–1702* (Brighouse, Yorks: 1881–5), vol. 3, p. 207.

2 E. J. Chimenson (ed.), *Elizabeth Montagu: Her Correspondence from 1720 to 1761* (London: 1906), vol. 1, p. 33.

3 A. Macfarlane (ed.), *The Diary of Ralph Josselin* (Oxford: 1976), p. 21.

4 R. Latham and W. Matthews (eds), *The Diary of Samuel Pepys* (London: 1971–), vol. 5, p. 10.

5 L. A. Marchand (ed.), *Letters and Journals of Lord Byron* (London: 1982), vol. 2, p. 58.

Part 7 Families

Carol Smart and Bren Neale, in Reading 23, discuss a situation that is becoming increasingly significant in the experience of children. In a society where divorce has become common, children as well as parents have to cope with and adapt to the consequences if a breakup of their parents' marriage occurs. The authors propose that it is a mistake to concentrate simply on the harm which comes to children through divorce. There are far more complexities involved than this. Just as important as whether marriage partners stay together – in some ways more important – is the nature of the parenting they provide. In many circumstances good parenting can continue even should a divorce occur.

Ulrich Beck and Elisabeth Beck-Gernsheim discuss the role of love in relationships and marriage. In traditional cultures marrying for love was extremely rare and unknown. In Western countries today, however, love is the prime source of the attachments that lead to sexual relationships and, quite often, marriage. However, love is an ambiguous and unsettled emotion – is it a substantial enough basis around which to build stable relationships? Beck and Beck-Gernsheim conclude that love can be an important basis of social corporation in relationships and in marriage, even if it to some extent becomes supplanted by routine and habit.

Among the changes now affecting modern societies few are more profound than those acting to transform the nature of personal life. Over the past several decades, in virtually all the industrialized countries, divorce rates have risen sharply, while the proportion of people in the 'orthodox' family (biological father and mother living with their children in the same household) has declined very substantially. There is a great deal of experimentation in personal life, and no one can be sure where patterns of family development will lead in the future. Reading 25 considers the implication of the changes happening in the family. Is the family indeed collapsing? The author considers comparative evidence from several different societies to assess this question.

Ray Pahl discusses in Reading 26 the significance of friendship in modern societies. Modern social life is more mobile and changeable than used to be the case – for instance, people changed jobs more frequently than they used to do and this might involve them moving geographically too. Friendship networks are a crucial way in which people sustain a sense of community through the changes that affect their lives. Families are smaller than they used to be, while higher levels of divorce mean that individuals shift between relationships more often. Friendship can be an important 'social glue' which gives us stable connections on which we can rely.

23 Constructing Post-divorce Childhoods

Carol Smart and Bren Neale

Introduction

Jim Walters: I think what worries me most is that they don't seem to have shown any signs of it affecting them. I am almost looking for something.

The concern expressed by this non-residential father captures exactly the framework of understanding which most parents in our sample adopted when talking about children after divorce. Although a number of parents felt that their children's problems pre-dated the divorce, even these felt that they had to talk about their children in the context of harm. Many of them had read books on the damage that divorce does to children and others had experienced their parents' divorce and wanted to save their own children from similar experiences. There was therefore an anticipation that the children would not escape unscathed, and many parents whose children were still outwardly happy, involved in social activities and doing well at school, were convinced that something would 'show' later in life.

This presumption of harm was so all-pervasive that we began to think it must be an additional burden for children to carry on behalf of their parents. Many children were whisked off to psychologists; parents had discreet talks with headteachers; school nurses were asked to talk to children; and a web of anxious surveillance was set up. The aim was undoubtedly to catch the children should they fall, but its omnipresence felt more like a trap from which the children would be lucky to escape. Moreover, the knowledge that divorce might cause harm produced a huge variety of responses from parents. For a couple who were social workers it meant that they had discussions with the children and that everything was planned in advance, allowing the children a say in arrangements which were based on the principles of co-parenting. For other parents it meant that the ex-spouse could be blamed for everything, because the spouse who made the decision to go was held responsible for all the actual and anticipated harm. For yet other parents, usually mothers, it meant that they stayed in oppressive or violent relationships for far too long because they did not want to harm the children. Finally, for other parents it meant that they became almost obsessive about their children's well-being in order to make up for perceived harms.

Knowing that divorce is thought to cause harm brought forth neither a unitary nor necessarily a very satisfactory response from parents. It certainly did not stop them divorcing because few parents, save those who were bitter and angry about being 'deserted', felt that couples should stay together for the sake of the children. Parents were therefore on the horns of a dilemma. They felt sure that their children would be harmed and therefore experienced extreme guilt, but they did not always know how to translate this worry into their everyday post-divorce parenting. Some parents thought that the best thing was to ensure that children maintained a relationship with both parents to the point of sharing the children physically, while others thought that the most important thing was stability and continuity with minimal emotional conflict. In this [discussion] we therefore want to focus on how parents managed and 'constructed' post-divorce childhood. We also want to consider the extent to which parents may have very different concepts of childhood and how to interact with children. It is, for example, often the case that the primary carer sees the child and also childhood rather differently to the contact parent, and even in co-parenting arrangements, crucial differences emerge. While these differences undoubtedly exist where marriages remain intact, they are less visible and (perhaps) more easily managed in those circumstances. Divorce highlights different styles of parenting and arguably creates new styles of childhood. These days more and more children spend time with parents in different households and are having to sustain relationships with parents who no longer live with them. Divided loyalties, which can perhaps be downplayed inside a family unit, become much more difficult to manage when a child is physically moving between her or his mother and father.

[. . .] Working through our data, we gradually came to think that the literature which focuses on the harms of divorce for children operates without a sufficiently nuanced grasp of all the different ways in which parenting (whether together or apart) operates. The myopic focus on divorce ignores the harm of certain types of parent/child relationship which are not dependent upon parents separating. We therefore came to think that it was important to understand how parents conceive of childhood. Parents do not all have the same ideas about how to raise children or how to prevent harm to children because they often have very different ideas about what a child is. They also vary in their views on whether a child experiences complex emotions and on the extent to which a child should be seen as more or less autonomous of his/her parents. This sort of complexity is not reducible to a simple judgement about 'good' and 'bad' parenting. It therefore follows that it is inappropriate to map this simple idea of 'good' parenting onto intact parents while conferring the adjective 'bad' on separated parents.

Unhappy family at home

Parenting styles and standards

How to raise children 'properly' is a deeply fraught and contested issue. There is, in general, little agreement about it and there is a rapid turnover in fashionable theories and practices. The huge range of titles in parentcraft and child development often displayed in bookshops and libraries suggests that parents are constantly in search of guidance and answers to problems. If there is no professional, political or personal agreement over something relatively straightforward like 'smacking' and physical punishment, then it is hardly surprising that there is no agreement over how to support and help a child through his or her parents' divorce.

Differences of standard and approach occur within households as well as across households. Where parents differ in approach this can itself bring about a divorce. Moreover, now that there is an emphasis on retaining the involvement of biological fathers in the care of their children after divorce, the issue of whether individual mothers and fathers have very different ideas on how children should be raised becomes much more critical. Children are now often faced with situations in which they not only have to accommodate to a new step-parent who may be living with them, but with a contact parent who also imposes a regime and set of standards and expectations on them. They may also receive care from another step-parent who lives with the non-residential parent and who also has different standards and expectations. A fairly typical picture might be a situation in which a girl is initially brought up in a two-parent household, primarily cared for by her mother with a somewhat distant father. On divorce, that father may become more involved with her if only because he spends more dedicated time with her. Her father may have repartnered and so, if she stays overnight or goes on holiday with him, she will experience care from yet another adult. Then if her mother repartners, she will be living with another adult who may adopt elements of a caring or parental role. The existence of step-brothers or step-sisters who may be treated quite differently obviously complicates this picture further. Parenting is therefore infinitely more complex now, and as a consequence childhood is changing too. Although we cannot comment directly on how the children of our sample of parents accommodated to these diverse patterns, we can identify how parents manage these new circumstances and what problems this causes them when they attempt to share responsibility for their children after divorce or separation.

With our sample of parents, some of the problems of living with different styles of parenting pre-dated the divorce and, where they were severe enough, were often part of the reason for the separation.

Jodie Hitchens: The thing was, I don't believe in smacking Alice. All right, she might get a tap on her bum sometimes if she's really overwrought, but I won't smack her if I can help it, I'll do it other ways. But he believes in the way his dad brought him up, which is a good clout over the head and a good hiding and then up to bed. I don't believe in that. I think he's got more into the idea of smacking kids [since he left] because they're boys that [his new partner] has got and he took over the father role of looking after them.

Nina Hester: She was twenty weeks old [and] he used to walk round the floor to scare the living daylights out of me. He used to have Jemma sat in the palm of his hand in a sitting position, legs crossed, hunched

... and he used to have his arm outstretched and he used to walk along the kitchen floor which was tiled and he used to say, 'I've never dropped one yet.'

Fathers who had been violent to their children did not necessarily lose contact with them. Sometimes mothers could not cope with children who were themselves becoming violent or who were seriously disturbed as a result of their early childhood and sent them to live with their fathers or, in one case, wished she had. In the case of Ginny Fry her son was frightened of his father, who had violent rages and would hit him and inflict severe punishment. Ginny, who was very worried about the situation, nevertheless wanted them to have some kind of relationship. She had therefore worked out an emergency code with her son so that if his father went into one of his rages, he would phone her and give the password. She would then drive over and collect him straight away. In this case the father was a solicitor. Ginny had to work very hard to sustain the relationship but not all mothers had her resources and her willingness to understand her husband's uncontrollable temper.

Differences in parenting styles and standards were not, of course, always as stark as this. They often concerned things like bedtimes, doing homework, being allowed to cross busy streets alone or to play in the street, cleanliness and things like being made to sit at table to eat rather than eating from a tray in front of the television. Delia Garrett, for example, had to tolerate her husband hiring violent videos to entertain her son. Anthony Dart insisted that when his son was with him he should be called by a name other than his given name because he was of mixed race and he did not want him to identify with his 'white' name. Even differences over the children's diet could cause considerable stress.

Erica Dawson: A typical example – my eldest son is not allergic to Coca-Cola but it hypes him up. So I cut it out of his diet altogether, he can have fizzy orange or lemonade but he doesn't drink Coke. When they went to their dad's house he would buy a bottle of Coke and Steven, being four or five would say, 'I don't have Coke, it hypes me up,' and he'd say 'That's ridiculous!

Your mother's picked that up off the television. She doesn't know what she's talking about, you drink it.' So he'd give him a couple of glasses of Coke and he'd come back to me and he'd be climbing up the wall!

James Grant: I think the way that Paula feeds them, if it isn't too patronizing to say, [it's] the way the working class would feed their children. It's loads of chips, loads of beans, loads of eggs. I tend to buy more fresh things, it's very rarely I buy anything in a tin, it isn't any good for them and I can't stand it so there's no distinct difficulties in that I have [sic] but it's not as if they're going to drop dead by it for the weekend.

Later James added:

I think that when you've got one system like this and one system like that, and neither of them is right or wrong, you know, that's just how it is, then I think it does make the children terribly confused in what to do and say in certain places. I mean, Paula will make Jimmy and William a sandwich and they can sit on the sofa and eat it and watch TV, I mean they don't even try it in here, you know!

Perhaps one of the most common and most frustrating things that our sample of parents faced was their children asserting that they would not do something (eat at table, do their homework, not swear) because the other parent did not make them do it. Almost all those who took a reasonable degree of responsibility for their children faced this at one time. Some parents would simply assert that they did not care what the children were allowed to do in the other house, they had to abide by the rules of whichever household they were in. Where parents were entirely co-operative they would often check with each other, and even have a joint meeting with the child if the issue was serious enough. While some parents could 'nip this behaviour in the bud', for others it was much more difficult. If they did not see the child very often they could not really assert authority, or if the child was not merely 'trying it on' but was quite badly disturbed it became a perennial nightmare. Pete Glenn, for example, wanted to cut down on the amount of contact James was having with his mother because of the effect it was appearing to have on him.

Pete Glenn: The only way is, like I say, they go on the Friday and cut the Wednesday out because James comes back on the Monday, he's boisterous but his arms are folded and he pulls a face if he doesn't get his way. Well that's [his mother], and he stamps around and I say, 'Come on, you've got to get your school work done.' 'No!', because his mum can't control him. So then Tuesday's OK, Wednesday I take him to school. He's away again till Thursday tea time, so I've got the same [thing on] Thursday. By Friday he's OK. He's away Saturday and Sunday; no wonder he wants to go, he just runs [wild], he just does what he wants.

This case is interesting because it is a residential father who is experiencing the problem of this kind of disruption. These sentiments are more usually uttered by mothers who suffer when their children return from action-packed weekends or any other time, having been spoilt by their fathers. It became increasingly apparent to us that what mattered most in this kind of tension between parents was the situation of the 'most responsible' parent. This did not always have to be the parent that the child was living with, although it almost always was. Thus we found that when fathers were put in the same structural position as that more commonly associated with mothers, they began to care about things like table manners and homework and bedtimes. They objected as much as mothers to children being kept up late or being taken to the pub.

Keith Minster: I think I've been more loving towards them, more soft with them, probably because I know that I'm the one looking after them and I've got to get them in bed on a night because if they're not then they're tired for school the next day. It's changed in that way, but you can't avoid it because it is me who's doing it.

We need therefore to consider the structure of post-divorce parenting and hence post-divorce childhood. Moving between parents who have very different standards and expectations can clearly cause problems for children. Many of the primary carers in our sample referred to the distress children feel at 'change-over' time. Often, because of the difficulties between parents, the handover was additionally difficult for children on an emotional level. One mother would meet her ex-husband in a motorway service station. This could lead to a kind of farce with her daughters refusing to get into his car, her virtually forcing them in (because she was worried about being blamed for alienating the children) and the girls simply getting out on the other side of the car before he could drive off. In another case a mother would wait outside Marks & Spencer for her ex-husband, who had to drive 150 miles in congested traffic and who was therefore often late, causing much distress, especially in the dead of winter. But she refused to let him come to the house. Other parents were able to work out that it was best if the mother took them to school on change-over day while the father would collect them. This gave the children a neutral space between the emotional worlds of their separated parents and they could move much more easily away from one parent and towards the other.

If a child showed emotional distress at the point of transition, this too could feed into the difficulties of the parental relationship. For example, we noted that if a child cried or became clingy on leaving their father, then it would often be interpreted as a clear sign that the child wanted to be with him and not their mother. In other words, the emotional difficulty of transition became a further point of contention rather than a catalyst for developing a less stressful 'exchange'. Some parents, it would seem, could not interpret their children's distress outside the framework of their own needs and interests. Thus, for some residential parents, a child's distress on returning from a contact visit was seen as a reason to cut down on contact, while for some non-residential parents it was a clear indication that the child's residence should be changed. Rather than making the problem easier for the child, the parents' hostilities therefore increased. But it is far too simple to suggest that parents simply acted selfishly when faced with these dilemmas. Sometimes reducing contact was the sensible thing to do, and sometimes children really did want to stay with the other parent and left to do so as soon as they were old enough. So, although some situations may look like parental selfishness on the surface, it was always unwise to assume this would inevitably be the case. Indeed one of the most fraught issues between parents after divorce was the question of whether one parent was manipulating the child to suit their own interests. Because post-divorce parenting is generally assumed to be motivated by a malevolent set of interests, we found that this accusation was regularly made, regardless of the circumstances.

[. . .]

24 The Normal Chaos of Love

Ulrich Beck and Elisabeth Beck-Gernsheim
Translated by
Mark Ritter and Jane Wiebel

[. . .]

Never before has marriage been built on such ephemeral and immaterial foundations. Men and women with good jobs are economically independent of family support. Their union no longer serves any political ends or the maintenance of dynasties or owning property as it did in the feudal hierarchy. Inherited ties, which used to be taken for granted, have slackened, and the couple working as a team becomes the exception; in short everything which used to be firm and preordained is vanishing. Instead one is supposed to seek and find in the macro-microcosm of life with the beloved everything that society previously assigned to various professions and often different parts of town: romantic love, keeping a mistress, comfortable affection, liberation from the shackles of adulthood and a humdrum life, being forgiven one's sins, refuge in family history and future plans, parental pride and pleasure and whatever other incompatibilities – with their enigmatic dragon's features – there may be.

Seen historically, in an era when men and women have lost their old political and economic certainties and moral guidelines one wonders why they are seeking their own private bliss in such a uniform way, marrying for love, of all things, while society in general suggests that differentiating is the answer. Marrying for love has existed only since the beginning of the industrial

revolution and was its invention. It is regarded as the most desirable goal although the social realities suggest exactly the opposite. Marriage has lost its stability but none of its attractiveness as a result of its metamorphosis from a means of passing on wealth and power into the airy version we know, nourished only on emotional involvement and the desire to find oneself. Despite and contrary to the 'bad' reality, the family and loving relationships continue to be idealized on every level of society (with slight behavioural differences), irrespective of income, education and age. Here is some evidence from research into working-class attitudes:

Interviewer:	'What does having a family and children mean to you?'
Mr Schiller:	'That there is some sense in life.'
Mrs Schiller:	'You know why you're there, you know what you're working for.'
Mr Xeller:	'To me, family means everything. I'd give up everything but that.'
Mrs Taler:	'Family and children are the main thing and the most important thing.'

There is scarcely anything else in the parents' lives which they describe so emphatically as the core of their lives. Only having a family and children gives existence a subjective 'purpose'.

This finding is both paradoxical and mysterious: the family is simultaneously disintegrating and being put on a pedestal. If one can draw conclusions about beliefs from how people behave, seventh heaven and mental torment seem to be very close neighbours in our ideal image of a loving couple. Perhaps they just live in different storeys – tower room and torture chamber – in the same castle. Above all some explanation must be found for the fact that so many people are yearning to have children, often to the exclusion of all other interests, while at the same time the birth-rate is declining. Equally, why does family life hold out so much appeal, promising personal salvation in a domestic paradise of companionship, parenthood and love, while there is also a sharp rise in the divorce rate? What induces the sexes to tear at each other's throats and still keep their high hopes of finding true love and personal fulfilment with this partner, or the next, setting standards which are so high that disappointment is almost inevitable?

These two poles, idealizing life as a couple and divorcing in thousands, represent two sides of a new faith quickly finding followers in a society of uprooted loners. Their hope rests in love, a powerful force obeying rules of its own and inscribing its messages into people's expectations, anxieties and behaviour patterns, leading them through marriage and divorce to remarriage.

It is as if love occupies its own different world separate from real life in the family and separate from the person whom it is supposed to help to greater happiness. According to its tenets someone who for the sake of true love sacrifices a marriage, family ties, parenthood, perhaps ultimately even the well-being of those dependent on him/her, is not committing a sin but merely obeying the rules, answering the call of the heart and seeking fulfilment for him/herself and others. He or she is not to blame; it would be wrong to cling to an order which does not value love highly enough:

Many people believe that one crisis in life is rather like any other. In fact, however, a divorce in a family with children is a disruption which cannot be compared with any other life crisis . . . When else do we have this overpowering urge to kill someone? When else are children used as weapons against their parents? In contrast to other crises, a divorce brings the most elementary human passions to the surface – love, hatred and jealousy . . . In most critical situations – earthquakes, floods, fire – parents instinctively get their children to safety before anything else. In the critical situation of a divorce, however, the children take second place for both mother and father; their own problems take priority. While divorce proceedings are under way parents neglect their children in almost every respect; domestic order breaks down and the children are left to themselves. Parents living apart spend less time with their children and have less empathy for their needs. In the panic of the upheaval naked egotism wins.[1]

The religious nature of our faith in love is clear in this striking parallel to Calvinism. The congregation was encouraged, in fact urged to make the world subservient to their own desire to please God, a message which implied breaking with tradition. Worshipping love in the modern way takes up this idea again, allowing or forcing us to break with family ties in order not to betray our personal search for genuineness, for true love. Abandoning one's own children for someone else is not a breach of love but a proof of it; idealizing love means pledging to break with all false forms of it. This illustrates the extraordinary power love already exerts over us as well as the contradictions of trying to live up to this ideal while coping with the mundane routine of ordinary life.

Such attitudes, wishing and hoping for the ultimate in love, constitute a belief, a religious state of mind, which must be clearly distinguished from behaviour, or what people actually do. In love as in Christianity there are pharisees, converts, atheists and heretics. And cynics often turn out to be disappointed and embittered adherents of an exaggerated faith in love. Because there are many contradictions between belief and action, it is vital to keep the two levels clearly separate. The assertions made here refer to our knowledge, our belief in love and hardly at all to behaviour which shows the opposite, or no matter how perversely results from it.

In addition there is a phenomenon which one could term the law of the inverse significance of faith and certainty. Anyone who feels comfortable in everyday life with a loving companion forgets how important this belief is to him/herself. Attention always focuses on uncertainties, and only when these crop up and certainty is banished does it become painfully obvious what a role love plays in designing our individual lives, even if we try to deny this.

How does this quasi-religious belief in love as the ultimate answer express itself if not in the ways people behave? Some would say: there are several priorities for me, love included, and then again love comes in so many shapes and sizes from passionate to maternal and companionable after seventeen years of marriage, homo- or hetero-sexual. One gauge of the intensity and power of love's claims on us, as we have said, lies in the divorce figures which unequivocally reveal what deep commitments are given up. [. . .] At the same time, however, research unanimously reveals an unshaken hankering for family and marriage, even though the 'Home Sweet Home' sign has been hanging rather crooked for some time. The number of remarriages after (early) divorce is also high. [. . .] Children of divorced parents strive particularly hard to make a happy family, a goal which they sadly often fail to achieve [. . .]

None of this reflects what actually happens in everyday life, highlighting the differences between how one would like life to be and how living at close quarters with other individuals actually is. While Weber investigated documents of the Calvinist faith for signs of inner asceticism, nowadays we would have to consult self-help books, therapeutic principles and transcripts of divorce proceedings to find signs of faith in true love.

Love as a latter-day religion

The essence of our faith in love can best be shown by comparing it with religion. Both hold out the promise of perfect happiness, to be achieved along similar lines. Each offers itself as a way of escaping from the daily grind, giving normality a new aura; stale old attitudes are tossed aside and the world seems suffused with new significance. In the case of religion all energy is directed towards another infinite reality, understood as the only true one and encompassing all finite life. In love this opening up of normal boundaries takes place both sensually, personally, in sexual passion and also in new perceptions of oneself and the world. Lovers see differently and therefore are and become different, opening up new realities for one another. In revealing their histories they recreate themselves and give their future a new shape. Love is 'a revolution for two', in overcoming antagonisms and moral laws which stand in their way they really prove their love. Inspired by their feelings, lovers find themselves in a new world, an earthly one but a realm of its own.[2]

Love 'as an archetypal act of defiance' (Alberoni): that is what modern love seems to promise, a chance of being authentic in a world which otherwise runs on pragmatic solutions and convenient lies. Love is a search for oneself, a craving to really get in contact with me and you, sharing bodies, sharing thoughts, encountering one another with nothing held back, making confessions and being forgiven, understanding, confirming and supporting what was and what is, longing for a home and trust to counteract the doubts and anxieties modern life generates. If nothing seems certain or safe, if even breathing is risky in a polluted world, then people chase after the misleading dreams of love until they suddenly turn into nightmares.

We are always vaulting over the apparently firm boundaries of everyday reality. Memory takes me back to myself when I was young. I wonder about the clouds and imagine a story behind them. I read a book and find myself in a different epoch; my head is full of scenes from someone's life who is now dead and I have never met; voices I have never heard are conversing in my inner ear. Among the extraordinary experiences in life love has a special status. Unlike illness and death it is sought for and not repressed, at least at this moment in our culture; it is immune to conscious or practical manipulation and cannot be produced on order. Those who hope to find it are looking for salvation here and now, and the 'hereafter' is in this world, with a voice, a body and a will of its own. Religion tells us there is a life after death; love says there is a life before death.

[...]

Love is communism within capitalism; misers give their all and this makes them blissful:

Falling in love means opening oneself to a new form of existence without any guarantee of achieving it. It is a rhapsody to happiness without any certainty that there will be a response . . . And if the answer does come from the person we love, then it seems something undeserved, a miraculous gift one never counted on getting . . . Theologians have their own term for this gift: grace. And if the other person, our beloved, says he or she loves us too and each is engrossed in the other, this is a blissful moment in which time stands still.[3]

Love is a utopia which is not ordained or even planned from above, from cultural traditions or sermons, but grows from below, from the power and persistence of sexual drives and from deep personal wishes. In this sense love is a religion unhampered by external meanings and traditions, its values lying in the depth of the lovers' attraction to one another and their subjective mutual commitment. No one has to become a member, and no one needs to be converted.

So our faith in love is linked to its lack of tradition; it comes after all the disappointing credos, and needs neither organizing committees nor party membership to be an effective subjective and cultural force. It is the outcome of sex being partially freed of taboos and wide disillusionment with other prescribed beliefs passed down to us. As befits modern social structures, there is no external moral agency responsible for love, but just the way the lovers feel for one another.

While a religion which lacks firm teaching usually vanishes, love is a religion without churches and without priests, and its continued existence is as certain as the tremendous force of sexual needs now freed of social disapproval. It cannot be organized, which also means it is independent, and its only place, despite all its cultural offshoots, is in the hearts of those involved; this makes it a non-traditional, post-traditional religion which we are hardly aware of because we ourselves are its temples and our wishes are its prayers.

Now that the old law-givers, the church, the state and traditional morality are on the retreat, even love can shed its old standard patterns and established codes. The result is a kind of positivism making norms out of individual preferences and values. This does not however reduce love's status as a force giving life purpose and meaning; on the contrary it confirms it. Here church and bible, parliament and government are merged into one – a matter of conscience guiding each person how to shape and structure his/her life. This is at least the ideal we share, this is how we would like it to be, even though in practical terms the solutions are often standard ones.

Because lovers can only rely on their own intuitions to guide them in matters of love, the whole process is a circular one, and so is any discussion of it. Therapists try to clarify these intertwined personal sufferings and experiences on general lines, but the very basic formula – I am myself – which is supposed to justify and explain everything else is [. . .] a peculiar attempt to define something in terms of itself. In his anlaysis of the language of love Roland Barthes reveals this circularity:

adorable/adorable
Not managing to name the specialty of his desire for the loved being, the amorous subject falls back on this rather stupid word: adorable, . . . Herein a great enigma, to which I shall never possess the key: Why is it that I desire So-and-so? Why is it that I desire So-and-so lastingly, longingly? Is it the whole of So-and-so I desire (a silhouette, a shape, a mood)? And, in that case, what is it in this loved body which has the vocation of a fetish for me? What perhaps incredibly tenuous portion – what accident? The way a nail is cut, a tooth broken slightly aslant, a lock of hair, a way of spreading the fingers while talking, while smoking? About all these folds of the body I want to say that they are adorable. Adorable means: this is my desire, insofar as it is unique: 'That's it! That's it exactly (which I love)!' Yet the more I experience the specialty of my desire, the less I can give it a name; to the precision of the

target corresponds a wavering of the name; what is characteristic of desire, proper to desire, can produce only an impropriety of the utterance. Of this failure of language there remains only one trace: the word 'adorable'.

... *Adorable* is the futile vestige of a fatigue, a fatigue of language itself. From word to word, I struggle to put 'into other words' the ipseity of my Image, to express improperly the propriety of my desire: a journey at whose end my final philosophy can only be to recognize – and to practice – tautology. *The adorable is what is adorable*. Or again I adore you because you are adorable, I love you because I love you.[4]

In fact those precious, holy sides of love are not just the outcome of our being besotted with ourselves. One has to look further into quite different fields, like education, scientific advances, world markets and technical risks if one wants to grasp why so many people plunge into a frenzy of love as if they were slightly insane. The outside world confronts us with a barrage of abstractions: statistics, figures, formulas, all indicating how imperilled we are, and almost all of them elude our comprehension. Loving is a kind of rebellion, a way of getting in touch with forces to counteract the intangible and unintelligible existence we find ourselves in.

Its value lies in the special, intense experiences it offers – specific, emotional, engrossing, unavoidable. Where other kinds of social contact are losing their hold, politics seem irrelevant, classes have faded into statistics, and even colleagues at work rarely find time for one another because their shifts and flexible working hours forbid it. Love, and especially the clashes it induces – from the 'eternal issue of the dishes' to 'what kind of sex', from parenting to tormenting each other with self-revelations – has a monopoly: it is the only place where you can really get in touch with yourself and someone else. The more impersonal life around you seems, the more attractive love becomes. Love can be a divine immersion in all kinds of sensations. It offers the same relief to a number-cruncher as jogging through the woods does to an office-worker – it makes you feel alive again.

A society short on traditions has produced a whole range of idols: television, beer, football, motorcycles, cordon bleu meals – something for every phase in life. You can join clubs or peace initiatives or keep up long-distance friendships to guarantee you still share some common ground with someone. You can hark back to old gods, or discover new ones, polish relics or read the stars. You can even insist on continuing the class struggle and sing about being free, although you know that such golden days, if they ever existed, are over.

What distinguishes love from these other escape routes is that it is tangible and specific, personal and now; the emotional upheavals cannot be postponed or handed on, and both sexes find themselves forced to react whether they want to or not. No one can decide to fall into or out of love, but might at any moment find themselves falling through the trap door into a new dimension.

Love is therefore not a substitute or a lightning conductor, nor is it a politically desirable export article or just a television advertisement. The boom in love reflects current living conditions and the anonymous, prefabricated pattern forced on people by the market relegating their private needs right to the end of the list.

Taking over from old categories like class and poverty, religion, family and patriotism there is a new theme, sometimes disguised as uncertainty, anxiety, unfulfilled and unfulfillable longings, sometimes sharply outlined and standardized in pornography, feminism and therapy, but gradually developing its own radiance, its own rhythms, opening up prospects much more alluring than the ups and downs of being promoted, having the latest computer or feeling underpaid.

'Being loved means being told "you do not have to die"' (Gabriel Marcel).[5] This glowing hope seems more delightful and irresistible the more we realize how finite, lonely and fragile our existence is. Illness and death, personal disasters and crises are the moments when the vows prove true or merely lies, and in this respect the secular religion of love can claim like other religions to give life sense and meaning. Or put the other way round, the idea of dying shatters normal life, making it seem highly suspect; in moments of pain and fear love acquires a new dimension. The brittle, carefully constructed shell cracks open – at least momentarily – and lets in questions like Why? and What for?, fed on memories of desperately missed togetherness.

As religion loses its hold, people seek solace in private sanctuaries. Loving is bound up with a hope which goes beyond basking in intimacy and sex. Making love in bed is one way; caring for one another in a sick-bed is another. Love's power is proven in its ability to cope with weakness, age, mistakes, oversights and even crime. Whether the promises 'for better, for worse' are actually kept is another question which applies just as much to other religions. Illness can result in a new kind of devotion; hidden behind the hope that we can compensate for our mistakes and shortcomings by lavishing love on the beloved is the belief that love is an act of confession, and often a gesture against a heartless society.

The analogy between love and religion giving our life a purpose comes to an end when love itself dies. The end of a loving relationship remains meaningless in this latter-day religion, or can acquire some meaning only if the lovers part 'for the sake of love', by mutual understanding. Perhaps for future generations changing lovers will be like changing jobs, and love mobility a version of social mobility, but at the moment the wrangling in the divorce courts points in the opposite direction.

Believing in love means being under the sway of the present, here and now, you and me, our mutual commitment, and how we live it. Delay is out of the question and so is asking for God's help or postponing happiness until the next life. There is no merciful heaven waiting where our disagreements and exaggerated expectations of one another are bound to be fulfilled, even if we fail in this world. Love is unrelenting and demands cash down.

Faith in love means you love your lover but not your neighbour, and your loving feelings are always in danger of turning into hate. Ex-lovers lose their home and even their residence permits; they have no right to asylum. Not being loved necessarily implies being rejected, a topic on which psychotherapists, acting as intensive care units for those ravaged by divorce, can write volumes. Faith in love produces two groups which fluctuate considerably; on the one hand there are the current lovers, quantitatively stable but varying in identity. On the other there is a group of ex-lovers which increases as the current lovers swap and change. People find themselves interwoven into networks of insiders and outsiders, the blessed and the no-longer-blessed, once closely related, now tenuously linked, all in search of a final satisfying love.

For all the similarities between love and religion, there are also enormous differences; love is a private cosmos, whereas religion is in alliance with the powers-that-be. Lovers are their own church, their own priests, their own holy scriptures, even if they sometimes resort to therapists to decipher these. They have to create their own rules and taboos; there is an infinite number of private systems of love, and they lose their magic power and disintegrate as soon as the couple cease to act as priests worshipping their belief in each other.

Love builds its nest out of the symbols lovers use to overcome their unfamiliarity with one another and to provide their relationship with a past. The nest is decorated as the focus of their togetherness, and turns into a flying carpet bearing their shared dreams. In this way the fetishes, the sacrifices, the ceremonies, the incense and the daily rites constitute the visible context within which we love. Instead of being officially sanctified and administered, this private faith is individually styled, invented and adorned: snuggling in Mickey Mouse and teddy symbols, agreeing everything yellow means love, inventing nicknames to use in our secret world, all these are efforts to counteract the nagging fear that it might end and all could be lost and forgotten.

Religion's horizon takes in this world and the next, the beginning and the end, time and eternity, the living and the dead, and is therefore often celebrated as immutable, untouched by time. Love's horizon, by contrast, is narrow and specific, consisting of a small world of you and me and nothing more, exclusive, apparently selfish, somewhere between unjust and cruel in its logic, arbitrary and outside the range of the law. Its imperatives cut across other wishes and its principles withstand any attempt to standardize them.

For these very reasons, however, love is the best ideology to counteract the perils of individualization. It lays stress on being different, yet promises togetherness to all those lone individuals; it does not rely on outdated status symbols or money or legal considerations, but solely on true and immediate feelings, on faith in their validity and on the person they are directed towards. The law-givers are the lovers themselves, phrasing their statutes with their delight in each other.

[. . .]

NOTES

1   J. Wallerstein and S. Blakeslee, *Gewinner und Verlierer* (Munich, 1989), pp. 28–9; = *Second Chances: Men, Women and Children a Decade after Divorce* (New York: Basic Books, 1987).

2   Francesco Alberoni, *Verliebtsein und lieben: Revolution zu zweit* (Stuttgart, 1983); = *Falling in Love* (New York).

3   Ibid., pp. 39–40.

4   R. Barthes, *Fragments: A Lover's Discourse* (New York, 1978), pp. 19, 20–1.

5   I am indebted to Christopher Lau for this quotation.

25 Home Sweet Home: The Debate About Family Values

The Economist

To European ears, America's 'family values' debate can sound shrill, even surreal. It is taken as a sign that the citizens of the new world remain considerably less sophisticated, and more moralistic, than those of the old. But Europe would do well to listen. In many American neighbourhoods, the family has collapsed: among households with children in poor inner cities, fewer than one in ten has a father in residence. If there are lessons from this awful experience, they are worth learning.

Many argue that the plight of the inner cities reflects a wider social malaise. America and Europe alike are witnessing profound changes in the structure of the family – increases in divorce and in births outside marriage. Great economic and social forces, combined with policy itself partly shaped by those forces, have weakened the link between parenthood and partnership. Compared with thirty years ago, it is easier for women to raise children without men, and for men to escape the burdens of fatherhood.

The weakening of that link has hurt children. Multi-generational studies in Sweden, Britain and America all seem to show that, compared with their peers of the same economic class, children in lone-parent families do less well in school, get in trouble more often and have more emotional and health problems. They are also more likely to become single parents themselves.

Demands for government to arrest the decline of the family are mounting. If governments were to heed these calls, what could they do?

Solo Swedes and German groupings

Governments act in ways that, intentionally or otherwise, affect the family: in this sense, every country has a 'family policy'. In Britain and America, these policies are a mess. To see how they might be changed, it is helpful to look at systems elsewhere. In Europe, the most distinctive approaches are those of Sweden and Germany. These start from very different assumptions about what such policy should be, but each acts upon a relatively coherent philosophy. Both manage to do moderately well by their children.

Sweden defines itself as a nation of individuals; its policy reflects that outlook. There is no married-couple's allowance, no tax deduction for children, no way to file jointly for income tax. Benefits are also assessed on an individual basis.

This treatment dates from reforms in the early 1970s. Sweden had a labour shortage and wanted to encourage married women into the job market. High marginal tax rates on joint filings, however, took an enormous bite out of a second income. By taxing both incomes independently, a major disincentive to work was removed; and as tax rates increased, two incomes became the norm. As a considered national policy to get women into work, it worked. Sweden has a higher proportion of working women than any other country. Everyone is expected to have a job. Mothers with young children generally work part-time.

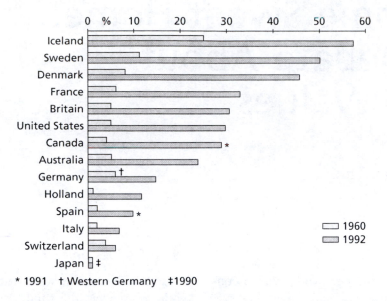

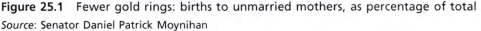

* 1991   † Western Germany   ‡1990

Figure 25.1   Fewer gold rings: births to unmarried mothers, as percentage of total
Source: Senator Daniel Patrick Moynihan

Swedes are not particularly religious, and with such an individualized tax structure it is no surprise that many couples do not bother to marry. About half the babies in Sweden are born to unwed mothers, though very few are born to young girls. And although nineteen out of twenty babies will go home to a father, many will not grow up with one. Half of Swedish marriages end in divorce, and unmarried parents split up three times as often as married ones. The result is that the number of lone-parent families as a proportion of all families with children has increased steadily, to 18 per cent in 1991.

The children in those families will not necessarily be in material need, though they do tend to be slightly worse off. Generous benefits mean that if one parent leaves, the other parent and children do not slip into poverty. Child support enforcement is ferocious. In 1990, only 6.8 per cent of Swedish children lived in families with less than half the average income. Though there are no premiums for children in the Swedish tax code, there are numerous state-supported goodies for them – parental leave, subsidized day care, leave to care for sick children and so on. This may be why

Swedish women have more children than their European sisters. It is the only OECD country in which the birth rate has increased since 1970.

Germany, by contrast, is a nation of families. People are legally required to help elderly parents and hard-up family members. There are tax allowances for dependants and a high level of child benefit. A minimum subsistence level for children is exempt from taxation.

Marriage is rewarded in the tax code. A parent who stays at home to care for a child can keep many of the perks of her job. And it is, normally, hers not his; the old idea of a woman's world dominated by '*Kinder, Küche, Kirche*' – children, kitchen and church – still persists, albeit to a diminishing extent. A full-time parent keeps her pension rights, and cannot be dismissed from her job for three years. When fathers fail to pay up, the state covers the child-support payment and enforces collection.

It is hardly surprising, given its dramatically different policies, that compared to Sweden Germany has: fewer births to unmarried mothers (figure 25.1); a higher rate of marriage; a divorce rate a third lower; a smaller percentage of children

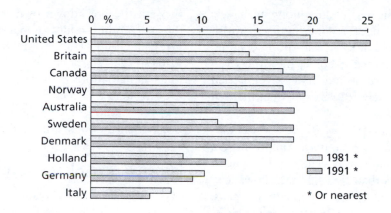

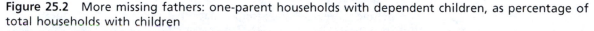

Figure 25.2 More missing fathers: one-parent households with dependent children, as percentage of total households with children

Sources: UNICEF; UN; US Bureau of Labor Statistics

being raised in one-parent families (figure 25.2); and a smaller percentage of women in the workforce. The gaps between the two countries are shrinking, though. Taxes and benefits have an effect on behaviour, but not a decisive one. If government policy was the only factor in such decisions, Sweden would never see a wedding.

Not back to basics

British family policy combines aspects of the Swedish and the German approaches without the coherence of either. The Tory government has preached 'back to basics', an alliterative nostrum not that far in feeling from Germany's three *Ks*. At the same time, its tax policies have been anything but encouraging to families with children, particularly those in which the father works and the mother stays at home. Since the late 1960s, Britain has steadily moved towards a tax system that treats adults as individuals, not as part of a family unit.

Critics say that these changes have made policy hostile to nuclear families. They have a point. Single adult occupiers pay 25 per cent less local council tax than a married or cohabiting couple, and those with children may be given higher priority for public housing. Taxes have increased more steeply for the married. In 1964 a married

couple with two children making the national average paid 9 per cent of its income in tax; now it pays 22 per cent, a faster rise than for single people or childless couples, The married-couple's tax allowance is probably doomed.

According to Patricia Morgan of London's Institute of Economic Affairs, a lone parent may end up with more income after tax than a working father with the same number of children and a dependent wife – even though in the latter case there is an additional adult in the house. Although Ms Morgan's conclusions have been hotly contested, there is little argument that, at lower levels of income, marriage becomes uneconomic. Parents with little money do better on benefit if they live apart than if they live together; boyfriends vanish when social workers come calling. As the Labour-affiliated Institute for Public Policy Research put it in a 1994 study, young mothers may be making a realistic assessment of the available options when they choose not to marry.

This realistic assessment lies behind the most dramatic change in patterns of marriage and parenting. While most British children live with their two natural, married parents, 20 per cent of households with children now contain only one parent. The majority of these single parents are divorced, but an increasing proportion never married, and many became mothers when very young (though the birth rate among teenagers has recently levelled off). One in three British births is out of wedlock. Half those children start life with no father at home; the others run an increased risk of losing him – unmarried fathers are more likely to walk out than married ones.

Almost three-quarters of those households depend on state income support, comprising the largest single group on benefit. Child benefit, itself less generous than the child tax allowance/family allowance it replaced in the mid-1970s, has been allowed to erode. In 1992 one in three British children lived in a poor household, three times the rate of 1979. More than half those poor children live in single-parent households.

America first

In America families are valued tremendously – so much so that most people will have at least two of them. Americans are religious, but have one of the highest divorce rates in the world. They are ambivalent about abortions but have a lot of them. Government has worked hard to make public policy as contradictory as private choices.

There is a marriage penalty at the middle to upper end of the income-tax schedule: married couples pay more tax than two single people with the same income. Under other conditions there is a marriage bonus. Divorce is easy. Three out of ten American children will sleep in a different home from their father tonight. Among black children, the rate is six out of ten.

Child benefits are low – the government spends four times as much on the elderly as on children, although old people are much better off. Lone parents are six times more likely to be poor than married couples. Benefits designed to alleviate that poverty have put the family under further strain. Until quite recently, women could not get income support if there was a man in the house. The welfare cheque, with its attendant medical benefits and food stamps, became considerably more valuable to have than a low-wage husband and father.

With the breakdown of marriages has come a breakdown in the idea of marriage as a precursor to family life. Half a million teenagers have babies every year; very few of them go home to their father. More than half the 5 m women on welfare started as teenage mothers. Their daughters often follow in their mothers' footsteps; their sons often follow in their fathers'.

When did you last see your father?

The only common thread to America's chaotic policies is that they are intended to allow adults freedom. That goal is now being questioned. There is widespread agreement that the design of America's modest safety net has helped to destabilize the family. Republican redesigns on offer include time limits and no increase in benefits for additional children; Democrats are talking about work requirements and group homes for teenaged mothers. Few, however, are talking about family policies that affect the middle class, such as state laws on divorce or the erosion of the dependants' allowance.

The problem with the American and British approach is not that benefits are too generous; they are stingy. The fundamental mistake is that fathers have been airbrushed out of the picture. Although there cannot be lone mothers without a roughly equivalent number of fathers lurking somewhere, the latter are mostly ignored.

Throughout the world, the lack of fathers is a key factor in the impoverishment of children. In Britain, almost half the single-parent families have incomes of £100 ($155) a week or less, compared with only 5 per cent of couples with children. This is not simply because the poor are more likely to become single parents. As the Rowntree Foundation, a British research organization, notes: 'Poverty is more obviously one of the consequences of breakdown than a cause.' The result of divorce or abandonment is often two poor households rather than a single struggling one. Children bear the brunt: when money is tight, studies show, parental discipline gets harsher and more arbitrary.

A father is not just a cash cow. Daniel Patrick Moynihan, a Democratic senator who has taken these problems seriously for thirty years, says that a community without fathers 'asks for and gets chaos'. As an American, he has been able to see that chaos for some time, but it is now visible elsewhere. There are neighbourhoods in Britain where more than two-thirds of homes with children lack fathers; some of Paris's wilder *banlieues* are not that different.

Humans have long childhoods in order to learn; they are very sensitive to the environment in which they grow up. In most societies, quite possibly throughout the evolution of the species, that environment has contained men – and, in particular, a man who is their mother's partner. If the environment is not like that but society tries to act as if it is, it should be no surprise that the child is affected in all sorts of ways. For boys, the absence of men can induce what sociologist Elijah Anderson calls 'hypermasculinity', characterized by casual, even predatory, sex and violence. Fatherless girls, like their brothers, tend to do less well in school and have greater difficulty in making the transition to adulthood; they are much more likely than girls who grew up with a father to be young and unmarried when they first get pregnant.

Asserting the value of fathers is not to say that lone mothers are rotten; it is to recognize that their children tend to have more of the kinds of social, economic and academic difficulties that a generous society would seek to spare them. But if that idea moves society to prefer faithful fatherhood, it will face two big problems: divorce and low pay.

At all levels of income, divorce destroys fatherhood. When men do not live under the same roof as their children, they find it more difficult to maintain a relationship. Researchers from Exeter, in Britain, found in a 1994 study that more than half the children of divorce did not see the non-custodial parent – almost always the father – on a regular basis. A quarter did not even know where he lived. Studies from other countries confirm that Britain's divorced fathers are not unique in their isolation from their children. Never-married fathers are even more remote. Stepfathers and boyfriends are, as a group, a poor substitute. They tend to offer less emotional and financial commitment than resident fathers. They are many times more likely to abuse the children with whom they live.

Low incomes may also discourage men from living with any family they have fathered. In the 1992–3 British Social Attitudes survey, men without an academic qualification were far more likely than those better educated to think that the husband's role was to earn money, and the wife's to stay at home. Unfortunately, many less-educated men cannot find work that pays enough to allow them to play this role. This is particularly true in Britain and America, less so in Sweden and Germany, where wage differentials are narrower.

In America, the earnings for black male high-school drop-outs fell by half, in real terms, in the period 1973–89. Roughly a third of all American men aged between 25 and 34 earn too little to lift a family of four out of poverty. American research has found that men's willingness to live as part of a family rises as their income does. When women get used to the idea that the state is a better breadwinner, they come to devalue fatherhood. 'How do you get a bloke to make a go of it with his girlfriend if the wage he can get is no more than welfare?' asks Frank Field, a Labour MP who chairs the House of Commons Select Committee on Social Security.

The Swedish response has been to nationalize the family. This may deal with the economic side of the problem. It is little help on the psychological front. And it is expensive. Britain and America, with their low tolerance for high taxes, are unlikely to choose the Swedish road. Nor are they likely to favour the heavy-handed approach that Germans accept. It should be possible, however, for these countries to build a consensus around three principles: first, that tax-and-benefit policies should not discriminate against the family; secondly, that fathers should be obliged to face up to their parental responsibilities; and thirdly, that the working poor should be given every opportunity to achieve financial self-reliance.

Proposed British legislation to make the welfare of children the first priority in divorce is a step in the right direction. Looking at ways to boost the take-home pay of working parents makes sense, as does getting lone mothers into work, something which Sweden does excellently, and which helps break down the belief that men must either be sole earner or nothing. Rules that are hostile to fathers staying with their families should be scrapped.

Even if all this was done, the effects might be disappointingly limited: far larger forces are at work. But incentives do matter. Sweden's marriage rate more than doubled in 1989 as couples married in order to take advantage of a one-off pension reform. Since people do respond to the tax-and-benefit structure, a systematic attempt to stop that response being socially destructive is not unreasonable. It is difficult for democratic government to create incentives so strong that they greatly change the behaviour of lots of people. But, as the effect of too many bad incentives in Britain and America has made it clear, it is not impossible.

26 On Friendship

Ray Pahl

Friendship may be seen as an increasingly important form of social glue in contemporary society. Young adolescents are well known to be heavily dependent on their peers for social support and self-identity, but now more people are culturally determined by their friends until much later in life. The early friend-dependent phase seems to be continuing through their twenties and thirties for an increasing proportion of the population, and, for the minority without partners, friends remain central throughout their lives.

The word 'friend' in English can cover a wide range of close informal relationships, so that its use without qualification can be highly ambiguous. The invitation to bring a friend to an exhibition may imply little more than knowing what name to write in the book at the entrance. At the other extreme, a special friend can share one's deepest thoughts, hopes and fears and provide 'another self' to share the vicissitudes of life. Something of the range of the forms and types of friendship will be explored [in this discussion]. It would be helpful if the reader is watchful for his or her taken-for-granted assumptions about what makes a friend a friend, recognizing that, whatever these may be, they are not universally shared. As the social and cultural context of friendship changes over time, so does the meaning of what it is to be a friend.

Those in the Western world who so avidly watch the TV soap opera *Friends* pick up new styles and modes of friendship, as well as finding that the actors resonate with their own experiences. The TV drama both reflects and creates modern forms of friendship.

Sociologists claim that, in modern Western societies, there is a growing centrality of personal communities as opposed to geographical or work-based communities. These personal communities may be geographically scattered and may change substantially as we move through the life-course. The teenager's 'need' for friends is of a different order from the 'need' of the socially isolated eighty-something. Our social convoy of significant others may change and fluctuate as we go through life.

The social *zeitgeist* of the early twenty-first century is democratic, anti-authoritarian and egalitarian. Family relationships are, inevitably, hierarchical, reflecting the differences between generations and the birth-order of siblings. Sociologists have shown that our social relationships with members of our families are heavily dependent on whether or not we get on with them. Family obligations, duties and responsibilities will be affected by whether we actually like the people concerned. While this has probably always been the case, people are more ready to acknowledge their preferences in their mix of chosen kin and non-kin friends.

The growth of an egalitarian ideology between partners means that these, too, are self-consciously more friend-like. Indeed, marriages and partnerships can break up as much through the finding of another more sympathetic, supportive and understanding friend as through refocused desire. Many women will be much more likely to be influenced by their closest female friend than by their mother-in-law – or even their own parents. Some commentators have gone so far as to see the emergence of 'families of choice' – a phrase that originated in the gay community but which adds potency to the idea of personal communities.

This [. . .] centrality of friends and friendship in contemporary society could be an important ingredient in the understanding of emerging social forms. The styles and symbols of contemporary culture are increasingly mediated through friends. Magazines of style and fashion are now more likely to surround their target consumers with friends, not family. The advertisement for Renault cars which showed a stylish father and daughter in collusion over their respective love lives is based on the assumption that the two are equals in their devotion to style. The young woman, Nicole, refers to her 'Papa' in a fond, sisterly, friend-like way. This is an exception that proves the rule: it nevertheless affirms that traditionally hierarchical relationships can be egalitarian and friend-like.

This modern focus on friends provides a challenge to conventional, traditional thinking about family and communities. Indeed, it was by my attempt to demythologize the idea of community that I was led to develop my interest in friends and friendship.

Over the last twenty or so years governments in the West have been increasingly concerned with social cohesion. Faced with rapidly rising divorce rates, the growth of juvenile crime, the apparent declining influence of parental authority, widespread feelings of insecurity among the elderly, declining involvement in local government and a host of other gloomy statistics purportedly indicating social decline, governments turned to sociologists for help and advice. Unwilling to acknowledge directly that increasing dependence on market forces and consumption is insufficient in itself to promote social solidarity, governments have responded to the beguiling promises of what has come to be known as 'communitarianism'.

The idea was encouraged in the United States of America in a book entitled *Habits of the Heart* by Robert Bellah and associates, which triggered off a debate about the decline of citizenship, moral responsibility and the relationship between character and society.[1] These American social scientists, and many others who followed them, notably Amitai Etzioni, argued for the need for some kind of moral regeneration reflecting what Bellah et al. describe as 'the tremendous nostalgia many Americans have for the idealised "small town". The wish for a harmonious community . . . is a wish to transform the roughness of utilitarian dealings in the market place, the courts and government administration into neighbourly conciliation. But this nostalgia is belied by the strong focus of American individualism on economic success. The rules of the competitive market, not the practices of the town meeting or the fellowship of the church, are the real arbiters of living.'

Ever since the Old Testament prophets, and probably before, there have always been those who have inveighed against the decadence of contemporary society, contrasting it with a more integrated and cohesive society in the past. There are many contemporary voices bemoaning the so-called breakdown of the family through divorce and the labour market pressures related to the intensification of work and the associated insecurities and stresses that impinge deleteriously on 'family life'. Likewise, social and geographical mobility, the decline of traditional industries and the development of new services more dependent on female labour have disrupted or broken down 'traditional' communities. However, there are other contemporary voices that question the cosiness of previous putative golden ages. Feuds between neighbours and families led to much bitterness, mistrust and, indeed, physical violence. The simmering hatreds of the former Yugoslavia are seen to be more typical of traditional than modern societies. Those sceptical of the warmth, trust and communal responsibility of times past see the freely chosen friend as the basis for a new form of social morality. [. . .] Friendships in the early modern period were more likely to be calculative exchange relationships than the mutual meeting of minds and spirits described in one way by Aristotle and in another by contemporary friend-focused people. [. . .]

There can be no going back, either to the authoritarian and patriarchal family, or to communities of deprivation and isolation. Isolated mining communities had certain strengths in their solidarities, but they also had material deprivation and female subservence. Unquestionably, twenty-first-century society is held together by qualitatively and quantitatively different social bonds from those more typical 300 years ago.

The crucial issue for those concerned with managing, governing and creatively understanding contemporary society is to know what, if anything, is replacing kinship obligations, civic responsibility and the mutual care and reciprocities engendered by being trapped in communities of fate. Evidently, strong social bonds do exist in some form, since the atomization of mass society based on individualized consumption is, in itself, an unlikely basis for social order. Whether or not these contemporary social bonds are becoming more firmly based on friends and friendship is an issue of fundamental importance.

Yet, perhaps surprisingly, there has been remarkably little scholarly concern with contemporary patterns and styles of friendship. This may be due partly to the fact that, [. . .] the term 'friend' is notoriously difficult to define and friendship is famously difficult for the authorities to tame or to control. The rights, obligations and duties of 'next-of-kin' can be clearly specified in family law in a way not so easily extended to 'best friend'.

Given the difficulties involved in advocating a return to the world we have lost, there is a need to understand the new basis for social connectedness. A widely held assumption, for which there is much empirical support, is that those societies which have better organized reciprocities and civic solidarity also have better schools, faster economic growth, better health and well-being and more effective government. The precise social mechanisms which underlie such correlations are not yet very clear. However, it is commonly agreed that a discussion of these issues is helpfully advanced under the umbrella of a new term – *social capital*. Robert Putnam has defined social capital as referring to 'features of social organisation such as networks, norms, and social trust that facilitate co-ordination and co-operation for mutual benefit.'

Defining, exploring and expanding the notion of social capital keeps many contemporary social scientists very busy, and, happily, there is no need to go into the complex niceties of their work here. It will suffice for present purposes for readers to be aware that a common ingredient in most discussions of social capital is the further notion of social network or social support. Friends and friendship are assumed to be part of any individual's salient social circle.

The term 'social network' is frequently taken to be a more precise way of describing social connectedness. The term has been much used and abused. Often people say they are 'networking' when all they are doing is adding new contacts to their address books. However, the analogy of a network carries with it the notion of interconnectedness. Thus, a family may be described as a social network since, presumably, all members of a family know each other. If one were representing links diagrammatically, with each individual represented as a dot on a piece of paper, then lines representing linkages could be drawn between each of the dots, providing a very close-knit network. However, even though each member of the family might be aware of each other member, it need not follow that the nature of the links is uniform. Some may be closer and see each other frequently; others may simply be aware of a tenuous tie of very minor social significance. The intensity, durability and other various qualitative and quantitative aspects of these linkages can be described or adduced.

Other social networks are more loose or ephemeral. Students at college may have a group of friends or acquaintances, some of whom know each other and others who do not. Some friends may know the parents or siblings of the person on whom the network is focused, others not. The student concerned may have a home-based network, a college-based network and later a work-based network, and so on. Careful analyses of these networks can become highly complex and, indeed, mathematically sophisticated. It will be evident that gathering the necessary information in order to carry out such network analyses can be hugely time-consuming and expensive. Understandably, perhaps, the quantitative analyses cannot explore the subtle nuances of each particular social relationship and the systems of classification have to be somewhat crude. Individuals may be designated simply as 'friends', 'neighbours', 'family', and so on. The fact that there are different kinds of friends is rarely considered, although, taking a crude index such as frequency of visiting, the relative importance of friends or family, *based on that criterion alone,* can be assessed. Thus, it can be shown in relation to various practical matters, such as finding a job, caring for or minding young children or being cared for when ill or very elderly, whether the help or support is more likely to be provided by friends or family. Such information is of interest, even though the precise definition of a friend – as opposed to other forms of social connectedness – remains elusive.

[. . .]

Basically, it seems likely that two quite distinct processes are taking place at the same time. On the one hand, friends may be taking over various social tasks, duties and functions from family and kin, simply out of practical necessity. Those who move away to new areas may do all they can to keep in touch with the family they leave behind. However, despite frequent visits, phone calls, e-mails, letters, and so on, in an emergency and for much day-to-day support, there can be no substitute for geographical propinquity. Caring for a sick child who has to be collected from school in an emergency almost certainly requires the help of a local friend. As women's participation in the labour force continues to rise, so grandmothers and aunts as well as mothers are torn by other responsibilities. The problems of distance and availability remain. There is increasing survey evidence to support the growing practical importance of friends.

The second process is the changing meaning of friendship. Our ideas of what it means to be a good friend, a close friend, a really close friend or a best friend are changing. Our expectations and aspirations are growing, and we are even prepared to judge the quality of our relationships with kin on the basis of some higher ideal of whether we can be closer to them as friends. This change in the meaning and quality of friendship is much harder to measure, since people themselves are only recently coming to terms with these changes and recognizing their significance. Evidently, it is hard to get coherent information from people about something which they are barely aware exists.

[. . .] I have begun researching on these problems [and] one thing can be said with certainty from the first round of interviews already completed. Respondents have little difficulty in describing their own personal communities and in recognizing that friends can be described as having different degrees of importance and significance for them at different stages of their lives. Some older respondents describe certain friends as being closer to them than their parents at later stages in the life-course. Some have special friends that mean more to them than anything else in life. Others have difficulty in recognizing any close friends at all. The diversity of ethnography with which we are faced presents daunting problems of analysis, but [I am] convinced that we are documenting something of singular significance for understanding the changing basis of social connectedness in contemporary society. [I] use the term 'social convoy' to describe the fluctuating form of an individual's personal community as he or she moves through life.

[. . .]

NOTE

1   Robert Bellah et al., *Habits of the Heart* (Berkeley: University of California Press, 1985).

Part 8

Crime and Deviance

Computers are becoming more and more important in our lives. Information technology is revolutionizing much of what we do. The rise of the internet is just one expression of this. However, there is a dark side to these developments – the rise of new forms of crime. In Reading 27, Tim Jordan and Paul Taylor discuss the rise of hacking. Hackers are individuals who illegally break into the computer systems of government, businesses or private individuals. Hackers are certainly not all criminals in the ordinary sense – most are not motivated by money, but by the challenge of illicitly breaking computer codes. As the authors show, hackers don't operate just as individuals – they form a community.

Richard Ericson and Kevin Haggerty, in Reading 28, analyse the development of electronic policing. With advances in information technology and communications, police use many new techniques in their struggle against crime. Police cars are now heavily wired, while a variety of electronic gadgets are used in direct crime detection. Police are also much more aware than they used to be of the role of the media in public reactions to crime and criminal investigation. Police in most

countries track media stories and try to achieve effective media discussion of policing issues. Specialized databases are used not just in relation to investigating crime but in deterring criminology too.

Ruaridh Nicoll, in Reading 29, pursues the connections between gender and violence. Most crimes of violence are carried out by men. Yet one of the offshoots of increasing gender equality is the rise of female violence. This reading discusses America's new all-female gangs. Violence, the author points out, is an intrinsic part of gang activities, whether male or female.

In Reading 30, Josie O'Dwyer and Pat Carlen consider the experience of women in prison. Women currently make up only a very small proportion of the total prison population in Britain, and apart from some illegal activities which are predominantly female (for instance, prostitution), the majority of offenders in all types of crime are men. Women's prisons, however, by no means form a benign environment: as O'Dwyer and Carlen describe them, such prisons are characterized by a good deal of violence and intimidation.

27 A Sociology of Hackers

Tim Jordan and Paul Taylor

Introduction

The growth of a world-wide computer network and its increasing use both for the construction of online communities and for the reconstruction of existing societies means that unauthorised computer intrusion, or hacking, has wide significance. The 1996 report of a computer raid on Citibank that netted around $10 million indicates the potential seriousness of computer intrusion. Other, perhaps more whimsical, examples are the attacks on the CIA world-wide web site, in which its title was changed from Central Intelligence Agency to Central Stupidity Agency, or the attack on the British Labour Party's web-site, in which titles like 'Road to the Manifesto' were changed to 'Road to Nowhere'. These hacks indicate the vulnerability of increasingly important computer networks and the anarchistic, or perhaps destructive, world-view of computer intruders. It is correct to talk of a world-view because computer intrusions come not from random, obsessed individuals but from a community that offers networks and support, such as the long running magazines *Phrack* and *2600*. At present there is no detailed sociological investigation of this community, despite a growing number of racy accounts of hacker adventures. To delineate a sociology of hackers, an introduction is needed to the nature of computer-mediated communication and of the act of computer intrusion, the hack. Following this the hacking community will be explored in three sections: first, a profile of the number of hackers and hacks; second, an outline of its culture through the discussion of six different aspects of

the hacking community; and third, an exploration of the community's construction of a boundary, albeit fluid, between itself and its other, the computer security industry. Finally, a conclusion that briefly considers the significance of our analysis will be offered.

In the early 1970s, technologies that allowed people to use decentred, distributed networks of computers to communicate with each other globally were developed. By the early 1990s a new means of organising and accessing information contained on computer networks was developed that utilised multi-media 'point and click' methods, the World-Wide Web. The Web made using computer networks intuitive and underpinned their entry into mass use. The size of this global community of computer communicators is difficult to measure but in January 1998 there were at least 40 million. Computer communication has also become key to many industries, not just through the Internet but also through private networks, such as those that underpin automated teller services. The financial industry is the clearest example of this; as John Perry Barlow says, 'cyberspace is where your money is'. Taken together, all the different computer networks that currently exist control and tie together vital institutions of modern societies; including telecommunications, finance, globally distributed production and the media. Analysis of the community which attempts to illicitly use these networks can begin with a definition of the 'hack'.

Means of gaining unauthorised access to computer networks include guessing, randomly generating or stealing a password. For example, in the Prestel hack, which resulted in the Duke of Edinburgh's mail-box becoming vulnerable, the hacker simply guessed an all too obvious password (222222 1234). Alternatively, some computers and software programmes have known flaws that can be exploited. One of the most complex of these is 'IP spoofing' in which a computer connected to the Internet can be tricked about the identity of another computer during the process of receiving data from that computer. Perhaps most important of all is the ability to 'social engineer'. This can be as simple as talking people into giving out their passwords by impersonating someone, stealing garbage in the hope of gaining illicit information (trashing) or looking over someone's shoulder as they use their password (shoulder surfing). However, what makes an intrusion a hack or an intruder a hacker is not the fact of gaining illegitimate access to computers by any of these means but a set of principles about the nature of such intrusions. Turkle identifies three tenets that define a good hack: simplicity, the act has to be simple but impressive; mastery, however simple it is the act must derive from a sophisticated technical expertise; and, illicit, the act must be against some legal, institutional or even just perceived rules.[1] Dutch hacker Ralph used the example of stealing free telephone time to explain the hack:

It depends on how you do it, the thing is that you've got your guys that think up these things, they consider the technological elements of a phone-booth, and they think, 'hey wait a minute, if I do this, this could work', so as an experiment, they cut the wire and it works, now *they're hackers*. Okay, so it's been published, so Joe Bloggs reads this and says, 'hey, great, I have to phone my folks up in Australia', so he goes out, cuts the wire, makes phone calls. He's a stupid ignoramus, yeah? (Ralph, hacker, interview)

A second example would be the Citibank hack. In this hack, the expertise to gain unauthorised control of a bank was developed by a group of Russian hackers who were uninterested in taking financial advantage. The hacker ethic to these intruders was one of exploration and not robbery.

But, drunk and depressed, one of the hackers sold the secret for $100 and two bottles of vodka, allowing organised criminals to gain the expertise to steal $10 million. Here the difference between hacking and criminality lay in the communally held ethic that glorified being able to hack Citibank but stigmatised using that knowledge to steal. A hack is an event that has an original moment and, though it can be copied, it loses its status as a hack the more it is copied. Further, the good hack is the object in-itself that hackers desire, not the result of the hack.

The key to understanding computer intrusion in a world increasingly reliant on computer-mediated communication lies in understanding a community whose aim is the hack. It is this community that makes complex computer intrusion possible and a never ending threat, through the limitless search for a good hack. It is this community that stands forever intentionally poised both at the forefront of computer communications and on the wrong side of what hackers see as dominant social and cultural norms.

Computer underground: demographics

Analysing any intentionally illicit community poses difficulties for the researcher. The global and anonymous nature of computer-mediated communication exacerbates such problems because generating a research population from the computer underground necessitates self-selection by subjects and it will be difficult to check the credentials of each subject. Further methodological difficulties involved in examining a self-styled 'outlaw' community that exists in cyberspace are indicated by the Prestel hacker.

There used to be a hacking community in the UK, the hackers I used to deal with 8 or 9 years ago were all based in North London where I used to live and there were 12 of us around the table at the local Chinese restaurant of a Friday night . . . within about 20 minutes of me and my colleague Steve Gold being arrested: end of hacking community. An awful lot of phone calls went around, a lot of discs got buried in the garden, and a lot of people became ex-hackers and there's really no-one who'll talk now.

(Schifreen, hacker, interview)

Demographic data is particularly difficult to collect from an underground community. However, some statistics are available. [. . .] After investigating the US police force's crackdown on the computer underground in the early 1990s, Sterling estimated there were 5,000 active hackers with only around 100 in the elite who would be 'skilled enough to penetrate sophisticated systems'.[2] For the same period, Clough and Mungo estimated there were 2,000 of 'the really dedicated, experienced, probably obsessed computer freaks' and possibly 10,000 others aspiring to this status.[3] Though no more than an indication, the best, indeed only, estimates for the size of the hacking community or computer underground are given by these figures.

Another means of measuring the size of the computer underground is by its effects. Though this cannot hope to indicate the actual number of hackers, as one hacker can be responsible for extensive illicit adventures, measuring the extent of hacking allows one indication of the underground's level of activity. Three surveys are available that generate evidence from the 'hacked' rather than hackers: the 1990 UK Audit Commission's survey, the 1993 survey conducted as part of this research project, and the 1996 WarRoom Research, information systems security survey. Results from all three sources will be presented, focusing on the amount of hacking.

The 1990 UK Audit Commission surveyed 1,500 academic, commercial and public service organisations in the United Kingdom. This survey found 5 per cent of academic, 14 per cent of commercial and 11.5 per cent of public service organisations had suffered computer intrusion. A survey was conducted as part of this research project (hereafter referred to as the Taylor survey) and received 200 responses, of which 64.5 per cent had experienced a hack, 18.5 per cent a virus only and 17 per cent no detected illicit activity. The 1996 WarRoom survey received 236

responses from commercial USA firms (*Fortune* 1,000 companies) of which 58 per cent reported attempts by outsiders to gain computer access in the 12 months prior to July 1996, 29.8 per cent did not know and 12.2 per cent reported no such attempts. The types of intrusions can be categorised as 38.3 per cent malicious, 46.5 per cent unidentifiable as malicious or benign and 15.1 per cent benign.[4]

The level of hacking activity reported in these surveys varies greatly between the Audit Commission on the one hand and the Taylor and WarRoom surveys on the other. A number of possibilities explain this. The lower level of hacking comes from a survey of UK organisations, while Taylor was over half from the USA and a third UK and WarRoom was solely USA. This might suggest a higher level of hacking into USA organisations, though this says nothing about the national source of a hack. Second, the Audit Commission survey has a much larger sample population and consequently should be more reliable. However, third, the WarRoom and Taylor surveys stressed the confidentiality of respondents. This is a key issue as organisations show a consistently high level of caution in reporting hacks. The WarRoom survey found that 37 per cent of organisations would only report computer intrusion if required by law, that 22 per cent would report only if 'everybody else did', that 30 per cent would only report if they could do so anonymously and only 7 per cent would report anytime intrusion was detected. From this perspective the Audit Commission survey may have under-reported hacking because it did not place sufficient emphasis on the confidentiality of responses. Fourth, the Taylor and WarRoom surveys were conducted later than the Audit Commission survey and may reflect rising levels of or rising awareness of hacking. Unfortunately, there is no way of deciding which of these factors explain the differences in reported levels of hacking.

The available statistics suggest the computer underground may not be very large, particularly in the number of elite hackers, but may be having a significant effect on a range of organisations. If the Taylor and WarRoom surveys are accurate nearly two-thirds of organisations are suffering hacks. To grasp the nature of hackers requires turning to the qualitative fieldwork conducted in this project.

Internal factors: technology, secrecy, and anonymity, membership fluidity, male dominance and motivations

To find 'hacker culture' you have to take a very wide view of the cyberspace terrain and watch the interactions among physically diversified people who have in common a mania for machines and software. What you will find will be a gossamer framework of culture.
(Marotta, hacker, interview)

The 'imagined community' that hackers create and maintain can be outlined through the following elements: technology, secrecy, anonymity, boundary fluidity, male dominance and motivations. Community is here understood as the collective identity that members of a social group construct or, in a related way, as the 'collective imagination' of a social group. Both a collective identity and imagination allow individuals to recognise in each other membership of the same community. The computer underground, or at least the hacking part of it, can be in this way understood as a community that offers certain forms of identity through which membership and social norms are negotiated. Even though some of these forms are externally imposed, the nature of Internet technology for example, the way these forms are understood allows individuals to recognise in each other a common commitment to an ethic, community or way of life. This theorisation draws on Anderson's concept of the imagined community and on social movement theories that see movements as dispersed networks of individuals, groups and organisations that combine through a collectively articulated identity. Anderson names the power of an imagined identity to bind people, who may never meet each other, together in allegiance to a common cause. Social movement theories grasp the way movements rely on divergent networks that are not hierarchically or bureaucratically unified but are negotiated between actors through an identity that is itself the subject of much of the negotiation. These perspectives allow us to grasp a hacking community that can use computer mediated communication to exist world-wide and in which individuals often never physically meet.

Technology

The hacking community is characterised by an easy, if not all-consuming, relationship with technology, in particular with computer and communications technology.

We are confronted with . . . a generation that has lived with computers virtually from the cradle, and therefore have no trace of fear, not even a trace of reverence.
(Professor Herschberg, academic, interview)

Hackers share a certain appreciation of or attitude to technology in the assumption that technology can be turned to new and unexpected uses. This attitude need not be confined to computer mediated communication. Dutch hacker Dell claimed to have explored the subterranean tunnels and elevator shafts of Amsterdam, including government fall-out shelters (Dell, hacker, interview), while Utrecht hacker Ralph argued hacking 'pertains to any field of technology. Like, if you haven't got a kettle to boil water with and you use your coffee machine to boil water with, then that in my mind is a hack, because you are using technology in a way that it's not supposed to be used' (Ralph, hacker, interview). It is the belief that technology can be bent to new, unanticipated purposes that underpins hackers' collective imagination.

Secrecy

Hackers demonstrate an ambivalent relationship to secrecy. A hack demands secrecy, because it is illicit, but the need to share information and gain recognition demands publicity. Sharing information is key in the development of hackers, though it makes keeping illicit acts hidden from law enforcement difficult. Hackers often hack in groups, both in the sense of physically being in the same room while hacking and of hacking separately but being in a group that physically meets, that frequents bulletin boards, on-line places to talk and exchange information. It is a rare story of a hacker's education that does not include being trained by more experienced hackers or drawing on the collective wisdom of the hacking community through on-line information. Gaining recognition is also important to hackers. A member of the Zoetermeer hacking group noted: 'Hacking can be rewarding in itself, because it can give you a real kick sometimes. But it can give you a lot more satisfaction and recognition if you share your experiences with others. . . . Without this group I would never have spent so much time behind the terminals digging into the operating system' (Zoetermeer, hackers, interview). A good hack is a bigger thrill when shared and can contribute to a hacker gaining status and access to more communal expertise. For example, access to certain bulletin boards is only given to those proven worthy.

A tension between the need to keep illicit acts away from the eyes of police and other authority figures but in front of the eyes of peers or even the general public defines hackers' relationship to secrecy. No hack exemplifies this more than a World-Wide Web hack where the object is to alter an internationally accessible form of public communication but at the same time not be caught. In the case of the Labour Party hack, the hacker managed to be quoted on the front page of UK national newspapers, by ringing up the newspapers to tell them to look at the hack before it was removed, but also kept his/her identity secret. A further example is that many hackers take trophies in the form of copied documents or pieces of software because a trophy proves to the hacking community that the hacker 'was there'. The problem is that a trophy is one of the few solid bases for prosecuting hackers. Ambivalence toward secrecy is also the source of the often-noted fact that hackers are odd criminals,

seeking publicity. As Gail Thackeray, one-time police nemesis of hackers, noted 'What other group of criminals . . . publishes newsletters and holds conventions?'

Anonymity

The third component of the hacking community is anonymity. As with technology what is distinctive is not so much the fact of online anonymity, as this is a widely remarked aspect of computer-mediated communication, but the particular understanding of anonymity that hackers take up. Anonymity is closely related to secrecy but is also distinct. Secrecy relates to the secrecy of the hack, whereas anonymity relates to the secrecy of a hacker's off-line identity. Netta Gilboa notes one complex version of this interplay of named and hidden identity on an on-line chat channel for hackers.

Hackers can log into the #hack channel using software . . . that allows them to come in from several sites and be on as many separate connections, appearing to be different people. One of these identities might then message you privately as a friend while another is being cruel to you in public.[5]

Gilboa experienced the construction of a number of public identities all intended to mask the 'real' identity of a hacker. A second example of this interplay of anonymity and publicity is the names or 'handles' hackers give themselves and their groups. These are some of the handles encountered in this research: Hack-Tic (group), Zoetermeer (group), Altenkirch (German), Eric Bloodaxe, Faustus, Maelstrom, Mercury, Mofo. Sterling notes a long list of group names – such as Kaos Inc., Knights of Shadow, Master Hackers, MAD!, Legion of Doom, Farmers of Doom, the Phirm, Inner Circle I and Inner Circle II. Hackers use names to sign their hacks (sometimes even leaving messages for the hacked computer's usual users), to meet on-line and to bolster their self-image as masters of the hack, all the while keeping their off-line identity secret.

Membership fluidity

The fourth quality of the hacking community is the speed at which membership changes. Hacking shares the characteristics ascribed to many social movements of being an informal network rather than a formally constituted organisation and, as such, its boundaries are highly permeable. There are no formal ceremonies to pass or ruling bodies to satisfy to become a hacker. The informal and networked nature of the hacking community, combined with its illicit and sometimes obsessional nature means that a high turnover of hackers occurs. Hackers form groups within the loose overall structure of the hacking community and these may aspire to be formally organised; however the pressures of law enforcement means that any successful hacking group is likely to attract sustained attention at some point.

People come and go pretty often and if you lay off for a few months and then come back, almost everyone is new. There are always those who have been around for years . . . I would consider the hacking community a very informal one. It is pretty much anarchy as far as rule-making goes. . . . The community was structured only within the framework of different hacking 'groups'. Legion of Doom would be one example of this. A group creates its own rules and usually doesn't have a leader . . . The groups I've been in have voted on accepting new members, kicking people out, etc.

(Eric Bloodaxe, hacker, member of
Legion of Doom, interview)

Gilboa claims that the future of hacking will be a split between lifelong hackers, often unable to quit because of police records and suspicion, and 90 per cent of hackers who will move on 'when they get a job they care about or a girlfriend who sucks up their time'.[6] A more prosaic, but equally potent, reason why the hacking community's membership is fluid is given by hacker Mike: 'if you stop, if you don't do it for one week then things change, the network always changes. It changes very quickly and you have to keep up and you have to learn all the tricks by heart, the default passwords, the bugs you need' (Mike, hacker, interview). The sheer speed at which computer communications technology changes requires a powerful commitment from hackers.

Male dominance

The fifth component of hacking culture is male dominance and an associated misogyny. Research for this project and literature on hackers fails to uncover any significant evidence of female hackers. Gilboa states, 'I have met more than a thousand male hackers in person but less than a dozen of them women'. This imbalance is disproportionate even in the field of computer-mediated communication. A number of factors explain the paucity of women generally in the computer sciences: childhood socialisation, where boys are taught to relate to technology more easily than girls; education in computers occurs in a masculine environment; and, a gender bias towards men in the language used in computer science. With these factors producing a general bias towards males in relation to computers, the drive towards the good hack exacerbates this as it involves a macho, competitive attitude. Hackers construct a more intensely masculine version of the already existing male bias in the computer sciences.

When Adam delved and Eve span . . . who was then the gentleman? Well, we see that Adam delves into the workings of computers and networks and meanwhile Eve spins, what? Programmes? Again, my wife programmes and she has the skills of a hacker. She has had to crack security in order to do her job. But she does it as her job, not for the abstract thrill of discovering the unknown. Even spin. Females who compute would rather spend their time building a good system than breaking into someone else's system.

(Mercury, hacker, interview)

Whether Mercury's understanding of differences between men and women is accurate or not, the fact that he, and many other hackers, have such attitudes means the hacking community will almost certainly feel hostile to women. Added to these assumptions of, at best, separate spheres of male and female expertise in computing is the problem that anonymity often fuels sexual harassment. 'The fact that many networks allow a user to hide his real name . . . seems to cause many males to drop all semblance of civilisation. Sexual harassment by email is not uncommon' (Freiss, hacker, interview). Gilboa, a woman, recounts an epic tale of harassment that included hackers using her on-line magazine as a 'tutorial' example of how to charge phone calls to someone else, taking over her magazine entirely and launching a fake version, being called a prostitute, child molester and drug dealer, having her phone calls listened to, her phone re-routed or made to sound constantly engaged and having her email read. One answer to Gilboa's puzzlement at her treatment lies in the collective identity hackers share and construct that is in part misogynist.

Motivations

Finally, hackers often discuss their motivations for hacking. They are aware of, and often glory in, the fact that the life of a dedicated hacker seems alien to those outside the hacking community. One result of this is that hackers discuss their motivations. These are sometimes couched as self-justifications, sometimes as explanations and sometimes as agonised struggles with personal obsessions and failures. However, whatever the content of such discussions, it is the fact of an ongoing discourse around the motivation to hack that builds the hacking community. These discussions are one more way that hackers can recognise in each other a common identity that provides a collective basis for their community. A number of recurring elements to these discussions can be identified.

First, hackers often confess to an addiction to computers and/or to computer networks, a feeling that they are compelled to hack. Second, curiosity as to what can be found on the world-wide network is also a frequent topic of discussion. Third, hackers often claim their off-line life is boring compared to the thrill of illicit searches in on-line life. Fourth, the ability to gain power over computer systems, such as NASA, Citibank

or the CIA web site, is an attraction. Fifth, peer recognition from other hackers or friends is a reward and goal for many hackers, signifying acceptance into the community and offering places in a hierarchy of more advanced hackers. Finally, hackers often discuss the service to future computer users or to society they are offering because they identify security loopholes in computer networks. Hackers articulate their collective identity, and construct a sense of community, by discussing this array of different motivations.

I just do it because it makes me feel good, as in better than anything else that I've ever experienced . . . the adrenaline rush I get when I'm trying to evade authority, the thrill I get from having written a program that does something that was supposed to be impossible to do, and the ability to have social relations with other hackers are all very addictive . . . For a long time, I was extremely shy around others, and I am able to let my thoughts run free when I am alone with my computer and a modem hooked up to it. I consider myself addicted to hacking . . . I will have no moral or ethical qualms about system hacking until accounts are available to the general public for free . . . Peer recognition was very important, when you were recognised you had access to more.

(Maelstrom, hacker, interview)

Maelstrom explores almost the whole range of motivations including curiosity, the thrill of the illicit, boredom, peer recognition and the social need for free or cheap access. By developing his own interpretation out of the themes of motivation, he can simultaneously define his own drives and develop a sense of community. It is this double movement, in which individual motivations express the nature of a community, that makes the discussions of motivations important for hackers. Finally, the motivations offered by perhaps the most famous of all hackers, Kevin Mitnick, provides another common articulation of reasons for hacking.

You get a better understanding of cyberspace, the computer systems, the operating systems, how the computer systems interact with one another, that basically was my motivation behind my hacking activity in the past. It was just from the gain of knowledge and the thrill of adventure, nothing that was well and truly sinister as trying to get any type of monetary gain or anything.

(Mitnick, hacker, interview)

[...]

External factors: the boundary between computer underground and the computer security industry

Hackers negotiate a boundary around their community by relating to other social groups. For example, hackers have an often spectacular relationship to the media. Undoubtedly the most important relationship to another community or group is their intimate and antagonistic bond to the computer security industry (CSI). This relationship is constitutive of the hacking community in a way that no other is. Put another way, there is no other social group whose existence is necessary to the existence of the hacking community. Here is a sample of views of hackers from members of CSI.

Hackers are like kids putting a 10 pence piece on a railway line to see if the train can bend it, not realising that they risk derailing the whole train.

(Mike Jones, security awareness division, Department of Trade and Industry, UK, interview)

Electronic vandalism.

(Warman, London Business School, interview)

Somewhere near vermin.

(Zmudsinski, system engineer/manager, USA, interview)

Naturally, hackers often voice a similar appreciation of members of CSI. For example, while admitting psychotic tendencies exist in the hacking community Mofo notes:

my experience has shown me that the actions of 'those in charge' of computer systems and networks have similar 'power trips' which need to be fulfilled. Whether this psychotic need is developed or entrenched before one's association with computers is irrelevant.

(Mofo, hacker, interview)

However, the boundary between these two communities is not as clear as such attitudes might suggest. This can be seen in relation to membership of the communities and the actions members take.

Hackers often suggest the dream that their skills should be used by CSI to explore security faults, thereby giving hackers jobs and legitimacy to pursue the hack by making them members of CSI. The example of a leading member of one of the most famous hacker groups, the Legion of Doom, is instructive. Eric Bloodaxe, aka Chris Goggans, became a leading member of the hacking community before helping to set up a computer security firm, Comsec, and later moving to become senior network security engineer for WheelGroup, a network security company. On the CSI side, there have been fierce debates over whether hackers might be useful because they identify security problems. Most striking, a number of CSI agencies conduct hacking attacks to test security. IBM employ a group of hackers who can be hired to attack computer systems and the UK government has asked 'intelligence agents' to hack its secure email system for government ministers. In the IBM case, an attempt at differentiating the hired hackers from criminal hackers is made by hiring only hackers without criminal records (a practice akin to turning criminals who have not been caught into police). Both sides try to assure themselves of radical differences because they undertake similar actions. For example, Bernie Cosell was a USA commercial computer systems manager and one of the most vehement anti-hackers encountered in this study, yet he admitted he hacked

once or twice over the years. I recall one incident where I was working over the weekend and the master source hierarchy was left read-protected, and I really needed to look at it to finish what I was doing, and this on a system where I was not a privileged user, so I 'broke into' the system enough to give myself enough privileges to be able to override the file protections and get done what I needed ... at which point I put it all back and told the systems administrator about the security hole.

(Cosell, USA systems manager, interview)

More famous is the catalogue of hacks Clifford Stoll had to perpetrate in his pursuit of a hacker, which included borrowing other people's computers without permission and monitoring other people's electronic communications without permission. Such examples mean that differences between the two communities cannot be expressed through differences in what they do but must focus on the meaning of actions. Delineating these meanings is chiefly done through ethical debates about the nature of hacking conducted through analogies drawn between cyberspace and non-virtual or real space.

CSI professionals often draw analogies between computer intrusion and a range of widely understood crimes. These analogies draw on the claim that a computer is something like a bank, car or house that can be 'got into'. Using this analogy makes it easy to understand the danger of hackers, that people who break into banks, schools or houses usually do so for nefarious purposes. The ethical differences between hackers and the CSI become clearly drawn. The problem with such analogies is that, on further reflection, hackers seem strange burglars. How often does a burglar leave behind an exact copy of the video recorder they have stolen? But this unreal situation is a more accurate description of theft in cyberspace because taking in cyberspace overwhelmingly means copying. Further, hacker culture leads hackers to publicise their break-ins, sometimes even stressing the utility of their break-ins for identifying system weaknesses. What bank robbers ring up a bank to complain of lax security? The simple analogy of theft breaks down when it is examined and must be complicated to begin to make sense of what hackers do.

There is a great difference between trespassing on my property and breaking into my computer. A better analogy might be finding a trespasser in your high-rise office building at 3am and learning that his back-pack contained some tools, some wire, a timer and a couple of detonation caps. He could claim that he wasn't planting a bomb, but how can you be sure?

(Cosell, USA systems manager, interview)

Cosell's analogy continues to draw on real world or physically based images of buildings being entered but tries to come closer to the reality of how hackers operate. However, the ethical component of the analogy has been weakened because the damage hackers cause becomes implied, where is the bomb? Cosell cannot claim there will definitely be a bomb, only that it is possible. If all possible illegal actions were prohibited then many things would become illegal, such as driving, because it is possible to speed and then hurt someone in an accident. The analogy of breaking and entering is now strong on implied dangers but weak on the certainty of danger. The analogies CSI professionals use continue to change if they try to be accurate. 'My analogy is walking into an office building, asking a secretary which way it is to the records room and making some Xerox copies of them. Far different than breaking and entering someone's home' (Cohen, CSI, interview). Clearly there is some ethical content here, some notion of theft of information, but it is ethically far muddier than the analogy burglary offers. At this point, the analogy breaks down entirely because the ethical content can be reversed to one that supports hackers as 'whistle-blowers' of secret abuses everyone should know about.

The concept of privacy is something that is very important to a hacker. This is so because hackers know how fragile privacy is in today's world. . . . In 1984 hackers were instrumental in showing the world how TRW kept credit files on millions of Americans. Most people had not even heard of a credit file until this happened . . . More recently, hackers found that MCI's 'Friends and Family' programme allowed anybody to call an 800 number and find out the numbers of everyone in a customer's 'calling circle'. As a bonus, you could also find out how these numbers were related to the customer . . . In both the TRW and MCI cases, hackers were ironically accused of being the ones to invade privacy. What they really did was help to educate the American consumer.[7]

The central analogy of CSI has now lost its ethical content. Goldstein reverses the good and bad to argue that the correct principled action is to broadcast hidden information. If there is some greater social good to be served by broadcasting secrets, then perhaps hackers are no longer robbers and burglars but socially responsible whistle blowers. In the face of such complexities, CSI professionals sometimes abandon the analogy of breaking and entering altogether; 'it is no more a valid justification to attack systems because they are vulnerable than it is valid to beat up babies because they can't defend themselves' (Cohen, CSI, interview). Here many people's instinctive reaction would be to side with the babies, but a moment's thought reveals that in substance Cohen's analogy changes little. A computer system is not human and if information in it is needed by wider society, perhaps it should be attacked.

The twists and turns of these analogies show that CSI professionals use them not so much to clearly define hacking and its problems, but to establish clear ethical differences between themselves and hackers. The analogies of baby-bashing and robbery all try to establish hacking as wrong. The key point is that while these analogies work in an ethical and community building sense, they do not work in clearly grasping the nature of hacking because analogies between real and virtual space cannot be made as simply as CSI professionals would like to assume.

Physical (and biological) analogies are often misleading as they appeal to an understanding from an area in which different laws hold. . . . Many users (and even 'experts') think of a password as a 'key' despite the fact that you can easily guess the password, while it is difficult to do the equivalent for a key.

(Brunnstein, academic, Hamburg University, interview)

The process of boundary formation between the hacking and CSI communities occurs in the creation of analogies by CSI professionals to establish ethical differences between the communities and their reinterpretation by hackers. However, this does not exclude hackers from making their own analogies.

Computer security is like a chess game, and all these people that say breaking into my computer systems is like breaking into my house: bull-shit, because securing your house is a very simple thing, you just put locks on the doors and bars on the windows and then only brute force can get into your house, like smashing a window. But a computer has a hundred thousand intricate ways to get in, and it's a chess game with the people that secure a computer.

(Gongrijp, Dutch hacker, interview)

Other hackers offer similar analogies that stress hacking is an intellectual pursuit. 'I was bored if I didn't do anything . . . I mean why do people do crosswords? It's the same thing with hackers' (J. C. van Winkel, hacker, interview). Gongrijp and van Winkel also form boundaries through ethical analogy. Of course, it is an odd game of chess or crossword that results in the winner receiving thousands of people's credit records or access to their letters. Hackers' elision of the fact that a game of chess has no result but a winner and a loser at a game of chess whereas hacking often results in access to privileged information, means their analogies are both inaccurate and present hacking as a harmless, intellectual pursuit. It is on the basis of such analogies and discussions that the famed 'hacker ethic' is often invoked by hackers. Rather than hackers learning the tenets of the hacker ethic, as seminally defined by Steven Levy, they negotiate a common understanding of the meaning of hacking of which the hacker ethic provides a ready articulation. Many see the hacker ethic as a foundation of the hacker community, whereas we see the hacker ethic as the result of the complex construction of a collective identity.

The social process here is the use of analogies to physical space by CSI and hackers to establish a clear distinction between the two groups. In these processes can be seen the construction by both sides of boundaries between communities that are based on different ethical interpretations of computer intrusion, in a situation where other boundaries, such as typical actions or membership, are highly fluid.

Conclusion

The nature of the hacking community needs to be explored in order to grasp the social basis that produces hacking as a facet of computer networks. The figures given previously and the rise of the World-Wide Web hack, offering as it does both spectacular publicity and anonymity, point to the endemic nature of hackers now that world-wide computer networks are an inescapable reality. Hackers show that living in a networked world means living in a risky world. The community found by this research articulates itself in two key directions. First there are a number of components that are the subject of ongoing discussion and negotiation by hackers with other hackers. In defining and redefining their attitudes to technology, secrecy, anonymity, membership change, male dominance and personal motivations, hackers create an imagined community. Second, hackers define the boundaries of their community primarily in relation to the Computer Security Industry. These boundaries stress an ethical interpretation of hacking because it can be difficult to clearly distinguish the activities or membership of the two communities. Such ethics emerge most clearly through analogies used by members of each community to explain hacking.

Hackers are often pathologised as obsessed, isolated young men. The alien nature of on-line life allows people to believe hackers more easily communicate with machines than humans, despite hackers' constant use of computers to communicate with other humans. Fear of the power of computers over our own lives underpins this terror. The very anonymity that makes their community difficult to study, equally makes hackers an easy target for pathologising. For example, Gilboa's experience of harassment outlined earlier led her to pathologise hackers, suggesting work must be done exploring the characteristics of hackers she identified – such as lack of fathers or parental figures, severe depression and admittance to mental institutions. Similar interpretations of hackers are offered from within their community,

'All the hackers I know in France have (or have had) serious problems with their parents' (Condat, hacker, interview). Our research strongly suggests that psychological interpretations of hackers that individualise hackers as mentally unstable are severely limited because they miss the social basis of hacking. Gilboa's experience is no less unpleasant but all the more understandable when the male dominance of the hacking community is grasped.

The fear many have of the power of computers over their lives easily translates into the demonisation of those who manipulate computers outside of society's legitimate institutions. Journalist Jon Littman once asked hacker Kevin Mitnick if he thought he was being demonised because new and different fears had arisen with society becoming increasingly dependent on computers and communications. Mitnick replied, 'Yeah . . . That's why they're instilling fear of the unknown. That's why they're scared of me. Not because of what I've done, but because I have the capability to wreak havoc'. The pathological interpretation of hackers is attractive because it is based on the fear of computers controlling our lives. What else could someone be but mad, if s/he is willing to play for fun on computer systems that control air traffic, dams or emergency phones? The interpretation of hackers as members of an outlaw community that negotiates its collective identity through a range of clearly recognisable resources does not submit to the fear of computers. It gains a clearer view of hackers, who have become the nightmare of information societies despite very few documented cases of upheaval caused by hackers. Hacking cannot be clearly grasped unless fears are put aside to try and understand the community of hackers, the digital underground. From within this community, hackers begin to lose their pathological features in favour of collective principles, allegiances and identities.

NOTES

1   S. Turkle, *The Second Self: Computers and the Human Spirit* (London: Granada, 1984), p. 232.

2 B. Sterling, *The Hacker Crackdown: Law and Disorder on the Electronic Frontier* (London: Viking, 1992), pp. 76–7.

3 B. Clough and P. Mungo, *Approaching Zero: Data Crime and the Computer Underworld* (London: Faber and Faber, 1992), p. 218.

4 WarRoom, '1996 Information Systems Security Survey', WarRoom Research, LLC, available at http://www.infowar.com/.

5 N. Gilboa, 'Elites, Lamers, Narcs and Whores: Exploring the Computer Underground', in L. Cherny and E. Weise, *Wired Women: Gender and New Realities in Cyberspace* (Seattle: Seal Press, 1996), pp. 102–3.

6 Ibid., p. 111.

7 E. Goldstein, 'Hacker Testimony to House Sub-Committee Largely Unheard', *Computer Underground Digest*, 5 (1993), p. 43.

28 Electronic Policing

Richard V. Ericson and Kevin D. Haggerty

[. . .]

Electronic infrastructures

The modern police organization equips its members with electronic technologies for tracing risks that threaten territories. Police cars have become mobile offices and technological laboratories. They are 'wired' with voice radios, cellular telephones, computer-assisted dispatch terminals, laptop computers, radar, video cameras, remote microphones, breathalyser equipment, fax machines, printers, and vehicle locators.

Patrol cars are sometimes incapable of handling this technological congestion. In some cases the front passenger seat is removed and the officer is left with technological partners rather than a human partner. In other cases the shotgun or other weapon harnessed between the driver's seat and the front passenger seat is removed, an action that signifies a shift from symbols of force to symbols of knowledge as power. The wired nature of the police car is evident even when one looks at the vehicle's exterior, which, because a separate antenna is required for each electronic device, takes on the appearance of an 'antenna farm.' A somewhat exasperated police executive said, 'We are already stretching the limits of the power source for a standard car. General Motors is currently trying to figure out how to increase the power load available for police cars just to run all our equipment. We may end up towing a diesel generator around behind the car!'

In addition to what they manage to fit into their patrol cars, police officers have access to other electronically equipped vehicles for tracing purposes. We accompanied a patrol sergeant in his van to a town house complex where some people were believed to have an illegal handgun. The equipment check-list for this van included various tracing devices such as printed and computer-generated city maps, a map of the complex, binoculars, a telescope, a polaroid camera, and special tools for wire-tapping. Some of this equipment was used to monitor the suspects while a strategy for forcibly entering the premises was developed. Among other things, a powerful telescope was used to peer into the premises and a remote wire-tapping device was attached to telephone lines to monitor calls.

Larger mobile surveillance and command vehicles are also available to map territories and what happens within them. A police organization we studied received a gift of a large truck from a private company. The organization decided to equip the truck with sophisticated electronic surveillance equipment, including full telephone facilities, wire-tapping and video surveillance devices, and television monitors to keep abreast of news coverage of critical events the police were involved in.

Police managers are acutely aware that major events are subject to the gaze of the news media and that news formats often govern how those events are understood and responded to. In consequence, they develop vehicles to trace how the news media trace events. One police organization had a large mobile home dedicated to the 'accommodation' of the news media at major events. As we toured this vehicle our police host commented that it was 'a place for them to get out of the cold. We find it better to accommodate them, to keep them informed about what is going on rather than having them cross over lines and try to find out for themselves. You find the odd one is not cooperative but generally they are OK.'

There are still other territory-mapping technologies that the police use to trace territorial populations and the risks those people pose and confront. Precinct and detachment profiles are developed to provide an overview of the territories and populations policed. One police organization had a five-page form for establishing precinct profiles, which required a description of the precinct's boundaries, roadways (length in kilometres), population characteristics (such as age structure and ethnic composition), and special problems. It also asked for information on police strategies for monitoring and dealing with problems in the precinct.

Many police organizations in Canada are buying computerized mapping systems that rely on American military technology adopted by the Canadian Department of National Defence. These systems allow territories to be broken down into ever smaller units, the smallest unit being only one square metre in size! Equipped with this technology, the patrol officer can obtain detailed knowledge of officially recorded crimes and other problems that have occurred in narrowly defined zones within a patrol area – blocks, buildings, and even parts of buildings. One system we examined identified population characteristics such as race. The police official who demonstrated this technology to us said, 'You can see where this would be a big help to the community police officer. He can come back to the station and search his specific area for crimes that have been occurring. He could get a geographic feel for the location of prostitution or sexual assault cases for a specific period if he wanted them.' When asked whether he saw difficulties arising from the fact that the system recorded only crimes officially known to the police, he replied, 'That is what is real for us. We can only deal with what is real not with crimes that we only think are occurring.'

Crime itself is defined by the police with reference to territories and the problems people create in such territories. For example, as part of a change to a new voice-entry system for reporting occurrences, a police organization revamped its entire reporting format and classification system. New classifications were developed for crime 'hot spots', such as residences where 'domestics' occurred and places in the public transit system where youths congregated and created trouble.

As we have noted, video surveillance devices are also used to trace risks to territories. The video production unit in one police organization was officially described as being 'equipped with a broadcast-quality camera and full editing facilities.' Such units produce public relations and police training videos, monitor major events such as demonstrations, and conduct surveillance of places and people.

Some police organizations have also placed video cameras in their patrol vehicles. During our fieldwork in one jurisdiction we witnessed the introduction of video cameras into patrol vehicles. The patrol officers we studied believed that the video cameras would serve many purposes. One interviewee remarked that these devices would be useful for 'Anything that your imagination could come up with.'

There was a firm belief in this jurisdiction that the video cameras would provide more-certain evidence. They would show a violator that the police 'had him' and thereby facilitate confessions and guilty pleas. As one officer said, 'If they have something to query, they cannot query it if it's involved with a taping. It's right there. There are no ands, ifs, or buts about it. It's cut and dried.'

Video cameras were also seen as useful for surveillance of suspects. They were used with radar to detect speeding vehicles, for the video image itself was able to display the speed of the target vehicle. They were also used to conduct surveillance outside a notorious club. People entering and leaving the club were filmed, and their licence plates and the criminal records of the vehicles' owners were checked on the police car's computer system. Video cameras were also believed to be helpful in identifying people involved in major disturbances such as riots, picket line confrontations, political demonstrations, bar fights, and noisy parties.

Another function of video cameras was as investigative tools for accident reconstruction. One officer imagined that in the long term videotaping might be one way to reduce the paper burden associated with major accident investigations: 'There is no amount of paper that you could shove into a court that would give you that great a view of "Here's where she died, here is where he came across." And you could still-frame those things and enlarge them up.'

Police video cameras come with an audio intrusion capacity. An officer can wear a transmitter on his or her belt and have any conversations relayed to his or her partner in the police vehicle some distance away. This capacity was seen by officers as especially useful for handling the always troublesome domestic disputes:

One guy's got a mike and the other guys can sit out in the car and listen. If things are getting out of hand they can go in; if they are not getting out of hand they can just sort of back off. Another thing is that you've got the 'record' on in the car and if the old guy is on the couch here and he yells, 'As soon as they leave, you slut, I'm going to beat your head in' – too bad, he's history. So then you can take him out and there's your evidence. It's all on tape. Actually, you could use it in a million different ways.

Video cameras in patrol vehicles offer opportunities for the police to produce training material that depicts actual instances of good and bad policing. Film from the same source can also provide exceptional visuals for televised police reality programs.

Like other police technologies, video cameras are potentially able to trace police officer activity. However, we found that there were a number of ways in which this capacity was circumvented. For example, officers might position the camera in a way that would produce a recording fashioned to induce the viewer to empathize with the officers rather than the suspect. As one officer declared, 'I'm not a great lover of Rodney King

or anything, but it will be nice to have the camera show our side of things for a change.'

The patrol officers maintain technical control over every aspect of taping. They can turn the tape recorder and microphone on and off as they choose. The tape recorder is kept in the trunk and the only key is fastened to the car's key-chain. Although tampering can be detected, officers can simply remove a troublesome tape, reinsert it, and six hours later the entire tape has been erased.

During our fieldwork a supervisor expressed a concern that the video system he was about to have installed would display the speed of the police vehicle as well as the speed of the vehicle being pursued. He worried that police vehicles would regularly be shown to be travelling at excessive speeds, even during routine patrols. For example, a police vehicle on radar patrol might be moving at 125 km/hr in a 100 km/hr zone, and the video system would register its excessive speed at the same instant that the patrol officer was 'catching' another speeding vehicle. The officer would thus be shown to be enforcing a law that he himself was breaking. The installer agreed to remove the speed display for the police vehicle, so that only the speed of the oncoming vehicle would be registered.

Still photography is also used regularly for surveillance. Polaroid cameras are employed to record suspects *in situ*. One police organization had a 'Noisy Party Reference Report' that called for each apprehended culprit to be photographed at the scene standing alongside the arresting officer. Next to the photograph were to be recorded the details of the place of arrest and the person arrested. Below the photograph was a space for a detailed description of the charges (if any) and the circumstances of arrest.

The same police organization took polaroids of all known prostitutes in order to make a record of the locations in which they worked. Notorious hotels frequented by drug dealers and fences as well as prostitutes were also sites for taking polaroids of anyone who regularly used the premises.

In visually recording risk in these ways, the police use the same technologies as the news media, and therefore can selectively supply the news media with material that the latter see as helpful. By the same token, the media sometimes produce material that helps the police find what they are after. The 'simulations' involved here are at times complex. During one of our ride-alongs a message appeared on the officer's computer screen warning that the robbery squad was filming a training video at a certain location, and that the staged robbery would include gunshots and other realistic features. This prompted the officer to recall a case in which one of his colleagues had noticed that a disqualified driver was in a television commercial driving a car. The officer proceeded to charge this person with driving while disqualified, which in turn was deemed newsworthy and resulted in further television coverage!

The police are also connected to a variety of electronic infrastructures that give them instant knowledge of people and places. Computer terminals in police vehicles provide immediate access to the Canadian Police Information Centre (CPIC) system, which maintains data on criminal records, outstanding warrants, and so forth. During their 'down time,' when they are not filling out reports, patrol officers conduct random checks on vehicles and people with the aid of the computer. We found that up to 15 per cent of shift time was spent on random checks of vehicles on the road or in parking lots. A licence plate check supplies the identity of the vehicle owner, and a check of the owner reveals whether he or she has a criminal record or is wanted on an outstanding warrant, either of which prompt further investigation. The only limits on such checks are the officer's time and keyboarding speed. The experience of using this technology was described by one of our interviewees, who had only recently received a computer terminal for his car:

It's right there beside you, and it takes two seconds to type a name and a date of birth and you can query anybody. Plus if you query somebody and get a hit on them you can send a message anywhere in Canada to any other CPIC terminal. You can ask if this is the person, if they want him or whatever the story is . . . You can go along and query plates as you drive around. You are constantly checking anything suspicious. Vehicles. People. If you stop somebody you can query them right on site. I have a tendency to drive down the street and query anybody. Just query vehicles as they go along . . . I do more haphazard queries now, because I could be driving down the road and could see a car that I just basically want to find out about them. Maybe I want to know who it is, who the car is. Maybe it's not doing anything at all, just driving down the road.

The computer terminal also provides links to data systems developed by other institutions. In many police jurisdictions there is a link to the provincial motor vehicle agency database, which provides information on driver's-licence status, vehicle registration, and vehicle safety inspections. There are also often links to municipal utility billing systems, which offer a convenient way to trace a person's address, telephone number, and credit history. These connections are facilitated in many jurisdictions by direct links between the patrol vehicle and police computers, but where such a system is not in place the telephone provides the necessary link. One officer remarked, 'We all retain certain contacts with different agencies. My pet people, my favourite one is the [provincial] power security because everyone has power. If I come across a house and want to know who lives in a certain place I call them up and talk to a guy in security. He'll go to his computer and I'll give him an address and he'll tell me who lives there.'

The police also maintain specialized databases on particular types of risks to territories. For example, the Canadian Bomb Data Centre collects reports on all bomb-related incidents in the country, which are categorized by target, official response, and the characteristics of the people who make the bomb threats. Callers are profiled according to such subtleties as accent, voice, speech patterns, diction, and manner, the goal being, in the words of one interviewee, 'tracking a serial bomber . . . [and tying] these incidents all back together in a forensic pattern.'

Police electronic infrastructures are also designed to intrude on private spaces. Police organizations retain specialists in what is variously called 'technical intrusion,' 'technical services,' and 'security engineering.' These specialists enter private locations to install surveillance equipment and conduct investigations. In one police organization the mandate of the Technical Services Unit was officially described as the provision of 'specialized electronic surveillance expertise to all areas of the [organization].' The Unit was required to 'administer and control Part VI of the Criminal Code [Invasion of Privacy] as well as fulfil all reporting requirements as requested by the Attorney General and Solicitor General . . . [and] through research and projective budgets, maintain a modern and technically advanced electronic surveillance capability.' Another organization had over forty employees in its unit, most of whom were technicians trained in community colleges and university-educated engineers. A member of this unit said one of its major purposes was to 'bug telephone lines, put room audio in, video surveillance, tracking, all that.'

In another unit we studied, the employees specialized in what was termed 'offensive assistance,' in other words, to invade private locations for the purpose of investigative tracing. A subgroup was dedicated to 'skilled forced entry,' such as how to 'circumvent a lock to get into a place so that the appropriate listening device could be installed.' A member of this subgroup told us how it had a research and development program for improving the technical expertise needed to ensure that entry could be effected as unobtrusively as possible, even in the face of resistance:

A: [We engage] in various types of research such as looking at skilled forced entry. Considering the times we live in, there are occasions when it is necessary to have a quick means to gain access where you might be looking at a barricaded door, that type of thing, and so they're involved in that type of research . . . how to go through a barricaded door . . . outside of taking a front-end

loader and driving through the side of the wall, which isn't very practical, it's been difficult.

Q: Doesn't look good on television.

A: No. You're absolutely right. So one of the things that they look into is various methods without the use of explosives which obviously isn't the way to go. I mean, you risk the injury to not only your police officers but also your people inside. So they look at various engineering issues like that.

Members of this unit were required to file a report on each incident of technical intrusion. The form was designed very much like a burglary report, except that it was the police who were breaking and entering. The officer would be asked to indicate, among other things, how he or she had effected entry, whether there had been an alarm system, whether there had been any locks or safety devices, and the 'type of attack,' to be described by the following fixed-choice responses: 'punch, pry, peel, chop, grind, drill, torch, thermal lance, explosives, clandestine.'

Such units try to centralize their electronic intrusion capabilities and the expertise in forced entry needed for their work. Their existence is based on an assumption that the average officer lacks the expertise needed to effect subtle forced entries and install electronic tracing devices. Nevertheless, officers outside these units do on occasion employ their own surveillance devices. A patrol officer informed us that he had been conducting surveillance of suspects whom he believed to be hiding two separate stashes of stolen goods. Since he could only observe one stash area at a time, he borrowed a friend's electronic baby-monitor to cover the other area. This device alerted him to the suspects' presence at the second stash, and he moved in to arrest them.

The expertise developed by these units is also used for 'counter-technical intrusion,' that is, protection against the electronic intrusions of others. One of our subjects described this specialization as 'methods and means of defeating and bypassing certain [electronic] systems.' She said much of the expertise is attained by attending scenes where 'electronic security systems have been bypassed or defeated in some method to commit a criminal act.' In addition to improving the compromised security system, the knowledge derived from such investigations is used to defeat efforts by others to electronically intrude on people and spaces under police protection.

Police organizations are charged with the responsibility of protecting secret or confidential knowledge held by various clients, especially members of municipal, provincial, or federal governments of which the police are a part. Therefore, technical intrusion and security engineering knowledge is used in patrolling access to spaces where confidential discussions occur. The task of experts in this area is revealed by an interviewee who talked about maintaining 'line security': 'With line security . . . we get into data encryption. Encrypt the data so that I can't break into that line, decode that signal this computer is receiving here to say everything is OK and then blackbox it . . . [this is similar to the way in which] ADT [a private security company] will sell you a double-A line for a bank which means it is encrypted and it does certain handshakings through the day and checks to make sure everything is OK.'

Of course not everything is so high tech. At the low tech end, police knowledge security units take an interest in rating shredders, document containers, and other devices that help to keep knowledge confidential. A security engineering specialist in one police organization described her testing of shredders for government 'in terms of the dimensions of the cut and various other physical requirements.' She also described a rating system for document containers: documents with lower risk potential if lost or stolen were placed in less secure boxes:

Probably more than occasionally there's been a tendency to err on the side of extreme caution when dealing with documents. For example, you might classify something at very high level when really all it talks about is something that wouldn't be harmful in the public interest or the national interest or wouldn't compromise anything. And so all that has an effect on your security containers because if you classify something very high then, of course, you need a container that will withstand the attacks and that kind of stuff. So now there's quite a reviewing of security requirements . . . if you have a container that only requires a minute of protection, it's a lot cheaper to build than one that requires twenty minutes.

[. . .]

29 Gang Babes Love to Kill

Ruaridh Nicoll

The scar on the woman's face was a neat, livid line running from her ear to her mouth and she wore it with pride. It was cut to show that she is part of a new women's gang emerging on the streets of Brooklyn.

There had been rumours about this new female club, in which members – instead of giving each other the customary beating that is usually enough to grant entry to an inner-city gang – cut their inductees' faces with a razor. The ultimate in self-loathing.

'It's pretty heavy when they start doing that to themselves', said Tony, who runs an organization of former gang members dedicated to taking kids off the streets. He has seen many things but this has taken him by surprise. His network of contacts threads New York's underworld, giving him running reports on the health of the city's ganglands.

Five years ago, girls in their early teens began joining America's inner-city gangs, attracted by the comfort of a group and the gangster image. For many, with their family lives destroyed by drugs, poverty and jail, gangs offered a sense of security, companionship and protection. They formed auxiliaries to the men's gangs and found that their status in the community suddenly shot up. 'They treated me like a little sister', said one inductee of her new gang pals. 'And if I ever had any problems, they'd help me out. I'd never had that before.'

America was shocked. The white population is used to the concept of the traditional gang made up of young, black males who expect to die violently before they are 20. But the idea of gangs of young girls, prepared to shoot, rob and sell drugs, does not fit easily into the American idea of femininity.

Yet violence is central to the girl gang phenomenon. The new Brooklyn scar-face gang shows that the violence is getting worse, and that much of it is aimed at themselves. When the gangs started forming, the girls mimicked the men by using watered-down versions of their initiation ceremonies. New members would be taken to some deserted spot where they would receive a beating for between ten seconds and three minutes. The damage would later be fixed with compacts and hairspray. If at some date in the future the inductee let the gang down, another beating would occur, but on this occasion there would be no set time limit.

Initially, their crimes were gang muggings, stealing jewellery and clothes that they could not afford themselves. 'I'd just see something I wanted so bad I'd just take it, I'd pull a knife, I'd just want things', said one 15-year-old. But as the new members have grown older, many have progressed to the killings carried out by the male gangs. A group of girls killed a 15-year-old on the New York subway for her earrings. 'The women can be as violent as the men, sometimes even more so', said a Brooklyn cop. 'When they are arrested for violent crime, they show no remorse.'

The number of girls arrested in New York for a serious felony has increased 10 per cent annually since the mid-1980s. In 1990 women made up 10 per cent of total gang membership; [in 1996] the figure is estimated to have risen beyond 15 per cent. Women are also heavily involved in drug dealing and violent crimes.

Across the Hudson River in New Jersey, where violent crime committed by women has seen a similarly dramatic rise in the past decade, a commission revealed forty-seven individual female gangs in the state. The gangs' names tell their own stories, displaying by turns self-loathing and humour – names like the 6th Street Whores, the Crochet Girls and the Wise Intelligent Sisters.

At the International Youth Organization in Newark three young mothers, one who had her first child when she was 15, talked about trying to get out of the poverty cycle. 'There is nothing out there to do but get into trouble', said Jenean Shiggs. 'When you try to do it the right way you see it's so much harder, you know there is an easier way.'

The United States Congress is currently cutting back welfare payments, increasing the squeeze on these teenage girls who are caught between the lack of job prospects, broken homes, and early pregnancy. 'It's going to get worse', said Dr Janice Joseph of Stockton State College in New Jersey. 'Ten years ago you never heard of girls in gangs, but now there are girls who if they want something from you they will kill for it.'

While many of the girls drop out of the gangs when they reach their twenties, often after they are arrested or have watched friends die, others go on to join more sophisticated gangs based in the big cities and involved in drug deals.

Nearly all the leading or 'corporate' gangs, as they are known, now have women members. For example, the Latin Kings, a huge organization born in a Chicago jail in the 1940s, has a women's corps, the Latin Queens.

Male gang members have begun to fear the women, who are starting to take key roles in many of the activities. One man, a contact of Tony's, who recently quit as a gang member, gave his own chilling conclusion on dealing with women in gangs: 'She'll set you up – men are like that with women – she'll draw you in, and then she'll kill you.'

30 Surviving in a Women's Prison

Josie O'Dwyer and Pat Carlen

Britain has six closed prisons for women: Holloway in London, Styal in Cheshire, Cookham Wood in Kent, a wing of Durham Prison, Cornton Vale just outside Stirling in Scotland and Armagh Prison in Northern Ireland.

For England and Wales there is one closed Youth Custody Centre, Bullwood Hall in Essex, and an open Youth Custody Centre, at East Sutton Park. There are three open prisons for women: Drake Hall in Staffordshire, Askham Grange in Yorkshire and East Sutton Park in Kent. The three remand centres which take women and girls are: Low Newton in Durham, Pucklechurch in Bristol and Risley in Cheshire. Scotland has no open prison for women as all penal facilities – remand wing, young prisoners' wing, Youth Custody Centre and prison – are concentrated on one site at Her Majesty's Institution, Cornton Vale. In Northern Ireland a separate part of Armagh Prison is used as the female young offenders' centre. Additionally, women on remand are often held for one night (or more) in police cells and, at various times, certain convicted women prisoners have been temporarily housed in one of the male institutions. Jose O'Dwyer has served sentences (or been remanded) at Pucklechurch, Bullwood Hall, Cookham Wood, Styal, Holloway and Mountjoy Gaol in Ireland. Although she is only 28 she has, since the age of 14, spent eight of those twenty-eight years in a variety of penal institutions, including approved school, Borstal, remand centre, and four closed prisons. And Josie has survived. The purpose of this [discussion], therefore, is to describe exactly how Josie did survive those years and, in telling the story of one

prisoner's survival, to describe also the violence, the injustices, the pain, the degradations and the other, different modes of survival (or not) which characterize British women's imprisonment.

On any day of the year around 1,500 women are held captive in British prisons. Many of them will be remand prisoners, only 27 per cent of whom will eventually receive a custodial sentence; over a quarter of the convicted women will be in prison for failing to pay a fine, and over half of them will be there for some minor crime of stealing. Of the remainder, less than 10 per cent of the convicted women will have been found guilty of violent crime and a sizeable number of prisoners in all categories will be those whose biographies embody accounts of all kinds of social, emotional and mental problems often either unrelated or related only tangentially to their criminal activities. A sizeable number of this latter group, too, will have either been brought up in institutions from an early age or will have been taken into either 'care' or the old Approved School system in their early teens. Either way these 'state-raised' children will have learned early on in their careers that the main name of the game in institutions is SURVIVAL.

Josie O'Dwyer is just one of the many women whose penal careers began at the age of 14 in circumstances which make a mockery of the terms 'care', 'training' and 'in the child's best interest'. Josie's account of her first taste of the penal system is one which is studded with references to feelings of fear and memories of violence. As a consequence of being apprehended by the police for 'breaking and entering' the full force of the penal and judicial machinery engulfed the adolescent Josie in a quick processing through police cell, prison remand wing and Approved School.

They took me in a police-car, up the motorway to Bristol. I was only little: aged 14, four-feet-ten inches in height and just six stone. It seemed a long journey from Exeter to Bristol and I was terrified, absolutely terrified. But I was stroppy with it. I had already spent the night in the police-cell at Exeter and I had been in a cell with a junkie who was really sick. I got myself in the top bunk and sat in the corner clutching a pillow; I actually chewed off the corner of that pillow watching this woman thrashing about. Then in the morning they took me to Pucklechurch. They had told me that it was a remand centre but it looked like a prison. I had thought that it was going to be a kids' home, maybe with bars on the windows so that I couldn't get out, but it wasn't, it was a real prison. They took me to the women's section and the police handed me over to the prison officers. All that I wanted to do was to curl up in a corner with something over my head and stay there, but I had to get undressed. I took my clothes off and put on this dressing-gown and I felt terrified. I've never felt such fear and yet the prison officers were being really nice to me compared with how I've seen them since with other people! They eventually coaxed me out with cigarettes and took me down this long corridor with cell doors on either side. They took me to a cell, locked me up for the night and came along in the morning and said that I was to go and see the Chief. I wouldn't get dressed though. I was still terrified, still had the dressing-gown over my head. Then I looked out of the window and I saw the prisoners exercising in the yard. I couldn't believe my eyes; I really thought that some of them were men! The prison officers kept coming in and encouraging me to go out and exercise – 'Come on, love' etc., but I would not go.

Josie was terrified and, as is often the case when people are afraid, she soon realized that one effective way to counter one's own fear is to inspire fear in others. Women's prisons, no less than men's, are places of violence; places where explicit violence is the necessary currency for efficient and healthy survival. In prison, moreover, the newcomer does not have to be predisposed to violence in order to engage in violent modes of behaviour – lessons in violence come at her from all sides.

In the cell next to me there was a Pakistani woman; I think that she was waiting to be deported. They had taken her baby away from her because she had kept trying to kill herself and the baby. She actually wrecked her cell, there was a lot of blood and I was terrified. Then I wrecked my own cell. I put all the windows out and smashed all the furniture. The officers came in and told me to take all my clothes off. Then they put me in this special dress and did something up at the neck so that it could not be taken off. It took me four hours to chew through it. I wouldn't come out of that cell for ten days and then I came out to go to church. After that the prison officers managed to coax me out for the last hour of Association and I was amazed at everyone wanting to mother me because I was so tiny. They gave me chocolates and they wanted me to sit on their lap. I didn't mind at all, I liked it. Then came the bombshell. I was told that I was being moved to the Approved School.

Within the penal system those who want to survive counter their own fear by inspiring fear in others and meet violence with violence or, better still, the threat of violence. Boredom and loss of freedom, however, call for different survival tactics and, in the case of children and young people held in less secure conditions, the most obvious way to regain their freedom and self-respect is to go straight back out, either over the wall or through the gate. Josie was eventually to find that, in fact, the senior Approved School provided a good academic education but when she first arrived there was no way that she intended to stay. She became a 'runner'.

Seventeen times I ran away from that school and seventeen times they took me back. Each time they took me back I spent twenty-four hours in the detention room. I eventually dislocated my knee jumping out of a window but I still tried to run away, on crutches! Next morning they gave me a skirt to put on, but I kept my jeans on and went for the nearest window, with tennis-rackets and anything else that came to hand. The school was in Bath and I used to run back to Truro. I don't know what I was running to really; it was just an instinct. If I could get out, I got out.

But Josie, recognizing that she, like many other runners, had in reality no one and nowhere to run to, eventually settled down to O-levels, horse-riding, forced religion (it was a convent school) and more lessons in the seamier side of life.

There were girls who had been through more than me, they had been prostitutes. It was mostly sex they talked about and sex was seen as a crime anyway, because we were in a convent school. Some of those girls went on to remand centres and then to Borstal.

When Josie left the school at 16 the process of her social isolation and stigmatization as a delinquent had already begun.

I was 16 when I left. I had never had a letter or a visit all the time that I had been there. I went back to Cornwall and tried for various jobs but they soon found out about my past, what I'd done and where I'd been, and they weren't prepared to forgive and forget. I used to sit for hours and stare into space. None of my friends understood; they all thought that I was mad. After about five months I took myself back to Bath and it was there that I overdosed – I just didn't know what to do next. Then I actually went breaking and entering with the full intention of getting myself nicked.

  I went to Borstal after I had been convicted on a burglary charge. They sent me off to Bullwood Hall along with two others and, again, I was terrified. This time there was real reason to be afraid. An air of viciousness pervaded the whole place. The tougher you were the better. If you weren't tough people insulted you and took your cigarettes off you. You had a dog's life. It's the way the prison officers ran it which made it like that. Inmates couldn't really retaliate, but having a go at an officer gave them some kind of credit. They tore up each other's photos and ripped up each other's clothes. I'd been on the Assessment Unit for about five days and it was my first night on the wing when I happened to be going for a bath that I saw one inmate being kicked by about five others. It was not done quickly to get it over with; they were actually thoroughly enjoying it. The message was 'Don't mix-it with us.' Everyone was frightened of everybody else. Anything could start off a fight. Everything or nothing. The officers could have stopped it if they'd wanted to. They could have run the place differently. They stood down on the ground floor and everything that went on that was bad went on either on the landings or in somebody's cell – and in the recess anyhow. Unless you were one of the toughest you were absolutely terrorized. Borstal was amazing. Whereas the grown women in Pucklechurch could take things

in their stride, in Borstal the slightest little thing could make someone hit the ceiling and the officers would just go in. There would be no 'Come on, dear, calm down.' None of that. They just went in and grabbed you and took you off down to the punishment block. You got the same treatment whatever you did so you knew that you might as well hit the roof, make a big show out of it and get some credit out of it.

At that stage Josie did not have time to think about the whys and wherefores of the viciousness which permeated Bullwood. She did not realize then that the viciousness was a product of the system itself rather than of the system's victims. She only had time to suss out how best to ensure her own survival.

You weren't allowed to do your sentence quietly. You survived by being the most vicious. But you couldn't just be vicious – you also had to have no fear, to be able to take the punishment and the lock-up. At first I was probably the most frightened. I was terrified. The whole place terrified me. The air was electric, always someone doing something, alarm bells going, a fight going on, screaming, shouting, banging. They used to sing 'A...G...G...R...O...' It was terrible – just bang, bang, bang, bang, bang. You *had* to scream, you had to let go. You just couldn't contain it within yourself. Every single day there was some sort of trouble and people were screaming out of the windows all the time in Bullwood. If one person started banging on the door the whole wing would take it up. I discovered that if I got all wound up, ready to blow, the whole wing would be all simmering, waiting for the action and it gave me credit. But it didn't just come from me, it was there all the time, just waiting for someone to set light to it. You had to have fights with the screws as they dragged you off to punishment because you were considered a sissy if you just walked there. Everyone struggled. They bent your arms so you tried to bite and you spat and kicked. They weren't exactly gentle either. Some of the officers were a little more vicious than the others so you worked out which ones to go for. You worked out who was soft, who was hard and who would hurt you most. So when you saw them coming at you – about eight or nine prison officers and a couple of men in the background – you tried to let the gentler ones get hold of you. To me it was just a game and you had to play the game well or you got hurt. Most of my stuff looked good, but it was all bravado, all for show, to give me more credit, so that I could survive. I never really hurt anyone.

[...] By the time Josie had finished her Borstal sentence she had completed her apprenticeship in violence and she was ready for bigger things. She knew that her Borstal days were over and, like many of the other Borstal girls, she knew also that the next stop would be prison.

Most of the girls had an idea that they were going on to prison anyway so you thought that whatever crimes you did when you were out, next time you went in you'd have more 'cred'. It was happening to me like that, though I didn't realize it at the time. But now when I go back and think, I think, 'Huh! What a wally!' Because when I came out of Borstal my ambition in life was to be the top dog, the most hardened criminal, the worst, the most vicious. There was no other reason to be alive as far as I was concerned. Anything outside wasn't going to give me a chance anyway, so if I was going to make it anywhere, it had to be in there.

Part 9

Race, Ethnicity and Migration

The classical sociologists – Marx, Durkheim and Weber – all believed that nationalism would decline with the further development of modern society. The advance of economic interdependence would make nationalists' beliefs seem archaic. Such has not proved to be the case. Nationalism remains a potent force in the contemporary world. In his contribution, Reading 31, Anthony Smith argues that both nations and nationalism can have a positive part to play in a globalizing world. Nationalism and national identity can of course often be divisive; but they can also provide a basis for social cohesion.

Ethnic divisions – divisions between groups based upon differences of culture and/or physical appearance – are frequently linked to profound social tensions and conflicts. There are few multicultural societies that have no history of antagonism between the members of their constituent ethnic communities. Lines of opposition and prejudice frequently centre upon 'racial' differences between whites and non-whites. In Reading 32, Frances Aboud discusses the development of ethnic awareness in childhood, concentrating upon 'racial' difference. She finds that ethnic awareness develops at an early age, although the differentiations that are drawn are complex and shift quite rapidly.

The prejudices which whites have entertained towards blacks have to be understood in a broad historical context. In substantial part their origins are bound up with Western expansionism and colonialism. Paul Gilroy, in Reading 33, emphasizes that the cultural development of black groups in Britain similarly has to be seen against an international backdrop. Black cultural styles in the United Kingdom form part of a 'diaspora' – a network of cultural connections and oppositions spanning many countries. Blacks in Britain, Gilroy argues, are linked by many ties to blacks elsewhere: something which is also the case, however, for whites within British culture.

Most Western European countries are becoming more multicultural, as immigration from North Africa, Asia and Eastern Europe becomes more widespread. As Reading 34 shows, such immigration often provokes great resistance within the countries to which immigrants come. Yet Western Europe in fact actively needs immigrants, to compensate for its low birth rates. Immigration usually has positive consequences for society. Immigrants mostly work hard and have a strong motivation to succeed. Moreover, the cultural beliefs and habits they bring with them can help introduce a healthy diversity into the wider society.

31 Nations and Nationalism in a Global Era

Anthony D. Smith

The idea that nations and nationalisms are likely to be here for some time to come, and that this has to do with nationalism's capacity for ensuring dignity and immortality, may seem both pessimistic and perverse when we consider the excesses and outrages for which nationalists are held responsible throughout the world. Commentators are fond of attributing to nationalism many of the conflicts which infest our planet, and they tend to assume that a world without nations will be free of the attendant ills of racism, fascism and xenophobia. A world without nations, they claim, will be a more stable and peaceful, as well as a more just and free world – a dream that is in fact common to liberals and socialists for whom the nation was at best a necessary stage in the evolution of humanity and at worst a violent threat and distraction.

I want to [examine briefly] the arguments against nationalism and demonstrat[e] why the nation and nationalism remain the only realistic basis for a free society of states in the modern world.

Nationalism: pro et contra

The arguments against nationalism are threefold: intellectual, ethical and geo-political.

(1) Intellectually, nationalism is held to be logically incoherent and its basic postulates untenable. These postulates are the principle of collective cultural identity, the principle of collective will and the doctrine of national boundaries.

As far as collective cultural identity is concerned, it is claimed that there are conflicting criteria for determining the national 'self'. These include language, religion, descent, customs and territory. As Max Weber showed long ago, no one of these criteria can be applied to all the collective cultural identities which claim to be or are recognized as 'nations'. In sub-Saharan Africa, for example, there is a series of overlapping 'selves', based on different criteria. Even within a single community, nationalists have espoused different criteria of the nation.[1]

The same difficulties surround the principle of the national 'will'. Apart from a daily plebiscite, there is no means of ascertaining its nature, or deciding whether it was in fact a true and free expression of the 'will of the people' or of the individuals who compose the nation. There is also the problem of deciding who shall count as 'the people'. It has been all too easy for demagogues to feel that they alone can interpret the popular will and decide who the people are.

Similar problems have attended the doctrine of national boundaries. For nationalists, these are usually self-evident; they coincide, as Danton claimed for France and Mazzini for Italy, with 'natural frontiers'. But it is easy to show that such frontiers are never natural, even when they have been longstanding or distinctive; South Tyrol, for example, remains a disputed area between Italy and Austria. Inhabitants of frontier areas have a habit of refusing to acknowledge the 'naturalness' of particular borders.

All this has led some scholars to conclude that there can be no consistent doctrine of nationalism, and that there are as many nationalisms as there are nations and nationalists. This seems to be an altogether erroneous reading of the ideo-logy of nationalism. The very fact that one can seek to analyse a set of sentiments, movements and ideas through a collective term, nationalism, suggests a certain commonality between the different expressions of these sentiments, movements and ideas. One need not deny the great variety of these expressions to concede an underlying pattern [that] is the 'core doctrine' of nationalism.

To grasp the misunderstanding in much of the critique of nationalism, it is necessary to remind ourselves of the main tenets of that doctrine and the basic ideals of nationalist movements. They are:

- The world is divided into nations, each with its own character and destiny.
- The nation is the source of all political power, and loyalty to the nation overrides all other loyalties.
- To be free, human beings must identify with a particular nation.
- To be authentic, each nation must be autonomous.
- For peace and justice to prevail in the world, nations must be free and secure.

The basic ideals that flow from these propositions are three: national identity, national unity and national autonomy. These are the goals, variously interpreted, of nationalists in every period and continent, just as the 'core doctrine' represents the *sine qua non* of nationalist beliefs, even when nationalists have added new motifs to apply the doctrine to the situation of their community. Together, the basic propositions and ideals suggest a working definition of nationalism as an 'ideological movement for the attainment and maintenance of autonomy, unity and identity on behalf of a population deemed by some of its members to constitute a "nation"'.[2]

From these propositions and ideals, there has emerged a set of symbols, myths and concepts which mark off the world of nationalism from other worlds of symbolism, mythology and discourse, and which have energized and comforted populations all over the world. Ceremonies, symbols and myths are crucial to nationalism; through them nations are formed and celebrated.

Now these propositions, ideals and definitions of nationalism and the nation make no mention of specific criteria of national identity. Any cultural element can function as a diacritical mark or badge of the nation – though it may make a considerable difference which is chosen in certain circumstances. One should not therefore castigate nationalisms for inconsistency on this score, since there is nothing in the core doctrine or ideals which lays down which cultural elements must serve as criteria of the national self. Similarly with the concepts of 'national will' and 'natural frontiers'. Nationalism does not have a theory of how the national will or the national boundaries may be ascertained; it requires other ideologies for that purpose, and so nationalism has been combined with all kinds of other movements and ideologies from liberalism to communism and racism. Nationalism's core doctrine provides no more than a basic framework for social and political order in the world, and it must be filled out by other idea-systems and by the particular circumstances of each community's situation at the time. To charge nationalism, therefore, with logical incoherence is to miss the point – and the power – of the ideological movement: nationalism combines a high degree of flexible abstraction with a unique ability to tap fundamental popular needs and aspirations, but it does not pretend to offer a comprehensive and consistent account of history and society.

(2) The ethical arguments against nationalism are, first, that it is necessarily extremist in nature; that its concern for cultural homogeneity leads to exclusiveness and social closure against minorities; and that it denies the independence, diversity and human rights of individuals.

There is considerable truth in some of these arguments, especially when applied to specific instances of nationalism. But, as general arguments, they need careful qualification. The idea that all nationalists are fanatical doctrinaires of the will and that every nationalism is extremist in nature is belied by the many movements, regimes and leaders that have been on the whole democratic, liberal and moderate; the cases of Masaryk and Czechoslovakia, Prat de la Riba and Catalonia, McDiarmid and Scotland and Snellman and Finland come to mind. Outside Europe, too, we can find cases of relatively moderate nationalism, if we allow for the very different social and political circumstances: in the Ivory Coast, Zambia, Ghana after Nkrumah, Tunisia, Egypt since Nasser, Turkey since Ataturk, early Indian nationalism, Japan since 1945, Mexico since Cárdenas. Though it cannot be claimed that many regimes in the states of Latin America, Africa and Asia are democratic or liberal, their failings cannot be attributed to nationalist extremism; many other factors account for the often non-democratic nature of these regimes. The important point is that nationalism comes in many forms and degrees; they cannot be lumped together under a single rubric of 'extremism'.

Moreover, not all nationalisms have equally striven for cultural homogeneity. What all nationalists demand is a single *public* culture. There are cases where they are happy to concede some degree of private culture for ethnic and religious minorities, provided these do not impinge too much on the national identity created by the public culture of the national state. These are not, as is often thought, only cases of civic nationalisms. As mentioned earlier, civic nations can be just as severe to minorities as ethnic nations. Rather, this tolerance tends to be found in the plural nations created by immigrant societies, though it is also possible to find some toleration of minority rights in dominant *ethnie* nations like Finland, Malaysia or the former Czechoslovakia.

Nor do all nationalisms deny basic human rights and individual diversity. This is more a function of the type of secondary nationalist ideology adopted. The 'core doctrine', while demanding primary loyalty to the nation, says nothing about diversity or human rights. It is in the 'organic' version of nationalism promulgated by the German Romantics that there is a tendency to see human beings simply as specimens of their national group; but it is a mistake to regard the German Romantic doctrine as normative for nationalism, if only because French Revolutionary doctrines have been even more influential, for example in Africa, where human rights are linked to national liberation. Nevertheless, while nationalism is patently not a democratic or liberal movement, the denial of nationalism's central tenets is likely to impede progress to human rights and democracy, as Engels observed about Polish nationalism.

(3) These arguments are also relevant to the main geo-political charge against nationalism: that it is destabilizing and divisive. Again, this is to overstate the case. Of course, one can point to particular cases of destabilization and division, of nationalists deliberately stirring up resentments among populations in ethnically mixed areas like Bosnia or the Caucasus. But, as the examples of the Soviet Union, Yugoslavia, Kurdistan and Ethiopia demonstrate, it is not nationalism *per se* that is responsible for the breakdown of states; nationalisms tend to emerge on the ruins of states that are, for other reasons as well as ethnic ones, no longer viable. In other cases, ethnic nationalisms may battle long and in vain, as has occurred with the Moro in the Philippines or the Nagas in India. Where states are for one reason or another no longer viable, nationalism may offer an alternative to the often unstable (because coercive) status quo, one that is more viable because it is better attuned to popular aspirations in particular regions. The divisiveness and destabilization of so many nationalisms is simply the other side of the coin of their popular, unifying and solidaristic dimensions. Nationalism cannot be held responsible for the rivalry of states, which long pre-dated the emergence of the doctrine. What nationalism has done is to ground the competition of sovereign states on a mass cultural base, thereby providing some social cohesion in periods of rapid social change; it did not invent that rivalry.

Necessity, functionality, embeddedness

From what I have said, it can be seen that while the charges laid against nationalism apply with force to specific doctrines and particular movements, they often either miss the point or overstate the case in regard to 'nationalism-in-general'.

In conclusion I want to set out briefly three arguments which together suggest both a qualified defence of the plural order of nations and the unlikelihood of any early supersession of nations and nationalism. These arguments are: that nationalism is politically necessary; that national identity is socially functional; and that the nation is historically embedded.

(1) [. . .] Given the plurality of recognized states since at least 1648, the introduction of nationalist principles since 1789 can be seen as underpinning, enlarging and humanizing the political order of the interstate system by basing it on cultural and historical criteria, that is, on the prior existence of historic culture-communities. These are popular communities whose culture and traditions express their aspirations as a community, and for whom nationalism seeks a place in the distribution of world power. That is why nationalisms so frequently strive against the existing states and interstate order, so as to make room for submerged and unrecognized culture-communities in a world of national states. Moreover, nationalists contend that each state in the plural world order should possess a distinctive political personality based on a separate and unique culture-community or nation. This became evident to others besides nationalists once the powers of the monarch had been eroded and transferred to the sovereign people. The question 'who are the people?' became unavoidable, and nationalism provided a general answer in the shape of a historic community of public culture, which the nationalists were helping to adapt and complete. Soon no other legitimation for an order of plural sovereigns, and no other source of political power, became acceptable.

It follows that nations and nationalisms remain political necessities because (and for as long as) they alone can ground the interstate order in the principles of popular sovereignty and the will of the people, however defined. Only nationalism can secure the assent of the governed to the territorial units to which they have been assigned, through a sense of collective identification with historic culture-communities in their 'homelands'. As long as any global order is based on a balance of competing states, so long will the principle of nationality provide the only widely acceptable legitimation and focus of popular mobilization. Since there is little sign that the competition of states, even in Europe, is being superseded by some completely new political order, the likelihood of the nation which forms the *raison d'être* of the state and its community of will being transcended remains remote. Even if a number of states were to pool their sovereignties and even if their national communities were to agree to federate within a single political framework, the nation and its nationalism would long remain the only valid focus and constituency for ascertaining the popular will. Elsewhere there is little sign of such federative activity, and a pluralist world of nations and national states remains the only safeguard against imperial tyranny.

(2) National identity, as opposed to other kinds of collective identity, is pre-eminently functional for modernity, being suited to the needs of a wide variety of social groups and individuals in the modern epoch. This is not primarily because nationalism is functional for an industrial society which requires armies of mobile, literate citizens for its effective operation. Rather, the myths, memories, symbols and ceremonies of nationalism provide the sole basis for such social cohesion and political action as modern societies, with their often heterogenous social and ethnic composition and varied aims, can muster. Nationalism is an ideology of historic territory, and it concentrates the energies of individuals and groups within a clearly demarcated 'homeland', in which all citizens are deemed to be brothers and sisters and to which they therefore 'belong'. By rehearsing the rites of fraternity in a political community in its homeland at periodic intervals, the nation communes with and worships itself, making its citizens feel the power and warmth of their collective identification and inducing in them a heightened self-awareness and social reflexivity.

As a result, individual members come to perceive the social functions of their dependence on the nation, including such collective needs as the preservation of their community's irreplaceable culture values, the rediscovery of its authentic roots, the celebration and emulation of its exemplars of heroic virtue, the re-creation of feelings of fraternity and kinship and the mobilization of citizens for common goals. From these needs, so often the themes of communal exhortations, flow the rituals and ceremonies, customs and festivals, traditions and symbols which commemorate and celebrate the nation in every generation. Their common purpose is to arouse in the citizens a national consciousness and generate a national will, and they achieve these ends through mass, public displays and vivid imagery. Though some brave souls may oppose particular national regimes, most of the citizens have shown themselves all too willing to participate in and celebrate the rites of the nation and accept the received narratives and myths of national identity. Defections have always been minimal and most members to this day continue to identify with the ideal version of the nation portrayed by nationalism.

Moreover, the sense of national identity is often powerful enough to engender a spirit of self-sacrifice on behalf of the nation in many, if not most, of its citizens. This is especially true of crises and wartime. Here one can witness the degree to which most citizens are prepared to endure hardships and make personal sacrifices 'in defence of the nation', to the point of laying down their lives willingly, often in vast numbers, as occurred in several of the combatant countries during both World Wars. Such self-sacrifice on this scale is unimaginable for any other kind of collective cultural identity and community in our epoch, except perhaps for a few religious communities, and it is the singular power of the nation in eliciting mass sacrifice that has made it so often the object of unscrupulous demagogues. By the same token, the nation has become the main vehicle of warfare and national identity, the chief justification for participation in lethal combat. England and Ireland; France and Germany;

Greece and Turkey; Israel and the Arabs; India and Pakistan; the Khmers and Vietnamese: the roll-call of ethno-national antagonisms in the modern epoch recalls how wars have strengthened national consciousness and how the mobilization of nations has changed the nature of warfare for ever.

All this in itself is insufficient to predict the persistence of national identity. As has been often demonstrated, the functionality of an institution or ideology is no proof of its continued presence or influence. At the same time, the many functions that national identity continues to perform need to be taken into account in assessing the vitality of contemporary nationalism.

(3) [. . .] The nation is historically embedded. It is the modern heir and transformation of the much older and commoner *ethnie* and as such gathers to itself all the symbols and myths of pre-modern ethnicity. Combining these pre-modern ties and sentiments with the explosive modern charge of popular sovereignty and mass, public culture, nationalism has created a unique modern drama of national liberation and popular mobilization in an ancestral homeland. The older myths of ethnic election – the belief in the conditional chosenness of certain communities whose divine privileges depended on the continued performance of their duties – have not withered away. Nationalism has given them a new lease of life, inspiring a yearning for collective regeneration in the homeland and for salvation of the national elect provided they repossess their authentic identity and ancestral soil, as has been so vividly demonstrated by Zionism and Armenian nationalism.

There are other examples of the historical embeddedness of the nation in much older ethnic frameworks. While the *idea* of the nation can be disembedded, generalized and transferred to milieux where there is no obvious historic *ethnie* or ancestral homeland, as in such heterogenous immigrant island communities as Trinidad and Mauritius, most actual nations have derived their power from their popular and political links with much older ethnic communities and identities. This has allowed nationalists to return, rediscover and reappropriate traditional customs, symbols and ceremonies, such as the Welsh *Eisteddfodau*, which despite several adaptations and changes, broadly followed the main lines of the medieval Welsh bardic contests which had gradually died out in the sixteenth century but had survived in the popular consciousness in the local 'almanack *eisteddfodau*'. Alternatively, religious elites may preserve older forms of celebration, such as the Jewish agricultural festivals of ancient Palestine which were kept from year to year by increasingly urbanized diaspora communities, to be revived as national festivals by the early Zionists on their return to Israel.

Heroes and sagas have also been reappropriated by modern nationalism for its own ends. Muhammad and Moses have ceased to be prophets and servants of God, and have become national leaders *par excellence*; mythological bards like Oisin (Ossian) and Vainamoinen have become exemplars of ancient Irish and Finnish national wisdom; the heroes of the *Ramayana* have become prototypes of Indian national resistance. What is of interest here is not the uses to which these ancient exemplars have been put by often unscrupulous leaders, but the fervour of the believing masses. The power of their identification with an ethnic past with its heroic myths and legends, symbols and values, is vital to the success of the nationalist enterprise. It is also decisive for the content of the ensuing nationalism. The ethnic past sets limits to the manipulations of the elites and provides the ideals for the restored nation and its destiny. In this way, the nation remains embedded in a past that shapes its future as much as any present global trends. The 'blocking presentism' of so much latterday analysis should not blind one to the continuing if sometimes hidden power of the nation's lineage, and to the persistence of particular ethnic ties and sentiments in which the nation is so often embedded.

But it is not simply the embeddedness of the nation as it is known today that is at issue; its destiny too owes its meaning and direction to successive interpretations of the ethnic past. It is this linking of ethno-history with national destiny that works most powerfully to uphold and preserve a world of nations. The modern nation has become what ethno-religious communities were in the past: communities of history and destiny that confer on mortals a sense of immortality through the judgement of posterity, rather than through divine judgement in an afterlife.

This ability to satisfy a more general craving for immortality marks out nationalism from other ideologies and belief-systems of the modern world. In some areas, it has enabled nationalism to ally itself with world religions like Islam or Buddhism; in others to substitute itself for crumbling traditions. In both cases, however, what sets out as essentially secular ideology and symbolism of culture and politics reveals a transcendental dimension, one that raises the individual above the earthly round and out of immediate time. In this sense, nationalism can be regarded as a 'religion surrogate' and the nation as a continuation, but also a transformation, of pre-modern ethno-religious community.[3]

[...]

NOTES

1   This article is based on a paper given to the conference on Nations and Citizens at the Centre for Philosophical Studies at King's College, London, in 1993; the latter part appears in Anthony D. Smith, 'Ties that Bind', *LSE Magazine*, 5/1 (1993), pp. 8–11. See M. Weber, *Essays in Sociology*, ed. Hans Gerth and C. Wright Mills (London: Routledge and Kegan Paul, 1947).

2   Louis Snyder, *The Meaning of Nationalism* (New Brunswick, NJ: Rutgers University Press, 1954). Walker Connor, 'A Nation is a Nation, is a State, is an Ethnic Group, is . . .', *Ethnic and Racial Studies*, 1/4 (1978), pp. 378–400.

3   Lionel Cliffe, 'Forging a Nation: The Eritrean Experience', *Third World Quarterly*, 11/4 (1989), pp. 131–47.

32 The Development of Ethnic Awareness and Identification

Frances Aboud

Applying an ethnic label correctly or identifying which person goes with a given ethnic label is usually measured by showing pictures or dolls from different ethnic groups and asking the child to point to, for example, the white, the black and the Native Indian person. A significant proportion of children make correct identifications at 4 and 5 years of age and this proportion increases with age. By 6 and 7 years the children reach close to 100 per cent accuracy especially when identifying whites and blacks. Two studies found that 3-year-olds were very inaccurate in that less than 25 per cent of them correctly pointed to the white and black when given those labels. However, 4- and 5-year-olds reached close to 75 per cent accuracy or better in both white and black samples. Most of these studies also indicate a significant improvement with age, suggesting that 3–5 are the critical years for acquiring this form of label awareness. By improvement, I mean that a larger proportion of children made accurate identifications. Older white and black children of 6, 7 and 8 years usually reached a level of 90–100 per cent accuracy.

[. . .] It is also between the ages of 5 and 7 years that white and Chinese Americans acquire the ability to identify Chinese people. However, the identification of Hispanics or Mexican Americans seems to be more difficult for both white and Hispanic children. They improved in accuracy between 4 and 9 years of age and reached asymptote around 9 or 10 years. Similarly, the identification of Native Indians by both white and Indian children was fairly good by 6 years of age but continued to improve during the next three years. Presumably the children were using features such as skin colour and hair type for whites and blacks and so found Hispanics, Indians and whites less distinctive in these features than whites and blacks.

The child's awareness of ethnic groupings also takes the form of perceiving certain similarities between members of the same group and perceiving certain differences between members of different groups. Vaughan gave children sets of three pictures of people and asked them which two were similar and different from the third. By 6 years of age the children had reached a level of 68 per cent accuracy and this improved to 83 per cent by 11 years.[1] Similarly, Katz, Sohn and Zalk asked children to rate the degree of similarity between pairs of people. At 8 years of age, white and black children rated same-ethnic pairs as more similar than different-ethnic pairs.[2] That is, two whites were perceived as very similar and two blacks were perceived as very similar despite their different facial features or different shades of skin colour. Black children rated two whites as slightly more similar than two blacks. However, a white and a black were always perceived as very different. An interesting result from the Katz et al. study was that in later years, perceptions of dissimilarity were not always based on race but were sometimes based on individual features such as emotional expression. In other words, the children had acquired perceptions of racial similarity and difference by 8 years, had continued to use these perceptions for the following three years, and then abandoned them at 11 or 12 years in favour of perceptions of individual features. Thus, we must keep in mind the fact that racial awareness is often overused when it is first acquired, but that it may lose its salience later on when other types of awareness become more useful.

Another method was used by Aboud and Mitchell to examine how children perceive similarities and differences among different ethnic members.[3] The Native Indian children in this study were first asked to place photographs of men from four different ethnic groups on a similarity board to indicate how similar the men were to themselves. Then a peer from each ethnic group was placed (one at a time) at the end of the board. The children were asked to repeat the rating procedure, this time to indicate how similar the men were to each ethnic peer. The children, who ranged from 6 to 10 years of age, accurately perceived the same-ethnic man as most similar to the peer and the three different-ethnic men as equally dissimilar. On a second task, they were asked whom each ethnic peer would most want as an uncle or brother. It was expected that these kinship selections would closely parallel the similarity ratings, as indeed they did.

When white children of the same age were given the same task they made a number of interesting errors. Younger children often made egocentric errors in that they assigned the uncle they wanted, a white uncle, to another ethnic peer. Both younger and older children also made mismatch errors in that they assigned an incorrect non-white uncle to the peer. These mismatches were especially frequent when the peer came from a disliked ethnic group, or when the peer, whether from their own or a disliked group, spoke his non-English native language (e.g. the Asian child spoke Chinese, the Hispanic Spanish and the white French). Perceptions of ethnic similarity or kinship received interference both from the child's

own strong preferences and from his or her strong dislikes. It seemed that the older children were able to control their own strong preferences but not their dislikes. The errors for the disliked group were probably due to a lack of knowledge or attention to details. [Another study] also found that children possessed least knowledge about national groups that they disliked. This lack of knowledge or attention to detail has manifested itself in several different ways. For example, in the Aboud and Mitchell study, many children chose the wrong, but not their ingroup, ethnic uncle. In [one] study, it was reported that British children from 7 to 11 years were egocentric in suggesting that a disliked outgroup peer would prefer a British person. The opposite was found by [another investigation], where more ingroup preference or ethnocentrism was attributed to disliked nationalities. The egocentric judgements of British children support Piaget's observations of Swiss children, but not the reports of North American children. Perhaps egocentrism persists longer when one is assigning preferences to national groups with whom one has little contact rather than ethnic groups living in one's community.

Vaughan found that children were able to categorize by race and to give appropriate labels to people only after they were relatively accurate at perceiving similarities.[4] He claimed that categorizing and labelling required certain cognitive skills, such as classification, that matured later than perceptual skills. For example, Vaughan asked children to sort white and Maori dolls by race. At 5 and 6 years of age, only 60 per cent of the children could do this correctly. However, by 7 years of age 85 per cent of the children were accurate, and 100 per cent were at 8 years. Similarly, when Vaughan showed them a doll and asked 'What sort of doll is this?' not until 7 years of age did a significant proportion of the children give the correct racial label: 85 per cent at 7 years of age and 100 per cent at 8 years.

Other researchers have used the sorting task but they have used it to measure the salience of race over other cues such as sex and age rather than as a measure of awareness of categories. [One group] presented children with pictures of people who varied in race, sex and age. The children sorted these pictures into two boxes of people who 'belong together'. Almost half the children sorted the people according to race; this was true for white, black and Asian children who ranged from 6 to 10 years of age. Sorting by race increased with age for the white children only. Given Vaughan's data, we cannot be sure whether the younger children sorted by sex or age because they were unable to sort by race or because sex and age were more salient to them. However, the older children were presumably capable of sorting by any one of the categories but chose race because it was the most salient. We might expect, then, that sorting by race or ethnicity increases from 4 to 7 years as children develop a cognitive awareness of racial categories. Whether it increases or decreases thereafter depends on the other categories available. Relative to sex and age, race remained salient for Davey's children. However, relative to personality or individual features, race became less salient for the white children in Katz et al.'s study.

A more mature form of ethnic awareness involves understanding that race and ethnicity are tied to something deeper than clothing and other superficial features. Adults think of a person's ethnicity as being derived from his or her family background. However, young children are not aware of this deeper meaning of ethnicity; they are fooled by superficial features. For example, not until the age of 9 or 10 do black children seem to be aware that a person remains black even though she puts on white make up or a blond wig, or even though she may want to be white. This deeper awareness manifests itself in many ways. One of these is constancy or the constant identification of a person's ethnicity despite transformations in superficial features. Aboud examined constancy by showing children a photograph of an Italian Canadian who was labelled as such. Then a sequence of four photos was shown of the Italian Canadian boy donning Native Indian clothing over the top of his ordinary clothes. In the final photo, the boy's appearance had changed except for his face. The children were asked to identify the boy in the final photo. Constancy was said to be present if the child said that he was Italian and not Indian (label), that he was more similar to photos of other Italian children than to photos of Indians (perceived similarity), and that he should be put into the pile of other Italians (categorization). Constancy increased from 5 to 9 years of age but was not really present until 8 years. Most children younger than 8 years thought the boy was Indian.

Furthermore, when asked if the boys in the first and last photos were the same person or two different persons, half the 6-year-olds said they were two different persons. Over 90 per cent of the 7-year-olds knew they were the same boy, but not until a year later did they attain ethnic constancy. Children of 8 years and older were certain that the boy was Italian and not Indian. Consistent with our previous discussion, the two cognitive identifications of labelling and categorization were more difficult than the perceived similarity identification. At 8 years they not only identified the boy as Italian but also inferred that he would prefer an Italian over an Indian playmate. However, although the 8- and 9-year-olds understood that ethnicity was deeper than clothing, they were not able to articulate the reason for this. When asked what makes a person Italian or Indian, only a few mentioned country of birth or family but most did not know.

Another manifestation of children's maturing awareness of ethnicity is that they understand the cause of skin colour. [One group] tested the notion that with age children dispense with their early view that skin colour is caused supernaturally or through arbitrary association (e.g. being American or being bad) and begin to understand that it is transmitted via a physical mechanism from parents to children. Children were asked. 'How is it that this person is white . . . this one black?' Their answers were coded in terms of seven levels of understanding the cause of skin colour. Children became aware that there were physical origins of a person's skin colour after the age of

7, though they did not make the link to parents till some time later. Understanding the physical basis of skin colour was acquired after they had mastered conversation. This awareness developed around the same time as identity constancy, measured here as the understanding that kinship remains constant despite a change in age and family size. It is clear, then, that ethnic constancy and a mature understanding of skin colour are later developments and require a fairly mature level of cognitive development. [It has been] found that this level of awareness [is] necessary for the decline in white children's prejudice towards blacks.

NOTES

1   G. M. Vaughan, 'Concept Formation and the Development of Ethnic Awareness', *Journal of Genetic Psychology*, 103 (1963), pp. 93–103.
2   P. A. Katz, M. Sohn and S. R. Zalk, 'Perpetual Concomitants of Racial Attitudes in Urban Grade Schoolchildren', *Developmental Psychology*, 11 (1975), pp. 135–44.
3   F. E. Aboud and F. G. Mitchell, 'Ethnic Role-taking: The Effects of Preference and Self-identification', *International Journal of Psychology*, 12 (1977), pp. 1–17.
4   Vaughan, 'Concept Formation'.

33 'There Ain't No Black in the Union Jack'

Paul Gilroy

As black styles, music, dress, dance, fashion and languages became a determining force shaping the style, music, dress, fashion and language of urban Britain as a whole, blacks have been structured into the mechanisms of this society in a number of different ways. Not all of them are reducible to the disabling effects of racial subordination. This is part of the explanation of how [black] youth cultures became repositories of anti-racist feeling. Blacks born, nurtured and schooled in this country are, in significant measure, British even as their presence redefines the meaning of the term. The language and structures of racial politics, locked as they are into a circular journey between immigration as problem and repatriation as solution, prevent this from being seen. Yet recognizing it and grasping its significance is essential to the development of anti-racism in general and in particular for understanding the social movements for racial equality that helped to create the space in which 'youth culture' could form. The contingent and partial belonging to Britain which blacks enjoy, their ambiguous assimilation, must be examined in detail for it is closely associated with specific forms of exclusion. If we are to comprehend the cultural dynamics of 'race' we must be able to identify its limits. This, in turn, necessitates consideration of how blacks define and represent themselves in a complex combination of resistances and negotiations, which does far more than provide a direct answer to the brutal forms in which racial subordination is imposed.

Black expressive cultures affirm while they protest. The assimilation of blacks is not a process of acculturation but of cultural syncretism.

Accordingly, their self-definitions and cultural expressions draw on a plurality of black histories and politics. In the context of modern Britain this has produced a diaspora dimension to black life. Here, non-European traditional elements, mediated by the histories of Afro-America and the Caribbean, have contributed to the formation of new and distinct black cultures amidst the decadent peculiarities of the Welsh, Irish, Scots and English. These non-European elements must be noted and their distinctive resonance must be accounted for. Some derive from the immediate history of empire and colonization in Africa, the Caribbean and the Indian subcontinent from where post-war settlers brought both the methods and the memories of their battles for citizenship, justice and independence. Others create material for the processes of cultural syncretism from extended and still-evolving relationships between the black populations of the overdeveloped world and their siblings in racial subordination elsewhere.

The effects of these ties and the penetration of black forms into the dominant culture mean that it is impossible to theorize black culture in Britain without developing a new perspective on British culture *as a whole*. This must be able to see behind contemporary manifestations into the cultural struggles which characterized the imperial and colonial period. An intricate web of cultural and political connections binds blacks here to blacks elsewhere. At the same time, they are linked into the social relations of this country. Both dimensions have to be examined and the contradictions and continuities which exist between them must be brought out. Analysis must, for example, be able to suggest why Afrika Bambaataa and Jah Shaka, leading representatives of hip-hop and reggae culture respectively, find it appropriate to take the names of African chiefs distinguished in anti-colonial struggle, or why young black people in places as different as Hayes and Harlem choose to style themselves the Zulu nation. Similarly, we must comprehend the cultural and political relationships which have led to Joseph Charles and Rufus Radebe being sentenced to six years' imprisonment in South Africa for singing banned songs written by the Birmingham reggae band Steel Pulse – the same band which performed to London's [Rock Against Racism] carnival in 1978.

The social movements which have sprung up in different parts of the world as evidence of African dispersal, imperialism and colonialism have done more than appeal to blacks everywhere in a language which could invite their universal identification. They have communicated directly to blacks and their supporters all over the world asking for concrete help and solidarity in the creation of organizational forms adequate to the pursuit of emancipation, justice and citizenship, internationally as well as within national frameworks. The nineteenth-century English abolitionists who purchased the freedom of Frederick Douglass, the distinguished black activist and writer, were responding to an appeal of this type. The eighteenth-century settlement of Sierra Leone by blacks from England and their white associates and the formation of free black communities in Liberia remain an important testimony to the potency of such requests. The back-to-Africa movements in America, the Caribbean and now Europe, Negritude and the birth of the New Negro in the Harlem Renaissance during the 1920s all provide further illustrations of a multi-faceted desire to overcome the sclerotic confines of the nation state as a precondition of the liberation of blacks everywhere.

Technological developments in the field of communication have, in recent years, encouraged this desire and made it more powerful by fostering a global perspective from the memories of slavery and indenture which are the property of the African diaspora. The soul singers of Afro-America have been able to send 'a letter to their friends' in Africa and elsewhere. The international export of new world black cultures first to whites and then to 'third world' markets in South America and Africa itself has had effects unforeseen by those for whom selling it is nothing other than a means to greater profit. Those cultures, in the form of cultural commodities – books and records – have carried inside them oppositional ideas, ideologies, theologies and philosophies. As black artists have addressed an international audience and blues, gospel, soul and reggae have been consumed in circumstances far removed from those in which they were originally created, new definitions of 'race' have been born. A new structure of cultural exchange has been built up across the imperial networks which once played host to the triangular trade of sugar, slaves and capital. Instead of three nodal points there are now four – the Caribbean, the US, Europe and Africa. The cultural and political expressions of new-world blacks have been transferred not just to Europe and Africa but between various parts of the new world itself. By these means Rastafari culture has been carried to locations as diverse as Poland and Polynesia, and hip-hop from Stockholm to Southall.

Analysis of the political dimensions to the expressive culture of black communities in Britain must reckon with their position within international networks. It should begin where fragmented diaspora histories of racial subjectivity combine in unforeseen ways with the edifice of British society and create a complex relationship which has evolved through various stages linked in different ways to the pattern of capitalist development itself.

The modern world-system responsible for the expansion of Europe and consequent dispersal of black slave labourers throughout Europe and the new world was from its inception an international operation. Several scholars have pointed to its uneasy fit into forms of analysis premised on the separation of its economic and cultural subsystems into discrete national units coterminous with nation states. The social structures and processes erected over the productive and distributive relations of this system centred on slavery and plantation society and were reproduced in a variety of different forms across the Americas, generating political antagonisms which were both international and transnational in character. Their contemporary residues, rendered more difficult to perceive by the recent migration of slave descendants into the centres of metropolitan civilization, also exhibit the tendency to transcend a narrowly national focus. Analysis of black politics must, therefore, if it is to be adequate, move beyond the field of enquiry designated by concepts which deny the possibility of common themes, motives and practices within diaspora history. This is where categories formed in the intersection of 'race' and the nation state are themselves exhausted. To put it another way, national units are not the most appropriate basis for studying this history, for the African diaspora's consciousness of itself has been defined in and against constricting national boundaries.

As the international slave system unfolded, so did its antithesis in the form of transnational movements for self-emancipation organized by slaves, ex-slaves and their abolitionist allies. This is not the place to provide a full account of these movements or even of the special place within them occupied by ideas about Africa. However, that continent has been accepted by many, though not all, who inhabit and reproduce the black syncretisms of the overdeveloped world as a homeland even if they do not aspire to a physical return there. Ties of affect and affiliation have been strengthened by knowledge of anti-colonial struggles which have sharpened contemporary understanding of 'race'. These feelings, of being descended from or belonging to Africa and of longing for its liberation from imperialist rule, can be linked loosely by the term 'pan-Africanism'. The term is inadequate as anything other than the most preliminary description, particularly as it can suggest mystical unity outside the process of history or even a common culture or ethnicity which will assert itself regardless of determinate political and economic circumstances. The sense of interconnectedness felt by blacks to which it refers has in some recent manifestations become partially detached from any primary affiliation to Africa and from the aspiration to a homogeneous African culture. Young blacks in Britain, for example, stimulated to riotous protest by the sight of black 'South Africans' stoning apartheid police and moved by scenes of brutality transmitted from that country by satellite, may not feel that shared Africanness is at the root of the empathy they experience. It may be that a common experience of powerlessness somehow transcending history and experienced in *racial* categories; in the antagonism between white and black rather than European and African, is enough to secure affinity between these divergent patterns of subordination. As Ralph Ellison pointed out long ago: 'Since most so-called Negro-cultures outside Africa are necessarily amalgams, it would seem more profitable to stress the term "culture" and leave the term "Negro" out of the discussion. It is not culture which binds the people who are of partially African origin now scattered throughout the world but an identity of passions.'[1]

[. . .] [These struggles] have, since the very first day that slaves set out across the Atlantic, involved radical passions rooted in distinctly African history, philosophy and religious practice. Passions which have, at strategic moments, challenged the political and moral authority of the capitalist world-system in which the diaspora was created. The ideologies and beliefs of new world blacks exhibit characteristically African conceptions of the relationship between art and life, the sacred and the secular, the spiritual and the material. Traces of these African formulations remain, albeit in displaced and mediated forms, even in the folk philosophies, religion and vernacular arts of black Britain.

NOTE

1   R. Ellison, *Shadow and Act* (New York: Random House, 1964), p. 263.

34 Europe Needs More Immigrants

The Economist

[. . .] The European popular imagination, it seems, is gripped by panic about foreigners: that there are too many of them pouring in, that there is certainly no need for any more. In short, that Europe is 'full up'.

Contrast that view, however, with some rather different observations. Because Europeans are not having enough babies and are living so long, the European Union would need to import 1.6 m migrants a year simply to keep its working-age population stable between now and 2050. With Europe's unemployment now falling, and its people increasingly sniffy about the sorts of jobs they are prepared to do, or too ill-equipped to do the high-tech ones being created, the continent's workforce is in need of renewal as never before. Immigrants tend to inject into stale, ageing countries fresh vitality, fresh energy and an uncommon willingness to work hard at unappealing jobs. How can Europe reconcile its economic need for more immigrants with its apparent political distaste for them?

In an ideal world, there would be no barriers to the free movement of people, between the various countries as within them. Indeed, one of the curiosities of migration is that, even where such barriers no longer exist, as within the EU, so few people choose to pack up their belongings, uproot their families, and trek off to settle in a foreign country. But human insecurities are not soothed by economic and demographic logic alone, nor even much by clear evidence that migrants are needed. Europeans seem to need reassurance that their jobs, their culture, their sense of identity are not somehow under threat.

The question is how to create a more liberal immigration regime that can still be made politically palatable on a continent as prone to xenophobia as Europe.

At present, Europe errs on the side of mean-mindedness. Since the 1970s, it has more or less shut its doors to primary immigration: that is, to economic migrants who might later bring their relations too. These days, many of those who settle permanently in the EU are the families of those who are already there. Yet, just as Europe has been busy bolting up its front door, so those seeking a better life in the rich countries of the Union have increasingly resorted to finding ways in round the back. Since the 1980s, there has been an upsurge in the numbers of people seeking political asylum, and – though they are difficult to measure – in the numbers of illegal immigrants.

Genuine refugees from persecution, as defined by the 1951 Geneva convention, should be welcomed in the EU without reservation. They should be confident of this welcome, and Europeans should be proud of it. Yet, and though it is politically incorrect to say so, even a cursory glance at the numbers of asylum claims judged to be false suggests that many of those hoping to gain entry as political refugees are economic migrants in disguise.

This is not to say that asylum-seekers 'shop around' for the best deal: research shows clearly that the chief reason they, like all migrants, head for one country rather than another is that they know people already there. Even if EU countries were to harmonise their provision for refugees, as they have promised to do, existing patterns would probably change little: the networks that draw asylum-seekers to, above all, Germany and Britain have taken on a life of their own.

What the many asylum claims do suggest, however, is that a clampdown on bogus refugees by itself is only a half-solution. In other words, economic migrants would not have to dress themselves up as refugees, nor to make those hazardous journeys crammed into the holds of rickety boats or the containers of long-distance lorries, if there were an alternative way of applying to get in legally – with some hope of success.

Fortress Europe

If the EU were to install a more orderly system of admitting economic migrants, both the high-tech ones it needs to fashion its software and the less skilled ones it needs to pick its lettuces and gut its chickens, would that really curb the numbers of illegals getting ready to make their dash across the continent's borders? That is one objection made by those who oppose the introduction of a more generous policy towards immigrants. It may be, they say, that today's image of Fortress Europe deters some of tomorrow's would-be migrants, and that a more liberal system to admit outsiders legally would only encourage yet others to slip in on the quiet. If so, however, it is a risk that Europe should be ready to take.

A more persuasive objection is that any regime that concentrated on luring the highly skilled would run the risk of robbing poorer countries of the people they are least able to do without. Yet even poor countries can benefit when émigrés send home the remittances they earn in the rich world.

Politicians face a choice. They can either pander to the fears of voters about being 'swamped' by outsiders, or they can seek to reassure them that those worries are only half-founded. As unemployment rates fall in most European countries, the task of reassurance ought to become easier. For the moment, however, Europe's politicians show little inclination to be brave. How many British politicians advertise the fact that, in terms of the number of asylum-seekers it accepts per head of population, Britain lies halfway down the EU table? How many German politicians remind their voters that as many foreigners, including lots of refugees, are now leaving Germany as are coming in? The greatest pity of all would be if the EU's governments at last managed to agree to a more orderly joint system of immigration, only to appeal to the lowest, most illiberal, common denominator.

Part 10

Class, Stratification and Inequality

Many sociologists argue that class is much less significant today than was the case in the past. Traditional class divisions have become largely eroded, while individuals increasingly pursue a diversity of lifestyles that cut across class boundaries. For instance, many middle-class as well as working-class people follow football. In Reading 35, Terry Nicholls Clark and Seymour Martin Lipset provide a succinct discussion of whether the concept of class still retains its relevance in sociology. They argue that by and large it does not. Societies today are too fragmentary for the notion of class to have much relevance. This does not mean that sociologists should forget about classes altogether. Class divisions still are important – for instance, class inequalities affect health, but class is not the dominant force it was.

All social systems are stratified – that is, material and cultural resources are distributed in an unequal fashion. In modern societies, class is the most significant (although by no means the only) form of social stratification. In spite of, or perhaps because of, its centrality in sociology there is no general agreement over how the concept of class should best be formulated.

Reading 36 compares the two most influential conceptions of class advanced in classical social thought, those of Karl Marx and Max Weber. According to Marx, class is above all linked to control of private property and 'surplus production'. Class relations are not just incidental to modern social orders, but

absolutely essential to them, as are mechanisms of class conflict. Weber accepted a good deal of Marx's viewpoint, but argued that economic factors other than ownership or control of property are important in determining class divisions. Class concerns the differential distribution of 'life-chances', and these are affected by economic influences such as the structure of labour markets as well as by who controls property in the means of production.

The idea of 'risk society' was introduced into sociology by the German thinker Ulrich Beck. Beck does not mean that our societies are more risky than in the past. Rather, we face a more open and fluid future and therefore have constantly to think in terms of risk. Individualism has in some part replaced class divisions, as is mentioned above, with the result that individuals have to make their own calculations about the future rather than passively accepting whatever the future might bring. The idea of risk society, Andy Furlong and Fred Cartmel assert in Reading 37, can help us – among many other areas – understand the experience of young people. Lacking the stable forms of group identity that exist in the past, young people enter a more fluid and uncertain world than their elders. In the world of work, for instance, a generation ago someone entering a job would expect to be in the same kind of work until the end of his or her career. Today there is much more fluidity in the job market, with very few jobs being for life.

Over recent years there has been much talk of the 'digital divide'. The division between those who have access to computers and to the internet might be just as significant as longer-established forms of economic division – a new version of the 'haves' and 'have-nots'. In the past, getting access to information technology was expensive. But the price of computers, mobile phones and other electronic appliances is coming down all the time. Preventing the emergence of a digital divide, the author argues in Reading 38, will depend much more upon education than anything else. We need to make sure that the school system is reformed sufficiently to allow everyone to benefit from the advantages of the new technologies.

35 Are Social Classes Dying?

Terry Nicholls Clark and Seymour Martin Lipset

New forms of social stratification are emerging. Much of our thinking about stratification – from Marx, Weber and others – must be recast to capture these new developments. Social class was the key theme of past stratification work. Yet class is an increasingly outmoded concept, although it is sometimes appropriate to earlier historical periods. Class stratification implies that people can be differentiated on one or more criteria into distinct layers, classes. Class analysis has grown increasingly inadequate in recent decades as traditional hierarchies have declined and new social differences have emerged. The cumulative impact of these changes is fundamentally altering the nature of social stratification – placing past theories in need of substantial modification.

This paper outlines first some general propositions about the sources of class stratification and its decline. The decline of hierarchy, and its spread across situses, is emphasised. The general propositions are applied to political parties and ideological cleavages, the economy, the family, and social mobility. These developments appear most clearly in North America and Western Europe, but our propositions also help interpret some of the tensions and factors driving change in Eastern Europe, the Soviet Union, and other societies.

We broadly follow Marx and Weber in understanding social class as social differentiation emerging from structured socio-economic life changes of distinct social categories of persons. Social classes can emerge from differential access to the means of production (as Marx stressed) or to trade or consumption (as Weber added). Class consciousness may be said to emerge if these social categories develop distinct subjective outlooks, culture and behaviour patterns. [. . .]

If one looks closely at class theories in recent decades, it is striking how much class has changed. This is not immediately obvious since most theorists claim direct descendance from Marx and Weber. But many have in fact fundamentally altered the concept of class towards what we term *the fragmentation of stratification*. Consider some examples of class theory and social stratification. Dahrendorf stressed that many lines of social cleavage have not erupted into class conflict.[1] For a Marxian revolution, the working class should suffer immiseration and grow more homogenous; capitalists should join in combat against them. But Dahrendorf points instead to the 'decomposition of labour': workers have become more differentiated by skill level – into skilled, semi-skilled and unskilled. Unions often separate more than join these groups. Perhaps even more important is the expansion of the 'middle class' of white-collar non-manual workers. Such a middle class was largely ignored by Marx; it was expected to join the capitalists or workers. Instead it has grown substantially, and differentiated internally, especially between lower-level salaried employees and managers. Dahrendorf might have abandoned the concept of class, but instead retained the term while redefining it to include all sorts of groups in political or social conflict: ' "class" signifies conflict groups that are generated by the differential distribution of authority in imperatively coordinated associations'.

Many writers have, like Dahrendorf, retained terms from Marx, while substantially changing their meaning. Erik Wright has sought to capture some of the same changes as Dahrendorf. He does so by developing a 12 category 'typology of class location in capitalist society' that includes: 1. bourgeoisie, 2. small employers, 4. expert managers, 5. expert supervisors, 8. semi-credentialled supervisors, and continues up to 12. proletarians. It explicitly incorporates not just ownership, but skill level, and managerial responsibility. It is striking that Wright, a self-defined Marxist, incorporates so much post-Weberian multi-dimensionality.[2] [. . .]

These analyses stress changes in work-place relations. Yet social relations outside the workplace are increasingly important for social stratification. If proletarians are visibly distinct in dress, food and life style, they are more likely to think of themselves, and act as, a politically distinct class. In the nineteenth and early twentieth century, this was often the case, as novels and sociologists report. The decreasing distinctiveness of social classes is stressed by Parkin, who holds that this brings the 'progressive erosion of the communal components of proletarian status'. Specifically, 'the absence of clearly visible and unambiguous marks of inferior status has made the enforcement of an all-pervasive deference system almost impossible to sustain outside the immediate work situation. It would take an unusually sharp eye to detect the social class of Saturday morning shoppers in the High Street, whereas to any earlier generation it would have been the most elementary task.'[3]

The same tendency toward fragmentation emerges from assessments of political leadership and power. The elitist and hierarchical assumptions that lie behind ruling class analysis as developed by Marx, Pareto and Mosca have been increasingly weakened. When Hunter's *Community Power Structure* appeared in 1953, it confirmed the view of many social scientists that upper-class power elites ruled. But over the next three decades, this class domination view was supplanted by a pluralistic, multi-dimensional conceptualisation. The paradigm change did not come easily: it cumulatively evolved from some 200 studies of national and community power, accompanied by considerable debates about power elites and class domination. Stressing historical changes, Shils suggests that by the late twentieth century 'these reflections seem to lead to the conclusion that Mosca's conception of a political class is no longer applicable in our contemporary societies'.

Should the social class concept be abandoned? In a 1959 exchange, Nisbet suggested that class 'is nearly valueless for the clarification of the data of wealth, power and social status in the contemporary United States'. Commenting on Nisbet in the same journal, Bernard Barber and O. D. Duncan both argued that his position had not been substantiated, and that a sharper analysis and evidence were necessary. This was over 30 years ago. Yet today class remains salient in sociologists' theories, and commentaries. We do not suggest it be altogether abandoned, but complemented by other factors. [. . .]

Many stratification analysts used class analysis longer and more extensively than empirically warranted due to their focus on Europe. Analysts of American society are often defensive, suggesting that America is somehow 'behind' Europe. Marxists were among the most outspoken in this regard, but not unique. However, things changed as new social movements emerged in the 1970s and 1980s. The United States then often seemed more a leader than a laggard. This seemed even more true in the dramatic changes of the late 1980s as the former communist societies, led by Eastern Europe, sought to throw off their central hierarchical planning and move toward free economic markets and political democracy.

What do these changes imply for theories of stratification? A critical point is that traditional hierarchies are declining; economic and family hierarchies determine much less than just a generation or two ago. Three general propositions state this argument:

(i) *Hierarchy generates and maintains rigid class relations. The greater the hierarchical (vertical) differentiation among persons in a social unit, the deeper its class divisions tend to become.*

Since the degree of hierarchy will vary with a society, we add:

(ii) *The greater the hierarchical differentiation in each separate situs (or separate vertical dimension, e.g. economic institutions, government organisations, and families), the most salient are class-defined patterns in informed social relations, cultural outlooks, and support for social change, such as support for social movements and political behaviour.*
(iii) *Conversely, however, the more the hierarchy declines, the more structured social class relations diminish in salience.* And the larger the number of situses which evidence declining hierarchy, the less salient are class relations in the society. As class conflict declines, there may be less conflict, or conflict may be organised along different lines (for instance, gender). Not all hierarchies generate counter-reactions. There must be sufficient acceptance of democratic processes to permit opposition to surface. And the more that legal structures, the media, and other institutions, permit or enhance the articulation of social conflict, the more can anti-hierarchical themes spread and win social support. [. . .]

We now consider separate situses of social stratification in terms of our three general propositions. In each situs we consider some of the specific dynamics by which social classes have declined. The cumulative effect, across situses, is emergence of a new system of social stratification.

Politics: less class, more fragmentation

Political behaviour is an ideal area to assess changes in stratification. It was central to Marx and Weber, it is highly visible today; it has been studied in detail; it permits tests of competing hypotheses, Lipset's *Political Man* stressed class politics in its first edition. But the second edition

focused on the declines in class voting. A striking illustration of this change is in the results from the 1940s to 1980s on the Alford Index of Class Voting. This index is based on the percentage of persons by social class who vote for left or right parties. For instance, if 75 per cent of the working class votes for the left, and only 25 per cent of the middle class does so, the Alford Index score is 50 (the difference between these two figures). The Alford Index has declined in every country for which data are available. [. . .]

What is replacing class? The classical left–right dimension has been transformed. People still speak of left and right, but definitions are changing. There are now two lefts, with distinct social bases. The traditional left is blue-collar based and stresses class-related issues. But a second left is emerging in Western societies (sometimes termed New Politics, New Left, Post-Bourgeois, or Post-Materialist), which increasingly stresses social issues rather than traditional political issues. The most intensely disputed issues for them no longer deal with ownership and control of the means of production. And in many socialist and even communist parties [. . .] supporters of these new issues are supplanting the old.

Political issues shift with more affluence: as wealth increases, people take the basics for granted; they grow more concerned with life style and amenities. Younger, more educated and more affluent persons in more affluent and less hierarchical societies should move furthest from traditional class politics. [. . .]

These trends are congruent with the 'post-industrial' trends identified by Daniel Bell and Alain Touraine, and the 'post-materialist' (earlier termed 'post-bourgeois') patterns identified by Ronald Inglehart – stressing 'self-actualisation' via aesthetic intellectual and participatory concerns. Scott Flanagan suggests a shift from traditional consciousness to libertarian consciousness. But one should not overstate the changes: Alan Marsh, analysing British data, finds that 'materialists' and 'post-materialists' do not differ in their concern for having enough money, which both share. The post-materialists, however, 'are distinguished by their relative youth, wealth, education and by their concern for ideology'.[4]

Economic organisation changes: sources of a new market individualism

One simple, powerful change has affected the economy: growth. And economic growth undermines hierarchical class stratification. Affluence weakens hierarchies and collectivism; but it heightens individualism. With more income, the poor depend less on the rich. And all can indulge progressively more elaborate and varied tastes. *Markets, ceteris paribus, grow in relevance as income rises.* But as such complexity increases, it grows harder to plan centrally; decentralised, demand-sensitive decision-making becomes necessary. These contrasts particularly affect(ed) centrally-planned societies like the Soviet Union. But they operate too for firms like General Motors or US Steel.

Many private goods come increasingly from more differentiated and sub-market-oriented small firms, especially in such service-intensive fields as 'thoughtware', finance and office activities. By contrast huge firms are in relative decline, especially for traditional manufacturing products like steel and automobiles. Some 2/3 of all new jobs are in firms with 20 or fewer employees, in many countries. These small firms emerge because they out-compete larger firms. Why? Technology and management style are critical factors.

The more advanced the technology and knowledge base, the harder it is to plan in advance and control administratively, both within a large firm and still more by central government planners. Technological changes illustrate how new economic patterns are no longer an issue of public versus private sector control, but bring inevitable frustrations for hierarchical control by anyone. As research and development grow increasingly important for new products and technologies, they are harder to direct or define in advance for distant administrators of that firm, and even harder for outsider regulators or political officials seeking to plan centrally (as in a Soviet five-year plan, to use an extreme case). Certain plastics firms

have as much as one-third of staff developing the chemistry for new products. Computers, biological engineering and robotics illustrate the dozens of areas that are only vaguely amenable to forecast and hence central control.

A major implication for social stratification of these economic changes is the decline in traditional authority, hierarchy and class relations. Current technologies require fewer unskilled workers performing routine tasks, or a large middle-management to coordinate them, than did traditional manufacturing of steel, automobiles, etc. High tech means increasing automation of routine tasks. It also demands more professional autonomous decisions. More egalitarian, collegial decision-making is thus increasingly seen as a hallmark of modern society, by analysts from Habermas and Parsons to Daniel Bell and Zbigniew Brzezinski, and to consultants in business schools who teach the importance of new 'corporate culture' – as illustrated by *In Search of Excellence*, the number one non-fiction best-seller in the United States for some time, and widely read by business leaders in the United States and Europe. Even Soviet scholars as early as 1969 noted 'a sweeping qualitative transformation of productive forces as a result of science being made the principal factor in the development of social production'. The occupations that are expanding are white-collar, technical, professional and service-oriented. The class structure increasingly resembles a diamond bulging at the middle rather than a pyramid. Higher levels of education are needed in such occupations; the numbers of students pursuing more advanced studies has rapidly increased in the past few decades.

The larger the extent of the market, the less likely are particularistic decisions (preference for family members, city residents, or nationals) likely to prevail. Local stratification hierarchies are correspondingly undermined as markets grow – regionally, nationally and internationally. The force of this proposition has grown in the 1970s and 1980s with the globalisation of markets for manpower, capital and sales. Big and small firms have experienced major consolidations – enhanced by the growth of multinationals, the 1970s oil boom and subsequent bust, leveraged buy-outs, the rise of the Eurodollar market, and world-wide trade expansion. The growth of the US economy has been fuelled by massive in-migration, especially from Mexico, Latin America and Asia. More immigrants came into the United States in the 1980s than in any decade since before World War I. These factors combine to undermine the familistic-quasi-monopolistic tradition of business hierarchy and class stratification patterns.

A slimmer family

Major trends here parallel those in the economy. The traditional family has been slimmed and hierarchical stratification has weakened. Family and intimate personal relations have increasingly become characterised by more egalitarian relations, more flexible roles, and more tolerance for a wider range of behaviour. The authoritarian paternalistic family is decreasingly the model for stratification in the rest of society. Fewer young people marry, they wed later, have fewer children, far more women work outside the home, divorce rates have risen, parents and grandparents live less often with children. Paralleling these socio-demographic changes are changes in attitudes and roles concerning the family. Children and wives have grown substantially more egalitarian in a very short period of time. Indeed attitudes towards the family have changed more than almost any other social or political factor in the past 20–30 years, especially to questions like 'Should women work outside the home?' The proportions of wives and mothers working in jobs outside the home have grown dramatically, first and especially in the United States, but in many European countries too.

The family has also grown less important as a basis of stratification in relation to education and jobs. Increased wealth and government support programmes have expanded choice to individuals, and cumulatively transferred more functions than ever away from the family. Families are thus decreasingly responsible for raising children and placing them in jobs. Fewer children work in family firms (farms, shops, etc.). US mobility studies from the late nineteenth century onward report few changes until the 1960s, but major changes since: Hout's replication of Featherman and Hauser showed that the effect of origin status on destination status declined by 28 per cent from 1962 to 1973 and by one-third from 1972 to 1985. Social mobility studies also show decreasing effects of parents' education and income in explaining children's occupational success. At the same time the independent effects of education have increased.

[. . .]

NOTES

1   R. Dahrendorf, *Class and Class Conflict in Industrial Society* (London: Routledge and Kegan Paul, 1959), pp. 157–206.
2   Erik Wright, *Classes* (London: Verso: 1985), pp. 64–104.
3   F. Parkin, *Marxism amd Class Theory: A Bourgeois Critique* (London: Tavistock, 1979), p. 69.
4   A. Marsh, 'The Silent Revolution, Value Priorities, and The Quality of Life in Britain', *American Political Science Review*, 69 (1975), p. 28.

36 Marx and Weber on Class

Anthony Giddens

According to Marx's theory, class society is the product of a determinate sequence of historical changes. The most primitive forms of human society are not class systems. In 'tribal' societies – or, in Engels's term, 'primitive communism' – there is only a very low division of labour, and such property as exists is owned in common by the members of the community. The expansion of the division of labour, together with the increased level of wealth which this generates, is accompanied by the growth of private property; this involves the creation of a surplus product which is appropriated by a minority of non-producers who consequently stand in an exploitative relation *vis-à-vis* the majority of producers. Expressed in the terminology of Marx's early writings, alienation from nature, which characterizes the situation of tribal society, yields place to an increasing mastery of the material world, whereby [human beings] both 'humanize' [themselves] and develop [their] culture; but the increasing dissolution of . . . alienation . . . is attained only at the price of the formation of exploitative class relationships – at the price of an increase in human self-alienation.

Marx was not always careful to emphasize the differences between capitalism and [the] forms of class system which have preceded it in history. While it is the case that all (written) history 'is the history of class struggles',[1] this most definitely does not mean that what constitutes a 'class' is identical in each type of class society (although, of course, every class shares certain formal properties which define it as such), or that the process of the development of class conflict everywhere takes the same course. Marx's rebuke to those of his followers who had assumed the latter is instructive in this respect. Several of the factors which characterized the origins of the capitalist mode of production in Western Europe in the post-medieval period existed previously in Ancient Rome, including the formation of a merchant/manufacturing class and the development of money markets. But because of other elements in the composition of Roman society, including particularly the existence of slavery, the class struggles in Rome took a form which resulted not in the generation of a 'new and higher form of society', but in the disintegration of the social fabric.[2]

The diverse forms and outcomes of class conflict in history explain the different possibilities generated by the supersession of one type of society by another. When capitalism replaces feudalism, this is because a new class system, based upon manufacture and centred in the towns, has created a sort of enclave within feudal society which eventually comes to predominate over the agrarian-based structure of feudal domination. The result, however, is a new system of class domination, because this sequence of revolutionary change is based upon the partial replacement of one type of property in the means of production (land) by another (capital) – a process which, of course, entails major changes in technique. While capitalism, like feudalism, carries 'the germ of its own destruction' within itself, and while this self-negating tendency is also expressed in the shape of overt class struggles, their underlying character is quite different from those involved in the decline of feudalism. Class conflict in capitalism does not represent the struggle of two competing forms of technique, but stems instead from the incompatibility of an existing productive technique (industrial manufacture) with other aspects of the 'mode of production' – namely, the organization of the capitalist market. The access of a new class to power does not involve the ascendancy of a new form of private property, but instead creates the conditions under which private property is abolished. The proletariat here is the equivalent of Saint-Simon's '*industriels*': because it becomes the 'only class' in society, its hegemony signals the disappearance of all classes.

The problem of Marx's usage of the term 'class' is complicated, given the fact that he does not provide a formal definition of the concept. In approaching this matter, it is valuable to make a distinction between three sets of factors which complicate discussion of the Marxian conception of class – factors which have not been satisfactorily separated in the long-standing controversy over the issue. The first of these refers simply to the question of terminology – the variability in Marx's use of the word 'class' itself. The second concerns the fact that there are two conceptual constructions which may be discerned in Marx's writings as regards the notion of class: *an abstract or 'pure' model of class domination*, which applies to all types of class system: and *more concrete descriptions of the specific characteristics of classes in particular societies*. The third concerns Marx's analysis of classes in capitalism, the case which overwhelmingly occupied his interests: just as there are in Marx 'pure' models of class, so there are 'pure' and 'concrete' models of the structure of capitalism and the process of capitalist development.

The terminological issue, of course, is the least significant of the three sets of questions here. The fact of the matter is that Marx's terminology is careless. While he normally uses the term 'class' (*Klasse*), he also uses words such as 'stratum' and 'estate' (*Stand*) as if they were interchangeable with it. Moreover, he applies the word 'class' to various groups which, in theoretical terms, are obviously only parts or sectors of 'classes' properly speaking: thus he speaks of intellectuals as the 'ideological classes', of the *Lumpenproletariat* as the 'dangerous class', of bankers and moneylenders as the 'class of parasites', and so on. What matters, however, is how far this terminological looseness conceals conceptual ambiguities or confusions.

The principal elements of Marx's 'abstract model' of class domination are actually not difficult to reconstruct from the generality of his writings. This model is a dichotomous one. In each type of class society, there are two fundamental classes. Property relations constitute the axis of this dichotomous system: a minority of 'non-producers', who control the means of production, are able to use this position of control to extract from the majority of 'producers' the surplus product which is the source of their livelihood. 'Class' is thus defined in terms of the relationship of groupings of individuals to the means of production. This is integrally connected with the division of labour, because a relatively developed division of labour is necessary for the creation of the surplus product without which classes cannot exist. But, as Marx makes clear in his unfinished discussion at the end of the third volume of *Capital*, 'class' is not to be identified with source of income in the division of labour: this would yield an almost endless plurality of classes. Moreover, classes are never, in Marx's sense, income groupings. Modes of consumption, according to Marx, are primarily determined by relations of production. Hence his critique of those varieties of socialism which are directed towards securing some kind of 'distributive justice' in society – which seek, for example, the equalization of incomes: such forms of socialism are based on false premises, because they neglect the essential fact that distribution is ultimately governed by the system of production. This is why it is possible for two individuals to have identical incomes, and even the same occupations, and yet belong to different classes; as might be the case, for example, with two bricklayers, one of whom owns his own business, while the other works as the employee of a large firm.

It is an axiom of Marx's abstract model of classes that economic domination is tied to political domination. Control of the means of production yields political control. Hence the dichotomous division of classes is a division of both property and power: to trace the lines of economic exploitation in a society is to discover the key to the understanding of the relations of super- and subordination which apply within that society. Thus classes express a relation not only between 'exploiters and exploited', but between 'oppressors and oppressed'. Class relations necessarily are inherently unstable: but a dominant class seeks to stabilize its position by advancing (not usually, of course, in a consciously directed fashion) a legitimating ideology, which 'rationalizes' its position of economic and political domination and 'explains' to the subordinate class why it should accept its subordination. This is the connotation of the much quoted assertion that:

The ideas of the ruling class are in every epoch the ruling ideas: i.e., the class which is the ruling *material* force of society, is at the same time its ruling *intellectual* force. The class which has the means of material production at its disposal, has control at the same time over the means of mental production, so that thereby, generally speaking, the ideas of those who lack the means of mental production are subject to it.[3]

In the abstract model, classes are conceived to be founded upon relations of mutual *dependence* and *conflict*. 'Dependence' here means more than the sheer material dependence which is presupposed by the division of labour between the classes. In Marx's conception, classes in the dichotomous system are placed in a situation of reciprocity such that *neither class can escape from the relationship without thereby losing its identity as a distinct 'class'*. It is this theorem, heavily influenced by the Hegelian dialectic, which binds the theory of classes to the transformation of types of society. Classes, according to Marx, express the fundamental identity of society: when a class succeeds in, for example, elevating itself from a position of subordination to one of domination, it consequently effects an overall reorganization of the social structure. In the dichotomous system, classes are not, of course, 'dependent' upon each other in the sense of being collaborating groups on a level of equality; their reciprocity is an asymmetrical one, since it rests upon the extraction of surplus value by one class from the other. While each class 'needs' the other – given the continued existence of the society in unchanged form – their interests are at the same time mutually exclusive, and form the basis for the potential outbreak of open struggles. Class 'conflict' refers, first of all, to the opposition of interests presupposed by the exploitative relation integral to the dichotomous class relationship: classes are thus 'conflict groups'. This is, however, a point at which Marx's terminology is again variable. Whereas in his normal usage a 'class' represents any grouping which shares the same relationship to the means of production, regardless of whether the individuals involved become conscious of, and act upon, their common interests, he occasionally indicates that such a grouping can be properly called a 'class' only when shared interests do generate communal consciousness and action. But there is not really any significant conceptual ambiguity here. On the contrary, by this verbal emphasis, Marx seeks to stress the fact that class only becomes an important social agency when it assumes a directly political character, when it is a focus for communal action. Only under certain conditions does a class 'in itself' become a class 'for itself'.

Most of the problematic elements in Marx's theory of classes stem from the application of this abstract model to specific, historical forms of society – that is to say, they turn upon the nature of the connections between the 'abstract' and 'concrete' models of class. The first question to consider in this respect is the relationship between the dichotomous class system, presupposed by the abstract model, and the plurality of classes which, as Marx admits, exist in all historical forms of (class) society. Although Marx nowhere provides an explicit discussion of this matter, there is no serious source of difficulty here. Each historical type of society (ancient society, feudalism and capitalism) is structured around a dichotomous division in respect of property relations (represented most simply in each case as a division between patrician and plebeian, lord and vassal, capitalist and wage-labourer). But while this dichotomous division is the main 'axis' of the social structure, this simple class relation is complicated by the existence of three other sorts of grouping, two of which are 'classes' in a straightforward sense, while the third is a marginal case in this respect. These are: (1) 'transitional classes' which are in the process of formation within a society based upon a class system which is becoming 'obsolete': this is the case with the rise of the bourgeoisie and 'free' urban proletariat within feudalism; (2) 'transitional classes' which, on the contrary, represent elements of a superseded set of relations of production that linger on within a new form of society – as is found in the capitalist societies of nineteenth-century Europe, where the 'feudal classes' remain of definite significance within the social structure. Each of the first two examples results from the application of two dichotomous schemes to a single form of historical society. They represent, as it were, the fact that radical social change is not accomplished overnight, but constitutes an extended process of development, such that there is a massive overlap between types of dichotomous class system. (3) The third category includes two principal historical examples: the slaves of the ancient world, and the independent peasantry of the medieval and post-medieval period. These are 'quasi-class groupings', in the sense that they may be said to share certain common economic interests; but each of them, for different reasons, stands on the margin of the dominant set of class relationships within the societies of which they form part. To these three categories, we may add a fourth 'complicating factor' of the abstract dichotomous system: (4) sectors or sub-divisions of classes. Classes are not homogeneous entities as regards the social relations to which they give rise: Marx recognizes various sorts of differentiations within classes.

It should be noted that none of these categories involves sacrificing the abstract conception of the dichotomous class system: but they do make possible the recognition of the existence of 'middle classes', which in some sense intervene between the dominant and the subordinate class. 'Middle classes' are either of a transitional type, or they are segments of the major classes. Thus the bourgeoisie are a 'middle class' in feudalism, prior to their ascent to power; while the petty bourgeoisie, the small property-owners, whose interests are partly divergent from those of large-scale capital, form what Marx sometimes explicitly refers to as the 'middle class' in capitalism. If the terminology is again somewhat confusing, the underlying ideas are clear enough. [. . .]

For the most significant developments in the theory of classes since Marx, we have to look to those forms of social thought whose authors, while being directly influenced by Marx's ideas, have attempted at the same time to criticize or to reformulate them. This tendency has been strongest, for a combination of historical and intellectual reasons, in German sociology, where a series of attempts have been made to provide a fruitful critique of Marx – beginning with Max Weber [. . .] As in Marx, we find in Weber's writings treatments of 'classes' and 'capitalist development' as abstract conceptions; and these can be partly separated from his specifically historical discussions of the characteristics of particular European societies.

In the two versions of 'Class, status and party' which have been embodied in *Economy and Society*,[4] Weber provides what is missing in Marx: an explicit discussion of the concept of class. There are two principal respects in which this analysis differs from Marx's 'abstract model' of classes. One is that which is familiar from most secondary accounts – the differentiation of 'class' from 'status' and 'party'. The second, however, as will be argued below, is equally important: this is that, although Weber employs for some purposes a dichotomous model which in certain general respects resembles that of Marx, his viewpoint strongly emphasizes a *pluralistic conception of classes*. Thus Weber's distinction between 'ownership classes' (*Besitzklassen*) and 'acquisition classes' (*Erwerbsklassen*) is based upon a fusion of two criteria: 'on the one hand ... the kind of property that is usable for returns; and, on the other hand ... the kind of services that can be offered on the market', thus producing a complex typology. The sorts of property which may be used to obtain market returns, although dividing generally into two types – creating ownership (*rentier*) and acquisition (entrepreneurial) classes – are highly variable, and may produce many differential interests within dominant classes:

Ownership of dwellings; workshops; warehouses; stores; agriculturally usable land in large or small-holdings – a quantitative difference with possibly qualitative consequences; ownership of mines; cattle; men (slaves); disposition over mobile instruments of production, or capital goods of all sorts, especially money or objects that can easily be exchanged for money; disposition over products of one's own labour or of others' labour differing according to their various distances from consumability; disposition over transferable monopolies of any kind – all these distinctions differentiate the class situations of the propertied . . .[5]

But the class situations of the propertyless are also differentiated, in relation both to the types and the degree of 'monopolization' of 'marketable skills' which they possess. Consequently, there are various types of 'middle class' which stand between the 'positively privileged' classes (the propertied) and the 'negatively privileged' classes (those who possess neither property nor marketable skills). While these groupings are all nominally propertyless, those who possess skills which have a definite 'market value' are certainly in a different class situation from those who have nothing to offer but their (unskilled) labour. In acquisition classes – i.e. those associated particularly with the rise of modern capitalism – educational qualifications take on a particular significance in this respect; but the monopolization of trade skills by manual workers is also important.

Weber insists that a clear-cut distinction must be made between class 'in itself' and class 'for itself': 'class', in his terminology, always refers to market interests, which exist independently of whether men are aware of them. Class is thus

an 'objective' characteristic influencing the life-chances of men. But only under certain conditions do those sharing a common class situation become conscious of, and act upon, their mutual economic interests. In making this emphasis, Weber undoubtedly intends to separate his position from that adopted by many Marxists, involving what he calls a 'pseudo-scientific operation' whereby the link between class and class consciousness is treated as direct and immediate. Such a consideration evidently also underlies the emphasis which Weber places upon 'status groups' (*Stände*) as contrasted to classes. The contrast between class and status group, however, is not, as often seems to be assumed, merely, or perhaps even primarily, a distinction between subjective and objective aspects of differentiation. While class is founded upon differentials of economic interest in market relationships, Weber nowhere denies that, under certain given circumstances, a class may be a subjectively aware 'community'. The importance of status groups – which are normally 'communities' in this sense – derives from the fact that they are built upon criteria of grouping other than those stemming from market situation. The contrast between classes and status groups is sometimes portrayed by Weber as one between the objective and the subjective: but it is also one between production and consumption. Whereas class expresses relationships involved in production, status groups express those involved in consumption, in the form of specific 'styles of life'.

Status affiliations may cut across the relationships generated in the market, since membership of a status group usually carries with it various sorts of monopolistic privileges. None the less, classes and status groups tend in many cases to be closely linked, through property: possession of property is both a major determinant of class situation and also provides the basis for following a definite 'style of life'. The point of Weber's analysis is not that class and status constitute two 'dimensions of stratification', but that classes and status communities represent two possible, and competing, modes of group formation in relation to the distribution of power in society. Power is *not*, for Weber, a 'third dimension' in some sense comparable to the first two. He is quite explicit about saying that classes, status groups and parties are all 'phenomena of the distribution of power'.[6] The theorem informing Weber's position here is his insistence that power is not to be assimilated to economic domination – again, of course, a standpoint taken in deliberate contrast to that of Marx. The party, orientated towards the acquisition or maintenance of political leadership, represents, like the class and the status group, a major focus of social organization relevant to the distribution of power in a society. It is, however, only characteristic of the modern rational state.

Weber's abstract discussions of the concepts of class, status group and party, while providing the sort of concise conceptual analysis which is missing in Marx, are nevertheless unfinished expositions, and hardly serve to do more than offer a minimal introduction to the complex problems explored in his historical writings. In these latter writings, Weber details various forms of complicated interconnection between different sorts of class relationships, and between class relationships and status group affiliations. In the history of the European societies, there has been an overall shift in the character of predominant types of class relationship and class conflict. Thus in ancient Rome, class conflicts derived primarily from antagonisms established in the credit market, whereby peasants and artisans came to be in debt-bondage to urban financiers. This tended to cede place, in the Middle Ages, to class struggles originating in the commodity market and involving battles over the prices of the necessities of life. With the rise of modern capitalism, however, relationships established in the labour market become of central significance. It is evident that for Weber, as for Marx, the advent of capitalism dramatically changes the character of the general connections between classes and society. The emergence of the labour contract as the predominant type of class relationship is tied to the phenomenon of the expansion of economic life, and the formation of a national economy, which is so characteristic of modern capitalism. In most forms of society prior to modern capitalism, even in those in which there is a considerable development of manufacture and commerce, status groups play a more important role in the social structure than classes. By creating various sorts of restriction upon enterprise, or by enforcing the monopolization of market privileges by traditionally established groups, status affiliations have in fact, as is shown in Weber's studies of the Eastern civilizations, directly inhibited the formation of modern capitalist production.

NOTES

1 K. Marx and F. Engels, 'Manifesto of the Communist Party', in *Selected Works* (London: 1968), p. 35.
2 K. Marx, *Capital*, vol. 3 (Moscow: 1959), pp. 582 ff.
3 K. Marx and F. Engels, *The German Ideology* (London: 1965), p. 61.
4 M. Weber, *Economy and Society* (New York: 1968), vol. 2, pp. 926–40, and vol. 1, pp. 302–7.
5 Ibid., vol. 2, p. 928.
6 Ibid., p. 927.

37 Capitalism without Classes

Andy Furlong and Fred Cartmel

In this article we look at the work of the influential German sociologist Ulrich Beck, and assess the relevance of his ideas by looking at some key changes in the experiences of young people. Beck's work represents an important break with classic Marxist and Weberian traditions insofar as he questions the continued relevance of social class and suggests that in the modern world risks have become individualised.

Beck's risk society

For Beck, many of the obstacles which we face in our daily lives are now regarded as a consequence of our individual actions rather than features of our class positions. These changes are seen as reflecting an historical transformation of Western societies which is as radical as the transition from medieval to modern society. Industrial society, based on the rational application of science, is being replaced by a new type of society which Beck refers to as the 'risk society'. Whereas industrial society was seen as a predictable and ordered social world, late modernity is perceived as a more dangerous and unpredictable place in which we are constantly confronted with risk.

Risks include the threat of nuclear war or environmental disasters, as well as a range of other risks which have to be negotiated in day-to-day life. Significantly, with a weakening of the social networks associated with the old order, people are forced to negotiate these new hazards as individuals rather than as members of a collectivity.

Over the past two decades, significant changes have occurred and in many different dimensions of social life we can find evidence of radical change. As these changes make life experiences more difficult to predict, sociologists have started to rethink the ways in which they conceptualise social divisions. On a theoretical level, these changes have been interpreted in a number of ways: some have tried to adapt traditional perspectives (such as those introduced by Marx, Weber and Durkheim); others have argued that we have entered a new, 'postmodern' epoch, in which patterns of behaviour and individual life chances have lost their predictability.

Postmodernists, such as Lyotard and Baudrillard,[1] argue that recent social changes have been so far-reaching that it is no longer possible to predict individual life chances or patterns of behaviour. Consequently, they reject the validity of social science as well as key concepts such as 'social class' and 'race'.

Beck also questions the usefulness of central sociological concepts, such as class. Although he argues that it has become increasingly difficult to predict human behaviour, he is somewhat more cautious than the postmodernists. For Beck, social divisions remain significant, and social inequalities are seen as likely to increase within the new social order. In the 'risk society', individuals remain subject to many different constraints, and, while in some ways social life has changed, we can also identify powerful continuities.

Risks for youth

In many respects, the study of youth provides an ideal opportunity to examine the relevance of

Beck's work: if the social order has changed and if social structures have weakened, we would expect to find evidence of these changes among young people making transitions from school to work. On the surface, changes have occurred which lend support to Beck's theory: in modern Britain, young people's life experiences have changed quite significantly. These changes affect relationships with family and friends, experiences in education and the labour market, leisure and lifestyles and the ability to become established as independent young adults.

Many of these changes are a direct result of the restructuring of the labour market, an increased demand for educated workers, flexible specialisation in the workplace, and social policies which have extended the period in which young people remain dependent on their families. As a consequence of these changes, young people today have to negotiate a set of risks which were largely unknown to their parents: this is true, irrespective of social background or gender.

Moreover, as many of these changes have come about within a relatively short period of time, points of reference which previously helped smooth the processes have become obscure and young people may feel that their lives are characterised by risk and uncertainty. Yet, despite significant changes, we suggest that inequalities associated with class, gender and race have remained firmly entrenched and that young people's experiences remain highly differentiated.

Individualisation and risk

Although Beck challenges the continued relevance of class analysis for an understanding of the distribution of life chances, he is not suggesting that social inequalities disappear or weaken within late modernity. Indeed, Beck admits that within Western societies social inequalities display 'an amazing stability',[2] and suggests that empirical research is unlikely to uncover significant changes. However, while social inequality continues to exert a powerful hold over people's lives, it increasingly does so at the level of the individual rather than the group or class. Whereas people once clearly shared life styles and key experiences with other members of their social class, today these regularities are much less visible. In other words, in late modernity life experiences have become much more varied and differentiated. As a consequence, people find it difficult to identify common patterns, and major life events tend to be linked to individual actions rather than to factors like social class, gender or race: a process Beck refers to as 'individualisation'.

As a result of this process of individualisation, Beck suggests that in late modernity it is not always possible to predict lifestyles, political beliefs or opinions by using information about occupations or family backgrounds. Because individual behaviour and lifestyles can no longer be predicted through concepts like social class, Beck describes the new epoch as 'capitalism *without* classes'.[3] The workplace, which was once central to an understanding of classes, becomes less of an arena for conflicts, and ascribed social differences, such as gender and racial inequalities, come to assume a greater significance.

While structures of inequality remain deeply entrenched, one of the most significant features of late modernity is the growing disjuncture between objective and subjective dimensions of life. Although people's life chances remain highly structured, they increasingly seek solutions on an individual, rather than a collective basis. With a tendency for risks to be individualised, Beck argues that in late modernity people increasingly regard setbacks and crises as individual shortcomings, rather than as outcomes of processes which are beyond their personal control. Unemployment, for example, may be seen as a consequence of a lack of skills on the part of the individual, rather than as the result of a general decline in demand for labour stemming from a world economic recession. Similarly, problems faced by school-leavers in less advantaged areas may be seen as a reflection of their lack of qualifications rather than a consequence of material circumstances and the lack of compensatory mechanisms within the school.

The individualisation of risk may mean that situations which would once have led to a call for political action are now interpreted as something which can only be resolved on an individual level through personal action. As a consequence, Beck argues that an increase in social inequality may be associated with an intensification of individualisation as more people are placed in difficult situations which they interpret as being due, in part, to their own failures. In the 'risk society', individual subjectivity becomes an important force and is often more significant than class position.

Young people and the risk society

If there is empirical evidence to support the claim that we are currently witnessing a significant transformation of the social world, then we would expect to find the most advanced representation of these changes in the experiences of young people. There is, in fact, plenty of evidence to support the claim that young people's life contexts have seen significant changes over the last two decades: changes which are closely linked to the transformation of the youth labour market, which was part of a broader process of economic change in Western economies, involving a shift from manufacturing to service industries.

The risks and opportunities which face young people in the age of late modernity are very different from those which were negotiated by their parents. In the 1960s and 1970s experiences in the school and the labour market were clearly related to social class. Those from working-class families tended to leave school at the minimum leaving age with few qualifications and made mass transitions to factories and building sites.

In the 1990s the traditional links between the family, school and work seem to have weakened and young people embark on journeys into adulthood which involve a wide variety of routes, many of which appear to have uncertain outcomes. Because there are many more pathways to choose from, young people may develop the impression that their own routes are unique and that the risks they face are to be overcome by them as individuals rather than as members of a collectivity.

These changes in the experiences of young people are clearly visible in education and the labour market: patterns of schooling today are very different from what they were in the 1970s, and the youth labour market has changed in such a way that it would be almost unrecognisable to members of previous generations. Today few young people make smooth transitions from school to work: unemployment has become much more common, even among graduates, and it is normal for those who leave full-time education before the age of 18 to spend time on government training schemes.

Changes in education

Does Beck's work help us to understand changes in young people's experiences of education? It is certainly true that changes have been dramatic (see figure 37.1). In 1973/74, around a third of 16-year-old males (35 per cent) and less than four in ten females (37 per cent) participated in some form of full-time education in England. By 1993/94 more than seven in ten 16-year-olds (70 per cent of males and 76 per cent of females) participated in full-time education. Similarly, full-time participation among 17- and 18-year-olds more than doubled during this period.[4]

These changes have not been confined to those from privileged class backgrounds. Young people from all social classes tend to remain in full-time education until a later age and, whereas higher education was once the preserve of a small elite, today it is rapidly becoming a mass experience. In the 1990s, even those with relatively few qualifications at the age of 16 frequently decide to remain in full-time education, although in many depressed areas this is partly because there are so few credible alternatives in the labour market.

However, despite the far-reaching nature of changing educational experiences, there is little evidence that the relationship between social class and scholastic performance has weakened. Data

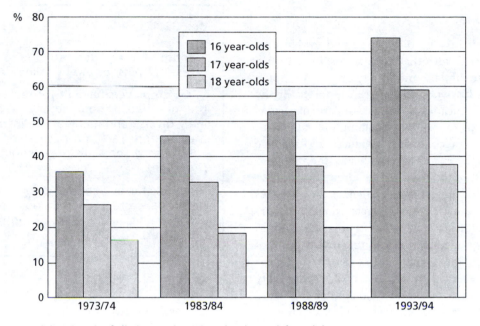

Figure 37.1 Participation in full-time education (male and female)

from a nationally representative youth cohort study has shown that among those who reached the age of 16, during the 1990/91 school year, staying-on rates varied from 84 per cent among young people with parents in professional, managerial and technical occupations to 51 per cent among those with parents working in semi- and unskilled and personal service occupations.[5]

Strong class-related differentials can also be found in relation to levels of attainment. In Scotland in 1991, for example, around four in ten young people from the lower working classes left school with a minimal level of qualifications, compared to just over one in ten from the professional and managerial classes. Similarly, almost half of the young people from the professional and managerial class achieved three or more Highers compared to less than one in five of those from the lower working class. Changing qualification profiles are shown by class and gender in figure 37.2, which shows quite clearly that despite an overall increase in the proportion of young people gaining three or more Highers, differentials remain strong.

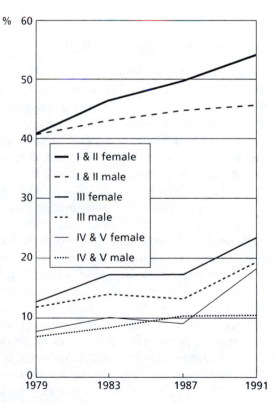

Figure 37.2 Young people in highest attainment band, by class

Educational change

Although it may be difficult to find evidence to support Beck's idea that class has lost its relevance in the age of late modernity, there are some aspects of his work which are supported in the context of educational change. In particular, educational experiences are becoming individualised, packaged as a consumer product. Performance 'league tables' encourage parents to 'shop around' for the best school for their children, and a growing range of educational credentials and courses may lead young people to treat educational services as products. In other words, changes in the delivery of education and the increased use of certification mean that young people and their parents are forced to take personal responsibility for educational outcomes. Consequently, failure is equated with poor choices or a lack of effort or talent rather than being seen as affected by social class.

Changes in the labour market

In the youth labour market as well as in education, changes have been dramatic. Whereas in 1977 more than seven in ten school-leavers had full-time jobs by the spring after leaving school, in 1991 less than three in ten had secured full-time jobs. Schemes have become central to an understanding of transitions from school to work, and young people now tend to follow much more complex routes into the labour market. These changes mean that the collectivised transitions which were once common among young people from working-class families have become much rarer as they begin to make transitions to a highly differentiated skill market as opposed to a relatively undifferentiated labour market.

The recession of the late 1970s and early 1980s was a turning point, marked by a radical change in the demand for youth labour. Prior to the late 1970s, there was a strong demand for relatively unqualified school-leavers in large industrial units: since the mid-1980s patterns of labour demand have changed significantly and opportunities for

> **Box 37.1**
>
> 'Choose life – get a job – get a career.' (*Trainspotting* by Irvine Welsh)
>
> 'Most employers haven't yet realised that the graduate labour supply is increasingly diverse and many of the institutions they ignore are producing graduates with exactly the skills they require.' (*The Guardian*)
>
> 'We look for evidence of good academic performance; a record of non-academic achievement; and a sense of motivation.' (Employer)

young workers are increasingly located in small work units. The demand for flexible specialisation and the increased use of part-time and temporary employment contracts have weakened collective employment experiences and can be associated with the process of individualisation and the sense of insecurity and risk identified by Beck.

However, despite significant changes in the labour market experiences of young people, risks continued to be distributed in a way which reflects social divisions characteristic of the 'traditional' order. In other words, it is still possible to predict labour market outcomes fairly accurately on the basis of social class and gender. At the same time, as a result of the diversity of routes between school and work, young people are faced with an increasing range of options which force them to engage with the likely consequences of their actions on a subjective level, In this sense, while labour market outcomes are best described in terms of continuity rather than change, young people often face these routes with a growing sense of unease and insecurity. Although transitional routes have remained highly stratified, these changes have again affected subjective orientations as the range of experiences encountered at this stage in the life cycle become much more individual.

Conclusion

The experiences of young people growing up in the late 1990s are quite different from those encountered by earlier generations. Life in late modernity involves subjective discomfort and uncertainty. Young people can struggle to establish adult identities, maintain coherent biographies and develop strategies to overcome various obstacles, but their life chances remain highly structured, with social class and gender being crucial to an understanding of experiences in a range of life contexts.

In our view, late modernity involves an essential continuity with the past: economic and cultural resources are still central to an understanding of differential life chances and experiences. The paradox of late modernity is that, although the collective foundations of social life have become more obscure, they continue to provide powerful frameworks which constrain young people's experiences and life chances.

While we reject the suggestion that traditional social divisions are becoming less powerful determinants of life chances, we accept Beck's conclu-

sion that one of the central characteristics of late modernity is a weakening of collective social identities. In our view the process of individualisation represents a subjective weakening of social bonds due to a growing diversity of life experiences. These changes are rejected in an individualisation of lifestyles and a convergence of class cultures which in turn make it more difficult to predict beliefs and opinions on using information on social class.

NOTES

1   D. Lyon, *Postmodernity* (Milton Keynes: Open University Press, 1994).
2   U. Beck, *Risk Society: Towards a New Modernity* (London: Sage, 1992), p. 91.
3   Ibid., p. 88.
4   A. Furlong and F. Cartmel, *Young People and Social Change: Individualization and Risk in Late Modernity* (Milton Keynes: Open University Press, 1997).
5   J. Payne, *Routes beyond Compulsory Schooling* (London: Employment Department, 1995).

38 Haves and Have-nots: How to Overcome the Digital Divide

The Economist

E-government is not just e-business on a larger scale. One of the most fundamental differences is that whereas businesses can, by and large, choose their customers, government cannot. The debate over the so-called 'digital divide' is like the ghost at the e-government feast. For e-government to succeed fully, the dream of Internet access for all has to become a reality.

Governments are well aware that large and expensive e-projects will command little support if only a privileged minority benefits. As David Agnew of the Toronto-based Governance in the Digital Economy Project, which is supported by eight big IT firms and 20 national and local governments, argues: 'If putting government online is just a way of reinforcing access for people who probably already have more opportunity to access government and decision-makers, then it hasn't really been much of an advance after all.'

When Arizona's Democrats held their state presidential primary online in March, it nearly did not happen – not because of security and authentication problems (although there were plenty of those), but because a pressure group called the Voting Integrity Project tried to have it banned. It almost persuaded a court that the vote would disenfranchise the state's minorities, so should be ruled illegal.

Raise the spectre of the digital divide with the technology vendors and e-government champions within the public sector, and their brows furrow with concern – but not for long. They are, after all, professional technology optimists. But they also genuinely believe that many of the barriers to near-universal Internet access are falling, at least in economically advanced countries (though it is worth remembering that half the world has never even made a telephone call). Survey after survey has found that the main barriers to access are the fear that it is too expensive, that computers are too complicated and that somehow the whole thing is not really relevant or useful. Those optimists argue that, one by one, each of those perfectly legitimate anxieties is being overcome.

What's the problem?

Too expensive? Internet-ready PCs can be bought for little more than $300 – less than the price of most televisions, a device that has found its way into 99 per cent of all American homes. Some Internet service providers (ISPs) are even giving PCs away in return for two or three years' subscription, and other firms offer free PCs to users who agree to be bombarded by advertisements while online. True, access fees and telephone call charges remain high in some countries, but unmetered local calls are spreading from America to Europe, and free ISPs are evolving a range of different business models.

Too complicated and unreliable? That will soon be fixed by the proliferation of non-PC devices

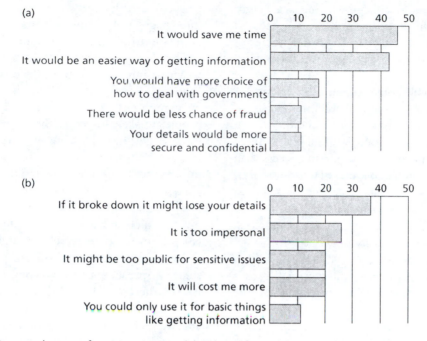

Figure 38.1 Pros and cons of e-government: (a) What, if anything, would be the benefits of being able to deal with government electronically? (b) What, if anything, would be the barriers to use of a government electronic delivery system?
Source: Performance and Innovation Unit, Cabinet Office/MORI, September 1998

which provide access to the web. Among them will be simple terminals that do nothing more than run a browser and take all their applications from the web. These will be found in places such as schools, community centres, libraries and anywhere else that needs a robust machine and has an 'always on' connection. An even simpler version is the kind of web kiosk with a touch-screen that is springing up in cities such as Singapore and Toronto.

Many people will be able to do as much business as they need over the Internet with inexpensive smart mobile phones, some of which will soon take the form of a wrist-watch that can be activated by speech rather than via a fiddly keypad. Many new mobile phones are already being loaded with WAP software and microbrowsers. Another way of getting online is by interactive digital television. Early services, such as BSkyB's Open in Britain, are still clunky, but the technology will improve, and the set-top box decoders will often come free.

The more extreme technology optimists, such as Adam Thierer of the conservative Heritage Foundation in Washington DC, say that the rapidly falling price of both computing power and bandwidth will in fact create a 'digital deluge', so any policies aimed at giving access to the 'information-poor' are quite unnecessary and may be counter-productive. It is a comforting view, but probably quite wrong.

The latest release of the US Department of Commerce's survey 'Falling Through the Net' paints a disturbing picture in which the digital divide between rich and poor, white and non-white, well-educated and under-schooled seems, if anything, to have widened significantly during the five years in which this information has been collected. Among the examples of the digital divide today, the survey found that:

- People with a college degree are eight times more likely to have a PC at home and 16 times more likely to have Internet access at home than those with an elementary school education.
- A high-income household in an urban area is 20 times more likely to have Internet access than a rural, low-income household.
- A child in a low-income white family is three times more likely to have Internet access than a child in a comparable black family, and four times more likely than if he were Hispanic.
- A wealthy household of Asian descent is 34 times more likely to have Internet access than a poor black household.
- A child in a two-parent white household is twice as likely to have Internet access as a child in a single-parent household. If the child is black, he is four times more likely to have Internet access than his single-parent counterpart.
- Disabled people are nearly three times less likely to have home access to the Internet than people without disabilities.

In other words, although Internet penetration has risen across all demographic groups, the digital divide remains only too real. It has also become a poignant proxy for almost every other kind of disadvantage and inequality in society.

Chalk and cheese

It would be hard to find a better real-life symbol for the digital divide than the gulf between Silicon Valley's leafy Palo Alto, home to dot.com millionaires, where the average house sells for nearly $700,000, and East Palo Alto, the desperate little town on the other side of Highway 101 that not long ago claimed America's highest murder rate. Palo Alto's website has 251 sections and is a paragon of e-government. Among many other things, it allows users to send forms to the planning department and search the city's library catalogue. During storms, it even provides live video footage of flood-prone San Francisquito Creek. East Palo Alto's site, by contrast, has only three pages, containing little more than outdated population figures and the address of City Hall.

The digital divide is not so much a question of access but of education. As Esther Dyson, an Internet pundit, puts it: 'You can put computers in community centres, but only the literate people are likely to go use them.' Simpler, cheaper ways of getting on to the web will help, as will content that seems relevant to those who shun the Internet today – after all, the mobile phone has conquered all social classes, thanks to its sheer usefulness and simplicity. But even with enlightened policies such as America's 'e-rate', which gives cut-price web access to schools and libraries, and the growing number of private–public partnerships to spread both technology and training in its use, there is a danger that the 'digital deluge' may reach only those parts where the grass is already green. The same people who have wired PCs today will collect all the fancy new web gadgets that are coming in, and the rest will continue to go without.

So what does this mean for e-government architects? First, as IBM's Todd Ramsey points out, they have to accept that some people, especially the elderly, will never want to deal with government – or indeed anyone else – online. That means some off-line channels will almost certainly have to be kept open for years after everything has moved on to the web. Second, they must find ways to allow even those diehards to benefit from the e-government transformation by improving the quality of the off-line channels and targeting them better. Not all the savings from electronic service delivery will be bankable.

Third, they need to think up incentives for those on the wrong side of the digital divide to take the leap. Government may be able to act as a catalyst in a way that the private sector cannot. What persuades most people to try the Internet is the promise that they will find something relevant to them. If the most convenient way of getting welfare benefits is online, a lot of people who had never thought of using the web will have a go.

Part 11

Poverty, Welfare and Social Exclusion

Like almost all other aspects of social life, poverty is being strongly influenced by globalization. So far, however, as Laura Buffoni points out in Reading 39, there has been little research on the connection between global influences and the experience of poverty. Buffoni interviewed a range of poorer people to investigate their experience of poverty against the background of global influences. She found that poorer people often are very well aware of wider global inequalities, which they compare to their own position. A variety of new forms of adaptation and coping have as a consequence emerged. William Julius Wilson looks in Reading 40 at the causes of the high rates of unemployment found in inner-city areas in the US. Many black people living in the inner city have never held a job. Such individuals, Wilson points out, are not counted in the employment statistics, because these statistics only concern individuals actively looking for work. The large majority of inner-city black unemployed people have simply given up actively searching for a job. High unemployment levels, Wilson maintains, have more serious consequences for neighbourhoods than poverty as such. Levels of crime and family breakdown tend to be high because people lack the status and involvements of an active work life. In inner-city families mothers have child-care responsibilities without much economic support and hence often become dependent on welfare payments. Men who are

long-term unemployed may become idle and shiftless. Lack of status and income from a job leads them to avoid domestic responsibilities too.

The welfare state – government-backed agencies that provide for social welfare through education, health care and social security – has its origins almost a century ago. Throughout most of the past century, until about the 1970s, welfare states in most industrial countries continued to expand. As the range of benefits paid out grew, however, the welfare system in many countries came under strain. Consider pensions, for example. People on average live far longer than they used to do. Many countries cannot afford the pension commitments they have set up. Over recent years it has been widely suggested that welfare provisions provided by government should be supplemented by those coming from the private sector. The contribution from Matthew Bishop in Reading 41 shows that adding in private resources is not without problems. It may simply be necessary to cut back upon the expectations that people have that benefits will automatically be provided for them whenever they are needed.

World economic inequalities today are very large. Such inequalities at the moment seem to be getting worse. As Martin Dickson shows in Reading 42, the average earnings of individuals in the US is over seventy times higher than that of citizens of the poorest countries in the world. Some less developed countries have improved their relative position over the past three decades or so – most notably the Asian 'tigers', such as Singapore, Taiwan or Hong Kong. However, on average the poorest countries in the world have got even poorer in relative terms over that period. We have a long way to go indeed if we are to create a world where wealth is shared out fairly evenly across nations.

39 Rethinking Poverty in Globalized Conditions

Laura Buffoni

The macro and the micro level

Poverty, with its local manifestations and interplay of global, regional (national) and local causes, can be considered as one of the phenomena in which the 'global' meets the 'local'. In this [article] it will be argued that:

1 polarization occurring at global (macro) level has dramatically increased in the last decades confirming the image of a 'North/South' divide, although the 'poles' might be scattered all over the globe;

2 because of the influence of globalization processes on individuals' everyday lives (defined as 'microglobalization'), poverty in 'affluent' societies has involved various ways of adaptation and forms of social coping, producing more complex patterns in the way poverty is perceived and experienced.

The focus [. . .] will be upon the latter aspect. By looking at people's life histories and at their subjective perception of poverty we can collect insights into the processes shaping the lives of individuals. I define poverty as the lack of material and cultural resources which restrict one's ability to socialize and, in a dynamic sense, as a 'trajectory' of progressive decline and of reduced availability of options in everyday life. How do these features change under globalized conditions? By collecting individuals' reflections and evaluations on poverty, I have attempted to gain information on the way and the extent to which external events and phenomena of social change, in this case microglobalization, have affected in one way or another (positively or negatively), the well-being of people and their access to material and cultural resources.

The discourse on 'consumption' and access to various lifestyles has a clear part to play in research on poverty. As globalization processes influence people's everyday lives in various ways, I think it is necessary to look beyond stereotypical images of the poor and not take for granted seemingly widespread patterns of consumption. Globalization has contributed to the increase of social polarization, but at the same time it has transformed class structures. Globalization has fractured consumption groups, on the one hand, creating new needs, on the other, cutting across traditional barriers of non-access. If globalization has an impact on stratification systems, it might well distort the manifestations of poverty and, in general, of access to resources: poverty in a global city or under 'globalized conditions' might be experienced by people who are in fact not marginalized or excluded and are still able to profit from and participate in various activities, thus alleviating the burden of poverty. On the other hand new forms of exclusion and marginalization could arise for those who do not seem to belong to the social category of the poor. The concepts of capability and functioning, as discussed by A. Sen, will be central to my analysis of poverty under globalized conditions, since they incorporate the notions of rights, quality of life and fulfilment, and the notion of freedom.[1]

Global economic trends have consequences on national economies and on people's well-being at local level. The actual regime of 'flexible accumulation', characterized by liberalization and privatization at global level, influences local economics and national welfare institutions. Furthermore the practice of 'global sourcing' pursued by transnational companies and the accelerated technological changes in production have an impact on the localization of production and on the international division of labour, thus creating areas of extreme labour fragility in many traditionally industrialized areas. But my intention here is to consider the issue from a different perspective.

I want to look at the way globalization has an impact on everyday life through its local manifestations. Globalization processes

1   inform people's values (globalism);
2   transform and/or increase access to images, information and commodities (globality);
3   influence people's mobility and their ability to maintain social relations across the globe (time/space compression); and
4   transform the interplay between local and global forces, thus changing the patterns of local communities.

It is from this perspective, that I will consider qualitative changes in the experience and perception of poverty in a specific locality of the world: London.

The global city: going beyond the dual city

Cities represent an ideal site for observing processes occurring within the wider society, especially changes in the relationship between people and their environment and among people themselves.

Through the media, the message becomes pervasive: credit cards, mobile phones, use of computer technology and leisure activities (in particular travelling) are given an image of familiarity, affordability and prestige, and at the same time they are presented almost as indispensable. But if it is true that many of these services become increasingly less expensive, the lack of capabilities may become more and more stigmatizing, even if they are based on built-up needs and not on necessities.

Globalization and the transition to an 'extended relativity'

Given the complex and heterogeneous nature of globalization processes, a definition of poverty under such circumstances has necessarily to be relative, although the 'boundaries' of this relativity are difficult to trace because they are rapidly shifting and not necessarily linked to a spatial dimension. A notion of poverty based on nationally consumed commodities or on a nationally defined poverty line does not represent a standard definition of who is poor any more. An increasing number of individuals know about and relate to poverty in different parts of the world, either through the media or personal experience. 'Global awareness' contributes to relating oneself to a wider social space.

Awareness about processes going on in the world (globalism) and knowledge about poverty worldwide might change individuals' perceptions of their own and others' poverty. An 'extended relativity' can be induced by the media, by travelling, by migrating, by relating to people coming from or living in various parts of the world. Furthermore, the co-existence of ethnic and cultural minorities within a dominant culture makes the notion of relative poverty more complex. Originally from 'poor' countries where they might have been relatively well-off, 'newcomers' may feel particularly marginalized and dispossessed in the 'new', host community. But the sense of loss and deprivation might be mitigated if a community of people with the same cultural origins and lifestyle is (re)created in the host country, and a stratification system (re)produced within the community itself.

On the other hand, time–space compression, enabling social relationships to be maintained at a distance, may reduce felt exclusion and the perception of social deprivation. Individuals may embark on new coping strategies and display enhanced capabilities through worldwide networking.

Poverty should be considered in terms of conditions of risk

The notion of risk is related to a condition of isolation and social exclusion. People who experience social isolation lack a 'safety net' in terms of adequate social and economic support networks, and they are therefore requested to display more flexible capabilities. When living in such a condition individuals find themselves just 'at risk of poverty' since any single negative event could result into a 'slipping' into a condition of poverty. In other words, an additional loss of resources could result in reduced possibilities of converting capabilities into useful functionings.

The interviews reported below represent examples of people who have a direct experience of poverty in the present or had it in the past, or people who, more than others, are at risk of poverty. For them, one single negative event or a minimal reduction of capabilities may result in a sudden, significant reduction of the quality of life and/or exclusion from social relations.

Sharing the world city: the use of space and the transcendence of boundaries

The variety of opportunities, both in terms of magnitude and range of activities, offered by the global city can be used in different ways by different actors, but still in some cases represents a viable resource for those who are worse-off. Free exhibitions can become a warm place for rough sleepers. Matinées or films on particular days of the week are accessible cultural/free-time resources for those living on income support or other forms of social assistance. International events like the Notting Hill Carnival can represent one important option of the global city, which gives the opportunity to participate in community life and express one's creativity, even if lacking material resources. So the global city, with its 'concessionary' opportunities and commodified leisure activities, contributes to the construction of a complex web of social activities, or 'sociospheres', which, though spatially very close, do not come in direct confrontation and therefore mask profound conditions of inequality.

The idea of the 'transcendence of boundaries' as manifested in the global city, with poverty and wealth co-existing side by side, can help us to relate the barriers of access and non-access to a spatial dimension. As we mentioned before, the 'transcendence' of boundaries implies the encounter of both poverty and wealth in the same locale, the global city. The same opportunities and areas are used at different times and/or with different aims, creating a system of 'shifting' purposes throughout the day or the week, but it is this difference in purpose and timing which reflects the uneven access to resources. Inhabiting the same locale makes it necessary for the poor and the better-off to negotiate the use of space. Space is negotiated in terms of its territorial organization (using the same locality for different purposes) and sequential order (inhabiting the same place at different times).

Spheres of access and non-access are redefined and eventually less intelligible, but not eliminated, and can be associated with the idea of 'time–space stratification': 'Time–space social stratification is the frame within which inequalities of access to resources and life chances are contained today which are more acute than any which prevailed during the period of class-based industrial society.'

Sociospheres of 'poverty' or 'wealth' can be (re)produced wherever people find themselves (re)located. In this sense the analysis of poverty in a global city is less dependent on the actual local settings, since spaces (and times) of the city are constantly negotiated and 'discovered' in terms of opportunities and resources.

Speaking poverty: meanings and perceptions of poverty in the world city

The interviews, carried out across London, present a variety of situations and conditions of people living 'at risk of poverty' (as previously discussed), or of people who, directly or indirectly, have and/or have had an experience of poverty. They present different types of social coping and various ways of experiencing unemployment, underemployment and homelessness. The social space of non-work is lived in ways that go beyond stereotypical images of impoverished worklessness. I selected these interviews to show active modes by which individuals make use of the resources available in their social worlds, and how they display a variety of capabilities which are converted in important functionings (participating in one's ethnic community activities, doing volunteer work, maintaining social relationships). They also show how perceptions of individuals' relative poverty might be constructed.

Apart from John, an old-age pensioner, and Bill, who is in daily interaction with other members of his family living in the area, the interviewees do not express a particular attachment to the specific locality they inhabit. Their indifference may also be described as 'disaffiliation': poverty and the everyday struggle for existence lead to a relative autonomy from a specific locale and to a detachment from the external world, if the locality itself cannot be converted into useful resources because of lack of money or other capabilities (a stable job, a fixed address). The local dimension can become relevant only if it offers opportunities of participation, for example a community activity involving members of the same ethnic group or other services (free meals, charity shops, cheap supermarkets). Toni, for example, has a particular relationship to Notting Hill, but he lives in a different area which he uses as a place from which to base his activities. For those who are worse-off and have been homeless or at risk of homelessness, a place to live, whether a bedsit, a hostel or a council house, is not a free choice. To the extent that choices on housing are taken by the 'administration of poverty' (social services or local council) poor people, sometimes only because they are unemployed, lose the ability to 'make territoriality', since decisions about their accommodation and spatial mobility in the city are taken outside of their sphere of control and without any possibility for negotiation.

Trained as a fishmonger in Hastings, Matthew, who is 30, came to London because he could not find a job on the coast, but lonely and unemployed he rapidly found himself on the street. The vicious circle of homelessness–unemployment–homelessness has been interrupted by Matthew since he started working for the *Big Issue*. He is now living in a council house in south-west London with no telephone and no TV, looking forward to a brighter future and considering himself among the lucky ones, since he feels he is relatively better off, both compared to people around him and relatively to people living in other parts of the world. In describing his own condition of poverty Matthew uses the 'traditional' relativity concept, and also refers to the contribution participation in social relationships can make to one's well-being:

I wouldn't class myself as rich. Well, I wouldn't say I am poor, poor. It is not like when you haven't got a pound in your pocket or poor when you are hungry and you haven't got nothing to buy food with. That is poverty. . . . But I have good food, I have a social life, I am not *that* poor, but I *am* poor. Compared to the normal, to the average, I am in the lower half, the lowest part. But if you have got friends and you have got no money you can always lend a fiver here and there. . . . Compared to the Third World, we are well-off countries, like America, England.

The image of the 'dual city' is recalled in Matthew's words, since the city is on the one hand a site of desolation and loneliness:

In these big cities everyone is for themselves, like America or here, you will always find people on the streets. I think if you go to the countryside, you won't find anything like that over there. Totally different people, kind to each other. Whereas in London it is such a big city and everyone is for themselves. They don't care about anybody else.

On the other hand, the city is a place for opportunities, where ideas from all over the world are collected, and where there is room for hope in a better future:

I can see the world definitely getting better. . . . You know, the *Big Issue* to me is a sensational idea. I mean, three years ago a homeless person never had the opportunity to get involved with a company like this . . . but for me . . . I was around on the streets and in hostels for nearly one year before I knew about the *Big Issue*. And the moment I found out about it I said: 'Yeah! it's a good idea'. I think that homelessness is getting better from this. I think a lot more people are paying attention. In America it's really good. We got the idea from America. It is sold in twelve different states over there. It is called *Streetwise, Streettalk* . . .

The idea of the *Big Issue* – and of street magazines in general – comes from the United States and is now to be found in various countries, adapted to local realities. It permits the creation of new forms of social coping for homeless and ex-homeless people, who use the magazine as a (temporary) way of access to material resources, whilst possibly planning other strategies and building up capabilities.

In some vendors' opinion the *Big Issue* must necessarily be a temporary experience, since they feel their image and condition of homelessness has been exploited, without any reward in terms of participating actively in the magazine itself. Denouncing a situation in which homeless people do all the distributive work and 'the staff' only are in charge of the production of the magazine, Joseph is very disillusioned and feels exploited by people who 'in reality do not care about the homeless', 'do their own business' and 'only for money'. None the less he uses the magazine as an easy way for making good money in his 'position' in Soho and relates to distant conditions of poverty, displaying a deep global (class?) consciousness. The slogan 'think globally, act locally', formulated some decades ago and still capturing the imagination of people across the globe, pervades Joseph's words, suggesting the possible creation of a 'world poverty movement' and the need for making people aware of conditions of poverty at the global level through acting locally:

I see a problem in our country: we must help ourselves before we help others. It's easier for me to see the people who are in front of me who are suffering, rather than people who are in another country suffering. I know they are there, I know they are suffering, but I can't reach out to them, if I can't reach out towards who is in front of me first. . . . Our commune at the moment acts locally. It is very smallsighted, because we must build up ourselves first. When we have become older, stronger, wiser and bigger, when we are ready, then we will reach out to other sites of the world. Hopefully, maybe, we can take children off the streets in Brazil where they are killed by despots and give them a holiday over in this country. . . . If we can help the homeless from other sites of the world to gather with the homeless of this country, then, maybe, those children together will have a better way of learning about each other than I have had in learning about others.

Toni, who came to London as a child, remembers his days in Trinidad and his direct experience of living in poverty and in 'hardship'. Now in his 40s, Toni is a freelance photographer, but most of his time and energy are spent working for the Notting Hill Carnival. Toni now has his own band and his council house in Acton has become more a workshop for the preparation of costumes than a home. The Carnival, as an opportunity for interaction between various cultures offered by the global city, gives Toni the opportunity to participate in the activities of the Trinidadian community and to fulfil his creativity. He distances himself from the hectic and unbearable rhythms of the city and from a commodified lifestyle:

People might see that as being laid-back. I remember my father jumping around and I mean . . . he got a stroke when he was in his 50s, because of the stress and all that. . . . You know, when I see people around me running and killing themselves on material things and unnecessary things, I just look at them . . . and prefer the way I am.

The concern about contemporary patterns of consumption is also mentioned by John, a 74-year-old pensioner who was in the building trade for most of his fifty-year-long working life. He is now retired but still works 'for friends'. John receives help from the council in order to pay the rent, but as he says 'that is the only thing I claimed in my life. I was never unemployed':

I've got the feeling that [despite] the commodities that people have in these days such as vacuum cleaners, fridges, washing machines – these 'luxuries of life' as I call them – living was better [in the old days] and people were more friendly.

John feels that he lives in an area where the sense of community has disappeared, although he has contacts with a few neighbours. His most important social relations are with his son and his son's family and with the friends in the local stamp club. The future of the stamp club has become a source of concern since 'the rents of the rooms are so high, and we had to close up'.

Living on a basic pension John finds various essential goods expensive, and considers himself a victim of the cuts in welfare spending. According to John, housing is the biggest problem. Food and clothing are also expensive but 'you look around' and 'find something cheaply'. The combination of age and low income limits John's access to relevant functionings in terms of social activities since it would be 'a bit too expensive if you went out for a meal'.

The older ones, they need a lot of heating. . . . They need more heat and clothes and things like that. . . . They cut out all this help one used to have with spectacles, dentures, things like that. You have to be on social security before you get just a little bit off. . . . Health is a problem with all these hospitals shutting down, kicking old people out. I think they want us to die so that they don't have to pay the pensions any more.

John knows about the outer world through the media which contribute to the building up of his own awareness and knowledge about the wider world: 'poverty is all over the place . . . also in wonderful America, but worse-off places are Haiti, China and India'. He seldom uses his bank account and has never had a credit card:

I won't touch a credit card. You get into debt too quickly. They keep sending them through and I keep cutting them up and throwing them away. I have heard of too many people who have gone into trouble. There are a few things I pay by cheque, like rent, but all the others I pay cash.

Elderly people seem really to be in the worst-off category, according to the perceptions of most interviewees. Julie, who is in her 70s and now living on her nurse's pension, talks of 'elderly people living on basic pensions':

I don't know how they can exist. Although social services gives free medicines, if you are just over you have to pay for a lot of things. Many people are too proud to ask for help and sometimes filling the forms and all the paraphernalia can be difficult and people feel they lose their dignity.

Even when dealing with the bureaucracy of social assistance, individuals need specific capabilities. In this sense elderly people are more disadvantaged, since capabilities belonging to the past – filling in forms, reading and writing a certain (bureaucratic) language, going to various offices – have to be recycled, and a possible failure in doing this may result in a sense of loss of dignity and self-confidence.

Julie's definition of (other's) poverty is absolute: 'poverty is not having enough to eat', but this poverty is not a far away one, it is near and experienced. Subsistence poverty, defined in terms of physical well-being, has not disappeared in affluent societies for those who live on a basic pension. But the problem is not only of maintaining one's well-being and efficiency, but a question of pride and dignity:

Everybody should have at least a little bit of good nourishment, but everything is so expensive. You can do without meat and eat other proteins, but fish is important. Eggs and butter are expensive. Basic things like clothes, bedlinen are so expensive. Maybe to spend £40 for clothes is not so much for someone who has a salary, but it is too much for someone living on a pension. Poverty is also about pride. Poverty is degrading.

As a major manifestation of global processes of social change, international migrations have generated a massive movement of people around the world, and have created new ways of assessing personal and others' well-being. Denzel, a former environmental officer who came from Mali nine years ago, has worked as a cleaner, petrol station attendant and mini-cab driver since his arrival in

London. Now doing a PhD, Denzel describes the process of globalization in terms of the diffusion of Western culture across Third World countries through the media and particularly education. The creation of new needs transforms the perception of well-being, and consequently of relative poverty.

The middle class in poor countries whose aspirations are blocked feels cheated. Poverty has to be considered relatively to the economic standards of the society you live in. But through education and communication the middle class has been exposed to different standards. So, although relatively to their own society they are not poor, their aspirations are blocked, since they cannot achieve the higher living standards they well know.

On the other hand, the lack of information and comparative data, making people relate only to their own reality, can have – according to Denzel – its advantages: 'the rural poor do not aspire to a different way of life; they do not feel cheated'. However, global forces inevitably expose people all over the world to cultural, economic and social processes which influence their lives, thus in some cases putting at risk their physical and cultural well-being, as Denzel says:

Communications and easy financial flows provoke the impoverishment of people because resources are calculated in terms of Western resources, US dollars. But, if I am a . . . tribesman why can't my richness be valued in terms of my resources, cattle and crops, rather than in US dollars?

Denzel supports quite a few people at home in Mali by regularly sending money to members of his family. He keeps contact by writing and sometimes by telephone if it is an urgent matter. For the time being he has not been back to Mali but his sister has come over to London.

Bill's 'living the world city' contrasts with the world of Joseph (see above) who lives in a commune for ex-homeless people, temporarily without telephone and electricity. Bill is a 40-year-old long-term unemployed person living in Elephant and Castle. He used to work in a quango but lost his job 'for political reasons', and got blacklisted from the Civil Service. He managed to get another job, but after a few months he injured his back badly and has not worked since. After nine years of invalidity pension, he was recently judged fit to work by a doctor, and is now back on income support (£45 a week). He lives in a Church Commission flat with his girlfriend who will soon have a baby. In the last nine years Bill has been engaged in volunteer jobs in the social welfare sector in the council estate next to his house. He also edits the journal of a sports association from a Macintosh computer which he has at home. With a lot of free time he 'reads all the time', goes to the library, free exhibitions and to the cinema sometimes on Monday when the price is £2, thus enjoying as much as he can the opportunities offered by the global city.

NOTE

1   Amartya Sen, 'Se in benessere non è il nostro bene', *Sole 24 Ore*, 296, suppl. (1990), p. 23.

40 When Work Disappears: New Implications for Race and Urban Poverty in the Global Economy

William Julius Wilson

[. . .]

Inner-city jobless poverty

There is a new poverty in American metropolises that has consequences for a range of issues relating to the quality of life in urban areas, including race relations. By the 'new urban poverty,' I mean poor, segregated neighbourhoods in which a majority of individual adults are either unemployed or have dropped out or never been a part of the labour force. This jobless poverty today stands in sharp contrast to previous periods. In 1950 a substantial portion of the urban black population in the United States was poor but they were working. Urban poverty was quite extensive but people held jobs. However, as we entered the 1990s most poor adults were not working in a typical week in the ghetto neighbourhoods of America's larger cities. For example, in 1950 a significant majority of adults held jobs in a typical week in the three neighbourhoods that represent the historic core of the Black Belt in the city of Chicago – Douglas, Grand Boulevard and Washington Park – the three neighbourhoods of Chicago that received the bulk of black migrants from the South in the early to mid-twentieth century. But by 1990 only four in ten in Douglas worked in a typical week, one in three in Washington Park, and one in four in Grand Boulevard. In 1950, 69 per cent of all males aged fourteen and over who lived in these three neighbourhoods worked in a typical week, and in 1960, 64 per cent of this group were so employed. However, by 1990 only 37 per cent of all males aged sixteen and over held jobs in a typical week in these three neighbourhoods.

The disappearance of work has adversely affected not only individuals and families, but the social life of neighbourhoods as well. Inner-city joblessness in America is a severe problem that is often overlooked or obscured when the focus is mainly on poverty and its consequences. Despite increases in the concentration of poverty since 1970, inner cities in the United States have always featured high levels of poverty, but the levels of inner-city joblessness reached during the first half of the 1990s was unprecedented.

I should note that when I speak of 'joblessness' I am not solely referring to official unemployment. The unemployment rate, as measured in the United States, represents only the percentage of workers in the *official* labour force, that is, those who are *actively* looking for work. It does not include those who are outside or have dropped out of the labour market, including the nearly six million males aged twenty-five to sixty who appeared in the census statistics but were not recorded in the labour market statistics in 1990.

These uncounted males in the labour market are disproportionately represented in the inner-city ghettos. Accordingly, in my book, *When Work Disappears*, I use a more appropriate measure of joblessness that takes into account both official unemployment and non-labour-force participation. That measure is the employment-to-population ratio, which corresponds to the percentage of adults aged sixteen and older who are working. Using the employment-to-population ratio we find, for example, that in 1990 only one in three adults aged sixteen and older held a job in the ghetto poverty areas of Chicago, areas with poverty rates of at least 40 per cent and that represent roughly 425,000 men, women and children. And in the ghetto census tracts of the nation's 100 largest cities for every ten adults who did not hold a job in a typical week in 1990 there were only six employed persons.

The consequences of high neighbourhood joblessness are more devastating than those of high neighbourhood poverty. A neighbourhood in which people are poor, but employed, is very different from a neighbourhood in which people are poor and jobless. In *When Work Disappears* I attempt to show that many of today's problems in America's inner-city ghetto neighbourhoods – crime, family dissolution, welfare, low levels of social organization and so on – are in major measures related to the disappearance of work.

It should be clear that when I speak of the disappearance of work, I am referring to the declining involvement in or lack of attachment to the formal labour market. It could be argued that in the general sense of the term 'joblessness' does not necessarily mean 'non-work.' In other words, to be officially unemployed or officially outside the labour market does not mean that one is totally removed from all forms of work activity. Many people who are officially jobless are none the less involved in informal kinds of work activity, ranging from unpaid housework to work in the informal or illegal economies that draw income.

Housework is work; baby-sitting is work; even drug dealing is work. However, what contrasts work in the formal economy with work activity in the informal and illegal economies is that work in the formal economy is characterized by, indeed calls for, greater regularity and consistency in schedules and hours. Work schedules and hours are formalized. The demands for discipline are greater. It is true that some work activities outside the formal economy also call for discipline and regular schedules. Several studies reveal that the social organization of the drug industry in the United States is driven by discipline and a work ethic, however perverse. However, as a general rule, work in the informal and illegal economics is far less governed by norms or expectations that place a premium on discipline and regularity. For all these reasons, when I speak of the disappearance of work, I mean work in the formal economy, work that provides a framework for daily behaviour because of the discipline, regularity and stability that it imposes.

In the absence of regular employment, a person lacks not only a place in which to work and the receipt of regular income but also a coherent organization of the present: that is, a system of concrete expectations and goals. Regular employment provides the anchor for the spatial and temporal aspects of daily life. It determines where you are going to be and when you are going to be there. In the absence of regular employment, life, including family life, becomes less coherent. Persistent unemployment and irregular employment hinder rational planning in daily life, a necessary condition of adaptation to an industrial economy.

Thus, a youngster who grows up in a family with a steady breadwinner and in a neighbourhood in which most of the adults are employed will tend to develop some of the disciplined habits associated with stable or steady employment – habits that are reflected in the behaviour of his or her parents and of other neighbourhood adults. These might include attachment to a routine, a recognition of the hierarchy found in most work situations, a sense of personal efficacy attained through the routine management of financial affairs, endorsement of a system of personal and material rewards associated with dependability and responsibility, and so on. Accordingly, when this youngster enters the labour market, he or she has a distinct advantage over the youngsters who grow up in households without a steady breadwinner and in neighbourhoods that are not organized around work; in other words, a milieu in which one is more exposed to the less disciplined habits associated with casual or infrequent work.

With the sharp recent rise of lone-parent families in the United States, black children who live in inner-city ghetto households are less likely to be socialized in a work environment for two main reasons. Their mothers, saddled with child-care responsibilities, can prevent a slide deeper into poverty by accepting welfare. Their fathers, removed from family responsibilities and obligations, are more likely to become idle as a response to restricted employment opportunities, which further weakens their influence in the household and attenuates their contact with the family. In short, the social and cultural responses to limiting constraints and changing norms are reflected in the organization of family life and patterns of family formation; there they have implications for labour force attachment as well.

Explanations of the growth of inner-city jobless poverty

What accounts for the much higher proportion of jobless adults in America's inner cities since the mid-twentieth century? An easy explanation would be racial segregation. However, a race-specific argument is not sufficient to explain recent changes in such neighbourhoods. After all, the historical black belt neighbourhoods that I have just discussed were *as segregated by skin colour in 1950* as they are today, yet the level of employment was much higher then. One has to account for the ways in which racial segregation interacts with other changes in society to produce the recent escalating rates of neighbourhood joblessness. Several factors stand out.

The disappearance of work in many inner-city neighbourhoods is in part related to the nation-wide decline in the fortunes of low-skilled workers. The sharp decline in the relative demand for unskilled labour has had a more adverse effect on blacks than on whites in the United States because a substantially larger proportion of African Americans are unskilled. Although the number of skilled blacks (including managers, professionals and technicians) has increased sharply in the last several years, the proportion of those who are unskilled remains large, because the black population, burdened by cumulative experiences of racial restrictions, was overwhelmingly unskilled just several decades ago.

The factors involved in the decreased relative demand for unskilled labour include the computer revolution (that is, the spread of new technologies that displaced low-skilled workers and rewarded the more highly trained), the rapid growth in college enrolment that increased the supply and reduced the relative cost of skilled labour, and the growing internationalization of economic activity, including trade liberalization policies which reduced the price of imports and raised the output of export industries. Whereas the increased output of export industries aids skilled workers, simply because skilled workers are heavily represented in export industries, increasing imports, especially those from developing countries that compete with labour-intensive industries (for example, apparel, textile, toy, footwear and some manufacturing industries) hurt unskilled labour, and therefore would have significant negative implications for American black workers. For example, 40 per cent of the workforce in the apparel industry is African American.

But, inner-city workers in the United States face an additional problem: the growing suburbanization of jobs. Most ghetto residents cannot afford an automobile and therefore have to rely on public transit systems that make the connection between inner-city neighbourhoods and suburban job locations difficult and time consuming. Although studies based on data collected before 1970 showed no consistent or convincing effects on black employment as a consequence of this spatial mismatch, the employment of inner-city blacks relative to suburban blacks has clearly deteriorated since then. Recent research, conducted mainly by urban and labour economists, strongly shows that the decentralization of employment is continuing and that employment in manufacturing, most of which is already suburbanized, has decreased in central cities, particularly in the Northeast and Midwest.

As pointed out in *When Work Disappears*, blacks living in central cities have less access to employment, as measured by the ratio of jobs to people and the average travel time to and from work, than do central-city whites. Moreover, unlike most other groups of workers across the urban/suburban divide, less educated central-city blacks receive lower wages than suburban blacks who have similar levels of education. And the decline in earnings of central-city blacks is related to the decentralization of employment, that is, the movement of jobs from the cities to the suburbs, in metropolitan areas.

Although the relative importance of the different underlying causes in the growing jobs problems of the less-skilled, including those in the inner city, continue to be debated, there is little disagreement about the underlying trends. They are unlikely to reverse themselves. In short, over a sustained period the labour market in the United States has twisted against disadvantaged workers – those with limited skills or education and/or from poor families and neighbourhoods – and therefore greatly diminished their actual and potential earnings.

Changes in the class, racial and demographic composition of inner-city neighbourhoods have also contributed to the high percentage of jobless adults in these neighbourhoods. Because of the steady outmigration of more advantaged families, the proportion of non-poor families and prime-age working adults has decreased sharply in the typical inner-city ghetto since 1970. In the face of increasing and prolonged joblessness, the declining proportion of non-poor families and the overall depopulation have made it increasingly more difficult to sustain basic neighbourhood institutions or to achieve adequate levels of social organization. The declining presence of working- and middle-class blacks has also deprived ghetto neighbourhoods of key resources, including structural resources, such as residents with income to sustain neighbourhood services, and cultural resources, such as conventional role models for neighbourhood children.

On the basis of our research in Chicago, it appears that what many high-jobless neighbourhoods have in common is a relatively high degree of social integration (high levels of local neighbouring while being relatively isolated from contacts in the broader mainstream society) and low levels of informal social control (feelings that they have little control over their immediate environment, including the environment's negative influences on their children). In such areas, not only are children at risk because of the lack of informal social controls, they are also disadvantaged because the social interaction among neighbours tends to be confined to those whose skills, styles, orientations and habits are not as conducive to promoting positive social outcomes (academic success, pro-social behaviour, employment in the formal labour market, etc.) as are those in more stable neighbourhoods. Although the close interaction among neighbours in such areas may be useful in devising strategies, disseminating information and developing styles of behaviour that are helpful in a ghetto milieu (teaching children to avoid eye-to-eye contact with strangers and to develop a tough demeanour in the public sphere for self-protection), they may be less effective in promoting the welfare of children in the society at large.

Despite being socially integrated, the residents in Chicago's ghetto neighbourhoods share a feeling that they have little informal social control over the children in their environment. A primary reason is the absence of a strong organizational capacity or an institutional resource base that would provide an extra layer of social organization in their neighbourhoods. It is easier for parents to control the behaviour of the children in their neighbourhoods when a strong institutional resource base exists and when the links between community institutions such as churches, schools, political organizations, businesses and civic clubs are strong or secure. The higher the density and stability of formal organizations, the less illicit activities such as drug trafficking, crime, prostitution, and the formation of gangs can take root in the neighbourhood.

A weak institutional resource base is what distinguishes high jobless inner-city neighbourhoods from stable middle-class and working-class areas. As one resident of a high-jobless neighbourhood on the South Side of Chicago put it,

Our children, you know, seems to be more at risk than any other children there is, because there's no library for them to go to. There's not a center they can go to, there's no field house that they can go into. There's nothing. There's nothing at all.

Parents in high-jobless neighbourhoods have a much more difficult task of controlling the behaviour of their adolescents, of preventing them from getting involved in activities detrimental to pro-social development. Given the lack of organizational capacity and a weak institutional base, some parents choose to protect their children by isolating them from activities in the neighbourhood, including the avoidance of contact and interaction with neighbourhood families. Wherever possible, and often with great difficulty when one considers the problems of transportation and limited financial resources, they attempt to establish contacts and cultivate relations with individuals, families and institutions outside the neighbourhood, such as church groups, schools and community recreation programmes.

It is just as indefensible to treat inner-city residents as super heroes who overcome racist oppression as it is to view them as helpless victims. We should, however, appreciate the range of choices, including choices representing cultural influences, that are available to inner-city residents who live under constraints that most people in the larger society do not experience.

[. . .]

41 Privatising Peace of Mind

Matthew Bishop

Will I have enough to live on when I retire? Will I get proper health care when I am sick, especially in old age? If I lose my job or become unable to work, will I end up in poverty or dependent on charity? These are big questions for everyone, and across the world they are being asked with growing apprehension.

Ever since 1889, when Otto von Bismarck, Prussia's 'Iron Chancellor', introduced the first state pension, people have increasingly looked to government to provide retirement income, health care and protection against poverty – which together are broadly called 'social insurance'. Britain got its first state pension in 1908, and its state-run National Health Service in 1948.

America's Social Security (the name for its state pension) was a product of the New Deal in the 1930s.

Some countries took this further than others. Sweden went to the interventionist extreme, and America to the laissez-faire opposite. Even so, there are remarkable similarities. Throughout the OECD, gross public spending on social insurance eats up half of total government budgets, and accounts for between a sixth and a third of GDP (see figure 41.1). But there is now a widespread sense that this system – dubbed the 'welfare state' in most countries (except America, where welfare is narrowly defined as aid to the poor) – is in crisis.

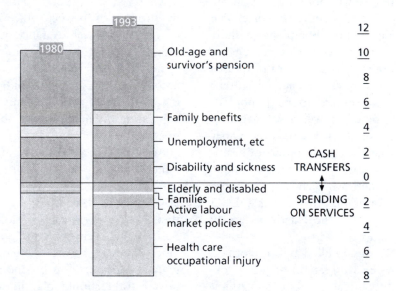

Figure 41.1 The mighty welfare state: OECD average transfers and spending as percentage of GDP

Problems, problems

So far, in rich countries, policymakers have been notably reluctant to reconsider from first principles what role the state should play in pensions, health care and the rest. (Some poorer countries, out of sheer necessity, have already had to be more adventurous.) Yet the time is ripe for a fundamental rethink. Today's systems of social insurance were devised for yesterday's world. When Bismarck invented the state pension, with a retirement age of 65, average life expectancy was 45. Now, in the OECD, it is 76 and rising – yet state pensions can still be claimed at 65 or even less.

When most welfare states were created, a large proportion of their population was poor. Not so today. In developed countries, most working adults pay tax, and most taxpayers will see some of their money redistributed to people less well-off than themselves. Moreover, social insurance in its present form was designed for a world in which men went out to work, women stayed at home and few people got divorced. Jobs were plentiful, and unemployment carried a strong social stigma.

The problems that have sapped public confidence in social insurance will not go away; on the contrary, they are about to get a lot worse. The so-called 'demographic time-bomb' has a short fuse. Populations in rich countries are ageing fast as the baby-boomer generation heads towards retirement and birth rates decline. If current social-insurance promises are to be honoured, spending on state pensions will have to go up steeply, which means a sharp rise in taxes. Older people are also by far the heaviest users of health care, which will increase the strain on public finances. Even in America, which relies far more on private health insurance than other OECD countries, health care for the elderly is largely paid for out of taxation.

The sort of tax rates implied by unreformed social-insurance systems threaten not just a loss of economic competitiveness, but something worse. As a new book, *Boomernomics*,[1] foretells it,

'Generational warfare erupts as the baby boomers' children and grandchildren revolt against punitive tax increases needed to care for the elderly boomers. Inflation makes an insidious comeback as government deficits and debt explode. Young investment strategists overseas dismiss the United States along with other G7 nations as poorly run nursing homes in terminal decline.'

In many countries, social insurance is being blamed for worsening some of the problems it was supposed to solve. In Germany, where over 10 per cent of the workforce is unemployed, high social-security contributions have become a severe tax on jobs. They already equal 20 per cent of an employee's gross income (half paid by the worker, half by the employer); at the height of the demographic squeeze, this is forecast to reach 30 per cent.

Meanwhile, benefits for the jobless may discourage the recipients from looking for work, making them increasingly dependent on the state; and aid to single mothers has been blamed, most loudly in America and Britain, for encouraging women to have children they cannot afford, and for discouraging marriage.

The most sensible way to rethink social insurance is to get away from all the ideology and instead ask, what works? This will not necessarily produce a perfect blueprint to suit every country. Any social-insurance system involves value judgments, and different societies have different values and different cultures that need to be accommodated. Yet these differences are easy to exaggerate, and there is plenty to be learnt from comparing different systems about what does, or does not, work.

Answering that question means being open-minded about the possibility that the private sector may replace much of what is now done by government, while admitting that there may be things that government can do better than private business, or even that only government can do. Since the state's role is now largely taken for granted, this survey will concentrate on the part private firms should play in social insurance in future.

On the face of it, that part should be large. Although they do not shout about it, governments are keen to shift more welfare provision into private hands to keep public spending under control and to avoid having to raise taxes or cut benefits. In many rich countries the private share of social insurance has been edging up in recent years.

Private bonanza?

Private firms, particularly insurers and fund-management companies, are licking their lips at the prospect of all that new business. The recent wave of mergers between insurers, banks, broker-ages and fund-management firms, and the rapid global expansion of American financial firms, were prompted partly by the expectation that individuals everywhere would be given more responsibility for managing their own affairs.

There are good theoretical grounds for thinking that competing, profit-seeking companies would not suffer from the more glaring weaknesses of state-provided social insurance. These range from monopoly problems, such as lack of choice, innovation and accountability to customers, to political interference. In reality, though, privatis-ing welfare faces many obstacles. The biggest of these, everywhere, is the electorate, which is generally opposed to privatisation, even though it also disapproves of higher taxes. But even leaving the voters to one side, not everybody in the priv-ate sector is convinced. Mark Boléat, director-general of the Association of British Insurers, fears that in all the talk of opportunities, 'there is perhaps a confusion between volume of business and profitability.' And recent examples of private provision replacing state social insurance have been a mixed success.

Some of this may be due to teething troubles, but the business of insurance is also notori-ously prone to market failure. Kenneth Arrow, a Nobel-prize-winning economist at Stanford Uni-versity, argues that the distortions to the alloca-tion of resources caused by 'the inherent difficulty in establishing certain markets for insurance' is 'one of the strongest criticisms of a system of freely competitive markets.'

One such market failure is 'adverse selection'. Buyers of insurance tend to have a better idea of how risky they are than the insurer, so if the premium is based on average risk, only people of average risk and above will buy the policy. That means the insurer will lose money. Another market failure is 'moral hazard'. Once insured, people will worry less about that particular risk, so they may take less care to avoid it than they would without insurance. That means insurers may end up paying out more than they expected. A further difficulty is that uncertainty about the size of future claims may make it impossible to set a realistic price for the insurance. This is a particular problem for policies providing cover far into the future.

In theory, at least, governments have a unique advantage in dealing with these market failures – though putting this into practice is another matter. Adverse selection can be overcome by making the insurance compulsory for everyone, thus allowing it to be profitable when priced for an average risk. A government's legal powers may enable it to reduce moral hazard by laying down strict rules on people's conduct once they are insured, and to monitor and enforce these rules more rigorously than a private firm could. The problem of uncertainty about future costs can be reduced by committing future generations of taxpayers to pick up whatever the bill turns out to be – though one of the main reasons that welfare states are now in difficulties is that the public is no longer convinced that future taxpayers will pay up.

Because of these market failures, the privatisa-tion of social insurance may often require some sort of government regulation to make it work. It has already become clear that getting this regulation right is crucial to the success of the transition, and that getting it wrong is all too easy.

Health care is much trickier. Market failures, particularly adverse selection and long-term un-certainty about costs, mean that, left alone, the private sector is likely to provide only limited health insurance that will fall short of most people's lifetime needs. There is a strong case for letting private firms provide the health care even if much of the funding comes from the taxpayer. And there may be scope for private health-care products that fall short of full insurance but give patients more choice, and confront them with some of the cost implications.

The biggest problem everywhere is to deflate the public's unrealistic expectations about how much care can be provided at a given level of expenditure, whatever the public–private split. The current crisis in the welfare state is due in large part to previous generations of voters' insistence that the state should play Santa Claus, and to politicians' unwillingness to disappoint them.

Reformers will also need to face up to some hard questions about the redistribution of wealth.

In most developed countries (though least so in America) a hefty transfer of money from rich to poor is at the heart of the social-insurance system. The private sector can channel voluntary redistribution through charity, but only the state can legally take money from the rich and give it to the poor. Any reform of the welfare state must spell out how much redistribution that will involve. Here, 'What works?' may not be the right question.

NOTE

1 William Sterling and Stephen Watts, *Boomernomics: The Future of your Money in the Upcoming Generational Warfare* (New York: Ballantine, 1998).

42 Global Inequality

Martin Dickson

Is global inequality getting worse or better? The question is simple but the answer is complicated, because it depends on the definition of inequality and the statistics used to measure it.

The most commonly used yardstick is gross domestic product per capita. It is far from perfect, since it does not show non-market measures of well-being, such as education, health and access to fresh water, nor can it accurately gauge the contribution of subsistence farming. However, it shows a broad correlation with other measures of well-being and, taking a long-term perspective, it shows world inequalities have been rising for nearly two centuries.

Until the industrial revolution in the west in the nineteenth century, there was relatively little inequality because there was so little economic growth. In 1820, the difference between the richest and poorest countries was a ratio of about three to one. Around that year, according to the United Nations Human Development Report, Britain's GDP per capita (in 1990 dollars) was roughly $1,765, while that of China, one of the world's poorest countries, was $523.

By 1992, the US, now the world's richest country, had GDP per capita of $21,558, while Ethiopia, among the poorest, had one of just $300 – a ratio of 72 to one. These extremes mask the fact that a significant number of countries have caught up, or narrowed the gap with, the most advanced nations in the period since the second world war – Japan had only 20 per cent of US income in 1950 but 90 per cent in 1992, while some states in southern Europe, the Middle East and Asia have also seen very big increases in income.

However, the very poorest nations have been getting relatively worse off for most of the post-war period. In 1960, according to the UN, the 20 per cent of the world's people in the richest countries had 30 times the income of the poorest 20 per cent, while by 1997 that had risen to 74 times. World Bank figures show a similar picture. The average per capita income of the poorest third of all countries fell from 3.1 per cent of the richest third to 1.9 per cent between 1970 and 1995, while the middle third suffered a decline from 12.5 to 11.4 per cent.

East Asia is the only region where incomes in low and middle income countries are converging towards incomes in richer countries, while in sub-Saharan Africa and the other least developed countries, per capita incomes today are lower than they were in 1970. Africa, in particular, has been hurt by a combination of poor infrastructure, skills and capital formation, along with war, misguided government policies and the ravages of disease, notably the Aids virus and malaria.

But is overall global income inequality still increasing? A recent paper by Andrea Boltho, of Oxford University, and Gianni Toniolo, of the University of Rome, claimed that it reached its maximum in the 1970s and has been shrinking as China and India, which together account for more than one third of the world population, have begun to grow rapidly. However, their arguments have been attacked by other economists on the grounds that their measurements are inaccurate, relying on too small a sample of countries, and are, anyway, not the best gauge of global income disparity, since they assume that every

Chinese and every American has the same national mean income.

Disparities of income within nations are certainly an important part of inequality measurement, and in China economic growth has been particularly uneven between the export-oriented coastal regions and the interior. Domestic income inequality has therefore increased sharply. A similar situation exists in the former communist states of eastern Europe and Soviet Union. In Russia, the share of income of the richest 20 per cent is 11 times that of the poorest 20 per cent. Income inequalities have also been growing in south-east Asian nations such as Indonesia and Thailand that had achieved high growth with improving income distribution and a reduction of poverty in earlier decades.

So, depending on the definition, global inequality is still rising, or has fallen marginally, thanks, in particular, to China's success. But as Nancy Birdsall, of the Carnegie Endowment for International Peace, has pointed out: 'It would take China almost a century of constant growth at its recent high rate just to reach the current level of US income per person.'

Whatever is happening to relative inequality, the number of people in absolute poverty – living on less than $1 a day is a popular yardstick – seems set to increase over the next two decades. World Bank figures show that some parts of the developing world have enjoyed levels of growth high enough to reduce absolute poverty in recent decades. In southern Asia, for example, the proportion of the population below the poverty line declined from 44.9 per cent in 1987 to 42.3 per cent in 1996 and is estimated at 40 per cent in 1998. But in others, such as Latin America and Africa, it has increased. Worldwide, the total population living on less than $1 a day has risen from 1.2bn in 1987 to around 1.5bn today, and if recent trends persist, it will reach 1.9bn by 2015.

Part 12 Modern Organizations

Economic prosperity does not necessarily conquer insecurity. The US is the richest country in the world and during the period from the early 1990s to the beginning of this century, the United States enjoyed a period of unprecedented economic growth. Yet many Americans, as the study by Steve Lohr shows (Reading 43), remain uncertain about their economic futures. Many fear that they could be laid off and they are right to sense this. For although the US has created new jobs, levels of job destruction are also high – therefore many people will be forced to move out of their current jobs even if new work is available. More employment is short-term than used to be the case.

Reading 44 from William H. Dutton discusses the impact of information technology and new communications technologies upon the structure of organizations. The new technologies make it possible for people to be in contact with one another in 'virtual space' – by means of computers, video links and conference phone lines, without having necessarily to meet physically. Modern business organizations are becoming networks. Networks tend to be more decentred than more traditional organizations. Traditional organizations were usually hierarchies, but networks are much 'flatter' – there isn't such a clearly defined line of authority. Networked organizations have great advantages over the more traditional types. They are more fluid, encourage innovation from below and are more adaptable to rapid social and technological change.

43 Though Upbeat on the Economy, People Still Fear for Their Jobs

Steve Lohr

Beth Cheney Mendes is well educated and well off. Ms. Mendes, a skilled nurse with a graduate degree from Yale University, and her husband, a bank executive, enjoy a six-figure income in Columbia, Conn.

The nearest brush Ms. Mendes, 37, has had with being laid off came five years ago when the private practice she worked for said it would be making cuts. She called a friend at Yale and had another job in 24 hours.

The economy, Ms. Mendes says, is healthy, but her experience has left her doubtful that any job can offer lasting security. 'You never know when you might be laid off,' she said.

Like Ms. Mendes, a growing number of Americans believe the economy is in good shape; even so, the number concerned about their own jobs has not changed significantly in the last year.

Their anxiety is not unfounded. A recent report by the Labor Department showed a high rate of layoffs from 1993 through 1995, even as unemployment was extremely low, with millions more jobs created than were wiped out. An analysis by The New York Times of the Labor Department figures found that the number of people laid off in 1995, the most recent year for which Government data are available, rose to nearly the peak reached in 1992, right after the last recession. Through November of this year, even after more than five years of economic recovery, the number of layoffs announced by companies had increased 14 per cent from a year earlier, according to one study.

The new findings confirm that layoffs have become a durable fixture of today's economy, occurring steadily in good times and bad. Three-quarters of all American households have seen a family member, friend, relative or neighbor lose a job since 1980. 'It makes you less secure and trusting of employers even after you get another job,' said Rich Kapatos of Aberdeen, Wash., who was laid off in 1989 and found another job within six months.

In a poll by The New York Times [of October 1996], 67 per cent rated the condition of the economy as fairly good or very good. That was up from 51 per cent in a New York Times poll that was conducted last December for a series of articles entitled 'The Downsizing of America,' published in March.

Despite the improvement, economic insecurity persists at virtually the level of a year ago, according to the new poll. And the job apprehension is spread remarkably evenly across society. [In 1996], 49 per cent of those polled said they were somewhat worried or very worried that someone in their household might be laid off within two or three years. [In 1995], 51 per cent said they were worried.

The finding of a gap between people's perceptions of economic health and of their own job security could easily be explained away early in a recovery, analysts say. Economic activity typically accelerates for a year or so before the job market firms up. 'But you wouldn't expect that gap now, well past five years into an economic expansion,' said Lawrence Katz, a labor economist at Harvard University.

Seventy per cent of those polled said they thought layoffs were not just a temporary problem in America but a feature of the modern economy that would continue permanently. [In 1995], 72 per cent said layoffs would continue permanently.

Just how the current level of job insecurity compares with years past is impossible to measure accurately. Comparable polls were not done in previous decades.

The issue of layoffs and job insecurity emerged briefly in the Presidential campaign, especially after Patrick J. Buchanan, whose message was laden with anti-corporate populism, won the Republican primary in New Hampshire in February [1996]. About that time, The Times and several other newspapers and magazines published prominent articles on layoffs.

Today the issue has faded from the nation's political debate and has lost the attention of many news organizations. But recent studies help explain the qualms still felt by many Americans in the midst of a generally healthy economy. Layoffs announced by companies increased 14 per cent through November, to 439,745, from 384,645 during the corresponding months a year ago, according to Challenger, Gray & Christmas. The consulting firm tracks publicly reported layoffs, so it tends to be a gauge only of cuts at larger companies. In the last few months, Challenger, Gray & Christmas reports, the pace of layoffs has eased.

Labor Department figures released in late October [1996] and analyzed by the Times show high rates of layoffs from 1993 through 1995 even though unemployment was low. In its series last March, the Times made projections of the layoff rate for 1994 and 1995 because the Government numbers for those years had not been tabulated. The Times projections were criticized by some economists and the Clinton Administration as little more than guesses and probably too high. In fact, the latest Labor Department numbers show, the Times projections were slightly lower than the official figures.

The Labor Department's October statistics, corrected from figures made public in August, indicated that 8.2 per cent of the labor force identified themselves as having lost a job involuntarily in the 1993–95 period, compared with 8.1 per cent in the Times projections. The layoff rate was significantly lower, at 5.7 per cent, during the years from 1987 through 1989, a period of roughly comparable unemployment rates.

In the huge American labor market, a difference of a few percentage points in the layoff rate translates into millions of workers – 10.1 million people laid off from 1993 through 1995 versus 6.7 million in 1987–89.

'Right now, the job-loss rate is higher than it was in the late 1980's,' said Henry Farber, a labor economist at Princeton University. 'We would have expected job losses to be much lower by now, given the low level of unemployment.'

Some economists emphasize that the high turnover – however wrenching for people who lose their jobs – is a byproduct of a fast-moving economy that has created far more jobs than it has destroyed in recent years. Yet others say that the elevated layoff rate also reflects the diminished bargaining power of workers in today's economy.

Since early 1992, America has generated 12.3 million net new jobs. In 1995, the number of new jobs created has outnumbered the ones wiped out at a rate of 208,000 a month. The American performance is the envy of the developed world, leaving the United States with far lower unemployment than many countries in Europe, where companies are often restrained by tax penalties and social pressure from laying off workers.

'The high job-loss rate in America is real and it's significant, but it is not the whole picture or even the general picture of the economy,' said Paul Krugman, an economics professor at the Massachusetts Institute of Technology. 'What economists call "labor market flexibility" is a euphemism for a certain amount of brutality. But it seems to be an unfortunate price we have to pay for having as dynamic an economy as we do.'

Many people laid off do suffer a loss in income, sometimes a sharp drop, notes Thomas Nardone, an economist at the Bureau of Labor Statistics in the Labor Department. So if higher levels of job loss do continue for years, the phenomenon should at least contribute to greater variability in incomes as more people move between jobs.

In [a] report, the Labor Department tracked the layoff, re-employment and earnings experiences of workers who had had a job for three years or more and were then laid off from 1993 through 1995. These so-called long-tenured workers, analysts say, are more likely to reflect trends in the labor market than are workers who frequently change jobs.

Of the long-tenured workers laid off, 74 per cent had found a job by February 1996. Still, only 34 per cent of them were making as much as or more than in their previous jobs. The rest, about two-thirds, were still looking for a job, were working part time, were self-employed or were working full time for less money than before.

Michael Rodgers was one of those hit hard by an unexpected layoff. In February 1994, Mr. Rodgers, now 40, was laid off from his job as manufacturing manager at a Pennsylvania chemical plant in a cost-cutting drive by Allied Signal. During his 14 years at Allied Signal, he had gone to school at night, earning a bachelor's degree and then an M.B.A. But the education did not shield him.

Mr. Rodgers sent out 240 résumés, and by the fall of 1994 he had a job as a manufacturing manager at a smaller company. The salary, though, was half the $75,000 he had been making at Allied Signal.

In the same year, Mr. Rodgers was divorced and, he says, nearly went bankrupt. The lost job and income, he says, contributed to both personal crises. But in 1995, he landed a better-paying job at another company.

Two months ago, Mr. Rodgers was hired as a manufacturing supervisor at a Philip Morris cigarette plant in Richmond. The job pays more than $50,000 a year with a chance for a bonus if he does well. Things are looking up for him now, but his recent experience brought a lesson. 'Nothing is secure,' he said.

The insecurity is pronounced for supervisors like Mr. Rodgers, according to a survey of 1,400 companies released in October by the American Management Association. The association found that among supervisors, the lowest level of management, two were laid off for every one hired. The biggest cuts, though, were made one level up, as three middle managers were let go for every one hired.

Yet as they lay off administrative workers, companies are also hiring to change the mix of skills of their work forces, trying to put more people directly at work developing products and selling them. The association's study found that companies are now hiring two technical and professional workers – a category that includes engineers, computer programmers and salespeople – for every one let go.

The highly publicized cuts at the largest corporations could be considered more symbolic than representative of the American labor market as a whole. After all, more than half of American workers are employed by companies with 500 workers or fewer. Still, the churning of the work force at many big companies contributes to the sense of insecurity.

'People worry about their own jobs, not jobs as a whole,' said Eric Greenberg, director of management studies for the American Management Association. 'In the current environment, a sense of job insecurity on the part of the individual is very rational.'

44 The Virtual Organization

William H. Dutton

The [information technology revolution] has created new electronically mediated opportunities for people to exchange information, meet, collaborate, work, and make decisions. This is of profound significance to all organizations because the new forms of access enabled by ICTs [Information and Communication Technologies] challenge many conventional management, organizational, and business structures and practices. For instance, ICTs question the need for 'line-of-sight' supervision in which managers monitor and supervise activities by being located close to subordinates, if not actually within view.

ICTs can overcome many constraints of time and distance to place organizations in the presence of critical information, people, and services. This can liberate creative, administrative, management, production, and distribution resources and processes from the constraints imposed by traditional organizational structures. It also reduces the role played by the need to share information in locating work at particular physical sites. That freedom should lead managers to rethink how they organize and run their businesses in order to be competitive in a networked economy.

The scope given by ICTs for re-engineering business processes and organizational responsibilities has opened up opportunities to create what management expert Charles Handy describes as 'virtual organizations' that 'do not need to have all the people, or sometimes any of the people, in one place in order to deliver their service. The organization exists, but you can't see it. It is a network, not an office.' Many highly successful networked organizations – some with no physical centre – demonstrate the potential for organizations to use ICTs to enable major change in the firm. They illustrate how essential ICTs have become to creating new products and services, enabling productivity improvements, and managing tele-access not only within and among firms, but also to consumers.

However, all organizations cannot expect to succeed by emulating models of the virtual organization, which, by virtue of their networking, appear to outsiders to be like most other traditional organizations that operate from a major headquarters and satellite branches – but in reality have little centralized physical presence (see box 44.1). There are other strategies for using ICTs to manage tele-access that can also competitively advantage certain organizations, such as supporting the vitality of large integrated firms. This [discussion] identifies the key opportunities and limitations of the virtual organization in the context of a broad analysis of the most effective ways in which tele-access can either be a barrier for a business or enable it to revitalize everything it does.

Enabling new organizational forms: the virtual organization

Electronic communications and the use of fixed and portable computers provide highly adaptable work spaces. These are the foundations on which virtual organizations can be built and rebuilt in a continuously shifting pattern of alliances over time and across space. Virtual enterprises could integrate business processes which encompass people

---

Box 44.1 The virtual organization: a technical, structural, and cultural vision

Networking through ICTs

- Substitutes electronic media for physical files and face-to-face meetings encourage more efficient sharing and gathering of information;
- focuses on face-to-face communication for building cohesion and trust;
- changes business processes to take advantage of the Internet and other ICT networks.

Restructuring to a decentralized network of companies

- uses networks to re-engineer and evolve structures of communication within and outside the organization;
- emphasizes horizontal coordination across functional, divisional, and company boundaries;
- creates jobs that span formerly separate functions and locations.

Building a team culture of trust and responsibility

- devolves authority and initiative;
- encourages workers to operate as trusting and cooperative team players;
- places high value on learning, change, and reorganizing to be responsible rather than on rules, procedures, and hierarchy.

Sources: Hammer and Champy (1993); Nohria and Berkley (1994: 115); Fulk and DeSanctis (1995: 340); Murray and Willmott (1997)

---

working for many different groups within and outside the company, including direct links to suppliers and customers. Boundaries of the organization and the units that compose them are becoming so permeable that a unit of a firm today could be replaced by an outside contractor from another part of the world tomorrow.

The enormous potential competitive power that can be unleashed by this enhanced flexibility and responsiveness depends largely on the strategic use of ICTs to support new patterns of tele-access. However, the excitement generated by tele-access innovations like the Internet has led to an overly deterministic portrayal of the virtual organization as a 'silver bullet' to solve all business problems. This is based primarily on a technical logic, derived from the escalating use of ICT networks, which ignores social and organizational constraints on fundamental change in the design and use of ICTs in organizations. These other factors mean that tele-access is also often used

successfully to facilitate the growth of large integrated firms. Nevertheless, for many enterprises the virtual organization can be a valuable approach to realizing the benefits of tele-access in order to reach new markets, open new channels to existing customers, transform existing products and services, and innovate in entirely new areas.

Imagine, for instance, entering a bookshop with over 2½ million volumes you can browse through before deciding what you want delivered to your door. This unlikely physical prospect is feasible on the Internet, as shown in 1995 when 'Amazon.com' opened a virtual bookshop on the Web – an innovation that other firms have emulated. An earlier example, based on telephone rather than computer networking, is provided by First Direct, a sort of a virtual bank established in 1989 by Midland, one of the UK's major banks. First Direct captured hundreds of thousands of customers, primarily among wealthier households, by delivering most of its services over the

---

Box 44.2   Intranets: private computer communication networks

A popular corporate innovation in the 1990s has been the private 'intranet', based on Internet and Web technology, such as the TCP/IP protocol and Web-like hypertext links and browsers. Intranets provide the benefits of the Internet in interconnecting diverse hardware and software. Its private ownership also enables much higher levels of security by creating electronic barriers such as passwords and security 'firewalls' – links to outside networks that are programmed to limit what kinds of access will be permitted by whom.

Booz Allen and Hamilton Inc., a major management consulting firm, has used a corporate intranet since 1995 to interconnect over 6,000 employees in 80 offices round the world. Whatever equipment is used locally, employees can get access to the same repository of information, containing thousands of documents cross-referenced by geography, industry, and topic. Its intranet also contains a directory of employees and their areas of specialization and skill, which allows quick identification and location of experts needed to form a consulting team for a particular client's requirements. E-mail and teleconferencing allow employees to engage in private and public discussions, for brainstorming, to ask questions, and to promote new ideas.

Source: http://home.netscape.com/ provides information on corporate intranets

---

telephone, twenty-four hours a day, seven days a week.

In addition to these technical changes, there are three related social and organization innovations that are essential to discussions of the virtual organization (see box 44.1).

1   *Networking* Telecommunication and computer-based communication systems are such a crucial element of virtual organizations that the overall approach is often referred to as 'the networked organization'. Networks can, for example, help managers develop new connections as individuals, generate more communication across, up, and down the organizational hierarchy, and create opportunities for new gatekeepers between the 'on-line' and 'off-line' worlds within the enterprise. [. . .] ICTs can be used to create new cross-functional 'virtual teams' spanning traditional departmental boundaries [. . .] and improve tele-access connections across firms. Both internal 'intranets' (see box 44.2) and inter-organizational networks, like the

Internet, are important tele-access media. Less than 10 per cent of companies in the UK, for example, were using an intranet by 1997, but this proportion is growing rapidly. These open up new 'electronic corridors' as channels of access, while they also create some electronic barriers to close off others, such as 'firewalls' (explained in box 44.2).

2   *Restructuring the organization* The virtual organization provides a strategy for downsizing, outsourcing, and transforming the business processes of the firm. Contracting out functions that are not among the core competencies of the firm can create more flexibility and lower costs. Likewise, the use of direct electronic data interchange (EDI) links between a manufacturer and a supplier to carry orders, invoices, and other key business transactions can facilitate the outsourcing of supply or manufacturing (see box 44.3). Outsourcing also presents a structural approach to managing the changing geography of the firm, creating more autonomous units that do not need to be managed directly.

Box 44.3   Electronic data interchange (EDI)

Inter-organizational linkages, such as that between a manufacturer and a supplier, can be facilitated by EDI systems that offer electronic interchange of data between computers, within or across organizations. EDI message standards permit companies with different types of hardware and software to exchange data. By creating a system in which networked machines communicate directly without requiring information to be re-entered by hand, the speed and accuracy of routine processes can be enhanced.

Colgate-Palmolive implemented an EDI software system in 1995 to link and organize data from all aspects of the company, including product shipments, schedules, balance sheets, and orders. For example, the software tracks when a shipment has left the factory, updates any data related to it, and alerts managers and technicians located hundreds of miles away. The goal is to track detailed demand in order to fine-tune production and delivery schedules to keep its inventory to a minimum. Tracking is done by monitoring the customers of Colgate-Palmolive's products, like Wal-Mart. As noted in the *Wall Street Journal*: 'If it works, no corner of its business will go untouched.'

---

3   *Building an appropriate 'learning-organization' culture*   Many advocates of virtual organizations stress that their approach is most likely to succeed within a culture which promotes cooperative teamwork at all organizational levels among individuals and groups who each have a great degree of local autonomy. Incentive systems, such as competitive contracting and pay rises based on team performance, have been developed to encourage this culture. Given a dependence on creating, disbanding, and recombining teams with new projects and strategies, proponents also emphasize the need for continuous learning and change.

[. . .]

Part 13

Work and Economic Life

The increasing use of computers and other electronic technologies makes it possible for more and more people to work from home rather than going to a physical workplace. Homeworking is becoming increasingly common. Given the instantaneous nature of modern communications, it is possible for people to work many miles away from wherever their companies' main offices are – perhaps even in a different country altogether. Attitudes towards homeworking differ, however. Some workers appreciate the fact of not having to make a journey to work and can make effective use of the greater autonomy and free time that they have. Others feel hemmed in at home and miss the more social environment of the workplace. In Reading 45 Nick Jewson and Alan Felstead suggest various ways in which homeworking can be made more palatable for those who find it difficult. One way, for example, is to establish a separate working area in the home, so that a boundary is maintained between work life and domestic life.

Chris Brewster, in Reading 46, discusses the changing shape of work careers. Some observers are suggesting that full-time, long-term jobs will become less and less common. In fact in the UK already less than 50 per cent of the working population are in such jobs. The same trends are observable in other industrialized countries. What seems on the face of it a problem – insecure careers – can also be an opportunity. If there is less and less lifetime work on offer, people might be able to develop more flexible and autonomous working careers.

David Lyon analyses in Reading 47 the possible implications of a further set of technological changes now affecting industrial production: the widespread use of information technology. Many have claimed that modern economies no longer depend centrally, as they once did, upon the production of manufactured goods; in place of manufacture, the production of information becomes a core resource. Lyon submits to critical scrutiny the idea that we are moving from an industrial order towards an 'information society'. As he says, it is impossible to resist the conclusion that information technology has already changed our lives significantly and is likely to alter them further in the future. Yet, as Lyon shows, upon examination the idea of the information society turns out to be a complicated one, and there is good reason to be cautious about some of the wilder claims which have been made about its potential consequences, good and bad.

45 New Ways of Working and Living

Nick Jewson and Alan Felstead

One of the first things everyone who studies sociology learns is that the rise of modernity meant the *separation* of home and work. Industrialisation and bureaucratisation generated separate spheres of social life around, on the one hand, the family and the domestic division of labour and, on the other, the social relations of production and paid employment. These divisions are commonly explained by saying that modern societies have institutions that are *more specialised* than those of the past and, as a result, a greater range of different types of institutions. All the classical sociologists commented on these processes, Émile Durkheim most explicitly.

The separation of home and work

In the past, home and work were more closely intertwined.[1] Production took place in farms and workshops that were also dwelling places. Domestic work and economic activity were much harder to disentangle: for example, childcare in the home was also an aspect of training and disciplining the junior workforce. With industrialisation, housework became more sharply divided from wage labour in the factory or office. So-called 'separate spheres' opened up. Workplaces became organised around formal and bureaucratic principles expressed in contracts, rules and regulations;

When work comes home

Table 45.1   Those who work at home (%)

	Mainly working at home	Employed workforce
Sex		
Women	69.3	44.7
Men	30.7	55.3
Type of job		
Manual	23	40
Non-manual	77	60
Employment status		
Employee	32	87
Self-employed	62	12
Unpaid family worker	6	1
Ethnicity		
White	96.8	95.1
Ethnic minority	3.2	4.9
Average age	46.1 years	38.8 years

Source: A. Felstead and N. Jewson, *In Work, at Home* (London: Routledge, 2000)

home became structured around informal personal dependencies and ideologies of love and affection.

These developments have, in turn, had enormous implications for a very wide range of aspects of our lives. Crucial dimensions of gender and age divisions are shaped by the separation of home and work. The organisation of cities, leisure, transport systems, social security payments and many other social policies rests on this separation, as do fundamental concepts of the public and the private, citizenship and personal life.

Homeworkers

There have always remained, of course, some ways of earning a living in which workplace and living space overlap. The lifestyles of those who run farmhouses, corner shops, guesthouses and pubs are examples. Throughout the modern period some aspects of routine manual and clerical work have been carried out in the home. 'Homeworkers', as they are called, have been among the most deprived and poorly paid members

of the workforce.[2] They have commonly been neglected in surveys and research studies – an invisible workforce hidden from public view within the private sphere of the home. Much 'homework' has been conducted in industries that have traditions of this kind of employment – such as clothing and textiles. Many of the workers are women with young children; migrant and ethnic minority communities are also heavily involved.[3]

New directions: It's 'hip' to work at home

In the closing decades of the twentieth century working at home began to take on a new significance and direction. From being perceived as a declining, marginalised and backward sector of the economy, quite suddenly working at home has begun to be presented as expanding, progressive and even fashionable. The evidence of this change is all around us.

The lifestyle sections of newspapers and magazines now commonly carry articles on the benefits and pitfalls of working at home (see Box 45.1).

Box 45.1   Working at home

Geoffrey Patterson spends 2 weeks a month working from his chalet in Verbier, Switzerland. For the other 2 weeks this president and chief executive of software house Teamphone stays in London and works in a conventional office. He enjoys this way of working. He can also easily check from Verbier how many phone calls his London staff are making.

'Businesses can't survive . . . without being flexible with their employees,' he says. 'Business needs people to be inspired. Some people need to work in a room with others; some don't. Some want rigid rules; some are better off working their own way. Employers need to be able to adapt.'

About 2 million UK workers are thought to be working in unorthodox patterns. BT's home-work consultancy suggests these numbers are doubling every two years. Neil McLocklin of BT thinks homeworking increases productivity.

'Companies find their absenteeism rate dwindles to virtually nothing for homeworkers. Very often when you're unwell, you're well enough to work but not well enough to travel to work. And if you spend more time working from home you are less likely to pick up bugs.'

John, a journalist and writer, left office employment and took up flexible home-based working 6 years ago. He would now jump at a traditional office job. He does not like the loneliness of homeworking. Other friends of his who work at home have become clinically depressed.

'You've got to be very disciplined – even more than when you're at work in an office. You've got to set the alarm and get up when it goes off. Writer's block does exist and it's terrible. In the office you have people there asking you if you haven't done something. Or they'll be asking why you aren't on the phone getting stories. Also, working from home, I've had people calling me at 7.30 a.m. and 1 a.m. You wouldn't like to be hanging around the office till then.'

(*The Observer*, 23 April 2000)

Furniture retailers routinely stock and advertise ranges of office equipment *for the home*. TV adverts depict people in paid employment in the home. Middle-class housing developments are beginning to be built with Internet connections as standard. Government departments are inundated with requests for data and advice about working at home.

The explanation for this reversal of attitude lies in a combination of recent social processes. Most significant among these are:

- globalisation;
- increasing flexibility of labour markets;
- changes in information and communications technologies (ICT);
- the growth of a knowledge-based economy.

Globalisation

The *globalisation of economic relationships* has made it possible to move economic activities around the world and for employers to seek out low-cost labour forces. This has been achieved by the breakup of different aspects of production processes into their constituent parts – manufacturing, assembly, research, marketing, administration etc. – and the location of each in parts of the world yielding maximum advantage to employers.

Flexibility in labour

Business survival makes it imperative to maximise productivity and profitability. Ways of working that cut costs are, therefore, extremely attractive to dynamic capitalist enterprises. This has resulted in a wave of interest in so-called *flexible* or *non-standard* ways of working. Across the world, businesses have turned to part-time, casual and freelance workers in order to cut labour costs. In Britain, governments of all shades have argued that flexible labour markets are the key to national survival.

Working at home has taken its place among these new forms of 'flexibility'. When workers are at home, parts of the production costs can often be transferred to the workers' own domestic budgets, for example costs of heating, lighting, storage and electric power for machines, thereby reducing employers' expenditures.

Manual and routine white-collar workers at home are low paid, very rarely unionised or even in contact with one another. 'Homeworkers' in the back streets of Third World cities, as well as in declining urban areas in the developed world, have often become part of global subcontracting chains that reach right up to some of the largest and best-known 'household name' companies.

The rise of information and communications technologies (ICTs)

These cost-saving measures may well also affect those in higher-status and more highly paid jobs. The big saving here is in office space. If professional and white-collar workers can be transferred to home as a base – even for only part of their working week – expensive offices can be sold off. Alternatively, business expansion can be accommodated without the need to invest in new buildings.

Computers, faxes and telephones are now cheap, portable and everywhere. New developments, such as video phones and digital television, will make communications technologies even more user-friendly. ICTs have made possible the emergence of the *teleworker*, seen by many pundits as the figure of the future.[4]

The prefix 'tele' means 'at a distance' or 'remote'. A teleworker is someone who works at a distance from the conventional workplace, using ICT to stay in touch with colleagues and clients. With a lap-top and a mobile phone the teleworker can, in principle, work almost anywhere – as anyone travelling by train or stuck in a motorway traffic jam can observe.

The knowledge-based economy

Now that ICT has come into our domestic environment, the separation of home and work has been put in doubt. It is now possible for millions of professional, administrative, managerial and technical workers to work at home easily, cheaply and efficiently. It is exactly these types of workers, *knowledge workers*, who are at the heart of a new type of economy, the *knowledge economy*, whose growth is rapidly outpacing that of manufacturing. The knowledge economy includes high-tech businesses (e.g. software companies and e-commerce), professional and technical services (e.g. insurance and legal services) and customer-facing personal services (e.g. business and research agencies). Much of this sector comprises small, self-employed freelancers (so-called *e-lancers*) working on and through the Internet. For them, home is a cheap and flexible place to work.

Good news, bad news . . .?

In the year 2000 about a quarter of the employed UK workforce work at home *some* of the time. If working at home is increasing, is it something we should welcome or deplore? There are differing views. Some commentators regard working at home as a thoroughly positive development and advocate its further growth. Others argue that those who work at home are among the most exploited and oppressed groups in the labour market, suffering the double burden of managing housework and paid work in the same space.

Part of the reason why these two contrasting images have flourished is that they refer to *different* kinds of people who work at home.

- The *optimistic* scenario focuses on professional and managerial teleworkers in highly paid jobs.

 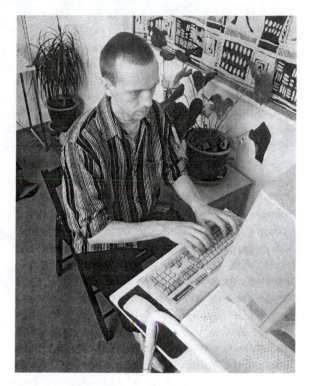

Is men's homeworking different from women's?
The old...

...and the new

These people often have large and comfortable houses and can afford childcare.
- The *pessimistic* scenario highlights the fate of routine, low-paid, manual and clerical workers.

There seems little doubt that the latter group experiences some of the *worst* conditions in the labour market. Surveys routinely show workers earning very low wages indeed and very rarely receiving even the most basic fringe benefits, such as paid holidays or pensions.[5] They often work in small houses and cramped spaces. Unable to afford childcare, they try to work and look after children at the same time. Often they are forced to work late at night or at weekends, thereby losing out on family and leisure time.

The experience of working at home is shaped by the kind of *management techniques* adopted by employers. 'High trust' methods of management are often adopted with those at the top end

of the labour market; workers are basically left alone to get on with their tasks. More coercive and 'low trust' methods are routinely applied to those in low-discretion jobs. Here, piece rates (pay by item produced) are often used, which drive workers to labour long hours to meet target incomes and obscure the low amounts they earn per hour.

There is a further reason why these two images flourish. For many, working at home is *both* good *and* bad news. They feel genuinely ambivalent about it. The *benefits* to the worker are the potential for increased control and independence. Those who work at home can often distribute their hours throughout the working day, taking time out for family commitments or even leisure breaks. They can create their own lifestyle – wear casual clothes, play their own music, eat their favourite foods, pace their own work, be available for domestic responsibilities and avoid unnecessary disruptions.

They do not have to spend time, money and energy commuting.

The *disadvantages* are the flip-side of these same possibilities. People who work at home can feel isolated and cut off from others, missing the camaraderie and support of the workplace and co-workers. They may be repeatedly interrupted by domestic events, whilst at the same time resenting the intrusion of outside forces of work into the private space of the home. The constant presence of their work close at hand may lead them to worry about meeting deadlines and to become 'workaholics'. They may also yearn for the variety that comes from getting out of the house.

So, dissolving the barriers between home and work offers exciting new possibilities but it also threatens to erode highly valued aspects of privacy and sociability. The home is often portrayed in popular accounts as a 'haven in a heartless world'. But in future, it seems, for many of us the heartless world will reach inside the domestic haven of the home. What are the implications for the new experience of home and work?

Surviving work at home

'Going to work' offers routines and disciplines which are not available to homeworkers. They have to invent and maintain their own routines and disciplines in their daily working lives in order to avoid the temptations of staying in bed or watching daytime TV.

Those who work at home have derived two different solutions to these challenges.

Recreate the workplace in the home

This typically means putting a spare room aside as an office or work station. When the door is closed, the worker may not be disturbed. Armstrong has illustrated the extraordinary lengths to which some teleworkers will go in order to defend themselves against interruptions,[6] for example, requiring the kids to phone mum working in the next room if they have something to say. It is not difficult to see how this 'segregation

option' can create family tensions and become difficult to maintain.

Take the 'integration option'

This involves working in the midst of the household, subject to all the to-ing and fro-ing that this entails, for example working on the dining-room table while the kids watch television. Here the worker is more accessible but the potentiality for interruptions is obvious. Working may involve a constant juggling act, with domestic chores threaded in and out of work tasks. Male homeworkers and those with higher incomes are more likely to adopt and sustain the 'segregation' approach. Female and lower-paid workers are more likely to find themselves committed to 'integration'.[7]

Home 'technologies of the self'

Whatever detailed strategy is adopted, those who work at home agree that it calls for a high degree of self-discipline and self-motivation. They set up boundaries dividing up times and spaces within and around the home. They become skilled at switching between different ways of relating to those around them: fending off intrusions; negotiating encroachments on family time; controlling links with the outside world; combating isolation; and managing their relative invisibility as workers. In short, there is a particular emotional approach, a psychological attitude and daily routine associated with working at home that emphasises self-monitoring and self-direction.

Conclusion

These developments in working at home mirror many other aspects of what Giddens calls 'late modernity'.[8] Late modernity is associated with heightened reflexivity and increased emphasis on self-control. Many social activities are *decontextualised*; that is, they are no longer tied down to local, traditional and fixed places. Instead, social activities become fluid in time and space. In the case of home and work, these processes may just be beginning. There is a long way to go yet, and some jobs will never be suitable to be done at home. However, for many of us the workplace as we have known it for a century or more is about to be fundamentally transformed.

NOTES

1 P. Laslett, The World We Have Lost (London: Methuen, 1983).

2 A. Felstead and N. Jewson, *In Work, at Home: Towards an Understanding of Homeworking* (London: Routledge, 2000).

3 A. Phizacklea and D. Wolkowitz, *Homeworking Women: Gender, Ethnicity and Class at Work* (London: Sage, 1995).

4 P. J. Jackson and J. M. Van Der Wielden (eds), *Teleworking: International Perspectives* (London: Routledge, 1998).

5 Felstead and Jewson, *In Work*.

6 N. Armstrong, 'Flexible Work in the Virtual Workplace', in A. Felstead and N. Jewson (eds), *Global Trends in Flexible Labour* (London: Macmillan, 1999).

7 Felstead and Jewson, *In Work*.

8 A. Giddens, *Modernity and Self Identity: Self and Society in the Late Modern Age* (Cambridge: Polity, 1991).

46 You've Got to Go with the Flow: The Changing Nature of Jobs

Chris Brewster

Only a minority of jobs in Britain now fits our idea of a 'normal' or 'real' job. We are only just beginning to understand the implications of this. [Since the late 1970s] the labour market in the UK has undergone more radical changes than occurred in the previous half a century. The nature of these has been so substantial – but comparatively so sudden – that many people still have only a vague idea what has happened.

Many employers, too, are only now beginning to understand the variety of ways, other than 'standard' employment, in which they can get work done; and many employees and potential employees are still struggling to realize that 'normal' jobs are frequently not on offer.

Less than 50 per cent of the working population in Britain has a full-time, long-term job with a traditional employment contract. Nor is the UK alone in this; although patterns of employment vary widely across Europe, the same trends are visible everywhere.

There has been a sharp rise in the variety of ways in which work is organized. We cannot describe it as 'the way people are employed' because many of these expanding forms of working arrangements (subcontracting, franchising, self-employment) break the link between work and employment.

The story is one of increases in almost every form of work – except the traditional full-time, long-term job. One million people have more than one job. Part-time work has more than doubled in the last fifteen years, and so has self-employment. Temporary employment and fixed-term contracts have significantly increased. And new working arrangements, such as job-sharing and annual hours contracts, have been established (Figure 46.1).

The increase in these forms of working is not just a matter of changes in the industrial structure: it is evidence of their spread into new areas. Shift working, for example, always existed in the emergency services and where manufacturers wanted to use expensive equipment over more than eight hours per day. It has now spread into shops which stay open in the evenings to meet customer requirements, and to offices concerned with global operations and which need to be in touch with people in different time zones. Similarly, subcontracting was always common in the construction industry, but it is now common in the computing, scientific and local authority sectors.

According to government statistics, around 27 million people now make up the UK's working population, of whom around 2.5 million are unemployed. The Trades Union Congress and others might argue that another several hundred thousand, who don't appear in the official statistics, should also be counted as out of work.

We know that unemployment is a significant problem for all European countries. In the UK, there are 1 million fewer men in jobs now than in 1990. Since 1990, the manufacturing sector

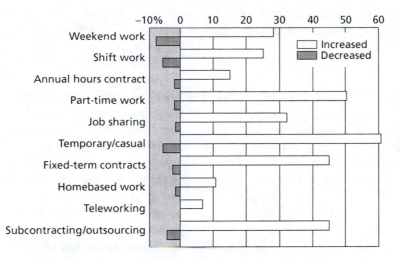

Figure 46.1 Flexible friends: percentage of organizations using flexible working practices, UK, 1995
Source: Chris Brewster, Cranfield

alone has lost almost a million jobs, although even in manufacturing there have been pockets of growth. British Aerospace, for example, has made well-publicized job reductions recently, while its former subsidiary, Rover, [. . .] increased jobs by 2,000 [in 1995]. And there is certainly growth in other sectors.

The world of work is changing and the range of options increasing. For employers, the need to think strategically becomes more important; to end the discussions about headcounts and to begin thinking about how to get the work done in the most cost-effective manner; and there is evidence that this is beginning to happen.

For employees and potential employees, the changes mean they have to be prepared to work in different ways and to be more flexible about their work arrangements. Already, a majority is in other than 'standard' or 'typical' employment. Also employees have realized that the days of a job for life have, in most cases, disappeared. Much more rapid movement in and out of work takes place now than it used to (around 10 per cent of the working population leave a job, and a roughly similar proportion start a job, every year). It is no surprise, therefore, to find that the job market is becoming more varied and more volatile. How

we deal with this situation will be one of the touchstones of social and economic success over the next few years.

Part-time working

In the past two years, well over two-thirds of all the jobs that have been created have been part-time jobs. Of those that are employed, about 6 million (one-quarter) have part-time jobs. Women fill more than eight out of ten of these, and research shows that most people are in part-time employment because they prefer to work that way.

Part-time working enables them to fit work in with other responsibilities, such as caring for young children or elderly relatives, which many see as a major part of their lives. Employers prefer it because it allows them to match the jobs on offer to the work that needs to be done. Not all work comes in neat, seven-and-a-half hour blocks; if the work a particular employer has only lasts for part of the day, why pay for a full day? Employers also know that if the tasks are not varied and interesting, employees find it easier to work with commitment and enthusiasm for a few hours rather than for a whole day. Nor do part-timers have to take time off for visits to the dentist or the doctor; so part-timers are more productive.

Temporary jobs

These account for well over 1.5 million employees, around 7.5 per cent of all jobs, including an additional 0.5 per cent increase last year. Few employers can predict whether a job will continue into the next decade; none can be sure that a particular recruit will succeed in a job – so it makes little sense to make a promise of permanent employment they may be unable to keep. A further 3 million people (more than 12 per cent) are self-employed, while more than 400,000 people are involved with some form of government-subsidized training.

Other options

A wide range of other forms of work exist, which sometimes overlap with part-time or temporary employment. Some involve quite small variations to the standard employment contract. But others are organized with no employment contract at all.

Shift working is not just becoming more widespread, it is also becoming less standardized. The days when nearly all shifts consisted of ten or twelve hours are gone. 'Twilight shifts', usually for women working in shops, are now widespread. Shifts can be of different and varying lengths, brought about by increasing pressures on managers, changing employee expectations, and the advent of computer programs which enable managers to organize and check that everyone works a specified number of hours, no matter how complicated the shift patterns.

Annual hours working has taken a firm foothold in recent years. If work in places such as travel agencies, food-processing firms and accounts departments is on a cyclical pattern, it makes little economic sense to employ staff for the same number of hours each day. Varying the hours to suit the work demand avoids paying for overtime in some periods – and also avoids the workers suffering boredom in others. Phillips, British Gypsum and some in the paper industry now pay their employees for the total number of hours they do during a year, while continuing to pay the same salary every month.

Job sharing is a form of part-time working where two people share the same full-time employment pattern. Job sharers working for Hewlett Packard, for example, guarantee that if one of them is away the other will fill in for them. The employer gets full cover for only a little extra cost.

Homeworking and teleworking have grown, but only a little. Some of the wilder predictions that large numbers of us would be working this way by the end of the decade will be wrong. Although the technology would allow this to happen, the predictions failed to take account of the necessary social side of work. More and more people will work at home, but the main growth will be among those who do so only occasionally, to complete a specific report or prepare for a meeting.

Term-time working has been successful at the NatWest bank. Female employees retain their contracts, without pay, during the school holidays, resuming their usual full- or part-time jobs during school terms.

Franchising, subcontracting and the use of consultants are all ways of getting work done without actually taking on the responsibility of employing people. The organization gets its work done (at a cost, of course), but without having to employ anyone extra. Those doing the work are either employed by other organizations or work for themselves.

Then, finally, there is the unlawful economy, or informal economy, which on any measure is a substantial part of the UK economy. Someone – although not you or me, of course – must be involved in making their living there.

47 Information Technology and the 'Information Society'

David Lyon

The 'information society' expresses the idea of a novel phase in the historical development of the advanced societies. Not just a 'postindustrial' society, but the advent of new social patterns is predicted, consequent upon a 'second industrial revolution' based above all on microelectronic technologies. A growing proportion of people, it is claimed, is involved in an unprecedented variety of information-related jobs. Scientific and technical workers gather and produce information, managers and supervisors process it, teachers and communications workers distribute it. From domestic life to international relations, and from leisure activities to industrial relations, no sphere of social activity is left untouched by this 'informatizing' process.

Notions such as Alvin Toffler's 'third wave' – virtually synonymous with 'information society' – have entered popular imagination. A television film has been made of the *Third Wave*, and in the UK, the 'Third Wave' is the slogan for a British Telecom advertising campaign. The 'information society' is increasingly used as a handy catch-all for focusing discussions of 'the future' as we approach the third millennium. Government policy also draws upon this concept, particularly with regard to education. The British are assured, for instance, that 'Our educational system will be a major, perhaps the dominant factor in ensuring the economic prosperity of the UK in a world-wide information society.'[1]

However, certain questions are too frequently left unanswered or treated only to oblique or opaque responses. What are the connections between new technology and society? To what extent and under what circumstances does technological potential become social destiny? Is it warranted to see an epochal social transformation in the kinds of economic and social restructuring currently taking place? And whether or not we are witnessing the emergence of a 'new kind of society', are its advocates correct to assume, as they often tend to, that the social effects of information technology are generally benign? [. . .]

All manner of vested interests are involved in [information technology] (IT), but the concept of the information society is all too often used in ways that obscure their role. Sometimes those interests are intertwined in ways that have yet to be carefully explored. The coincidence that defence funding supports so much research in IT *and* that the world of IT frequently excludes women deserves just such exploration. Technology in general is undoubtedly associated with maleness, socially and culturally; IT no less so.

Secondly, the information society concept papers over not only the cracks but also opposing movements in society. Underlying contradictions are even less likely to be exposed than inequalities and conflicts on the surface. Opposing movements may be seen, for instance, in the IT context, along the fault-line of information as public good versus saleable commodity. The real threats of current IT development to public service broadcasting and to public libraries are manifestations of deeper dynamics of opposition.

Thirdly, the coming of the information society is viewed (by its popular proponents at least) as an entirely natural occurrence. It is the obvious way forward. The future lies with IT. The new technologies must be 'whole-heartedly embraced', declare the captains of industry. This is why educational systems have to be reorientated, the market unshackled and high-technology research and trading deals engineered. It is also why Luddism has to be stamped out.

This particular ideological aspect – information society as a natural and logical social advance – is further buttressed by the typically Western belief in progress via unlimited economic accumulation. What Shallis calls 'silicon idolatry' resonates with this still-strong belief. As Bob Goudzwaard observes, if indeed this faith is a driving force within economic and technological expansion then two things follow. One, the 'overdevelopment' of both spheres comes as no surprise, and two, it is 'accompanied by an expectation of happiness that relativises anything that might raise objections against them'.[2] [. . .]

Anyone worried about the encroaching tyranny of technocratic power embodied in IT should not ignore countervailing movements also present in contemporary societies. True, the information society idea is strong and popular, but there are many for whom it is remote and unreal, and yet others who regard it with suspicion and hostility. For them, the critique of ideology may itself appear as a less than central task; more urgent is actual resistance to the adoption of new technology. Examining forms of resistance – particularly the 'Luddism' scathingly referred to above – is one thing, however; joining the quest for alternatives is another. I shall argue that both strategies are required if the information society as depicted here is not to become a self-fulfilling prophecy.

The intrusion of IT into numerous areas of life – only this week I discovered that my plastic card could buy a train ticket at the local station and that my office is soon due to be connected with a central IBM computer – has revived interest in Luddism as a mode of opposing technology. While some use it as an epithet to be directed at all 'anti-progressives' who quite irrationally wish to 'put the clock back' by refusing to adapt to new technology, others – both conservative and radical – willingly accept the label as correctly portraying their stance. 'If Luddite means the preservation of all that is good from the past and the rejection of things that destroy good', says Michael Shallis, 'then I would welcome the term.' [. . .]

What form should be taken by 'alternative visions' to the 'information society' idea? At least two criteria should be satisfied. One, the normative basis of the alternative(s) must be made clear. Two, the different levels on which intervention might take place, and modes whereby policies may be implemented, must be indicated. This involves offering practical examples of altered practice and of the potential for choice in technological innovation.

Technocratic thought, especially that embodied in today's computer logic, tends to minimize or exclude debate about ethics. Discussion of 'alternatives' brings this into the foreground. Unfortunately, [. . .] an ethic suited to the global and long-term aspects of today's technology is largely lacking. The ethics of the personal is far better developed. That said, once it is recognized that the 'information society' gives the false impression that we are entering an *entirely* novel social situation, then certain long-trodden ethical paths become pertinent.

A further problem here is the relative lack of contexts within which such moral debate may take place. Professions, for instance, have always provided such opportunities (even though they have sometimes been self-interestedly abused). Medicine, involving 'technologies of the body', has traditionally been hedged by moral qualification, dating back to the Hippocratic oath. Today's computer professionals evidence a very low level of membership or interest in any comparable organizations.

It may be that IT raises new moral problems. The ease with which data can be permanently and untraceably erased may be one, the way in which privacy is invaded by computers, another. But among the most pressing issues is that of the status of information itself. This raises old questions about the proper relation between data, information, knowledge and a fourth category, which has a low profile today, wisdom. But IT gives their ethical consideration a new urgency, and also connects them with another cluster of problems to do with property: information as a commodity. 'Information' is produced for sale in the market-place. But what should rightly be defended as 'public information', as a 'resource'? What should be the limits to commodification?

The second criterion is that of realism about strategies. It is all very well for 'processed' (read 'alienated') San Francisco office-workers to parade the streets wearing cardboard visual display terminals over their heads, but such demonstrations do not exhaust the possibilities of strategic action relating to IT. The kind of realism required is that which connects possibilities for alternative action with actual conditions in a given social context. Despite the apparent cohesiveness of the 'information society' vision, it is unlikely that alternatives to it will be similarly homogeneous.

Although it may be possible theoretically to show how modern societies are increasingly divided between classes of people with and without control over and access to information, in real life their struggles are on numerous and often unconnected fronts. The labour process and industrial relations offer some obvious examples of appropriate strategies. New Technology Agreements, for whatever reason they are introduced,

may be used to monitor and control the process of adapting to new technologies. Demonstrations of automation and robotics whose introduction does not de-skill or displace labour are vital here.

Other strategies run through a spectrum including formal political activity within existing parties, involvement in the political process by social movements, attempts to influence communications or educational policy and local grass-roots action. Legislative change, such as data protection, clearly requires activity of the former sort. But concern for IT alternatives may also be expressed in conjunction with other movements. In Britain, the 'Microsyster' organization attempts to redress the gender imbalance within IT, while 'Microelectronics for Peace' encourages the fostering of alternatives to military developments, mainly within the big IT transnationals. Similar organizations, such as the American 'Computer Professionals for Social Responsibility', exist elsewhere.

NOTES

1 Information Technology Advisory Panel, *Learning to Live with IT* (London: HMSO, 1986).
2 B. Goudzwaard, *Aid for the Overdeveloped West* (Toronto: Wedge, 1975), p. 4.

Part 14 — Government and Politics

Most modern industrial societies regard themselves as democracies. But what exactly is democracy? This issue is taken up by David Beetham and Kevin Boyle in Reading 48. Democracy, the authors argue, does not just belong to the sphere of government as such. Democratic principles can be involved in decision-making in any kind of organization. We can, and should, relate democracy in government to the level of democratic development of other institutions in society.

In his contribution to this part, Ernest Gellner (Reading 49) addresses the issue of the nature of nationalism and its relation to the modern state. Nationalism, he proposes, is essentially a theory of political legitimacy, by means of which ethnic boundaries are made subordinate to the overall political integration of the state. Sentiments of nationalism, and the boundaries of nation states, he stresses, do not necessarily coincide; hence the impact of nationalist beliefs can foster the disintegration as well as the cohesion of states.

There is no democracy without political parties. In democratic systems parties compete for a share of the vote in order to decide who shall govern a country. For the past several decades, however, parties in most countries seemed to have been on the decline. Rates of party membership have declined, while the proportion of voters who say they have no fixed affiliation to any party has risen deeply. Yet, as Reading 50 makes clear, the level of party decline can be exaggerated.

Moreover, even if membership has declined, parties remain the chief vehicle for organizing political interests and the bigger parties still normally sustain high levels of finance. Parties will be with us for a long time yet.

All democratic systems are nationally or regionally based. But many of the forces which influence our societies today are much more wide-ranging, connected as they are with global events and issues. Can we produce a form of democratic governance appropriate for the globalized world in which we now live? Economic exchange has now gone massively beyond the boundaries of any particular society, but democratic institutions so far have not. The giant corporations, such as those involved in the media world, are able to dominate large aspects of the world economy and shift people and resources around more or less at will. It might seem as though we simply have to give up on our capacity to govern globalism. Yet Benjamin Barber in Reading 51 suggests that we should not be too pessimistic. Civic organizations and social movements can help counter undemocratic global forces. Governments are forced to take note of the activities of civic groups, as are corporations. In a globalizing world what corporations do is continually under the gaze of such groups who, by means of modern information systems, are able to chart out what they do in any part of the world. Governments working collaboratively in the global arena can also still exert a great deal of power.

48 What is Democracy?

David Beetham and Kevin Boyle

Throughout our lives we are members of different groups or associations, from families, neighbourhoods, clubs and work-units to nations and states. In all such associations, from the smallest to the largest, decisions have to be taken for the association as a whole: about the goals to be pursued, about the rules to be followed, about the distribution of responsibilities and benefits between members. These can be called *collective* decisions, in contrast to *individual* decisions taken by people on behalf of themselves alone. Democracy belongs to this sphere of collective decision-making. It embodies the ideal that such decisions, affecting an association as a whole, should be taken by all its members, and that they should each have equal rights to take part in such decisions, Democracy, in other words, entails the twin principles of *popular control* over collective decision-making and *equality of rights* in the exercise of that control. To the extent that these principles are realized in the decision-making of any association, we can call it democratic.

Defining democracy in this way makes two things clear at the outset. The first is that democracy does not just belong to the sphere of the state or of government, as we usually tend to think of it. Democratic principles are relevant to collective decision-making in any kind of association. Indeed, there is an important relation between democracy at the level of the state and democracy in the other institutions of society. However, because the state is the most inclusive association, with the right to regulate the affairs of society as a whole, the ability to raise compulsory taxation and the power of life and death over its members, democracy at the level of the state is of crucial importance. It is with democratic government, therefore, that we shall be mostly concerned.

The second point about our definition is that democracy is not an all-or-nothing affair, which an association possesses either in full or not at all. It is rather a matter of degree; of the extent to which the principles of popular control and political equality are realized; of greater or lesser approximations towards the ideal of equal participation in collective decision-making. Conventionally we have come to call a state 'democratic' if its government is accountable to the people through competitive election to public office, where all adults have an equal right to vote and to stand for election, and where civil and political rights are legally guaranteed. However, no such state in practice realizes the two principles of popular control and political equality as fully as it might. To that extent the work of democratization is never ended; and democrats everywhere are involved in struggles to consolidate and extend the realization of democratic principles, whatever regime or political system they happen to live under.

There are many reasons why democracy should be valued. Democracy aims to treat all people equally. 'Everyone to count for one and none for more than one', wrote the English legal theorist Jeremy Bentham in his attack on the aristocratic view that some people's lives were intrinsically more valuable than others. The principle of equality requires not only that people's interests should be attended to equally by government policy, but also that their views should count equally.

'We give no special power to wealth,' spoke an Athenian in one of Euripides' plays; 'the poor man's voice commands equal authority.' Critics of democracy have always objected that the mass of people are too ignorant, too uneducated and too short-sighted to take any part in determining public policy. To this democrats answer that the people certainly need information and the time to make sense of it, but are perfectly capable of acting responsibly when required to do so. Just as we expect all adults to take responsibility for directing their own personal lives, so they are also capable of taking a share in decisions affecting the life of their society.

Democratic government is more likely than other types of government to meet the needs of ordinary people. The more say people have in the direction of policy, the more likely it is to reflect their concerns and aspirations. 'The cobbler makes the shoe', went the ancient Athenian saying, 'but only the wearer can tell where it pinches.' It is ordinary people who experience the effects of government policy in practice, and only if there are effective and consistent channels of influence and pressure from below does government policy reflect this experience. However well-intentioned the holders of public office may be, if they are immune from popular influence or control, their policies will be at best inappropriate to people's needs and at worst self-serving and corrupt.

Democracy relies upon open debate, persuasion and compromise. The democratic emphasis on debate assumes not only that there are differences of opinion and interest on most questions of policy, but that such differences have a right to be expressed and listened to. Democracy thus presupposes diversity and plurality within society as well as equality between citizens. And when such diversity finds expression, the democratic method of resolving differences is through discussion, through persuasion and compromise, rather than by forceful imposition or the simple assertion of power. Democracies have often been caricatured as mere 'talking shops'. However, their capacity for public debate should be seen as a virtue rather than a vice, since it is the best means for securing consent to policy, and is not necessarily inconsistent with decisive action.

Democracy guarantees basic freedoms. Open discussion, as the method for expressing and resolving societal differences, cannot take place without those freedoms that are enshrined in conventions of civil and political rights: the rights of free speech and expression, of association with others, of movement, of security for the person. Democracies can be relied on to protect these rights, since they are essential to their own mode of existence. At best such rights allow for the personal development of individuals and produce collective decisions that are better for being tested against a variety of argument and evidence.

Democracy allows for societal renewal. By providing for the routine and peaceful removal of policies and politicians that have failed or outlived their usefulness, democratic systems are able to ensure societal and generational renewal without the massive upheaval or governmental disruption that attends the removal of key personnel in non-democratic regimes.

The idea that ordinary people should be entitled to a say in the decisions that affect their lives is one that has emerged as an aspiration in many different historical societies. It achieved a classical institutional form in Athens in the fifth and fourth centuries BC. From the early fifth century onwards, when property qualifications for public office were removed, each Athenian citizen had an equal right to take part in person in discussions and votes in the assembly on the laws and policies of the community, and also to share in their administration through jury service and membership of the administrative council, which were recruited in rotation by lot. The example of this first working democracy has been a reference point and source of inspiration to democrats ever since. The fact that it coincided with a period of Athenian economic and naval supremacy, and with an enormous flourishing of creative arts and philosophical enquiry, put paid to the idea that giving ordinary people a say in their affairs would produce either a society of drab uniformity or irresponsible government, as the critics of democracy have often asserted.

Athenian democracy was both more and less democratic than the democracies we know today. It was more democratic in that citizens took part in person in the main decisions of the society ('direct democracy'), whereas today's representative democracies are indirect, and citizens stand at least at one remove from the decision-making processes of government and parliament. For direct democracy to be possible requires a relatively small citizen body capable of being accommodated in a single place of assembly, and one with enough time free from other responsibilities to be able to grasp the evidence and arguments necessary to make an informed political decision. Neither requirement for direct democracy is met by the citizen bodies of today, though there is scope for their involvement in direction decision-making at national level in elections and referenda, and for more continuous participation in decision-making at very local levels.

Athenian democracy was less democratic than democracies of today, however, in that citizenship was restricted to free-born males; it excluded women, slaves and resident foreigners, these groups ensuring the continuity of the domestic and productive work necessary to enable the male citizens to engage in political activity. So the active participation of a direct democracy was only possible at all because the citizenship was restricted. 'The people' certainly ruled, but they did so from a position of privilege.

It is worth recalling that similar restrictions on citizenship existed in most Western parliamentary systems until well into the twentieth century. The principle made famous by the French Revolution that 'all political authority stems from the people' was not intended to include all the people. Thus it is only in this century that women and propertyless males have been granted the suffrage in most Western countries; and even today not all adult residents of a country are entitled to vote in its elections, however much they may contribute to its economy.

Can a representative system be really democratic? The eighteenth-century political theorist Rousseau thought not. In a representative system, he argued, people are only free once every few years at election time; thereafter they revert to a position of subordination to their rulers which is no better than slavery. This is an extreme version of the characteristic left-wing or radical criticism that representative systems are not properly democratic, in contrast to the right-wing objection that they give people too much say.

The simple response is that a representative system is the best system yet devised for securing popular control over government in circumstances where the citizen body is numbered in millions and has not the time to devote itself continuously to political affairs. The theory is that the people control the government by electing its head (president or prime minister) and by choosing the members of a legislature or parliament that can exercise continuous supervision over the government on the people's behalf, through its power to approve or reject legislation and taxation. This popular control is only effective, however, to the extent that elections are 'free and fair', that government is open, and that parliament has sufficient powers in practice to scrutinize and control its actions.

Although elections are the principal means by which people have a say in government policy in a representative system, they are not the only means. People can join associations to campaign for and against changes in legislation; they can become members of political parties; they can lobby their representatives in person. Governments in turn can be required to consult those affected by their policies or a selected cross-section of the electorate. In practice, few representative governments are immune to expressions of public opinion such as are regularly provided by opinion polls or through the press, radio and television. Yet all these channels of popular influence are ultimately dependent upon the effectiveness of the electoral process. Governments will only listen seriously to the people when there is a realistic possibility that they will be turned out of office if they do not.

So popular control in a representative system is secured by the direct influence people exercise over the direction of government policy and personnel at elections, through the continuous supervision exercised over government by a representative assembly or parliament and by the organized expression of public opinion through a variety of channels, which governments have to take into account.

What about the second democratic principle [...] that of political equality? A representative system involves inequality at least in this respect, that it gives a small number of the population the right to take political decisions on behalf of the rest. Within these limits, however, political equality can be achieved to the extent that there is an effective equal right for all citizens to stand for public office, to campaign on public issues and to obtain redress in the event of maladministration; and that the electoral system gives equal value to each person's vote. In practice most representative democracies do not fully satisfy these criteria, since political equality is substantially qualified by systematic differences in the wealth, time, access and other resources possessed by different groups of the population. It is one of the tasks of democrats in a representative system to find ways to reduce the political impact of these differences, as well as to make more effective the various mechanisms of popular control over government.

In a large society people can exercise little public influence as individuals, but can in association with others. Political parties bring together those who share similar views and interests to campaign for political office and influence. They perform a number of different functions. For the *electorate* they help simplify the electoral choice by offering broad policy positions and programmes between which to choose. For *governments* they provide a reasonably stable following of political supporters to enable them to achieve their programmes once elected. For the *more politically committed* they provide an opportunity for involvement in public affairs, a means of political education and a channel for influencing public policy.

49 Nations and Nationalism

Ernest Gellner

Nationalism is primarily a political principle, which holds that the political and the national unit should be congruent.

Nationalism as a sentiment, or as a movement can best be defined in terms of this principle. Nationalist *sentiment* is the feeling of anger aroused by the violation of the principle, or the feeling of satisfaction aroused by its fulfilment. A nationalist *movement* is one actuated by a sentiment of this kind.

There is a variety of ways in which the nationalist principle can be violated. The political boundary of a given state can fail to include all the members of the appropriate nation; or it can include them all but also include some foreigners; or it can fail in both these ways at once, not incorporating all the nationals and yet also including some non-nationals. Or again, a nation may live, unmixed with foreigners, in a multiplicity of states, so that no single state can claim to be *the* national one.

But there is one particular form of the violation of the nationalist principle to which nationalist sentiment is quite particularly sensitive: if the rulers of the political unit belong to a nation other than that of the majority of the ruled, this, for nationalists, constitutes a quite outstandingly intolerable breach of political propriety. This can occur either through the incorporation of the national territory in a larger empire, or by the local domination of an alien group.

In brief, nationalism is a theory of political legitimacy, which requires that ethnic boundaries should not cut across political ones, and, in particular, that ethnic boundaries within a given state – a contingency already formally excluded by the principle in its general formulation – should not separate the power-holders from the rest.

The nationalist principle can be asserted in an ethical, 'universalistic' spirit. There could be, and on occasion there have been, nationalists-in-the-abstract, unbiased in favour of any special nationality of their own, and generously preaching the doctrine for all nations alike: let all nations have their own political roofs, and let all of them also refrain from including non-nationals under it. There is no formal contradiction in asserting such non-egoistic nationalism. As a doctrine it can be supported by some good arguments, such as the desirability of preserving cultural diversity, of a pluralistic international political system and of the diminution of internal strains within states.

In fact, however, nationalism has often not been so sweetly reasonable, nor so rationally symmetrical. It may be that, as Immanuel Kant believed, partiality, the tendency to make exceptions on one's own behalf or one's own case, is *the* central human weakness from which all others flow; and that it infects national sentiment as it does all else, engendering what the Italians under Mussolini called the *sacro egoismo* of nationalism. It may also be that the political effectiveness of national sentiment would be much impaired if nationalists had as fine a sensibility to the wrongs committed by their nation as they have to those committed against it.

But over and above these considerations there are others, tied to the specific nature of the world we happen to live in, which militate against any impartial, general, sweetly reasonable nationalism.

To put it in the simplest possible terms: there is a very large number of potential nations on earth. Our planet also contains room for a certain number of independent or autonomous political units. On any reasonable calculation, the former number (of potential nations) is probably much, *much* larger than that of possible viable states. If this argument or calculation is correct, not all nationalisms can be satisfied, at any rate at the same time. The satisfaction of some spells the frustration of others. This argument is further and immeasurably strengthened by the fact that very many of the potential nations of this world live, or until recently have lived, not in compact territorial units but intermixed with each other in complex patterns. It follows that a territorial political unit can only become ethnically homogeneous, in such cases, if it either kills, or expels, or assimilates all non-nationals. Their unwillingness to suffer such fates may make the peaceful implementation of the nationalist principle difficult.

These definitions must, of course, like most definitions, be applied with common sense. The nationalist principle, as defined, is not violated by the presence of *small* numbers of resident foreigners, or even by the presence of the occasional foreigner in, say, a national ruling family. Just how many resident foreigners or foreign members of the ruling class there must be before the principle is effectively violated cannot be stated with precision. There is no sacred percentage figure, below which the foreigner can be benignly tolerated, and above which he becomes offensive and his safety and life are at peril. No doubt the figure will vary with circumstances. The impossibility of providing a generally applicable and precise figure, however, does not undermine the usefulness of the definition.

Our definition of nationalism was parasitic on two as yet undefined terms: state and nation.

Discussion of the state may begin with Max Weber's celebrated definition of it as that agency within society which possesses the monopoly of legitimate violence. The idea behind this is simple and seductive: in well-ordered societies, such as most of us live in or aspire to live in, private or sectional violence is illegitimate. Conflict as such is not illegitimate, but it cannot rightfully be resolved by private or sectional violence. Violence may be applied only by the central political authority, and those to whom it delegates this right. Among the various sanctions of the maintenance of order, the ultimate one – force – may be applied only by one special, clearly identified and well centralized disciplined agency within society. That agency or group of agencies *is* the state.

The idea enshrined in this definition corresponds fairly well with the moral intuitions of many, probably most, members of modern societies. Nevertheless, it is not entirely satisfactory. There are 'states' – or, at any rate, institutions which we would normally be inclined to call by that name – which do not monopolize legitimate violence within the territory which they more or less effectively control. A feudal state does not necessarily object to private wars between its fief-holders, provided they also fulfil their obligations to their overlord; or again, a state counting tribal populations among its subjects does not necessarily object to the institution of the feud, as long as those who indulge in it refrain from endangering neutrals on the public highway or in the market. The Iraqi state, under British tutelage after World War I, tolerated tribal raids, provided the raiders dutifully reported at the nearest police station before and after the expedition, leaving an orderly bureaucratic record of slain and booty. In brief, there are states which lack either the will or the means to enforce their monopoly of legitimate violence, and which none the less remain, in many respects, recognizable 'states'.

Weber's underlying principle does, however, seem valid *now*, however strangely ethnocentric it may be as a general definition, with its tacit assumption of the well-centralized Western state. The state constitutes one highly distinctive and important elaboration of the social division of labour. Where there is no division of labour, one cannot even begin to speak of the state. But not any or every specialism makes a state: the state is the specialization and concentration of order maintenance. The 'state' is that institution or set of institutions specifically concerned with the enforcement of order (whatever else they may also be concerned with). The state exists where specialized order-enforcing agencies, such as police forces and courts, have separated out from the rest of social life. They *are* the state.

Not all societies are state-endowed. It immediately follows that the problem of nationalism does not arise for stateless societies. If there is no state, one obviously cannot ask whether or not its boundaries are congruent with the limits of nations. If there are no rulers, there being no state, one cannot ask whether they are of the same nation as the ruled. When neither state nor rulers exist, one cannot resent their failure to conform to the requirements of the principle of nationalism. One may perhaps deplore statelessness, but that is another matter. Nationalists have generally fulminated against the distribution of political power and the nature of political boundaries, but they have seldom if ever had occasion to deplore the absence of power and of boundaries altogether. The circumstances in which nationalism has generally arisen have not normally been those in which the state itself, as such, was lacking, or when its reality was in any serious doubt. The state was only too conspicuously present. It was its boundaries and/or the distribution of power, and possibly of other advantages, within it which were resented.

This in itself is highly significant. Not only is our definition of nationalism parasitic on a prior and assumed definition of the state: it also seems to be the case that nationalism emerges only in milieux in which the existence of the state is already very much taken for granted. The existence of politically centralized units, and of a moral–political climate in which such centralized units are taken for granted and are treated as normative, is a necessary though by no means a sufficient condition of nationalism.

By way of anticipation, some general historical observations should be made about the state. Mankind has passed through three fundamental stages in its history: the pre-agrarian, the agrarian and the industrial. Hunting and gathering bands were and are too small to allow the kind of political division of labour which constitutes the state; and so, for them, the question of the state, of a stable specialized order-enforcing institution, does not really arise. By contrast, most, but by no means all, agrarian societies have been state-endowed. Some of these states have been strong and some weak, some have been despotic and others law-abiding. They differ a very great deal in their form. The agrarian phase of human history is the period during which, so to speak, the very existence of the state is an option. Moreover, the form of the state is highly variable. During the hunting-gathering stage, the option was not available.

By contrast, in the post-agrarian, industrial age there is, once again, no option; but now the *presence*, not the absence of the state is inescapable. Paraphrasing Hegel, once none had the state, then some had it, and finally all have it. The form it takes, of course, still remains variable. There are some traditions of social thought – anarchism, Marxism – which hold that even, or especially, in an industrial order the state is dispensable, at least under favourable conditions or under conditions due to be realized in the fullness of time. There are obvious and powerful reasons for doubting this: industrial societies are enormously large, and depend for the standard of living to which they have become accustomed (or to which they ardently wish to become accustomed) on an unbelievably intricate general division of labour and co-operation. Some of this co-operation might under favourable conditions be spontaneous and need no central sanctions. The idea that all of it could perpetually work in this way, that it could exist without any enforcement and control, puts an intolerable strain on one's credulity.

So the problem of nationalism does not arise when there is no state. It does not follow that the problem of nationalism arises for each and every state. On the contrary, it arises only for *some* states. It remains to be seen which ones do face this problem.

The definition of the nation presents difficulties graver than those attendant on the definition of the state. Although modern man tends to take the centralized state (and, more specifically, the centralized national state) for granted, nevertheless he is capable, with relatively little effort, of seeing its contingency, and of imagining a social situation in which the state is absent. He is quite adept at visualizing the 'state of nature'. An anthropologist can explain to him that the tribe is not necessarily a state writ small, and that forms of tribal organization exist which can be described as stateless. By contrast, the idea of a man without a nation seems to impose a far greater strain on the modern imagination. [. . .]

A man must have a nationality as he must have a nose and two ears; a deficiency in any of these particulars is not inconceivable and does from time to time occur, but only as a result of some disaster, and it is itself a disaster of a kind. All this seems obvious, though, alas, it is not true. But that it should have come to *seem* so very obviously true is indeed an aspect, or perhaps the very core, of the problem of nationalism. Having a nation is not an inherent attribute of humanity, but it has now come to appear as such.

In fact, nations, like states, are a contingency, and not a universal necessity. Neither nations nor states exist at all times and in all circumstances. Moreover, nations and states are not the *same* contingency. Nationalism holds that they were destined for each other; that either without the other is incomplete, and constitutes a tragedy. But before they could become intended for each other, each of them had to emerge, and their emergence was independent and contingent. The state has certainly emerged without the help of the nation. Some nations have certainly emerged without the blessings of their own state. It is more debatable whether the normative idea of the nation, in its modern sense, did not presuppose the prior existence of the state.

What then is this contingent, but in our age seemingly universal and normative, idea of the nation? Discussion of two very makeshift, temporary definitions will help to pinpoint this elusive concept.

1   Two men are of the same nation if and only if they share the same culture, where culture in turn means a system of ideas and signs and associations and ways of behaving and communicating.
2   Two men are of the same nation if and only if they *recognize* each other as belonging to the same nation. In other words, *nation maketh man*; nations are the artefacts of men's convictions and loyalties and solidarities. A mere category of persons (say, occupants of a given territory, or speakers of a given language, for example) becomes a nation if and when the members of the category firmly recognize certain mutual rights and duties to each other in virtue of their shared membership of it. It is their recognition of each other as fellows of this kind which turns them into a nation, and not the other shared attributes, whatever they might be, which separate that category from non-members.

50 Are Political Parties Empty Vessels?

The Economist

What would democracy look like if there were no political parties? It is almost impossible to imagine. In every democracy worth the name, the contest to win the allegiance of the electorate and form a government takes place through political parties. Without them, voters would be hard put to work out what individual candidates stood for or intended to do once elected. If parties did not 'aggregate' people's interests, politics might degenerate into a fight between tiny factions, each promoting its narrow self-interest. But for the past 30 years, political scientists have been asking whether parties are 'in decline'. Are they? And if so, does it matter?

Generalising about political parties is difficult. Their shape depends on a country's history, constitution and much else. For example, America's federal structure and separation of powers make Republicans and Democrats amorphous groupings whose main purpose is to put their man in the White House. British parties behave quite differently because members of Parliament must toe the party line to keep their man in Downing Street. An American president is safe once elected, so congressmen behave like local representatives rather than members of a national organisation bearing collective responsibility for government. Countries which, unlike Britain and America, hold elections under proportional representation are different again: they tend to produce multi-party systems and coalition governments.

Despite these differences, some trends common to almost all advanced democracies appear to be changing the nature of parties and, on one view, making them less influential. Those who buy this thesis of decline point to the following changes:

People's behaviour is becoming more *private*. Why join a political party when you can go fly-fishing or surf the web? Back in the 1950s, clubs affiliated to the Labour Party were places for Britain's working people to meet, play and study. The Conservative Party was, among other things, a marriage bureau for the better-off. Today, belonging to a British political party is more like being a supporter of some charity: you may pay a membership fee, but will not necessarily attend meetings or help to turn out the vote at election time.

Running out of ideas

Politics is becoming more *secular*. Before the 1960s, political struggles had an almost religious intensity: in much of Western Europe this took the form of communists versus Catholics, or workers versus bosses. But ideological differences were narrowing by the 1960s and became smaller still after the collapse of Soviet communism. Nowadays, politics seems to be more often about policies than values, about the competence of leaders rather than the beliefs of the led. As education grows and class distinctions blur, voters discard old loyalties. In America in 1960, two out of five voters saw themselves as 'strong' Democrats or 'strong' Republicans. By 1996 less than one in three saw themselves that way. The proportion of British voters expressing a 'very strong' affinity with one party slumped from 44 per cent to 16 per cent between 1964 and 1997. This process of '*partisan de-alignment*' has been witnessed in most mature democracies.

The erosion of loyalty is said to have pushed parties towards the *ideological centre*. The political extremes have not gone away. But mainstream parties which used to offer a straight choice between socialists and conservatives are no longer so easy to label. In the late 1950s Germany's Social Democrats (SPD) snipped off their Marxist roots in order to recast themselves as a *Volkspartei* appealing to all the people. 'New' Labour no longer portrays itself as the political arm of the British working class or trade-union movement. Bill Clinton, before he became president, helped to shift the Democratic Party towards an appreciation of business and free trade. Neat ideological labels have become harder to pin on parties since they have had to contend with the emergence of what some commentators call *post-material issues* (such as the environment, personal morality and consumer rights) which do not slot elegantly into the old left-right framework.

The *mass media* have taken over many of the information functions that parties once performed for themselves. 'Just as radio and television have largely killed off the door-to-door salesman,' says Anthony King, of Britain's Essex University, 'so they have largely killed off the old-fashioned party worker.' In 1878 the German SPD had nearly 50 of its own newspapers. Today the mass media enable politicians to communicate directly with voters without owning printing presses or needing party workers to knock on doors. In many other ways, the business of winning elections has become more capital-intensive and less labour-intensive, making political donors matter more and political activists less.

Another apparent threat to the parties is the growth of *interest and pressure groups*. Why should voters care about the broad sweep of policy promoted during elections by a party when other organisations will lobby all year round for their special interest, whether this is protection of the environment, opposition to abortion, or the defence of some subsidy? Some academics also claim that parties are playing a smaller role, and

think tanks a bigger one, in making policy, Although parties continue to draw up election manifestos, they are wary of being too specific. Some hate leaving policymaking to party activists, who may be more extreme than voters at large and so put them off. Better to keep the message vague. Or why not let the tough choices be taken by *referendums*, as so often in Switzerland?

Academics have found these trends easier to describe than to evaluate. Most agree that the age of the 'mass party' has passed and that its place is being taken by the 'electoral-professional' or 'catch-all' party. Although still staffed by politicians holding genuine beliefs and values, these modern parties are inclined to see their main objective as winning elections rather than forming large membership organisations or social movements, as was once the case.

Is this a bad thing? Perhaps, if it reduces participation in politics. One of the traditional roles of political parties has been to get out the vote, and in 18 out of 20 rich countries, recent turnout figures have been lower than they were in the 1950s. Although it is hard to pin down the reasons, Martin Wattenberg, of the University of California at Irvine, points out that turnout has fallen most sharply in countries where parties are weak: Switzerland (thanks to those referendums), America and France (where presidential elections have become increasingly candidate- rather than party-centred), and Japan (where political loyalties revolve around ties to internal factions rather than the party itself). In Scandinavia, by contrast, where class-based parties are still relatively strong, turnout has held up much better since the 1950s.

Running out of members

It is not only voters who are turned off. Party membership is falling too, and even the most strenuous attempts to reverse the decline have faltered. Germany is a case in point. The Social Democrats there increased membership rapidly in the 1960s and 1970s, and the Christian Democrats responded by doubling their own membership numbers. But since the end of the 1980s mem-

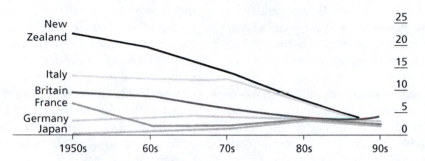

Figure 50.1 The few not the many: party members as percentage of electorate

Source: Susan E. Scarrow, Center for German and European Studies Working Paper 259, University of California, Berkeley

bership has been falling, especially among the young. In 1964 Britain's Labour Party had about 830,000 members and the Conservatives about 2 m. By 1997 they had 420,000 and 400,000 respectively. The fall is sharper in some countries than others, but research by Susan Scarrow of the University of Houston suggests that the trend is common to most democracies (see figure 50.1). With their membership falling, ideological differences blurring, and fewer people turning out to vote, the decline thesis looks hard to refute.

Or does it? The case for party decline has some big holes in it. For a start, some academics question whether political parties ever really enjoyed the golden age which other academics hark back to. Essex University's Mr King points out that a lot of the evidence for decline is drawn from a handful of parties – Britain's two main ones, the German SPD, the French and Italian Communists – which did indeed once promote clear ideologies, enjoy mass memberships, and organise local branches and social activities. But neither of America's parties, nor Canada's, nor many of the bourgeois parties of Western Europe, were ever mass parties of that sort. Moreover, in spite of their supposed decline, parties continue to keep an iron grip on many aspects of politics.

In most places, for example, parties still control *nomination for public office*. In almost all of the mature democracies, it is rare for independent candidates to be elected to federal or state legislatures, and even in local government the

proportion of independents has declined sharply since the early 1970s. When state and local parties select candidates, they usually favour people who have worked hard within the party. German parties, for example, are often conduits to jobs in the public sector, with a say over appointments to top jobs in the civil service and to the boards of publicly owned utilities or media organisations. Even in America, where independent candidates are more common in local elections, the parties still run city, county and state 'machines' in which most politicians start their careers.

Naturally, there are some exceptions. In 1994 Silvio Berlusconi, a media tycoon, was able to make himself prime minister at the head of Forza Italia, a right-wing movement drawing heavily on his personal fortune and the resources of his television empire. Ross Perot, a wealthy third-party candidate, won a respectable 19 per cent vote in his 1992 bid for the American presidency. The party declinists claim these examples as evidence for their case. But it is notable that in the end Mr Perot could not compete against the two formidable campaigning and money-raising machines ranged against him.

This suggests that a decline in the membership of parties need not make them weaker in *money and organisation*. In fact, many have enriched themselves simply by passing laws that give them public money. In Germany, campaign subsidies to the federal parties more than trebled between 1970 and 1990, and parties now receive between

20 per cent and 40 per cent of their income from public funds. In America, the paid professionals who have taken over from party activists tend to do their job more efficiently. Moreover, other kinds of political activity – such as donating money to a party or interest group, or attending meetings and rallies – have become more common in America. Groups campaigning for particular causes or candidates (the pro-Republican Christian Coalition, say, or the pro-Democrat National Education Association) may not be formally affiliated with the major party organisations, but are frequently allied with them.

The role of the mass media deserves a closer look as well. It is true that they have weakened the parties' traditional methods of communicating with members. But parties have invested heavily in managing relations with journalists, and making use of new media to reach both members and wider audiences. In Britain, the dwindling of local activists has gone hand-in-hand with a more professional approach to communications. Margaret Thatcher caused a stir by using an advertising firm, Saatchi & Saatchi, to push the Tory cause in the 1979 election. By the time of Britain's 1997 election, the New Labour media operation run from Millbank Tower in London was even slicker.

Another way to gauge the influence of parties is by their *reach* – that is, their power, once in office, to take control of the governmental apparatus. This is a power they have retained. Most governments tend to be unambiguously under the control of people who represent a party, and who would not be in government if they did not belong to such organisations. The French presidential system may appear ideal for independent candidates, but except – arguably – for Charles de Gaulle, who claimed to rise above party, none has ever been elected without party support.

The fire next time

Given the cautions that must be applied to other parts of the case for party decline, what can be said about one of the declinists' key exhibits, the erosion of ideological differences? At first sight,

this is borne out by the recent movement to the centre of left-leaning parties such as America's Democrats, New Labour in Britain, and the SPD under Gerhard Schröder. In America, Newt Gingrich stoked up some fire amongst Republicans in 1994, but it has flickered out. The most popular Republican presidential hopefuls, and especially George W. Bush, the front-runner, are once again stressing the gentler side of their conservatism.

Still, the claim of ideological convergence can be exaggerated. It is not much more than a decade since Ronald Reagan and Mrs Thatcher ran successful parties with strong ideologies. And the anecdotal assumption that parties are growing less distinct is challenged by longer-term academic studies. A look at the experience of ten western democracies since 1945 (*Parties, Policies and Democracy*, Westview Press, 1994) concluded that the leading left and right parties continued to keep their distance and maintain their identity, rather than clustering around the median voter in the centre. Paul Webb of Britain's Brunel University concludes in a forthcoming book (*Political Parties in Advanced Industrial Democracies*, Oxford University Press) that although partisan sentiment is weaker than it was, and voters more cynical, parties have in general adapted well to changing circumstances.

Besides, even if party differences are narrowing at present, why expect that trend to continue? In Western Europe, the ending of the cold war has snuffed out one source of ideological conflict, but new sparks might catch fire. Battered right-wing parties may try to revive their fortunes by pushing the nationalist cause against the encroachments of the European Union. In some places where ideas are dividing parties less, geography is dividing them more. Politics in Germany and Britain has acquired an increasingly regional flavour: Labour and the Social Democrats respectively dominate the north, Conservatives and Christian Democrats the south. Disaffected *Ossis* are flocking to the Party of Democratic Socialism in eastern Germany. Britain, Italy, Canada and Spain have strong separatist parties.

So there is life in the party system yet. But the declinists are on to something. The Germans have a word for it. One reason given for the rise of Germany's Greens in the 1980s and America's Mr Perot in 1992 was *Parteienverdrossenheit* – disillusionment with mainstream parties that seemed to have abandoned their core beliefs and no longer offered meaningful choices. A 'new politics' of citizens' protests appeared to be displacing conventional politics.

In the end, far from undermining the domination of the parties, the German Greens ended up by turning themselves into one and joining the government in an uneasy coalition with the SPD.

The balance of evidence from around the world is that despite all the things that are changing them, parties continue to dominate democratic politics.

Indeed, there are grounds for wondering whether their continuing survival is more of a worry than their supposed decline. Is it so very comforting that parties can lose members, worry less about ideas, become detached from broader social movements, attract fewer voters and still retain an iron grip on politics? If they are so unanchored, will they not fall prey to special-interest groups? If they rely on state funding instead of member contributions, will they not turn into creatures of the state?

51 Globalizing Democracy

Benjamin R. Barber

Can globalism be governed? Or, as a first step, can we start by building a global civil society? Until recently, one could look in vain for a global 'we, the people' to be represented. That is now changing. There is another internationalism, a forming crystal around which a global polity can grow. Effective global governance to temper the excesses of the global market does not yet exist; however, international activism by nongovernmental organizations (NGOs) has made some surprising gains. People who care about public goods are working to recreate on a global scale the normal civic balance that exists within democratic nations. Consider the following:

A young woman named Jody Williams, with celebrity help from a princess (sadly deceased), creates a worldwide civic movement for a ban on land mines that actually enacts a treaty.

A Bangladeshi visionary, Mohammed Yunus, develops an idea for microfinancing, which makes mini-loans to women in third world societies, which at once jump-starts enterprise and liberates women from traditional servitude.

Striking fear into retired tyrants everywhere, European public opinion and spirited English law lords make possible the arrest of a Chilean ex-dictator. Ill health got Pinochet temporarily off the hook, but the Chilean Supreme Court has lifted his immunity and the tocsin has sounded. Dictators are no longer safe in their retirement havens.

Women's groups from around the world meet in Beijing in a demonstration of international solidarity that asks nothing of national governments and everything of civic institutions that are powerfully reinforced by their actions.

Multiplying coalitions of workers, environmentalists, students, and anarchists use the Internet to fashion a decentralized, nonideological resistance to the International Monetary Fund (IMF) and the World Trade Organization (WTO), effectively capturing media attention by taking to the streets in Seattle, Washington, D.C., and London. [. . .]

Citizen groups use 'Good Housekeeping seal' methods to underwrite safe fisheries ('dolphin-safe tuna') and rug manufacturers without child labor (Rugmark), while students at Duke University initiate a movement to ensure that campus sports apparel is not manufactured in child-exploiting sweatshops.

The market-friendly, stealth Multilateral Agreement on Investment that would further erode national attempts to regulate foreign investment is subjected to broad citizen scrutiny and indefinitely deferred.

Global Internet communication among groups facilitated by organizations like Peter Armstrong's oneworld.org and Globalvision's new mediachannel.org supersite are diverting the new telecommunications from pure commerce to the public interests of global civil society.

Europe responds as 'Europe' to a coalition between Austria's traditional parties and Jörg Haider's reactionary Freedom Party, signaling the potency of an emerging transnational public opinion operating across state boundaries.

Hundreds of NGOs gather in new international organizations like CIVICUS, the World Forum on Democracy, and Transparency International, and begin to develop the kind of civic networking across nations that corporations have enjoyed for decades, courtesy of the World Economic Forum at Davos, Switzerland.

President Clinton offers the corporate leaders at Davos a 'wake-up call' reminding them that there are 'new forces seeking to be heard in the global dialogue,' progressive forces that want to democratize rather than withdraw from the new world order.

What is afoot here? Davos is a good place to begin. For nearly 30 years, the world's multiplying multinational corporations, transnational banks, and speculators have met every February in the Swiss ski resort to network, strategize, and acquire legitimacy by mixing with invited statesmen and intellectuals. Davos has been a fit symbol for an international arena in which the 'three-legged stool' of government, civil society, and the private-market sector on which stable democracies are said to rest has been transformed into a tottering toadstool held up by a thick and solitary economic stem.

Markets have escaped the boundaries of eroding national frontiers and become global, but governing organizations have not. This has created a perilous asymmetry: Global economics operate in an anarchic realm without significant regulation and without the humanizing civic institutions that within national societies rescue it from raw social Darwinism. National boundaries have become too porous to hold the economy in, but remain sufficiently rigid to prevent democracy from getting out and civilizing the larger world. We have globalized our economic vices – crime, drugs, terror, hate, pornography, and financial speculation – but not our civic virtues. The result has been a growing tension between the beneficiaries of globalization and just about everyone else, a tension symbolized by the unrest in Seattle [. . .], and in Washington, D.C., and London [in 1999].

Yet while it has not yet attracted the attention of the media (inured to good news and prefer-

ring to celebrate globalization uncritically and treat resistance to it as Luddism or worse), the new millennium has in fact brought new efforts at overcoming the global imbalance. In June more than a dozen democracies – including not only the center-left regimes led by Bill Clinton, Lionel Jospin, Gerhard Schröder, and Tony Blair, but also South Africa, Argentina, Brazil, and Chile – met in Berlin to discuss how they might redress international injustices. A few weeks later, nearly 100 nations met in Warsaw under the somewhat hyperbolic banner of the 'community of democracies' – are there really 100 'democracies' in the world? fifty? twenty!? – to seek an even broader consensus for a democratic concert of nations.

More to the point, they met for the first time together with a fledgling transnational civil society – a parallel forum supported by Freedom House, Poland's Stefan Batory Foundation, and George Soros (author of a remarkable new critique of globalization called *Open Society*), with the title World Forum on Democracy. This forum assembled a company of NGOs, foundations, and intellectuals committed to strengthening global civil society; it underscored its novelty by actually holding a joint dinner and several meetings in common with the foreign ministers, who were eventually presented with a document in effect announcing, 'Here we are, and we want to be heard.' The World Forum plans biennial meetings, with work groups gathering more frequently, but it is by no means the only civil society umbrella group seeking a serious hearing on the global scene.

Last fall the National Endowment for Democracy had already convened the first of what were to be a series of global meetings of its own, the next of which will be in São Paulo. Other global civic umbrella groups playing on this turf (finally it is valuable enough to be the venue of turf wars!) include the aforementioned CIVICUS, a group of more than 500 NGOs that has been meeting for a half-dozen years; Transparency International, a German-based civic group focusing on monitoring corruption; and the Aventis

Foundation's Triangle Forum on the global future, which met in the middle of July at Robert Wilson's Watermill Center on Long Island for another of a series of trilateral discussions among businesspeople, politicians, NGO representatives, scholars, and (uniquely) artists, including Watermill's creator, Robert Wilson.

All this activity suggests we are entering a new era in which global markets and servile governments will no longer be completely alone in planning the world's fate. And just in time. While President Clinton showed at Seattle that he could talk eloquently about civic and human dilemmas of globalism (in a speech that upset his advisers), there has been no meaningful follow-up. On the contrary, with his fast-track legislation (failed) and his opening to China (apparently successful), Clinton is accelerating a headlong rush to global laissez-faire. Likewise Bush and Gore.

The asymmetries resulting from the rapid globalization of markets in the absence of any commensurable globalization of political and civic institutions are largely ignored by elected officials, even those of the center-left. Ripped from the box of the nation-state, which traditionally acted as its regulator and civilizer, capitalism turns mean and anarchic. The market sector is privileged; the political sector is largely eclipsed (when not subordinated to the purposes of the market); the private is elevated above the public, which is subjected to ruthless privatization at every turn. Liberty itself is redefined as the absence of governmental authority and hence an exclusively market phenomenon, while coercion and dependency are associated with government even when (especially when) government is democratic.

The difficulty nation-states have with globalization comes not just from the force of what is happening in the international arena but from ideological developments within nation-states. The push toward privatization is bipartisan. This is not decentralization – the devolution of power down the democratic public ladder to provinces, municipalities, and neighborhoods – but de-democratization, the shifting of concentrated power at the highest levels from public to private hands. Power shifted from authorities that were hierarchical but also public, transparent, and accountable, to authorities that remain hierarchical but are private, opaque, and undemocratic.

In the unfettered high-tech global market, crucial democratic values become relics. Indeed, because globalization is correctly associated with new telecommunication technologies, the globalized and privatized information economy is constructed as an inevitable concomitant of post-sovereign, postmodern society.

Media concentration versus democracy

Nowhere are the asymmetries of the new globalism more evident than in media mergers like Disney/ABC, Viacom/CBS, Verizon (Bell Atlantic/GTE), and AOL/Time Warner/CNN/EMI. These mergers present a challenge not just to economic competition in the domain of goods, labor, and capital, but to democracy and its defining virtues. These include free and autonomous information (guaranteed by the independent existence of plurally owned media), social and political diversity (guaranteed by genuine pluralism in society), and full participation by citizens in deciding public policies and securing public goods (guaranteed by a robust public domain). When Congress passed the Telecommunications Act of 1996 – the first major piece of legislation dealing with new media since the Federal Communications Act of 1934 – it effectively ceded the modern information economy to the private forces that control global markets.

The new monopolies are particularly insidious because while monopolies of the nineteenth century were in durable goods and natural resources, and exercised control over the goods of the body, new information-age monopolies of the twenty-first century are over news, entertainment, and knowledge, and exercise control over the goods of the mind and spirit. When governments control information and news, we call it totalitarianism; when monopolistic corporations control them, we call it free market strategy.

The impact on diversity is misleading because sources of content and information delivery appear to be multiplying. Superficially, this trend is pluralist and empowering. Analysts argue that AOL and Time Warner cover different consumer bases, and the new partners, Steve Case of AOL and Gerald Levin of Time Warner, both promise to pursue 'open access' on cable so that the owners of 'pipes' that carry content do not become monopoly gatekeepers. But it is hardly clear between AOL and Time Warner who actually represents the pipes and who the content. AOL controls online content but as a Web server is also a monolithic Web portal. Time Warner wanted the deal to get its content on the Web; it is a content provider but, via hard cable installations, also controls pipes. AOL wanted the deal to get its Net services on fast hard-wired cable (it currently depends on snail-speed telephone lines). To suggest there is no real overlap, to suggest there is other than one audience and one information market, is to badly misunderstand the technology and to muddy the real issues of monopoly and globalization in the new information society – as, ironically, the Disney corporation's assault on the merger cogently argues.

Indeed, the whole point of 'convergence' is to eliminate the features that separate hardware and software, the carriers and the content, until there is a seamless stream of information and entertainment entering your home: one medium, one content, one audience. Telephones, computers, televisions, VCRs, DVDs, video stores, and content companies are the segmented way of the past. The new media company must control them all; in an economy that demands integration and convergence, this means they must control (own) one another.

Monopoly is not an accidental outcome but a necessary condition of doing business in this new world. Vertical integration is a condition of synergy. When Bill Gates insists his integration of an Internet portal into his Windows operating system is a 'natural' extension of his original product, he is being truthful. But the truth he tells is that convergence means monopoly, and synergy

means vertical integration; that a capitalism still defined by real diversity, genuine competition, differential markets, and multiple firms is an anachronism – these are practices of the industrial past that have no place in the postindustrial information-economy future.

Now this may all represent a new and powerful logic of an information economy that dictates its own imperatives. But no one has spent much time trying to think about how this new economic logic in which private monopoly is a public good impacts the traditional logic of the democratic society, which holds that private monopoly is a public bad. There were good reasons for thinking that many newspapers and magazines were better than a few when the founders wrote the First Amendment. There were good reasons for thinking that broadcast media were public utilities over which the public had special claims when legislators wrote the Federal Communications Act of 1934. There were good reasons for thinking that diversity of content and pluralism of culture were integral virtues of a democratic society when America embraced multiculturalism in the 1980s and 1990s.

Does a change in private technological and economic logic mean that the public logic of democracy must accommodate itself uncomplainingly to that change? Or is it technology and the information economy that need to be reassessed and revised to meet our public goals and common goods as a democratic people? Should private logic dominate public logic in democracy? Are Steve Case, Gerald Levin, and Ted Turner appropriate unelected representatives to shape America's destiny as an information society? Will their decisions become de facto legislation for the rest of the world? These troublesome questions cannot be answered in the context of national politics. The real challenge is whether we can address the erosion of democracy in the asymmetrical setting of global markets, where such civic and political tools as are available to us within nations have gone missing.

Yet the outlook is not quite so pessimistic as the diagnosis suggests. Why? Because there is an emerging international alternative to global markets in new transnational civic organizations and social movements, and there are still political strategies that can oppose privatization within nations and then help nation-states reassert control over the global economy through traditional 'concert of nations' approaches. After all, the IMF and the WTO are not supranational organizations, but the tools of groups of powerful nations. They will bend to the will of democratic governments, if leading governments can once again represent the public interests of their sovereign peoples and can find ways to cooperate.

Transnational civil society

The marketplace functions effectively within nation-states because it is only one of three sectors. The private-business sector is not only balanced by the public-government sector, but the two are in turn mediated by a civil society that, like government, is public and composed of communities and other collective associations, but like the market is voluntary and free. Within nation-states, it is not the market alone but this stable tripod of governmental, civic, and private institutions that generates liberty and produces the pluralistic goods of free society. Rip the market from its nesting place in nation-states, however, and you have wild capitalism – wild not in itself (it is supposed to be aggressively competitive) but because in globalizing it slips the civilizing embrace of its nation-state hosts.

The turmoil in Seattle at the end of last year and in Washington, D.C., and London [. . .] arose from frustration. The protectionist backlash bespeaks a deep insecurity in the face of a world out of control – an exaggerated nightmare of a world in which American soldiers serve under foreign command, Islamic fundamentalists conspire to wage terror on the American heartland, jobs hemorrhage abroad, immigrants inundate the nation and rend its fragile unity. Far from suggesting common cause between American protestors and the wretched of the earth elsewhere, however, this backlash can look like an American

version of Jörg Haider's politics of fear. As Egypt's Economy Minister Youssef Boutros-Ghali said, 'The world is not represented on the streets of Seattle. The truth is, most of the world's population was inside the conference in Seattle, not outside.'

Yet the democratic world really is out of control because the instruments of benign control – democratic governing institutions – simply do not exist in the international setting, where markets in currency, labor, and goods run like engines without governors. Happily, the rising internationalism of transnational civic institutions and social movements promises a measure of countervailing power in the international arena and serves as an alternative to the reactionary politics of Pat Buchanan or Jean-Marie Le Pen.

These civic efforts – the work of citizens rather than governments, or the work of governments reacting to citizens (and not just their own) – embody a global public opinion in the making, a global civic engagement that can alone give the abstraction of international politics weight. The outreach of citizens and civic groups can make entities like 'Europe' more than a mere function of economic and security concerns. Coteries of NGOs, the shifting voice of global public opinion, and the emergent hand of the international rights movement may not be the equal of multinational corporations or international banks, but they represent a significant starting place for countervailing power. They put flesh on the bare bones of legalistic doctrines of universal rights. James Madison noted that a declaration of rights is a paper fortress from which it is impossible to defend real rights. Rights depend on engaged citizens and a civic space where their activities are possible. These new transnational civic spaces offer possibilities for transnational citizenship and hence an anchor for global rights.

A concert of nations

Even so, these transnational civic projects should not fool us into thinking that Amnesty International or Médecins Sans Frontières are the equivalent in clout of AOL Time Warner or the IMF. International markets spin out of control not just because the economy has been globalized, but because, nation by nation by nation, we have conspired in the transfer of sovereignty from popular hands that are transparent and accountable to private hands that are neither. We remain transfixed by privatization on the Thatcher/Reagan/Blair/Clinton model, and so we are unable to avail ourselves of the many potential control mechanisms already in place. We bemoan the absence of governance and international regulation over free markets, though in truth the international institutions most often vilified are ultimately instruments of sovereign nations acting in concert. Their subservience to multinational corporations and powerful banking and financial interests reflects not just some historically inevitable erosion of sovereignty but the willed sellout of sovereign peoples to the myths of privatization. As international civil society grows stronger, it can become a source of countervailing democratic pressure on national governments.

Technically, like the United Nations, the WTO is itself a creature of nation-states. Like the IMF and many other market institutions, it could be regarded as the exoskeleton of international governance. But privatization – globalization's nasty twin – has robbed the nations that nominally control it of their democratic will, and they appear to be servants rather than masters of the new global corporate sovereigns. With animals running the zoo, those who seek such public goods as environmental protection, transparency, accountability, labor safety, and the protection of children look in vain for keepers and finally settle for theatrics, raising a ruckus rather than effecting a change.

Were they to agree on policy, the leading industrial nations could probably work their will at the IMF and the WTO. Ironically, although global markets do erode national sovereignty, a reassertion of national sovereignty as a consequence of domestic political campaigns aimed at challenging privatization could go a long way toward controlling global markets. Currently, the WTO treats national 'boycotts' of imported goods, even when they are motivated by legitimate safety or environmental or child-labor concerns, as illegal. Its members can change these provisions. Third world nations worry with reason that first world environmental and safety and minimum wage concerns are a way of putting a human face on protectionism. By imposing impossible-to-meet standards, the United States can win back jobs from developing nations. But if first world governments agreed to pay the price of meeting those standards, they would win the support of third world governments in regulating global capitalism and improving standards worldwide.

National sovereignty is said to be a dying concept, but it is a long way from dead. Sovereign nations remain the locus of democratic society and the only viable powers capable of opposing, subduing, and civilizing the anarchic forces of the global economy. International civil society, the emerging global alternative to world markets, needs the active support of sovereign states for its fragile new institutions to have even a modest impact. Working together as they began to in Berlin and Warsaw in June, progressive forces within the democracies can increase the voice of civil society in how the world is organized and governed – but only if citizens and the new president they elect in November begin to listen to that voice in earnest.

Part 15 Mass Media and Communications

The media have an enormous influence on our lives – not only through the factual information they provide, as in the news, but in more subtle ways. People who watch soap operas, for example, may identify with the actors they watch and use them as role models for their own lives. Innumerable discussion groups for soap opera fans exist on the internet. In Reading 52, Nancy Baym discusses the significance of some of these. As she joined in with the groups, she found that she had entered a virtual community in which she not only got emotional rewards but was able to pursue intensive debates about characters and plots in the soap operas. On the basis of her participant observation in the groups, she rejects the idea that soap opera fans are merely passive consumers of culture living their lives through their favourite characters. Participants mostly provided witty and perceptive comments, not only on the soap operas themselves but on their relation to their own lives.

In Reading 53, James Slevin takes a general look at the history of the internet and its contemporary influence. The internet began as a military project within the US Department of Defense. In the late 1960s the department developed a new computer network designed to facilitate communication among its various sections. The idea was to enrich decision-making by the pooling of information and by expanding opportunities for individuals within the organization to interact with each other electronically. Following this, the internet moved into universities. Scientists and scholars made use of it to communicate with one another and to gain access to scholarly resources. Subsequently, businesses began to see the commercial applications of the internet and started to build new forms of connection and modes of searching for available information. Over recent years the internet has spread very rapidly, although most users are still at the present time concentrated in the US. Many businesses have reorganized their internal structures around 'intranets' – internet systems which are private to the organization in question. No one knows where the internet will lead, as the technology is probably only in its early period of development. But it has already affected many areas of social life and its impact is bound to spread further. It may eventually be even more important in less developed countries than in the developed ones. For an example, where people can gain access to the internet without the use of computers or wiring (for instance, by mobile phones), people in less developed countries can tap in directly to enormous educational and informational resources.

In Reading 54 John B. Thompson emphasizes that the reception of the 'messages' conveyed through the mass media is an actively organized one. Audiences respond to media messages selectively and in a critical fashion. The term 'mass' in mass media, Thompson points out, is somewhat misleading: media audiences may be very large, but they are also highly differentiated.

52 Tune in, Log on
Soaps, Fandom and Online Community

Nancy K. Baym

My daily routine in graduate school went something like this. When I was done teaching, taking my classes, and doing the readings or whatever else had to be done that day, I curled up on my couch, rewound the videotape, and (making liberal use of the fast-forward button) watched my soaps. Later, I turned on my computer and logged on to rec.arts.tv.soaps (r.a.t.s.), a Usenet newsgroup distributed through the Internet. Once 'there' – in my tiny study nook with the computer before me – I read the many messages that had been posted about my soaps, sometimes sending my own. The r.a.t.s. newsgroup transformed my understanding of computers; for the first time, I saw them as social tools. The more time I spent reading and posting to r.a.t.s., the less the collection of written messages seemed like lines of glowing green text. I saw in them instead a dynamic community of people with unique voices, distinctive traditions, and enjoyable relationships. Reading r.a.t.s. began to influence me as I viewed the soap opera. I began to think of how those others would react, the types of discussion each episode would provoke, and what I might have to add. Soap viewing had become the base on which witty, sociable women and men had built an interpersonal realm rich with strong traditions and a clear group identity.

When I began to think of r.a.t.s. as a 'community,' I gravitated toward that term primarily for its warm, emotional resonance. When I decided a few months later to add scholarly inquiry to my recreational use of r.a.t.s., I was led by the question of how people who rarely (if ever) met face-to-face, whose participants came and left, and who seemed to have such a limited communication medium managed to create not just a social world but a social world that felt like community? The case of r.a.t.s. demonstrates the types of communicative practices through which online places come to feel like communities and gives us grounded ways in which to think about the much theorized but underexamined phenomenon of online community. The tale of r.a.t.s. as an online community is one of three this [study] has to tell.

Early research on computer-mediated communication (CMC) generally identified its defining feature as anonymity and the consequences of that anonymity for social interaction as negative. More recent work has continued to focus on anonymity, stressing the novel opportunities to develop alternative identities or to enhance the ones we already have. It certainly is true, at least so far, that race, rank, physical appearance, and other features of public identity are not immediately evident. Neither are emotional reactions such as laughter or expressions of disgust. Gender, although generally apparent, is not always known with certainty. Scholars who focused on the lack of contextual cues and feedback in task-oriented communication argued that because of this enhanced anonymity, participation becomes more evenly distributed across group members. Consensus becomes more difficult to achieve when everyone is willing to talk. Anonymity also was taken to remove social norms and to increase *flaming* or antagonistic attacks on other users. Recent work has been less damning of online social potential, sometimes celebrating its liberating possibilities and other times investigating its ability to make people seem more likable.

Although the term *virtual community* has become common parlance, [. . .] when one goes to the scholarly literature in search of what makes an online group a community and how online community works, one tends to find instead autobiographical accounts of online life or ideological arguments about whether these groups are 'real' communities or good or dangerous for offline communities. Speculation abounds, but comprehensive frameworks grounded in empirical evidence about what happens within online communities still are in short supply. This [analysis] is an effort to fill that void, offering ways in which to think about online communities that are grounded in close study rather than in personal reflection.

The second story in this [discussion] is about r.a.t.s. as an audience community, in particular a soap opera fan community. Online communities have formed around thousands of topics; r.a.t.s. is one of the many hundreds formed around the mass media. Much like online communities, audience communities have been better discussed and theorized than documented. The cultural studies work that has examined (often soap opera) audiences and the more recent research into random or fan culture have built a strong case for the importance of audience interaction about mass media. This work leads us to understand the mass media in the context of the everyday lives of interconnected individuals. However, audience researchers rarely have ventured into the spontaneous interpersonal communication in which people perform their identities as audience members and, hence, have given us too little insight into how the mass media are appropriated for interpersonal purposes. Looking closely at what r.a.t.s. participants do as they discuss the soap, and how they build relationships with one another and identities for themselves in the process, forces us to rethink our understanding of what it means to be a fan,

especially as more audience members go online to discuss the mass media and to create fan Web sites.

I came to r.a.t.s. as a soap fan who had long recognized the social significance of my engagement with soap operas. From its beginnings, my soap watching had been situated within social relationships. In many cases, watching soaps or discussing them with housemates and acquaintances was integral to the development of our friendships. I became a soap fan at 15 years old, when I took a luxurious summer foray into the working class with my first job as a hotel maid. I was trained by an older woman who had worked there for years. For 2 weeks, we worked together. The official skills she taught included making beds with 'hospital corners,' getting pillows into their cases with ease, and using clever tricks to make bathtub faucets sparkle. My unofficial socialization included an explanation of all the characters on *General Hospital*, their relationships, and their current story lines. The entertainment came in handy in the repetitive job of room cleaning, but I also quickly discovered another advantage of watching: It gave an academic brat like me something easy yet involving to discuss with the people who worked there year-round, people with whom I seemed to have little in common.

Given that I have a modicum of self-respect, I also came to r.a.t.s. prepared to think favorably of soaps and their fans. Any soap fan knows, however, that not everyone conceptualizes soaps as worthwhile or soap fans as intelligent. The pervasive stereotype about soaps and their viewers ensures that no one has to justify dismissing soap operas as mindless melodrama or imagining that they appeal primarily to vulnerable women living vicariously through them. Before I became a fan, I too assumed that soap operas were for other, less intelligent (or affluent) people. As a child, the only soap viewer I knew looked after the children around the corner while their parents worked. My earliest soap opera memory is the opening screen of *As the World Turns* flickering in the children's living room; I remember thinking that this woman must be lazy if she was watching the soaps. The class difference between this domestic laborer and me, combined with my meager understanding of domestic labor, surely enhanced my sense that soaps were for other, lesser people. I have since discovered that the soap fans are not Them but rather Us. We all are members of audience communities of one sort or another, although some of the materials around which we organize might be granted higher social status. Instead of asking what is wrong with people that would make them want to watch soaps, the far more interesting question is how audience members, in this case soap viewers, 'use the mass media to structure and articulate our relations with one another and to make the world intellectually meaningful, aesthetically pleasing, and emotionally compelling.'

Audience communities and online communities co-opt mass media for interpersonal uses. Grappling with the social nature of these new types of community requires understanding them not just as online communities (organized through a network) or as audience communities (organized around a text) but also as communities of practice organized, like all communities, through habitualized ways of acting. Viewed in this way, the limits and possibilities of computer networks and mass media texts are preexisting contexts that become meaningful only in the ways in which they are invoked by participants in ongoing interaction. The focus is on how networks and texts are transformed into socially meaningful fields through interaction that is ongoing and patterned in subtle yet community-constituting ways. From a practice perspective, the key to understanding online and audience communities is to focus on the communicative patterns of participants rather than on the media through and in response to which members coalesce. Thus, the third story this [discussion] has to tell is that of r.a.t.s. as a community of practice. [. . .]

The structure of Usenet and rec.arts.tv.soaps

Had I gone online in 1984, I could have been among the first to participate in r.a.t.s. In 1990,

when I did go online, r.a.t.s. was one of a few thousand newsgroups distributed through the Usenet computer network, which piggybacks onto the Internet. When it was developed during the 1970s, the network's original function was to enable computer scientists to share programs between North Carolina and California. As it became Usenet, it quickly outgrew both that narrow population and narrow function, distributing thousands of primarily recreational discussion forums. Although less famous than the World Wide Web, America Online's chat rooms and folders, or the interactive real-time conversation spaces known as multi-user domains (MUDs) and multi-user domains object oriented (MOOs), Usenet is arguably the oldest, largest, most widely accessible, and most widely used network for interactive online discussion. The scholarly research into Usenet (and other forms of computer-mediated communication) has been scattered across multiple disciplines and takes a wide variety of approaches. [. . .]

Soap viewers were among the first to appropriate the Internet for recreational use, but they were not alone in flocking to Usenet. By 1993, Usenet linked at least 3 million users at more than 100,000 sites across the United States and throughout most of the world. Although no one seems to be able to keep track of the Internet's growth, there surely are exponentially more sites today. During the early 1990s, nearly all Usenet sites were mainframe computers at universities or colleges, computing and software companies, and scientific laboratories, both government and private. Since then, the growth in commercial Internet service providers, especially America Online, has led to millions of individuals accessing Usenet through personal accounts at a cost of approximately $20 (U.S.) per month.

Like much online activity, the precise history of soap opera discussion on the Internet is not well documented. The r.a.t.s. newsgroup is one of Usenet's oldest groups and was one of the first (if not *the* first) Internet sites specifically dedicated to soap operas. It began when it split off from the general television newsgroup, then called net.tv. As the few original participants who still were there when I arrived told the group's history (something they did only when asked), the non-soap fans became annoyed at the excessive soap opera discussion, and the soap opera fans moved to create their own group, which was named net.tv.soaps. The earliest record of the group is a traffic report from late October 1984 that reported that during the 2 weeks prior to that date, the group had distributed 11 messages. The 'rec.arts' was substituted for 'net' in 1986 as newsgroups multiplied and the hierarchical system used to name them expanded.

The most popular of Usenet's groups always have been those that discuss recreational and social issues. This is demonstrated by statistics gathered by Brian Reid through 1994 and posted to Usenet. In the 20 most *read* discussion groups in March 1993, for example, his figures show that a quarter of the messages (4,629) were in groups discussing social issues ranging from political activism to Indian culture. Nearly a fifth of the messages were in groups discussing sex. If figures on readership tap users' curiosities, then figures on the number of messages each group generates tap users' creative investments. In the highest *volume* discussion groups, half of the messages (24,983) were about social issues such as Indian culture, abortion, homosexuality, and guns. Another two fifths of the messages (20,025) in these high-traffic groups were in fan groups that discussed sports, television shows, and movies.

As is apparent to anyone who remembers how recently no one had heard of it, the Internet has grown tremendously. To see the figures on Usenet's growth, however, still is stunning. Consider these statistics collected by Rick Adams about the messages passing through uunet, one of the larger networks through which Usenet runs. In the fall of 1984 when r.a.t.s. began, there were only 158 groups and a mere 303 daily posts in all groups combined. When I arrived in 1990, Usenet was huge, distributing about 1,231 newsgroups that contained a daily average of 6,055 posts, nearly 20 times more than was the case 6 years earlier. Since 1990, the Web has become the most

Table 52.1   Biweekly numbers of posts to rec.arts.tv.soaps, 1984–1993

2-week period ending . . .	Number of posts in rec.arts.tv.soaps
October 23, 1984	11
October 22, 1985	8
October 22, 1986	32
October 22, 1987	68
October 27, 1988	231
October 22, 1989	427
October 8, 1990	696
October 23, 1991	1,037
October 23, 1992	1,685
September 8,1993	2,412

After 1994, these types of statistics no longer were collected.
Source: R. Adams, news.lists (newsgroup).

visible aspect of the Internet. However, the Web has scarcely inhibited Usenet's growth, and indeed, it probably has boosted it given that Usenet can be accessed through the Web. In 1997, statistics on the size of Usenet from an Internet service provider called Erol's indicate a daily average of 682,144 posts, 113 times as many as in 1990 and 2,251 times as many as in 1984.

The r.a.t.s. newsgroup never has been one of Usenet's most read groups, generally ranking between 200th and 300th among groups in estimated readership. However, from its modest beginnings during its first 4 years, r.a.t.s. traffic has expanded exponentially. Consider the number of posts to r.a.t.s. in consecutive 2-week periods 1 year apart over a 10-year period, as shown in table 52.1. By the fall of 1993, so many messages were passing through r.a.t.s. each day that printing them would have taken nearly a 1½-inch-thick stack of letter-sized paper. By 1994, the traffic on r.a.t.s. had grown to be so unmanageable that it was further subdivided into three groups: rec.arts.tv.soaps.abc, rec.arts.tv.soaps.cbs, and rec.arts.tv.soaps.misc. These three offshoot groups now carry a biweekly average of as many as 6,104 posts (2,744, 1,568, and 1,792 average messages, respectively). [. . .]

There is no consensus on how many Usenet groups exist now, but there are at least 30,000, each of which is identified by topic. The contents of each newsgroup are electronic letters called *posts* or *articles*. These are contributed by individuals from personal accounts. With the exceptions of some site restrictions and some moderated groups, these articles can be any length and are not censored prior to distribution. These posts are the sole constitutive elements of a Usenet group. Without messages, there is no newsgroup. Until DejaNews (http://www.deja.com) began archiving Usenet on the Web in 1995, the only places any messages were stored were the accounts and hard drives of ambitious individuals.

In the simplest sense, there are two ways in which to interact with any newsgroup including r.a.t.s. *Lurkers* read without ever contributing or contributing only rarely. *Posters* write messages. People lurk and post through programs called *newsreaders*, which keep track of which articles already have been read, allow people to edit what they will read, and allow people to reply to posted messages and to create new lines of discussion. Anyone with access to Usenet and the minor expertise it requires can read the recent contributions to a newsgroup or add one's own. One consequence of this is that the groups cannot exclude anyone with access from participating; except in moderated groups, there are no group participants with the power to exclude others. However, as many have noted, users are largely preselected by external social structures. Furthermore, groups may use social pressure to drive out undesirables.

When people read newsgroups, they see only the articles that have arrived at their sites since they last read. Participants need not be online simultaneously; they can read and respond at different times. Thus, the temporal structure of all Usenet newsgroups is that of an ongoing asynchronistic meeting. Messages are stored at each site for a time period left to the sites' system administrators to decide, usually no longer than a couple of weeks. Until the old messages are removed, readers can check in at their convenience to read or respond to what messages have arrived. The asynchronous structure of r.a.t.s. distinguishes Usenet from the real-time Internet interaction that takes place on Internet relay chat.

Although people often experience Usenet interaction as akin to talk, one of the ways in which this asynchronous online interaction is very different from talk is that posts, the equivalent of conversational turns, appear to the newsgroup reader as a list rather than as a temporally situated sequence. The potential for conversational chaos is not hard to see; imagine a party in which everyone wrote their utterances and set them up in a row. It would seem nearly impossible to create coherent threads of conversation, let alone attribute messages to particular speakers or link them to particular prior turns. Usenet and the newsreader programs used to access it provide a number of structural features that help to organize the groups and minimize this type of chaos. Two particularly important elements of the structure are the headers and the quotation system. Here is a sample post:

```
From
news.cso.uiuc.edu!ux1.cso.uiuc.edu!howgard.redkin.aps.
net!allik!
herdfine.university.EDU!nntp.university.EDU!walter!far
gate
Sat May 8 20:07:18 CDT 1993
Article: 100045 of rec.arts.tv.soaps
Newsgroups: rec.arts.tv.soaps
Path:
news.cso.uiuc.edu!ux1.cso.uiuc.edu!howgard.redkin.aps.
net!allik!herdfine.university.EDU!nntp.university.EDU!
walter!fargate
From: fargate@herdfine.university.EDU (Susan Fargate)
Subject: Re: AMC: Tad/Ted
Message-ID:
<1993May5.024010.6295@gordon.university.EDU>
Sender: news@gordon.university.EDU (Sir Headlines)
Organization: Science Dept, University.
References: <1993May3.231122.28337@IRO.UMontreal.CA>
<13669006@pccupp.cap.pc.com>
Date: Wed, 5 May 93 02:40:10 GMT
Lines: 25

In article <136690006@pccupp.cap.pc.com>
Beth@pccupp.cap.pc.com (Beth Hunter) writes:

>Hi Everyone,
>
>I'm still way behind on AMC (getting less as my
>post-work activities schedule is lighter in
>May), but am I missing something here? Are we
```

```
>supposed to believe that Ted Orsini looks
>exactly like Tad Martin?????????
>
> The Ted Orsini story was based on the fact that
>Nola's kid disappeared as a child. It would not
>therefore be a requirement that the guy (our
>tadski) who shows up on her doorstep look
>exactly a certain way, similar coloring should
>be enough.
>Obviously, I'm missing something, since the
>writers wouldn't actually expect me to believe
>anything as unlikely as them being identical.
>Right? :-)
>
I agree Beth, but the Erica-turned-30 storyline was
enough to convince me that 'believability' is not a
prerequisite for a storyline. It bugs me because it
is hard to get swept up in any sort of suspense
knowing that your hypotheses (based on logic) are
bound to fall short of the writers' whims, but then
again, I have been watching for 14 years so it must
not bug me too much!
—
Susan Fargate  fargate@herdfine.university.EDU
```

The headers provide information about the message's route through the sites, the newsgroup(s) to which it has been sent, the sender of the message, the subject, a unique identification number, the machine and organization of origin, other posts referenced in the message, when the post was sent, and its length. Other lines, such as summary lines, can be added at the time of posting. Headers automatically accompany every post; it is impossible to send a post *without* headers, although some newsreaders allow one to read without seeing all header lines.

The lines labeled 'From' and 'Subject' are perhaps most important in creating a sense of conversational coherence because newsreaders index these two to create their menus. The from line identifies the sender. Although fake and anonymous addresses can be used, in general, providing the sender's e-mail address helps to make the sender accountable for his or her behavior in that it allows others to send e-mail directly to a sender who offends. Especially prolific posters emerge as personalities in any newsgroup. Thus, their names in the from line invoke implications for those familiar with the contributors. This familiarity allows regular readers to form expectations about the messages and select which ones to read. Readers can go straight to the posts from those they like or can skip posts from those they dislike. They can even create *KILL files*, which cause their newsreaders to automatically eliminate messages from selected individuals. The subject line also is a major organizational resource for Usenet social situations. Chosen by the sender, or automatically replicated in responsive posts, the line is intended to make explicit the message's topic (although the topics may change sooner than the subject lines in ongoing discussions).

The opportunity to title posts gives rise to labeling practices that help to structure the group. For example, one of the most basic organizational problems for r.a.t.s. is that very few people follow every soap opera, yet all soap operas are discussed in the same group. Thus, although the newsgroup's concern with the general topic of daytime serials defined the external boundaries of the group, that concern was too broad to meet the separate interests within the group. To negate this problem, participants created a conventionalized system to segment the group by using the initials of each soap opera in the subject line. For example, a post about *All My Children* (*AMC*) might carry the subject line 'AMC: Carter and Natalie,' whereas one about *Days of Our Lives* (*DOOL*) might read 'DOOL: Update for Thursday.'

Because people tend not to read posts about soap operas they do not watch, r.a.t.s. is in many ways not a single group; instead, it comprises nearly a dozen subgroups, each of which discusses one serial (and each of which has its own personality). In 1992, when I collected most of my data, *AMC* and *DOOL* discussion constituted about half of the messages. Table 52.2 summarizes the distribution of posts and posters in terms of which soap operas they discussed, based on an analysis of subject lines during 10 months of r.a.t.s. posts. Thus, the discourse on r.a.t.s. is made coherent in part through the use of headers that segment the messages by soap opera and then by sender and topic.

Another essential Usenet resource for creating conversational coherence is the quotation system

Table 52.2   Participation in rec.arts.tv.soaps by soap opera in 10-month period

Soap opera	Number of posts and percentage	Number of posters and percentage
All My Children	8,665 (27)	481 (21)
Days of Our Lives	7,537 (23)	308 (13)
The Young and the Restless	3,436 (11)	276 (12)
As the World Turns	2,972 (9)	192 (8)
Santa Barbara	2,531 (8)	162 (7)
Guiding Light	2,390 (7)	234 (10)
General Hospital	1,779 (6)	228 (10)
Another World	1,133 (4)	154 (7)
One Life to Live	874 (3)	131 (6)
The Bold and the Beautiful	551 (2)	104 (4)
Loving	385 (1)	62 (3)
Total	32,253 (100)	2,332 (100)

Percentages are in parentheses. Percentages do not add to 100 due to rounding.

used to reference previous messages, demonstrated in the post quoted earlier. When a post is a reply (usually indicated in the subject line with 'Re:'), many newsreaders automatically insert a line immediately below the headers that provides the identification number of the prior post and explicitly attributes authorship to that quotation based on its from line. Quoted words are marked with angle brackets (>) in the left margin, just as they are in most e-mail software. This ability to embed previous messages within a new post allows posts to be chained together in an ongoing interactive thread of discussion.

The interaction within Usenet messages is a novel hybrid between written, oral, interpersonal, and mass communication. Like writing, there is no body movement, vocal tone, rate, or volume. However, some nonverbal cues are available as writers on Usenet, like those in other forms of writing, exploit 'aspects of graphic form such as spelling, punctuation, typography, and layout for expressive purposes.' Participants are temporally separated, as they are in writing. As a result, Usenet writers cannot assume that all readers will have read the messages to which they are responding or that all readers will be able to tell to which message Usenet writers are responding. Usenet's quotation system, which allows writers to replicate whole or partial prior turns within their own messages, helps to mitigate the potential noncoherence of Usenet discourse by explicitly marking topics and creating an orientation to specific previous messages.

Despite the similarities to writing, r.a.t.s. participants experience their own interaction as 'talk.' The comment of one r.a.t.s. participant that she likes r.a.t.s. because 'I enjoy having some people to talk about the show with' exemplifies the naturalness with which people apply a talk metaphor to online language use. Although r.a.t.s. participants do describe themselves as 'reading' rather than 'listening,' they characterize their own messages as 'sharing' or 'expressing' and never as 'writing.' Like speech, Usenet is interactive and contextualized. Writers can assume who many of their readers will be and that they will share many referents, will be reading within a few days, and will be able to respond. Like interpersonal communication, messages may be built off the comments of particular individuals, have consequences for one-on-one relationships, and be highly personalized. However, like mass communication, Usenet interaction always is written for a large audience and is affected by and affects the writers' public images and the image of the group as a whole. This overlap between interpersonal and mass communication provides the potential for otherwise disconnected individual voices to establish a community. [. . .] participants draw on these structural resources to create the practices, norms, relationships, and identities that come to define the group.

[. . .]

53 The Internet and Society

James Slevin

[. . .]

The emergence of the internet

The origin of the internet is firmly rooted in the circumstances of the Cold War, a period during which nuclear conflict featured as potentially the most immediate and catastrophic of all global dangers. The launch of Sputnik 1 on 4 October 1957 by the Soviet Union spawned a very specific fear: if nations were capable of launching space satellites, they might also be capable of launching long-distance nuclear attacks. Although state security was never seriously threatened by this event, it did contribute to the setting up of the Advanced Research Projects Agency (ARPA) within the United States Department of Defense.

ARPA: the Advanced Research Projects Agency

The agency's task was to establish and maintain a worldwide lead in science and technology. Its first director, however, defined the agency's role almost completely in military terms, and failed to recognize the importance of cutting-edge research taking place in the nation's universities at that time. This misjudgement was to threaten the continuation of the agency during its early years, and in 1958, ARPA saw many of the projects and programmes it had initiated transferred to the National Aeronautics and Space Administration (NASA). Consequently, the agency was forced to rethink its mission or face being abolished.

The Advanced Research Projects Agency's reputation as an innovative research institution only really began in 1961 when Jack Ruina was appointed as its director. He decentralized the structure of the agency and redefined its role as a body supporting and funding the work carried out by teams of researchers on special projects. One of the most important research programmes supported by the agency involved the investigation of techniques and technologies for interlinking computer networks of various kinds. The objective was twofold: first, to develop a communication network which would facilitate the exchange of information between various research centres involved in ARPA projects, and second, to allow participants in the network to share scarce computer resources. The creation of this so-called ARPANET in 1969 has become widely recognized as the origin and advent of the internet.

A number of developments in the history of computer-mediated communication were fundamental to the success of the ARPANET project. The first was the idea of communicating with computers at a distance. In September 1940, George Stibitz had decided to demonstrate a calculator to a meeting of the American Mathematical Society. The complex machine took up lots of space, so rather than transporting it to the meeting with the risk of it getting damaged, Stibitz set up a teletype terminal so that the calculator could be used remotely via a telegraph connection.

A second development was that computers had to be seen as more than just devices for solving mathematical problems. In 1945, Vannevar Bush published an article, 'As We may Think', in which he described the 'Memex', a communication system for storing and retrieving information.

A third, and crucial, development for setting up the ARPANET was the invention of packet-switching communication technology. Packet-switching involves the breaking down of digitized information into packets or blocks that are labelled to indicate both their origin and their destination, and the sending of these from one computer to another. The advantages of packet-switching are twofold. First, network resources are used more efficiently because a single channel can carry more than one transmission simultaneously. Second, communication is more robust because information can still reach its destination even if a large portion of the network is not functioning. The packets bypass the problem by taking a different route to their destination. The number of possible routes is referred to as the network's level of redundancy. The higher the level of redundancy, the greater the safety margin and thus the more robust a network is.

The technology necessary for packet-switching was developed independently at a number of research centres around the world, for example, at the National Physical Laboratory in Great Britain, and the Massachusetts Institute of Technology and the RAND Corporation in the United States. Of these, the research done by Paul Baran at the RAND Corporation deserves particular attention. Baran had been commissioned by the United States Air Force to do a study on how the military could maintain control over its missiles and bombers in the aftermath of a nuclear attack. In 1964 he proposed a communication network with no central command or control point. In the event of an attack on any one point, all surviving points would be able to re-establish contact with each other. He called this kind of network a distributed network. It was from this RAND Corporation study that the false rumour started that the ARPANET was somehow directly and primarily related to the building of a communication network which would be resistant to nuclear attack.

While Baran had been conducting his study into packet-switching, Joseph Licklider had been appointed to head the computer research programme at ARPA. As a psychologist with a background in hearing and speech research at MIT, he was mainly interested in computers as communication devices. Licklider saw networking not so much as a way of connecting computers, but as a way of connecting people. In his paper 'Man–Computer Symbiosis' he had already explored the idea of interconnected networks of information storage and retrieval centres supporting the team effort of groups and individuals. These ideas were reflected in his work for ARPA as he continued to decentralize the activities of the agency, setting up research contracts and bringing together computer scientists from MIT, Stanford, the University of California at Los Angeles, Berkeley and a number of companies. He nicknamed his dispersed team of scientists the 'intergalactic network'. Licklider later extended this concept to mean a globally interconnected network which would allow all participants to access and use information and programs from any site, When Licklider left ARPA in 1964 the name of the research programme he had led changed from 'Command and Control Research' to the 'Information Processing Techniques Office'. This change symbolizes and reflects both the changes that had taken place in ARPA as an organization and the changing role of computers in human activity.

In 1968, ARPA awarded the contract to build the ARPANET to Bolt, Beranek and Newman, a consulting firm in Cambridge, Massachusetts, specializing in information systems. Licklider, who had returned to work at MIT, claimed that in a few years individuals would be able to communicate more effectively through the digital computer than face to face. He wrote:

we are entering a technological age in which we will be able to interact with the richness of living information . . . We want to emphasize something beyond its one-way transfer: the increasing significance of the jointly constructive, the mutually reinforcing aspect of communication – the part that transcends 'now we both know a fact that only one of us knew before.' When minds interact, new ideas emerge.[1]

Although there were clearly definite conceptions as to the use of computer-mediated communication, this is not to say that all those involved were fully aware of the possibilities. Within ARPA opinions diverged as to the necessity of a decentralized computer network to promote new opportunities for horizontal communications between the various research centres. This is well documented by Hafner and Lyon, who explain that few of ARPA's researchers wanted to participate in such a project. 'This attitude was especially pronounced among researchers from the East Coast universities, who saw no reason to link up with campuses in the West.' Individual researchers located in the various centres could not understand that others had information relevant to their work or that they themselves had material others wanted to see. In any case, they argued, researchers could always read each other's reports. A very different perspective, however, emerges from the account given by Hafner and Lyon, describing the terminal room attached to the suite of Bob Taylor, director of the Information Processing Techniques Office at ARPA headquarters:

There, side by side, sat three computer terminals, each a different make, each connected to a separate mainframe computer running at three separate sites . . . Each of the terminals in Taylor's suite was an extension of a different computing environment – different programming languages, operating systems. . . . Each had a different log-in procedure; Taylor knew them all. But he found it irksome to have to remember which log-in procedure to use for which computer. And it was still more irksome . . . to remember which commands belonged to which computing environment.[2]

From the ARPANET to the internet

The ARPANET was launched at the end of 1969, creating the first long-haul computer network and connecting four sites: the University of California at Los Angeles, the Stanford Research Institute in Menlo Park, California, the University of California at Santa Barbara, and the University of Utah. These sites did not remain alone for long. Within sixteen months there were more than ten sites with an estimated 2,000 users and at least two routes between any two sites for the transmission of information packets.

A public demonstration of the ARPANET was held during the first International Conference on Computer Communications in Washington DC in October 1972. Representatives from projects in countries such as Great Britain, Sweden, Norway, Japan, France, Canada and the United States were present. The gathering highlighted the beginnings of networking elsewhere in the world and resulted in the setting up of the InterNetwork Working Group which was to begin to discuss global interconnectivity. The first international connections were soon to be set up with Norway and Great Britain. At a conference held in Brighton in 1973, data was sent by satellite to Goonhilly Downs in Cornwall and from there by cable via the University of London, so that delegates could use the ARPANET as if they were themselves in the United States.

An important part of the ARPANET was the Network Control Protocol which governed how packets of data were to be transmitted from one computer to another. Because the ARPANET was the only network being used, a very high level of reliability could be achieved. With the advent of global information infrastructures, however, involving the connecting up of a variety of computer networks, the same sender-to-receiver reliability could not be provided. Weak connections were the cause of transmission errors and different networks often used incompatible protocols. A new protocol was therefore needed, one which would allow individual networks to be designed separately in order to meet local requirements while still allowing distant users to communicate with each other. On a global scale this would have to be achieved without the need for any kind of direct control or intervention.

The answer was first introduced by Bob Kahn in 1972, the same year in which ARPA was renamed DARPA, the Defense Advanced Research Projects Agency. It involved the idea of so-called open architecture networking. Kahn and Vint Cerf, who had been involved in the original

Network Control Protocol development, set to work on what would become the Transmission Control Protocol/Internet Protocol (TCP/IP). The TCP organized the data into packages, put them into the right order on arrival at their destination, and checked them for errors. The IP was responsible for the routing of packages through the network. By 1983 all networks connected to the ARPANET had to make use of TCP/IP and the old Network Control Protocol was replaced entirely. From then on, the collection of interconnected and publicly accessible networks using the TCP/IP protocols came to be called the 'internet'.

The emergence of the internet, however, is not only the outcome of military and scientific endeavour, and the activities of big business. The invention of the modem and the development of the Xmodem protocol in the late 1970s by two Chicago students allowed for the transfer of information between computers over the regular telephone system. Using such technology, computer networks which had so far been excluded from connecting to ARPANET, or other backbone systems, were now also able to communicate with each other. In its restricted way it pointed to the existence of a wider potential demand for computer-mediated communication and to the wide range of situations in which it could be successfully used. The modem, together with the advent of the personal computer, particularly contributed to the development and worldwide proliferation of electronic notice boards such as bulletin board systems (BBSs) and electronic discussion forums such as USENET. The internet, however, with its global reach and local call accessibility, soon surpassed the opportunities offered by such networks, whereupon many of them became connected to the internet themselves.

The internet constellation

By 1983 the open nature of the ARPANET was causing a concern for security. It was therefore split into the MILNET, which would serve military operational requirements, and the ARPANET,

which continued to support research needs. However, during the 1980s the ARPANET's role as a long-haul network or backbone providing an important link between networks was gradually taken over by the network of supercomputing centres (NSFNET) set up by the National Science Foundation. In 1990 the ARPANET was decommissioned and taken out of service altogether.

Like the Joint Academic Network in Great Britain, NSFNET prohibited the use of its backbone for purposes other than research and education. However, the 'acceptable use policy' which governed the use of NSFNET did allow its commercial use on a local and regional level. This generated revenue which was then used to lower the subscription fees and make the network more accessible to smaller academic institutions. This exclusion of long-distance commercial traffic stimulated and speeded up the growth of competitive private backbone networks.

[. . .]

Most individuals and small businesses access the internet by connecting to the host computer of an internet service provider (ISP) where they hold an account. Such connections can be made from homes or places of work via a telephone line or other cable facilities. Access is also possible via terminals placed in public spaces, such as airport and hotel lounges, internet cafés and on street corners. Large and medium-sized organizations often have direct access to the internet.

From the mid-1990s the development of the internet took a new turn as a growing number of large and medium-sized organizations started running the TCP/IP protocols on their intra-organizational communication networks. These private internets are called 'intranets'. Smaller intranets may be confined to connecting up computers in a single building; larger ones may connect up computers into a system which spans the globe. For security purposes, intranets are shielded from the outside world by so-called firewalls. These protection systems often allow for the exchange of information with the internet via so-called 'gateways'. A group of organizations can also use the TCP/IP protocols on their inter-organizational networks. These private networks are called 'extranets' and allow organizations to exchange data with each other. By 1997 the market for intranets and extranets was growing annually at a rate of 40 per cent worldwide and 60 per cent in the United States. This rate of increase prompted the view that the intranet market would exceed the size of the internet market by a ratio of two to one. [. . .]

Many internet service providers have extended their services to include intranets and extranets, supplying them with a full range of value-added services such as network backbones and network security. Internet service providers thus vary greatly in size and in the services they offer. Some are major global online services, such as Microsoft Network, America On-line, and CompuServe. Others have fewer than a thousand subscribers and act only as intermediaries – leasing line capacity from larger providers and telecommunication companies who own the long-haul network facilities. This situation, however, is changing rapidly as many of the small and medium-sized ISPs are taken over by a small number of big corporations seeking to become one-stop suppliers of telecommunication and internet services.

Probably one of the most globally consequential events in this field at the end of the millennium, with repercussions stretching well beyond the top end of the market, involved the acquisitional activities of WorldCom. Its dealings meant that it was set to carry more than half of all internet backbone traffic, control more than half of all direct connections to the internet, and lease line capacity to two-thirds of all internet service providers. All major telecommunication players, and indeed governments, are having to respond strategically to these kinds of developments. It is feared that a few powerful organizations will be able to charge internet service providers prohibitive fares for leasing lines, exclude certain users and interfere with content and also with the speed at which information is transmitted over sections of the networks, giving some users an unfair advantage over others.

[. . .]

NOTES

1 Zona Research, http://www.zonaresearch.com.
2 Katie Hafner and Matthew Lyon, *Where Wizards Stay up Late* (New York: Simon and Schuster, 1966), pp. 12–13.

54 Mass Communication, Symbolic Goods and Media Products

John B. Thompson

The advent of mass communication, and especially the rise of mass circulation newspapers in the nineteenth century and the emergence of broadcasting in the twentieth, has had a profound impact on the modes of experience and patterns of interaction characteristic of modern societies. For most people today, the knowledge we have of events which take place beyond our immediate social milieu is a knowledge largely derived from our reception of mass-mediated symbolic forms. The knowledge we have of political leaders and their policies, for instance, is a knowledge derived largely from newspapers, radio and television, and the ways in which we participate in the institutionalized system of political power are deeply affected by the knowledge so derived. Similarly, our experience of events which take place in contexts that are spatially and temporally remote, from strikes and demonstrations to massacres and wars, is an experience largely mediated by the institutions of mass communication; indeed, our experience of these events as 'political', as constitutive of the domain of experience which is regarded as politics, is partly the outcome of a series of institutionalized practices which endow them with the status of news. The role of the media is so fundamental in this regard that it would be partial at best to portray the nature and conduct of politics at a national and international level without reference to the processes of mass communication.

In this [discussion] I want to begin to explore some of the ways in which the advent of mass communication has transformed the modes of experience and patterns of interaction characteristic of modern societies. [. . .]

Let me begin by analysing some of the general characteristics of what is commonly called 'mass communication'. It has often been pointed out that, while 'mass communication' is a convenient label for referring to a broad range of media institutions and products, the term is misleading in certain respects. It is worth dwelling for a moment on some of the respects in which this term can lead astray. The expression 'mass' derives from the fact that the messages transmitted by the media industries are generally available to relatively large audiences. This is certainly the case in some sectors of the media industries and at some stages in their development, such as the mass circulation newspaper industry and the major television networks. However, during other periods in the development of the media industries (e.g. the early newspaper industry) and in some sectors of the media industries today (e.g. some book and magazine publishers), the audiences were and remain relatively small and specialized. Hence the term 'mass' should not be construed in narrowly quantitative terms; the important point about mass communication is not that a given number or proportion of individuals receive the products, but rather that the products are available in principle to a plurality of recipients. Moreover, the term 'mass' is misleading in so far as it suggests that the audiences are like inert, undifferentiated heaps. This suggestion obscures the fact that the messages transmitted by the media industries are received by specific individuals situated in particular social–historical contexts. These individuals attend to media messages with varying degrees of concentration, actively interpret and make sense of these messages and relate them to other aspects of their lives. Rather than viewing these individuals as part of an inert and undifferentiated mass, we should leave open the possibility that the reception of media messages is an active, inherently critical and socially differentiated process.

If the term 'mass' may be misleading in this context, the term 'communication' may also be, since the kinds of communication generally involved in mass communication are quite different from those involved in ordinary conversation. I shall examine some of these differences in the course of the following discussion. Here I shall call attention to one important difference: namely, that mass communication generally involves a one-way flow of messages from the transmitter to the receiver. Unlike the dialogical situation of a conversation, in which a listener is also a potential respondent, mass communication institutes a fundamental *break* between the producer and receiver, in such a way that recipients have relatively little capacity to contribute to the course and content of the communicative process. Hence it may be more appropriate to speak of the 'transmission' or 'diffusion' of messages rather than of 'communication' as such. Yet even in the circumstances of mass communication, recipients do have some capacity to contribute, in so far as recipients are also consumers who may sometimes choose between various media products and whose views are sometimes solicited or taken into account by the organizations concerned with producing and diffusing these products. Moreover, it is possible that new technological developments – such as those associated with fibre optic cables – will increase the interactive capacity of the medium of television and give viewers greater control over the transmission process, although the extent to which this will become a practical reality remains to be seen.

In the light of these preliminary qualifications, I want to offer a broad conceptualization of mass communication and to highlight some of its key characteristics. We may broadly conceive of mass communication as *the institutionalized production and generalized diffusion of symbolic goods via the transmission and storage of information communication*. By conceiving of mass communication in terms of the production and diffusion of symbolic goods, I wish to stress the importance of viewing mass communication in relation to the institutions concerned with the commodification of symbolic forms. What we now describe as mass communication is a range of phenomena and processes that emerged historically through the development of institutions seeking to exploit new opportunities for the fixation and reproduction of symbolic forms. I [. . .] want to analyse mass communication in a more theoretical way by focusing on the following four characteristics: the institutionalized production and diffusion of symbolic goods; the instituted break between production and reception; the extension of availability in time and space; and public circulation of symbolic forms. [. . .]

The first characteristic of mass communication is *the institutionalized production and diffusion of symbolic goods*. Mass communication presupposes the development of institutions – that is, relatively stable clusters of social relations and accumulated resources – concerned with the large-scale production and generalized diffusion of symbolic goods. These activities are 'large-scale' in the sense that they involve the production and diffusion of multiple copies or the provision of materials to numerous recipients. This is rendered possible by the fixation of symbolic forms in technical media and by the reproducibility of the forms. *Fixation* may involve processes of encoding whereby symbolic forms are translated into information which can be stored in a particular medium or material substratum; the symbolic forms may be transmitted as information and then decoded for the purposes of reception or consumption. The symbolic forms diffused by mass communication are inherently *reproducible* in the sense that multiple copies may be produced or made available to numerous recipients. The reproduction of forms is generally controlled as strictly as possible by the institutions of mass communication, since it is one of the principal means by which symbolic forms are subjected to economic valorization. Forms are reproduced in order to be exchanged on a market or through a regulated type of economic transaction. Hence they are *commodified* and treated as objects to be sold, as services to be paid for or as media which can facilitate the sale of other objects or services. In the first instance, therefore, mass communication should be understood as part of a range of institutions concerned, in varying ways, with the fixation, reproduction and commodification of symbolic forms.

A second characteristic of mass communication is that *it institutes a fundamental break between the production and reception of symbolic goods*. These goods are produced for recipients who are generally not physically present at the place of production and transmission or diffusion; they are, literally, *mediated* by the technical media in which they are fixed and transmitted. This characteristic is not, of course, unique to mass communication: the fixation and transmission of symbolic forms on papyrus or stone also involved a break between production and reception. But with the rise of mass communication, the range of producers and receivers affected by this process has greatly expanded. Moreover, as I noted earlier, the mediation of symbolic forms via mass communication generally involves a one-way flow of messages from the producer to the recipient, such that the capacity of the recipient to influence or intervene in the processes of production and transmission or diffusion is strictly limited. One consequence of this condition is that the processes of production and transmission or diffusion are characterized by a distinctive form of *indeterminacy*. Symbolic forms are produced for audiences and transmitted or diffused in order to reach these audiences, but these processes generally take place in the absence of a direct and continuous monitoring of the audiences' responses. In contrast to face-to-face interaction, where the interlocutors can question one another and observe one another's responses, in mass communication the personnel involved in the production and

transmission or diffusion are generally deprived of immediate feedback from the recipients. Since the economic valorization of mass-mediated symbolic forms may depend crucially on the nature and extent of reception, the personnel involved typically employ a variety of strategies to cope with this indeterminacy. They draw upon past experience and use it as a guide to likely future outcomes; they use well-tried formulas which have a predictable audience appeal; or they try to obtain information about recipients through market research or through the routine monitoring of audience size and response. These and other techniques are institutionalized mechanisms which enable personnel to reduce the indeterminacy stemming from the break between production and reception, and to do so in a way which concurs with the overall aims of the institutions concerned.

A third characteristic of mass communication is that *it extends the availability of symbolic forms in time and in space*. Again, this characteristic is not unique to mass communication: all forms of cultural transmission involve some degree of space–time distanciation. But the media of mass communication generally involve a relatively high degree of distanciation in both space and time; and with the development of telecommunications, space–time distanciation is severed from the physical transportation of symbolic forms. The transmission of symbolic forms via telecommunications – for example, via a network of terrestrial and satellite relays – enables the institutions of mass communication to achieve a high degree of spatial distanciation in a minimal amount of time. Moreover, since the symbolic forms are generally fixed in a relatively durable medium, such as paper, photographic film or electromagnetic tape, they also have extended availability in time and can be preserved for subsequent use. The space–time distanciation involved in mass communication is also affected by the conditions under which symbolic forms are received and consumed. By virtue of the instituted break between production and reception, the nature and extent of distanciation may depend on the social practices and technical conditions of reception. For example, the extension of availability of a book in time and space may depend as much on the ways in which the book is received – whether it is recommended or ignored, incorporated into curricula or actively suppressed, and so on – as [. . .] on the channels of diffusion and the nature of the technical medium itself. Similarly, the extension of availability of a television programme or film may depend on whether potential recipients have the technical means to receive the programme, whether the scheduling concurs with the social organization of their everyday lives, and so on.

A fourth characteristic of mass communication is that *it involves the public circulation of symbolic forms*. The products of mass communication are produced in principle for a plurality of recipients. In this respect, mass communication differs from forms of communication – such as telephone conversations, teleconferencing or private video-recordings of various kinds – which employ the same technical media of fixation and transmission but which are orientated towards a single or highly restricted range of recipients. This basic difference between established forms of mass communication and other forms of electronically mediated interaction may be called into question by the increasing deployment of new communication technologies, but this is a development which has yet to be fully realized. As the institutions of mass communication have developed hitherto, their products circulate within a 'public domain', in the sense that they are available in principle to anyone who has the technical means, abilities and resources to acquire them. While the nature and scope of this public domain may be unlimited in principle, it is always limited in practice by the social–historical conditions of production, transmission and reception. The institutions of mass communication often aim to reach as large an audience as possible, since the size of the audience may directly affect the economic valorization of the products concerned. Today the audiences for some films and television programmes may amount to hundreds of millions of viewers worldwide; a single Christmas Day television broadcast can command more than 30 million viewers in Britain alone. The nature and scope of the audiences for the products of mass communication vary enormously from one medium to another, and from one product to another within the same medium. The ways in which these products are appropriated by the recipients – whether, for example, they are appropriated by a collective gathering in a cinema or by a private viewing in the home – also vary considerably, depending on the medium, the product, the channels of diffusion and the social and technical conditions of reception. One consequence of the intrinsically public character of media products is that the development of mass communication has been accompanied by attempts to exercise control, on the part of state authorities and other regulatory bodies, over the institutions of mass communication. The very capacity of these institutions to make symbolic forms available to a potentially vast audience is a source of concern for authorities which seek to maintain order and regulate social life within the territories under their jurisdiction.

Part 16 Education

For many years boys were on average more successful at all levels of education than girls. Over the past few years, however, this relationship has started to go into reverse – girls get better results at primary and secondary schools. This change is discussed by Eirene Mitsos and Ken Browne in their contribution (Reading 55). Why have boys become 'under-achievers'? Several factors are probably involved. Women have more autonomy in many areas of their lives than in the past – and this has helped raise the self-esteem and expectations of girls. In addition, schools have placed a strong emphasis upon gender equality in the classroom. Finally, job opportunities for boys, especially in less skilled work, have diminished, while women's employment has expanded, particularly in the service sector. Some boys have become disengaged from, or hostile to, educational values.

The intrinsic value and social importance of education are not always evident to those obligated to attend schools – more specifically, children from underprivileged backgrounds, who often see the authority system of the school as oppressive rather than liberating. Paul Willis's study (Reading 56) describes the outlook of a group of working-class boys ('the lads') in a school in Birmingham. The lads feel alienated from the dominant culture of the school and seek every opportunity to challenge or contest it. They have developed an informal culture of their own, the main tenets of which diverge radically from the orthodoxy of the school. The lads seek every opportunity, Willis points out, to frustrate the formal objective of the school, which is to make pupils 'work'.

Higher education is currently expanding in the most remarkable way. Over the past several decades higher education in the industrial countries has been transformed from an elite system to a mass one. On average some 50 per cent of the population of 18 to 23-year-olds are enrolled in some form of higher education in these countries. There is a direct correlation between the wealth of a country and the proportion of its population in higher education. Middle-income countries have only 21 per cent of 18 to 23-year-olds in higher education, while the poorest countries have on average only 6 per cent. Higher education in the future looks likely to be transformed by the internet and other forms of new communication systems. A new entity is coming into being, the 'virtual university', where courses are taught online rather than in physical classrooms. No one knows as yet how these developments will affect conventional universities. Most such universities are developing internet-based systems of learning alongside their orthodox teaching and research. But it is at least possible that internet-based learning will to some extent supplant traditional campus based universities in the future. Globalization also increases competitiveness in higher education as universities across the world compete with each other to get the best students and faculty and do so increasingly within a globalized marketplace, as discussed in Reading 57.

55 Gender Differences in Education:

The Underachievement of Boys

Eirene Mitsos and Ken Browne

There are marked differences between the sexes in education. Until the late 1980s, the major concern was with the underachievement of girls. This was because, while girls used to perform better than boys in the earlier stages of their education, from GCSE-level they tended to fall behind, being less likely than boys to get the three A-levels required for university entry and less likely to go into higher education. However, in the early 1990s girls began to outperform boys in all areas and at all levels of the education system. The main problem today is with the underachievement of boys, although there are still concerns about the different subjects studied by boys and girls. There are also concerns that girls could do even better if teachers spent as much time with girls as they are forced to do with boys.

The facts

Girls do better than boys at every stage in National Curriculum SAT (Standard Assessment Test) results in English, maths and science, and they are now more successful than boys at every level in GCSE, outperforming boys in every major subject (including traditional boys' subjects – design, technology, maths and chemistry) except physics. In 1995–96, 49.3 per cent of girls got five or more GCSEs (grades A–C) compared to 39.8 per cent of boys (see figure 55.1). In English at GCSE, the gender gap is huge, with nearly two thirds of girls getting a grade A–C, compared to less than half of boys.

A higher proportion of females stay on in post-16 sixth form and further education, and post-18 higher education. Female school leavers are now more likely than males to get 3 or more A-level passes (see figure 55.1), and more females than males now get accepted for full-time university degree courses.

But problems still remain for girls . . .

Despite this general pattern of girls outperforming boys, problems do still remain for girls. As figure 55.2 and table 55.1 show, girls still tend to take different subjects from boys, which influences future career choices. Broadly, arts subjects are 'female', science and technology subjects 'male'. This is evident at GCSE-level, but becomes even more pronounced at A-level and above. Girls are therefore less likely to participate after 16 in subjects leading to careers in science, engineering and technology. Girls tend to slip back between GCSE and A-level, achieving fewer high-grade A-levels than boys with the same GCSE results.

There is little evidence that the generally better results of girls at 16 and above lead to improved post-school opportunities in terms of training and employment. Women are still less likely than men with similar qualifications to achieve similar levels of success in paid employment, and men still hold the majority of the positions of power in society.

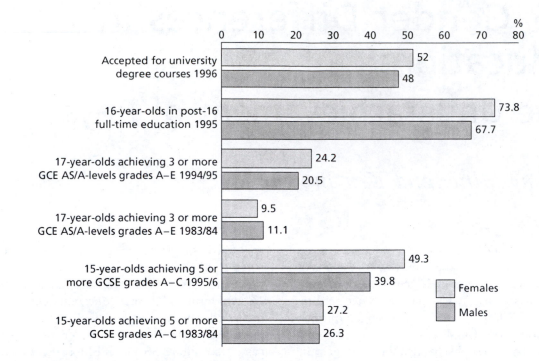

Figure 55.1   Some male and female differences in education

Source: Data from *Separate Tables*, DFEE, 1997, and UCAS Annual Report, 1996

Boys will be boys . . .

. . . and girls will be girls?

In the 16–59 age group in the population as a whole who are in employment or are unemployed, men tend to be better qualified than women. However, this gap has decreased among younger age groups, and can be expected to disappear if females keep on outperforming males in education.

Explaining gender differences in education

The change to girls outperforming boys is still a fairly recent development, and research to explain it is still at an early stage. There are some suggested explanations for the huge improvement in the performance of girls, the under-performance of boys and the subject choices that continue to separate males and females.

First, the *women's movement* and *feminism* have achieved considerable success in improving the rights and raising the expectations and self-esteem of women. They have challenged the traditional stereotype of women's roles as housewives and mothers, and this means that many women now look beyond the housewife/mother role as their main role in life.

Second, the work of sociologists in highlighting the educational under-performance of girls in the past led to a greater emphasis in schools on *equal opportunities*, in order to enable girls to fulfil their potential more easily. These policies included, amongst others, monitoring teaching and teaching materials for sex bias to help schools to meet the needs of girls, by encouraging 'girl-friendliness', not only in male-dominated subjects but across the whole range of the experience of girls in schools. Teachers are now much more sensitive about avoiding *gender stereotyping* in the classroom; this may have overcome many of the former academic problems which girls faced in schools.

Third, the number of 'male' jobs, particularly in semi-skilled and unskilled manual work, has been declining in recent years, while there are growing *employment opportunities* for women in the service sector. As a consequence, girls have become more ambitious and are less likely to see

---

Box 55.1   Boys' underachievement in English

Research carried out in Coventry showed that one of the main reasons why boys do not do as well as girls in English is because of their attitudes to the subject and to reading. Boys saw English as a 'feminine' subject that was 'alien' to their way of thinking and working: they felt 'uncomfortable', while in science they felt 'safe'. 'Science is straightforward. You don't have to think about it. There are definite answers . . . You feel safe in science.' English, on the other hand, 'is about understanding, interpreting . . . you have to think more. There's no definite answer . . . the answer depends on your view of things.'

This shows how boys' view of English is related to the way they are socialised into their gender roles: middle-class men's position in society – the fact that they occupy the positions of economic, political and ideological power – means that men have to be seen as strong, sure of themselves, always being right and always in control. English is a subject where the boundaries are not clearly defined. One of the boys interviewed said: 'That's why girls do English (at A-level) because they don't mind getting things wrong. They're more open about issues, they're more understanding . . . they find it easier to comprehend other people's views and feelings.' This also reinforces the idea that women are the 'understanding', the 'caring' sex.

Men use language to protect their independence and to negotiate status; women, on the other hand, use language to seek confirmation, to make human connections and to reinforce intimacy. This division between facts and emotions is reflected in the differing natures of the two subjects. Those students were articulating this.

Source: Adapted from E. Mitsos, 'Classroom Voices', *English and Media Magazine*, 33 and 34 (1995).

---

having a home and family as their main role in life. Many girls growing up today have mothers working in paid employment, who provide positive role models for them. Many girls now recognise that the future involves paid employment, often combined with family responsibilities. Sue Sharpe found in *Just like a Girl* in 1976 that girls' priorities were 'love, marriage, husbands, children, jobs and careers, more or less in that order'. When she repeated her research in 1994, she found that these priorities had changed to 'job, career and being able to support themselves'. These factors may all have provided more incentives for girls to gain qualifications.

Fourth, there is mounting evidence that girls work harder, are more conscientious and are *better motivated* than boys. Girls put more effort into their work and spend more time on doing their homework properly. They take more care with the way their work is presented and they concentrate more in class. (Research shows that the typical 14-year-old girl can concentrate for 3 to 4 times as long as her fellow male students.) Girls are generally better organised: they bring the right equipment to school and meet deadlines for handing in work. It has been suggested that these factors may have helped girls to take more advantage of the increasing use of coursework in GCSE, A-level and GNVQ. Such work often requires good organisation and sustained application, and girls do better than boys in these respects.

Finally, by the age of 16, girls are estimated to be *more mature* than boys by up to two years. Put simply, this means that girls are more likely to view exams in a far more responsible way, recognise their seriousness and the importance of the academic and career choices that lie ahead of them.

Table 55.1   (a) GCSE achievements of 15-year-old males and females by subject group, entries, and pass rate (% achieving grades A–C) in England by the end of 1994/95. (b) GCE A-level achievements of male and female candidates by subject group, entries, and pass rate (% achieving grades A–E) in England by the end of 1994/95

(a) Subject group	Male entries	Pass rate (%)	Female entries	Pass rate (%)	(b) Subject group	Male entries	Pass rate (%)	Female entries	Pass rate (%)
Sciences[a]	824,112	44.9	799,817	47.3	Sciences[a]	122,173	81.5	80,376	81.9
Social sciences[b]	380,515	46.1	335,439	53.1	Social sciences[b]	101,283	77.2	114,047	76.2
Arts[c]	897,733	48.3	981,576	63.6	Arts[c]	65,096	86.2	129,206	88.5
Total number of students entering any subject					General studies	28,520	85.1	28,230	78.8
	274,893	68.5	267,414	79.2	Total students entering any subject	317,072	81.4	351,859	82.2

[a] Includes subjects like Biology, Physics, Chemistry, Single/Double science, Mathematics, Computer studies, Craft, Design and technology, and Home economics

[b] Includes subjects like Business studies, Geography, History, Area studies, Economics, Humanities, Social studies, Physical education and Vocational studies

[c] Includes subjects like Art and design, English, English literature, Drama, Communication studies, Foreign languages, Classical studies, Music, Creative arts and Religious studies

Source: Data from *Separate Tables*, DFEE, 1997

Why do boys underachieve?

Many of the reasons given above also suggest why boys may be underachieving. However, there are some additional explanations. First, there is some evidence that staff are not as strict with boys as with girls. They are more likely to extend deadlines for work, to have *lower expectations* of boys, to be more tolerant of disruptive, unruly behaviour from boys in the classroom and to accept poorly presented work.

Second, boys are generally *more disruptive* in classrooms than girls. They may lose classroom learning time because they are sent out of the room or sent home. Four out of every five permanent exclusions from schools are boys: most of these are for disobedience of various kinds and usually come at the end of a series of incidents.

Third, boys appear to gain 'street cred' and peer-group status by not working, and some develop almost an *anti-education*, anti-learning subculture, where schoolwork is seen as 'unmacho'. This may explain why they are less conscientious and lack the persistence and application required for exam success, particularly with the new coursework styles of assessment. This subculture was first discussed over 20 years ago by Paul Willis in *Learning to Labour* and was rediscovered by Stephen Byers, the schools minister, in January 1998, when he said, 'We must challenge the laddish, anti-learning culture which has been allowed to develop over recent years and should not simply accept with a shrug of the shoulders that boys will be boys.'

Fourth, the *decline in traditional male jobs* is also a factor in explaining why many boys are under-performing in education. They may lack motivation and ambition because they may feel that they have only limited prospects and that getting qualifications won't get them anywhere anyway, so what's the point in bothering? These changing employment patterns and unemployment have resulted in a number of (predominantly white) boys and men having lowered expectations, a low self-image and a lack of self-esteem. This inevitably leads boys to attempt to construct a positive self-image away from achievement and towards 'laddish behaviour' and aggressive 'macho' posturing in attempts to draw attention to themselves.

The interrelationship between the home, the community and schools becomes clear here. Beatrix Campbell showed in her book *Goliath* how, in the climate of underfunding and cut-backs in community provision in the early 1990s, funds are focused on the troublesome boys who destroy communities, rather than on the people who struggle to maintain those communities – who are mainly women. Educational research has shown the same pattern, where teachers' time is spent mostly on the troublesome boys, rather than on the girls who are keen to learn and to get on with their schooling. This suggests that girls may still be underachieving, even if they are not doing so in relation to the boys.

Feeling and behaving differently

Boys and girls feel differently about their own ability. Research by Michael Barber at Keele University's Centre for Successful Schools reveals that 'more boys than girls think that they are able or very able, and fewer boys than girls think they are "below average"'. Yet GCSE results show these perceptions to be the reverse of the truth. Boys feel that they are bright and capable but at the same time they keep stating that they don't like school and that they don't work hard. Girls, on the other hand, lack confidence in their ability, feel undervalued and see teachers spending more time with the boys than with them.

More research is coming to the conclusion that the differences in the achievement of girls and boys is due to the differing ways in which the genders behave and spend their spare time. To simplify and generalise: while boys run around kicking footballs, playing sports or computer games and engaging in other aspects of 'laddish' behaviour, girls are more likely to read or to stand around talking. Girls relate to one other by *talking*, while boys often relate to their peers by *doing*. The value of talking, even if it is about the heartthrob of Year 11, is that it uses a key skill that is needed at school and in many non-manual, service-sector jobs: verbal reasoning. Peter Douglas argues: 'School is essentially a linguistic experience and most subjects require good levels of comprehension and writing skills.' Further research is revealing a picture of boys as viewing the crucial reading and linguistic skills as 'sissy'.

Boys don't like reading

Girls like reading while boys don't: boys see reading as a predominantly feminine activity, which is boring, not real work, a waste of time and to be avoided at all costs. The interrelationship between society and schooling is clear here. Reading is 'feminised' in our culture: women are not only the main consumers of reading in our society, but they also carry the responsibility for disseminating reading – it is women who read, talk about and 'spread the word' about books. The consequences of this are that there are very few positive role models for boys. Research has shown that boys tend to stop being interested in reading at about the age of eight.

Girls and boys also tend to read different things: girls read fiction while boys read for information. Schools tend to reproduce this gendered divide: fiction tends to be the main means of learning to read in the primary school years and this puts girls at an early advantage.

Why do males and females still tend to do different subjects?

As figures 55.1 and 55.2 and table 55.1 show, there is still a difference between the subjects that males and females do at GCSE and above. Females are still more likely to take arts subjects, like English literature, history, foreign languages and sociology, and males are more likely to take scientific and technological subjects – particularly at A-level and above (even though girls generally get better results when they do take them). This is despite the National Curriculum, which makes maths, English and science compulsory for all students. However, even within the National Curriculum, there are gender differences in option

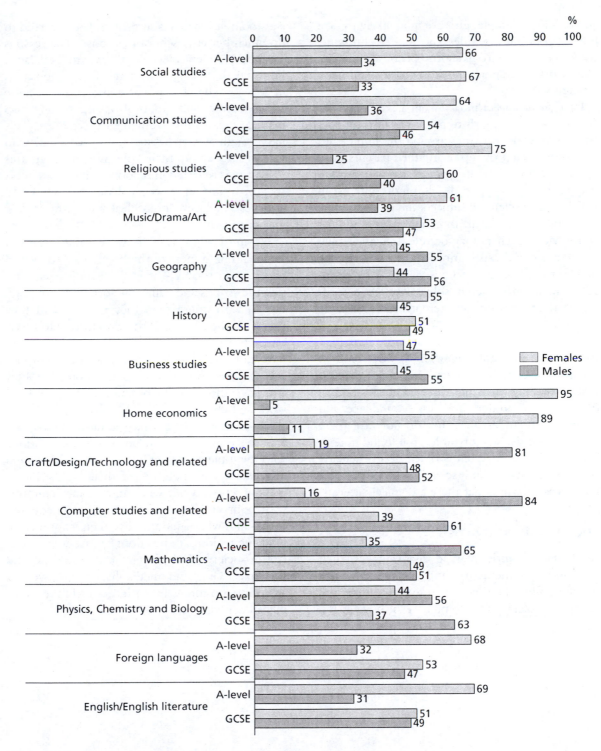

Figure 55.2 Percentage of entries by subject and sex, GCSE and A-level

Source: Data from *Separate Tables*, DFEE, 1997

choices. For example, girls are more likely to take home economics, textiles and food technology, while boys are more likely to opt for electronics, woodwork or graphics. How can we explain these differences?

First, *gender socialisation* from an early age encourages boys and girls to play with different toys and do different activities around the home, and they very often grow up seeing their parents playing different roles in the home. Such socialisation may encourage boys to develop more interest in technical and scientific subjects and to discourage girls from taking them. In giving subject and career advice, teachers may be reflecting their own socialisation and expectations and reinforcing the different experiences of boys and girls by counselling them into different subject options, according to their own gender stereotypes of 'suitable subjects'.

Second, science and the science classroom is still seen as mainly '*masculine*'. Boys tend to dominate science classrooms – grabbing apparatus first, answering questions directed at girls and so on, which all undermine girls' confidence and intimidate them, so that they do not take these subjects. Gender stereotyping is still found in textbooks, with the 'invisibility' of females particularly obvious in maths and science textbooks. This reinforces the view that these are 'male' subjects.

The male identity crisis

In the face of girls' marked disadvantages, such as underrating themselves and lacking confidence in their ability, getting less of teachers' time and having to tolerate the dominance of boys in the classroom, it is perhaps surprising that they tend to do much better at school than boys. The reasons for boys' underachievement have to be placed firmly in the changing nature of men's position in society. The change has come about because of economic and political changes, but also because of a rise in women's expectations. This has brought on an *identity crisis* for men, who feel unsure about their role and position: this insecurity is reflected in schools, where boys don't see the point in working hard and trying to achieve. The future looks bleak and without clear purpose to them.

We must not forget, however, that it is still men who hold most of the highly paid, powerful positions in society – it is still mainly men who pull the strings and 'run' our society. Women go out to work more than they used to and they now make up about half the workforce. However, research has shown that in the home gender roles have not changed that much: women now not only go out to paid work a lot more, but they still have the majority of the burden of housework and childcare.

We cannot predict what the future holds, but it is to be hoped that women will not continue with the triple burden of housework, childcare and jobs that increasingly reflect their high achievement at school, while working-class men continue with poor employment prospects or unemployment and while middle-class men continue to hold the majority of positions of power and control in society. 'Girl power' needs to go beyond the Spice Girls and media hype, with women achieving positions in society which are commensurate with their educational achievements.

56 Dossing, Blagging and Wagging:
Countercultural Groups in the School Environment

Paul E. Willis

On a night we go out on
the street
Troubling other people.
I suppose we're anti-social,
But we enjoy it.

The older generation
They don't like our hair,
Or the clothes we wear
They seem to love running
us down,
I don't know what I would
do if I didn't have the gang.
(*Extract from a poem by Derek
written in an English class*)

[. . .] Counterschool culture is the zone of the informal. It is where the incursive demands of the formal are denied – even if the price is the expression of opposition in style, micro-interactions and non-public discourses. In working-class culture generally opposition is frequently marked by a withdrawal into the informal and expressed in its characteristic modes just beyond the reach of 'the rule'.

Even though there are no public rules, physical structures, recognized hierarchies or institutionalized sanctions in the counterschool culture, it cannot run on air. It must have its own material base, its own infrastructure. This is, of course, the social group. The informal group is the basic unit of this culture, the fundamental and elemental source of its resistance. It locates and makes possible all other elements of the culture, and its presence decisively distinguishes 'the lads' from the 'ear'oles'.

The importance of the group is very clear to members of the counterschool culture.

[In a group discussion]
Will: [. . .] we see each other every day, don't we, at school [. . .]
Joey: That's it, we've developed certain ways of talking, certain ways of acting, and we developed disregards for Pakis, Jamaicans and all different . . . for all the scrubs and the fucking ear'oles and all that [. . .] We're getting to know it now, like we're getting to know all the cracks, like, how to get out of lessons and things, and we know where to have a crafty smoke. You can come over here to the youth wing and do summat, and er'm . . . all your friends are here, you know, it's sort of what's there, what's always going to be there for the next year, like, and you know you have to come to school today, if you're feeling bad, your mate'll soon cheer yer up like, 'cos you couldn't go without ten minutes in this school, without having a laff at something or other.

PW: Are your mates a really big important thing at school now?

–   Yeah.

–   Yeah.

–   Yeah.

Joey: They're about the best thing actually.

The essence of being 'one of the lads' lies within the group. It is impossible to form a distinctive culture by yourself. You cannot generate fun, atmosphere and a social identity by yourself. Joining the counterschool culture means joining a group, and enjoying it means being with the group:

[In a group discussion on being 'one of the lads']

Joey: [. . .] when you'm dossing on your own, it's no good, but when you'm dossing with your mates, then you're all together, you're having a laff and it's a doss.

Bill: If you don't do what the others do, you feel out.

Fred: You feel out, yeah, yeah. They sort of, you feel, like, thinking the others are . . .

Will: In the second years . . .

Spanksy: I can imagine . . . you know, when I have a day off school, when you come back the next day, and something happened like in the day you've been off, you feel, 'Why did I have that day off', you know, 'I could have been enjoying myself'. You know what I mean? You come back and they're saying, 'Oorh, you should have been here yesterday', you know.

Will: [. . .] like in the first and second years, you can say er'm . . . you're a bit of an ear'ole right. Then you want to try what it's like to be er'm . . . say, one of the boys like, you want to have a taste of that, not an ear'ole, and so you like the taste of that.

Though informal, such groups nevertheless have rules of a kind which can be described – though they are characteristically framed in contrast to what 'rules' are normally taken to mean.

PW: [. . .] Are there any rules between you lot?

Pete: We just break the other rules.

Fuzz: We ain't got no rules between us though, have we?

[. . .]

Pete: Changed 'em round.

Will: We ain't got rules but we do things between us, but we do things that y'know, like er . . . say, I wouldn't knock off anybody's missus or Joey's missus, and they wouldn't do it to me, y'know what I mean? Things like that or, er . . . yer give 'im a fag, you expect one back, like, or summat like that.

Fred: T'ain't rules, it's just an understanding really.

Will: That's it, yes.

PW: [. . .] What would these understandings be?

Will: Er . . . I think, not to . . . meself, I think there ain't many of us that play up the first or second years, it really is that, but y'know, say if Fred had cum to me and sez, 'er . . . I just got two bob off that second year over there', I'd think, 'What a cunt', you know.

[. . .]

Fred: We're as thick as thieves, that's what they say, stick together.

There is a universal taboo among informal groups on the yielding of incriminating information about others to those with formal power. Informing contravenes the essence of the informal group's nature: the maintenance of oppositional meanings against the penetration of 'the rule'. The Hammertown lads call it 'grassing'. Staff call it telling the truth. 'Truth' is the formal complement of 'grassing'. It is only by getting someone to 'grass' – forcing them to break the solemnest taboo – that the primacy of the formal organization can be maintained. No wonder, then, that a whole school can be shaken with paroxysms over a major incident and the purge which follows it. It is an atavistic struggle about authority and the legitimacy of authority. The school has to win, and someone, finally, has to 'grass': this is one of the ways in which the school itself is reproduced and the faith of the 'ear'oles' restored. But whoever has done the 'grassing' becomes special, weak and marked. There is a massive retrospective and ongoing reappraisal among 'the lads' of the fatal flaw in his personality which had always been immanent but not fully disclosed until now:

[In a group discussion of the infamous 'fire extinguisher incident' in which 'the lads' took a hydrant out of school and let it off in the local park]

PW: It's been the biggest incident of the year as it's turned out, hasn't it?

Joey: It's been blown up into something fucking terrific. It was just like that [snapping his fingers], a gob in the ocean as far as I'm concerned when we did it, just like smoking round the corner, or going down the shop for some crisps.

PW: What happened [. . .]?

– Webby [on the fringes of the counterschool culture] grassed.

Joey: Simmondsy had me on me own and he said, 'One of the group owned up and tried to put all the blame on Fuzz'. But he'd only had Webby in there.

Spanksy: We was smoking out here.

Spike: He's like that, you'd got a fag, hadn't you [to Fuzz].

Spanksy: And Webby asks for a drag, so he give Webby the fag. Rogers [a teacher] walked through the door, and he went like that [demonstrating] and he says, 'It ain't mine sir, I'm just holding it for Fuzz'.

Will: Down the park before, [. . .] this loose thing, me and Eddie pulled it off, didn't we, me and Eddie, and the parky was coming round like, he was running round, wor'he, so me and Eddie we went round the other side, and just sat there, like you know, two monkeys. And Webby was standing there, and the parky come up to him and says, 'Come on, get out. Get out of this park. You'm banned'. And he says, he walks past us, me and Eddie, and he says, 'I know you warn't there, you was sitting here'. And Webby went, 'It warn't me, it was . . .', and he was just about to say summat, warn't he?

Eddie: That's it, and I said, 'Shhh', and he just about remembered not to grass us.

Membership of the informal group sensitizes the individual to the unseen informal dimension of life in general. Whole hinterlands open up of what lies behind the official definition of things. A kind of double capacity develops to register public descriptions and objectives on the one hand, and to look behind them, consider their implications, and work out what will actually happen, on the other. This interpretative ability is felt very often as a kind of maturation, a feeling of becoming 'worldlywise', of knowing 'how things really work when it comes to it'. It supplies the real 'insider' knowledge which actually helps you get through the day.

PW: Do you think you've learnt anything at school, has it changed or moulded your values?

Joey: I don't think school does fucking anything to you [. . .] It never has had much effect on anybody I don't think [after] you've learnt the basics. I mean school, it's fucking four hours a day. But it ain't the teachers who mould you, it's the fucking kids you meet. You'm only with the teachers 30 per cent of the time in school, the other fucking two-thirds are just talking, fucking pickin' an argument, messing about.

The group also supplies those contacts which allow the individual to build up alternative maps of social reality, it gives the bits and pieces of information for the individual to work out himself what makes things tick. It is basically only through the group that other groups are met, and through them successions of other groups. School groups coalesce and further link up with neighbourhood groups, forming a network for the passing-on of distinctive kinds of knowledge and perspectives that progressively place school at a tangent to the overall experience of being a working-class teenager in an industrial city. It is the infrastructure of the informal group which makes at all possible a distinctive kind of *class* contact, or class culture, as distinct from the dominant one.

Counterschool culture already has a developed form of unofficial bartering and exchange based on 'nicking', 'fiddles', and 'the foreigner' – a pattern which, of course, emerges much more fully in the adult working-class world:

Fuzz: If, say, somebody was to say something like, 'I'm looking, I want a cassette on the cheap like'. Right, talk about it, one of us hears about a cassette on the cheap, y'know, kind of do the deal for 'em and then say, 'Ah, I'll get you the cassette'.

Cultural values and interpretations circulate 'illicitly' and informally just as do commodities.

Opposition to the school is principally manifested in the struggle to win symbolic and physical space from the institution and its rules and to defeat its main perceived purpose: to make you 'work'. Both the winning and the prize – a form of self-direction – profoundly develop informal cultural meanings and practices. By the time a counterschool culture is fully developed its members have become adept at managing the formal system, and limiting its demands to the absolute minimum. Exploiting the complexity of modern regimes of mixed ability groupings, blocked timetabling and multiple RSLA options, in many cases this minimum is simply the act of registration.

[In a group discussion on the school curriculum]
Joey: [. . .] of a Monday afternoon, we'd have nothing right? Nothing hardly relating to school work, Tuesday afternoon we have swimming and they stick you in a classroom for the rest of the afternoon, Wednesday afternoon you have games and there's only Thursday and Friday afternoon that you work, if you call

that work. The last lesson Friday afternoon we used to go and doss, half of us wagged out o' lessons and the other half go into the classroom, sit down and just go to sleep [. . .]
Spanksy: [. . .] Skive this lesson, go up on the bank, have a smoke, and the next lesson go to a teacher who, you know, 'll call the register [. . .]
Bill: It's easy to go home as well, like him [Eddie] . . . last Wednesday afternoon, he got his mark and went home [. . .]
Eddie: I ain't supposed to be in school this afternoon, I'm supposed to be at college [on a link course where students spend one day a week at college for vocational instruction].
PW: What's the last time you've done some writing?
Will: When we done some writing?
Fuzz: Oh are, last time was in careers, 'cos I writ 'yes' on a piece of paper, that broke me heart.
PW: Why did it break your heart?
Fuzz: I mean to write, 'cos I was going to try and go through the term without writing anything. 'Cos since we've cum back, I ain't dun nothing [it was half way through term].

Truancy is only a very imprecise – even meaningless – measure of rejection of school. This is not only because of the practice of stopping in school for registration before 'wagging off' (developed to a fine art among 'the lads'), but also because it only measures one aspect of what we might more accurately describe as informal student mobility. Some of 'the lads' develop the ability of moving about the school at their own will to a remarkable degree. They construct virtually their own day from what is offered by the school. Truancy is only one relatively unimportant and crude variant of this principle of self-direction which ranges across vast chunks of the syllabus and covers many diverse activities: being free out of class, being in class and doing no work, being in the wrong class, roaming the corridors looking for excitement, being asleep in private. The core skill which articulates these possibilities is being able to get out of any given class: the preservation of personal mobility.

[In a group discussion]

PW: But doesn't anybody worry about your not being in their class?

Fuzz: I get a note off the cooks saying I'm helping them [. . .]

John: You just go up to him [a teacher] and say, 'Can I go and do a job'. He'll say, 'Certainly, by all means', 'cos they want to get rid of you like.

Fuzz: Specially when I ask 'em.

Pete: You know the holes in the corridor, I didn't want to go to games, he told me to fetch his keys, so I dropped them down the hole in the corridor, and had to go and get a torch and find them.

For the successful, there can be an embarrassment of riches. It can become difficult to choose between self-organized routes through the day.

Will: [. . .] what we been doing, playing cards in this room 'cos we can lock the door.

PW: Which room's this now?

Will: Resources centre, where we're making the frames [a new stage for the deputy head], s'posed to be.

PW: Oh! You're still making the frames!

Will: We should have had it finished, we just lie there on top of the frame, playing cards, or trying to get to sleep [. . .] Well, it gets a bit boring, I'd rather go and sit in the classroom, you know.

PW: What sort of lessons would you think of going into?

Will: Uh, science, I think, 'cos you can have a laff in there, sometimes.

This self-direction and thwarting of formal organizational aims is also an assault on official notions of time. The most arduous task of the deputy head is the construction of the timetables. In large schools, with several options open to the fifth year, everything has to be fitted in with the greatest of care. The first weeks of term are spent in continuous revision, as junior members of staff complain, and particular combinations are shown to be unworkable. Time, like money, is valuable and not to be squandered. Everything has to be ordered into a kind of massive critical path of the school's purpose. Subjects become measured blocks of time in careful relation to each other. Quite as much as the school buildings the institution over time is the syllabus. The complex charts on the deputy's wall show how it works. In theory it is possible to check where every individual is at every moment of the day. But for 'the lads' this never seems to work. If one wishes to contact them, it is much more important to know and understand their own rhythms and patterns of movement. These rhythms reject the obvious purposes of the timetable and their implicit notions of time. The common complaint about 'the lads' from staff and the 'ear'oles' is that they 'waste valuable time'. Time for 'the lads' is not something you carefully husband and thoughtfully spend on the achievement of desired objectives in the future. For 'the lads' time is something they want to claim for themselves now as an aspect of their immediate identity and self-direction. Time is used for the preservation of a state – being with 'the lads' – not for the achievement of a goal – qualifications.

Of course there is a sense of urgency sometimes, and individuals can see the end of term approaching and the need to get a job. But as far as their culture is concerned time is importantly simply the state of being free from institutional time. Its own time all passes as essentially the same thing, in the same units. It is not planned, and is not counted in loss, or expected exchange.

57 Globalization and Concurrent Challenges for Higher Education

Jan Sadlak

A cautiously optimistic vision of the future of the world can be summarized as follows: 'The society that mankind will inhabit in the 21st century is being shaped by new and powerful forces that include the globalization of economic activity, the growing importance of knowledge as a prerequisite for participation in fundamental human activities and the increasing democratization of political systems'.[1] Education, in general, and higher education (HE), in particular, has been an important factor in laying the foundations for such an evolution of society. It is expected that HE will play a prominent role also with regard to globalization and how this concept will evolve. Will globalization be a starting point for a more coherent vision of global problems and a more equitable use of what we all produce and consume, or it will be the epitome of the globalized *laissez-faire* flow of capital, goods, entertainment and information?

Whatever specific characteristics we tend to associate with the concept of 'globalization', it is an expression of 'new geopolitics' in which a control over territory is of lesser importance than the control of and access to all kinds of markets, the ability to generate and use knowledge and the capacity to develop new technology and human resources. As such, 'globalization' becomes not only a complex interlinking of various (and not only economic) processes but also a sombrely dominant framework for anxious peering into our future as individuals and members of society. This [discussion] tries to look, foremost from the global perspective, at how the recent developments, still persisting imbalances, changing conditions and challenges facing HE can relate to this irreversible but not yet conclusively positive prospect for internationalization in the years to come.

Quantitative paradigm

The mounting statistics on student population attest to the fact that extraordinary effort is being expended on a global scale in expanding the HE enterprise. All societies, whether modern or modernizing, post-industrial or developing, are experiencing increasing demand for access to HE, foremost in order to respond to an increasing requirement for trained citizens for an economy which more and more depends upon knowledge-related skills and the ability to handle information. Without assuming monopoly, only HE institutions can produce such citizens in big numbers and of varied kinds.

The number of students in HE in the world increased from 51 million in 1980 to about 82 million in 1995, representing an increase of 61 per cent. In a majority of highly industrialized countries, around 50 per cent of the typical HE-bound age group of 18–23 are enrolled in various types of HE institution. According to data from the World Bank, there is a clear correlation between the level of participation in HE and economic development, which on average is 51 per cent in the Organization for Economic Cooperation and Development (OECD) countries, compared with 21 per cent in middle-income countries and 6 per cent in low-income countries.[2] On a worldwide basis the overall ratio has increased from 12.2 per cent in 1980 to 16.2 per cent in 1995.

A closer look at the pace with which the process of transformation from a relatively elitist to a mass HE system took place is also worthwhile. For example, in 1955 in France there were less than 150,000 students. Today, there are about 2,169,000 students which represents more than 46 per cent of 18–23 age group. In Germany, student numbers have increased by 80 per cent since 1977. At present, the number of students exceeds such coveted professional/social groups as farmers in a majority of OECD countries. All these are signs of enormous systemic changes in which demography plays an important but not a decisive role.

By no means is this trend limited to highly industrialized countries. For example, in the last 25 years the number of students in HE in Saudi Arabia increased more than 21 times. Many rapidly developing countries, especially those in South East Asia, plan to increase the proportion of school-leavers going into HE to levels which would be similar to those of the most advanced countries. The same tendency is observable also in most countries of Central and Eastern Europe where the level of participation in HE is still below the 30 per cent mark.

At present, in some 20 countries the number of students enrolled in HE exceeds 1 million. Of these 20, at least half are developing countries. And this has been achieved only in the course of the last decade or so. The similarity of the pace of this development with that of urban growth in those countries is quite striking.

However, when presenting these trends, it is also necessary to bear in mind the still existing inequality of access to HE between various countries and regions. It must be recalled that despite the progress achieved in this area, young people's opportunities to pursue HE in sub-Saharan Africa are 17 times lower than in the industrially developed countries, nowadays often described

as 'the North', and are on average four times lower for young people in *all* the developing countries. (The end of communism as a global ideological force and the end of the East–West confrontation brought about changes in the configuration of the so-called regions. It resulted in the world being seen in a bipolar configuration in which the countries which belong to the non-aligned movement, together with developing countries, have reoriented themselves to become the South, while the rest of the countries, especially those in Europe and North America, have been grouped to become the North. The ascendance of the trading blocs has only reinforced this perspective.)

Overall, the policy of wide access to HE is nowadays more a rule than an exception. The argument for the continuation of this policy is based, among other things, on estimations concerning the evolution of labour markets which show that in the course of the next decade some 40 per cent of all jobs in the industrialized countries will require 16 years of schooling and training. For the developing countries the argument is similar as it looks as if one of the characteristics of the next century will be further internationalization of economic relations and further development of technology. To this end it is almost an imperative that more and more people must master science and technology as well as information.

Already in the late 1970s, James Perkins, for many years the chairman of the International Council for Educational Development (ICED) and the former president of Cornell University, in a lucid analysis of principal axioms determining the quantitative development of HE, noted that 'in every society entry to higher education must be open to a minimum percentage of the entering age group if that society is to grow and survive. This percentage varies according to different opinions, but it would seem that a range of between 12 and 18 per cent of the age group constitutes a reasonable number'. He also gives a stern warning that 'Any society that does not give at least 12 per cent of the age group access to post-secondary education does not have a chance to survive in the type of future that lies ahead.'[3] It is worth keeping in mind arguments brought by Perkins when, under a banner of due concern for priority and efficiency of educational investment, the role of HE is de-emphasized.

Informational paradigm

In the context of the [present] topic, it is hard to omit new information and communication technology which gives a practical dimension to being 'global' and not only with regard to HE. The greatest contributor to rapid multi-faceted globalization which can be most directly attributed to academia is probably the Internet, which was developed as a result of researchers' desire for rapid and low-cost communication. In the course of recent years it has become a powerful economic and cultural instrument. Together with other wonders of new information and telecommunication technology, we are rapidly observing profound changes in the way students acquire knowledge and scientists carry out their work and communicate among themselves on local, national and international levels.

The term 'university without walls' which was often used in the 1970s to promote not only new educational technology but also the idea of political and cultural openness in HE becomes a pragmatic high-tech reality, symbolized by another term – the virtual university. The number of such virtual institutions offering virtual degrees is steadily increasing. According to some estimates, in the United States alone there are about 300 colleges and universities offering this form of HE studies and over 1 million students are now plugged into the virtual classroom. It is also estimated that the number of 'cyberstudents' will more than triple by the turn of the century. There are more and more signs that distant and traditional forms of studying are merging and mutually supplementing each other. Besides offering an alternative means of getting a degree, this type of studying can be an effective form of providing retraining and upgrading of courses without involving too much of a break from professional employment or time-consuming travel to the campus. In order to be able to take full advantage of marvellous informational tools, members of the academic community must not only have the right equipment but continue to develop their symbolic analytical skills.

There is no need to worry that the traditional academic work of teaching, studying and research in a conventional institution of HE is going to disappear altogether. Being together and talking to other students, teachers and researchers is going to be an academically and socially essential part of intellectual and professional development for as long as we can foresee. There is however no doubt that virtual education is an alternative to mainstream provision of HE. Some argue that it also will bring sorely needed competition to conventional HE. It might also be an answer when dealing with still unmet demand for HE, particularly in the developing countries, because, as John Daniel, the vice-chancellor of the Open University argues, 'Merely to keep student participation rates constant in the developing world, one sizeable new university has to open every week to meet the demands of the young and growing population.'[4] Obviously, in a situation where very few developing countries can afford to fund at appropriate levels already existing HE institutions, new technology can be a logical option. What remains problematic is how much those countries will be able to sustain their indigenous knowledge capacity in order to be able to produce educational software adequate to their own needs. It should also be pointed out that the globalized circulation of information might not be an all-inclusive partnership, especially in those cases when academic recognition and traditional not-for-profit circulation of knowledge within the academic community will be replaced by 'for-profit' activities.

International versus global university cooperation

It is not too presumptuous to claim that there is more 'international content' within an average university than within a transnational, globally operating corporate organization. This derives from the very nature of HE learning and academic work which imposes the seeking of relevance and confirmation not only on local or national but also on global levels. The long history of the universities shows that intellectual self-sufficiency and inward-looking parochialism lead to a decline of HE and its institutions. A desire to know and understand 'others' brings many people to the doors of universities. A growing number of HE institutions articulate in their mission their commitment to internationalization. This takes a multitude of forms which makes assessing them, particularly at the supra-institutional level, quite difficult, with the exception of international student mobility.

According to recent studies by the United Nations Educational, Scientific and Cultural Organization (UNESCO), in 1995 more than 1.5 million foreign students were enrolled for HE study in the 50 major host countries. More than 800,000 students from less developed regions were enrolled for third-level study in a foreign country, as were more than 150,000 students from the former communist countries of Central and Eastern Europe and Euro-Asian countries of the former Soviet Union. About 440,000 students from more developed regions were enrolled for HE in another country.

If this aspect of internationalization of HE is a remarkable development, the pattern of student flows across national boundaries has hardly become more globally balanced. As in past years, more than three-quarters of all foreign study takes place in just ten host countries: the United States (more than 30 per cent of all foreign students), France (more than 11 per cent), Germany (about 10 per cent), the United Kingdom (about 9 per cent), the Russian Federation (about 5 per cent), Japan (more than 3 per cent, i.e. 3.5 per cent), Australia (about 3 per cent), Canada (less than 2.5 per cent), Belgium (less than 2.5 per cent) and Switzerland (about 2 per cent), followed by two other countries, Austria and Italy, with almost the same number of foreign students as Belgium,

at around 25,000. With the exception of one, all these 'host countries' are members of the OECD, once again confirming the direct correlation between economic strength and the capacity of educational and scientific systems.

A number of countries have adopted a policy of increasing their international student population. As a result of this decision, countries such as Germany, the United Kingdom, Japan and Australia reported an increase of more than 10 per cent. It is worth pointing out that the most rapid growth took place in China where the number of foreign students increased by more than 27 per cent, from 3,250 in 1985 to 22,617 in 1995.

It is much less encouraging to see a continuous imbalance of participation with regard to student mobility in sub-Saharan African countries. With the exception of South Africa, no other country of this region is among the 50 major host countries. And when analysing the number of students abroad as a percentage of national enrolment, once again, only one country – Cameroon – is among the group of 50 'major countries of origin'. It can be argued that if a national system of HE responds sufficiently to student demand then there is no need to undertake study abroad. This would be an encouraging conclusion but it is more likely that this situation is the result of the generalization of poverty in and the declining financial capacity of those countries to send their nationals to study abroad. As a result, they reduce their collective capacity to develop a deeper understanding of cultures, technologies, languages and business methods, or to build personal networks. Long seen as a plus for intellectual and cultural diversity, foreign students have now become a part of 'economic competitiveness' in the global economy. It is the very reason why such an organization as the European Commission has launched well-structured and relatively well-founded student mobility schemes such as ERASMUS and SOCRATES which allowed some 500,000 students in member states of the EU to spend a meaningful period of their studies in another country of the European

Union. Other organizations or treaties such as the NAFTA, ASEAN, APEC and Mercorsur encourage student mobility within their member states. There is a risk that despite globalization or maybe because of it, we might move away from multilateral cooperation towards more controllable bilateral cooperation. This would sooner rather than later lead to a significant number of members of the international community being excluded from active participation in the globalized economy, international scientific and cultural exchanges, etc.

There tends to be a strong conviction that one means of better preparing future graduates for the demands of an increasingly international, professional life is to provide them with more opportunities to study and live abroad. The personal, educational and ultimately social benefits are difficult to measure but it is often acknowledged that studying abroad results in:

- acquiring new knowledge and competencies;
- improving knowledge of a foreign language;
- familiarization with new teaching methods as well as new scientific equipment, organization of laboratories, etc.;
- opportunities to purchase new books, software, etc.;
- establishing new personal contacts, professional networking;
- familiarization with another country, its institutions and their functions;
- personal development and building of self-confidence.

Gradually, internationalization is making strides in fields which were perceived as foremost national domains, such as quality assessment and accreditation. Such initiatives as Universitas 21, which is run from the University of Melbourne and which brings together a group of large but more or less similar profile public universities round the world (in Australia, Canada, New Zealand, Singapore, the United Kingdom and the United States) to accredit each other and share external examiners, will be followed by other types of global network.

Conclusions

History shows that social and economic development is rarely an outcome of one, however powerful, factor or encompassing concept, and 'globalization' is only one such factor. There are several others which are no less important or less complex. UNESCO's *Policy Paper for Change and Development in Higher Education* (1995) identifies, in addition to globalization, several other trends which are directly or indirectly shaping the development of HE. These are:

- Democratization, which brought about the collapse of many totalitarian regimes, the steady advance of democratic forces, the development of civil society and progress in the respect for human rights.
- Regionalization, as groups of states associate themselves in order to facilitate trade and economic integration. The other form of regionalization is that within existing states. All these regional arrangements are also making inroads in matters of education, culture, scientific cooperation and academic labour markets.
- Polarization of inequalities, resulting in a widening gap between rich and poor countries and within the various categories of society.
- Marginalization and fragmentation, which, due to various forms of underdevelopment, foment social and cultural exclusion and divide whole communities along ethnic, tribal or religious lines.[5]

Globalization is a relatively new phenomenon and some of its processes are just beginning to show at local, national and international levels. We have only just started to organize our international life in a way which will allow us to deal with the problems associated with this multifaceted phenomenon. Globalization does not have to be seen as a downward-pointed megadesign threatening cultural diversity or insatiable globalized commercialism. It is true that it can reduce local and national sovereignty particularly in economic and financial areas. But it can work to the advantage of social and economic development in many developing countries and disadvantaged groups in our society. It might help us to understand and accept that the world continues to undergo immense transformations and is beset by problems which can and must be dealt with on a worldwide basis. It brings much closer to our collective attention, through traditional media, satellite television and Internet-based networks, what is going on in the world.

As in the past, HE is going to be involved in searching for a response to the above challenges not least because universities and other HE and academic institutions have become central in modern society and their role has shifted from being a *reflection* of social, cultural and economic relationships to being a *determinant* of such relationships. This will only be reinforced by an advancement of science and its growing role in our biological, economic and social lives.

The frank acknowledgement that globalization has become a permanent feature of our social, economic and cultural space is essential in order to take advantage of what it can offer as well as to avoid the perils it may involve. I think society can expect that universities and other HE institutions will try to reflect on how globalization affects our society and its institutions. Why? Because universities are one of those places conducive to a development and gestation of theories, ideas, and innovations. Primarily through critical examination, they are enhancing our individual and collective ability for selection and application of ideas in all spheres of social, cultural, technical and economic activity. These functions of universities, without minimizing their traditionally central roles in teaching, learning, and scholarship, are important as they are one of the major determinants of how successful we are all going to be in dealing with the challenges and opportunities brought by globalization. It is the mission of global organizations like UNESCO to promote the global vision of HE in which people are enabled to function in their personal, professional and community lives, and are able to be perpetuators and repositories of knowledge, ideas and local and national cultural traditions.

NOTES

1   UNESCO, *Adult Education in a Polarizing World* (Paris, UNESCO, 1997), p. 7.

2   World Bank, *Higher Education: The Lessons of Experience* (Washington, DC: World Bank, 1994).

3   J. Perkins, 'Four Axioms and Three Topics of Common Interest in the Field of Higher Education', in *The Contribution of Higher Education to the Development of Changing Societies* (Bucharest: UNESCO/CEPES, 1977), p. 134.

4   J. Daniel, 'The World Cuisine of Borderless Knowledge', *Times Higher Education Supplement*, 9 August 1996, p. 14.

5   UNESCO, *Policy Paper for Change and Development in Higher Education* (Paris: UNESCO, 1995).

Part 17 Religion

Secularization means a decline in religious beliefs and practice. Sociologists are agreed that most modern societies have become largely secularized. In the US, for example, rates of church attendance are much lower than they were years ago in the industrial countries. Yet the idea that religion will become of only marginal importance has proved to be wrong. Most of the population continues to believe in God, as Malcolm Hamilton shows in Reading 58. In countries outside the West, religion often remains a very strong influence indeed. Even within the developed countries a decline in belief in orthodox religion is quite frequently balanced by upsurges of interest in new religious groups. The secularization thesis therefore has to be treated with caution.

In Reading 59 Akbar Ahmed and Hastings Domman discuss Islamic religion in the context of globalization. Globalization has affected religion, even in more traditional countries, as much as any other institution. Notions drawn from Islam – such as *fatwa*, which literally means a sermon – are now quite well known in the West as a result of the impact of the media. However, these notions are often completely detached from the meaning they have for Muslim believers.

Andrew Brown in Reading 60, discusses the question of gender and religion. While the Anglican church has now admitted women priests, the Roman Catholic church still bans women from ordination to the priesthood. At least for the moment, the Pope and other major church leaders seem determined to resist the growing demand for equal female rights within the religious sphere. Brown suggests, however, that the promotion of equal rights for women within the religious domain should be seen as part of the more general process of social democratization, and in that sense in the end is likely to prove irresistible.

58 Secularisation?
Now You See it, Now You Don't

Malcolm Hamilton

When a fundamental change takes place in society it is not unusual for sociologists to disagree about the exact nature of the change and its implications, but it is not usually the case that they disagree that the change has taken place. This, strangely, is the case with secularisation.

From the start, the study of secularisation has been beset by intense debates about whether secularisation has occurred at all. The consequence of this is that some sociologists of religion find themselves trying to explain and account for developments which, according to other sociologists, have not taken place. For some, secularisation is one of the more profound changes to have affected our society over the last century or so while, for others, it is an illusion or a myth.

Religion and modernity

Not so long ago it was almost the received wisdom that religion was of steadily declining significance in modern industrial societies, in terms both of its public role and of its importance in the private lives of individuals. In other words, such societies were thought to be essentially secular in nature and increasingly so (see table 58.1).

This secularisation thesis was bound up with the idea that modernity gives no room to religious

Table 58.1 Christian church membership in Britain, 1900–1990

Year	All Protestant Total (m)	Roman Catholic Total (m)	All Christian Total (m)	All Christian Ratio	All Christian % of adult population
1900	5.4	2.0	7.4	100	30
1930	7.1	2.8	9.9	133	29
1950	6.1	3.5	9.6	129	25
1970	5.2	2.7	7.9	107	19
1990	3.4	2.2	5.6	76	12

For comparability, the 1970 and 1990 Catholic figures are for mass attendance on an average Sunday. As the proportion of 'observant' Catholics has steadily declined over the century from over 80 per cent to less than 40 per cent, 1900, 1930 and 1950 data have been left as the total Catholic population. If they had also been adjusted, the decline in percentage of total adult population who are church members would be slightly but not significantly less dramatic.

Sources: P. Brierley, *A Century of British Christianity: Historical Statistics 1900–1985 with Projections to 2000*, Research Monograph 14 (MARC Europe, 1989); R. Currie, A. D. Gilbert and L. Horsley, *Churches and Churchgoers: Patterns of Church Growth in the British Isles since 1700* (Oxford University Press, 1977); P. Brierly and V. Hiscock, *UK Christian Handbook 1994/95* (Christian Research Association, 1993)

belief. In a society increasingly based upon the rational mastery of nature through science and technology, systems of ideas and beliefs that make reference to supernatural or non-material beings, powers and entities, or which are founded upon the view that there is a transcendental dimension of reality, have no place.

The foremost scholar taking this view is Bryan Wilson, whose *Religion in Secular Society* was published in 1966. A more recent statement of the secularisation thesis has been put forward by Steven Bruce, especially in his *Religion in the Modern World*. It is a view that has its roots in the Enlightenment of the eighteenth century, which not only placed enormous emphasis upon reason and human progress through rational understanding of the workings of nature but often saw religion as a major impediment to such advance.

More recently, the secularisation thesis has been seriously questioned and challenged. Hadden and Stark, for example, have described secularisation as a contemporary myth. An early opponent of the secularisation thesis was David Martin in such books as *The Religious and the Secular*. The pendulum has, in fact, swung the other way. The bedrock of Enlightenment optimism concerning human reason and progress has been breaking up under the impact of postmodern forces; religion is seen as very much on the agenda and part of modern society, if in very altered, diverse and unfamiliar forms. Some, however, hold out against the trend and cling tenaciously to the secularisation thesis.

What is religion?

One of the main reasons for this peculiar situation of disagreement about whether such an important development has actually occurred or not is that there is little agreement among sociologists on the question of what religion is. In order to support the claim that religion is of diminishing significance in modern society and that modern society is fundamentally secular in nature, one has first to define what religion is.

Those who oppose the idea that religion is of diminishing significance in modern society have frequently pointed out that while traditional church religion may be weakening, religion as such, which they conceive much more broadly than traditional church religion, is not necessarily following the same path or doomed to the same fate. If we think of religion as traditional church religion it is not difficult to make out a case that it is of decreasing importance in modern society; if religion is much broader than this and includes such things as, for example, deep commitment to and respect for one's country and its institutions, devotion to a style of rock music or to a particular football team, then religion may be, in this form, as vibrant a part of modern life as traditional church religion was at any time in the past. The supporters of the secularisation thesis reply that, on the other hand, there is a danger that religion may be defined so broadly that it can be found behind every bush and under every stone.

What is secularisation?

A second reason for the disagreement about whether religion is declining in modern society is that secularisation itself is conceived in very different ways by proponents and opponents of the secularisation thesis. There is a broad range of meanings of the term secularisation as used by various theorists. This range stretches from, at one extreme, the complete disappearance of religion, which writers such as Marx and Freud anticipated, to such things as the separation of church and state and removal of the influence of religion and religious bodies from public life and affairs, at the other.

Bryan Wilson's definition of secularisation as the 'process by which religious institutions, actions and consciousness lose their social significance' illustrates well typical contemporary meanings of the term. If we think of secularisation in the broader and more radical sense, it is easier to dispute that it is occurring; if we think of secularisation in the latter and narrower sense, then in certain countries and circumstances it is much

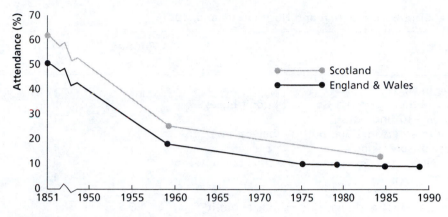

Figure 58.1 Adult church attendance in Britain, 1851–1989

Sources: P. Brierley (1980) *Prospects for the Eighties: From a Census of the Churches in 1979*, Bible Society; P. Brierley and F. Macdonald (1985) *Prospects for Scotland: From a Census of the Churches in 1984*, The Bible Society of Scotland: P. Brierley (1991) *Prospects for the Nineties: Trends and Tables from the English Church Census*, MARC Europe: British Parliamentary Papers (1970) 1851 Census, *Great Britain, Report and Tables on Religious Worship 1852–3*, repr. Irish University Press; British Parliamentary Papers (1854) *Religious Worship and Education, Scotland, Report and Tables*, HMSO.

more convincing to argue that it is, in fact, a major feature of modern society and the way in which it is developing.

Secularisation theorists often complain that their opponents misrepresent them, attributing to them far more radical versions of the thesis than they in fact espouse. Anti-secularisation theorists tend to retort that secularisation theorists have simply shifted their ground, retreating into weaker and weaker versions of it.

The historical importance of religion

A third difficulty underlies the disagreement about secularisation. In order to say that religion is less significant than it was in the past we have to be able to say how important it was in the past. Critics of the secularisation thesis often claim that our knowledge of the past is either not adequate to enable us to make such a claim reliably or that people in the past were not as religious as we imagine them to be. It is often simply assumed, they argue, that in the past most people attended church regularly, accepted the tenets of religious

belief and placed them at the centre of their lives. Such an assumption is unfounded, according to these critics, who produce historical evidence of indifference to and lack of involvement in religion in many areas and communities.

Secularisation theorists in their turn point to the obvious centrality of religion and of the church or churches in public affairs, in local communities and in many spheres of life in the past. They argue that, even if the masses were not as Christian as supposed, there was, however, a survival of folk belief and practice.

Good, reliable and detailed historical data is, of course, necessary to resolve such disputes but is, at the same time, difficult to come by. Perhaps more promising would be to measure trends during more recent decades by the use of surveys. The problem here has been to find a good measure of religious belief and conviction, participation and so on. Church attendance, for example, has declined dramatically over the course of the twentieth century (figure 58.1) but this does not necessarily mean that religious belief has declined.

Table 58.2 Belief in God in Britain and Northern Ireland, 1991

	Position	Britain (%)	Northern Ireland (%)
'I don't believe in God'	1	10	1
'I don't know whether there is a God and I don't believe there is any way to find out'	2	14	4
'I don't believe in a personal God but I do believe in a higher power of some kind'	3	13	4
'I find myself believing in God some of the time but not at other times'	4	13	7
'While I have doubts, I feel that I do believe in God'	5	26	20
'I know God really exists and I have no doubts about it'	6	23	57
'I don't know' and 'No answer'	7	2	7

Source: 1992 British Social Attitudes Survey

Table 58.3 'What is God?', Britain, 1947–1987 (%)

	1947	1957	1987
'There is a personal God'	45	41	37
'There is some sort of spirit or vital force which controls life'	39	37	42
'I am not sure that there is any sort of God or life force'	16	—	—
'I don't know what to think'	—	16	—
'I don't really think there is any sort of spirit, God or life force'	—	6	—
'Don't know', other, or neither	—	—	21

Sources: G. H. Gallup (ed.), The Gallup International Public Opinion Polls; Great Britain 1937–1975 (Random House, 1976); M. Svennevig, I. Haldane, S. Speirs and B. Gunter, Godwatching: Viewers, Religion and Television (John Libbey/IBA, 1989)

Who believes in God?

Surveys have often asked whether respondents believe in God (tables 58.2 and 58.3). The figures have, on the whole, shown a persistence of rather high rates of belief in God or some supernatural entity or force, despite very low rates of church attendance (although there is considerable variation from one country to another, one social group to another and over time). On this basis the opponents of secularisation tend to stake their claim. The supporters of secularisation, on the other hand, point out that assent to such a belief does not mean that it has any consequences for behaviour, is held with any conviction or has any real meaning. They argue that it is slightly more respectable to say that you believe in God. In a situation where there is uncertainty about the existence of God and low salience of the idea of a God, many people will say yes to the question rather than no.

What the surveys show is not that people are still religious but that they have a propensity to say yes to this sort of survey question. Surveys might also ask whether they ever pray. A much higher proportion of those surveyed will say that they pray sometimes than say that they attend church, but it is often not clear what they mean by 'praying'. At a time of great stress or anxiety people may find themselves asking God for help,

Table 58.4 Beliefs in Britain, 1957–1991 (%)

	1957	1981	1987	1991
Sin	—	69	51	—
Soul	—	59	50	—
Heaven	—	57	48	46
Life after death	54	45	43	27
Devil	34	30	31	24
Hell	—	27	29	24

Sources: G. H. Gallup (ed.) (1976) *The Gallup International Public Opinion Polls; Great Britain 1937–1975*, Random House; D. Gerard (1985) 'Religious attitudes and values', in M. Abrams, D. Gerard and N. Timms *Values and Social Change in Britain*, Macmillan, pp. 50–92; M. Svennevig, I. Haldane, S. Speirs and B. Gunter (1989) *Godwatch: Viewers, Religion and Television*, John Libbey/IBA; *1991 British Social Attitudes Survey*.

but it does not follow that they really believe that such help would or could be forthcoming or even that there is any God who would or could intervene in the course of affairs and change them in desired ways.

For what they are worth, such surveys show that, in general, institutional religion of the traditional church kind has been very much in decline in most modern industrialised countries, with the most notable exception of the United States. In Britain, fewer people are church members or attend church, the number of clergy has fallen, their pay has declined and they have lower status. Fewer children are christened or attend Sunday School. Fewer marriages are conducted in church.

Believing without belonging

Surveys show, on the other hand, that there seems to be a survival of some sort of belief of a religious kind and, although such things as belief in God have declined somewhat, a majority of the population still assent to such beliefs as they do to that of some form of life beyond death (hell, however, is distinctly out of fashion); (see tables 58.3 and 58.4). Grace Davie has character-

ised this sort of situation in Britain as 'believing without belonging'.

For pro-secularisation theorists such as Steve Bruce this is evidence rather of a weakening commitment to a religious outlook, slowed down by a lingering nostalgic fondness for it.

Roy Wallis and Steve Bruce, drawing upon the work of Bryan Wilson, have updated the theory of secularisation as a development rooted in modernity. Three processes have promoted secularisation in the modern world, according to Bruce: *social differentiation, societalisation* and *rationalisation*.

Social differentiation is the set of processes by which specialised roles and institutions concerned with very specific functions develop; for example, institutions to handle education, health and welfare, all of which were once the concern of the church.

Societalisation refers to the process by which more and more aspects of life come under the influence of broad levels of social organisation such as the state and are decreasingly matters for the local community. Religion, according to Bryan Wilson, stems from the community whose identity and life it celebrates and legitimates. As this community becomes less significant in the impersonal conditions of modern life religion loses its significance.

Rationalisation refers to all those developments which have seen the rise to prominence of science and technology in the modern world. Rationalisation is a notion drawn from the work of Max Weber, who saw it as a peculiarly strong force in Western culture linked to the Christian tradition.

Peter Berger has developed this idea, seeing the roots of secularisation in the rise of rationality which was given a particularly strong impetus by the Protestant Reformation. In this sense, for Berger, Christianity has ultimately been its own gravedigger. It generated a conception of God so transcendent and distant that He ceased to have much relevance for this world and for life in it. Protestantism focused attention on this life and upon work and the pursuit of prosperity. Berger here follows Max Weber's famous Protestant ethic thesis, which holds that capitalism was greatly nourished by the ethic of Protestantism.

Once in existence, this expansive, thrusting, dynamic economic system infected the entire globe. The rationality it was based upon and the science and technology that it ultimately gave rise to became independent forces in their own right, impacting generally upon all societies and cultures exposed to them.

The secularisation of churches

For these theorists religion in the modern world has been marginalised and privatised. The traditional churches, in so far as they survive, do so only by secularising from within. This has occurred, for example, in the case of the Church of England, in which much of the traditional Christian belief has been relinquished by a large part of the clergy and the congregations: the virgin birth, hell, even God as a real force external to ourselves.

Such developments have not stemmed the decline in membership or attendance, however. Ironically, it is the more traditional and conservative churches which are successful in retaining their membership and in some cases, especially the independent charismatic churches, greatly increasing it. There are, however, marked variations in the extent to which the process can be observed, the United States being a major and, for the secularisation theorists, very awkward instance.

For Bruce, the United States and other regions where traditional religion remains vibrant, such as Poland and Ireland (especially Northern Ireland), can be explained as exceptional instances of either cultural defence or cultural transition. Northern Ireland is a good example of a group, the Protestant community, which feels threatened by the surrounding culture and clings to its religion as an expression and defence of its own distinctiveness.

In the United States we observe a situation of immense and very rapid change in terms of demography, ethnic and racial composition, technology and conditions of life. In this melting pot religion has often provided the means of handling cultural transition and of providing stability and identity, thereby easing the process of integration and adaptation, as it often does for immigrant communities in Britain and European countries.

For Bruce, then, religion may remain for periods of time at the centre of social life where it has work of this kind to do; work, that is, other than its primary task of relating the individual to the supernatural.

Against this view critics of the secularisation thesis argue that there seems still a great deal of such work for religion to do. These and other 'exceptions' could be seen to be the norm. Change is ubiquitous and is always unsettling. Further than this, most secularisation theory has been in the context of the Western world.

Secularisation outside the western world

There seems little evidence of secularisation outside the developed world. The real test lies in developed and industrialised non-Western countries and cultures. Japan gives considerable support to the anti-secularisation theorists since it is highly developed but does not seem to show much weakening of religion. This might suggest that secularisation is largely a Christian phenomenon rather than a feature of modernity; but another way of looking at the data from the Western world is to see that it is predominantly Europe that is secular. This may reflect the long history of anti-clericalism in Europe, bound up as it was with political revolution and emancipation. Once freed from such hangovers, as was the case in the United States, religion can flourish.

If change is threatening and unsettling and if the anxieties associated with change find their expression in religion, then we ought to see the emergence of new religious responses to this anxiety. This is precisely what many critics of the secularisation thesis believe they observe.

New religions

Another major difficulty that secularisation theorists have had to deal with is the rise of a multitude of new religious movements, sects and cults as well as quasi- and fringe religious practices, many of which are grouped together under terms such as 'New Age' or the 'Human Potential Movement'. Traditional, organised, institutionalised religion may be in decline, the anti-secularisation theorists concede, but in its place we observe the emergence of new forms of religion, some of which do not look very much like religion until we examine them a little more closely.

The response of the secularisation theorists to this phenomenon has been, first, to point out that the rise of new religious movements and sects comes nowhere near compensating for the decline of membership of the traditional churches. Second, these phenomena are ephemeral, marginal and relatively trivial in the extent to which they affect people's lives.

For Bryan Wilson it is the very marginality and ephemerality of such things which testifies to the difficulty of upholding seriously a religious view in the contemporary world. Sects may have a profound impact upon the small numbers who become involved in them; cults and movements such as New Age represent a re-enchantment and re-magicalisation of the world but more as a hobby or pastime than as a serious religious commitment. They are relatively unorganised and privatised activities destined to remain on the fringes of society.

Conclusion

In conclusion, the evidence for secularisation is ambivalent and can be read either in favour of or against the secularisation thesis. We observe at the same time a loss of the supernatural element in traditional religion and, in certain quarters, a re-magicalisation of the world; we see secularisation within some churches while more traditional and conservative churches flourish; new religious movements and sects grow up at a bewildering pace, yet they involve only small numbers of people and remain marginal. It is a picture of instability, change and, above all, diversity, which reflects fundamental contradictions in our present condition: on the one hand, a widespread need to believe in something and, on the other, scepticism about anything incompatible with scientific rationality, antipathy to dogma and religious authority and affirmation of individualism and freedom to question and to choose.

As for the eventual outcome, if there is one, the jury is likely to be out for some time. We cannot yet answer the question: 'Is religion declining or just changing?' Changes of the scale we are concerned with are measured not in decades but in hundreds of years. Stark and Bainbridge argue that secularisation is a cyclical process. According to them, we are now passing out of a trough of religious decline and moving into the upswing. Secularisation is a self-limiting process in which a decline in traditional religion calls forth new forms of faith and belief. Certainly, as with many social developments, no one supposes that secularisation follows a smooth path. Religious revivals often interrupt the process of change. Only time will tell whether Stark and Bainbridge are correct and whether the current upswing will continue or be followed by a yet deeper trough.

59 Islam in the Age of Postmodernity

Akbar S. Ahmed and Hastings Donnan

Islamic studies – or the study of Muslim groups and their religion Islam – has been changing dramatically in the last decades. Until recently, Islamic studies was largely the exotic focus of a relatively small group of academics who wrote books about it mainly for one another's consumption. Many of these intellectuals were based in the West, and few of these were Muslims. The Muslim voice itself was seldom heard outside the Muslim world. This has been changing, partly in response to the fact that the lives of many ordinary Muslims have been changing, and partly as a reflection of the equally dramatic changes taking place in the world more generally. Many factors can explain this, and this [study] sets out to trace both their impact on Muslims and the latter's responses to them.

Globalization

Firstly, we consider the phenomenon sometimes referred to as globalization. Since it is not always clear that people mean the same thing when they talk about globalization – some talk about globalization theory, others about a global process defined with varying degrees of precision – it is as well to be clear at the outset about how the term is used here. By globalization we principally refer to the rapid developments in communications technology, transport and information which bring the remotest parts of the world within easy reach. For instance, today if a development takes place in New York it can be relayed instantly across the world to Cairo or Karachi. A good example of this process of globalization is the controversy surrounding Salman Rushdie which began in the late 1980s in the United Kingdom with the publication of *The Satanic Verses*. Within hours, developments in the United Kingdom – in Bradford and London – provoked responses in Islamabad and Bombay. Indeed, people died as they protested against the book. Government pronouncements, media chat shows, editorials, vigils and protests reflected the heated debate. Never before in history had such developments taken place in this manner and at such speed.

One consequence of the globalization process is the necessity to look at Islamic studies not as an esoteric or marginal exercise but as something that concerns the global community. We are thus forced to look at Muslims in different parts of the world not as the preserve of specialist scholars but as an ever-present and ubiquitous reality that relates to non-Muslims in the street. And let us not forget the truly global nature of Muslim society which totals something like one billion people living in about 50 countries with significantly some ten to fifteen million living in the USA and Europe. Issues of migration arise from this reality. Here Muslims face major problems as immigrants, including racism.

Owing to the developments in and around Islam, words such as *fatwa* (a sermon), *jihad* (struggle, including armed effort), *ayatollah* (highly learned scholar and cleric) are now common in the West. The tabloids have popularized these words and they have entered the English language. This again is a consequence of the Western media using or misusing words and adopting and adapting them to the local usage. It also reflects the interplay and interchange of ideas between Islam and the West. An earlier example of borrowing is the word *mughal*, which signified the great Mughal emperors and dynasty of India and is now used for any powerful person, and particularly to refer to business tycoons ('moguls'). Another earlier example is harem, which in Arabic designates a female sanctuary to which only close male relatives have access but which in English often suggests only the voluptuous and licentious exploitation of women. It is clear, then, that borrowing of this kind has been going on for some time. Indeed, the process of globalization itself might be said to have a long history, even if the term is of fairly recent currency.

Like much of the rest of the world, Muslims and the West have long been interconnected through international trade and economic exchange (or exploitation), locked together in what has been referred to as the 'economic world-system'. An embryonic form of late twentieth-century globalization might thus be discerned in the collaborations between the representatives of colonial power and the indigenous élites who helped them to rule. Indeed, there are those who consider this period of human history to be one stage – and not necessarily the first stage – in the development of what we now call globalization. For example, it has been suggested that the historical path to current global complexity has passed through five phases, beginning in the early fifteenth century. Globalization is thus not necessarily the wholly novel phenomenon, unique to the latter half of this century, that some commentators appear to imply. As a process it is of considerable historical depth, and as a theory it exhibits all the notions of 'system' and 'stages of growth' which distinguish its forerunner, world-systems theory. Nevertheless, and most commentators appear to agree, late twentieth-century globalization does seem different from earlier forms in certain important respects.

For one thing, the historical connections between nations have generally been previously understood largely in terms of an *economic* world-system. The economic content of international

contact has thus been emphasized at the expense of the *cultural* flows which were obviously also taking place alongside the material exchanges; indeed, the place of 'culture' in analyses of global interconnections such as world-systems theory is a matter of some disagreement, with some alleging that it has mostly been left out. But there are obviously many examples of collaborations between colonials and locals which involved much more than just political and economic cooperation; thus when the values of gentlemanly behaviour and fair play arrived in India as a cultural export from Victorian and Edwardian England, they were quickly adopted by those – such as the Parsis – who wished to please their then colonial masters. But while these cultural flows clearly existed in the past, they never seem to have been an end in themselves, and they have usually been of less interest to scholars than the material realities which underpinned them.

Today the emphasis has shifted and it is the cultural flows between nations which above all else seem to typify the contemporary globalization process (or its current phase). These cultural flows are not, of course, detached from economic and political realities. Because of their origins, some flows – mainly those in 'the West' – have more force than others and so reach a wider audience. Accordingly, there has been much discussion about the possible homogenization of culture – the move towards a 'global culture' in which everyone will drink the same soft drinks, smoke Marlboro cigarettes, and emulate JR. Such an homogenization of culture has been questioned from a number of perspectives, and the situation is certainly more complex than is sometimes supposed. Firstly, the notion of a hegemonic global cultural centre dispensing its products to the world's peripheries is more often assumed than described; and even if there is such a thing, it is not clear that its exports have any more significance to those they reach than its exports of a generation or two ago. Secondly, even though the same cultural 'message' may be received in different places, it is domesticated by being interpreted and incorporated according to local values. And finally, cultural flows do not necessarily map directly on to economic and political relationships, which means that the flow of cultural traffic can often be in many different directions simultaneously. We shall return to these points later.

The globalization process today is also marked by the accelerated pace at which informational and cultural exchanges take place, and by the scale and complexity of these exchanges. Facilitated by the new technologies, it is the sheer speed, extent and volume of these exchanges that have engaged popular imagination, and that seem to have led to globalization being so often represented, if perhaps a little glibly, by the VCR. Cheater lists an impressive array of such technologies from electronic mail to the satellite dish, and although these are clearly not accessible to all, they have obviously been directly or indirectly responsible for exposing many different sorts of people to new influences.[1] Such technologies are able to uncouple culture from its territorial base so that, detached and unanchored, it pulsates through the airwaves to all those with the means to receive it.

Whatever the ultimate outcome might be – greater homogeneity or heterogeneity of culture – and this is hotly disputed, the contemporary phase of globalization has thus resulted in more people than ever before becoming involved with more than one culture. It is perhaps this which above all else captures the sense in which the term is used here.

Diaspora

Of course, it is not just technologies which carry culture across national boundaries; people clearly do as well, and the twentieth century has witnessed dramatic developments in the ease with which people cross from one state to another. Moreover, unlike the population movements of the past, these post-industrial diasporas occur in a world where even the old 'geographical and territorial certainties seem increasingly fragile'; thus

today's diasporas seem much less likely to have 'stable points of origin, clear and final destinations and coherent group identities'.

These changes have resulted in diasporas of various kinds: that of the cosmopolitan academic parodied by Lodge (in a book whose very title – *Small World* – plays on the sense of compressed global space characteristic of globalization, that of the international business/management/design consultant, and that of the migrant labourer and refugee.[2] The former – who are always on the move – have given rise to the so-called 'third cultures', while the latter – often in search of a new home – have resulted in the linguistically, culturally and socially heterogeneous communities now typical of many parts of the globe. Muslims are represented in all these groups, and this [study] tries to deal with each: peripatetic intellectuals as well as labour migrants. [It addresses] directly the question of how people manage the cultural uncertainties typical of such poly-ethnic situations and of how Islam is moulded to 'foreign' settings.

It has often been noted that Islam explicitly encourages and even enjoins certain forms of travel, and that the movement of Muslims from one part of the world to another, whatever the purpose, resonates with the historical foundations of their religion. But here too globalization seems to have greatly encouraged this willingness to move, and has added a dimension to it. Transformations of the world economy brought about by the globalization of markets and labour under late capitalism have resulted in enormous numbers of people moving round the globe in search of work. Muslims constitute a large proportion of this population movement. It is in this manner that Muslim societies have today become part and parcel of Western countries. Muslim doctors and engineers live as American or British citizens. Their children have no intention of going back to their place of origin. The study of this Muslim diaspora raises both empirical and conceptual issues.

Since the bulk of Muslim migrant labour has settled abroad on a permanent basis, it is important to now look at these societies as local, as indigenous not as the other, the exotic or the Oriental, in Edward Said's words.[3] Thus Said's Orientalism is dated in this new theoretical frame and we need to move beyond its position. Although pointing to something important – that is, the imbalance or asymmetry between Islam and the West and the continuing prejudice, stereotypes and caricatures created of Islam by the West – Said's position has created serious intellectual problems, principally because of the manner in which it has been received and applied. It has led to a cul-de-sac. 'Orientalism' itself has become a cliché, and third world literature is now replete with accusations and labels of Orientalism being hurled at critics and at one author by another at the slightest excuse. This has had a stultifying effect on the dispassionate evaluation of scholarship. Thus, for example, in the passion generated by the debate what has been missed out is the great contribution of many Orientalist scholars. The writings of Ibn Khaldun, Ibn Battuta, or the Mughal emperor Babar come to us only through the painstaking scholarship of Orientalists who spent a life-time deciphering notes in Asian languages and sitting in remote libraries. For them it was a labour of love. To dismiss their work as simply Orientalism or as an attempt to suppress or subjugate Muslim peoples denies an important truth. Unfortunately, after Edward Said, that is how many Muslim writers do see the work of the Orientalists. If research on contemporary Muslim societies is not to be similarly dismissed as the most recent manifestation of Orientalism, it is clearly imperative to introduce conceptual innovations which both surmount the limitations of Islamic studies as identified by Said, and transcend the shortcomings of his own analysis. This would seem to be possible only by contextualizing local versions of Islam within global structures.

Sensitive and innovative research seems particularly critical for understanding the Muslim diaspora. The diaspora has led to the oft-remarked quest for identity and authenticity, particularly for those who find themselves abroad but also,

to some extent, for those who remain behind and who now find that their culture, transported to new settings, is being defined and practised in novel and sometimes disturbing ways. The empirical issues raised by diaspora thus chiefly revolve around questions of identity and the vulnerability of having to redefine the self in a world which seems constantly on the move. The hyphen of hyphenated identities like that of British-Muslim or American-Muslim, for example, both reflects and obscures the necessary conjunction of disparate cultural traces brought together in the act of 're-membering' and 're-creating'.

In the zone of the culturally displaced, Muslims in the diaspora experience a range of practical, psychological and pragmatic difficulties. [. . .] These include the problems of establishing enduring relationships with the opposite sex, of contracting acceptable marriages, and of adapting religion to a new life. But they also include the problems of negotiation with other Muslims and agreeing with them on the meaning of Islam on foreign soil. After all, Muslims who migrate are not only often in a minority in their place of destination, where they must encounter the cultures of the majority, but they also come from different sectarian and cultural traditions themselves. In some cases, as with Turkish Alevis in Germany for example, residence abroad may permit a greater freedom of religious expression. Thus the diaspora has released these Alevis from what they see as Sunni hegemony in Turkey, as well as enabling them to substantially reverse their hierarchically subordinate position to Sunni Turks based in Germany.

But the diaspora raises issues of identity and direction at 'home' too, among those faced with the fantasy if not the reality of moving and among those who now find their 'local cultures less pervasive, less to be taken for granted, less clearly bounded toward the outside' than they perhaps once were. Migrants return to their place of origin not only with novel versions of the world which challenge the views of those who never left [. . .] but also on occasion with fossilized and outmoded versions of what they left behind: ways of dressing, behaving, believing and so forth which have been developed and reshaped in their absence but which they have lovingly and carefully preserved intact while abroad. Either way, old certainties are challenged. To draw again on Fischer and Abedi writing about Iran, but to slightly modify their focus, the Muslim world and the Muslim habitations abroad 'mirror each other at acute or oblique angles, mutually affecting each other's representations, setting off mutating variations'. The very elasticity of the diasporic tie thus ensures the reciprocal redefinition of identity at both ends of the migratory chain as elements of culture rebound first this way and then that. Renewed attempts to define proper behaviour for Muslim women in Cairo and Lahore, and to establish an Islamic basis for the state in Malaysia [. . .] might thus be interpreted as a search for identity which is at least partially stimulated by the Muslim diaspora.

The detachment of culture from territory which is entailed by diaspora, with its generation of cultures with no clear anchorage in any one space has unleashed powerful forces which affect us all and not just those most directly involved. According to Appadurai, for example, it is this deterritorialization which is 'now at the core of a variety of global fundamentalisms, including Islamic and Hindu fundamentalism'. The 'problems of cultural reproduction for Hindus abroad' Appadurai suggests, have become 'tied to the politics of Hindu fundamentalism at home'.[4] The same could easily and realistically be said of the Muslim diaspora, with the added complication that, unlike the Hindus, Muslims abroad do not even share a common homeland. It is in this sense that the new Islamic movements in the Arab world [. . .] must be seen in the context of the Muslim diaspora. Indeed, the politics of all Muslim countries in this postmodern age must similarly be seen within a global frame.

[. . .]

NOTES

1   A. Cheater, 'Globalization and the New Technologies of Knowing: Anthropological Calculus or Chaos?', pp. 3–4; paper presented to the Association of Social Anthropologists Decennial Conference, St Catherine's College, Oxford. Cited with the permission of the author.

2   D. Lodge, *Small World* (Harmondsworth: Penguin Books, 1985).

3   E. Said, *Orientalism* (Harmondsworth: Penguin Books, 1978).

4   A. Appadurai, 'Disjuncture and Difference in the Global Cultural Economy', *Public Culture*, 2/2 (1990), pp. 1–24, p. 11.

60 And the Word Was All Male

Andrew Brown

Pope John Paul II has once more addressed his 'Venerable Brothers in the episcopate' on the infinitely troublesome subject of women. In a letter to bishops published [in 1966], he reiterated the Roman Catholic Church's ban on the ordination of women to the priesthood. 'Wherefore, in order that all doubt may be removed regarding a matter of great importance . . . in virtue of my ministry of confirming the brethren, I declare that the Church has no authority to confer priestly ordination on women and that this judgement is to be definitively held by all the Church's faithful.'

This is about as authoritative as a pope can get without claiming infallibility. The curious phrase 'confirming the brethren' is a reference to Luke 22: 32, where Jesus tells Peter that he has prayed that his faith may not fail; and that he in turn is to strengthen the faith of his brothers. Since the root of the papacy's power is the claim that the pope today is the linear successor of Peter, the use of this phrase entails a claim that John Paul II is faithfully transmitting the will of Jesus in this matter.

'The question is one of discerning the mind of the Lord. In his treatment of women, Our Lord emphasised their dignity without conforming to the prevailing customs of the time, yet he still did not choose them as apostles', explained Monsignor Philip Carroll, the General Secretary to the Bishops' Conference of England and Wales.

This is the letter that some Catholic feminists have been dreading, since they think it makes it a great deal more difficult for any subsequent pope to change his mind on the issue. Others are more upbeat. One, who did not want to be named, said: 'The more feminist people are, the less distressed they are, because it's so ridiculous; there's nothing new.'

In fact, the latest papal letter ties in with the signals that have been coming from the Catholic church in recent years. The English translation of the new catechism, which has just been published, was delayed for nearly two years by the successful attempts of American anti-feminists and their allies in the Vatican to remove 'inclusive' language from it. The inclusive language in the original draft was never about God, but about men and women, or 'men' as the Vatican calls them. Even this was too much of a concession for the Vatican, which found an elderly archbishop in Tasmania to rewrite the whole thing without reference to modern usage. The rewriting reaches an exquisite climax on page 500, where the devout reader learns that 'everyone, man and woman, should acknowledge and accept his sexual identity'.

The pattern is one of almost pathological hostility to feminism. It was especially clear in reactions to the one concession the Vatican has made in recent years to any sort of feminist sentiment: the decision [. . .] that women could serve as altar girls. This only regularized what had been the practice in many dioceses, yet it was greeted with hysterical outrage by the anti-feminist political right in America.

Any weakening of the laws that exclude women from the priestly domain of the altar threaten, it seems, all order in the church.

Otherwise, the line has been clear ever since *Humanae Vitae*, the encyclical banning artificial birth control that was produced in 1968. *Humanae Vitae*, too, was only reaffirming the teaching of the church throughout previous ages. It marked a watershed, though, for two reasons: first, it followed a really intense period of consultation and research by a specially appointed commission, whose members had decided, rather to their own surprise, in favour of contraception within marriage, before the pope overruled them; second, after he had overruled them, most Catholics in the developed world carried on using contraception exactly as if nothing had happened.

Humanae Vitae has had almost no effect on the birth-rate in countries where Catholics have access to some form of contraception. But it has had a shattering effect on papal authority.

It has vastly weakened the church's ability to resist abortion by tangling two very different issues together. For many intelligent self-reliant women who grew up as Catholics, it was simply too much to be told the meaning of sex by celibate old men. They have left the church, concluding that since it is obviously wrong about this, it must be wrong about everything else. Similarly, the choice of bishops has been drastically diminished, since any suspicion that a man doubts the teaching is a bar to promotion in the church.

However strange this attitude of passionate resistance to plain justice and common sense may seem, it is not new. There is almost an exact parallel in the attitude that the Catholic Church adopted in the last century. Then, the object of its scorn and hatred was democracy rather than feminism.

For most of the latter half of the [nineteenth] century and the first half of [the twentieth], successive popes did all they could to stamp out the idea that discussion had any place in the discovery of truth. Free Thought, in the sense of atheism, was confused with free thought in the sense of unsupervised, or grown-up thought (a conclusion that suited the atheists as much as anyone else).

In 1861 Pope Pius IX solemnly denounced the theory that a pope 'ought to reconcile and adjust himself with progress, liberalism and modern civilisation'. Papal infallibility was defined (infallibly) in 1870. The papacy gloried in being chief among the forces of reaction. In 1961, however, at the Second Vatican Council, all this came tumbling down, or seemed to. The church had been full of progressives all along, we discovered; and only a tiny minority under Archbishop Lefebvre left in protest against the great renewal.

Humanae Vitae represents the hinge at which the Vatican, without perhaps even realizing it, stopped struggling against democracy, and started to struggle against feminism instead. There are, of course, anti-democratic elements involved in the struggle against artificial contraception. But it is primarily a struggle against feminism; against the dignity and moral sense of women. The same attitude lies behind the pope's repeated defence of a celibate priesthood.

If this parallel is correct, then it should be most heartening for women who want their granddaughters to have the option of becoming priests. After all, the resistance to democracy did crumble when it was safe for the church to drop its guard: no one, it could be argued, has done more to spread democracy than the present pope, who played such a large part in the fall of Communism. In 2094, perhaps, onlookers may be arguing that no one has done more for women's rights than the pope. But not before.

Part 18

Cities and Urban Spaces

In Reading 61 Tom Horlick-Jones discusses new aspects of risk created by the interdependent nature of a highly advanced technological society. The new 'megacities' – cities with populations above 8 million – present many new hazards. For instance, the release of nerve gas by terrorists in the Tokyo underground in 1994 put many thousands of people at risk. Natural hazards like earthquakes can be much more dangerous than before if they happen in areas containing millions of people.

Urban areas differ massively in terms of their socio-economic characteristics. In many cities affluent and poor neighbourhoods exist side by side. Those in the most impoverished areas normally lack any kind of contact with their wealthier neighbours, while those who are well off never visit the poor neighbourhoods. The impoverishment of some neighbourhoods, as Anne Power shows in Reading 62, takes the form of a downward spiral. As areas become rundown, those who stay there do so because they can't move anywhere else; at the same time the quality of education declines and job opportunities diminish.

61 Urban Disasters and Megacities in a Risk Society

Tom Horlick-Jones

Much concern has been expressed about the disaster vulnerability of the new 'megacities' in developing countries. [...] These rapidly growing urban developments, with populations (according to the UN definition) exceeding 8 million, combine structural poverty and fragile infrastructures to create a worrying susceptibility to the impact of natural hazards. Events like the gas explosions in Mexico City (1984) and Guadalajara (1992) warn of the potential for technological disasters in such cities.

In contrast, megacities in the technologically advanced countries, cities like London and New York, are commonly regarded as relatively free of such concerns. But is this the case? What trends, if any, are creating greater vulnerability or resilience to hazards in these urban environments? Cities like Los Angeles and Tokyo continue to be exposed to potential earthquake hazards, and the [1995] Kobe earthquake revealed extensive vulnerability, despite use of advanced building codes. The [...] Tokyo underground railway nerve gas release, together with events such as the New York City World Trade Center bombing [in 1993], demonstrated the vulnerability of complex urban infrastructures not only to terrorist attack, but also, perhaps, to technological failure.

The modern city may present relative freedom from risk for some, yet for others it conjures up a host of 'man-made' and social risks. David Harvey has nicely characterized this contradictory environment:

The city is the high point of human achievement, objectifying the most sophisticated knowledge in a physical landscape of extraordinary complexity, power, and splendour at the same time as it brings together social forces capable of the most amazing sociotechnical and political innovation. But it is also the site of squalid human failure, the lightning rod of the profoundest human discontents, and the arena of social and political conflict.[1]

Paradoxically, these cities present both a rich array of potential hazards and relative safety. They also provide an arena in which certain visions of doom are selected for special attention and concern, leading Douglas and Wildavsky to ask 'are the dangers increasing or are we more afraid?'[2]

The perception of risks is now recognized as being framed in social and cultural formations [...] and the consequent mismatch between 'objective' measures of potential harm and degree of risk aversion has been the subject of much discussion. The degree to which modern urban environments can be said to be more or less safe is, then, a matter deeply fashioned by the politics of risk tolerability.

This recognition certainly does not deny the potential physical harms associated with a given risk. Rather, it reflects the extent to which risk perception and resulting decision-making [are] deeply embedded in cultural consciousness and practices. Indeed a direct correspondence has been observed between patterns of risk adjustment identified in the classical geographical literature and the distinct risk-handling behaviour of specific lifestyles.

It has been argued that the 'late modern' post-industrial societies, in which the megacities to be considered in this [discussion] are embedded, are experiencing profound structural changes which will have an increasingly significant impact on the way risk is regarded and handled. Writers such as Beck and Giddens have begun to map out the contours of societal forms in which risk plays a central role. However, as Beck puts it: 'It is not clear whether it is the risks that have intensified, or our view of them. Both sides converge, condition each other, strengthen each other, and because risks are risks in knowledge, perceptions of risks and risks are not different things, but one and the same.'[3]

This conception of the 'Risk Society' poses an important challenge to our understanding of risk tolerability and the practice of risk management. It has important implications for hazard adjustment in megacity environments.

Urban systems and risks

To what extent do physical hazards pose serious difficulties for megacities in the developed world? Adopting a relatively flexible definition of 'megacity' leads to consideration of about half a dozen cities – New York City, Tokyo, Los Angeles, London, Paris and possibly Osaka and Moscow [. . .] This [discussion] will focus on the first four. Together they offer an interesting series of similarities and contrasts with regard to a number of relevant factors, including age of infrastructure, spatial distribution, built environment and exposure to natural hazards.

A city may be regarded as a complex nexus of socio-technical systems, all interacting with shared physical and socio-economic environments. Risks may be posed by technological failures, such as train crashes, natural agents – perhaps the result of winds or floods – or by social activity, such as crime. All may be regarded as resulting from the undesirable outputs of such systems [. . .]

The scale and complexity of these cities together with their population densities can generate physical vulnerability to unusual perturbations [. . .], for example the disruption that can be produced by freak weather conditions. This effect is, however, rather unpredictable. The 1992 'urban nightmare' of a 'Jumbo' jet crash in Amsterdam produced relatively little damage beyond the immediate vicinity of the crash site; however, it generated disruption necessitating a complex process of crisis management.

The literature on technological systems failure is of relevance here, there being a multitude of opportunities for the 'incubation' of latent failures and many examples of tightly coupled subsystems with the potential for complex interactions. Indeed, Sylves and Pavlak have suggested that the failure of elaborate security and safety systems following the World Trade Center bombing may have been characteristic of one of Perrow's 'normal accidents'.[4]

Studies of New York City and London reveal the range of possible risks posed by extensive transport infrastructures, places that attract large crowds, such as shopping and entertainment centres, and industrial hazards, whether at fixed sites or in transit. The built environment complicates matters considerably, with the substantial resource implications of infrastructure maintenance, the possibility of major fires, evacuation difficulty from high-rise structures and the problem of road congestion sometimes leading to gridlock.

Exposure to extremely violent perturbations presented by natural hazards is relatively limited for New York City and London. However, the 1992 and 1993 East Coast storms presented major difficulties for New York City, and development on the London floodplain has heightened the risk of severe flash flooding. The catastrophic risk to London presented by Thames tidal flooding is significantly reduced by the Thames Barrier, although the effectiveness of this measure may be challenged by the impact of global warming early in the [twenty-first] century.

Both Los Angeles and Tokyo have suffered massive destruction from earthquakes in the past; however, the degree of protection to earthquake hazard that can be afforded by advanced building codes was graphically demonstrated in Los Angeles early in 1994, where, despite the collapse of a section of interstate highway, a 6.6-Richter-scale earthquake resulted in relatively few casualties. It has been suggested that the same level of protection does not apply to Tokyo, which possesses significantly more vulnerable infrastructure [. . .] although studies of the impact of the [1995] Kobe earthquake may provide useful lessons for future preparations, and prompt appropriate action. Direct comparisons between North America and Japan may, however, be misleading in view of possible differences in the utilization of building techniques.

Paradoxically, the ageing infrastructures of New York City and London, spared by most violent disruptions (with the exception of the World War II 'Blitz'), present a range of risks from leaks, structural weaknesses and other failures. These potential hazards arise from the interaction between socio-technical systems and their socio-economic environments, which, it has been suggested, can erode the systems in such ways as to create a metastability to sometimes apparently innocuous perturbations. Such 'real-world' features of urban hazard management can prove particularly intractable and the resource implications of maintaining complex socio-technical systems may be significant. In times of financial stringency or economic turbulence ensuring the safe functioning of such systems may be more difficult than expected [. . .]

Changes in risk profiles

Whilst some city structures tend to receive inadequate levels of investment and maintenance, powerful economic forces can drive rapid developments in the built environment and associated new infrastructures. This is particularly true in the dramatic changes in urban form associated with global economic restructuring that have occurred in the four cities in question over recent years. All have been transformed into so-called 'postmodern urban landscapes' by these processes, the term reflecting radical social, cultural and spatial changes. All these changes may have important implications for disaster vulnerability,

manifesting themselves in the gentrification of the older megacities like London and New York, and the creation of a 'Disney World'-like form of a 'stage set for consumption' in Los Angeles.

Whereas London and New York City possess concentrated, high-rise centres, the evolution of Los Angeles has followed a more decentralized pattern over a wide geographical area. A relentless process of suburbanization has increased the proportion of city dwellers exposed to wildfire, landslide and flood hazards, whilst an associated extensive road transport infrastructure has led to severe air pollution.

New York City, London and Tokyo now form the apex of the organization and management of the world economy. This development is based especially upon the rapid growth of the international financial market and the trade in services. A host of support industries has developed to facilitate these activities, bringing significant changes to the local economies of these cities. In terms of urban form, the need for management and servicing of a huge and complex volume of financial transactions leads to high building densities, rapid building of high-rise offices and extremely high land prices. Massive telecommunication infrastructures have also been introduced. These dramatic changes bring new potential for complex system failures in parts of the urban infrastructure.

The Cold War may have ended; however, the former possibilities of aerial bombardment or nuclear attack have been replaced by 'para-warfare', or terrorism, as the major threat of hostile attack. The February 1993 World Trade Center bombing in New York City and, two months later, the huge amount of damage created by the City of London bombing, together with the [1995] nerve gas attack in Japan and bombing of the Federal building in Oklahoma City in 1998 have demonstrated the possible scale of such events. Bombings of industrial plant or transport systems, for example, invalidate conventional risk assessments, yielding results that can be radically different in nature, likelihood and severity from accidents.

The social dimension

Processes of gentrification of once-poor parts of London, New York City and Tokyo have taken place, together with the development of associated shopping and entertainment facilities, like South Street Seaport in Manhattan and Covent Garden in London. Yet the glittering glass palaces of the financial institutions and the conspicuous consumption of fashionable stores are but one side of these cities. Recent changes have sharpened the contrasts behind the new well-off and an increasingly marginalized poor. Homelessness is now present in London, New York City and Tokyo and, as Sassen puts it, 'How many times do high-income executives have to step over the bodies of homeless people till this becomes an unacceptable fact or discomfort?'[5]

In Los Angeles, staggering contrasts of wealth exist in a city that combines high-tech industry with extensive areas of virtual shanty town characterized by drugs, crime and violence. The recent riots were indicative of the level of inter-ethnic and class tensions in some parts of the city and its suburbs.

The influence of the socio-economic environment on these urban systems is profound. Consider fire risk. Research in both the United States and Britain has demonstrated the correlation between the high frequency of fires and resulting casualties with those parameters of poverty associated with the urban inner city: the unemployed, those on low wages, single parents, the old, those living in overcrowded, shared accommodation or in rented or local authority accommodation. These are the people most likely to fall victim to domestic fire. Direct comparisons with cities in Japan, for example Tokyo, might, however, be misleading in view of the use of wood-based construction and high prevalence of fires.

These categories of urban dwellers, together with the homeless, are also most exposed to risks resulting from various criminal activities, whether drug-driven, interethnic violence and so on (*New Statesman & Society*, 1988). They are extremely vulnerable to the hostile environments created by a range of natural and technological hazard agents.

Vulnerability for urban dwellers is not, however, simply a matter for the poor. The relatively wealthy are exposed to certain risks by virtue of their work or leisure activities. Flying, commuting by train, enjoying a party on a river boat, going to the theatre by underground railway or working in a high-rise office block can all be risky activities.

Clearly a wide variety of risks and vulnerability to hazard exists in these cities. The new concentration of built environment, financial investment and associated infrastructure has brought the possibility of massive losses. A sharpened division between rich and poor has generated 'risk ghettos' that expose classically vulnerable groups to relatively high levels of risk. Turbulent socioeconomic environments erode the resilience of complex socio-technical systems leading to the unexpected effects of 'system vulnerability'.

Urban living in a risk society

The economic changes responsible for the restructuring in urban form discussed above also provide some of the sources of turbulence that may be responsible for eroding the resilience to failure of a multitude of urban systems. In social terms, they also contribute towards shifting risk *perception* into a position of central importance by encouraging the development of 'reflexivity'.[6] Such changes create significant uncertainties and doubts, and, as Giddens put it: 'To live in the "world" produced by high modernity has the feeling of riding a juggernaut.'[7] So he describes the experience of contemporary life, referring primarily to the technologically advanced societies, with their bewildering doubts and multiple risks. It is a theme developed at length by Beck [. . .] in his celebrated work on the so-called 'Risk Society'; a recognition of transitions taking place from postindustrial societies to new societal forms in which the perception and management of hazards and risks become a central organizing dynamic.

Beck's 'risks' are not, however, the traditional blights on humanity such as disease, famines, natural hazards or other 'Acts of God'. Rather, they are the (actual or perceived?) uncontrollable and dysfunctional side-effects of technology, 'the dark side of progress'.[8] According to these theories, the emergence of 'Green' politics is one significant outcome of social processes that erode trust in institutions and produce uncertainties about identities and ways of life. Of course, such processes are rather more complex, with 'Green' politics also being associated, for example, with the rise of a 'knowledge class' with distinct cultural characteristics.

It has been argued that the concept of disaster in the technologically advanced societies has been socially constructed from traditional notions relating to catastrophic events. Building upon themes explored by Giddens and Beck, this work concludes that the social and political impact of contemporary 'disasters' corresponds with a release of repressed existential anxiety resulting from a perceived betrayal by trusted individuals or institutions. Blaming mechanisms are used to restore trust [. . .]; however, the events fuel the imagery of the 'nightmare' and the generalized sense of threat. In practical terms, the social impact of such events may be out of all proportion with the physical harms generated by them.

The media seem to have an important role to play in amplifying certain risks and 'disasters' for special attention. Indeed, urban disasters form powerful motifs in works of fiction, and the imagery of the *Towering Inferno* and other such stories are used by the media to retell topical stories, complete with associated myths. Reality begins to mirror fiction, as in the London *Evening Standard*'s coverage following the October 1992 'Jumbo' crash in Amsterdam. 'Like a plane disaster movie' read the headlines. 'Here they lived in fear of a disaster from the jets that roared overhead. Here they died, when the nightmare became true.'

Since the work of Weber it has been recognized that cities play a key role in social change.

Harvey reminds us that 'Big cities have long been important arenas of cultural production, forcing-grounds of cultural innovation, centres of fashion and the creation of "taste".'[9] One might conclude that the advanced megacities, bringing together a variety of risks and potential 'modern disasters' with the most pronounced worries and uncertainties of the Risk Society, play a central role in creating new patterns of behaviour with regard to risk in the technologically advanced countries. How might such changes manifest themselves? Can they be observed today?

The implications for adjustment to hazard

[. . .] Burton et al. in their classical examination of adjustment to environmental hazards, argued that urbanization leads to vulnerability to natural hazards.[10] They observed that urban dwellers appear to be less sensitive to the possibility of extreme natural events than rural people. This, they note, might reflect a preoccupation with other, apparently more pressing, problems associated with urban life.

Kirby suggests that such vulnerability arises from a combination of an economic imperative and a belief that 'civilization' leads to the safety of almost any location. Indeed, urbanization is based on the use of technology, which in turn is legitimated by ideas of control. The city is, then, a zone where technological risks are under control. The key question now seems to be what happens to individual and collective hazard adjustment strategies when trust in such controlling influences is eroded.[11]

In the advanced societies adjustment to hazard has largely been determined by institutions that are related to individuals by power and trust relationships. If such trust is eroded, then it follows that individual and small-group adjustment strategies may begin to be adopted. If so, what form will they take? Horlick-Jones and Jones drawing on the work of Mary Douglas and her collaborators, have discussed the cultural roots of risk aversion strategies embedded as they are in chosen ways of life, leading to a number of distinct approaches – denial, passive acceptance, action to reduce future losses and radical action to remove the risk.[12]

In practice, individual actions will be constrained by personal circumstances and a range of contextual factors. Such factors also contribute to the social framing of risk perception. Individuals are exposed to a portfolio of risks, from the mundane to the catastrophic, and corresponding sources of information are integrated into a pragmatic assessment of contingencies and possibilities.

The emergence of 'Green' politics would correspond to some individuals adopting the 'radical action to remove the risk' strategy. Changes in insurance-purchasing behaviour, for example, could be an indicator of the influence of an 'action to reduce further losses' strategy. There is clearly a need for more empirical investigations in order to investigate possible evidence for these hypotheses, in particular ethnographic-type investigations of community risk perception, the design of which recognizes the social and cultural framing effects in risk perception and handling.

Turning now to the role of hazard and emergency management agencies, it is important to consider how their behaviour might be affected by social changes in risk perception behaviour. The planning agendas of such organizations are determined by a combination of resource constraints, the experience of day-to-day crises and the political dynamics of risk tolerability. The impact of past disasters may be very significant in shaping institutional agendas [. . .] and arguably such processes may shift hazard adjustment in unhelpful ways if they provide a 'distorting lens' that skews priorities away from hazards that generate less 'dread' in the imagination of the public, politicians and administrators.

Perhaps this point needs to be developed a little. Many spectacular 'modern disasters' arise from technological failures of one sort or another, and they tend to produce an intense 'zone of harm' of rather limited geographical extent. There are important counter-examples, of course, such as the [1996] Chernobyl nuclear power station accident. Nevertheless, a host of train and aircraft crashes, sports ground tragedies and sundry fires and explosions do generate rather different patterns of harm from, for example, the impact of a range of natural hazard agents, although, of course, such impacts can themselves precipitate technological failures.

The point here is that geographically large-scale hazards, producing both acute and chronic effects, may require rather different forms of emergency response from local, acute catastrophes. It has been suggested that discontinuous shifts occur in the resource burden of responding to progressively greater-scale contingencies.

Equally, various sorts of unusual contingencies may present challenges that exceed capabilities corresponding to the usual and the routine. In megacities such as London and New York, the dynamism, speed of change and concentration of activities lead to the routine occurrence of emergencies of one sort or another. Whilst regular response to such 'routine' emergencies assists the development of effective operational procedures, it does tend to reinforce a view that major crises require simply an extended application of day-to-day emergency procedures. Such unusual contingencies may require extensive and co-ordinated response, [with] scale problems described above, unanticipated effects and considerable situation uncertainties [. . .]

Finally, the insurance industry may [prove] both an interesting indicator and [a] significant player as the impact of the Risk Society makes its presence felt more keenly in megacity environments. Concern about losses resulting from fires in large urban supermarkets has [in 1994] been expressed by the industry (*Financial Times*) together with a warning that cover against flooding in London may be increasingly difficult to obtain. Changing perceptions of risk clearly play a central role in the operation of the industry, and concerns about the potential losses in the developed megacities may lead to the disappearance of some cover and the need to develop new, preventive, risk management strategies.

Conclusions

Global economic restructuring has impacted on the physical form, socio-economic environment and socio-cultural structures of developed megacities in complex and interacting ways, as gentrified wealth and relative safety from physical harm exist in close proximity to 'risk ghettos'. An increased propensity for the spectacular failure of socio-technical systems combines with a social fluidity and insecurity to create 'modern disasters'; events with significant social and political impact such as catastrophes become media spectacle.

Such events erode trust in institutional risk management and generate a convoluted risk politics as individuals and small groups tend to adopt a fragmented range of risk management strategies, whilst hitherto hegemonic institutions come under pressure to address those contingencies associated with popularly perceived 'dread', resulting in possibly distorted risk management priorities.

Clearly these conclusions have potentially very important implications for hazard adjustment in the megacities of the developed world. There is an urgent need for more empirical investigation of the hypotheses discussed [here].

Finally, it is important to note that the risk politics in developed countries discussed in this paper is associated with powerful global processes. These will impact in significant ways on the vulnerability to both natural and technological hazards of the megacities of the developing world, leading to an even sharper contrast between developed and developing countries. Beck argues in graphic terms that this impact will rebound upon the wealthy countries, as the poor ones 'become the breeding grounds of an international contamination, which, like the infectious diseases of the poor in the cramped medieval cities, does not spare even the wealthy neighbourhoods of the world community.'[13]

NOTES

1 D. Harvey, *The Urban Experience* (Oxford: Basil Blackwell, 1989).

2 M. Douglas and A. Wildavsky, *Risk and Culture* (Berkeley: University of California Press, 1982).

3 U. Beck, *Risk Society* (London: Sage, 1992), p. 55.

4 R. Sylves and T. Pavlak, 'The World Trade Center Disaster: A Normal Accident?', in T. Horlick-Jones (ed.), *New York City and Urban Emergency Management*, special issue of *Disaster Management*, 6/3 (1994).

5 S. Sassen, *The Global City: New York, London, Tokyo* (Princeton, NJ: Princeton University Press, 1991).

6 A characteristic of 'late' (or 'high') modernity in which, in sociological terms, agency is progressively freed from structure. A number of authors have pointed to the negative aspects of this fragmentation of traditional social structures; however, recent work has suggested that reflexivity may have a number of positive effects. In particular, it may bring a 'deepening of the self', in which new possibilities emerge for individuals to reflect critically upon their social conditions of existence.

7 A. Giddens, *The Consequences of Modernity* (Cambridge: Polity, 1990).

8 Beck, *Risk Society*.

9 D. Harvey, 'Introduction', in S. Zukin, *Loft Living* (London: Radius, 1988).

10 I. Burton, R. Kates and G. White, *The Environment as Hazard* (New York: Oxford University Press, 1978).

11 A. Kirby, 'Towards a New Risk Analysis', in A. Kirby (ed.), *Nothing to Fear: Risk and Hazards in American Society* (Tucson: University of Arizona Press, 1990).

12 T. Horlick-Jones and D. K. C. Jones, 'Communicating Risks to Reduce Vulnerability', in P. Merriman and C. Browitt (eds), *Natural Disasters: Protecting Vulnerable Communities* (London: Thomas Telford, 1993).

13 Beck, *Risk Society*.

62 Poor Areas and Social Exclusion

Anne Power

Social exclusion is about the inability of our society to keep all groups and individuals within reach of what we expect as a society. It is about the tendency to push vulnerable and difficult individuals into the least popular places, furthest away from our common aspirations. It means that some people feel excluded from the mainstream, as though they do not belong. For a long time this has meant that inner city areas, and some large outlying council estates, increasingly vacated by people who can find an alternative, became a receptacle for problems.

Social exclusion is almost entirely an urban problem. The 100 most deprived local authority areas in [Britain] are all urban and the 20 most deprived are all in major industrial conurbations and inner London. We have to start from where we are – cities concentrate and intensify social problems. The social exclusion agenda is an urban agenda.

Cities are made up of neighbourhoods and their fortunes are locked together. The success of cities depends on successful neighbourhoods, and therefore the urban agenda – an attempt to reverse the urban exodus and overcome social exclusion – focuses on neighbourhoods as well as cities and regions. They are intrinsically interconnected.

Neighbourhoods are physical areas within which people organise their lives, base a significant portion of their social time and therefore connect with the world outside the home. Urban neighbourhoods usually cover around 2,000 homes, 5,000 people, a typical primary school catchment. Neighbourhoods often have sharp boundaries, either physical or atmospheric, but the layers of neighbourhood life are like an onion with a tight core and a loose outer skin.

Neighbourhoods have three interlocking aspects: the home and immediate surroundings – the elements people pay as much as they can to secure; services such as shops and schools which reflect the social composition of the neighbourhood; and the neighbourhood environment, giving an intangible but powerful signal of who we are and how we should behave. Neighbourhoods offer a sense of familiarity and security to the people who live there, which counters fear of the unknown, even where the neighbourhood is poor, run-down or unpopular.

Neighbourhoods can break down if the three elements – home, services, environment – are disrupted to a point where security disintegrates. If decline is very rapid, then even the sense of familiarity can go. It is the issue of neighbourhood breakdown and rescue that concerns government because school failure and crime – their top social preoccupations – are neighbourhood problems. Poor education and crime fuel the movement outwards, creating large rifts in society and leaving much poorer neighbourhoods behind. [. . .]

Area problems – people or place?

Will we [in the UK] succeed where the Americans have failed so disastrously?

In America individual success is more important than area conditions, with the consequent acceptance of appalling inner city ghettos, high

Table 62.1 Intrinsic and acquired characteristics of poor areas

Intrinsic area characteristics	Condition	Outcomes
Location and transport links	Poor access	Low status
Physical style and ownership	Segregated community	Low value
Environment	Unattractive, poor quality	Low desirability
Economy	Low investment	Low mix

Acquired area characteristics	Condition	Outcomes
Population mix	Low status deters more ambitious	Concentrated poverty
Reputation and history	Image activates fear	Rejection and isolation
Standards and services	Performance is poor	Deteriorating conditions
Poor supervision	Low morale reduces incentives	Negative behaviour
Weak informal controls	Intimidation prevents action	Withdrawal

levels of violence and many human casualties. A strong racial divide is tolerated in the belief that individuals can progress out of ghettos.

In Europe, including Britain, success is more commonly measured by area improvement alongside individual progress. This seems a more logical approach since there is little doubt that areas affect people as well as people affecting areas. The strongest and simplest proof of the interaction of people and areas lies in the very different cash values that attach to near-identical properties in different types of area.

Property values are dictated by neighbours and neighbourhoods – in other words the character of an area influences our choice, as much as who we are influences where we can choose to live. Some places are inherently difficult and unattractive to live in; this impacts strongly on people, determining who moves in, who stays and who moves out, creating people-based characteristics, alongside physical conditions. Table 62.1 shows this interaction of inherent and acquired area characteristics, making people and place equally important in the creation of and struggle against social exclusion. Areas often have a mix of these characteristics; occasionally all the characteristics are clustered together.

Areas that were once valuable – our industrial inner cities – can become redundant, semi-abandoned, ransacked, a true nightmare for the people stranded within seriously depleted communities. But these same areas can also regain value, without losing their 'character', if we can change some of the intrinsic or acquired features. For we do build and sustain, or run down and destroy, our urban neighbourhoods ourselves – we are responsible for social exclusion and its reversal.

Some neighbourhood characteristics are easier to change than others. Change in one element can have a knock on effect on others. For example, the environment and economy of Islington, one of the poorest inner London boroughs, gradually changed over the 1970s after the lifting of slum clearance orders, and the cancellation of road widening blight. Islington council in the 1970s became a pioneer in the renovation of Georgian and Victorian street property. Whole blighted, tumble-down streets were revived, giving birth to that controversial idea – gentrification – now strongly supported as 'mixed communities'. The loss of light engineering was replaced by a booming service economy. Islington is still the 10th most deprived local authority in the country but

The top 20 local authorities on the government's new index of deprivation in rank order

1 Liverpool
2 Newham
3 Manchester
4 Hackney
5 Birmingham
6 Tower Hamlets
7 Sandwell
8 Southwark
9 Knowsley
10 Islington
11 Greenwich
12 Lambeth
13 Haringey
14 Lewisham
15 Barking and Dagenham
16 Nottingham
17 Camden
18 Hammersmith and Fulham
19 Newcastle upon Tyne
20 Brent

Source: Department of the Environment, Transport and the Regions, 1998

it no longer has the intense concentrations of the poorest neighbourhoods that it had because area conditions have changed.

I use Islington as an example to underline that areas can improve, alongside significant individual poverty. Islington still has extremely serious problems, some of the worst performing schools in the country, a level of violence in some areas that has tyrannised whole communities, a tension between the extremes of wealth and poverty that may prove hard to hold together. None the less few would argue that Islington would have been better for the poor, more inclusive, if it had been bulldozed and rebuilt as large council estates, the Labour government's plan for it after the war. The list taken from the government's *Index of Local Deprivation* (1998) shows how Islington fits within the most deprived boroughs in the

country – all urban with many inner London or other big city councils.

Poverty concentrations

We have argued that areas are intrinsically unequal and therefore attract very different people. This inequality of areas shows up in distance from work, contrasting tenures, unequal schools and environment. It is inevitable that more vulnerable people with less economic clout will be concentrated in areas of greater difficulty, with lower opportunities. In other words poor conditions and poor people group together. Far more seriously poorer neighbourhoods also tend to group together, forming large poverty clusters within cities. Thus we have, not just isolated poor neighbourhoods, but whole swathes of cities dominated by exclusionary problems.

We have identified the 5 per cent of wards with the highest levels of workless households and the highest concentrated deprivation, based on what the population as a whole believes is the minimum necessary to escape deprivation. The concentration of poverty and worklessness within the poorest areas is double the national average. [...] Poor areas are much more deprived on all measures of deprivation than other more popular areas.

[...] This is important. Figure 62.2 shows the regional concentrations of poverty.

The clustering of poverty areas is so strong in some cities that large continuous tracts of concentrated poverty develop. Only 40 of the 284 highest poverty wards in the country are 'lone' wards within a local authority. The rest are grouped in 51 'poverty clusters' within cities. Most areas of the country do not have any high poverty wards, though most have *smaller* poorer neighbourhoods.

Clustering is by definition an urban problem. [This research] shows that 91 per cent of the people living in poverty wards are concentrated in inner cities, industrial and ex-industrial areas, inner London and ex-coal mining areas. Figure 62.3a underlines the large numbers of people

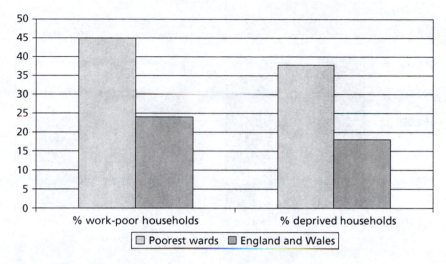

Figure 62.1 The poorest wards in England and Wales
Source: CASE (1998)

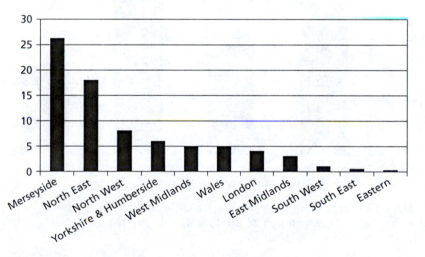

Figure 62.2 Percentage of regional population living in poverty wards
Source: CASE (1998)

grouped within poverty clusters, over quarter of a million in Liverpool. Figure 62.3b shows the proportion of some borough populations concentrated in poverty clusters. In Tower Hamlets it reaches 57 per cent.

The impact of poverty clusters in cities

Clusters of poverty matter because all the disadvantages associated with poverty are more concentrated and more extensive, therefore escape becomes more difficult. Large poverty clusters within cities often have a long history and attract powerful stigma, making them hard to change. They work to limit people's chances in many ways:

- there are less obvious routes out, so more people feel trapped;
- depression and low morale are more common, resulting in lower levels of organisation

(a)

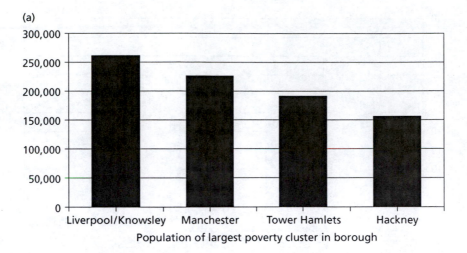

Population of largest poverty cluster in borough

(b)

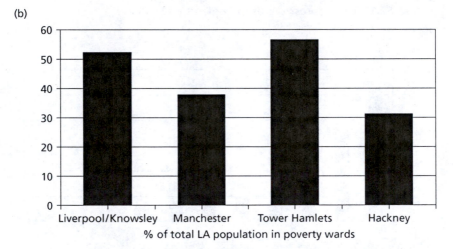

% of total LA population in poverty wards

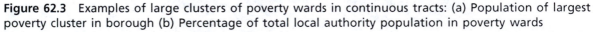

Figure 62.3 Examples of large clusters of poverty wards in continuous tracts: (a) Population of largest poverty cluster in borough (b) Percentage of total local authority population in poverty wards

and initiative and higher levels of frustration, aggression and other negative behaviour;

- parenting is more difficult because of this;
- children's social learning is heavily influenced by surroundings and negative examples;
- schools suffer from low expectations resulting in lower performance and lower employment prospects; they also suffer more disruptive behaviour and higher pupil turnover;
- the high concentration of low-skilled people leads to intense competition for a shrinking pool of low-skill jobs, resulting in lower wages and often complete withdrawal from the labour market;

- the difficulties in accessing jobs help create high levels of early retirement, disability and economic inactivity;
- lower cash incomes affect shops and other services as well as home conditions and ability to support extra activities.

The larger and longer-running the area problems, the stronger the cumulative impact becomes, leading to the flight of those more able to go

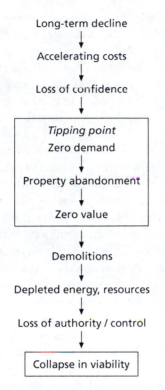

Figure 62.4 Tipping point in neighbourhood decline

and gradual loss of control resulting from chronic instability. Tipping into chaotic decline becomes more likely as the backbone of a neighbourhood weakens. This makes some areas subject to eventual abandonment.[1]

These 'clustering' impacts on people's life chances and on neighbourhood conditions have wider consequences. Being poor in an area with many poor people and poor conditions generates a gradual loss of confidence in 'the system'. In the largest poverty cluster in Newcastle for example, only one in ten people vote. In Hackney and Liverpool the performance of local government has been a source of scandal over several decades. Area depletion leads to inadequate political representation and reduced competition for the role of Councillor. This is now a serious problem in the poorest inner city authorities including inner London. Many conventional forms of involvement do not operate. A sense of failure, rejection

and shame over where people live and belong grows. This undermines hope of change and prevents neighbourhoods from offering that sense of security and commitment that ensure vitality. If not reversed, it leads to a collapse in the housing market at the bottom. [...]

Neighbourhood collapse

A new phenomenon, the complete disintegration of inner city neighbourhoods within some of the biggest poverty clusters is gathering pace across our major cities. It is driven by five interlocking factors:

- The long run movement away from conurbations, although slowing in the 80s and 90s, is still continuing. It creates serious *pressures on green fields* all over the country. Inner cities lose more people than the wider conurbations, particularly in the poorest neighbourhoods. Whole streets and estates in towns of the North West, North East, West Midlands, South Wales, Yorkshire, Humberside and Clydeside are emptying. But the migration outwards is selective.

- Cities have *double the proportion of council housing* and half the proportion of owner occupation compared with the national average. In the poorest neighbourhoods three-quarters or more of homes are for rent, compared with a third elsewhere. This helps explain many of the large poverty clusters. Demolition of large, unpopular, under-occupied council estates has accelerated in the 90s, including in London. Large estates of social housing are difficult to manage and often difficult to live in, particularly for families with children. Council estates have become increasingly unpopular and stigmatised as they became tied to slum rehousing, then became housing of last resort for people who might otherwise become homeless. By the 1980s, a vast stock of about 10,000 large council estates – nearly 4 million homes – was seen as a fail-safe to house the poor in an increasingly unequal society.

The low level of management and repair both reflect and help cause this negative image.

- Many people are *unwilling to risk ownership* in the most acutely declining areas, even when good quality houses with gardens carry massive discounts under the Right to Buy for council tenants. The concentrated poverty prevents many from considering it since the resale value is often zero. Therefore few risk buying. In the areas where owner occupation is most needed to hold onto aspiring households, there is too little real opportunity to buy.

- The collapse of major industries and the outward flow of new investment to the greener and more spacious city hinterland has *devastated city job markets*. In cities like Manchester, Glasgow and Newcastle, up to three-quarters of manual jobs have gone. Hackney has one of the highest unemployment rates in the country. A large population of low-skilled unemployed males is trapped, while women take up many of the new, often part-time, service jobs. Better off people leap-frog the city and commute in, rather than live within declining neighbourhoods. Neighbourhood polarisation then becomes extreme.

- The loss of traditional patterns of work, family and neighbourhood has *fuelled the breakdown of social infrastructure*. Educational performance is only one fifth the national average, while crime, and particularly violence can be four times higher. Truancy, disorder and youth disaffection undermine efforts at improvement in schools (Power and Tunstall, 1997). Security is minimal and most forms of guarding such as caretaking have been cut or withdrawn.

The live political debate on social exclusion constantly returns to conditions within these poorest areas, because multiple problems are so highly concentrated within them. The much higher incidence of neighbourhood conflicts, anti-social behaviour, youth crime, street disorder, disrupted classrooms, shuttered shop-fronts and abandoned property in poorer neighbourhoods is reflected in much higher levels of neighbourhood dissatisfaction.[2] It follows the collapse in confidence and informal controls.

An area can slide from marginal viability towards cumulative collapse. It can happen in deprived areas of prospering cities such as London as well as in declining industrial areas, such as Manchester or Newcastle. It is a problem across cities world-wide as their fortunes rise and fall but it is most acute in older industrial cities, such as in Britain. The Crime and Disorder Act of 1998 proposed significant new powers to restrain anti-social behaviour and serious child offending, precisely because social conditions have disintegrated in some of the highest poverty areas.[3]

[. . .] Considerable political controversy [was provoked] around the new powers to evict families for anti-social behaviour. The truth is that social controls have broken down to such a point that only strong security and enforcement measures can contain the fall-out. On their own, these powers are of course insufficient. But they do give a powerful signal to an intimidated community that the wider society cares. The Act also uses the law more even-handedly than in the past to protect vulnerable groups within vulnerable areas from gross abuse, usually by criminals. It is an important beginning to the process of inclusion and greater equality.

Abandonment

Within declining inner neighbourhoods we now experience accelerating turnover of occupants and growing empty property; private withdrawal and growing empty spaces; trouble in the vacuum of collapsing demand. Council tenants generally move less often than other people, but in cities they move more frequently and in the poorest neighbourhoods, most frequently of all. The instability can become unmanageable as figure 62.5 suggests.

In practice many estates are already so unpopular as to be non-viable. Only the very poor, the most vulnerable, move in to replace the more ambitious, more stable residents who feel

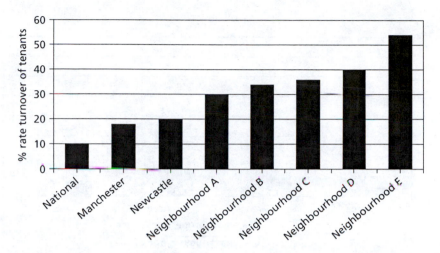

Figure 62.5 Turnover rate in council housing creating severe management problems in the poorest neighbourhoods
Source: Power and Mumford, *The Slow Death of Great Cities*

forced to move in search of greater security. Once abandonment gathers pace it affects all tenures. Some new housing association property has already been demolished in cities in the North through a collapse in demand. Owner occupied streets are also being demolished and some abandoned properties are taken over by private landlords, then let on 100 per cent government subsidy through housing benefit. [. . .]

The land problem

The breakdown of inner city neighbourhoods is creating demand for a different type of housing in different types of neighbourhood, fuelling planning pressures, building pressures and market supply. As a result land is now being released ahead of demand, anticipating and helping accelerate the urban exodus while creating the ugly problem of sprawl.

There is an unsustainable triple process that results from acute area decline:

- thinning out the poorest inner city neighbourhoods which have lost their original purpose;
- depleting older cities more generally;

- building outwards on green land at even higher environmental cost to all. [. . .]

Britain is extensively built up around all the major conurbations. The higher the land value, the more carefully we use it. Thus London produces 85 per cent of new units on brown-field sites because there is little alternative given the distances and the green belt. This explains both the high levels of concentrated deprivation and the higher than average level of social mixing in most parts of the capital. London is rapidly expanding its use of recycled sites and increasing its generally low density to more sustainable levels. In contrast, Manchester, Birmingham, Newcastle, Glasgow and Liverpool have very large expanses of low value brown-field sites but spread their new buildings into the suburban and semi-rural hinterland, thus creating intense problems of sprawl, and depopulation.

The extremes of low demand in cities are coupled with the over-release of green-field land for building. If *current* planning permissions and land releases are kept in place, the large double conurbation of Greater Manchester and Merseyside, is building houses faster than the disputed household projections would require. It has a land

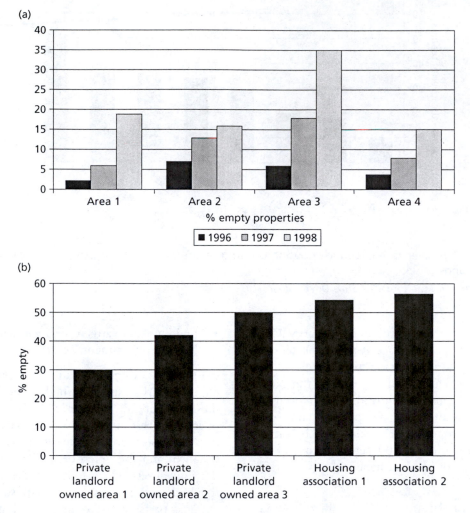

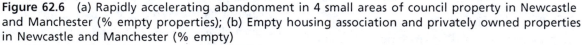

Figure 62.6 (a) Rapidly accelerating abandonment in 4 small areas of council property in Newcastle and Manchester (% empty properties); (b) Empty housing association and privately owned properties in Newcastle and Manchester (% empty)

Source: Power and Mumford, *The Slow Death of Great Cities*

supply in the pipeline around ten times the level of projected demand. Yet little account is taken of the large stock of empty but sound property and the disproportionate supply of inner city brown-field land. Figure 62.7 illustrates the scale of the oversupply of land matched by the extraordinary levels of empty property.

Urban sprawl is gobbling up land far faster than we want, yet our planning system is wedded to mechanistic household projections, low density

and the over-release of land, trapped between the powerful lobbying forces of builders, aspiring families, housing providers, rural protectionists and urbanites. In our crowded country we continue to spill out of cities, while our depleted inner areas spiral. Therefore urban problems lock into the land problem. As long as people with choice can move out relatively cheaply to safe havens of low-density houses, we are unlikely to seek the avant-garde solutions we need to our urban

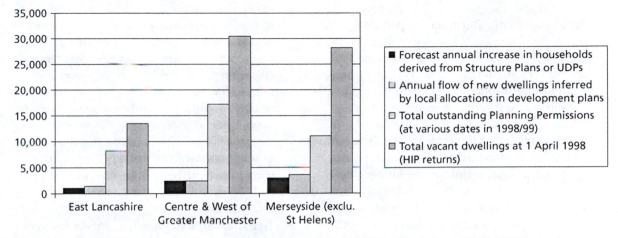

Figure 62.7 Figures for housing provision based on household projections, actual building, current planning permissions and empty dwellings

Source: Social Exclusion Unit/DETR, *Unpopular Housing: National Strategy for Neighbourhood Renewal*, Report of Policy Action Team 7 (London: DETR)

problems or to attract sufficient urban pioneers back into the collapsing inner neighbourhoods.

It is an irony of wealthy societies that spreading out from cities destroys the two objectives that lower density aims to achieve – more manageable cities through lower crowding; and easier access to the green lungs of the city, the countryside. In practice it results in impoverished city neighbourhoods and low-density housing developments in green fields. The Urban Task Force argued in its report to the government [in summer 1999] that we have no choice but to tackle the land problem and increase density as it affects city neighbourhoods and country villages alike.

City neighbourhoods can be too dense, particularly if they are poor. But our poor neighbourhoods are now too empty, leaving them prey to insecurity, illegal activity and acute depletion of basic services. If we raise our density to a moderate 50 houses per hectare, from our current average of less than 25, we will halve at a stroke our use of green-field land, and begin to recreate a critical mass of people in urban areas that will reinvigorate public transport, education and other services. Islington has around 100–200 homes per hectare and is lastingly popular as its property values show.

Higher densities work with sensitive, skilled, creative urban design. Lower densities often fail through lack of connection. The government chose Richard Rogers, the international architect, to head up the Urban Task Force, precisely because it recognises that the physical and the social dynamics of areas go hand in hand.

Solutions

To reverse exclusion by area which fuels green sprawl, we have to make inner neighbourhoods attractive to far more people. Given that households are much smaller than a generation ago, we have to fit in *many more* households, simply to keep enough *people* for neighbourhoods to work – [. . .] shops, buses, doctors, schools, police depend on a critical mass of people and do *not* survive sprawl. So what might work? There are several ways forward that could be implemented by changes in *how* we do things. They require energy and commitment rather than vast cash.

- Many cities are now planning large-scale demolition. Demolition of structurally sound and often physically attractive, renovated property appears inevitable in the face of zero demand and zero market value, however outrageous it seems. But planning permission to build ever more outside cities may be driving the problem of abandonment and demolition within. We should *halt land releases* in areas of housing surplus and abandonment, and should create stronger incentives to renovate cities.

- Cleaner, brighter, safer, livelier streets, restored Victorian monuments, canals and warehouses, glamourous new buildings, are luring people back into city centres. Private loft apartments and quayside flats are selling vigorously for high prices within a mile of the emptying city neighbourhoods I have described. If there is *demand for high quality, carefully secured homes in city centres*, then surely we can apply this approach to inner neighbourhoods, attracting urban pioneers who currently choose commuting.

- Since 1930 council housing has gone to those in greatest need. This has created intense polarisation, made much worse by the loss of traditional jobs, the break-up of traditional family patterns, the rapid expansion of owner occupation and the increase in inequality in the 1980s. Is there a way of preventing ghettoisation? Maximising choice and freedom in council housing, attracting broader income groups, encouraging family and social ties, increasing security and maintenance, breaking up one-class estates into more mixed areas, preventing racial concentrations in the worst estates, are all possible if we *change the way council housing is owned, managed and let*.[4]

- Many inner city neighbourhoods have high concentrations of ethnic minorities. These areas are crowded and under pressure; but they tend to be more entrepreneurial than many mainly white inner neighbourhoods. The future of cities depends on *supporting and integrating minority communities* within more vibrant, more popular neighbourhoods, alongside the often collapsing white areas.

- Residents within acutely declining areas face an increasingly precarious future. Some argue for new clearances and a clean-sweep approach to regeneration. Many defend their neighbourhoods and hang on for a better future. *Clean-sweep solutions are immensely damaging to community ties*, costly and therefore impossible to implement in the several thousand acutely declining neighbourhoods. Holding onto people, developing micro-initiatives within neighbourhoods, *restoring, beautifying and upgrading cities* is surely a more realistic vision than the large-scale disruption of past and often current urban regeneration programmes.

- New Deal for Communities, the government's neighbourhood flagship, will help about 50 neighbourhoods – renewal programmes only ever target a tiny number at a time. We need practicable fundable schemes across every town and city in Britain. The Social Exclusion Unit's 'strategy for neighbourhood renewal' should include *neighbourhood 'supremos' to troubleshoot and sort problems out from a local base*. They need to be backed by *neighbourhood wardens and supercaretakers* to secure and sustain improved conditions.

[. . .]

NOTES

1 CASE [Centre for Analysis of Social Exclusion], *Persistent Poverty and Lifetime Inequality: The Evidence*, proceedings from a workshop held at HM Treasury, chaired by Professor John Hills. CASE report 5, London School of Economics, and HM Treasury Occasional Paper 10.

2 Urban Task Force, *Towards an Urban Renaissance* (London: DETR, 1999).

3 A. Power and K. Mumford, *The Slow Death of Great Cities: Urban Abandonment or Urban Renaissance* (York: Joseph Rowntree Foundation, 1999).

4 A. Power, *Estates on the Edge* (London: Routledge, 1999).

Part 19

Population Growth and Ecological Crisis

In Reading 63 Scott Lash and his colleagues discuss controversies about the use of nuclear power. In so doing they analyse how late people respond to and interpret scientific findings. The authors show that none of the groups involved in responding to potential contamination understood each others views satisfactorily. Government officials failed to understand aspects of local farming; scientists ignored farmers' local knowledge and carried out experiments which the farmers knew to be ill-prepared ; the farmers involved themselves only partly understood the ideas coming from the 'experts'.

It used to be believed that there was an intrinsic conflict between policies concerned with the environment and those to do with economic growth. In recent years we have discovered that economic development and job creation can be compatible with environmental care. Ernst von Weizsäcker and his colleagues in Reading 64 argue that by employing the right technologies we can both increase economic efficiency and reduce ecological damage. They describe their ideas as 'factor four' – meaning that we can generate twice as much wealth as we do at the moment by using half the resources we currently consume.

Reading 65 discusses the influence of migration in the contemporary world. Large-scale migrations have happened at many points in history. For instance during the slave trade of 200–300 years ago many millions of people were transported from Africa to North and South America to work as slaves. Large-scale movements of population remain very common today, fuelled mainly by the desire of people to move between countries or continents in search of a better life. The US remains the main host society for immigrants from around the world but there are increasing levels of immigration into the West European countries. Although immigration often promotes hostile responses from those living in the countries to which people move, most evidence suggests that immigration has positive consequences, since it adds to economic vitality and cultural diversity.

63 Risk, Environment and Modernity:

Towards a New Ecology

Scott Lash, Bronislaw Szerszynski and Brian Wynne

[...]

[The author Wynne] studied the responses of sheep farmers in Cumbria, a mountain area of north-west England, who had been subjected to administrative restrictions on sheep movements and sales due to radioactive contamination caused by the fallout from the 1986 Chernobyl nuclear accident. The farmers interacted over some years, but most intensely for a year or two, with scientists from a variety of agencies who were responsible for official views of the behaviour of the radio-activity, and of the likely duration of the restrictions. These interactions, between a relatively well defined lay public and a particular, but fairly typical, form of expert system, illuminate several more general points about the social basis of scientific knowledge and its public credibility, and about the nature of lay knowledge.

After initial denials of any problems in the UK from the radioactive fallout, in June 1986 the UK Ministry of Agriculture imposed a sudden blanket ban on the movement and sale of sheep from defined areas in hill regions such as the Lake District of northern England. This was potentially ruinous to what was a marginal and economically fragile sector of British farming, because these farmers depended for almost all of their annual income on being able to sell a large crop of surplus lambs from midsummer onwards. Not only would their income be devastated, but they would be unable to feed this lamb flock if it was forced to remain in their hands, because these hill areas comprise mainly meagre grazing on open mountains and only very limited valley grass, which would 'become a desert in days', as one farmer put it, if the lambs were not moved on. Thus wholesale slaughter of sheep flocks was on the agenda, with long-term ruin of the hill-farming economy and its distinct culture.

These dire threats were alleviated when the Ministry announced that the ban would be only for three weeks, a period which would return the situation to normal well before the annual sales would begin. This reassuring projection was based on prevailing scientific assumptions about the behaviour of radiocaesium in the environment. According to those beliefs the fallout would be washed off the vegetation which sheep grazed, into the soil where it would be absorbed and 'locked up' chemically, unavailable for any further mobility and possible return to vegetation and the sheep food chain. Thus a once-through model of contamination was involved, and this meant that there would be no further dose to the sheep after the first flush. Thus measured body burdens of radiocaesium in sheep were assumed to be peak levels which would decay according to the biological half-life. Since the biological half-life for caesium in sheep was about 20 days, it was estimated that the contamination levels would fall below levels at which action was required, within three weeks. This view was expressed by the experts with utter confidence unqualified by any hint of uncertainty.

Given the crucial importance of avoiding anything more than such short-term restrictions, the shock announcement in July 1986 that the three-week ban would have to be extended for the indefinite future was a stunning contradiction of previous reassurances and even denials of any problem at all from scientists, officials and ministers. Contrary to scientific beliefs and pronouncements, measured levels had shown no decrease, and an urgent reappraisal of existing understanding was begun. In order to allay rising fears of the imminent collapse of hill farming, the restrictions were altered so as to allow sheep from the contaminated area to be sold, so long as they were marked with a stipulated dye which marked them as unfit for human consumption. Thus they could at least be sold and moved out of the grazing-poor and contaminated hill area, even though they could not be sold for slaughter until deemed clear. It was expected that once the sheep were on uncontaminated land, this would not be long.

It is a point of general importance to observe just how completely controlled by the exercise of scientific interpretation the farmers felt themselves to be. Thus if they sold their marked sheep and avoided their overpopulation and possible starvation, they lost money badly in the markets because these sheep were blighted – indeed so were those that were unmarked but still from the affected area. This social reality was not recognised by the experts until a great deal of upset and loss of credibility had been caused amongst the farmers. Yet if they held on to the sheep, the farmers could only survive by incurring large extra imported-feed costs as well as build-up of disease and other problems. Still believing in their short-term model of the high levels of radiocaesium, the scientists continued to advise the farmers to hold on just a little longer, expecting the restrictions to be removed soon, even if later than originally thought. Caught whichever way they turned, many farmers still followed this advice despite the evidence of expert mistakes; but their

hopes were dashed as the early removal of restrictions promised by the experts never materialised.

It gradually became clear that the 'three weeks only' scientific judgement which had been translated into public policy commitments and predictions had been a mistake, but this became evident only over the following years, as more research and debate ensued. The predictions of only a three-week-long problem had been based on the assumed existence of alkaline clay soils (on which much of the original observations had been made). In such soils the behavioural properties of radiocaesium envisaged by the scientists do indeed occur. The problem was that the scientists had overlooked the essentially localised nature of this knowledge, because clay soil was not a universal condition, and in other soils such as those in the hill areas, very different behaviour prevailed. In these areas acid peaty soils predominated, and in such soils radiocaesium remains chemically mobile, hence available for root uptake from the soil, back into the vegetation which the sheep grazed. Thus, because they had assumed that the knowledge drawn from particular conditions was universal knowledge, the scientists did not understand that in these conditions the sheep were exposed to continual recontamination and hence probably much longer-term restrictions.

In the heat of the crisis over the Chernobyl accident and the restrictions, it arose as an issue whether there had been an innocent scientific mistake or a deliberate attempt to cover up knowledge of a longer-term problem, so as to avoid public reaction. Even the admission of a mistake was never made clearly and unambiguously. But in addition a further issue took off from this. At the outset of the restrictions a large area the size of the county of Cumbria was included. Within three months this had been reduced to a small crescent-shaped area in the mountains near the coast, and just downwind from the huge international Sellafield nuclear reprocessing complex. When this area persisted with high levels of contamination, against the confident predictions of the scientists, given its position various people began to ask whether the measured contamination had really been from Sellafield rather than Chernobyl, and had actually existed unnoticed or concealed by the expert authorities. Given Sellafield's notoriety as a discharger of radioactive contamination into the environment and the history of the world's worst civil nuclear accident in 1957 in a reactor on this site, this was by no means a frivolous suggestion. The 1957 fire was known to have spewed radiocaesium and other radioactive materials over this same area, and had resulted in the banning of milk sales for some weeks afterwards. Some local farmers even argued that the government and the nuclear industry had known all along but had been waiting for a convenient alibi for this environmental contamination; Chernobyl provided it.

Scientists dismissed these suggestions as unfounded, and pointed to what they regarded as unambiguous scientific proof, in the radioactive 'fingerprint' of the radiocaesium samples collected from the environment. The radiocaesium emitted from nuclear fission processes is made up of two isotopes of caesium-134 and caesium-137. The latter has a half-life of about thirty years while the former's is about one year. In nuclear fuel of a given level of burn-up the ratio of caesium-137 to caesium-134 fission products will be the same, but as they age with passage of time, the ratio increases due to the different half-lives. In fresh Chernobyl deposits it was about 2 : 1, whereas for typical Sellafield emissions (from reprocessed fuel often stored for many years on site before processing) or old 1957 accident emissions, the ratio would be about 12 : 1. The two isotopes emit gamma radiation of different specific frequencies, thus according to the scientists there was a clear means of distinguishing the two possible sources in the radioactive fingerprints of samples. The scientists asserted – again without any hint of uncertainty – that the origin of the contamination found in the environment was Chernobyl, and not Sellafield. This did not persuade the farmers, and it is worth examining the grounds of their scepticism.

First, they had just experienced the experts as having committed a huge mistake over the predictions of contamination, having expressed that mistaken view unqualified by any sense of uncertainties, and not having admitted any mistake. In this case also there was much more uncertainty in the technical process of discriminating between different sources than the experts' confident assertions implied. Actual soil samples contained mixed deposits, so that measured isotope ratios involved combined isotope intensities and assumptions about the precise ratio from any single source. It was later admitted that sampled deposits typically contained 50 per cent Chernobyl radiocaesium, and 50 per cent from 'other sources', which meant Sellafield and atmospheric weapons testing fallout. This was quite a significant move in the direction of the sceptical farmers' beliefs, from the initial expert assertion of certainty about Sellafield's innocence.

In addition to direct observation of Sellafield's position and the otherwise unexplained and unanticipated persistent crescent of contamination around it, the lay public also noted various elements of institutional 'body-language' which placed the experts' claims to credibility in question. The exaggerated certainty of official science was one element, but so too was the way that questions about environmental data from the affected area before 1986, which were designed to test the claim that the levels had not been high before that, were deflected to either data from after 1986, or data from other areas. This suggested that either there were data which showed the suspected high levels but which were being covered up, or there were no data at all, in which case there had been gross negligence considering that this was an area that had been affected by the 1957 fire. The choice of judgement of the expert authorities seemed to be either corruption or complacent incompetence.

The historical experience of secrecy and misinformation by official institutions also acted as a direct evidentiary input to the existing risk issue. Effectively recognising that they had to trust the experts and could not independently generate knowledge of the environmental hazards, the public had good reason from past experience of social relationships with what were to them the same institutions, not to invest that trust. This reinforced the evidence from the current issue. Yet feeling mistrustful of the experts, they were nevertheless realistic enough to recognise pervasive dependency on them, and often spoke and behaved *as if* they trusted them. A typical farmer's assessment was: 'The scientists tell us it's all from Chernobyl. You just have to believe them – if a doctor gave you a jab up the backside for a cold, you wouldn't argue with him, would you?' In other words, we might look as if we trust them, but just because we have no choice but to 'believe' them doesn't mean we don't have our own beliefs.

A further factor involved in the public's evaluation of the scientific knowledge-claims was the way in which the official experts neglected elements of the local situation, including specialist farming knowledge, which were relevant to the understanding and social management of the crisis. Thus the scientists did not understand the implications of the restrictions on hill sheep farming, and appeared not to recognise the need to learn. For example, they assumed that farmers would be able to bring sheep down from the high fells where contamination was highest, to the relatively less contaminated valley grass, and thus reduce levels below the action thresholds. This and other expert misconceptions were scornfully dismissed by the farmers as utterly unrealistic. Outbursts of frustrations at the experts' ignorance occurred often, here in response to their assumption that straw would make up for the drastic shortage of grazing:

[The experts] don't understand our way of life. They think you stand at the fell bottom and wave a handkerchief and all the sheep come running. . . . I've never heard of a sheep that would even look at straw as a fodder. When you hear things like that it makes your hair stand on end. You just wonder, what the hell are these blokes talking about?

In addition, farmers' specialist knowledge of local environmental conditions and sheep behaviour was ignored by the experts, much to the provocation of the farmers. The scientific knowledge constructed out of field observations began life as highly uncertain and uneven – the farmers watched scientists decide in apparently arbitrary ways where to sample mountainsides or fields with huge variations of readings, and they helped scientists as they changed their recorded monitoring readings of sheep contamination by changing the background reading, or the way the monitor was held to the sheep. Yet these kinds of uncertainty and open-endedness were obliterated by the time the knowledge returned to that same public as formal scientific knowledge in official statements.

Many of the conflicts between lay farmers and scientists centred on the standardisation built into routine structures of scientific knowledge. The quantitative units involved often encompassed several farms and even valleys with one measurement or value, when the farmers knew and could articulate various significant differences in environment, climate factors, management practices, etc., between neighbouring farms, indeed even on a single farm. These variations often reflected substantial elements of skill and specialist identity on the part of the farmers, yet they saw these wiped out in the scientific knowledge and the ignorant or insensitive ways it was deployed. A typical lament indicated this conflicting embryonic epistemological orientation, which was connected to a conflict between central administration and bureaucracy and a more informal, individualist and adaptive culture: 'This is what they can't understand. They think a farm is a farm and a ewe is a ewe. They just think we stamp them off a production line or something.'

In other cases the scientists ignored the farmers' informal expertise when they devised and conducted field experiments which the farmers knew to be unrealistic. An example was an experiment intended to examine the effects of bentonite spread on affected vegetation in reducing sheep contamination. The experiment involved penning sheep in several adjacent pens on similarly contaminated grazing, and spreading different specified amounts of bentonite over each pen area, then measuring contamination levels in the sheep, before and at intervals after. The farmers immediately observed amongst themselves that these experiments would be useless because hill sheep were unused to being penned up, and would 'waste' in such unreal conditions – that is, they would lose condition and their metabolisms be deleteriously affected, thus confounding the experiment. This was a typical arena in which expert knowledge and lay knowledge interacted and directly conflicted over the appropriate design of scientific experiments.

After a few months the scientists' experiments were abandoned, though the farmers' criticisms were never explicitly acknowledged. In this and other cases, also for example over the levels of recognised uncertainty and standardisation, the lay public were involved in substantive judgement of the validity of scientific commitments. Much of this conflict between expert and lay epistemologies centred on the clash between the taken-for-granted scientific culture of prediction and control, and the farmers' culture in which lack of control was taken for granted over many environmental and surrounding social factors in farm management decisions. The farmers assumed predictability to be intrinsically unreliable as an assumption, and therefore valued adaptability and flexibility, as a key part of their cultural identity and practical knowledge. The scientific experts ignored or misunderstood the multidimensional complexity of this lay public's problem-domain, and thus made different assumptions about its controllability. In other words, the two knowledge-cultures expressed different assumptions about agency and control, and there were both empirical and normative dimensions to this.

This example corresponds with many others in which expert and lay knowledge cultures interact, [...] Dickens found similar underlying factors involved in conflicts between weather forecasting scientists and lay publics over the prediction of extreme weather events such as hurricanes.[1] Martin also identified essentially the same cultural dimensions of conflict between the knowledges of working-class women and biological scientists about menstruation.[2] These were not a matter of lay public 'cultural' responses to 'meaning-neutral' objective scientific knowledge, but of cultural responses, to a *cultural* form of intervention – that is, one embodying particular normative models of human nature, purposes and relationships.

Many other studies of the interactions between scientific expertise and lay publics support this kind of analysis. These [...] studies show the following common features:

- scientific expert knowledge embodies assumptions and commitments of a human kind, about social relationships, behaviour and values;
- it also embodies problematic 'structural' or epistemic commitments, for example about the proper extent of agency, control and prediction, or of standardisation;
- it neglects and thus denigrates specialist lay knowledges;
- at a secondary level it then defines lay resistances as based on ignorance or irrationality rather than on substantive if unarticulated objections to these inadequate constructions of lay social identity which the expert discourses unwittingly assume and impose;
- thus a further reinforcement takes place, of tacit public ambivalence about being dependent on social actors (experts) who engender such alienation and social control;
- hence the fundamental sense of risk in the 'risk society', is risk to identity engendered by dependency upon expert systems which typically operate with such unreflexive blindness to their own culturally problematic and inadequate models of the human.

[...]

NOTES

1 P. Dickens, *Society and Nature: Towards a Green Social Theory* (New York and London: Harvester/Wheatsheaf, 1992).

2 E. Martin, *The Woman in the Body* (Milton Keynes: Open University Press, 1989).

64 Factor Four:
Doubling Wealth – Halving Resource Use

Ernst von Weizsäcker, Amory B. Lovins and L. Hunter Lovins

Exciting prospects for progress

'Factor Four', in a nutshell, means that resource productivity can – and should – grow fourfold. The amount of wealth extracted from one unit of natural resources can quadruple. Thus we can live twice as well – yet use half as much.

That message is both novel and simple.

It is novel because it heralds nothing less than a new direction for technological 'progress'. In the past, progress was the increase of labour productivity. We feel that *resource productivity* is equally important and should now be pursued as the highest priority.

Our message is simple, offering a rough quantitative formula. This [study] describes technologies representing a quadrupling or more of resource productivity. Progress, as we have known at least since the Earth Summit at Rio de Janeiro in 1992, must meet the criterion of sustainability. *Factor Four* progress does.

The message is also *exciting*. It says that some aspects of that efficiency revolution are available now at *negative* cost; that is, profitably. Much more can be made profitable. Countries engaging in the efficiency revolution become stronger, not weaker, in terms of international competitiveness.

That is not only true for the industrialised countries of the North. It is even more valid for China, India, Mexico or Egypt – countries that have a great supply of inexpensive labour but are short of energy. Why should they learn from the US and from Europe how to waste energy and materials? Their journey to prosperity will be smoother, swifter and safer if they make the efficiency revolution the centrepiece of their technological progress.

The efficiency revolution is bound to become a global trend. As is always the case with new opportunities, those who pioneer the trend will reap the greatest rewards.

Moral and material reasons

Changing the direction of progress is not something a *book* can do. It has to be done by people – consumers and voters, managers and engineers, politicians and communicators. People don't change their habits unless they have good reasons for doing so. Motivation needs to be experienced as compelling and urgent by a critical mass of people, otherwise there won't be enough momentum to change the course of our civilisation.

The reasons for changing the direction of technological progress are both moral and material. We trust that most readers share our view that preserving physical support systems for humankind is a high moral priority. The ecological state of the world demands swift action. [. . .] We avoid the language of doom and gloom, but we do present some disturbing ecological facts and trends. These should be established if we want to say something in quantitative terms about the necessary answers. We shall demonstrate that gaps as large as a factor of four are opening before us which need to be closed.

If these gaps aren't closed, the world may run into unprecedented troubles and disasters. Avoiding them may seem like a formidable task. Can such gigantic gaps be closed at all? This question leads us to the good news. The gaps can be closed. *Factor Four* is at the heart of the answer. Best of all, we shall discover very strong *material* reasons for changing the direction of technological progress.

Countries starting at once will reap major benefits. Countries that hesitate are likely to suffer formidable losses of their capital stock which will quickly become obsolete as resource efficiency trends take hold elsewhere.

Efficiency cure for the wasting disease

Why do we believe this? Essentially because we see our society in the grip of a severe but curable illness. It is not unlike the disease our grandparents called 'consumption' because it made its victims waste away. Today's economic tuberculosis consumes neither our bodies nor our resources (used energy and resources stay behind as unproductive pollution), but its effect on people, nations and the planet is just as deadly, costly and contagious.

We have been told that industrialisation has resulted from increasing levels of efficiency and productivity. Human productivity has certainly multiplied manyfold since the beginning of the Industrial Revolution. We have increased our productive capacities by substituting resources for human labour. Yet that substitution has now gone too far, over-using such resources as energy, materials, water, soil and air. Gains in 'productivity' pursued in this way are thus overwhelming the living systems that provide our resource base and must also assimilate the detritus of our civilisation.

A currently popular line of rhetoric maintains that any solution to these environmental problems will be very costly. That is wrong. What makes it wrong is the revolution in resource efficiency that this [study] is all about. Correcting the imbalances between how we use people and resources, improving resource efficiency and healing the 'wasting disease' represent, in fact, major economic opportunities. Much of the cure is not painful but soothing to both natural systems and the social fabric of global civilisation.

When people think of waste, they consider their household garbage, exhaust gases from their cars and the containers of rubbish outside businesses or construction sites. If you were to ask how much material is wasted each year, most people would admit that a certain percentage is wasted, but not a great deal. Actually, we are more than ten times better at wasting resources than at using them. A study for the US National Academy of Engineering found that about 93 per cent of the materials we buy and 'consume' never end up in saleable products at all. Moreover, 80 per cent of products are discarded after a single use, and many of the rest are not as durable as they should be. Business reformer Paul Hawken estimates that 99 per cent of the original materials used in the production of, or contained within, the goods made in the US become waste within 6 weeks of sale.

Most of the energy, water and transportation services we consume are wasted too, often before we get them; we pay for them, yet they provide no useful service. The heat that leaks through the attics of poorly insulated homes; the energy from a nuclear or coal-fired power station, only 3 per cent of which is converted into light in an incandescent lamp (70 per cent of the original fuel energy is wasted before it gets to the lamp, which in turn converts only 10 per cent of the electricity into light); the 80–85 per cent of a car's petrol that is wasted in the engine and drivetrain before it gets to the wheels; the water that evaporates or dribbles away before it gets to the roots of a crop; the senseless movement of goods over huge distances for a result equally well achieved more locally – these are all costs without benefits.

This waste is unnecessarily expensive. The average American, for example, pays nearly US$2,000 a year for energy, either directly purchased for the household or embodied in businesses' goods and services. Add to that wasted metal, soil, water, wood, fibre and the cost of moving all these materials around, and the average American is wasting thousands of dollars every year. That waste, multiplied by 250 million people, yields at least a trillion dollars per year that is needlessly spent. Worldwide, it may even approach US$10 trillion, every year. Such waste impoverishes families (especially those with lower incomes), reduces competitiveness, imperils our resource base, poisons water, air, soil and people, and suppresses employment and economic vitality.

The efficiency cure

Yet the wasting disease is curable. The cure comes from the laboratories, workbenches and production lines of skilled scientists and technologists, from the policies and designs of city planners and architects, from the ingenuity of engineers, chemists and farmers, and from the intelligence of every person. It is based on sound science, good economics and common sense. The cure is using resources efficiently; doing more with less. It is not a question of going backward or 'returning' to prior means. It is the beginning of a new industrial revolution in which we shall achieve dramatic increases in resource productivity.

Ways of doing this have significantly increased in the past few years, opening up wholly unexpected opportunities for business and society. This [study] is an introduction, description and call to action on behalf of these opportunities in advanced resource efficiency. It shows practical, often profitable ways to use resources *at least four times as efficiently as we do now*. Or to put it another way, it means we can accomplish everything we do today as well as now, or better, with only one-quarter of the energy and materials we presently use. This would make it possible, for example, to double the global standard of living while cutting resource use in half. Further improvements on an even more ambitious scale are also rapidly becoming feasible and cost-effective.

Doing more with less is not the same as doing less, doing worse or doing without. Efficiency does not mean curtailment, discomfort or privation. When several presidents of the US proclaimed that 'energy conservation means being hotter in the summer and colder in the winter', they were not talking about energy *efficiency*, which should make us *more* comfortable by improving buildings so that they provide better comfort whilst using less energy and less money. To avoid this common confusion, this [study] avoids the ambiguous term 'resource conservation' and instead uses 'resource efficiency' or 'resource productivity'.

Seven good reasons for resource efficiency

We have given somewhat abstract moral and material reasons for moving into efficiency. Now we will become more concrete by offering seven compelling reasons for doing exactly that.

1 *Live better* Resource efficiency improves the quality of life. We can see better with efficient lighting systems, keep food fresher in efficient refrigerators, produce better goods in efficient factories, travel more safely and comfortably in efficient vehicles, feel better in efficient buildings, and be better nourished by efficiently grown crops.

2 *Pollute and deplete less* Everything must go somewhere. Wasted resources pollute the air, water or land. Efficiency combats waste and thus reduces pollution, which is simply a resource out of place. Resource efficiency can greatly contribute to solving such huge problems as acid rain and climatic change, deforestation, loss of soil fertility and congested streets. By themselves, energy efficiency plus productive, sustainable farming and forestry practices could make up to 90 per cent of

today's environmental problems virtually disappear, not at a cost but – given favourable circumstances – at a profit. Efficiency can buy much time in which we can learn to deal thoughtfully, sensibly and sequentially with the world's problems.

3 *Make money* Resource efficiency is usually profitable: you don't have to pay now for the resources that aren't being turned into pollutants, and you don't have to pay later to clean them up.

4 *Harness markets and enlist business* Since resource efficiency has the potential of being profitable, much of it can be implemented largely in the marketplace, driven by individual choice and business competition, rather than requiring governments to tell everyone how to live. Market forces can theoretically drive resource efficiency. However, we are still confronted with the considerable task of clearing barriers and reversing daft incentive structures that keep the market from working fully.

5 *Multiply use of scarce capital* The money freed up by preventing waste can be used to solve other problems. Developing countries in particular, with less of their capital sunk in inefficient infrastructure, are in an excellent position to multiply the use of scarce capital. If a country buys equipment to make very energy-efficient lamps or windows, it can provide energy services with less than a tenth of the investment that would be required to buy more power stations instead. By also recovering that investment at least three times faster and reinvesting it elsewhere, the services rendered by the invested capital can rise more than 30-fold. (Some calculations show savings far higher still.) For a good many developing countries this could be the only realistic way to achieve prosperity in a reasonable timespan.

6 *Increase security* Competition for resources causes or worsens international conflict. Efficiency stretches resources to meet more needs, and reduces unhealthy resource dependencies that fuel political instability. Efficiency can reduce international sources of conflict over oil, cobalt, forests, water – whatever someone has that someone else wants. (Some countries pay in military costs, as well as directly, for their resource dependence: one-sixth to one-quarter of the US's military budget is earmarked for forces whose main mission is getting or keeping access to foreign resources.) Energy efficiency can even indirectly help block the spread of nuclear bombs by providing cheaper and inherently non-military substitutes for nuclear power plants and their dual-purpose materials, skills and technologies.

7 *Be equitable and have more employment* Wasting resources is the other face of a distorted economy that increasingly splits society into those who have work and those who don't. Either way, human energy and talent are being tragically misspent. Yet a major cause of this waste of people is the wrong and profligate thrust of technological progress. We are making ever fewer people more 'productive', using up more resources and effectively marginalising one-third of the world's workforce. We need a rational economic incentive that allows us to employ more people and fewer resources, solving two critical problems at the same time. Businesses *should sack the unproductive kilowatt-hours, tonnes and litres rather than their workforce.* This would happen much faster if we taxed labour less and resource use correspondingly more.

[. . .]

What's so new about efficiency?

Efficiency is a concept as old as the human species. Much human progress, in all societies, has been defined by new ways to do more with less. A great deal of engineering and business is about using all kinds of resources more productively, but for the past 150 years much of the technological effort of the industrial revolution has been devoted to increasing *labour productivity, even if that required more generous use of natural resources.* Recently, however, resource efficiency has undergone such a conceptual and practical revolution that most people haven't yet heard about its new potential.

Ten years ago, the main news about how to do more with less was the speed of technological improvement. Since the oil crisis of the 1970s, we have learnt in each half-decade how, in principle, we could use electricity about twice as efficiently as before. Each time, that doubled efficiency would theoretically cost two-thirds less. Similar progress continues today – less through new technologies than through better understanding of how to choose and combine existing ones. Progress in making resource efficiency bigger and cheaper is thus quite dramatic. It is, in fact, somewhat comparable to the computer and consumer electronics revolution, where everything is continually becoming smaller, faster, better and cheaper. But the energy and material resource experts typically have not yet begun to think in terms of ever-increasing energy efficiency. The talk in official energy policy organisations seems still to concentrate on questions such as how much coal should be displaced by nuclear power and at what price – questions of supply that the demand-side revolution increasingly renders outdated and irrelevant.

The prejudice remains widespread that saving more energy will always cost more. The usual belief is that, beyond the familiar zone of 'diminishing returns', there will be a wall beyond which further savings are prohibitively expensive. This was historically found to be true both for resource savings and for pollution control, and it fitted nicely with traditional economic theory.

Yet today, not only are there new technologies, but there are also new ways of linking them together so that in principle, *big savings can often be had even more cheaply than small savings*. When a series of linked efficiency technologies are implemented in concert with each other, in the right sequence and manner and proportions (just like the stages in a good recipe), there is a new economic benefit to be reaped from the whole that did not exist with the separate technological parts.

[. . .]

65 The Effect of Migrants in the Labour Market

The Economist

From the beginning, migration has been one of the most conspicuous features of human history. Humanity did not appear simultaneously all over the earth but, according to the current scientific consensus, first evolved in Africa, and from there spread far and wide. Even after mankind had populated most of the planet, migration continued to play a decisive role in history down the centuries, as people contended for territory and the resources that go with it.

In many of history's biggest movements of people, the migrants were not volunteers. In the 17th and 18th centuries 15m people were taken as slaves from Africa and shipped to Brazil, the Caribbean and North America. In the 19th century, between 10m and 40m indentured workers ('coolies', often no better than slaves) were sent in vast numbers around the world, mainly from China and India.

[The twentieth] century's wars in Europe and Asia displaced millions more. But perhaps the most intense episode of migration-under-duress in modern times occurred after the partition of India in 1947, when 7m Muslims fled India for the new state of Pakistan and 7m Hindus fled in the opposite direction.

As individuals, not merely as members of races or religions in flight, people have always travelled in search of a better life. Between the middle of the 19th century and the start of the second world war 60m people left Europe and moved overseas – to the United States (which received 40m of them), Canada, Latin America, Australia, New Zealand and South Africa. Much of this movement was guided by economic calculation. Most modern migration is of this kind, though nowadays the pull is high wages rather than cheap land.

For the past century or so, the pattern of migration has shifted a good deal, with changes in government policy playing a key role. Until 1914 governments imposed almost no controls. This allowed the enormous 19th-century movement of migrants from Europe to North America. The United States allowed the entry of anybody who was not a prostitute, a convict, a 'lunatic' – or, after 1882, Chinese.

Travel within Europe was largely uncontrolled: no passports, no work-permits. Foreign-born criminals could expect to be deported, but that was the extent of immigration policy. The only questions were whether migrants could afford the journey and, having arrived, be better off than at home.

Between 1914 and 1945, partly reflecting security concerns, migration was curtailed. Many countries excluded immigrants – including refugees from Hitler's Germany – on openly racist grounds. America's Congress passed laws aiming to preserve the country's racial and religious make-up.

After 1945 came another great change. Many European countries faced labour shortages. Their immigration laws by and large were not repealed, but were enforced much more liberally. Governments actively recruited immigrants for jobs in their expanding industries. Migration surged again, now not mainly from Europe to North America but from the developing countries to the rich ones.

The next big change came in the 1970s. The rich countries were no longer growing quickly and struggling with labour shortages. Recession came to Europe and America, and immigration rules were tightened again. This more restrictive regime continues to apply.

Counting heads

It is difficult to say how much migration is going on. Official definitions of 'migrant' vary, and migrants on any definition are difficult to count.

However, according to estimates in *The Work of Strangers*, a study by Peter Stalker published by the International Labour Organisation, roughly 80m people live today in countries they were not born in. Another 20m live in foreign lands as refugees from natural disasters or political oppression. Each year sees another 1½ m or so emigrate permanently, and perhaps another 1m seek temporary asylum abroad. By historical standards, these numbers are large in absolute terms, but small in relation to the now much larger populations of the receiving countries (see figure 65.1).

The United States remains much the world's biggest recipient. It gets about as many permanent immigrants as every other country in the world added together: 720,000 in 1995, down from a peak of nearly 2m in 1991. Germany, easily the main receiving country in Europe, had roughly 800,000 immigrants in both 1994 and 1995, but its definition of 'immigrant' is much broader than America's and includes many temporary workers.

The underlying trend of economic migration reflects two countervailing forces. As the cost of travel drops and incomes rise in developing countries, migration becomes easier. On the other hand, in poor countries with fast-rising incomes the incentive to move shrinks. The net effect in the early years of industrialisation tends to be higher migration. Despite the tightening of rules in many rich countries during the 1970s, immigration did increase somewhat during the 1980s and early 1990s. New restrictions have slowed this expansion in the past few years (see figure 65.2).

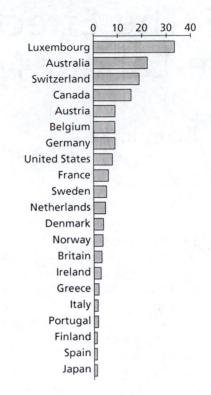

Figure 65.1 Home from home: foreign population as percentage of total population, 1995
Source: OECD

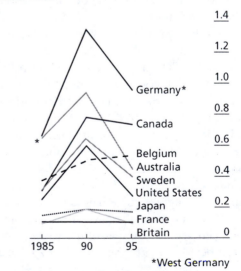

Figure 65.2 On the wane: inflows of immigrants as percentage of population
Source: OECD

Table 65.1 Melting pots: country of origin of immigrants '000, 1995

Australia		Britain	
New Zealand	12.3	Pakistan	6.3
Britain	11.3	India	4.9
China	11.2	United States	4.0
Ex-Yugoslavia	7.7	Bangladesh	3.3
Hong Kong	4.4	Nigeria	3.3
India	3.7	Australia	2.0

Canada		France	
Hong Kong	31.7	Algeria	8.4
India	16.2	Morocco	6.6
Philippines	15.1	Turkey	3.6
China	13.3	United States	2.4
Sri Lanka	8.9	Tunisia	1.9
Taiwan	7.7	Ex-Yugoslavia	1.6

Japan		United States	
China	38.8	Mexico	89.9
Philippines	30.3	Ex-Soviet Union	54.5
United States	27.0	Philippines	51.0
South Korea	18.8	Vietnam	41.8
Brazil	11.9	Dominican Rep.	38.5
Thailand	6.5	China	35.5

Source: OECD

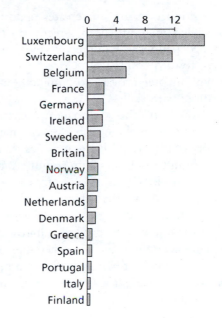

Figure 65.3 What mobility? EU-born population as percentage of total population, 1995
Source: OECD

Has there ever been a global market for labour? During the 19th century, arguably there was. Otherwise, the United States could not have expanded at anything like the rate it did. Nowadays, there is no real market, such is the severity of restrictions in force. The interplay of these rules and other factors gives rise to complicated migratory patterns. Each receiving country has its own sources: the links are often historical as well as economic or geographical. Earlier generations of migrants form networks that help new ones to overcome legal obstacles; and today's tighter rules tend to confine immigration to family members of earlier 'primary' migrants.

Mexico is the main source of migrants to the United States, with about 90,000 permanent (legal) settlers in 1995. But the former Soviet Union and the Philippines, taken together, supplied even more during that year – 55,000 and 51,000 respectively (see table 65.1).

Citizens of European Union countries are free to work anywhere within the EU. This is presumably promoting the flow of economic migrants within the EU, but it is difficult to be sure of the effect (see figure 65.3). The proportion of EU citizens in each member-country's foreign-born population varies widely – from 25 per cent in the Netherlands to 89 per cent in Luxembourg – and any tendency for this share to rise has lately been overshadowed by the influx of new immigrants from Central and Eastern Europe.

Another new trend is a worldwide shift towards migration of highly skilled workers. Again this reflects the interplay of economics and regulation. As multinational companies expand, they develop their own internal markets for skilled workers.

The expansion of trade also creates opportunities for skilled migrants, both directly (in trade-related occupations) or indirectly (by changing attitudes towards 'abroad'). Governments also prefer high-income arrivals, so immigration rules favour those with skills.

The growth of the multinational enterprise seems likely to spur the next big development in the history of migration. Big companies want the freedom to shift employees from country to country, and to use citizens of one country to alleviate skills shortages in another. This will be not so much a quantitative change (which governments would resist in any case) but a qualitative one – namely, greater migration of workers-plus-skills, or 'human capital'. If a truly global market for labour ever reappears, it is likely to be for highly skilled workers only.

Migration may not be new, but it has become more controversial than for many years. On the face of it, immigration brings a variety of benefits to the receiving country. An important one for many rich countries is demographic. The average age of the advanced economies' populations is rising. Immigration tends to lower it, because most migrants are young. This improves the ratio of active workers to retired people, so taxes can be lower than otherwise.

Against this, a common view is that immigrants compete for jobs which would otherwise have gone to nationals, reducing wages and/or employment prospects for the indigenous workers. This sounds plausible – surely an increase in the supply of labour must reduce wages or increase unemployment? The truth is more complicated.

Jobs and wages

Immigrants are consumers as well as producers, so they create jobs as well as taking them. And the work they do need not be at the expense of native workers. Immigrants often hold jobs (as domestic servants, for instance) that natives are unwilling to accept at any feasible wage.

Also, immigrants sometimes help to keep industries viable that would otherwise disappear altogether, causing employment to fall. This was the conclusion, for instance, of a study of the Los Angeles garment industry in the 1970s and 1980s. And when immigrants working for low wages do put downward pressure on natives' wages, they may raise the (real) wages of natives in general by keeping prices lower than they otherwise would be.

In theory, then, the net effect of immigration on native wages is uncertain. Unfortunately, most of the empirical research on whether immigrants make natives worse off in practice is also inconclusive – except that the effect, one way or the other, seems small. Most of this research has been done in America: if there were any marked influence on wages, that is where you would expect to find it, given the scale of immigration and the tendency of the newcomers to concentrate in certain areas. But most studies have found that the impact, if any, is very slight.

Many studies have compared wages and employment in areas with many immigrants to wages and employment in areas with few. For instance, one examined the impact of the sudden and notorious inflow of refugees to Miami from the Cuban port of Mariel in 1980. Within the space of a few months, 125,000 people had arrived, increasing Miami's labour force by 7 per cent. Yet the study concluded that wages and employment among the city's natives, including the unskilled, were virtually unaffected.

Another study examined the effect of immigration on wages and employment of those at the bottom of the jobs ladder – unskilled blacks and hispanics. It found that a doubling of the rate of immigration had no detectable effect on natives (although the wages of the previous group of immigrants, presumably those in closest competition with the newcomers, saw their relative wages fall by 2½ per cent).

The most recent work, admittedly, has tended to question these findings. This new strand of research is linked to recent work on the effects of trade on wages, and especially on wage inequality. Using more detailed statistics and more sophisticated methods than the earlier studies, this work has tended to find that immigrants' wages take longer to rise to the level of natives' wages than had been supposed. This implies a more persistent downward pressure on the host economy's labour market.

Typically these studies find that immigration does depress unskilled natives' wages – to a small extent. But even these new results (which are by no means unchallenged) need to be kept in perspective. Nearly all economists would agree that the effects of immigration are insignificant in relation to other influences.

In his 1997 book *Trade and Income Distribution*, William Cline reviews the literature on globalisation and wages. In general, Mr Cline's estimates tend to the pessimistic end of the range. Nonetheless he finds that of all the forces acting to lower unskilled wages relative to skilled, immigration is the weakest.

According to his estimates, immigration would by itself account for a fall of two percentage points in the ratio of unskilled to skilled wages in America between 1973 and 1993. Technological change, acting to reduce the demand for unskilled labour, and a category called 'unidentified factors' pushing the same way would each account for a much greater fall of nearly 30 percentage points.

It seems safe to conclude, despite the uncertainties, that fears over the economic effects of immigration are much exaggerated.

Part 20
Sociological Research Methods

In Reading 66 Mike Moores discusses the role of experiments in sociology. At first sight it might seem as though experimentation is virtually impossible in sociology, because most social life can't be brought into the laboratory. Moores points out that it is possible effectively to conduct 'field experiments' – research in real-life situations where there is a strong element of experimental manipulation of key variables. He gives several examples of how fruitful field experiments have already been.

The survey method is used as widely as fieldwork in social research. Surveys are usually carried out by means of questionnaires, either administered directly by the researcher, or sent by post to the individuals concerned. Other variations include telephone or tape-recorded interviews orientated towards a fixed range of questions. In Reading 67, Catherine Marsh gives a general description of the survey method and also points out that it is widely used in other disciplines besides sociology.

In Reading 68 Robert A. Georges and Michael O. Jones provide a general interpretation of the nature of fieldwork. Fieldwork research, they stress, cannot be carried on in the way in which a natural scientist might conduct an experiment in a laboratory. The researcher must interact with, and gain the confidence of, those whose activities form the concern of the investigation. Fieldworkers face many problems, including the possibility that their research endeavours might have a strong impact upon their own personal attitudes and identity (a phenomenon which, however, some authors argue is actively desirable: the situation should be one of mutual communication).

Joanna Mack and Stewart Lansley (Reading 69) employed the survey method in their investigation of poverty in the United Kingdom. Surveys of the poor formed the basis of the celebrated work by Charles Booth, who in the late nineteenth century first brought to public consciousness the level and extent of poverty in London. Mack and Lansley say that their own study reveals an important point about conceptions of poverty today: that most people now interpret poverty not in terms of the minimal material requirements for subsistence, but in terms of a minimal standard of living which everyone living in the country should rightfully expect to achieve.

66 Sociologists in White Coats:

Experiments in Sociology

Mike Moores

If you look through most major textbooks for sociology at A or AS level, you find that the chapters on research methods tend to be very similar. In particular, a lot of time is spent dealing with what might be called 'majority methods' (i.e. those that tend to be most used, such as interviews, questionnaires and participant observation) and then give very little attention to what we might call 'minority methods'. In this latter category we might include methods such as content analysis and case-studies. However, there is one particular sociological method that the standard textbooks often say very little about – experimentation.

It is not surprising, then, that students do not write much about _experiments in sociology_ in their examination answers – and often there is scope to do this. [. . .] So, we might call experimentation in sociology a 'neglected' method in many ways. However, it is a valid way of studying social behaviour, and there could be benefits to students if they learn more about the method, apply this knowledge appropriately and evaluate experimentation's usefulness as a research technique.

Experiments in natural sciences

Interestingly, our starting point for looking at experimentation happens to be outside sociology. Natural sciences – say, physics and chemistry – are traditionally associated with experimentation, and we can learn a great deal by comparing their experimental approach with that used by sociologists.

Perhaps the key feature of positivist experimentation in subjects like physics is that the work takes place in a laboratory. (In the next section we will see how important it is to distinguish positivist laboratory experiments from sociological field experiments). In this context, we immediately think of scientists controlling variables, quantifying data, testing hypotheses, isolating causal links, minimising subjectivity and so on, all of this with high levels of reliability and validity!

Obviously, this rather stereotyped view of what scientists do has been challenged by a number of critics, especially in relation to the idea that natural scientists can suspend their personal values in carrying out experimentation. However, the essential features of a lot of positivist laboratory work coincide with many of the above characteristics. Let's look at some of these essential features.

Controlling variables

When natural scientists carry out their research in laboratories, the issue of _controlling variables_ is of crucial importance. More specifically, experimentation usually involves manipulating one _independent variable_ and creating change in the _dependent variable_. This is actually more straightforward than it sounds! Remember that natural scientists work in a controlled context or environment. This means that they can alter one factor (or variable) in a given situation and measure how this affects a related factor. What is important, of course, is that all *other* factors are held constant (or controlled) and are not allowed to contribute to any change which might occur. For example, if scientists want to examine the effect of a special diet (the independent variable) on the aggressiveness of laboratory rats (the dependent variable), they can only do so effectively if they control all other variables involved. So, laboratory temperature, the age of the rats involved, their sex, etc., must all be controlled if the true relationship between the two specified variables is to be understood.

Once this research design has been established, it is clearly possible to measure any changes which happen. This means that natural science experimentation offers the possibility of *quantifying data*, which will usually be done in specific units of measurement.

As the experimentation process continues, the central aims of the researcher become realisable. The first of these is the aim of *testing a hypothesis*. In many respects, a hypothesis is an 'educated guess' about relationships between variables. In our example, it might be hypothesised that a certain type of diet will increase the aggressiveness of laboratory rats. The measured results of the experiment will decide whether the hypothesis should be accepted or rejected or, put another way, validated or refuted. If the hypothesis is validated, it means that the researcher has achieved another of his/her central aims – that of *isolating a causal link*. In other words, it can be said with certainty that a 'cause and effect relationship' between two variables has been established. What is more, the whole process of experimentation has been carried through in a way which minimises subjectivity, i.e. the values of the researcher have been kept out of the process and objectivity has been achieved, as far as is humanly possible.

In addition, natural scientists argue that experimentation has a high level of *reliability* (it offers the possibility of other researchers repeating or replicating the study to test out the findings and to check for flaws in the research design or process) and a high level of *validity* (it offers results which tell us something about the phenomenon being studied, rather than about a related phenomenon). All in all then, experimentation can be seen as the 'essential' *positivist* method. (Students might like to refer to Lawson for a more critical consideration of the natural science experimental model.[1]) [. . .]

Sociological field experiments

A point of *irony* is necessary as a starting point for this section. From the above consideration of natural scientific experimentation, it is obvious that it is based on a positivist view of the world. The irony is that, in sociology, the method of experimentation is most likely to be used by researchers who adopt a *non-positivist* view of the social world. This point is important. [One] should realise that experiments in sociological research are used in particular contexts (i.e. in naturally occurring 'in the field' settings) and that they represent an attempt to explore the issues which preoccupy non-positivist or 'interpretive' sociologists: roles, group dynamics, rules, etc. – the processes that underpin everyday social life, in other words. You can see that these types of experiments are very different from those carried out in laboratories.

To illustrate the key and recurrent features of sociological field experiments I have selected three studies to discuss. [. . .] What the studies share is their attempt to 'flush out' the mechanisms by which social groups operate – the sets of expectations that govern our behaviour, whether we are aware of them or not. Adopting this strategy inevitably means disturbing 'normal' social patterns, as we shall see.

Study 1   D. L. Rosenhahn: 'On Being Sane in Insane Places'

In this study eight pseudo-patients (or 'false' patients), using false names and fabricated biographies, had themselves admitted to 12 mental

institutions across the United States.[2] This group consisted of people from a range of professions; none had any real symptoms of mental illness. The aim of the experiment was to test out how effectively and consistently psychiatrists applied the criteria for diagnosing individuals as 'mentally ill'.

The pseudo-patients all complained of 'hearing voices'. All were judged to be suffering from schizophrenia (except one, who was diagnosed 'manic-depressive'). They stayed in hospital for, on average, 19 days. Whilst in hospital, they behaved as normally as they possibly could – a point noted very well by 'genuine' patients. Nevertheless, when they were discharged, the hospital authorities released them as 'schizophrenic in remission' (i.e. temporarily not suffering from the symptoms) rather than completely cured. Whilst in hospital the pseudo-patients were administered over 2,000 pills (most of which were not taken).

As a follow-up experiment, one hospital was informed that more pseudo-patients were 'on their way'. The hospital was asked to try to identify them. Judgements were made on about 200 new patients and one fifth were thought to be pseudo-patients. Actually, no pseudo-patients had presented themselves.

Study 2   H. Garfinkel: Studies in Ethno-methodology

In this volume Garfinkel (1967) outlines a series of experiments he conducted.[3] Each of these is designed to 'disrupt' everyday interaction in specific contexts in order to highlight the unspoken (and usually unquestioned) norms and assumptions on which 'normal' social interaction is based. In one particular experiment Garfinkel asked his undergraduate students to spend short periods at home behaving as, or playing the role of, lodgers, rather than sons or daughters – an extremely simple research strategy, but one with dramatic consequences. As his students gradually introduced the 'lodger role-playing' into family life, chaos developed.

As their sons and daughters became more polite and distant, formally asking if it was OK to get a snack from the fridge, for example, parents became angry and confused. Clearly, they found it difficult to cope with this new aspect of their child's behaviour: normal patterns of expectations between family members were being frustrated. Garfinkel had 'unpicked' family interaction by getting one family member to play 'out of role'. Students were asked: 'What's gotten into you?' and were accused of being selfish and inconsiderate. Social order was restored when parents had the experiment explained to them, but we can assume that some resentment lingered on in the minds of the parents.

Study 3   R. Rosenthal and L. Jacobson: Pygmalion in the Classroom

In this experiment the researchers visited a San Francisco elementary school;[4] they claimed to have developed a new IQ test which could predict which children were likely to become 'high-attainers' in the very near future. Teachers were told that about 20 per cent of a particular age-group would come into this category of 'very able children' and were invited by the researchers to administer the IQ test. Once this had been done, Rosenthal and Jacobson informed the teachers which pupils the test had identified as most likely to become high-attainers. In fact, the names had been selected at random.

Over a period of 18 months, the researchers visited the school regularly and found that the 'named' children had, in fact, improved significantly in their school work – more than could be explained purely by chance. Rosenthal and Jacobson explained this dramatic improvement in performance in terms of increased or raised teacher expectation of the children in question.

So this experiment identified a central *variable* in pupil attainment – the role of the teacher in shaping the child's self-image.

Looking back over the three experiments considered, we can summarise the features of sociological field experiments.

Field experiments

- Clearly, field experiments present *ethical* problems for the researcher. Is it right to deceive members of the social groups involved? Is it fair to manipulate their behaviour?
- In some cases, experiments involve *risk* for the researcher. Individuals can get angry about the new and often strange situations sociological experiments place them in (as with the parents in Garfinkel's experiment).
- This methodology obviously means that the researcher relinquishes a large degree of *control* once the experiment is under way. In this respect, the researcher has to settle for whatever outcome he or she obtains.
- This method, for all of its faults, represents a tremendously *effective* way of 'getting inside' group behaviour, generating interesting qualitative data in a naturally occurring context and allowing interpretive sociologists to get 'close to their subject matter'.

Experiments in student coursework

Now that you are familiar with the idea of field experiments, your might consider building this method into your own research. You might want to try out some experimentation relating to, say, personal space and gender. Are males more uneasy about close (non-sexual) contact from 'same-sex' peers than females? How would you set up an experiment to test this? Always remember the points about ethics and risk mentioned above, but also the point about this method having many advantages, too. Whatever your topic in your coursework, the experimental approach should be possible, given careful thought and planning.

And finally . . .

To conclude, then, we have to say that sociologists who use experimentation are unlikely to wear white coats! It's not *that* sort of experimentation. Nevertheless, it is a method with credibility, and it is often, quite simply, a very interesting way of studying society.

NOTES

1 T. Lawson, *Sociology for A-Level* (London: Collins, 1993), pp. 7–16.

2 D. L. Rosenhahn, 'On Being Sane in Insane Places', *Science* (1973), p. 179; repr. in M. Bulmer (ed.), *Social Research Ethics* (New York: Holmes and Meier, 1982).

3 H. Garfinkel, *Studies in Ethno-methodology* (Englewood Cliffs, NJ: Prentice Hall, 1967).

4 R. Rosenthal and L. Jacobson, *Pygmalion in the Classroom* (New York: Holt, Rinehart and Winston, 1968).

67 The Value of the Survey Method

Catherine Marsh

The word ['survey'] has a long tradition in the English language, and developed from being the fact of viewing or inspecting something in detail (as in a land survey) to the act of doing so rigorously and comprehensively, and finally to the written results. The idea of the social survey started with this connotation of the collection of social facts, but has undergone an evolution such that nowadays the survey method is a way not just of collecting data but also of analysing the results.

A survey refers to an investigation where:

1 systematic measurements are made over a series of cases yielding a rectangle of data;
2 the variables in the matrix are analysed to see if they show any patterns;
3 the subject matter is social.

In other words, surveys have a particular method of data collection, a particular method of data analysis and a particular substance.

The only restriction made on the survey as a method of collecting data is to insist that it be systematic, looking at more than one *case*, be it individuals, hospitals, countries or whatever, and measuring the same variables on each case, so that you end up with each case having one and only one code for each variable. The data could come from observation, from fixed-choice responses to a postal questionnaire, from content analysis of newspapers, or from postcoding tape-recorded depth interviews. The important thing is that there is more than one case and that variation between cases is considered systematically. 'Survey analysis' involves making causal inferences from some kind of passive observation

programme. The word 'survey' *is* sometimes used to refer to such investigations as a split-ballot question-wording trial, where there has been an experimental manipulation, but I think it is clearer if we use the word 'experiment' to describe such investigations.

Surveys and experiments are the only two methods known to me to test a hypothesis about how the world works. The experimenter intervenes in the social world, does something to a set of subjects (and usually also refrains from doing that thing to a set of controls) and looks to see what effect *manipulating* variance in the independent variable has on the dependent variable. If the subjects have been assigned in some fashion to control and experimental groups, the experimenter can be sure that it is what she did to the independent variable that has produced any differences between the groups.

The survey researcher has only made a series of observations; to be sure, as we shall come on to argue, these cannot be seen as passive reflections of unproblematic reality, but they must be logically distinguished from the manipulation that the experimenter engages in. The only element of randomness in the survey design comes in random selection of cases; *random sampling does not achieve the same result as random allocation into control and experimental groups.* The survey researcher may have a theory which leads her to suspect that X is having a causal effect on Y. If she wants to test this, she has to measure X and Y on a variety of different subjects, and infer from the fact that X and Y covary that the original hypothesis was true. But unlike the experimenter, she cannot rule out the possibility *in principle* of there being a third variable prior to X and Y and causing the variance in both; the experimenter knows that the relationship is not spurious because she knows exactly what produced the variance in X – *she* did.

In other words, in survey research the process of testing causal hypotheses, central to any theory-building endeavour, is a very indirect process of drawing inferences from already existing variance in populations by a rigorous process of comparison. In practice, one of the major strategies of the survey researcher is to control for other variables that she thinks might realistically be held also to produce an effect, but she never gets round the purist's objection that she has not definitively established a causal relationship. Furthermore, although having panel data across time certainly helps with the practical resolution of the problem of how to decide which of one's variables are prior to which others, it does not solve the logical difficulty that, in principle, any relationship which one finds may be explained by the operation of another unmeasured factor.

Finally, the subject matter of the surveys that sociologists are interested in is always social. Many different disciplines collect systematic observational data and make inferences from it. Biologists looking at correlations between plant growth and different types of environment, psychologists coding films of mother–child interactions, or astronomers drawing inferences about the origins of the universe from measurements of light intensity taken now are all performing activities whose logic is similar to that of the social survey analyst, but they would not describe their studies as 'surveys'. [. . .]

Surveys have a lot to offer the sociologist. Since experimentation cannot be used to investigate a wide range of macrosocial processes, there is often no alternative to considering variation across cases in a systematic fashion. Since the processes of determination in the social world are subjective in important ways, involving actors' meanings and intentions, the survey researcher has to face the task of measuring these subjective aspects. It is not easy. Perhaps the most misguided and damaging of all the criticisms that have been made of survey research was C. W. Mills's contention that their design and implementation involved no sociological imagination, but only the mechanical skills of techniques following time-honoured formulae. Nor are surveys cheap. Because of the ever-present danger of faulty inference from correlational data, measurements of all the possible confounding variables must be made, and the sample size must be large enough to ensure adequate representation of cases in the subcells created in analysis.

The survey method is a tool. Like any tool, it is open to misuse. It can be used in providing evidence for sociological arguments or, as in any aspect of sociology, it can be used for ideological constructions. Surveys are expensive, so it tends to be people with power and resources who have used them most heavily.

68 The Human Element in Fieldwork

Robert A. Georges and Michael O. Jones

Two facts about the nature of fieldwork are seldom recognized, acknowledged or discussed. First, as individuals move from the planning to the implementation stages of their field research, they discover that they must engage continuously in a process of clarifying for others and for themselves just who they are, what it is they want to find out and why they wish to obtain the information they seek from the individuals they choose as subjects. Second, as fieldworkers interact with their selected subjects, they are confronted with the necessity of being willing and able to compromise. Unlike laboratory scientists, who can control the phenomena that are the focal points of their investigations by controlling the environments and conditions under which these phenomena are examined, individuals whose research plans call for them to study other human beings while interacting with them in non-laboratory settings must surrender a certain amount of the independence and control they enjoy while they are generating their fieldwork projects. For to gain the co-operation of those from whom they need to learn if they are to succeed in their endeavours, fieldworkers must explain, again and again, their identities and intentions in meaningful and acceptable ways. In seeking assistance, fieldworkers implicitly request permission to assume, and indicate their willingness to accept, a subordinate, dependent status *vis-à-vis* those they have chosen to study.

That fieldworkers must become largely dependent upon their research subjects is one of the ironies of fieldwork, creating a source of tension as fieldwork projects are implemented. The irony stems from the fact that while it is fieldworkers who elect to study others rather than others who choose to be studied by fieldworkers, it is the subjects who are knowledgeable, and the fieldworkers who are ignorant, about the phenomena or behaviours that fieldworkers decide to study. For their project plans to succeed, therefore, fieldworkers must be willing to learn and subjects to teach; and the pupil is necessarily subordinate to the teacher. Tensions arise because fieldworkers' conceptions of themselves as subordinate to their subjects conflict with their images of themselves as investigators to whom research subjects are subordinate. Dealing with this conflict creates an ambivalence with which both fieldworkers and subjects must cope. This coping requires clarifying identities and intentions for, and compromising with, both others and self.

Feelings of ambivalence that require fieldworkers to clarify identities and intentions and to compromise arise not only from the conflict between images of self as both independent and dependent, or dominant and subordinate, in their relations with their chosen subjects, but also from differences between themselves and their subjects that fieldworkers conceive to be significant. The differentiation may be based on any one of some combination of such factors as sex, age, race, nationality, native language, religious background, occupation, social or economic status, living environment, relative degree of technological know-how or overall lifestyle. The greater the significance of differences that fieldworkers conceive to exist between themselves and their chosen subjects, the greater the amount of conflict and ambivalence that is apt to arise, and the greater the number of clarifications and compromises that is likely to occur. [. . .]

Because they plan fieldwork projects and commit themselves to carrying them out, fieldworkers understandably feel that they have the right to become privy to the kinds of information they set out to obtain; yet they are also aware that their selected subjects are under no obligation to provide that information. Similarly, individuals may determine in advance that the successful implementation of their fieldwork projects is dependent upon their filming, photographing, tape-recording, sketching or making written records of the phenomena or behaviours they have singled out for study; yet they know that those they have chosen to study are not obliged to permit such activities. Individuals may also decide that to accomplish the objectives set forth in their research plans, they must interact on a day-to-day basis and for an extended period of time with their chosen subjects; yet they are also cognizant of the fact that subjects are not required to welcome, accept, accommodate or co-operate with them. Fieldworkers tend to assume as well that subjects have a responsibility to keep interview appointments, provide honest and full answers to questions and submit willingly to any tests or experiments that are part of research designs; yet they also know that their subjects' principal time commitments are not to the fieldworker, but rather to those whose relationships with them are permanent instead of temporary, and that subjects need not tell or do anything unless they choose to tell or do it, regardless of its importance to the fieldworker's aims. In fieldwork involving people studying people at first hand, in sum, rights and responsibilities cannot be legislated by the fieldworker, but must instead be negotiated by fieldworkers and subjects. The negotiating is continuous and requires repeated clarification and compromise.

69 Absolute and Relative Poverty in Britain:

An Illustration of Survey Work

Joanna Mack and Stewart Lansley

There has been a long tradition that has tried to define poverty narrowly in terms of health, aiming either for a universal standard or for a standard relative to a particular moment in time. There has been an equally long tradition that has seen a person's needs as being culturally and socially, as well as physically, determined. It is a view that recognizes that there is more to life than just existing. Two hundred years ago the economist Adam Smith wrote:

By necessaries, I understand not only commodities which are indispensably necessary for the support of life but whatever the custom of the country renders it indecent for creditable people, even of the lowest order, to be without. A linen shirt, for example, is strictly speaking not a necessity of life. The Greeks and Romans lived, I suppose, very comfortably though they had no linen. But in the present time . . . a creditable day-la-bourer would be ashamed to appear in public without a linen shirt, the want of which would be supposed to denote that disgraceful state of poverty.

This theme was adopted and first used for a more practical purpose by Charles Booth in his pioneering surveys of poverty in London from the late 1880s to the turn of the century. He defined the very poor as those whose means were insufficient 'according to the normal standards of life in this country'. [. . .]

The essentially relative nature of poverty is immediately obvious when viewing people's stand-ards of living in these broader terms. Purchases of consumer durables are specific to each genera-tion, or even each decade, and activities involving social participation have no meaning outside the society in which people live. This has long been recognized; Karl Marx wrote in 1849: 'Our needs and enjoyments spring from society; we measure them, therefore, by society and not by the objects of their satisfaction. Because they are of a social nature, they are of a relative nature.' [. . .]

[Yet] a body of opinion has persisted that places emphasis only on 'absolute' poverty. The fact that the poor in Britain today are better off than the poor of the past, and than the poor of other countries today, is seen to devalue their prob-lems. Dr Rhodes Boyson, as Minister for Social Security, gave his view of 'relative' poverty to the House of Commons in a debate on the rich and the poor called by the opposition:

Those on the poverty line in the United States earn more than 50 times the average income of someone in India. That is what relative poverty is all about. . . . Apparently, the more people earn, the more they believe poverty exists, presumably so that they can be pleased about the fact that it is not themselves who are poor.

Others, in contrast, have argued that the facts of starvation in the poorest countries of the world and the intense deprivations suffered by the poor of the past are not relevant to the problems of the poor of the industrialized world today. Tony Crosland, for example, argued not just for the importance of a concept of 'primary' poverty but also that

poverty is not, after all, an absolute, but a social or cultural concept. . . . This demands a relative, subjective view of poverty, since the unhappiness and injustice it creates, even when ill-health and malnutrition are avoided, lies in the enforced deprivation not of luxuries indeed, but of small comforts which others have and are seen to have, and which in the light of prevailing cultural standards are really 'conventional necessities'.

During the 1960s this view became widely accepted, as a result – at least in part – of the work of Professor Peter Townsend. For the last thirty years, Townsend has argued that poverty can only be viewed in terms of the concept of 'relative deprivation'. In his studies of poverty he has refined this concept, culminating in his 1969 survey of living standards. In his report of this comprehensive and influential study, Townsend defined poverty as follows:

Individuals, families and groups in the population can be said to be in poverty when they lack the resources to obtain the types of diet, participate in the activities and have the living conditions and amenities which are customary, or are at least widely encouraged or approved, in the societies to which they belong.

Although something like this definition of poverty would now be widely accepted, there remains immense room for debate about what exactly it means.

The central brief given to MORI, the survey specialists commissioned by London Weekend Television to design and conduct the *Breadline Britain* survey, was as follows:

The survey's first, and most important, aim is to try to discover whether there is a public consensus on what is an acceptable standard of living for Britain in 1983 and, if there is a consensus, who, if anyone, falls below that standard.

The idea underlying this is that a person is in 'poverty' when their standard of living falls below the minimum deemed necessary by current public opinion. This minimum may cover not only the basic essentials for survival (such as food) but also access, or otherwise, to participating in society and being able to play a social role.

The survey established, for the first time ever, that a majority of people see the necessities of life in Britain in the 1980s as covering a wide range of goods and activities, and that people judge a minimum standard of living on socially established criteria and not just the criteria of survival or subsistence.

Table 69.1 lists the thirty-five items that were tested, ranked by the proportion of respondents identifying each item as a 'necessity'. This ranking shows that there is a considerable degree of social consensus. Over nine in ten people are agreed about the importance of the following basic living conditions in the home:

- heating;
- an indoor toilet (not shared);
- a damp-free home;
- a bath (not shared); and
- beds for everyone.

The right of everyone, regardless of income, to exactly these sorts of basic minima was a key objective of postwar housing policy until the recent sharp cutbacks in public-sector housing investment.

The survey also found a considerable degree of consensus about the importance of a wide range of other goods and activities. More than two-thirds of the respondents classed the following items as necessities:

- enough money for public transport;
- a warm waterproof coat;
- three meals a day for children;
- self-contained accommodation;
- two pairs of all-weather shoes;
- a bedroom for every child over 10 of different sex;
- a refrigerator;
- toys for children;
- carpets;
- celebrations on special occasions such as Christmas;

Table 69.1   The public's perception of necessities

Standard-of-living items in rank order	% classing item as necessity	Standard-of-living items in rank order	% classing item as necessity
1 Heating to warm living areas of the home if it's cold	97	18 New, not second-hand, clothes	64
2 Indoor toilet (not shared with another household)	96	19 A hobby or leisure activity	64
3 Damp-free home	96	20 Two hot meals a day (for adults)	64
4 Bath (not shared with another household)	94	21 Meat or fish every other day	63
5 Beds for everyone in the household	94	22 Presents for friends or family once a year	63
6 Public transport for one's needs	88	23 A holiday away from home for one week a year, not with relatives	63
7 A warm waterproof coat	87	24 Leisure equipment for children e.g. sports equipment or a bicycle	57
8 Three meals a day for children	82	25 A garden	55
9 Self-contained accommodation	79	26 A television	51
10 Two pairs of all-weather shoes	78	27 A 'best outfit' for special occasions	48
11 Enough bedrooms for every child over 10 of different sex to have his/her own	77	28 A telephone	43
12 Refrigerator	77	29 An outing for children once a week	43
13 Toys for children	71	30 A dressing gown	40
14 Carpets in living rooms and bedrooms	70	31 Children's friends round for tea/a snack once a fortnight	37
15 Celebrations on special occasions such as Christmas	70	32 A night out once a fortnight (adults)	36
16 A roast meat joint or its equivalent once a week	67	33 Friends/family round for a meal once a month	32
17 A washing machine	67	34 A car	22
		35 A packet of cigarettes every other day	14

Average of all 35 items = 64.1

- a roast joint or its equivalent once a week; and
- a washing machine.

This widespread consensus on what are necessities clearly reflects the standards of today and not those of the past. In Rowntree's study of poverty in York in 1899, for a family to be classed as poor 'they must never spend a penny on railway fare or omnibus'. In Britain in the 1980s, nearly nine in ten people think that such spending is not only justified but a necessity for living today.

70 Conversation Analysis

John Heritage

The inception and development of conversation analysis as a distinctive field of research is closely linked with problems surrounding the tendency for ordinary language descriptions to gloss or idealize the specifics of what they depict. This tendency is inherent in the use of type concepts in the social sciences irrespective of whether the types are produced by 'averaging' as recommended by Durkheim[1] or by explicit idealization as proposed by Weber in his various methodological writings. In an early paper, Sacks criticized the use of both of these categories of type concepts in sociology on the grounds that they necessarily blur the specific features of the events under investigation.[2] The result, he argued, is that sociological concepts and generalizations can have only a vague and indeterminate relationship with any specific set of events. This, in turn, inhibits the development of sociology as a cumulative body of knowledge because, given this indeterminacy, it can be difficult to decide whether a specific case in fact supports or undermines a given sociological generalization.

Sacks's response to this problem was a deliberate decision to develop a method of analysis which would keep a grip on the primary data of the social world – the raw material of specific, singular events of human conduct:

When I started to do research in sociology I figured that sociology could not be an actual science unless it was able to handle the details of actual events, handle them formally, and in the first instance be informative about them in the direct ways in which primitive sciences tend to be informative, that is, that anyone else can go and see whether what was said is so. And that

is a tremendous control on seeing whether one is learning anything. So the question was, could there be some way that sociology could hope to deal with the details of actual events, formally and informatively? . . . I wanted to locate some set of materials that would permit a test.[3]

Sacks's work on tape-recorded conversation was initiated in deliberate pursuit of this methodological aim:

It was not from any large interest in language or from some theoretical formulation of what should be studied that I started with tape-recorded conversation, but simply because I could get my hands on it and I could study it again and again, and also, consequentially, because others could look at what I had studied and make of it what they could, if, for example, they wanted to be able to disagree with me.[4]

The contemporary methodology of conversation analysis has maintained Sacks's pioneering focus on the details of actual interactions and his effort to forestall the process of idealization. Its insistence on the use of data collected from naturally occurring occasions of everyday interaction is paralleled by a corresponding *avoidance of a range of other research methodologies as unsatisfactory* sources of data. These include: (1) the use of interviewing techniques in which the verbal formulations of subjects are treated as an appropriate substitute for the observation of actual behaviour; (2) the use of observational methods in which data are recorded through field notes or with pre-coded schedules; (3) the use of native intuitions as a means of inventing examples of interactional behaviour; and (4) the use of experimental methodologies involving the direction or manipulation of behaviour. These techniques have been avoided because each of them involves processes in which the specific details of naturally situated interactional conduct are irretrievably lost and are replaced by idealizations about how interaction works.

A range of considerations inform this preference for the use of recorded data over subjects' reports, observers' notes or unaided intuition or recollection. Anyone who has examined conversational materials will be highly conscious of the deficiencies of such resources by comparison with the richness and diversity of empirically occurring interaction. For example, although the following sequence is by no means extraordinary, it is difficult to imagine its invention by a social scientist.

(1) (NB:VII:2)[5]
    E: = Oh honey that was a lovely luncheon
          I shoulda ca:lled you s:soo::ner but I: I:
    M: ((f)) Oh:::
    E: lo:ved it. It w's just deli:ghtfu:l.
    M: (   )   Well =
    M: = I w's gla d   you (came).
    E: 'nd yer f: friends 're so da:rli:ng, =
    M: = Oh::::: it w'z:
    E: e-that P- a:t isn'she a do::ll?
    M: iYe-
          h isn't she pretty,
          (.)
    E: Oh: she's a beautiful girl. =
    M: = Yeh I think she's a pretty girl.
    E: En' that
          Reinam'n::
          (.)
    E: She SCA:RES me. =

Not only is it impossible to imagine the above being invented, it is similarly inconceivable that it could be recollected in such detail either by an ethnographer or by an actual participant. And, even if it could be recollected, it could not be heard again and again. Moreover, as Sacks notes, it can be difficult to treat invented or recollected sequences as fully persuasive evidence for analytic claims.[6] And even if they are accepted, such inven-

tions or recollections can tell us nothing about the frequency, range, variety or typicality of the conversational procedures within the fragment.

The intuitive invention of data is subject to an additional problem which has nothing to do with complexity, but everything to do with the way unaided intuition tends to typify the ways interaction happens. Consider (2) below:

(2) A: I have a fourteen-year-old son.
     B: Well that's alright.
     A: I also have a dog.
     B: Oh I'm sorry.

Although (2) is simple enough, it is not the way we imagine interaction happens. If it had been invented, it might have been used to show what is meant by incoherent interaction. But in fact (2) is taken from a conversation in which the would-be tenant of an apartment (A) is describing circumstances to the landlord (B) which might disqualify the rental and, viewed in this context, the datum is perfectly coherent and sensible. The myriad ways in which specific contexts (e.g. particular social identities, purposes and circumstances) are talked into being and orientated to in interaction vastly exceed the comparatively limited, and overwhelmingly typified, powers of imaginative intuition.

A similar range of issues arises in relation to experimentally produced data. The success of social-psychological experiments is strongly dependent on the experimenter's ability to identify, control and manipulate the relevant dependent and independent variables. Not only is this extremely difficult to accomplish without some form of experimenter contamination, but also it is unlikely that an experimenter will be able to identify the range of relevant variables without previous exposure to naturally occurring interaction. Moreover, without such exposure the experimenter will find it difficult to extrapolate from experimental findings to real situations of conduct, nor will it prove easy to determine which (if any) of the experimental findings are artefacts of the experimental situation, since such a determination can only be achieved by systematic comparison with naturally occurring data. In sum, the most straightforward procedure has been to work with naturally occurring materials from the outset. Naturally occurring interaction presents an immense range of interactional variations in terms of which systematic comparisons may be used both to check and to extend particular analyses.

Thus the use of recorded data is an essential corrective to the limitations of intuition and recollection. In enabling repeated and detailed examination of the events of interaction, the use of recordings extends the range and precision of the observations which can be made. It permits other researchers to have direct access to the data about which claims are being made, thus making analysis subject to detailed public scrutiny and helping to minimize the influence of personal preconceptions or analytical biases. Finally, it may be noted that because the data are available in 'raw' form they can be reused in a variety of investigations and can be re-examined in the context of new findings. All of these major advantages derive from the fact that the original data are neither idealized nor constrained by a specific research design or by reference to some particular theory or hypothesis.

NOTES

1 É. Durkheim, *The Rules of Sociological Method* (London: Routledge and Kegan Paul, 1982 [1897]).

2 H. Sacks, 'Sociological Description', *Berkeley Journal of Sociology*, 8 (1963), pp. 1–16.

3 H. Sacks, unpublished lectures, transcribed and indexed by G. Jefferson (University of California at Irvine, 1964–72).

4 Ibid.

5 Transcription conventions: a single left bracket [indicates the point of overlap onset; a single right bracket] indicates the point at which an utterance or utterance part terminates *vis-à-vis* another; (.) indicates a tiny 'gap' within or between utterances . . . probably no more than one-tenth of a second; :: colons indicate prolongation of the immediately prior sound – the length of the colon row indicates length of the prolongation; WORD upper case, indicates especially loud sound.

6 H. Sacks, 'Methodological remarks', in J. M. Atkinson and J. C. Heritage (eds), *Structures of Social Action: Studies in Conversation Analysis* (Cambridge: Cambridge University Press, 1984).

Part 21 Theoretical Thinking in Sociology

Most sociologists either stress that social phenomena are independent of the intentions and reasons individuals have for what they do, or emphasize such reasons and intentions to the exclusion of structural influences. As suggested in Reading 71, we need to develop an outlook in sociological theory which acknowledges the structural features of social systems, yet gives full recognition to the significance of 'meaningful' action. Such a perspective implies a reassessment of the relation between sociology and common-sense beliefs, since such beliefs are core elements of the meaningful activities of social actors.

Ulrich Beck's concept of 'risk society' has been referred to in several earlier readings in this volume. It has proved to be one of the most important theoretical concepts in sociology in recent years. For Beck the theme connects to a broad analysis of modernization. In the industrial era modernization was a 'simple' process – an accumulation of social and economic changes which simply 'happened'. In the contemporary information era modernization has become 'reflexive'. Beck means by this that we constantly have to pay attention to monitoring the consequences of the changes we experience. Managing risk, on both a personal and an institutional level, is a key part of this process of reflexivity.

Jürgen Habermas is one of the most influential of current social thinkers. Although Habermas is primarily a philosopher, his works have had a major impact in sociology. Habermas seems to keep alive Marx's idea that we need to study society in a critical way with a view to structural reform. Critical theory today, Habermas acknowledges, can't draw much direct inspiration from Marx, since following the fall of communism in the Soviet Union and Eastern Europe Marxism is largely a lapsed project. A critical theory of society today must be orientated to creating a just and humane society within an essentially capitalistic framework.

71 Sociology and the Explanation of Human Behaviour

Anthony Giddens

The 'sociological' direction of modern philosophy involves a recovery of the everyday or the mundane. Our day-to-day activities are not merely inconsequential habits, of no interest to the student of more profound matters, but on the contrary are relevant the explication of quite basic issues in philosophy and in social science. Common sense is thus not to be dismissed as merely the inertia of habit or as a set of semi-formulated ideas of no importance to social analysis. To develop this observation further, however, we have to enquire a little more deeply into what common sense is. We cannot necessarily understand the term 'common sense' in a common-sense way.

Although no doubt more finely honed distinctions could be made, I shall distinguish two basic meanings of 'common sense'. One of these I call 'mutual knowledge' and separate from what can simply be called 'common sense' understood generically. By mutual knowledge I refer to knowledge of convention which actors must possess in common in order to make sense of what both they and other actors do in the course of their day-to-day social lives. Meanings are produced and reproduced via the practical application and continued reformulation in practice of 'what everyone knows'. As I would understand it, the programme of ethnomethodology consists in the detailed study of the nature and variations of mutual knowledge. Mutual knowledge refers to the methods used by lay actors to generate the practices which are constitutive of the tissue of social life. It is in substantial part non-discursive. That is to say, to use [Ludwig] Wittgenstein's phrase, it consists of the capability to 'go on' in the routines of social life.

Not having any place for a concept of mutual knowledge, naturalistic social science presumes that the descriptive terminology of social analysis can be developed solely within professionally articulated theories. But in order to generate valid descriptions of social life, the sociological observer must employ the same elements of mutual knowledge used by participants to 'bring off' what they do. To be able to generate veridical descriptions of social activity means in principle being able to 'go on' in that activity, knowing what its constituent actors know in order to accomplish what they do. [. . .] The implications of the point are rich. All social analysis has a 'hermeneutic' or 'ethnographic' moment, which was simply dissolved in traditional mainstream social science.

There is one way in which a grasp of the inescapably hermeneutic character of social science provides an answer to the question of its enlightening possibilities. That is to say, we might suppose [. . .] that what is 'new' in social science concerns only descriptions of forms of life (either in unfamiliar settings in our own culture, or in other cultures). In the view of the naturalistic social scientist, of course, the claim that social analysis can be no more than ethnography is absurd [. . .] But it is a proposition that deserves to be taken seriously. For there is a sense in which lay agents must always 'know what they are doing' in the course of their daily activities. Their knowledge of what they do is not just incidental but is constitutively involved in that doing. If they already not only do know, but in at least one sense *must* know what they are doing, it might seem that social science cannot deliver 'findings' with which the actors involved are not already familiar. At a minimum we must accept that the conditions under which the social sciences can deliver enlightenment to lay actors are more complex than was presumed in naturalistic social science.

What forms, then, might such enlightenment assume? The following considerations provide the basis of an answer.

1 It has to be accepted that the ethnographic tasks of social science are indeed fundamentally important. That is to say, all of us live within specific cultures which differ from other cultures distributed across the world, and from others 'recoverable' by historical analysis. In modern societies we also all live in specific contexts of larger cultural totalities. The 'news value' of the ethnographic description of culturally alien settings is certainly a significant element in social science.

2 Second, social science can 'display' – that is, give discursive form to – aspects of mutual knowledge which lay actors employ non-discursively in their conduct. The term 'mutual knowledge' covers a diversity of practical techniques of making sense of social activities, the study of which is a task of social science in its own right. As I have already mentioned, it can be construed as the task of ethnomethodology to provide such a 'display' of the taken-for-granted practicalities of our conduct. We might also instance, however, the writings of Erving Goffman as of singular importance in this respect. Perhaps more than any other single writer, Goffman has made clear how complicated, how subtle – but how routinely managed – are the components of mutual knowledge. We might also remark that the whole of linguistics is concerned with the 'display' of mutual knowledge. Linguistics is about what the language user

knows, and must know, to be able to speak whatever language is in question. However, most of what we 'know' in order to speak a language, we know non-discursively. Linguistics tells us what we already know, but in a discursive form quite distinct from the typical modes of expression of such knowledge.

3 A matter of very considerable significance – social science can investigate the unintended consequences of purposive action. Actors always know what they are doing (under some description or potential description), but the consequences of what they do characteristically escape what they intend. A nest of interesting problems and puzzles is to be found here, and I shall only discuss them briefly. Naturalistic versions of social science depend for their cogency upon the observation that many of the events and processes in social life are not intended by any of the participants involved. It is in the 'escape' of social institutions from the purposes of individual actors that the tasks of social science are discovered. In this respect we must in some part continue to defend the version of social science advanced by the 'mainstream' against more 'interpretative' conceptions. A characteristic failing of those traditions of thought which have done most to bring into focus the significance of mundane social practices is that they have ignored altogether the unintended consequences of social activity. But it would be futile to imagine that the issue was adequately handled in naturalistic social science. For the naturalistic sociologist, the unintended character of much social activity is wedded to the view that social life can be analysed in terms of the operation of factors of which social actors are ignorant. But it is one thing to argue that some of the main parameters of social activity are unintended by those who participate in that activity; it is quite another to presume that, consequently, individual agents are acted upon by 'social causes' which somehow determine the course of what they do. Far from reinforcing such a conclusion, a proper appreciation of the significance of the unintended consequences of action should lead us to emphasize the importance of a sophisticated

treatment of the purposive nature of human conduct. What is unintentional cannot be even characterized unless we are clear about the nature of what is intentional; and this, I would argue, also presumes an account of agents' reasons.

There are several different types of enquiry that relate to the role of unintended consequences in human action. For example, we might be interested in asking why a singular event occurred in spite of no one's intending it to occur. Thus a historian might pose the question: why did World War I break out, when none of the main parties involved intended [its] actions to produce such an outcome? However, the type of question with which naturalistic social scientists have traditionally been preoccupied concerns the conditions of social reproduction. That is to say, they have sought to demonstrate that social institutions have properties which extend beyond the specific contexts of interaction in which individuals are involved. The connection between functionalism and naturalism has specific application here. For the point of functional explanation has normally been to show that there are 'reasons' for the existence and continuance of social institutions that are quite distinct from the reasons actors might have for whatever they do.

In recent years, partly as a result of a renewed critical examination of functionalism, it has become apparent that an account of institutional reproduction need not, and should not, have recourse to functional interpretations at all. Human social systems do not have needs, except as counterfactually posited 'as if' properties. It is perfectly appropriate, and often necessary, to enquire what conditions are needed for the persistence of a given set of social institutions over a specified period of time. But such an enquiry invites analysis of the mechanics of social reproduction, it does not supply an explanation for them. All large-scale social reproduction occurs under conditions of 'mixed intentionality'. In other words, the perpetuation of social institutions involves some kind of mix of intended and unintended outcomes of action. What this mix is, however, has to be carefully analysed and is historically variable. There is a range of circumstances which separate 'highly monitored' conditions of system reproduction from those involving a feedback of unintended consequences. The monitoring of conditions of system reproduction is undoubtedly a phenomenon associated with the emergence of modern society and with the formation of modern organizations generally. However, the intersection between intended and unintended consequences in respect of institutional reproduction is variable and in all instances needs to be concretely studied. A double objection can be made to explaining social reproduction in terms of statements of the form 'the function of x is . . .'. The first is, as already stated, that such a statement has no explanatory value, and can only be rendered intelligible when applied to social activity in the form of a counterfactual proposition. The second is that the statement is ambiguous in respect of intentionality. In conditions in which reproduction is 'highly monitored', the tie between purposes (of some agents) and the continuity of social institutions will be direct and pervasive. Where an unintended feedback operates, the mechanics of the reproduction process will be quite different. It is normally essential to distinguish the difference.

72 Risk Society: Towards a New Modernity

Ulrich Beck
translated by *Mark Ritter*

On the logic of wealth distribution and risk distribution

In advanced modernity the social production of *wealth* is systematically accompanied by the social production of *risks*. Accordingly, the problems and conflicts relating to distribution in a society of scarcity overlap with the problems and conflicts that arise from the production, definition and distribution of techno-scientifically produced risks.

This change from the logic of wealth distribution in a society of scarcity to the logic of risk distribution in late modernity is connected historically to (at least) two conditions. First, it occurs – as is recognizable today – where and to the extent that *genuine material need* can be objectively reduced and socially isolated through the development of human and technological productivity, as well as through legal and welfare-state protections and regulations. Second, this categorical change is likewise dependent upon the fact that in the course of the exponentially growing productive forces in the modernization process, hazards and potential threats have been unleashed to an extent previously unknown.[1]

To the extent that these conditions occur, one historical type of thinking and acting is relativized or overridden by another. The concepts of 'industrial' or 'class society', in the broadest sense of Marx or Weber, revolved around the issue of how socially produced wealth could be distributed in a socially unequal and *also* 'legitimate' way. This overlaps with the new *paradigm of risk society* which is based on the solution of a similar and yet quite different problem. How can the risks and hazards systematically produced as part of modernization be prevented, minimized, dramatized, or channeled? Where they do finally see the light of day in the shape of 'latent side effects', how can they be limited and distributed away so that they neither hamper the modernization process nor exceed the limits of that which is 'tolerable' – ecologically, medically, psychologically and socially?

We are therefore concerned no longer exclusively with making nature useful, or with releasing mankind from traditional constraints, but also and essentially with problems resulting from techno-economic development itself. Modernization is becoming *reflexive*; it is becoming its own theme. Questions of the development and employment of technologies (in the realms of nature, society and the personality) are being eclipsed by questions of the political and economic 'management' of the risks of actually or potentially utilized technologies – discovering, administering, acknowledging, avoiding or concealing such hazards with respect to specially defined horizons of relevance. The promise of security grows with the risks and destruction and must be reaffirmed over and over again to an alert and critical public through cosmetic or real interventions in the techno-economic development.

Both 'paradigms' of inequality are systematically related to definite periods of modernization. The distribution of socially produced wealth and related conflicts occupy the foreground so long as obvious material need, the 'dictatorship of scarcity', rules the thought and action of people (as today in large parts of the so-called Third World). Under these conditions of 'scarcity society', the modernization process takes place with the claim of opening the gates to hidden sources of social wealth with the keys of techno-scientific development. These promises of emancipation from undeserved poverty and dependence underlie action, thought and research in the categories of social inequality, from the class through the stratified to the individualized society.

In the welfare states of the West a double process is taking place now. On the one hand, the struggle for one's 'daily bread' has lost its urgency as a cardinal problem overshadowing everything else, compared to material subsistence in the first half of [the twentieth] century and to a Third World menaced by hunger. For many people problems of 'overweight' take the place of hunger. This development, however, withdraws the legitimizing basis from the modernization process, the struggle against obvious scarcity, for which one was prepared to accept a few (no longer completely) unseen side effects.

Parallel to that, the knowledge is spreading that the sources of wealth are 'polluted' by growing 'hazardous side effects'. This is not at all new, but it has remained unnoticed for a long time in the efforts to overcome poverty. This dark side is also gaining importance through the overdevelopment of productive forces. In the modernization process, more and more *destructive* forces are also being unleashed, forces before which the human imagination stands in awe. Both sources feed a growing critique of modernization, which loudly and contentiously determines public discussions.

In systematic terms, sooner or later in the continuity of modernization the social positions and conflicts of a 'wealth-distributing' society begin to be joined by those of a 'risk-distributing' society. [...] That means that two types of topics and conflicts overlap here. We do not *yet* live in a risk society, but we also no longer live *only* within the distribution conflicts of scarcity societies. To the extent that this transition occurs, there will be a real transformation of society which will lead us out of the previous modes of thought and action.

Can the concept of risk carry the theoretical and historical significance which is demanded of it here? Is this not a primeval phenomenon of human action? Are not risks already characteristic of the industrial society period, against which they are being differentiated here? It is also true that risks are not an invention of modernity. Anyone who set out to discover new countries and continents – like Columbus – certainly accepted 'risks'. But these were personal risks, not global dangers like those that arise for all of humanity from nuclear fission or the storage of radioactive waste. In that earlier period, the word 'risk' had a note of bravery and adventure, not the threat of self-destruction of all life on Earth.

Forests have also been dying for some centuries now – first through being transformed into fields, then through reckless overcutting. But the death of forests today occurs *globally*, as the *implicit* consequence of industrialization – with quite different social and political consequences. Heavily wooded countries like Norway and Sweden, which hardly have any pollutant-intensive industries of their own, are also affected. They have to settle up the pollution accounts of other highly industrialized countries with dying trees, plants and animal species.

It is reported that sailors who fell into the Thames in the early nineteenth century did not drown, but rather choked to death inhaling the foul-smelling and poisonous fumes of this London sewer. A walk through the narrow streets of a medieval city would also have been like running the gauntlet for the nose, 'Excrement piles up everywhere, in the streets, at the turnpikes, in the carriages . . . The façades of Parisian houses are decomposing from urine . . . the socially organized constipation threatens to pull all of Paris into the process of putrescent decomposition'. It is nevertheless striking that hazards in those days assaulted the nose or the eyes and were thus perceptible to the senses, while the risks of civilization today typically *escape perception* and are localized in the sphere of *physical and chemical formulas* (e.g. toxins in foodstuffs or the nuclear threat).

Another difference is directly connected to this. In the past, the hazards could be traced back to an *under*supply of hygienic technology. Today they have their basis in industrial *over*production. The risks and hazards of today thus differ in an essential way from the superficially similar ones in the Middle Ages through the global nature of their threat (people, animals and plants) and through their *modern* causes. They are risks *of modernization*. They are a *wholesale product* of industrialization, and are systematically intensified as it becomes global.

The concept of risk is directly bound to the concept of reflexive modernization. *Risk* may be defined as a *systematic way of dealing with hazards and insecurities induced and introduced by modernization itself*. Risks, as opposed to older dangers, are consequences which relate to the threatening force of modernization and to its globalization of doubt. They are *politically reflexive*.

Risks, in this meaning of the word, are certainly as old as that development itself. The immiseration of large parts of the population – the 'poverty risk' – kept the nineteenth century holding its breath. 'Threats to skills' and 'health risks' have long been a theme of automation processes and the related social conflicts, protections (and research). It did take some time and struggle to establish social welfare state norms and minimize or limit these kinds of risk politically. Nevertheless, the ecological and high-tech risks that have upset the public for some years now, which will be the focus of what follows, have a new quality. In the afflictions they produce they are no longer tied to their place of origin – the industrial plant. By their nature they endanger *all* forms of life on this planet. The normative bases of their calculation – the concept of accident and insurance, medical precautions, and so on – do not fit the basic dimensions of these modern threats. Atomic plants, for example, are not privately insured or insurable. Atomic accidents are accidents no more (in the limited sense of the word 'accident'). They outlast generations. The affected even include

those not yet alive at the time or in the place where the accident occurred but born years later and long distances away.

This means that the calculation of risk as it has been established so far by science and legal institutions *collapses*. Dealing with these consequences of modern productive and destructive forces in the normal terms of risk is a false but nevertheless very effective way of legitimizing them. Risk scientists normally do so as if there is not the gap of a century between the local accidents of the nineteenth century and the often creeping, catastrophic potentials at the end of the twentieth century. Indeed, if you distinguish between calculable and non-calculable threats, under the surface of risk calculation new kinds of *industrialized, decision-produced incalculabilities and threats* are spreading within the globalization of high-risk industries, whether for warfare or welfare purposes. Max Weber's concept of 'rationalization' no longer grasps this late modern reality, produced by successful rationalization. *Along with the growing capacity of technical options [. . .] grows the incalculability of their consequences.* Compared to these global consequences, the hazards of primary industrialization indeed belonged to a different age. The dangers of highly developed nuclear and chemical productive forces abolish the foundations and categories according to which we have thought and acted to this point, such as space and time, work and leisure time, factory and nation state, indeed even the borders between continents. To put it differently, in the risk society the unknown and unintended consequences come to be a dominant force in history and society.[2]

The social architecture and political dynamics of such potentials for self-endangerment in civilization will occupy the center of these discussions. The argument can be set out in five theses:

1 Risks such as those produced in the late modernity differ essentially from wealth. By risks I mean above all radioactivity, which completely evades human perceptive abilities, but also toxins and pollutants in the air, the water and foodstuffs, together with the accompanying short- and long-term effects on plants, animals and people. They induce systematic and often *irreversible*

harm, generally remain *invisible*, are based on *causal interpretations*, and thus initially only exist in terms of the (scientific or anti-scientific) *knowledge* about them. They can thus be changed, magnified, dramatized or minimized within knowledge, and to that extent they are particularly *open to social definition and construction*. Hence the mass media and the scientific and legal professions in charge of defining risks become key social and political positions.

2 Some people are more affected than others by the distribution and growth of risks, that is, *social risk positions* spring up. In some of their dimensions these follow the inequalities of class and strata positions, but they bring a fundamentally different distributional logic into play. Risks of modernization sooner or later also strike those who produce or profit from them. They contain a *boomerang effect*, which breaks up the pattern of class and national society. Ecological disaster and atomic fallout ignore the borders of nations. Even the rich and powerful are not safe from them. These are hazards not only to health, but also to legitimation, property and profit. *Connected* to the recognition of modernization risks are *ecological devaluations and expropriations*, which frequently and systematically enter into contradiction to the profit and property interests which advance the process of industrialization. Simultaneously, risks produce *new international inequalities*, firstly between the Third World and the industrial states, secondly among the industrial states themselves. They undermine the order of national jurisdictions. In view of the universality and supra-nationality of the circulation of pollutants, the life of a blade of grass in the Bavarian Forest ultimately comes to depend on the making and keeping of international agreements. Risk society in this sense is a world risk society.

3 Nevertheless, the diffusion and commercialization of risks do not break with the logic of capitalist development completely, but instead they raise the latter to a new stage. There are always losers but also winners in risk definitions. The space between them varies in relation to different issues and power differentials. Modernization risks from the winners' points of view are *big business*.

They are the insatiable demands long sought by economists. Hunger can be sated, needs can be satisfied, but *civilization* risks are a *bottomless barrel of demands*, unsatisfiable, infinite, self-producible. One could say along with Luhmann that with the advent of risks, the economy becomes 'self-referential', independent of the surrounding satisfaction of human needs. But that means: with the economic exploitation of the risks it sets free, industrial society produces the hazards and the political potential of the risk society.

4 One can *possess* wealth, but one can only be *afflicted* by risks; they are, so to speak, *ascribed* by civilization. [Bluntly, one might say: in class and stratification positions being determines consciousness, while in risk positions *consciousness determines being*.] Knowledge gains a new political significance. Accordingly the political potential of the risk society must be elaborated and analysed in a sociological theory of the origin and diffusion of *knowledge about risks*.

5 Socially recognized risks, as appears clearly in the discussions of forest destruction, contain a peculiar political explosive: what *was* until now *considered unpolitical becomes political* – the elimination of the causes in the industrialization process itself. Suddenly the public and politics extend their rule into the private sphere of plant management – into product planning and technical equipment. What is at stake in the public dispute over the definition of risks is revealed here in an exemplary fashion: not just secondary health problems for nature and mankind, but the *social, economic and political consequences of these side effects* – collapsing markets, devaluation of capital, bureaucratic checks on plant decisions, the opening of new markets, mammoth costs, legal proceedings and loss of face. In smaller or larger increments – a smog alarm, a toxic spill, etc. – what thus emerges in risk society is the *political potential of catastrophes*. Averting and managing these can include a *reorganization of power and authority*. Risk society is a *catastrophic* society. In it the exceptional condition threatens to become the norm.

[. . .]

73 Introduction to Habermas

David Held

[...]

[Jürgen] Habermas conceives of his project as an attempt to develop a theory of society with a practical intention: the self-emancipation of people from domination. Through an assessment of the self-formative processes of the human species, Habermas's critical theory aims to further the self-understanding of social groups capable of transforming society. While the status he ascribes to his enterprise has changed, and a greater emphasis has been placed in recent times on what he calls its 'empirical-theoretical' or 'empirical reconstructive' tasks, critical theory remains designed to help in the making of history 'with will and consciousness'. In order to defend the idea of a critical theory of society, Habermas has been concerned systematically to develop its philosophical underpinnings. This involves a reconstruction of some of the central theses of classical Greek and German philosophy: the inseparability of truth and virtue, of facts and values, of theory and practice. The project is defined as a 'struggle for the critical soul of science' and 'the scientific soul of criticism'.

The imperative to reformulate critical theory derives its force, for Habermas, from the 'course of history'. He maintains that twentieth-century history is characterized by a number of major developments in socialist and capitalist societies. The degeneration of the Russian revolution into Stalinism and technocratic social management; the failure hitherto of mass revolution in the West; the absence of mass proletarian revolutionary class consciousness; the frequent collapse of Marxist

theory into either a deterministic, objectivistic science or a pessimistic cultural critique: all, he holds, are important features of recent times. He sees structural changes in capitalist society as having altered both its appearance and its essence. State intervention grows; the market-place is supported and replaced; capitalism is increasingly 'organized'; instrumental reason and bureaucracy, seeming ever to expand, threaten the public sphere, the sphere in which political life is discussed openly by a reasoning public. Habermas contends that in light of these events, doubt can be cast on the validity of Marx's work, the general Marxian framework and on many other well known theories of society. He finds it necessary, therefore, to assess, and in fact reformulate, the major traditions of social thought.

The events of the 1960s, particularly the advent of the student movement, also had a significant impact on his thinking. Initially, Habermas was a leading spokesman for the movement and, in fact, for all those who sought a radical democratization of society. However, by the late 1960s, he had become estranged from the movement's leading groups. He was critical of what he saw as their departure from their original democratic and non-authoritarian goals. Instead of struggling for an expansion of the sphere of freedom and initiative, they were working, he believed, to impose new restrictions on thought and action. The students in turn criticized Habermas for, among other things, failing to become involved in actual struggles, retreating into theoretical reflection, and for uniting theory and practice in theory only. Since this time Habermas appears to have put less emphasis on the practical-political aspects of his programme. He has sought to defend and elaborate his theoretical interests, only pointing occasionally to their practical implications.

[. . .]

Habermas's project: an overview of fundamental concepts

[. . .] Habermas's views have changed over time and, indeed, are still in the process of development. He often gives his positions a tentative and programmatic status – they are part of an on-going project. The positions he elaborated and defended in his important *Knowledge and Human Interests* (1968) have been modified and, in many cases, substantially reworked. His conception of the logical structure of critical theory has altered and with it his view of the nature of social science. [. . .]

A major concern of Habermas's [. . .] has been the spread of instrumental reason to many areas of social life. The rise of technocratic consciousness, with its disintegrative effect on the public sphere, is discussed at two fundamental levels. At the level of social theory Habermas argues that the increasing tendency to define practical problems as technical issues threatens an essential aspect of human life; for technocratic consciousness not only justifies a particular class interest in domination, but also affects the very structure of human interests. Accordingly, reflection on this state of affairs must, on Habermas's account, 'penetrate beyond the level of particular historical class interests to disclose the fundamental interests of mankind as such'.

[. . .]

Like Horkheimer, Habermas contends that knowledge is historically rooted and interest-bound. But he understands this in quite different terms from his predecessor. In *Knowledge and Human Interests* and *Theory and Practice*, Habermas develops the theory of cognitive interests (or knowledge-constitutive interests), the important first stage in his elaboration of the relationship of knowledge to human activity. In more recent work he has extended this inquiry and formulated the theory of 'communicative competence'. These complex theories have been developed in order to justify the critical enterprise.

The theory of cognitive interests is concerned with uncovering the conditions for the possibility of knowledge. While accepting the need to understand knowledge as the result of the constituting activity of the cognizing subject, Habermas rejects the [. . .] approach of locating such activity in an ahistorical, transcendental subject. Rather, starting with an essential tenet of historical materialism – that history, social reality and nature (as known) are all a product of the constituting labour of the human species – Habermas understands knowledge in light of the problems man encounters in his efforts to 'produce his existence and reproduce his species being'. The conditions of the constitution of knowledge which determine 'the structure of objects of possible experience', are the historical material conditions in which the development of the species has occurred.

It is Habermas's contention that the human species organizes its experience in terms of *a priori* interests, or cognitive interests or knowledge-guiding interests. That there is a 'basis of interests' follows, he argues, from an understanding of humans as both toolmaking and language-using animals: they must produce from nature what is needed for material existence through the manipulation and control of objects and communicate with others through the use of intersubjectively understood symbols within the context of rule-governed institutions. Thus, humankind has an interest in the creation of knowledge which would enable it to control objectified processes and to maintain communication. There is, however, on his account, a third interest: an interest in the reflective appropriation of human life, without which the interest-bound character of knowledge could not itself be grasped. This is an interest in reason, in the human capacity to be self-reflective and self-determining, to act rationally. As a result of it, knowledge is generated which enhances autonomy and responsibility [. . .]; hence, it is an emancipatory interest. Cognitive interests, which are the transcendental conditions of knowledge, are themselves naturalistically grounded. That is, the rule systems governing the activities of the species 'have a transcendental function but arise from actual structures of human life'. Habermas accords to the category of 'cognitive interests' a somewhat problematic status as 'quasi-transcendental'.

The end point of this analysis – of the mode in which reality is disclosed, constituted and acted upon – is a trichotomous model of the human species' *interests* ('anthropologically rooted strategies for interpreting life experience'), *media* (means of social organization) and *sciences*. The interests are the technical, the practical and the emancipatory. These unfold in three media, work (instrumental action), interaction (language) and power (asymmetrical relations of constraint and dependency) and give rise to the conditions for the possibility of three sciences, the empirical-analytic, the historical-hermeneutic and the critical. It is one of Habermas's central claims that these three sciences only systematize and formalize the procedures required for the success of human activity.

The theory of cognitive interests, as developed in *Knowledge and Human Interests*, represents Habermas's initial attempt to specify the relation between knowledge and human activity. He has recently recognized, however, the need to examine this relation further – particularly, the distinction between processes of constitution and justification. This he attempts to do in the theory of communicative competence.

In this theory Habermas argues that all speech is oriented to the idea of a genuine consensus – a discursively achieved consensus – which is rarely realized. The analysis of consensus, he claims, shows this notion to involve a normative dimension, which is formalized in the concept of what he calls 'an ideal speech situation'. A consensus attained in this situation, referred to as a 'rational consensus', is, in Habermas's opinion, the ultimate criterion of the truth of a statement or of the correctness of norms. The end result of this argument is that the very structure of speech is held to involve the anticipation of a form of life in which truth, freedom and justice are possible. On Habermas's account, the critical theory of society makes this its starting point. Critical theory is, therefore, grounded in a normative standard that is not arbitrary, but 'inherent in the very structure of social action and language'. It is just this anticipation of an ideal form of discourse which can be used as a normative standard for a critique of distorted communication. It is Habermas's contention that in every communicative situation in which a consensus is established under coercion or under other similar types of condition, we are likely to be confronting instances of systematically distorted communication. This is, in his view, the contemporary formulation of ideology. [. . .] The process of emancipation [. . .] entails the transcendence of such systems of distorted communication. This process, in turn, requires engaging in critical reflection and criticism. It is only through reflection that domination, in its many forms, can be unmasked.

[. . .]

Human beings' capacity for freedom is dependent, on Habermas's account, on cumulative learning in theoretical and practical activity. Through such learning, knowledge is generated that makes possible the technical mastery of the natural and social world and the organization and alteration of social relations; that is, the expansion of the sphere of 'sensuous human activity' or praxis. Habermas analyses praxis (both in his early and later writings, but more clearly in his later writings) as a complex consisting of two key parts – work (or instrumental action, purposive-rational action) and interaction (or communicative interaction). [. . .]

Table 73.1 The analysis of praxis

	Work	Interaction
Orientation	technical control over objectified processes	mutual understanding
Co-ordinating elements	rational decision procedures (involving e.g. preference rules, decision maxims) and efficient use of technical knowledge	intersubjectively recognized norms and rules (reciprocity and consensus predominate)

	Work bounded by interaction: strategic action	
Orientation	calculated pursuit of individual interests	
Co-ordinating elements	rational decision strategies interlocked in a framework of norms and intersubjectively recognized rules of procedure	

Under the categories of 'work' and 'interaction' attention is directed to issues concerning, respectively, the technical mastery of the natural and social worlds and the organization of social relations.

Habermas takes as central to his theory of social evolution the claim that through work and interaction the human species evolves in two separate but interrelated dimensions, namely the development of the forces of production and the development of normative structures of interaction. In both these dimensions 'cumulative processes are involved which allow a direction to be perceived'. Figure 73.1 outlines some of the main elements of this process.

Habermas's ideas about social evolution provide the framework within which he examines the development of specific societies or social formations. Part of this project involves the identification of first, the 'possibility spaces' – the potential avenue of development – which a society's 'core structures' open to evolution; and second, the crisis tendencies to which such structures are vulnerable. Although Habermas is concerned to investigate pre-civilization (primitive communities) and traditional societies, his main focus hitherto has been on modern capitalism. He explores, in particular, the way 'advanced' (or, as he sometimes calls it, 'late' or 'organized') capitalism is susceptible to 'legitimation crisis' – the withdrawal from the existing order of the support or loyalty of the mass of the population as their motivational commitment to its normative basis is broken. It is Habermas's contention that the seeds of a new evolutionary development – the overcoming of capitalism's underlying class contradiction – can be uncovered in this and other related crisis tendencies.

From the above sketch it can be seen that Habermas's work covers an extraordinary range of problems. It is his ultimate objective to provide a coherent framework within which a large number of apparently competing approaches to the social sciences can be integrated; these include the critique of ideology, the perspective of action theory, the analysis of social systems and evolutionary theory. It is also his hope that the framework will provide a basis for bringing together the interests and findings of the ever more fragmented, individual disciplines within the social sciences. [. . .]

Marx's category of 'sensuous human activity', or praxis, involves two types of structured activities:

Work, or purposive-rational action (the dimension of activity in which the human species – through the manipulation and control of objects – produces from nature what is needed for its material existence)

Language, or communicative action (the dimension of activity in which the human species communicates through the use of intersubjectively understood symbols within the context of rule-governed institutions)

The human species has the capacity to learn. It is unable not to learn:

through the generation and application of technical knowledge there is development of the forces of production

through the generation and application of practical and moral knowledge there are changes in structured interaction (the relations of production, for instance)

The human species evolves in these two dimensions. In each there is a logic of development which has its own dynamic and which cannot be reduced to the other. The logics can be reconstructed in terms of:

cumulative growth in technical and scientific knowledge

the pattern of reflexivity, universality of beliefs, and discursiveness in the sphere of practical life

Figure 73.1   Learning and evolution

Acknowledgements

The author and publishers wish to thank the following for permission to use copyright material:

Frances Aboud for material from *Children and Prejudice* by Frances Aboud, Blackwell Publishers (1988);

Philip Allan Updates for M. Moores, 'Sociologists in white coats', *Sociology Review*, 7:3 (1998); A. Furlong and F. Cartmel, 'Growing up in a risk society', *Sociology Review*, 7:2 (1997); M. Hamilton, 'Secularisation', *Sociology Review*, 7:4 (1998); N. Jewson and A. Felstead, 'When work comes: new ways of working and living', *Sociology Review*, 10:1 (2000); and S. Hunt and N. Lightly, 'A healthy alternative', *Sociology Review*, 8:3 (1999);

Ashgate Publishing Ltd for material from Paul E. Willis, *Learning to Labour: How working class kids get working class jobs*, Gower (1977);

Benjamin R. Barber for 'Globalizing Democracy' by Benjamin R. Barber, *The American Prospect*, 11.9.00;

Blackwell Publishers for Tim Jordan and Paul Taylor, 'A sociology of hackers', *The Sociological Review*, 48 (1998) pp. 756–76. Copyright © 1998 The Editorial Board of Sociological Review; and Zygmunt Bauman, *Thinking Sociologically*, Blackwell Publishers (1990);

Crown copyright © material is reproduced under HMSO Class Licence C01W0000283 with the permission of the Controller of HMSO;

Peter F. Drucker for material from 'Beyond the information revolution' by Peter Drucker, *Atlantic Monthly*, October (1999);

The Economist Newspaper Ltd for 'Home Sweet Home: The debate about family values', *The Economist*, 9.9.95, pp. 25–7. Copyright © The Economist Newspaper Ltd, London 1995; Paul Hewitt and Jane Warren, 'Are Men Necessary?', *The Economist*, 23.12.95. Copyright © The Economist Newspaper Ltd, London 1995; 'The proper study of mankind', *The Economist*, 29.6.00. Copyright © The Economist Newspaper Ltd, London 2000; William Dutton, 'Europe needs more immigrants', *The Economist*, 4.5.00. Copyright © The Economist Newspaper Ltd, London 2000; 'Haves and Have-nots: How to overcome the digital divide', *The Economist*, 22.6.00. Copyright © The Economist Newspaper Ltd, London 2000; 'Empty vessels?', *The Economist*, 22.7.99. Copyright © The Economist Newspaper Ltd, London 1999. 'Privatising peace of mind', *The Economist*, 22.10.98. Copyright © The Economist Newspaper Ltd, London 1998; and 'Workers of the world', *The Economist*, 30.10.97. Copyright © The Economist Newspaper Ltd, London 1997;

Earthscan Publications Ltd for material from Ernst von Weizsacker, Anthony B. Lovins and L. Hunter Lovins, *Factor Four: Doubling Wealth – Halving Resource Use*, pp. xviii–xxv;

Economic and Social Research Council for material from Anne Power, 'Poor Areas and Social Exclusion' in *Social Exclusion and the Future of Cities*, CASE paper 35;

Financial Times Ltd for Martin Dickson, 'Global inequality', *Financial Times*, 22.9.00. Copyright © The Financial Times Ltd 2000;

The Foreign Policy Centre for material from David Held and Anthony McGrew, David Goldblatt and Jonathan Perraton, *Globalization*;

The Free Press, a Division of Simon & Schuster, Inc. for material from Erving Goffman, *Behavior in Public Places: Notes on the Social Organization of Gathering* (1963). Copyright © 1963 by The Free Press;

Anthony Giddens for material from *The Class Structure of the Advanced Societies* by Anthony Giddens, 2nd edition, Unwin Hyman (1980);

The Guardian and Observer News Service for Chris Brewster, 'You've got to go with the flow', *The Guardian*, 22.4.95; and Ruaridh Nicoll, 'Gang babes love to kill', *The Observer*, 12.11.95;

HarperCollins Publishers for material from Ray and Dorothy Porter, 'Sickness and Health in Pre-Modern England', in *In Sickness and in Health: The British Experience 1650–1850*, eds. Ray and Dorothy Porter, Fourth Estate (1985);

The Independent for Andrew Brown, 'And the word was all male', *The Independent*, 31.5.95;

Kluwer Academic Publishers for Tom Horlick-Jones, 'Urban disasters and megacities in a risk society', *Geojournal*, 37:4 (1995) pp. 329–34;

Christian Heath for material from 'Embarrassment and Interactional Organization' by Christian Heath in *Erving Goffman: Exploring the Interaction Order*, eds. Paul Drew and Anthony Wootton, Polity (1988) pp. 136–60;

Eirene Mitsos and Ken Browne for 'Gender differences in education: The underachievement of boys' by Eirene Mitsos and Ken Browne, *Sociology Review*, 8:1 (1998);

The New York Times for Steve Lohr, 'Though upbeat on the economy, people still fear for their jobs', *The New York Times*, 12.19.96. Copyright © 1996 The New York Times Co;

Open University Press for material from Jan Sadlak, *The Globalization of Higher Education*, ed. Peter Scott (1998) pp. 100–5;

The Orion Publishing Group Ltd for material from Jeremy Rifkin, *The Biotech Century*, Victor Gollancz;

Oxford University Press for material from William H. Dutton, *Society on the Line: Information Politics in the Digital Age* (1999) pp. 114–18. Copyright © William Dutton 1999; and with the University of Toronto Press for Richard V. Ericson and Kevin D'Haggerty, *Policing the Risk Society* (1997) pp. 135–44. Copyright © Richard V. Ericson and Kevin D. Haggerty 1997;

Oxford University Press, Inc. for material from C. Wright Mills, *The Sociological Imagination* (1959). Copyright © 1959 Oxford University Press, Inc. renewed 1987 by Yaraslava Mills;

Palgrave for material in Rosamund Billington, 'What is Culture?' in *Culture and Society*, eds. Rosamund Billington et al., Macmillan (1991) pp. 1–9; and Gillian Dunne, *Lesbian Lifestyles* (1997) pp. 181–7;

Pearson Education Ltd for material from Terry Nicholls Clark and Seymour Martin Lipset, 'Are Social Classes Dying?' in *Conflicts about Class*, eds. David J. Lee and Bryan S. Turner, Longman (1996). Copyright © Addison Wesley Longman Ltd 1996;

Peters Fraser & Dunlop Ltd on behalf of the Estate of the author for material from Ernest Gellner, *Nations and Nationalism*, Blackwell Publishers (1983). Copyright © 1983 The Estate of Ernest Gellner;

Polity for material from John Heritage, *Garfinkel and Ethnomethodology* (1984); John B. Thompson, *Ideology and Modern Culture: Critical Social Theory in the Era of Mass Communication* (1990); Pat Carlen, *Criminal Women: Autobiographical Accounts* (1985); David Lyon, *The Information Society* (1988); David Beetham and Kevin Boyle, *Introducing Democracy*, pp. 1–9; James Slevin, *The Internet and Society* (2000) pp. 28–34; Anthony S. Smith, *Nations and Nationalism in a Global Era* (2000) pp. 147–59; Carol Smart and Bren Neale, *Family Fragments* (1999) pp. 87–95; Sarah Nettleton, *The Sociology of Health and Illness* (1995) pp. 58–66; Ray Pahl, *On Friendship* (2000) pp. 1–9; Anthony Giddens, *Social Theory and Modern Sociology* (1987); and with Suhrkamp Verlag for Ulrich Beck and Elizabeth Beck-Gernsheim, *The Normal Chaos of Love / Das Normale Chaos Der Liebe*, trans. Mark Ritter and Jane Wiebel (1995) pp. 172–81. Copyright © Suhrkamp Verlag Frankfurt am Main 1990;

Sage Publications, Inc. for material from Nancy K. Baym, *Tune In, Log On: Soaps, Fandom, and Online Community*, pp. 1–14; and George Ritzer, *The McDonaldization of Society*, 2nd edn, Pine Forge Press, pp. 1–11;

Sage Publications Ltd for material from Scott Lash, Bronislaw Szerszynski and Brian Wynne, *Risk, Environment and Modernity*, pp. 62–8; and Ulrich Beck, *Risk Society: Towards a New Modernity* (1997) pp. 19–24;

Taylor and Francis Group Ltd for material from William Julius Wilson, 'When work disappears: new implications for race and urban poverty in the global economy', *Ethnic and Racial Studies*, 22:3 (1999) pp. 480–5; Catherine Marsh, *The Survey Methods: The Contribution of Surveys to Sociological Explanation*, Routledge

(Allen & Unwin); Joanna Mack and Stewart Lansley, *Poor Britain*, Routledge (1985); Akbar S. Ahmed and Hastings Donnan, *Islam, Globalization and Postmodernity*, Routledge, pp. 1–7; Laura Buffoni, 'Rethinking poverty in globalized conditions' in *Living the Global City*, ed. John Eade, Routledge (1997) pp. 110–23; Jane Pilcher, *Women in Contemporary Britain: An Introduction*, Routledge (1999) pp. 4–14; and Paul Gilroy, *There Ain't No Black in the Union Jack: The Cultural Politics of Race and Nation*, Routledge (Unwin Hyman);

Thames and Hudson Ltd for material from Michael Young, *The Metronomic Society: Natural Rhythms and Human Timetables* (1988);

UNESCO for material from David Beetham and Kevin Boyle, *Introducing Democracy: 80 Questions and Answers* (1995) pp. 1–9. Copyright © UNESCO 1995;

University of California Press for material from Robert Georges and Michael Owen Jones, *People Studying People: The Human Element in Fieldwork* (1980). Copyright © 1980 The Regents of the University of California; and David Held, *Introduction to Critical Theory: Horkheimer to Habermas* (1980) pp. 250–9. Copyright © 1980 David Held;

Every effort has been made to trace the copyright holders but if any have been inadvertently overlooked the publishers will be pleased to make the necessary arrangement at the first opportunity.

Picture Credits

83 Hulton Getty

88, 89 Simon Spilsbury Illustration

98 (top) Thomas Raupacah / Still Pictures / Argus Fotoarchiv GmbH

98 (bottom), 99 © Topham Picturepoint

104 Mark Edwards / Still Pictures

124 Image Bank

243 © 2000 Topham / Image Works

247 (left) © Topham Picturepoint

247 (right) © John Phillips / Photofusion

302 © Sarah Saunders / Photofusion

303 © Jacky Chapman / Format

379 © Jacky Chapman / Format

Index

THE
STATE
OF THE
WORLD
ATLAS

NINTH EDITION

Completely revised & updated

DAN SMITH

New Internationalist

www.newint.org

This State of the World ninth edition first published in 2013
by New Internationalist

New Internationalist
55 Rectory Road, Oxford, OX4 1BW
www.newint.org

Myriad Editions
59 Lansdowne Place, Brighton BN3 1FL
www.MyriadEditions.com

3 5 7 9 10 8 6 4 2

Edited and co-ordinated for Myriad Editions by
Jannet King and Candida Lacey
Designed by Isabelle Lewis and Corinne Pearlman
Maps and graphics by Isabelle Lewis
Cover by New Internationalist/Myriad Editions

A CIP catalogue record for this book is available from the
British Library.
ISBN: 978-1-78026-121-8

Printed and bound in Hong Kong on paper produced from sustainable sources
by Lion Production under the supervision of Bob Cassels, The Hanway Press, London

Contents

ABOUT THE AUTHOR

Dan Smith is Secretary General of the London-based international peacebuilding organization International Alert, and former Director of the International Peace Research Institute in Oslo. He has also held fellowships at the Norwegian Nobel Institute and Hellenic Foundation for Foreign and European Policy and was, for over a decade, the Chair of the Institute for War and Peace Reporting.

He is the author of *The State of the Middle East,* as well as successive editions of *The State of the World Atlas* and *The Atlas of War and Peace.* At International Alert he produced the path-breaking *A Climate of Conflict* (2007) report on the links between climate change, peace, and war. He is regularly invited to advise governments and international organizations on policies and structures for peacebuilding, including through his membership of the Advisory Group for the UN Peacebuilding Fund, of which he was Chair until 2011.

He was awarded the OBE in 2002, and blogs on international politics at www.dansmithsblog.com

Introduction

Ours is a period of change – continual, multi-form, and multi-level – technical, scientific, economic, and political.

Scientific discovery feeds into technical innovation at dizzying speed, changing how we communicate with each other, what we can know about far-flung parts of the world and how quickly we can know it, how we do business, what we understand about the natural world and how the human brain works, how many diseases we can cure, and the kinds of energy supply we can utilise. In every corner of our lives as individuals and as communities and societies, there is change.

THE THREE GREAT CHANGES

The theme is repeated in the big global picture. Five major issues and how the world – its leaders, governments, companies, international organizations, individuals, everybody – responds to them will define our future. To take them on, change is needed. And three great changes at approximately ten-year intervals over the past two decades will set the terms and the tone of how that response shapes up.

In the 1980s, the Cold War seemed stuck fast, likely to be a long-enduring feature of world politics. Yet in half a year in 1989 its basic components unravelled, and in a second series of events the Soviet Union came to an end in five swift months of 1991.

For the 1990s, then, the USA seemed set to enjoy a golden age as the sole superpower while its allies basked in the security it generated. Those comfortable assumptions were detonated in 2001, not only by the force of the 9/11 terror attacks on New York and the Pentagon, but by the wide-reaching, aggressive, and ultimately self-defeating, US "war on terror". The golden age was gone and there was a widespread sense of insecurity as the 9/11 attacks were followed by others in Bali, Madrid, London, and elsewhere, as well as by the wars in Afghanistan and Iraq.

Underneath that, however, was a different kind of security. Economic growth and prosperity seemed broadly dependable. There were winners and losers as always, but for most people in the rich world times were pretty good, and for many people in poorer countries conditions were also improving a little.

Much of that was destabilized by the third great change of the recent era, as unsustainable patterns of lending and borrowing fed a shattering credit crunch in 2007 and 2008, triggering recession and a financial catastrophe whose full effects had not played out some four or five years later.

If we look back over those 20 years, we can see how quickly confidence about the future can be generated and then lost. We need something rather better than that moodiness, something more stable and persistent, if we are going to be successful in facing up to the five big challenges we face as a global community: wealth and poverty, war and peace, rights and respect, and the health both of the people and of the planet.

WEALTH & POVERTY

The world is marked by large inequalities of wealth. Multiple further inequalities flow from that starting point – dramatically different degrees of access to education, health care, good food, clean water, sanitation, reasonable housing. Though the proportion of the world's population that lives in the extreme poverty of less than $1 a day is declining, progress is slow and more than one-third of all people live on less than $2 a day. The benefits of economic growth are not being distributed evenly or anything like it, and at the same time the model of economic development is environmentally unsustainable.

At the start of the century, world leaders undertook to make a major new effort to help developing countries move forward. In the confident spirit of that time, more money was committed and targets were set with a fixed date of 2015. These Millennium Development Goals have guided Western countries' official development assistance ever since. In the much less confident spirit in which these donor governments are working a decade on, still reeling from the economic aftershocks of 2008, it is clear that there has been progress but the targets will not be met. And some of the most significant economic development and alleviation of poverty in the last decade seems to have owed very little, if anything, to the Millennium Development Goals.

Above all, on the economic front, the events of 2008 and since have generated a growing realization of another axis of change. For a long time it has been recognized that the economic output of China and India was growing much more quickly than that of Europe and the USA. China's eventual assumption of the position as the world's largest economy – and India's as the third largest, with the USA staying second – has been long anticipated. Whether that makes them in a meaningful sense two of the three wealthiest countries is another matter, because their output per person remains much lower than in the USA and Europe. There is, nonetheless, a distinct political weight that comes with economic size. And the effect has been emphasized because, while the USA's recovery from 2008 has been halting and uncertain, Europe has faced a serial crisis and renewed recessions. The contrast with China has only served to emphasize its rise. The European Union's combined economic scale remains huge; it is the largest single market in the world. But the combined political weight of its member states, which has always seemed less than the sum of its parts, has diminished because of the political leaders' seeming inability to find a solution to Europe's problems that retains credibility for more than a few months.

WAR & PEACE

This is not a peaceful world, and yet it is more peaceful today than at any time since before the First World War and, some argue, ever. Military spending remains high, and armed conflict remains a major cause of death, yet by comparison with earlier times, there are markedly fewer wars and they are less lethal. There has been an avalanche of peace agreements in the two decades since the end of the Cold War, and a major, sustained if quiet effort not only to make peace, but then to lay the foundations for long-term peace in conflict-affected countries.

It would be wrong to look at the issues of war and peace and declare job done. In many countries, it is not so much a case of having achieved peace as, rather, of bottling up conflict. Indeed, declaring job done prematurely is a repeated failing of the Western governments who often offer themselves as custodians of peace processes in war-torn countries. In many countries, there are patterns of violent conflict that are from a different mould than civil wars. They are generated by, and reinforce, a dangerous intersection between crime and politics, and in several cases they revolve around the trade in illegal narcotics or other illegal and massively profitable enterprises. The main international institutions on which we rely for responding to armed conflicts are strikingly ill-prepared for this kind of violent conflict. A high United Nations representative can be sent to negotiate with even the most despicable of dictators, but the same space and the same role does not exist between a government and a drug lord.

There is, further, a risk that the number of civil wars could increase. The environmental, demographic, and economic pressures are there. The United Nations has become quite adept at generating norms that manage violent conflict, but a new round of conflict pressures might encounter a deficient response because the governments that have tended to fund peace efforts include several that have been hard hit by economic crisis. With repetitive demands for bailing out countries and banks, these governments may simply conclude they have too many competing calls on economic resources for it to be politically feasible to support long-term peacebuilding. If no new actors appear to take their place, the peacebuilding enterprise could collapse.

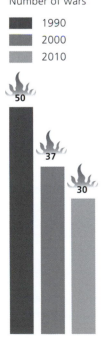

Two decades of growing peace

Number of wars

- 1990
- 2000
- 2010

50

37

30

These are all risks – the potential is there. Even so, if the United Nations as an organization and those governments that have been particularly committed to the work of ending armed conflicts can stay focused and keep their efforts properly resourced, there is every reason to expect a reasonably successful record of building peace to continue.

RIGHTS & RESPECT

This is the ninth edition of this atlas. The last one before this came out in 2008. At that time, 43 per cent of the world's population lived in established democracies. In this atlas, it is recorded that in 2012 48 per cent live in established democracies.

For all its flaws, viewed from the perspective of ordinary citizens and their shared interests, democracy is by far the best, most stable, and freest political system. It is based on a bargain that concedes power to the state as long as it is accountable to the people. It is a system in which the social and economic elite has to accept constraints on its power. When it works properly, it protects us from the negative consequences of our own short-sightedness and tunnel vision. And it does so on the basis of our consent. It is the system that has, on average, been associated with the most successful economies.

It is, however, like peace, a trend and benefit that needs safeguarding; it cannot be taken for granted. Achieving democracy is perilous, and is closely associated with violent conflict. And when it is well established and the struggle to achieve it has been forgotten, it often seems barely to be taken seriously by those who could most benefit from it. In countries that have recently entered a democratic transition, there will always be false friends of democracy, ready to try for power that way if that's all that's possible, but to grab and hold it against the democratic will if that becomes possible. Similarly, in the established democracies there are always economic and social elites who are content with democracy as long as they can rig its rules in their favour, but are ready to cry foul if it ever threatens to rule against them.

These fake and shallow supporters of democracy reveal themselves by trying to call the language of rights into service for one segment of society and not for others, or by claiming exemptions from national and international legal responsibilities whenever it suits them.

HEALTH OF THE PEOPLE

Without our good health, what can we do? Providing for our own and each other's health is fundamental to us, both as individuals and as social beings.

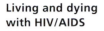

**Living and dying
with HIV/AIDS**

Adults and children
1990–2010

---- new HIV Infections

—— AIDS-related deaths

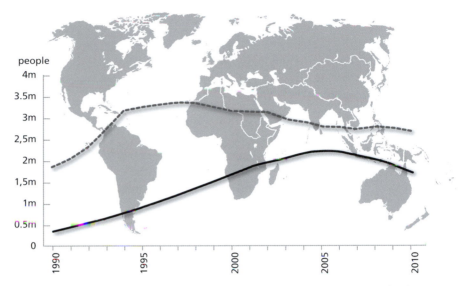

Many societies do not generate the wealth required to be able to look after the health of the people on a more or less fair basis. Others have the resources but the political and social will to do so is lacking. Challengingly, even where and when the resources are available and are deployed to provide health care for all, that is no guarantee that our patterns of behaviour will be healthy. For that is a matter of personal responsibility and individual action; government can make it easier or harder, can educate the citizens or neglect the issues, but in the end it is impossible to enforce healthy behaviours.

Even so, people's health is improving. There is still too much suffering from curable and preventable conditions and, in many countries, the way that mental and psychological disorders are handled primarily by silence and taboo is as big a health scandal as any. But medical science is advancing, the sequencing of the human genome has been worked out, the genetics of cancers are being unlocked, and new treatments are being and will be developed. The progress is encouraging but there is further to go because many of these conditions have social causes – lifestyle diseases whether of poverty or spreading prosperity. What is required now is to increase the capacity to address those causes.

HEALTH OF THE PLANET

On top of all this, there is growing awareness about the unfolding crisis in the natural environment. Compared to the other events that have shaped the spirit of our time, changes in the natural environment are slow moving. By the standards of 21st-century political culture, they do not deserve the name of crisis at all – but the timescale in which they should be understood is much longer than a four- or five-year political cycle, which is the maximum we are used to thinking in.

Of the five key issues that we must as a world community resolve in order to prosper, our relationship to the natural environment is the most tangled, the one in which knowledge is most essential to understanding, and the one that has the highest stakes – yet the one on which we seem unable to act on the scale that is needed. Though we cannot yet make out all the details of the interaction between different components of this crisis – between the different ways in which we are damaging the environment – we can clearly see the critical moment bearing down on us. Yet generating a united and viable response is currently beyond us. Calm reflection reveals that, on the basis of what we currently know, there is time to act effectively as long as we act now. But each day that passes increases the depth and scale of change that is required.

PROBLEMS & SOLUTIONS

These five key challenges are in principle all amenable to solution. In one sense, that is illustrated simply by there being successful approaches to significant aspects of three of the five. Problems remain in the realms of war and peace, rights and respect, and people's health, but progress is visible. There is less war, though violent conflict persists. There is more democracy and more respect for human rights, though abuses persist and the transition is often dangerous. Improvements in treatment for many of the major ailments are available, though lifestyle diseases are on the increase. Undernourishment is slowly reducing as a problem, but obesity – perhaps a different kind of malnutrition – is now a global epidemic.

What holds us back from pressing through to greater improvements on these three fronts and to sorting out at least some of the big issues of wealth, poverty, and the natural environment is the condition of our politics and our international political institutions. In Europe in the years since 2008 we have seen signs of a breakdown in the fundamental relationship between citizens and state – the implicit bargain that power is both real and accountable. There is now such a deep resentment about taxpayers being forced to pay the cost of the failings, incompetence and, in some cases, apparent crimes in the major banks that it is building towards refusing consent to be governed. The social and economic elite has shown a combination of incompetence and the arrogance of impunity, and would-be political leaders continue to cosy up to that elite so shamelessly that they are threatening the continued viability of the contract of government.

It is, in the end, unlikely that this will erupt into any kind of revolution and, if it does, the odds are that it will be profoundly unpleasant for ordinary people. But it is the kind of deep-seated problem that may make it next to impossible to generate new policies and approaches to prevent environmental degradation and successfully address the other major issues.

Our enemies in trying to generate new and better approaches are inequality, unfairness and social exclusion, short termism, and blinkered allegiance to norms and policies that used to be functional. Anything and everything that limits the amount of knowledge that can be brought to bear on a problem, and the number of knowledge-holders that can get engaged, is an obstacle. Part of this problem resides in the limitations of the institutions we have developed to regulate our affairs. We need new ones. There is energy available that has not yet been harnessed and connected to engines of change. The old power formats are creaking but the new ones have not yet emerged.

KNOWING THE WORLD

Getting things more or less right on these five issues will be done by international agreement or not at all, for no single government can handle – or should even dream of handling – the whole set of issues alone, and much of it will in turn be based on shared knowledge and understanding.

Of course, knowledge is not the same as wisdom. You can know all the facts and still not be able to act wisely. But without knowledge, it is harder to be wise – even if what wisdom tells us is that knowledge is very often provisional and that we cannot wait to have certainty about every fact before we act.

DAN SMITH
LONDON, JULY 2012

THE PROBLEM WITH MAPS

The aim of this atlas is to look at the world through the lens of world problems. That means mapping those issues onto the world – and there we encounter the standard problem of atlases. Because the world is virtually a sphere, it cannot be accurately depicted on a flat, rectangular piece of paper. Peel an orange and flatten out the skin and the problem is immediately understandable. Choices and compromises must accordingly be made – choices, essentially, about how to be inaccurate. These choices are packaged into the projection of the world that is utilised in drawing the map.

The most widely seen world maps use projections that retain the shapes of the continents and islands, and therefore wildly distort their size. The first and most famous of these projections is the one developed by the 16th-century Flemish cartographer, Gerardus Mercator. Using that projection, the sizes of regions far from the equator are exaggerated. Thus Europe looks bigger than it is, while China and India look smaller. The most notorious distortion of area in Mercator is that Greenland looks similar in size to Africa, which is actually 14 times bigger than Greenland. Mercator's choice of projection was determined in part by his wish, as the sub-title of the original atlas put it, to produce an aid for navigators. Navigation was at the forefront of Europe's advance into the world from the 15th through the 18th centuries. It was the scientific precondition for sailing to far-flung destinations for trade and conquest.

There have been numerous attempts over succeeding centuries to correct the illustrative weakness in the Mercator projection. The best known today is the one proposed in 1973 by Arno Peters, drawing on work in the 19th century by a Scottish clergyman, James Gall. The Peters or Gall-Peters projection is more accurate on the size of different regions but distorts the world's appearance in other ways. There are geographers who believe the depiction of the world on rectangular pieces of paper should be stopped.

Below: Myriad's world map based on the Winkel Tripel projection, and a cartogram based on population size.

The projection employed in this atlas makes a different set of choices and compromises. It is the Winkel's Tripel, first used in 1913, compromising between the three elements of area, direction, and distance. Distortion is not completely eliminated but is minimized. The curved lines of latitude and longitude make the projection useless for navigators, but the result is fairer and reasonably familiar, especially since it was adopted by the US National Geographic Society in 1998.

ACKNOWLEDGEMENTS

The atlas is the work of a team. Jannet King has been the editor, assiduous and detailed in her work, and respectful of a wayward author's prerogatives. Isabelle Lewis provides the basic cartographic design work without which the whole atlas approach would be impossible, and throughout showed her talent for coming up with innovative ways of displaying the information. The overall look and feel of the atlas is down to the design coordination of Corinne Pearlman. Candida Lacey ran and coordinated the Myriad team and was always a joy to work with. Elizabeth Sarney was an extremely diligent research assistant without whom the basic research for the atlas could not have been done; she also offered insightful comment on the draft layouts for displaying the data. Nicolle Nguyen made sure I stayed up to par on my day job and was another source of comment and feedback on draft designs. Ilaria Bianchi and Selena Mirams were a responsive focus group at a critical stage. Åsa Frankenberg provided thoughtful reflections on the look and functioning of the spreads, and was a source of strength throughout. Felix Smith-Frankenberg reminded me of what life is about at moments when I thought it only consisted of missed deadlines. I thank all of you unreservedly.

PHOTOGRAPHS

The publishers are grateful to the following for permission to reproduce their photographs on the following pages: 18 © Mark Henley / Panos Pictures; 30 Mexico City: Milan Klusacek / iStockphoto; New York: Candida Lacey; London: Ivan Mateev / iStockphoto; Paris: JB Russell / Panos Pictures; Lagos: George Osodi / Panos Pictures; Sao Paulo: AM29 / iStockphoto; 31 Istanbul: George Georgiou / Panos Pictures; Karachi: Giacomo Pirozzi / Panos Pictures; Shanghai: Manfred Leiter; Tokyo: Wikimedia Commons / Chris 73; Jakarta: Martin Adler / Panos Pictures; Cairo: ictor/ iStockphoto; Mumbai: Candida Lacey; Tehran: Frank van den Bergh / iStockphoto; 36 Ian Teh / Panos Pictures; 56 Iva Zimova / Panos Pictures; 74 Philippe Lissac / Panos Pictures; 88 Teun Voeten / Panos Pictures; 104 Alvaro Leiva / Panos Pictures; 120 Dieter Telemans / Panos Pictures.

Below: The world map based on the Mercator, Gall and Peters projections.

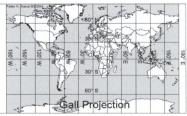

PART ONE
WHO WE ARE

This is the age of more, most, and never before. There are more people, living in more countries, and more of us living in cities, than at any time in the past.

It is only 200 years ago – less than a blink of an eye in the timescale of the planet, and not much more than a blink in the timescale of human beings walking the planet – that the world's human population passed the 1 billion mark. Today there are just over 7 billion of us. At that time, some 3 per cent – just 30 million people – lived in cities. Today, the corresponding figure is about 50 per cent, or some 3.5 billion people.

Current projections are that these figures and percentages will all increase. World population is expected to grow, as will the proportion of us who live in cities. The total expected population increase by 2030 – about another 2 billion people – is about the same as the expected rise in the urban population, as increasing numbers are born in cities or move there.

Humanity has never before experienced demographic change on such a huge scale. The movement from the countryside to the cities in the industrial revolution two centuries ago has nothing on this. The migration from Europe to the New World of the Americas from the mid-19th century to the early 20th numbered some 30 million. In the first ten years of this century, global population grew by some 100 million a year and urban population even faster.

But the issue is not just population increase. There is the matter of resources. According to one estimate, our seven-times-larger population compared to 1810 produces 50 times as much in economic output, and uses 60 times as much water and 75 times as much energy. Seen in a longer timescale going back to the beginning of recorded history some 5,000 years ago, that astonishing increase in the production of wealth is as wholly unprecedented and wildly abnormal as the increase in population itself.

The figures testify to the creativity unleashed through the industrial revolution. They are the evidence against fears, widely expressed over the past two centuries, that population increase must end in starvation and mass misery.

It is no new thought, however, to wonder how long this growth of output and consumption can be sustained, to question what may happen as the emerging economies of China, India, Brazil, and other countries, with increasing economic growth in Africa and many parts of Asia, successfully produce and consume ever-increasing amounts of everything, just as we have done in Europe, North America, and Japan.

This growth in production both owes much to, and has fed, the extraordinary growth in human knowledge over the past 200 years – as, indeed, does the underlying population growth because of the improvements in public health that have made it possible. Whether knowledge generates wisdom is, as we all know, questionable. But if we are seeking to compare ourselves to the past in the effort to understand who we are today, one thing is that we are better educated. We know more and, despite the way it may seem, we understand more.

Among other knowledge, we know more about each other than ever before. There is more travel and more communication, leading to more encounters and more information. As we encounter each other, we see our diversity – of background, race, ethnicity, belief – and how we handle that diversity will have much to say about whether we will in the end be able to rise successfully to the great challenges we face today. It is possible to see every day how the encounter between people and groups of diverse backgrounds can be on the one hand a benefit – a source of interest, pleasure, or mutual gain – or on the other hand a source of danger and potential loss – of jobs, fellow-feeling in the community, or security.

It is paradoxical how we are divided and united by our needs. Because so many of our needs are the same, there is a risk of clashing over our attempts to meet them. And when there is a possibility of clashing and sides get chosen, we are more likely to choose the side that looks, sounds, feels, and thinks like us. Perhaps if our needs were as diverse as we are, they would mesh and be complementary.

Especially when communities are under pressure, the need to band together against the outsider gets stronger. The multiple sources of change in today's world are a constant source of pressure and thus of danger. Those who once sought world government based on the recognition of all that we have in common are destined for disappointment. We have chosen instead to be divided, creating more and more independent countries and following different faiths.

Yet there is also plenty of evidence that different ethnicity and faith do not prevent people living together peacefully. As more of us cram into cities, bringing our different traditions and social norms into close proximity, being able to draw on that part of humanity's experience will become more and more important.

The States of the World

Some of our sense of who we are comes from where we were born and grew up – our countries, most of which are quite recent creations. In 1945 the United Nations was founded by just 51 states, some of which were not fully independent at the time (and the defeated states in World War II were initially excluded). Today, the UN has 193 members.

Over the past century, states have won, lost, and regained independence, often against a background of war and bloodshed. Some have become formally independent before achieving real independence; with others, it has been the other way round. This atlas shows many ways – economic, environmental, political – in which independent states do not have full sovereignty in the modern world – yet the evidence is clear that sovereignty is a highly desirable political commodity. The age of forming new states is not yet over.

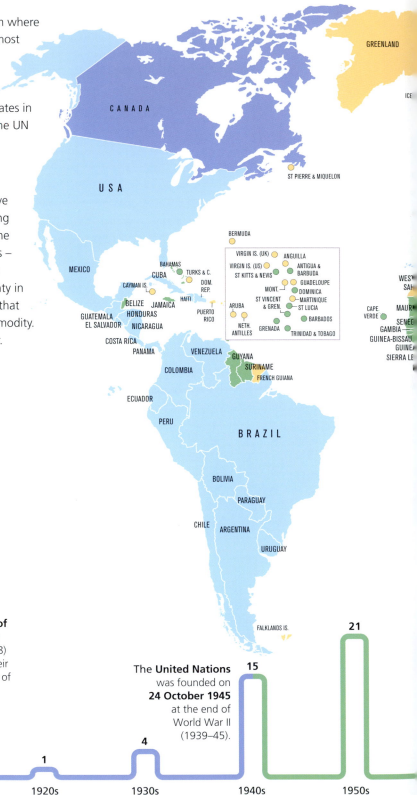

State formation
Number of states gaining effective independence in each decade

48 pre 1900

8 1900s

The defeat of Austria-Hungary and of the Ottoman Empire in World War I (1914–18) led to the breakup of their empires and the creation of new European and Middle Eastern states.

7 1910s

1 1920s

4 1930s

The **United Nations** was founded on **24 October 1945** at the end of World War II (1939–45).

15 1940s

21 1950s

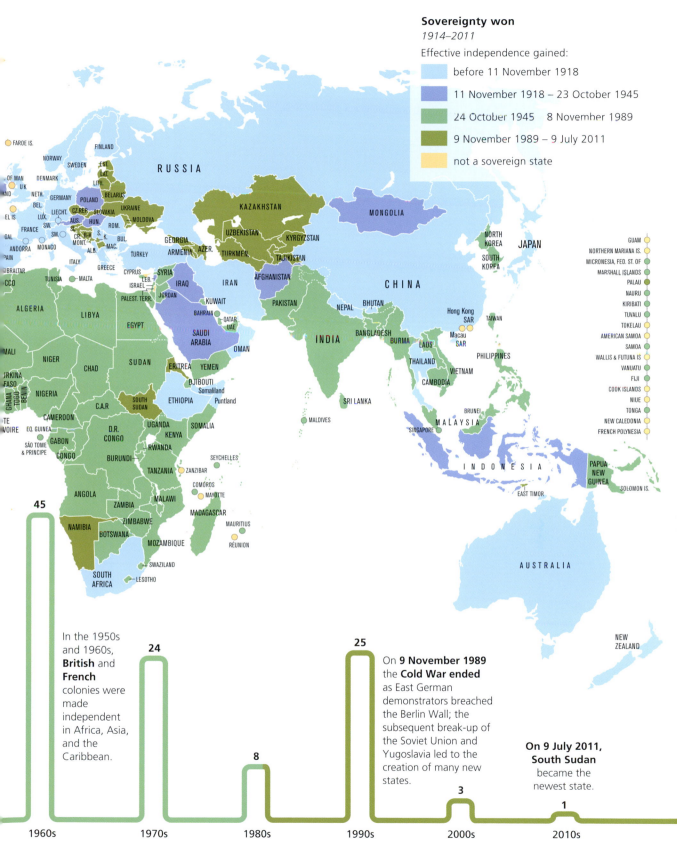

Sovereignty won
1914–2011
Effective independence gained:

before 11 November 1918

11 November 1918 – 23 October 1945

24 October 1945 – 8 November 1989

9 November 1989 – 9 July 2011

not a sovereign state

In the 1950s and 1960s, **British** and **French** colonies were made independent in Africa, Asia, and the Caribbean.

On **9 November 1989** the **Cold War ended** as East German demonstrators breached the Berlin Wall; the subsequent break-up of the Soviet Union and Yugoslavia led to the creation of many new states.

On **9 July 2011**, **South Sudan** became the newest state.

45

24

8

25

3

1

1960s   1970s   1980s   1990s   2000s   2010s

Population

The global population is still growing, although the rate of increase is beginning to slow compared with that of the last 50 years. In 2010 the average number of babies born to each woman was 2.5; in 1990 it was 3.2.

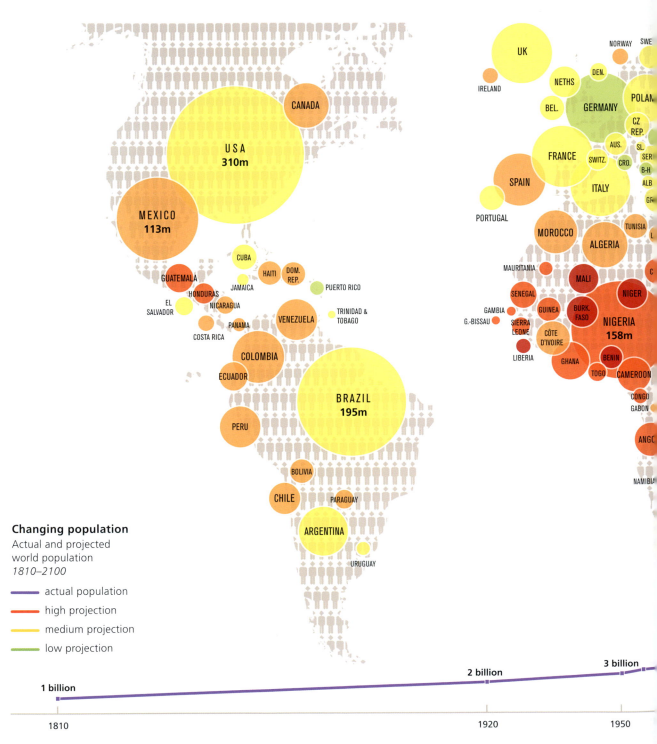

Changing population
Actual and projected
world population
1810–2100

— actual population
— high projection
— medium projection
— low projection

1 billion

2 billion

3 billion

1810

1920

1950

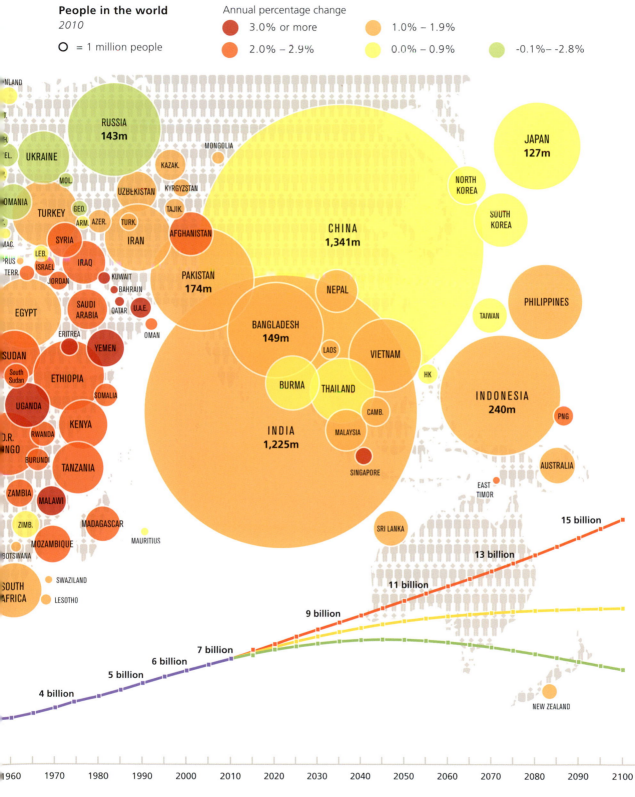

People in the world
2010

◯ = 1 million people

Annual percentage change

🔴 3.0% or more   🟠 1.0% – 1.9%

🟠 2.0% – 2.9%   🟡 0.0% – 0.9%   🟢 -0.1%– -2.8%

RUSSIA **143m**

UKRAINE

MONGOLIA

KAZAK.

MOL.

UZBEKISTAN

KYRGYZSTAN

TAJIK.

OMANIA

TURKEY

GEO.

ARM. AZER.

TURK.

AFGHANISTAN

SYRIA

IRAN

CHINA **1,341m**

JAPAN **127m**

NORTH KOREA

SOUTH KOREA

LEB.

ISRAEL

IRAQ

JORDAN

KUWAIT

BAHRAIN

PAKISTAN **174m**

NEPAL

PHILIPPINES

TAIWAN

EGYPT

SAUDI ARABIA

QATAR

U.A.E.

OMAN

BANGLADESH **149m**

LAOS

VIETNAM

ERITREA

YEMEN

SUDAN

South Sudan

ETHIOPIA

SOMALIA

BURMA

THAILAND

INDONESIA **240m**

PNG

UGANDA

KENYA

RWANDA

CAMB.

MALAYSIA

INGO

BURUNDI

TANZANIA

INDIA **1,225m**

SINGAPORE

AUSTRALIA

ZAMBIA

MALAWI

ZIMB.

MADAGASCAR

EAST TIMOR

MAURITIUS

SRI LANKA

MOZAMBIQUE

BOTSWANA

SOUTH AFRICA

SWAZILAND

LESOTHO

15 billion

13 billion

11 billion

9 billion

7 billion

6 billion

5 billion

4 billion

NEW ZEALAND

1960   1970   1980   1990   2000   2010   2020   2030   2040   2050   2060   2070   2080   2090   2100

Life Expectancy

Average life expectancy has never been higher, and continues to grow as general levels of health and public sanitation continue to improve.

In southern Africa, the proportion of the population infected by HIV/AIDS was 12 to 30 times the world average during the 2000s. This has combined with other diseases to reduce average life expectancy in the region.

Being homeless in England cuts life expectancy by 30 years to just 47, one year less than in Afghanistan and Central African Republic.

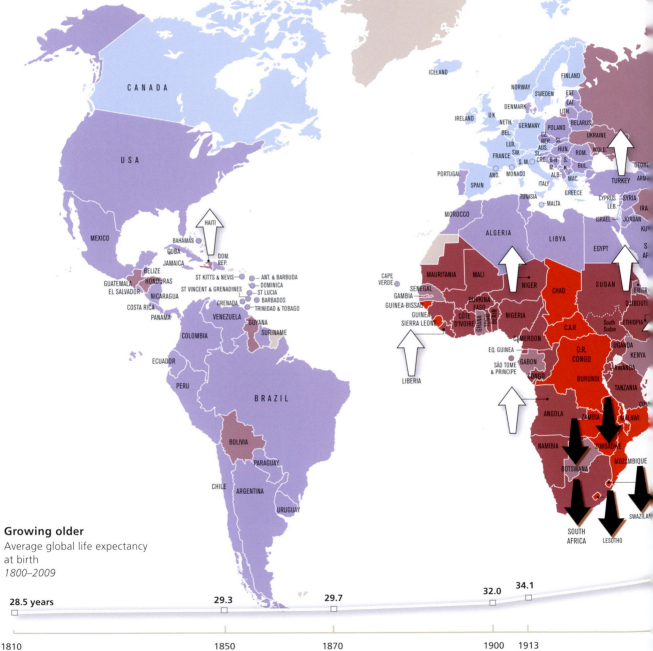

Growing older
Average global life expectancy at birth
1800–2009

28.5 years		29.3		29.7		32.0	34.1
1810		1850		1870		1900	1913

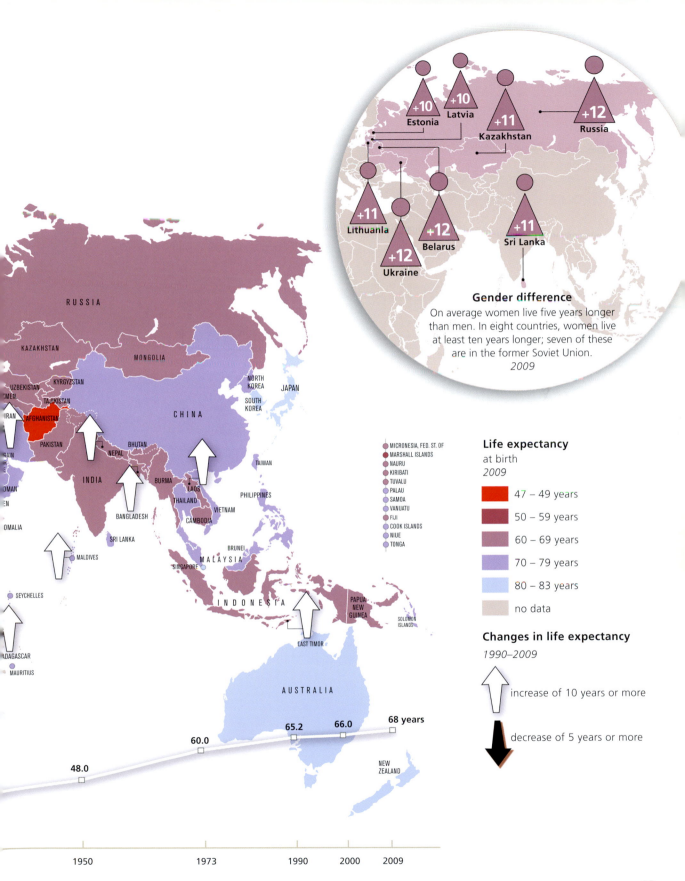

Gender difference

On average women live five years longer
than men. In eight countries, women live
at least ten years longer; seven of these
are in the former Soviet Union.
2009

+10 Estonia
+10 Latvia
+11 Kazakhstan
+12 Russia
+11 Lithuania
+12 Ukraine
+12 Belarus
+11 Sri Lanka

RUSSIA

KAZAKHSTAN

MONGOLIA

NORTH KOREA

JAPAN

SOUTH KOREA

UZBEKISTAN
KMER.
KYRGYZSTAN
TAJIKISTAN
AFGHANISTAN
IRAN
PAKISTAN
BHUTAN
NEPAL
INDIA
BURMA
THAILAND
BANGLADESH
CAMBODIA
VIETNAM
LAOS
CHINA
TAIWAN
PHILIPPINES

RAIN
OMAN
OMALIA
SRI LANKA

MALDIVES

SEYCHELLES

ADAGASCAR
MAURITIUS

SINGAPORE
MALAYSIA
BRUNEI
INDONESIA
PAPUA NEW GUINEA
SOLOMON ISLANDS
EAST TIMOR

AUSTRALIA

NEW ZEALAND

MICRONESIA, FED. ST. OF
MARSHALL ISLANDS
NAURU
KIRIBATI
TUVALU
PALAU
SAMOA
VANUATU
FIJI
COOK ISLANDS
NIUE
TONGA

Life expectancy
at birth
2009

🟥	47 – 49 years
🟥	50 – 59 years
🟪	60 – 69 years
🟦	70 – 79 years
🟦	80 – 83 years
⬜	no data

Changes in life expectancy
1990–2009

⬆ increase of 10 years or more

⬇ decrease of 5 years or more

48.0
60.0
65.2
66.0
68 years

1950   1973   1990   2000   2009

Ethnicity & Diversity

Part of human diversity lies in our membership of large groups – nations, ethnic groups, races, tribes, clans. How these are defined varies from one culture to another. How important they are varies both from one person to the next and from time to time. Groups take on the most explicit importance for their members when they are or feel threatened – whether by day-to-day discrimination and ill treatment or by traumatic events as in war.

National ceremonies such as independence days, martial anniversaries and royal weddings offer rituals for coming together in spirit to renew identity bonds. For the rest of the time, ethno-national and racial identities tend to be little considered even though a lot of life is quietly shaped by them. Ethnic and national differences are often part of war but there are far more instances of diverse groups living peacefully together.

Ethnic and national identity is at stake in

50%

of 21st-century wars

215

million
people live outside their country of birth

Migrants
People living in country other than that in which they were born as a percentage of total population
2010

less than 10%
10% – 29%
30% or more
no data

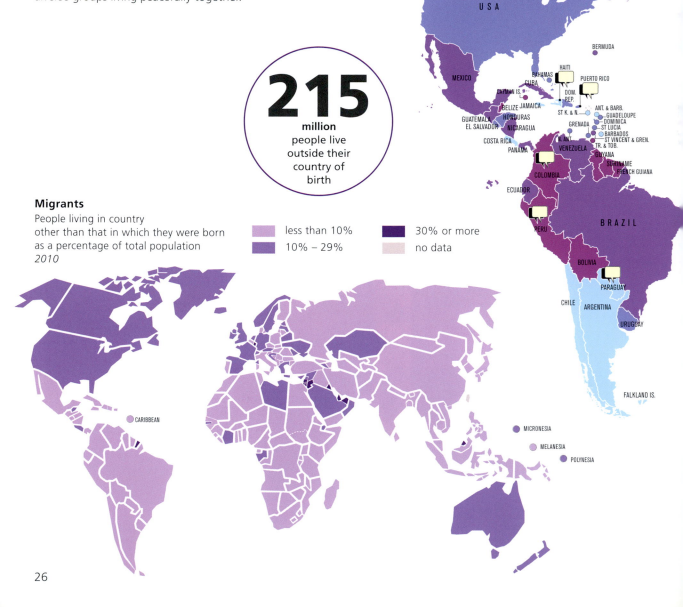

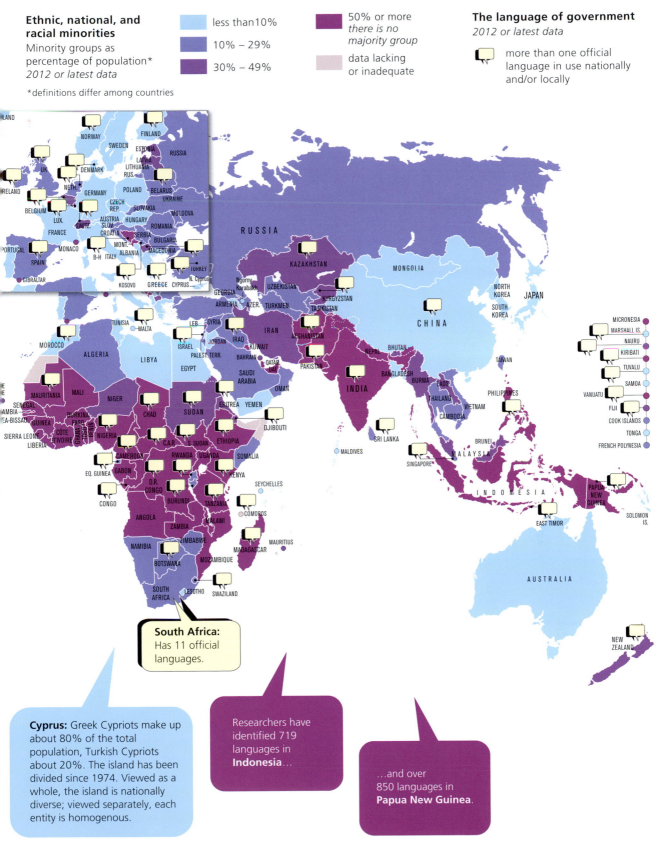

Ethnic, national, and racial minorities

Minority groups as percentage of population*
2012 or latest data

*definitions differ among countries

- less than 10%
- 10% – 29%
- 30% – 49%
- 50% or more *there is no majority group*
- data lacking or inadequate

The language of government

2012 or latest data

more than one official language in use nationally and/or locally

South Africa: Has 11 official languages.

Cyprus: Greek Cypriots make up about 80% of the total population, Turkish Cypriots about 20%. The island has been divided since 1974. Viewed as a whole, the island is nationally diverse; viewed separately, each entity is homogenous.

Researchers have identified 719 languages in **Indonesia**…

…and over 850 languages in **Papua New Guinea**.

Religious Beliefs

The vast majority of people profess a religious faith. Although professing a faith on a population census form and actually practising it are two very different things, their faith is, for many, a basic marker of identity. Shared religious conviction can unite people where other things divide them, and even between different faiths there is significant ethical common ground and a shared openness to the spiritual and immaterial.

But religious identity coincides with other markers of identity – regional, national, ethnic, and cultural. When and where religious leaders cannot or will not restrain the way in which adherents to different faiths express their differences, conflicts can overheat and explode. Some of the world's most brutal violence is – and has been throughout history – inflicted in the name of religion. And some of the worst violence is over differences within the same religion: between Protestants and Catholic Christians, or between Sunni and Shi'a Muslims. Yet common to all major religions is the over-riding value of peace.

Faithful countries
Countries with largest populations of Christians and Muslims

Christians   Muslims

Non-believers
People who profess no religion as a percentage of population
2005

- 20% or more
- 10% – 19.9%
- fewer than 10%

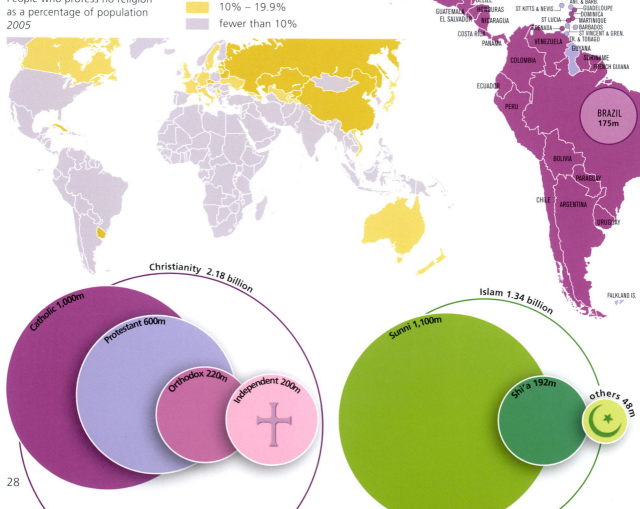

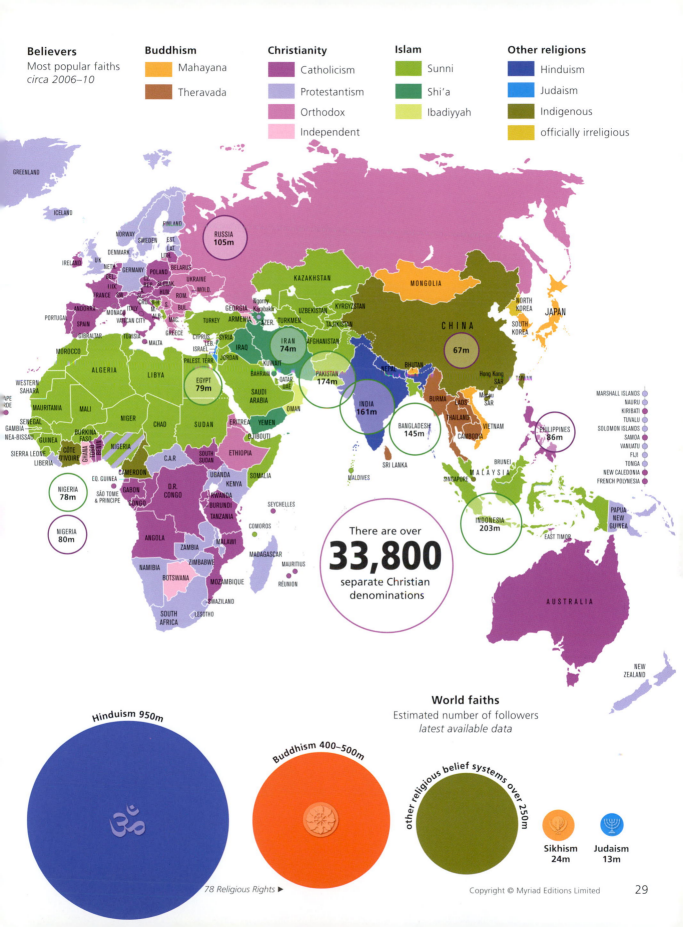

Believers

Most popular faiths
circa 2006–10

Buddhism
- Mahayana
- Theravada

Christianity
- Catholicism
- Protestantism
- Orthodox
- Independent

Islam
- Sunni
- Shi'a
- Ibadiyyah

Other religions
- Hinduism
- Judaism
- Indigenous
- officially irreligious

RUSSIA 105m

CHINA 67m

EGYPT 79m

IRAN 74m

PAKISTAN 174m

INDIA 161m

BANGLADESH 145m

PHILIPPINES 86m

NIGERIA 78m

NIGERIA 80m

INDONESIA 203m

MARSHALL ISLANDS
NAURU
KIRIBATI
TUVALU
SOLOMON ISLANDS
SAMOA
VANUATU
FIJI
TONGA
NEW CALEDONIA
FRENCH POLYNESIA

There are over
33,800
separate Christian
denominations

World faiths
Estimated number of followers
latest available data

Hinduism 950m

Buddhism 400–500m

other religious belief systems over 250m

Sikhism 24m

Judaism 13m

78 Religious Rights ▶

Literacy & Education

Literacy is simultaneously a functional need for modern societies, a basic tool for individual advancement, and a personal source of knowledge, access to the world and satisfaction. Thanks to a major international effort, trends in the last decade have been positive. Although there remain places where adult illiteracy rates are still over 50 per cent of the population, and in Africa and some other areas, progress in secondary and tertiary education remains slow, primary education, where the foundations are laid, has registered real forward movement.

Nonetheless, the challenge remains steep. The UN estimates that the world needs 8 million more primary school teachers by 2015 in order to achieve its Millennium Development Goal for education. Of these, 6 million are required simply to replace others who will leave the teaching profession, while 2 million are necessary extra teachers. And of those 2 million, more than half are needed in Sub-Saharan Africa.

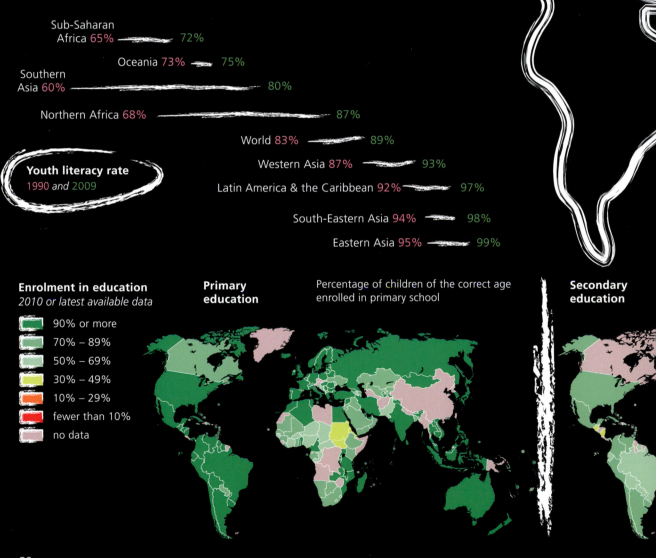

Haiti

Sub-Saharan Africa 65% — 72%

Oceania 73% — 75%

Southern Asia 60% — 80%

Northern Africa 68% — 87%

World 83% — 89%

Western Asia 87% — 93%

Latin America & the Caribbean 92% — 97%

South-Eastern Asia 94% — 98%

Eastern Asia 95% — 99%

Youth literacy rate
1990 *and* 2009

Enrolment in education
2010 or latest available data

- 90% or more
- 70% – 89%
- 50% – 69%
- 30% – 49%
- 10% – 29%
- fewer than 10%
- no data

Primary education

Percentage of children of the correct age enrolled in primary school

Secondary education

Adult illiteracy
As percentage of adult population
2010 or latest available data

70% or more
50% – 69%
35% – 49%

Morocco
Mauritania
Senegal
Gambia Mali Niger
Guinea- Burkina Chad
Bissau Faso
Guinea Nigeria
Sierra Côte Togo
Leone d'Ivoire Benin
Liberia

Ethiopia
South
Sudan
Central
African
Republic

Pakistan Nepal
Bhutan
Yemen India
Bangladesh

Madagascar

Mozambique

Papua New
Guinea
East
Timor

20%
of adults
are illiterate,
two-thirds of
them women

Percentage of children of the correct
age enrolled in secondary school

**Tertiary
education**

Percentage of young people enrolled
in tertiary college

Urbanization

Today 51 per cent of the world's people live in cities. In 1800 just 3 per cent were urban dwellers. Projections suggest between 60 and 70 per cent of the world's population will live in cities by 2030. New urbanization is largely concentrated in the developing countries. Most major cities in Europe are static or declining in size, partly because improved transport and communications are reducing the economic benefits of concentrating large numbers of people in a few places. In developing countries, however, big cities remain magnets for people seeking livelihoods when they can no longer sustain themselves in the countryside.

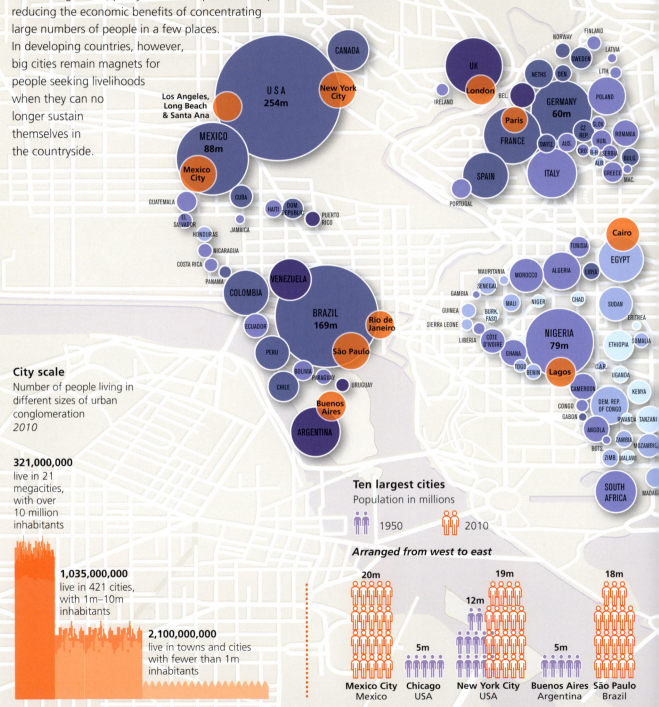

City scale

Number of people living in different sizes of urban conglomeration
2010

321,000,000
live in 21 megacities, with over 10 million inhabitants

1,035,000,000
live in 421 cities, with 1m–10m inhabitants

2,100,000,000
live in towns and cities with fewer than 1m inhabitants

Ten largest cities
Population in millions

1950   2010

Arranged from west to east

20m — Mexico City, Mexico
5m — Chicago, USA
12m / 19m — New York City, USA
5m — Buenos Aires, Argentina
18m — São Paulo, Brazil

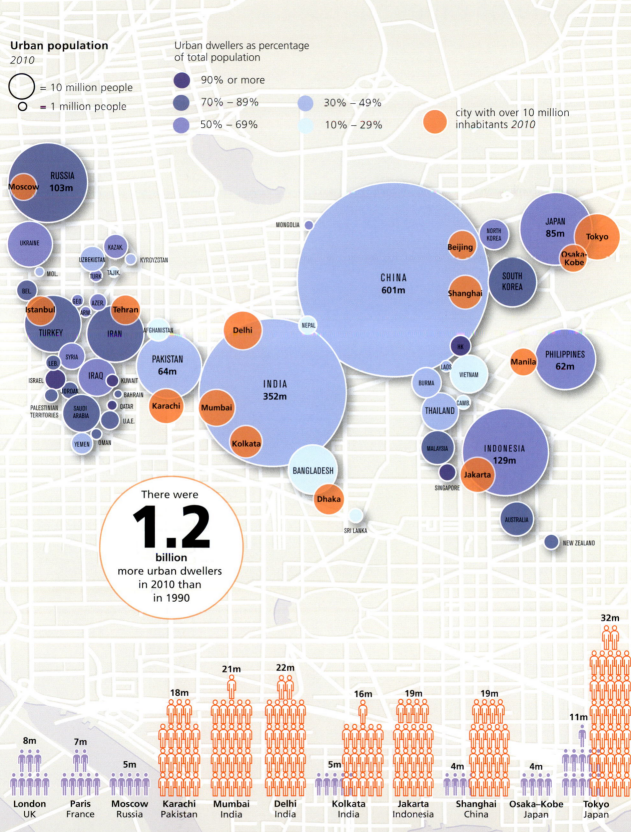

Urban population
2010

○ = 10 million people

○ = 1 million people

Urban dwellers as percentage
of total population

● 90% or more
● 70% – 89%
● 50% – 69%
● 30% – 49%
● 10% – 29%

● city with over 10 million
inhabitants *2010*

RUSSIA
103m
Moscow

UKRAINE

KAZAK.

UZBEKISTAN
MOL.
TURK.   TAJIK.   KYRGYZSTAN

BEL.

GEO.   AZER.
ARM.

Istanbul
TURKEY   Tehran
                IRAN
                AFGHANISTAN

SYRIA
LEB.
ISRAEL   IRAQ
JORDAN   KUWAIT
                BAHRAIN
PALESTINIAN   QATAR
TERRITORIES   SAUDI   U.A.E.
              ARABIA
YEMEN   OMAN

PAKISTAN
64m
Karachi

MONGOLIA

CHINA
601m

Beijing

NORTH
KOREA

Shanghai

NEPAL

Delhi

INDIA
352m

Mumbai

Kolkata

BANGLADESH

Dhaka

HK

LAOS
BURMA   VIETNAM

THAILAND

CAMB.

MALAYSIA

SINGAPORE

SRI LANKA

JAPAN
85m   Tokyo

Osaka-
Kobe

SOUTH
KOREA

Manila   PHILIPPINES
         62m

INDONESIA
129m
Jakarta

AUSTRALIA

NEW ZEALAND

There were

1.2

billion
more urban dwellers
in 2010 than
in 1990

32m

London
UK — 8m

Paris
France — 7m

Moscow
Russia — 5m

Karachi
Pakistan — 18m

Mumbai
India — 21m

Delhi
India — 22m

Kolkata
India — 16m

Jakarta
Indonesia — 19m

Shanghai
China — 19m

Osaka–Kobe
Japan — 4m / 4m

Tokyo
Japan — 11m / 32m

5m (Kolkata)

Diversity of Cities

The diversity of cities is as great as the diversity of the world. They hold, display, and generate great wealth – and equally great poverty. They are places of danger, and equally of opportunity, as continued urban migration shows. Worldwide, just under a billion people are believed to live in slums, almost one-third of the urban population.

London, UK

Population: 13m/7.8m • Area: 8,400/1,570

- More than 300 languages are spoken in London.
- It has the world's oldest and second most extensive underground railway network.

Paris, France

Population: 10m/2.2m • Area: 2,800/105

- 20% of Parisians were born outside France.
- The city receives 28 million tourists a year, 17 million from outside France.

London
Paris

New York City, USA

Population: 17m/8.2m • Area: 8,700/790

- About 45% of New Yorkers speak a language other than English at home.
- The urban legend of alligators in Manhattan sewers grew in the 1960s based on a colourful account by a retired city official.

New York

Mexico City, Mexico

Population: 20m/9m • Area: 7,300/1,490

- Mexico City sits on a drained lake-bed of saturated clay that is subsiding as it continues to dry: in 100 years, parts of the city have sunk about 9 metres.
- Its metro system is the world's fourth largest and cheapest to use.

Mexico City

Lagos, Nigeria

Population: 13m • Area: 1,000

- Lagos has no overall city administration.
- The city population is growing at the rate of 1 new person every 2 minutes.

Lagos

São Paulo, Brazil

Population: 18m/11m • Area: 8,500/1,500

São Paulo

- "Sampa" is the world's largest Japanese city outside Japan, the largest Spanish city outside Spain, the largest Lebanese city outside Lebanon.

Comparative wealth of city dwellers

Number of hours someone needed to work for the average city wage in order to buy an iPod Nano (8GB version) in 2009

New York
9 hours

Tokyo
12 hours

London
11 hours

Paris
15 hours

São Paulo
46.5 hours

Istanbul
56 hours

Shanghai
56.5 hours

◀ 32 Urbanization

Cities around the world
2011 or most recent data

Size of metropolitan area:

- metro area = 1,000 km² (outer ring)
- city area = 100 km² (inner ring)

Population density: people per square kilometre:
- 20,000 or more
- 10,000 – 19,999
- 6,000 – 9,999
- 3,000 – 5,999
- fewer than 3,000

Istanbul, Turkey
Population: 13m • Area: 5,300

- Istanbul has 18% of Turkey's population and produces over 25% of national GDP.
- Its population grew tenfold in the second half of the 20th century.

Karachi, Pakistan
Population: 18m • Area: 3,500

- As Pakistan's financial and commercial capital, Karachi contributes 25% of national tax revenue.
- The city's population grows at the rate of 1 person a minute.

Shanghai, China
Population: 19m • Area: 6,300

- Shanghai has the world's most extensive underground railway network.
- It has the world's busiest container port.
- The Shanghai Stock exchange ranks third in the world by trading volume.
- 99% of residents are Han Chinese.

Tehran, Iran
Population: 13m/9m • Area: 1,300/730

- Tehran's population has grown fivefold in 50 years.
- Air pollution (80% cars, 20% industrial) kills about 10,000 people a year; in 2006, 3,600 died in the month of October alone.

Mumbai, India
Population: 21m/14m • Area: 2,350/660

- 16 major languages are widely spoken in Mumbai.
- With less than 2% of India's population, Mumbai pays over 33% of its taxes.
- About half of residents live in unregistered accommodation and lack sanitation.

Tokyo, Japan
Population: 32m/13m • Area: 8,000/2,100

- 99% of Tokyo's population is Japanese by birth.
- 40% of the city is built on landfill.

Cairo, Egypt
Population: 17m/6.7m • Area: 6,600/453

- Almost 20% of Cairo's buildings date from 1997 or later.
- 60% of the population is aged under 30.
- Up to 25,000 people a year die from air pollution.

Jakarta, Indonesia
Population: 19m/10m • Area: 5,100/740

- 40% of Jakarta is below sea level.
- At least 35% and perhaps as many as 80% of residents lack a clean water supply.
- All Jakarta's rivers are polluted – 71% heavily.

Map labels: Istanbul • Tehran • Cairo • Karachi • Mumbai • Shanghai • Tokyo • Jakarta

Jakarta 3 hours	Mexico City 95 hours	Cairo 105 hours	Mumbai 177 hours

PART TWO
WEALTH & POVERTY

The two decades up to 2008 were hardly still waters in the global economy, and the sense of safety and certainty about the economy that opinion-leaders and policy-makers in the rich countries often expressed was always somewhat shallow and misleading. There was a severe downturn at the turn of the 1980s into the 1990s, followed by Japan's lost decade, and the costs and upheavals in eastern Europe and the former Soviet Union as they went through a massive economic transformation, then an Asian economic crisis in the late 1990s and the collapse of many new technology companies in the early years of this century. And in the countries where there was more or less steady economic growth, there were plenty of losers as well as winners, while global poverty persisted. But there was also an unmistakable – and now absent – sensation of forward movement, a confidence that economic problems were open to relatively straightforward solutions, and trust in many countries that the hands on the economic tiller were competent and dependable.

Today it feels so very different. And in the change of conditions brought about by economic events since 2008, it is sometimes hard to disentangle what has really changed and what not. As always, not everybody gains and loses equally. One line of inequality has been narrowing and there is every reason to expect it to continue to do so: the old idea of a sharp division in the world between rich countries and poor countries no longer holds in the same form. The contrasts are now more subtle, as other lines of inequality are getting broader. Some countries are richer than others, but in the rich countries there remains much poverty. India is no longer one of the poorest countries, not even when wealth is measured per head of the population. But there are more people living in poverty in India than in any other country. Worldwide, the number of people living below $1 a day is declining, but the number on less than $2 a day is over 2.5 billion – more than one person in three in the global population.

World leaders committed themselves at the start of the century to a major effort at international social and economic development, with the richer countries pledging to spend more on aiding development. Promises were made and targets set for achievement by 2015. The record is mixed: development spending has increased, though that has been slowed by the economic downturn, and there has been considerable progress on some indicators in some countries. By and large the targets will not be met; they now seem to have been not only too ambitious but also flawed by being generic. Countries are different from each other; the policies that work in one place fail elsewhere. It is in particular countries that are affected by violent conflict and political instability where the millennium development effort is failing most comprehensively.

Among the factors that hold back some countries is their pervasive corruption. But it should not be thought that this is only a problem of poor, developing countries. A significant contribution to corruption in those countries is made by businesses headquartered in the financial capitals of the northern world.

And when looking at how the banks have performed – borrowing and lending up to 2008 in amounts and ways they could not keep track of, running a cosy system of mis-selling poorly understood financial products and fixing interest rates to their own benefit, their top managers paying themselves vast bonuses then seeking government hand-outs when their incompetence caught up with them, and then carrying on with the big bonuses – the concept of legalized corruption comes to mind.

The economic crash highlighted a global imbalance, in which the USA borrowed and spent while China saved and lent. On a smaller scale the same imbalance existed between Germany and much of the rest of Europe. But the USA had more collateral. This crisis has been a knock, a profound one, for the USA – but not the shattering disaster it is turning out to be in some parts of Europe.

Out of the crash of 2008, while Europe has stumbled into one hole after another, the USA has limped, several times seeming to pull itself clear of the wreckage only to fall back, while China has walked tall and the Indian economy has performed only a little less impressively. Yet, like the USA, the rising economic powers may be slowed and hindered by Eurozone stagnation. Globalization has harnessed everybody's economic fates together.

An economic system that has previously been marked not only by perpetual forward motion but by astonishing resilience has taken a terrible buffeting. So far the politicians have no solution. Each crisis summit is the solution, so it is declared, until the next one. In all probability, the resilience of the system will reassert itself over time – but most likely at high cost for ordinary people in many countries. There seems little doubt that less painful recovery requires new institutions to protect us all from the malign influence of short-term greed and the tunnel vision it generates.

Income

Despite the economic crash of 2008 and the recessions, depressions, and crises that have happened since, growth in the world's annual economic output continues to outpace by far the growth in world population. Yet extreme poverty persists.

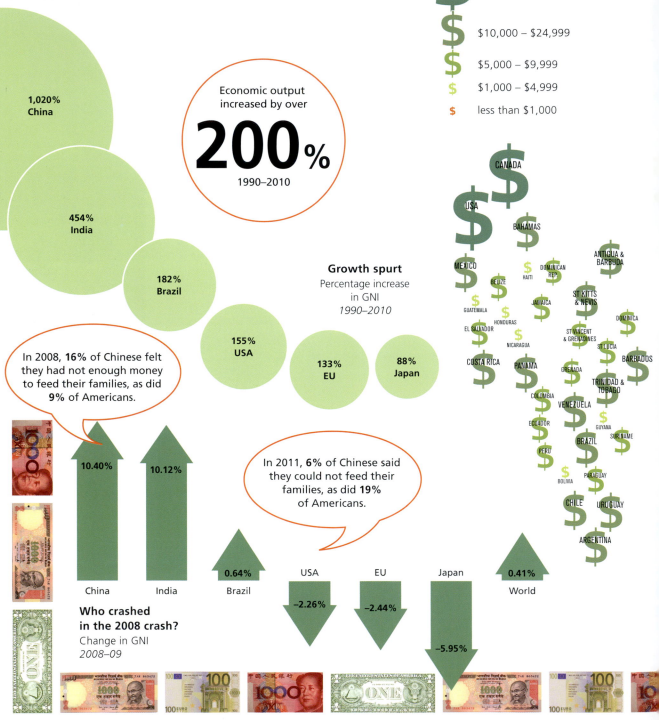

Gross National Income
Per capita
2010 or latest available data
PPP$

$ $25,000 or more

$ $10,000 – $24,999

$ $5,000 – $9,999

$ $1,000 – $4,999

$ less than $1,000

Economic output increased by over

200%

1990–2010

1,020%
China

454%
India

182%
Brazil

Growth spurt
Percentage increase in GNI
1990–2010

155%
USA

133%
EU

88%
Japan

In 2008, **16%** of Chinese felt they had not enough money to feed their families, as did **9%** of Americans.

In 2011, **6%** of Chinese said they could not feed their families, as did **19%** of Americans.

CANADA
USA
BAHAMAS
MEXICO
ANTIGUA & BARBUDA
HAITI DOMINICAN REP
BELIZE
GUATEMALA
JAMAICA
ST KITTS & NEVIS
HONDURAS
EL SALVADOR
ST VINCENT & GRENADINES
DOMINICA
NICARAGUA
ST LUCIA
COSTA RICA
PANAMA
GRENADA
BARBADOS
TRINIDAD & TOBAGO
COLOMBIA
VENEZUELA
ECUADOR
GUYANA
PERU
BRAZIL
SURINAME
BOLIVIA
PARAGUAY
CHILE
URUGUAY
ARGENTINA

10.40%
China

10.12%
India

0.64%
Brazil

USA
−2.26%

EU
−2.44%

Japan
−5.95%

0.41%
World

Who crashed in the 2008 crash?
Change in GNI
2008–09

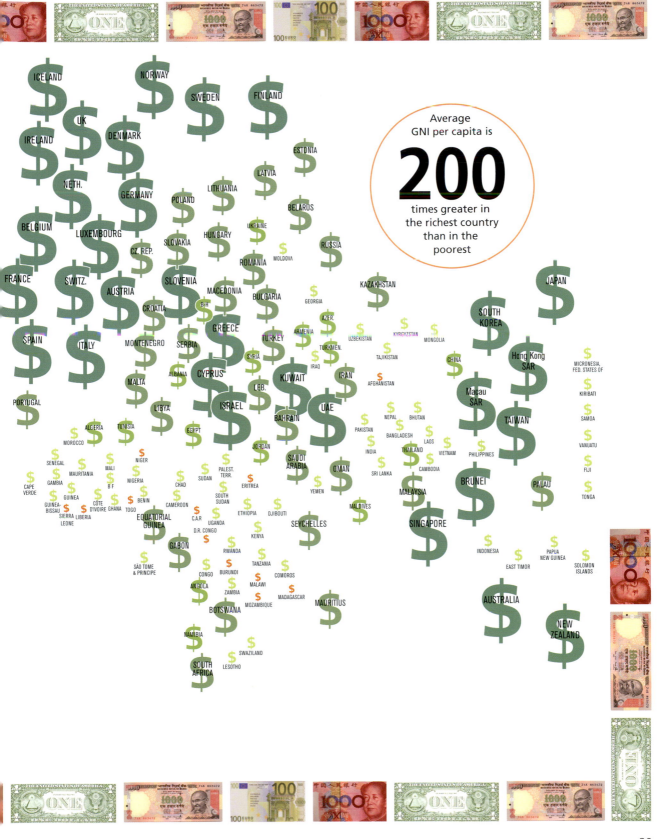

Average GNI per capita is

200

times greater in the richest country than in the poorest

Copyright © Myriad Editions Limited

Inequality

The Gini index measures the degree to which the distribution of wealth within a country is different from a perfectly equal distribution. The higher the index, the greater the inequality.

Billionaires were hit hard by the global crash in 2008. They have recovered quickly.

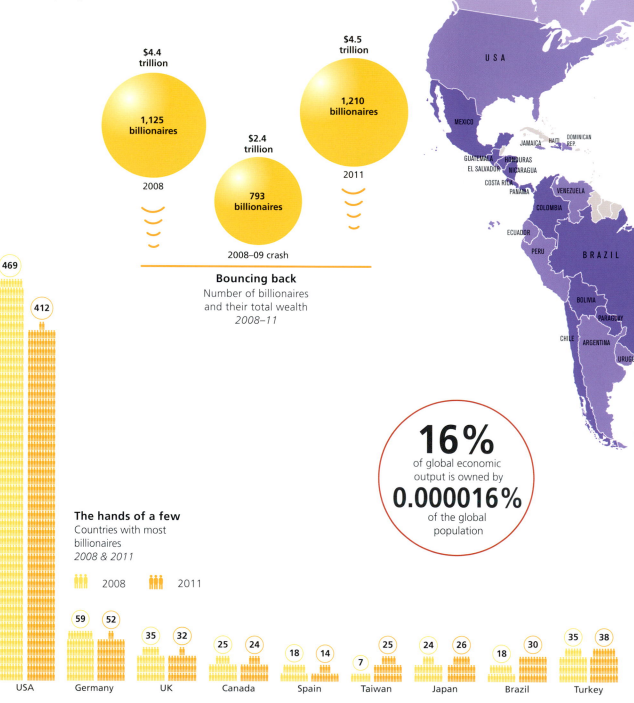

$4.4 trillion

1,125 billionaires

2008

$2.4 trillion

793 billionaires

2008–09 crash

$4.5 trillion

1,210 billionaires

2011

Bouncing back
Number of billionaires and their total wealth
2008–11

The hands of a few
Countries with most billionaires
2008 & 2011

2008   2011

16%
of global economic output is owned by
0.000016%
of the global population

Country	2008	2011
USA	469	412
Germany	59	52
UK	35	32
Canada	25	24
Spain	18	14
Taiwan	7	25
Japan	24	26
Brazil	18	30
Turkey	35	38

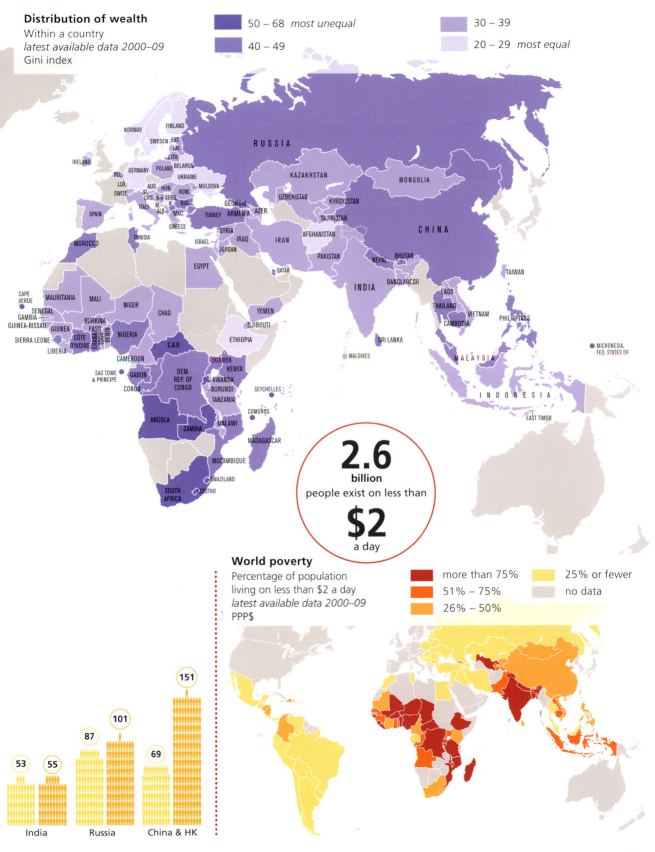

Distribution of wealth

Within a country
latest available data 2000–09
Gini index

50 – 68 *most unequal*	30 – 39
40 – 49	20 – 29 *most equal*

NORWAY
FINLAND
SWEDEN EST.
LAT.
LITH.
IRELAND
GERMANY POLAND BELARUS
BEL. UKRAINE
LUX. AUS. HUN.
SWITZ. SL. B-H SERB. MOLDOVA
CRO. M-K BUL.
ITALY ALB. MAC.
SPAIN GREECE
GEORGIA
TURKEY ARMENIA AZER.
MOROCCO SYRIA
TUNISIA ISRAEL IRAQ IRAN
JORDAN
EGYPT QATAR

RUSSIA
KAZAKHSTAN
MONGOLIA
UZBEKISTAN
KYRGYZSTAN
TAJIKISTAN
AFGHANISTAN CHINA
PAKISTAN
NEPAL BHUTAN
INDIA BANGLADESH
TAIWAN
LAOS
THAILAND VIETNAM
CAMBODIA PHILIPPINES

CAPE VERDE
SENEGAL MAURITANIA MALI NIGER
GAMBIA CHAD
GUINEA-BISSAU GUINEA BURKINA
SIERRA LEONE CÔTE FASO NIGERIA YEMEN
D'IVOIRE TOGO BENIN DJIBOUTI
LIBERIA GHANA ETHIOPIA
SRI LANKA
CAMEROON C.A.R.
SAO TOME GABON UGANDA MALDIVES
& PRINCIPE KENYA
CONGO DEM. RWANDA
REP. OF BURUNDI
CONGO TANZANIA SEYCHELLES
ANGOLA MALAWI COMOROS
ZAMBIA
MOZAMBIQUE
MADAGASCAR
SWAZILAND
SOUTH LESOTHO
AFRICA

MICRONESIA,
FED. STATES OF

MALAYSIA

INDONESIA
EAST TIMOR

2.6
billion
people exist on less than
$2
a day

World poverty

Percentage of population
living on less than $2 a day
latest available data 2000–09
PPP$

more than 75%	25% or fewer
51% – 75%	no data
26% – 50%	

151
101
87
69
53 **55**

India   Russia   China & HK

Quality of Life

There is more to happiness than wealth alone – yet rich countries inevitably offer a higher quality of life.

The happiness league
Percentage of people who gave their current and future life high scores
2005–09

- more than 50%
- 26% – 50%
- 25% or fewer
- no data

> How do I feel about my current life, and how do I envisage my life in five years' time?

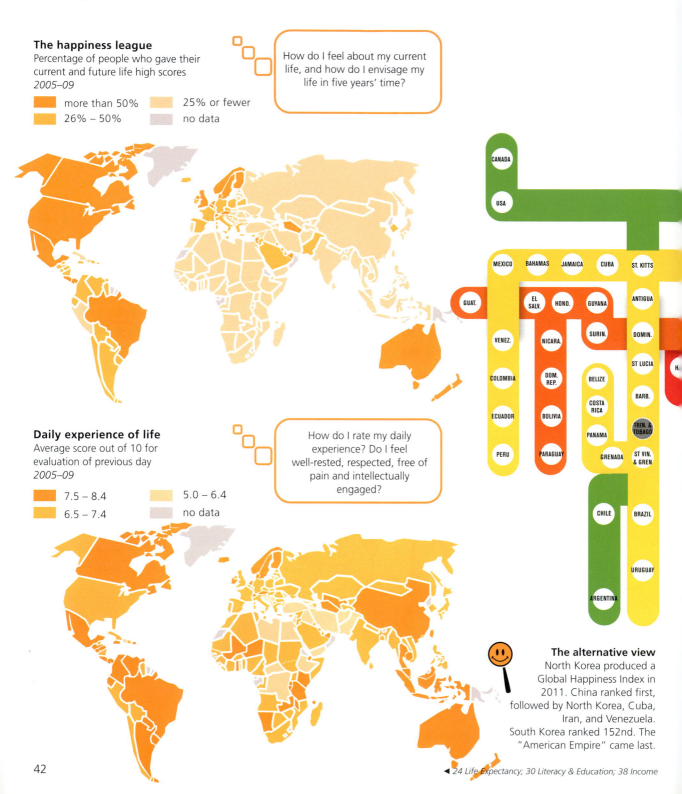

Daily experience of life
Average score out of 10 for evaluation of previous day
2005–09

- 7.5 – 8.4
- 6.5 – 7.4
- 5.0 – 6.4
- no data

> How do I rate my daily experience? Do I feel well-rested, respected, free of pain and intellectually engaged?

The alternative view
North Korea produced a Global Happiness Index in 2011. China ranked first, followed by North Korea, Cuba, Iran, and Venezuela. South Korea ranked 152nd. The "American Empire" came last.

◀ 24 Life Expectancy; 30 Literacy & Education; 38 Income

Relative human development

Score on the Human
Development Index (HDI)
2011

The Human Development Index (HDI) scores countries according
to the life expectancy and educational level of their populations,
and the national income per capita.

- 🟢 very high
- 🟡 high
- 🟠 medium
- 🔴 low

⚫ HDI ranking much lower than
Gross National Income ranking.
This suggests a country uses less
than the average proportion of
national wealth to improve quality
of life

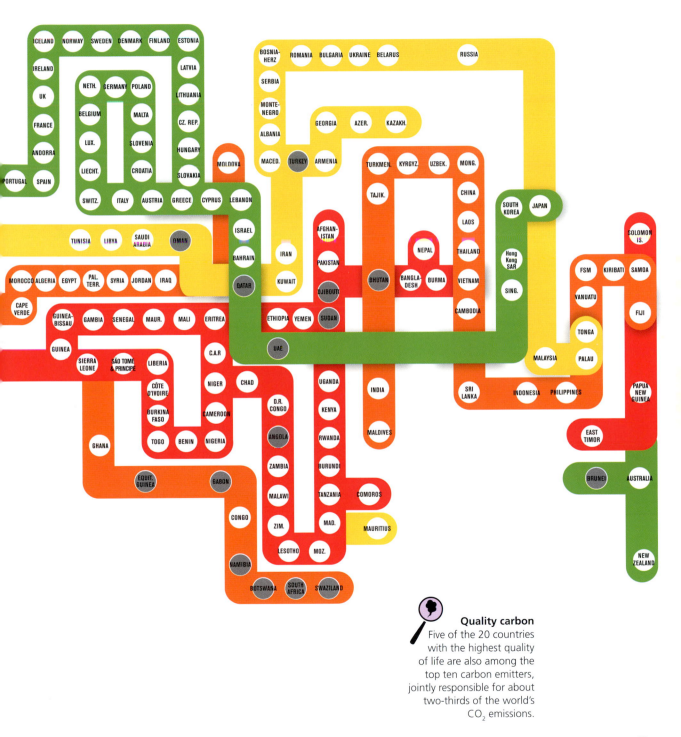

Quality carbon
Five of the 20 countries
with the highest quality
of life are also among the
top ten carbon emitters,
jointly responsible for about
two-thirds of the world's
CO_2 emissions.

Transnationals

Transnational corporations represent enormous wealth and therefore power. Comparing countries' Gross National Income (GNI) with the revenue of some of the giants of the corporate world is salutary.

The largest corporation is Walmart. Only 27 countries have a GNI larger than its revenue, and some 50 countries have populations smaller than Walmart's global workforce. Operating in scores of countries, the biggest companies have interests that reach far beyond any single national loyalty.

Corporate wealth

Gross National Income (GNI) compared with the annual revenue of selected transnationals
2010 or latest available data

country's GNI larger than revenue of any transnational	
country's GNI smaller than: **Walmart** ($421.8 billion) but bigger than: Nestlé	Walmart employs 2.1 million people and sells to 100 million customers a week. Its 2010 sales revenue exceeded the combined GNI of the world's 62 smallest economies. 80% of its suppliers are in China. A legal case, started in 2000, sued Walmart for discrimination against 1.5 million current and former women employees. In 2011, the US Supreme Court dismissed the case on the grounds that the women could not pursue it as a single group.
country's GNI smaller than: **Nestlé** ($105.3 billion) but bigger than: Kraft Foods	Nestlé operates in 86 countries and has 30% of the global market for baby food. The way it sells substitutes for breast milk remains controversial. An international boycott started by consumer activists in 1977 is still active in over 100 countries.
country's GNI smaller than: **Kraft Foods** but bigger than: McDonald's	Kraft sells in 170 countries. 40 of its brands are more than a century old. It started in 1903. Its first-year losses amounted to $3,000 and one horse. In 1915 the company invented pasteurized processed cheese.
country's GNI smaller than: **McDonald's** ($24.1 billion)	McDonald's employs 1.7 million people and operates in 119 countries. It serves 68 million customers a day – more than the population of France or the UK.
no data	

Wheel of Fortune
Changes to Fortune magazine's ranking of largest corporations
2011

Fortune Global 500 2011

39 new to list include:
- 15 Chinese
- 7 European
- 5 South Korean

among 39 dropped from list
- 20 European
- 11 US
- 5 Japanese

◀ 38 Income

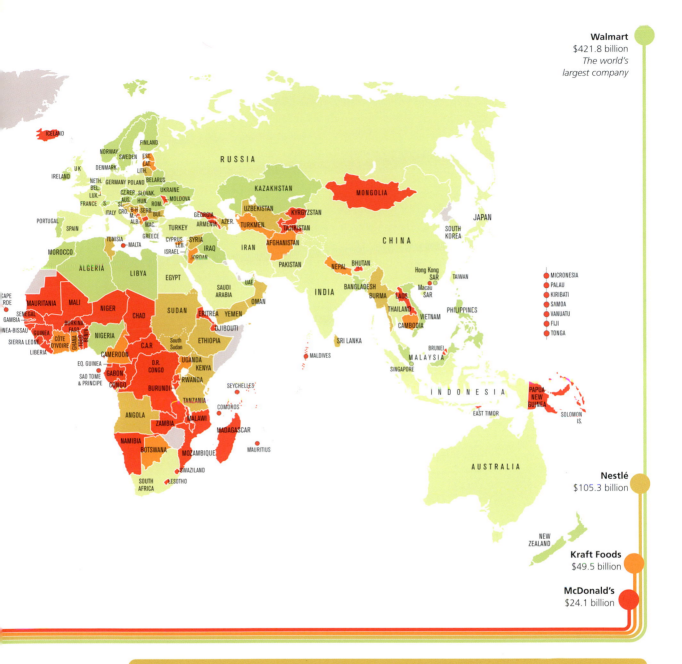

Walmart
$421.8 billion
The world's largest company

MICRONESIA
PALAU
KIRIBATI
SAMOA
VANUATU
FIJI
TONGA

Nestlé
$105.3 billion

Kraft Foods
$49.5 billion

McDonald's
$24.1 billion

Profitability

The profits of these selected major companies are larger than the GNI of each of these countries
2010

Nestlé:
$32.84bn
≥ GNI of 82 countries

Paraguay • Trinidad & Tobago • Luxembourg • Cambodia • Honduras • Albania • Botswana • Estonia • Cyprus • Macau SAR • Senegal Macedonia • Georgia • Mozambique • Democratic Republic of Congo • Burkina Faso • Madagascar • Jamaica • Brunei • Gabon

Microsoft:
$18.76bn
≥ GNI of 62 countries

Mauritius • Zambia • Armenia • Equatorial Guinea • Papua New Guinea • Nicaragua • Mali • Laos Tajikistan • Namibia • Benin • Chad

Apple:
$14.01bn
≥ GNI of 50 countries

Congo • Malawi • Rwanda • Moldova • Haiti • Kyrgyzstan • Niger • Malta Guinea • Mongolia • Iceland • Bahamas • Montenegro • Mauritania • Swaziland Togo • Barbados • Sierra Leone • Lesotho • East Timor • Suriname • Fiji • Bhutan Central African Republic • Burundi • Eritrea • Guyana • Maldives • Gambia Djibouti • Belize • Cape Verde • Seychelles • St Lucia • Antigua & Barbuda Guinea-Bissau • Liberia • Solomon Is • St Vincent & The Grenadines • Vanuatu Grenada • St Kitts & Nevis • Dominica • Comoros • Samoa • Tonga • Micronesia Kiribati • São Tome & Príncipe • Palau

Banks

Bank failures lay behind the financial crash of 2008 that has fed the recessions and depression since then. There were failures in two senses: in the technical sense that some banks did not have enough assets to meet their liabilities; and in the ordinary sense that they and the people who ran them, as well as those who regulated them, failed. They didn't do their jobs properly. The top bankers, however, with only a few exceptions, have weathered the storm and continue to receive vast salaries and bonuses.

The consequences of that dual failure are so far-reaching because the banks are so big and because money and credit are fundamental to the functioning of a modern economy. When the credit system goes bust, it threatens to take the money system down with it. The peak (so far) of the fear this creates has been found in the Eurozone – 17 disparate members of the European Union who chose to enter a monetary union. Because of this fear, the current history of the Eurozone is a series of crisis meetings – another summit, another national bail-out.

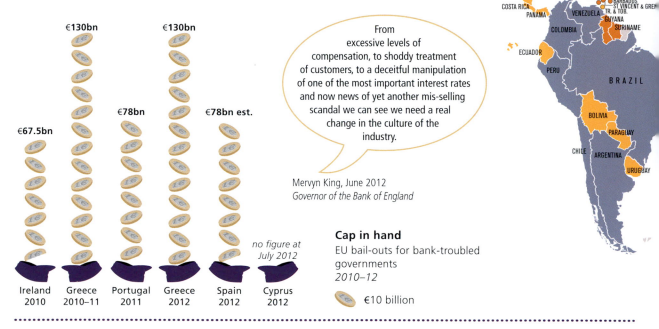

€130bn   €130bn

€67.5bn   €78bn   €78bn est.

| Ireland 2010 | Greece 2010–11 | Portugal 2011 | Greece 2012 | Spain 2012 | Cyprus 2012 |

no figure at July 2012

From excessive levels of compensation, to shoddy treatment of customers, to a deceitful manipulation of one of the most important interest rates and now news of yet another mis-selling scandal we can see we need a real change in the culture of the industry.

Mervyn King, June 2012
Governor of the Bank of England

Cap in hand
EU bail-outs for bank-troubled governments
2010–12

€10 billion

Peaks and troughs of the banking crisis

2008 Iceland: Following the collapse of all three major commercial banks, Iceland effectively went bankrupt. The prime minister of the time has been convicted for negligence.

2008 UK: Economic bail-out commitment peaked at **£4.5 trillion** in loans, spending & guarantees.

2009 USA: Commitment to economic rescue peaked at **$12.8 trillion** in loans, spending & guarantees.

2011 Bank boss bonuses: Banks' average share price and revenues dropped in all financial centres AND top banks awarded their chiefs **$12.8m** on average – **11.9% more** than in 2010.

2012 Spain: As the banking crisis accelerated to bail-out, Spanish escorts **banned sex** with bankers until they started lending to small business and families.

2008   2009   2011   2012

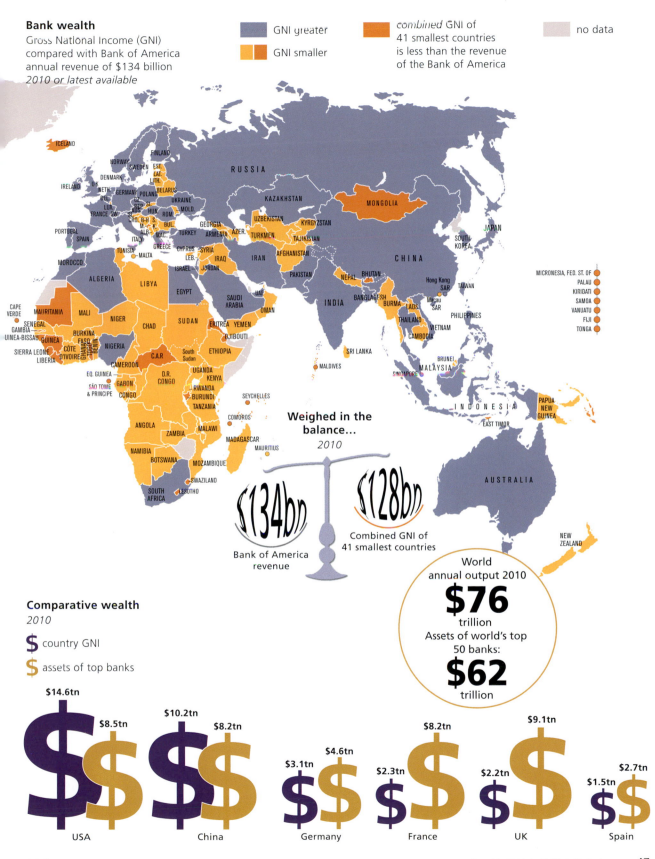

Bank wealth

Gross National Income (GNI) compared with Bank of America annual revenue of $134 billion
2010 or latest available

GNI greater

GNI smaller

combined GNI of 41 smallest countries is less than the revenue of the Bank of America

no data

Weighed in the balance...
2010

$134bn
Bank of America revenue

$128bn
Combined GNI of 41 smallest countries

World annual output 2010
$76 trillion
Assets of world's top 50 banks:
$62 trillion

Comparative wealth
2010

$ country GNI

$ assets of top banks

$14.6tn	$8.5tn	$10.2tn	$8.2tn	$3.1tn	$4.6tn	$2.3tn	$8.2tn	$2.2tn	$9.1tn	$1.5tn	$2.7tn
USA		China		Germany		France		UK		Spain	

Corruption

Corruption is everywhere – officials taking bribes, companies and individuals evading taxes. It weakens governments and weakens public trust in them. Transparency International provides an index of corruption that is highly regarded, if often controversial, based on the perceptions of the citizens of the countries concerned.

The strength of the shadow economy is one indicator of a corrupt society. Although it may involve activities that are themselves legal, the failure to report the financial gains from those activities to the country's tax authorities – tax *evasion* – is illegal. It steals about 25 per cent of potential global tax revenue. Tax *avoidance*, on the other hand, is legal. It exploits loopholes in the law, differences between national laws, and the existence of tax havens. It probably costs as much if not more.

The shadow economy
Economic activities unreported to tax authorities as percentage of the formal economy
average for 1999–2007

- 51% – 66%
- 36% – 50%
- 21% – 35%
- 9% – 20%
- no data

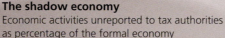

The shadow economy represents more than 60% of total output in Bolivia, Georgia, and Zimbabwe.

CANADA

USA

MEXICO

BAHAMAS
CUBA
DOMINICAN REP.
PUERTO RICO
JAMAICA
HAITI
HONDURAS
GUATEMALA
EL SALVADOR
NICARAGUA
COSTA RICA
PANAMA
ST VINCENT & GRENADINES
DOMINICA
ST LUCIA
BARBADOS
TRINIDAD & TOBAGO
VENEZUELA
GUYANA
SURINAME
COLOMBIA
ECUADOR
PERU
BRAZIL
BOLIVIA
PARAGUAY
CHILE
ARGENTINA
URUGUAY

BAHAMAS

CAPE VERDE

MALTA

MALDIVES

SINGAPORE

COMOROS

MAURITIUS

FIJI

Level of corruption

Score according to Corruption Perceptions Index 2010

1.0 – 2.5	*highly corrupt*	
2.6 – 5.0	*significantly corrupt*	
5.1 – 7.5	*reasonably clean*	
7.6 – 10.0	*very clean*	
	no data	

Estimate of assets held legally in tax havens:

$21 trillion

Estimate of revenue lost to illegal tax evasion:

$3 trillion

5.9 billion
people live in countries considered significantly corrupt

Debt

The credit crunch of 2007 to 2008 that turned into the economic crash of 2008 to 2009 that became the fiscal catastrophe of 2010 and beyond has been fuelled by the unsustainable and unrepayable debt of governments, private companies, and individuals. But not everywhere and everyone is equally indebted. American borrowing had largely been thanks to China's willingness to lend, leading to a major imbalance between the mountain of savings in China and the pits of debt in the USA.

In Europe, governments responded to the magnitude of debt with austerity policies. Banks, having lent too much, cut back sharply on loans. The combined result of the original ills and this remedy was economic slowdown and unemployment, financial crises and new bail-outs every few months, and growing political uncertainty.

In the USA, the treatment applied to the economic problem was less harsh, but recovery was slow, and confidence about the future was low.

Current account balance
2010 or latest available data
US$

Deficit of:

- $470 billion
- $11 billion – $68 billion
- $1 billion – $10 billion
- $999 million deficit – $999 million surplus

Surplus of:

- $1 billion – $100 billion
- $166 billion – $305 billion
- no data

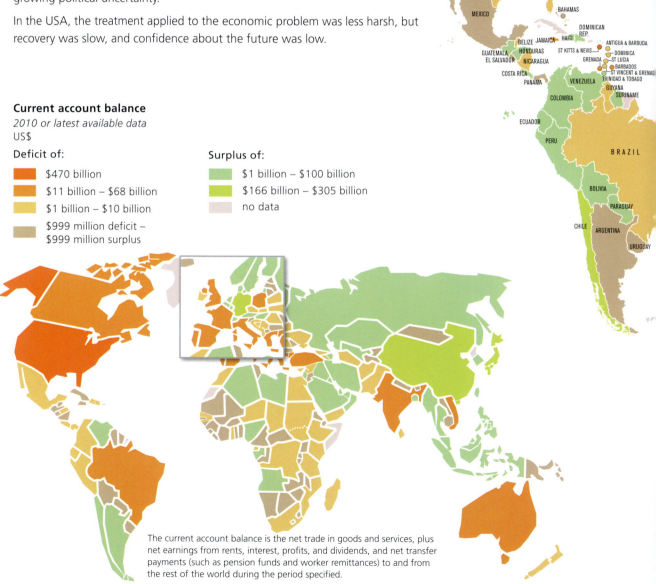

The current account balance is the net trade in goods and services, plus net earnings from rents, interest, profits, and dividends, and net transfer payments (such as pension funds and worker remittances) to and from the rest of the world during the period specified.

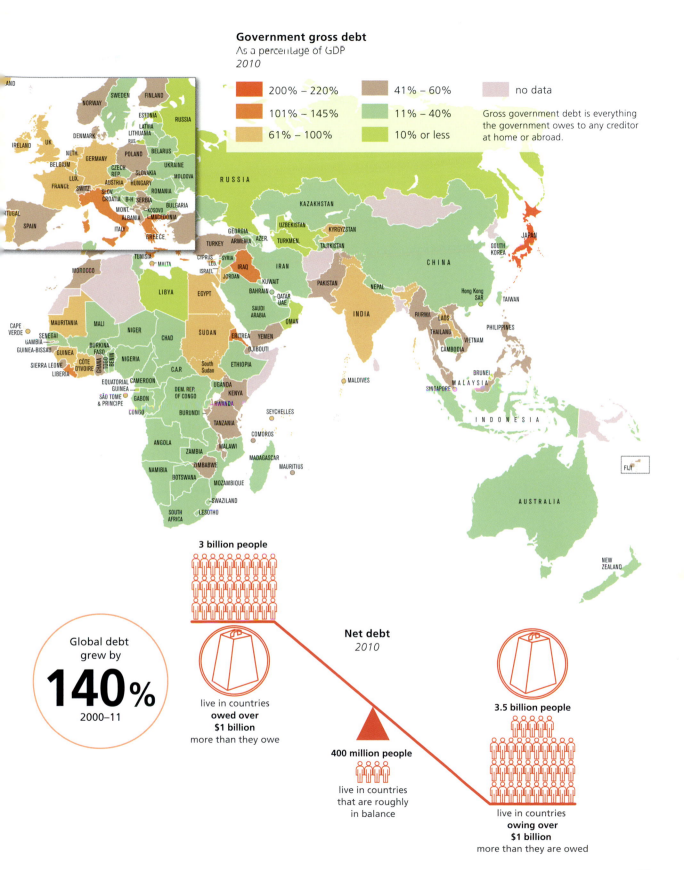

Government gross debt
As a percentage of GDP
2010

200% – 220%	41% – 60%
101% – 145%	11% – 40%
61% – 100%	10% or less
no data	

Gross government debt is everything the government owes to any creditor at home or abroad.

3 billion people

Net debt
2010

live in countries
**owed over
$1 billion**
more than they owe

Global debt grew by

140%

2000–11

400 million people

live in countries
that are roughly
in balance

3.5 billion people

live in countries
**owing over
$1 billion**
more than they are owed

Tourism

Tourism is a sorely needed source of income for many countries. In the Middle East and North Africa, a third of export income is earned through tourism. And for many Caribbean and Pacific islands, the tourist dollar represents more than 40 per cent of the country's income. Tourism often threatens the natural and architectural beauty that attracts the visitors. It is a potent form of cultural invasion, and in extreme circumstances armed groups have declared tourists to be legitimate targets for attack.

2000:
723
million
tourist trips

Economic significance of tourism
2010 or latest available data

Countries where earnings from overseas visitors as percentage of export earnings is:

more than 40%

21% – 40%

BAHAMAS
DOMINICAN REPLUBIC
JAMAICA ANTIGUA & BARBUDA
BELIZE HAITI DOMINICA
ST KITTS & NEVIS ST LUCIA
GRENADA BARBADOS
ARUBA
ST VINCENT & GRENADINES

Canada 27m
UK 59m
Germany 72m
Russia 37m
USA 61m
Portugal 21m
France 21m
Italy 29m
Poland 50m
China 48m
Hong Kong 82m

Departures
Countries generating highest number of overseas trips
2010 or latest available data

20 million

2010:
940
million
tourist trips

2030
projected:
1,800
million
tourist trips

CROATIA
ALBANIA ARMENIA
GREECE SYRIA
MOROCCO LEBANON JORDAN
PALESTINIAN
TERRITORIES
CAPE
VERDE EGYPT
GUINEA-BISSAU
LIBERIA
SÃO TOME
& PRINCIPE
RWANDA
TANZANIA
MADAGASCAR
MAURITIUS
ETHIOPIA
UGANDA
SEYCHELLES

NEPAL
Macau SAR
CAMBODIA
MALDIVES

SOLOMON
ISLANDS
SAMOA
VANUATU FIJI
TONGA
FRENCH
POLYNESIA

UK
28m

Germany
24m

Russia
24m

Ukraine
21m

France
77m

Austria
21m

USA
60m

Spain
52m

Italy
43m

Turkey
26m

China
51m

Mexico
21m

Malaysia
24m

Arrivals
Countries attracting highest
number of overseas trips
2010 or latest available data

20
million

53

Goals for Development

In 2000, the UN summit agreed the Millennium Declaration – aspirations for the new century. The following year the narrower, measurable Millennium Development Goals (MDGs) set out what the grand ambitions meant in practice, with 2015 as a target date for achieving them.

The MDGs have encouraged increased aid for development (though its continued growth is put in doubt by the tough economic environment), and have helped focus international effort onto important goals in health and education. But the record is mixed, partly because the MDGs are not equally applicable in all countries with widely differing circumstances. Conflict-affected countries have needs the MDGs do not address. And success in reducing global poverty is not due to the MDGs but to China's spectacular economic growth.

Millennium Development Goals
Progress achieved 2001–11 compared to targets whose benchmark is 1990

- target already met or expected to be met by 2015
- progress insufficient to reach target if prevailing trends persist
- no progress, or deterioration
- missing or insufficient data

Goal 1 Eradicate extreme poverty and hunger
Selected target: Reduce $1 a day poverty by half

World poverty is falling mainly due to Chinese economic growth. In a troubled global economy, progress in Africa, South Asia, and Latin America is behind. ◀ 40 *Inequality;* ▶ 92 *Malnutrition*

Goal 2 Achieve universal primary education
Target: Universal primary schooling

There is progress overall but much too slow to meet the target. There have been dramatic increases in Africa but the situation is static elsewhere. ◀ 30 *Literacy & Education*

Overseas aid
Total aid disbursed *1990–2009*
and breakdown by donor *2009*

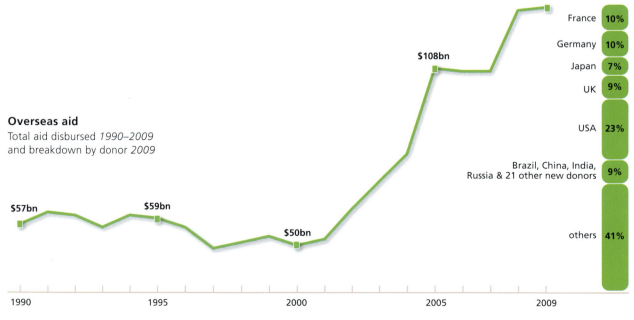

$57bn $59bn $50bn $108bn $128bn

France	10%
Germany	10%
Japan	7%
UK	9%
USA	23%
Brazil, China, India, Russia & 21 other new donors	9%
others	41%

1990   1995   2000   2005   2009

◀ 30 *Literacy & Education;* 40 *Inequality*

Goal 3 Promote gender equality and empower women
Selected target: Increase women's paid employment

There have been significant gains in girls' education (and this target will be met on time) and slow improvements in women's economic and political participation. ▶ 84 *Women's Rights*

Goal 4 Reduce child mortality
Target: Reduce mortality of under-five-year-olds by 66%

There has been progress everywhere, and global child mortality has fallen by one third; children in rural areas face much higher risk than urban children.

Goal 5 Improve maternal health
Selected target: Reduce maternal mortality by 75%

Based on very vague data, maternal mortality seems to be reducing (34% down by 2008) except in Africa, but even as a global average the goal looks unachievable.

Goal 6 Combat HIV/AIDS, malaria, and other diseases
Target: Halt and reverse spread of tuberculosis

New HIV infections are declining – especially in Africa. Malaria deaths are 20% down. The incidence of tuberculosis is falling in Africa, and treatment is increasingly available. ▶ 98 *HIV/AIDS*

Goal 7 Ensure environmental sustainability
Selected target: Reduce forest loss

Despite progress, the world faces an environmental crisis. It has gone beyond safe margins on some key issues, and there is little sign of world agreement on a new course. ▶ 110 *Water Resources*; 114 *Waste*

Goal 8 Develop a global partnership for development
Selected target: Make internet widely accessible

There has been increased aid, reduced debt burdens, and more transfer of technology – but terms of trade remain unfavourable to poorer countries.

PART THREE
WAR & PEACE

Peace is one of the great but quiet good news stories of our time though it is a long way from being a smooth or perfect picture. Using consistent definitions, there were 50 armed conflicts in 1990 and 30 in 2010; a brief upsurge of wars in the early 1990s was followed by a sustained downward trend in the number of armed conflicts each year. It was fairly consistent until about 2006 but now seems to have bottomed out.

Though there is no certain information about war deaths, it does also seem true that while war remains one of the major causes of death worldwide, there is not only less war, but it is also less lethal than before. Nonetheless, the human costs remain extremely high, as 30 million refugees may attest, with long-term economic damage and, as one of the major after-effects of armed conflict, an increased risk that it will happen again.

The decline in armed conflict worldwide reflects a general pattern of being less inclined to inflict cruelty on fellow human beings, and less inclined to accept it when it happens. A much smaller proportion of people die violent deaths than a few hundred years ago. The decline in the number of wars has not just happened as part of a long historical trend, however; it is the result of an enormous effort. One study records a total of 646 peace agreements signed between 1990 and the end of 2007, considerably more in less than two decades than had been arrived at in the previous two centuries.

The benefits of the peace-making enterprise since 1990 are clear, but what is less obvious is whether it has addressed the underlying causes of armed conflict, or succeeded only in addressing symptoms without going further.

The situation in a country can be described as peaceful when people are able to have their conflicts without violence. Conflict is not only an apparently inevitable part of life, it is also often necessary, productive, and progressive. Many improvements in the conditions of ordinary people and almost all increases in political rights and freedoms were gained only by conflict. But if change is available only through violence, it is all too often tainted by the very acts that win it. The problem, in short, is not conflict – it is violent conflict.

Being able to have conflicts without threat of violence is what many of our most important institutions are for – courts, parliaments and assemblies, laws and government. When these are backed by other institutions that make it possible for people to be consulted about decisions that directly affect their lives, the whole builds into an implicit contract of accountable authority.

To achieve this, ordinary people need to be able to participate in shaping the way we are governed – primarily through elections to representative bodies. We need enough income and assets for a dignified life, and we need freedom from fear of physical or psychological threat. We need a fair and efficient justice system based on equality before the law and we need the agents of security such as the police to work with and for the people rather than to prey on us. And finally we need our well-being to be upheld and advanced through access both to services such as clean water, education, and health care, and to common goods, such as a sense of community. Lying behind these factors of a peaceful society are values of inclusivity and fairness. This is a view of society in which the greatest good is served by a balance between the collective good and the individual's well-being, and thus between the rights and responsibilities of individuals. Peace agreements offer an opportunity for countries afflicted by violent conflict to find a way towards this process of self-sustaining peace.

This is the direction of travel in some parts of the world. But there are also reasons for concern. Though the number of armed conflicts has declined, 1.5 billion people live in countries experiencing political and social instability and large-scale criminal violence. In these countries, not a single Millennium Development Goal has been achieved, and probably none will be by 2015, the MDG target date. The intersection of crime, politics, and business leads to intractable violent conflicts for which current international institutions are not really suited, neither in mandate, skills, nor mind-set. It is rarely possible for the International Red Cross to find humanitarian space between a state and a criminal. The UN's high representatives and other potential mediators have no mandate there either. Yet the scale of death and destruction inflicted in such cases may be as bad as in any armed conflict.

Furthermore, the decline in the number of armed political conflicts should not lead anyone to think something irreversible has happened. Potentially competing and clashing demands for natural resources could lead, especially against a background of social instability, to a resurgence in the number of civil wars. If that happens while the economic depression retains its grip, it is an open question whether the international organizations and governments that have hitherto been willing to fund peace-making, peacekeeping, and peacebuilding, will still have the energy and resources to continue.

War in the 21st Century

The period since the end of the Cold War in 1989 is an era of growing peace – yet there has never been more global awareness of the problem of armed conflict. The war horrors in Afghanistan, Iraq, Sudan, Syria, and elsewhere have grabbed international attention; even when international intervention does not happen it is discussed. There is a feeling abroad that something has to be done.

Less widely noticed has been a gradual, uneven, but over time unmistakeable, decline in the number and ferocity of armed conflicts. It is no comfort to those who suffer amidst some of the most appalling brutality humans can devise, but the fact is that overall the world has been getting safer. The tougher economic times that have followed the financial crash of 2008 suggest it may get harder to sustain that progress.

Beyond national borders
Most war-fighting by states outside their borders was done in just three wars.

■ location of war
■ participating states

Dem Rep Congo, early 2000s:
Angola, Burundi, Chad, Namibia, Rwanda, Sudan, Uganda, Zimbabwe

Afghanistan from 2001:
Australia, Belgium, Canada, Denmark, France, Georgia, Germany, Italy, Netherlands, Norway, Turkey, UK, USA

Iraq from 2003:
Australia, Poland, UK, USA

50 wars in 1990
30 in 2010

The Americas

At war

Presence of open armed conflict
for political goals with continuity
between clashes
2000–mid-2012

has experienced armed conflict within national borders 2000–11

armed conflict active within national borders during first half of 2012

has *also* fought war outside national borders 2000–12

has *only* fought war outside national borders 2000–12

has not experienced armed conflict within national borders 2000–12

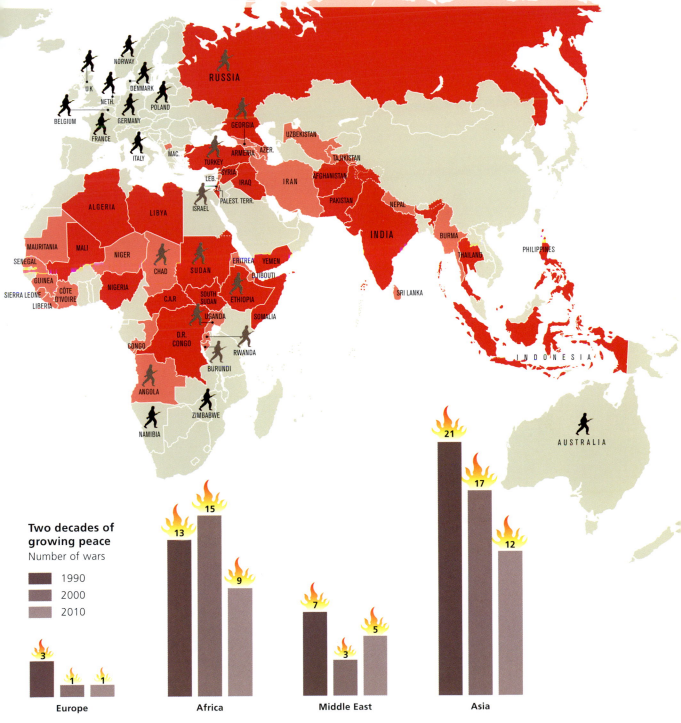

NORWAY

UK

DENMARK

NETH.

BELGIUM

GERMANY

POLAND

FRANCE

ITALY

MAC.

RUSSIA

GEORGIA

TURKEY

ARMENIA

AZER.

UZBEKISTAN

TAJIKISTAN

SYRIA

LEB.

IRAQ

IRAN

AFGHANISTAN

ISRAEL

PALEST. TERR.

PAKISTAN

NEPAL

INDIA

ALGERIA

LIBYA

MAURITANIA

MALI

NIGER

CHAD

SUDAN

ERITREA

YEMEN

DJIBOUTI

SENEGAL

GUINEA

SIERRA LEONE

CÔTE
D'IVOIRE

LIBERIA

NIGERIA

C.A.R.

SOUTH
SUDAN

ETHIOPIA

SOMALIA

UGANDA

D.R.
CONGO

RWANDA

BURUNDI

CONGO

ANGOLA

ZIMBABWE

NAMIBIA

BURMA

THAILAND

PHILIPPINES

SRI LANKA

INDONESIA

AUSTRALIA

Two decades of growing peace

Number of wars

- 1990
- 2000
- 2010

Europe
3
1
1

Africa
13
15
9

Middle East
7
3
5

Asia
21
17
12

62 Military Muscle; 66 Casualties of War; 68 Refugees; 80 Human Rights ▶

Copyright © Myriad Editions Limited

Warlords, Ganglords, & Militias

While the number and intensity of wars between states have declined, new problems have come into view – the proliferation of non-state armed forces and the number of armed conflicts in which the state has no part.

The power of private armies and the risk of non-state wars grow when and where the state's ability to impose order is weak – and in some parts of some countries the state is essentially absent for extended periods. This may happen because of the impact of war, or through the corruption of the state, or because it simply cannot afford to obtain the equipment and train the forces it would need in order to control its territory. Many militias continue to operate long after the war is over.

In those circumstances, local leaders emerge, often enriching themselves by controlling key economic activities – small-scale mining, as in eastern DRC, or the narcotics trade, as in Colombia, Mexico, and Central Asia. If the state does reappear with a campaign to restore its authority, its soldiers all too often become part of the problem, terrorizing civilians with theft, rape, and other human rights abuses.

One common abuse in which militias lead the way is recruiting children to fight, often forcibly, always with a brutal, traumatizing impact on the children's lives – even if they survive the war.

Mexico and Colombia: Drug money provides criminal cartels with weapons and power.

MEXICO

GUATEMALA

HONDURAS

COLOMBIA

ECUADOR

BRAZIL

Colombia

Côte d'Ivoire

Nigeria

Chad

C.A.R

Sudan

S. Sudan

Uganda

Dem. Rep. of Congo

Burundi

Somalia

Iraq

Afghanistan

Pakistan

Nepal

India

Burma

Thailand

Sri Lanka

Philippines

Child soldiers
Used by non-state armed forces
mid 2000s

Nigeria: Police report that the group usually referred to as Boko Haram is responsible for at least 1,200 deaths since 2009.

Democratic Republic of Congo: Many insurgent groups were integrated into the country's army in 2009. In 2012, some groups mutinied and pulled out of the national army.

Nepal: There are thought to be between 50 and 100 armed groups active in the south-east of the country.

Non-state armed forces
Estimated strength
2010–12

10,000 or more	unknown strength
fewer than 10,000	no known non-state armed force

armed conflict fought between non-state forces
2002–12

Military Muscle

World military spending in 2011 was approximately $1.5 trillion. Regular armed forces had just over 20 million personnel. About 20,000 nuclear warheads were stockpiled.

With the end of the Cold War, many people believed there would be a major peace dividend. Military spending did indeed decline, but was protected against deeper cuts in the 1990s by several factors. Zones of political tension and military rivalry persisted; military spending was supported by entrenched interests and justified by residual security fears. And some Western states were attracted by the paradoxical idea of enforcing peace – using armed force against states such as Yugoslavia and Iraq, whose leaders' regional ambitions destabilized peace and security.

With the turn of the century, hopes of a renewed peace dividend were swamped by the US response to 9/11 – and by the response of other states to the renewed US willingness to project force. The global economic crisis has tightened the public purse strings, but interests, fears, and rivalries still combine to keep military spending buoyant.

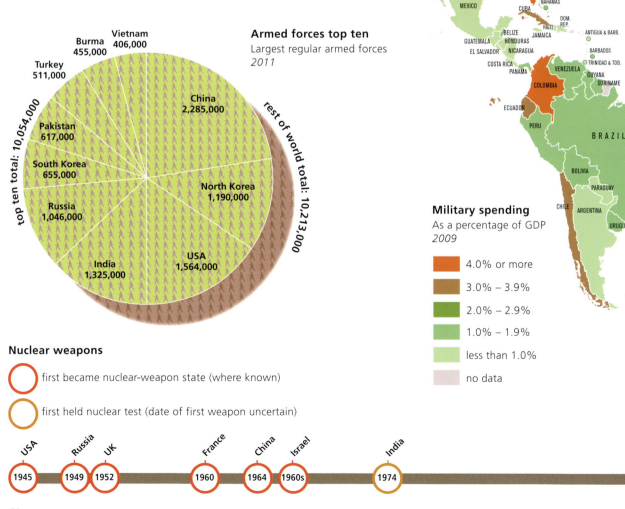

$526,271m

$441,561m

$668,604m

USA

Armed forces top ten
Largest regular armed forces
2011

top ten total: 10,054,000

Vietnam 406,000
Burma 455,000
Turkey 511,000
Pakistan 617,000
South Korea 655,000
Russia 1,046,000
India 1,325,000
China 2,285,000
North Korea 1,190,000
USA 1,564,000

rest of world total: 10,213,000

CANADA

USA

MEXICO
BAHAMAS
CUBA
DOM. REP.
HAITI
BELIZE
JAMAICA
GUATEMALA
HONDURAS
EL SALVADOR
NICARAGUA
COSTA RICA
PANAMA
ANTIGUA & BARB.
BARBADOS
TRINIDAD & TOB.
VENEZUELA
GUYANA
COLOMBIA
SURINAME
ECUADOR
PERU
BRAZIL
BOLIVIA
PARAGUAY
CHILE
ARGENTINA
URUGUAY

Military spending
As a percentage of GDP
2009

- 4.0% or more
- 3.0% – 3.9%
- 2.0% – 2.9%
- 1.0% – 1.9%
- less than 1.0%
- no data

Nuclear weapons

first became nuclear-weapon state (where known)

first held nuclear test (date of first weapon uncertain)

USA 1945
Russia 1949
UK 1952
France 1960
China 1964
Israel 1960s
India 1974

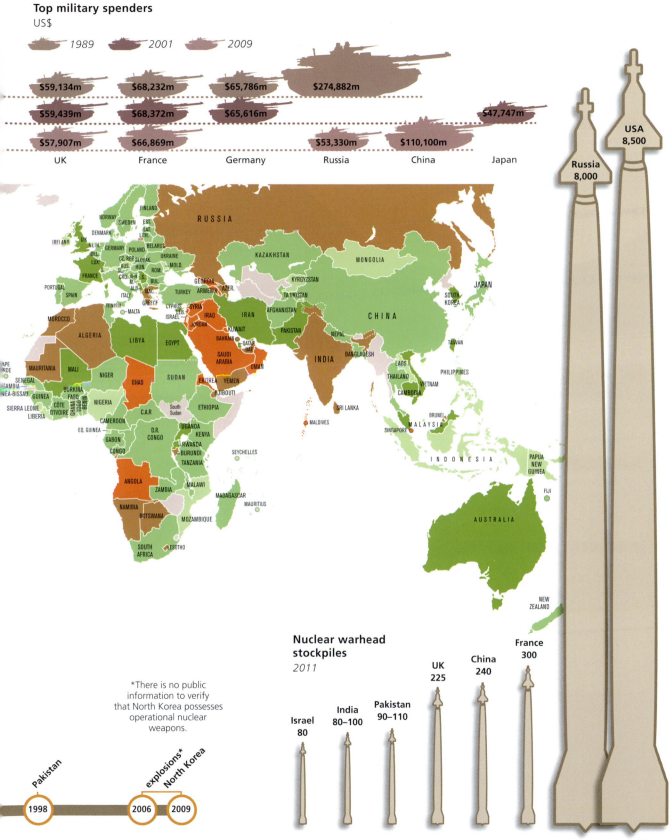

Top military spenders
US$

1989 *2001* *2009*

$59,134m	$68,232m	$65,786m	$274,882m		
$59,439m	$68,372m	$65,616m			$47,747m
$57,907m	$66,869m		$53,330m	$110,100m	
UK	France	Germany	Russia	China	Japan

Nuclear warhead stockpiles
2011

Israel 80

India 80–100

Pakistan 90–110

UK 225

China 240

France 300

Russia 8,000

USA 8,500

*There is no public information to verify that North Korea possesses operational nuclear weapons.

Pakistan 1998

explosions* 2006

North Korea 2009

The New Front Line

Warfare constantly evolves. Global travel and communications allow different kinds of attack and response. Drones and special forces are now the instruments of choice for the most powerful, terror attacks remain the top tactical option for the less powerful but determined, and a race is on for cyber supremacy.

- **drones**
- **cyber**
- **special forces**
- **terrorism/piracy**

Global cyber attack, 2011: The biggest reported series of cyber attacks to date hit 72 organizations including:
- The governments of Canada, India, S. Korea, Taiwan, Vietnam, USA
- The UN secretariat in Geneva
- The Association of South-East Asian Nations
- The International Olympic Committee and the World Anti-Doping Agency
- Defence contractors and hi-tech companies

Estonia, 2007: A series of a "distributed denial of service" (DDoS) attacks originating from Russia disrupted government departments and interrupted access to emergency services.

USA, 9/11: Al-Qaeda terrorists crash three airliners into the World Trade Center and the Pentagon, killing 2,973 people of more than 50 nationalities.

London, UK, 2005: Four suicide bombers on public transport kill 52 people.

Terror and the economy: Each act of terror costs the country where it takes place about 0.4% of annual GNI.

USA, 9/11: Estimated cost to al-Qaeda of attack on the World Trade Center and Pentagon: $0.5m. Estimated cost to USA of responding, including rebuilding and counter-terror measures, approximately $3.3tn. Cost ratio: 1:7,000,000

London, UK, 2012: UK's counter-intelligence director illustrated cyber threat by reference to an unnamed major UK company that lost around $1.35bn in a hostile cyber attack.

Piracy global cost: Including theft, insurance, damage, preventive measures, and response: approximately $2bn a year.

Madrid, Spain, 2004: Bombs on four trains kill 191 people.

Piracy around the globe, 2012: The International Maritime Bureau warned shipmasters about the following piracy hotspots: coasts of Ecuador and West Africa; Red Sea, Gulf of Yemen; Indian Ocean from Oman to Madagascar as far east as the Maldives; coasts of Bangladesh and Indonesia; Malacca Straits, Singapore Straits.

Cyber Command, 2010: USA appoints first general in charge of cyber warfare. 30,000 US troops reassigned to cyber warfare missions.

Libya, 2011: Former UK special forces soldiers fought with rebels to topple the Gaddafi regime.

Beslan, Russia, 2004: Chechen fighters hold children and parents hostage in school. 336 hostages and 30 Chechens killed when Russian security forces storm school.

Georgia, 2008: As the Russian–Georgian war started, Russian nationalists mounted a "distributed denial of service" (DDoS) attack on Georgia – flooding government websites with bogus enquiries so as to overwhelm and crash them.

US military, Middle East, 2008: At a US military base in the Middle East, memory sticks containing a self-propagating worm were deliberately left in a washroom. One or more soldiers broke regulations by putting one in a military laptop. US Central Command was infected; the clean up took 14 months.

Somalia: Piracy has grown into a local "industry". In 2000, Somali pirates were responsible for 5% of global attacks; by 2009 this had risen to 52%. In June 2012 they were holding 13 vessels and 185 hostages.

Somalia, 2007–12: Up to 169 civilians killed by US drone strikes.

Kampala, Uganda, 2010: Ethiopian group al-Shabab detonated bombs in a bar where people were watching the football World Cup, killing 76 people.

Abbottabad, Pakistan, 2011: US Special Forces assassinated Osama bin-Laden 9½ years after 9/11.

Pakistan, 2007: Karachi, October: Bomb kills 140 supporters of ex-Prime Minister Benazir Bhutto. Rawalpindi, December: Bhutto and 28 supporters killed in further attack.

Pakistan, 2004–12: 332 reported US drone strikes, with a total death toll estimated at about 3,000, including 300 to 800 civilians and as many as 175 children.

Afghanistan, 2012: 30 US drone attacks on civilian homes in first 6 months of the year.

Iran, 2010: 30,000 government computers and some centrifuges in Iran's nuclear enrichment plant were deactivated by Stuxnet virus, widely believed to originate from USA and Israel.

Iran, 2012: Flamer, the most sophisticated cyber worm yet created, was allegedly designed in Israel. Targeted Iranian officials' computers, wiping out hard drives, and forcing some oil terminals to go offline. Bluetooth capability allowed it to leap from an infected laptop to other devices.

Virtual manoeuvres, 2011, 2012: US and Chinese officials jointly played cyber war games.

Mumbai, India, 2008: 10 terrorists mount three-day attack, focusing on two hotels, the main train station and a Jewish centre, killing 166 people.

North Korea, 2012: A senior US officer is reported saying that US and South Korean special forces have parachuted into North Korea to gather intelligence about underground military installations. Report is officially denied.

Xinjiang, China, 2008: Separatists reportedly attacked a group of around 70 policeman on a training run with machetes and grenade, killing 16 people. **2011:** 18 people died in a series of alleged terrorist attacks in the city of Kashgar.

China, 2009: China's special forces join a public military parade for first time.

China, 2010: China claimed it was hit by nearly 500,000 cyber attacks, almost half originating overseas: 15% from the USA and 8% from India.

Bali, 2002: 200 holidaymakers killed in al-Qaeda bomb attack.

Casualties of War

We have less certain knowledge about casualties than about almost any other aspect of war. Figures for battle deaths are concocted for propaganda – to claim success or blame, and to argue for or against outside intervention. Strip that away and uncertainties remain, caused by the power of rumour and the rudimentary systems of information in many war-torn zones.

About 600,000 deaths have been recorded as directly caused by violent conflicts from 2000 through 2010. That is almost certainly well below the real total. Statistical methods vary, and as a result the Peace and Conflict Research Department at Uppsala University, generally regarded as authoritative on global figures, includes an estimate for deaths in Iraq that is only 10 to 15 per cent of that provided by Iraq Body Count, usually regarded as authoritative on Iraq. One group of research centres proposed figures for 2004 to 2007 about double Uppsala's global estimates.

The confusion is even greater about indirect deaths caused by disease as health facilities are destroyed in war, or by the crime that erupts out of the chaos. One reasonable estimate is that, on average, indirect deaths are about four times as high as direct deaths – but there is no certain information.

The effects of war are long lasting. An average of 30 years of economic growth is lost through a civil war, and the country's international trade takes on average 20 years to recover. People who might otherwise have grown up healthy are born into poverty, malnutrition, and ill health. And one effect of war is war itself; 90 per cent of contemporary armed conflicts are old conflicts coming back.

1.5 billion
people live in countries under the threat of large-scale organized violence

CANADA

U S A

MEXICO

JAMAICA HAITI

HONDURAS

GUYANA

COLOMBIA

ECUADOR

PERU

BRAZIL

BOLIVIA

Death toll
By type of conflict
2000–10

Non-state conflict: an armed conflict that does not actively involve the state but other, non-state groups.

73,000

One-sided violence: organized and sustained attacks on defenceless civilians by the state or an armed group.

114,000

Armed conflict: politically motivated violence between the state and another party, involving armed force.

411,000

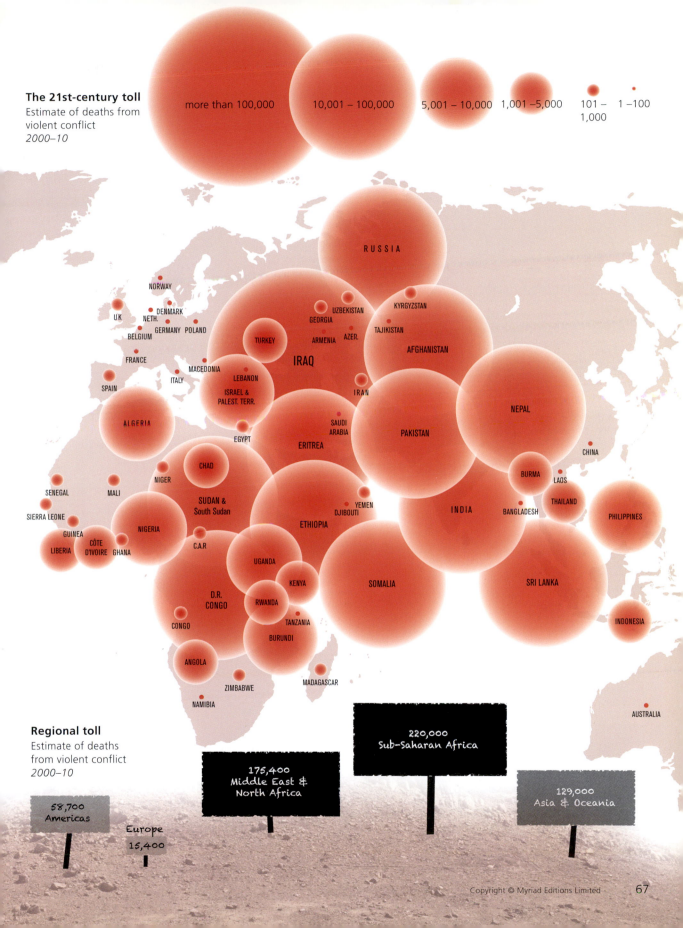

The 21st-century toll
Estimate of deaths from violent conflict
2000–10

more than 100,000

10,001 – 100,000

5,001 – 10,000

1,001 –5,000

101 – 1,000

1 –100

RUSSIA

NORWAY
DENMARK
UK
NETH.
BELGIUM GERMANY POLAND
FRANCE
ITALY
SPAIN
MACEDONIA
TURKEY
GEORGIA
UZBEKISTAN
ARMENIA AZER.
KYRGYZSTAN
TAJIKISTAN
AFGHANISTAN
LEBANON
ISRAEL &
PALEST. TERR.
IRAQ
IRAN
ALGERIA
EGYPT
SAUDI ARABIA
ERITREA
PAKISTAN
NEPAL
CHINA
CHAD
BURMA
LAOS
SENEGAL
NIGER
MALI
SUDAN &
South Sudan
YEMEN
DJIBOUTI
INDIA
BANGLADESH
THAILAND
PHILIPPINES
SIERRA LEONE
ETHIOPIA
GUINEA
LIBERIA
CÔTE
D'IVOIRE GHANA
NIGERIA
C.A.R
UGANDA
KENYA
SOMALIA
SRI LANKA
D.R.
CONGO
RWANDA
CONGO
TANZANIA
BURUNDI
INDONESIA
ANGOLA
ZIMBABWE
MADAGASCAR
NAMIBIA
AUSTRALIA

Regional toll
Estimate of deaths
from violent conflict
2000–10

220,000
Sub-Saharan Africa

175,400
Middle East &
North Africa

129,000
Asia & Oceania

58,700
Americas

Europe
15,400

67

Refugees

30 million people are unable to return to their homes because of war or repression. Many have been made refugees more than once. Some refugee populations now include the grandchildren of those who originally fled.

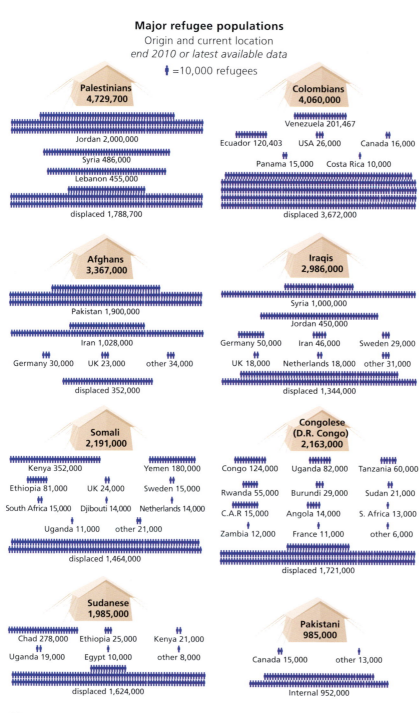

Major refugee populations
Origin and current location
end 2010 or latest available data

🚹 =10,000 refugees

Palestinians
4,729,700

Jordan 2,000,000

Syria 486,000

Lebanon 455,000

displaced 1,788,700

Colombians
4,060,000

Venezuela 201,467

Ecuador 120,403   USA 26,000   Canada 16,000

Panama 15,000   Costa Rica 10,000

displaced 3,672,000

Afghans
3,367,000

Pakistan 1,900,000

Iran 1,028,000

Germany 30,000   UK 23,000   other 34,000

displaced 352,000

Iraqis
2,986,000

Syria 1,000,000

Jordan 450,000

Germany 50,000   Iran 46,000   Sweden 29,000

UK 18,000   Netherlands 18,000   other 31,000

displaced 1,344,000

Somali
2,191,000

Kenya 352,000   Yemen 180,000

Ethiopia 81,000   UK 24,000   Sweden 15,000

South Africa 15,000   Djibouti 14,000   Netherlands 14,000

Uganda 11,000   other 21,000

displaced 1,464,000

Congolese (D.R. Congo)
2,163,000

Congo 124,000   Uganda 82,000   Tanzania 60,000

Rwanda 55,000   Burundi 29,000   Sudan 21,000

C.A.R 15,000   Angola 14,000   S. Africa 13,000

Zambia 12,000   France 11,000   other 6,000

displaced 1,721,000

Sudanese
1,985,000

Chad 278,000   Ethiopia 25,000   Kenya 21,000

Uganda 19,000   Egypt 10,000   other 8,000

displaced 1,624,000

Pakistani
985,000

Canada 15,000   other 13,000

Internal 952,000

Displaced
Number of people who have fled their homes but remain in their own country
end 2010

Some **14 million** people are **internally displaced**.

◀ 58 War in the 21st Century; 60 Warlords, Ganglords, & Militias

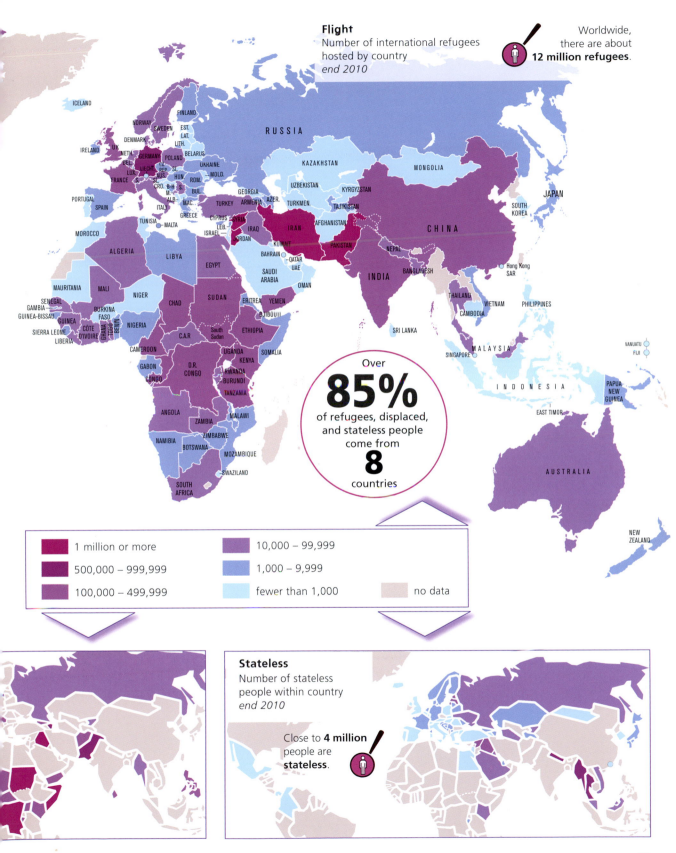

Flight
Number of international refugees hosted by country
end 2010

Worldwide, there are about **12 million refugees**.

Over **85%** of refugees, displaced, and stateless people come from **8** countries

	1 million or more		10,000 – 99,999
	500,000 – 999,999		1,000 – 9,999
	100,000 – 499,999		fewer than 1,000	no data

Stateless
Number of stateless people within country
end 2010

Close to **4 million** people are **stateless**.

Peacekeeping

There are nearly 100,000 UN peacekeepers, counting police as well as military personnel. The number of missions increased rapidly following the end of the Cold War in 1990, not because there were suddenly more wars (although the number did increase in the early 1990s), but because the end of the confrontation between the USA and the Soviet Union freed the United Nations to do more.

For the same reason, there were more agreements for peacekeeping forces to support. A UN study found that in the first 12 or so years after the end of the Cold War, as many peace agreements were signed as in the previous 200 years.

The number of peacekeeping missions plateaued in the mid-2000s and, although the trend is not yet clear, it looks as though it is now tailing off. This is partly an indication that several peacekeeping missions have been successfully accomplished – but may also be a sign that rich states are less willing to pay for peacekeeping in tougher economic times.

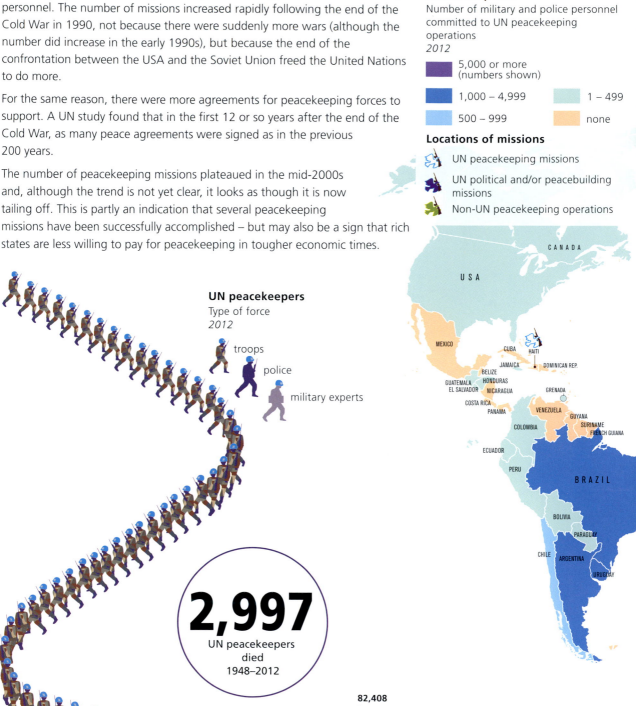

Forces for peace
Number of military and police personnel committed to UN peacekeeping operations
2012

- 5,000 or more (numbers shown)
- 1,000 – 4,999
- 500 – 999
- 1 – 499
- none

Locations of missions

- UN peacekeeping missions
- UN political and/or peacebuilding missions
- Non-UN peacekeeping operations

UN peacekeepers
Type of force
2012

- troops
- police
- military experts

2,997
UN peacekeepers died
1948–2012

82,408 troops

70

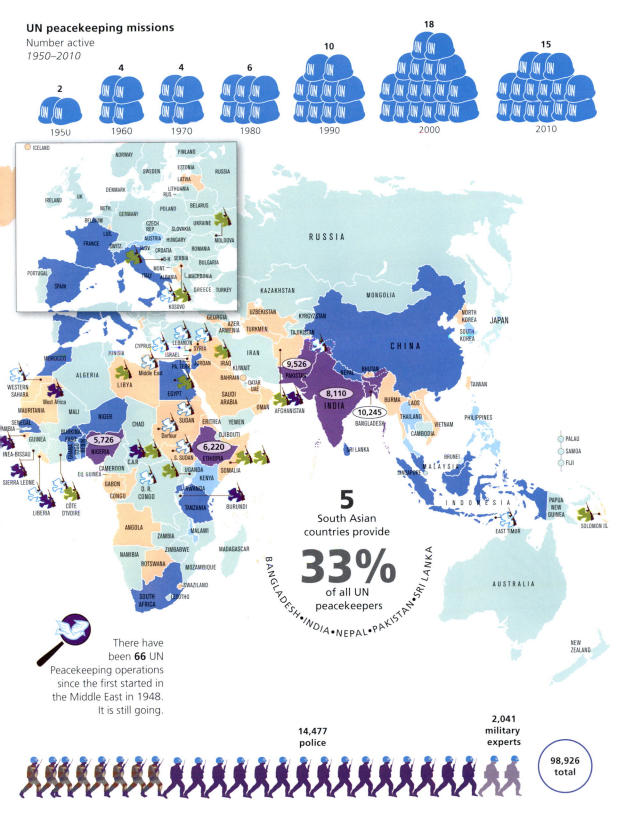

UN peacekeeping missions
Number active
1950–2010

2	4	4	6	10	18	15
1950	1960	1970	1980	1990	2000	2010

9,526 PAKISTAN

8,110 INDIA

10,245 BANGLADESH

5,726 NIGERIA

6,220 ETHIOPIA

5
South Asian
countries provide

33%
of all UN
peacekeepers

BANGLADESH • INDIA • NEPAL • PAKISTAN • SRI LANKA

There have
been **66** UN
Peacekeeping operations
since the first started in
the Middle East in 1948.
It is still going.

**14,477
police**

**2,041
military
experts**

**98,926
total**

Global Peacefulness

Discussion of armed conflict and peace almost always focuses heavily on what goes wrong and why. The Global Peace Index is an independent attempt to make sense of the other, too often neglected, part of the discussion – what goes right and why. The Index ranks countries according to their peacefulness, looking both at peace at home (government stability, democratic values, community relations, and trust between citizens) and peace in foreign relations (propensity to war, military spending, commitment to UN operations).

The Index is based on the idea that helping people and governments to understand what creates peaceful relations is a significant step towards making it possible for the world to be more peaceful.

If the USA were as peaceful as Canada, it would save $360 billion of public and private spending.

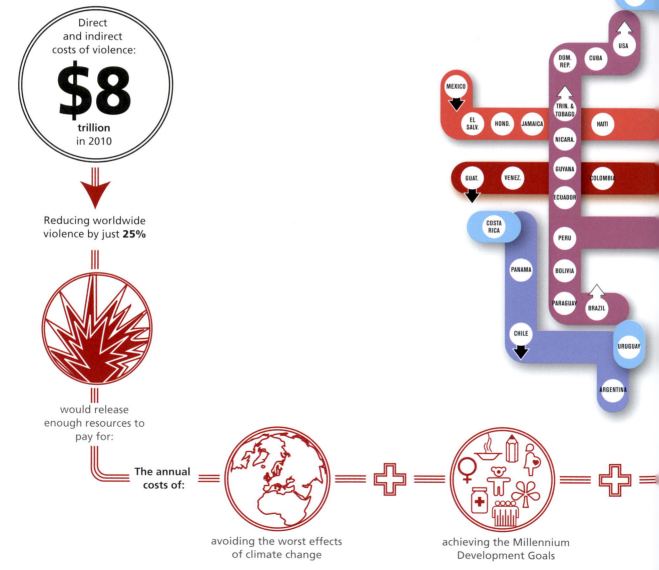

Direct and indirect costs of violence:

$8 trillion in 2010

Reducing worldwide violence by just **25%**

would release enough resources to pay for:

The annual costs of:

avoiding the worst effects of climate change

achieving the Millennium Development Goals

CANADA
USA
DOM. REP.
CUBA
MEXICO
TRIN. & TOBAGO
EL SALV.
HOND.
JAMAICA
HAITI
NICARA.
GUYANA
GUAT.
VENEZ.
COLOMBIA
ECUADOR
COSTA RICA
PERU
PANAMA
BOLIVIA
PARAGUAY
BRAZIL
CHILE
URUGUAY
ARGENTINA

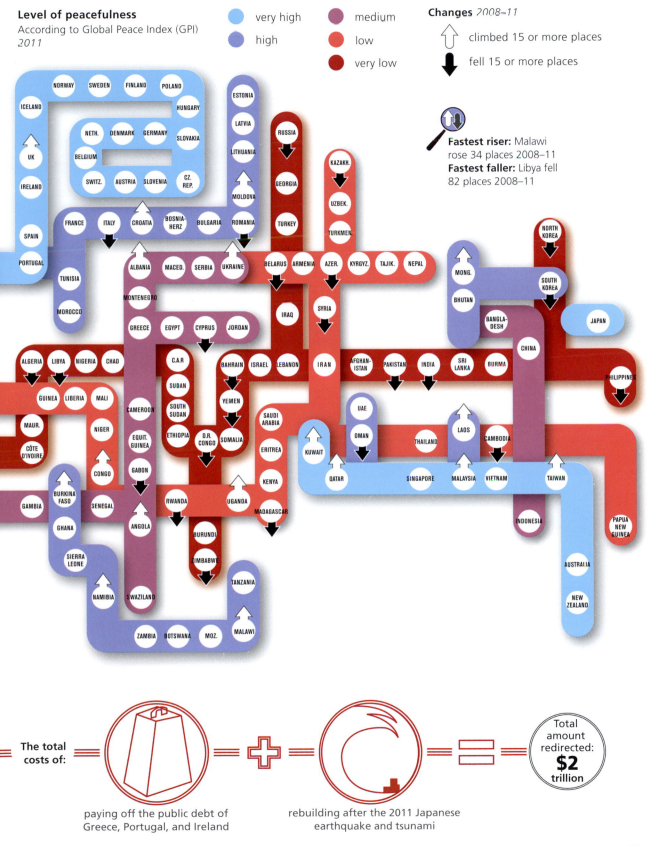

Level of peacefulness
According to Global Peace Index (GPI)
2011

- very high
- high
- medium
- low
- very low

Changes *2008–11*

↑ climbed 15 or more places

↓ fell 15 or more places

Fastest riser: Malawi
rose 34 places 2008–11
Fastest faller: Libya fell
82 places 2008–11

The total costs of:

+

paying off the public debt of
Greece, Portugal, and Ireland

rebuilding after the 2011 Japanese
earthquake and tsunami

=

Total
amount
redirected:
$2
trillion

PART FOUR
RIGHTS & RESPECT

Protection from both economic depredation and the threat of violent conflicts derives from laws developed on the basis of the common good. When laws are made by a process that represents and responds to the interests of the majority, and are therefore accepted rather than imposed, then it can be said that social order is based on the rule of law. Then the contract between citizen and state upholds accountable authority. Such societies are more resilient, and the majority of people fare better, than when power is arbitrary and laws are made by an elite minority for their own interests.

Ours is an age of growing democracy – at least when measured by the number of countries that are now established democracies, and the percentage of the world population that lives in them. Governing in this way is a relatively new development in human history. The trend of history has only been moving in that direction for one or two centuries, and until the last 20 to 25 years it would have been impossible to think of democratic government as the global norm.

The transition from dictatorship to democracy is perilous. The upsurge of wars in the early 1990s came at the same time as the states that emerged out of the former Soviet Union and ex-Yugoslavia were making their way – some of them – towards democracy. Those who expect to be disadvantaged by that transition almost always resist the change if they can. It is hard for there to be any peaceful way of pursuing the ensuing conflict when the institutions that might keep it peaceful are themselves being fought over. The democratic wave that swept the Middle East in 2011 and into 2012 was accompanied everywhere by violence, with open civil war in Libya and Syria.

But it is not only the transition to democracy that is of concern. Even today, in countries that are established democracies, it is not certain that it is irreversibly entrenched. Democratic countries in the years since 2008, most notably in Europe, have witnessed a fragmentation of political norms and social consensus. This is in large part a direct result of the economic problems of the day, with unemployment on the increase, especially for young people, and the economic future looking bleak. It also builds on a much longer and slower erosion of the vitality of democracy. In many established democracies, though there continue to be surges of political energy on major, mobilizing issues, political participation is not at all high. Exercising the vote is as far as the vast majority of citizens' political participation goes, and there is not always a solid majority of people who go out and vote.

Democracy is a system that says to the holders of government power, "You might be wrong – so we reserve the right to check on you every few years and replace you if need be." And in some systems it says to the highest holders of government power, "Regardless of whether you get it right or wrong, you'll be out in a few years." This must generate a degree of humility compared to holders of power under other systems. And it is that humility among the leaders that is the greatest and most precious characteristic of not just a democratic system but of democratic culture.

When that humility seems to diminish and the arrogance of power takes hold in elected leaders and on a whole governing class, that is when it is time to take care. That is when the strength and the authenticity of democratic institutions may start to be eroded by stealth.

A good litmus test of the rule of law is respect for human rights. Beyond law as a system of justice, of controls and constraints, human rights law upholds fairness in society, based on mutual respect. In order to work, it has to be universal – fairness for all, mutual respect among all.

When some people are declared to be second-class citizens – whether on the basis of race, skin colour, ethnicity, gender, sexual preference, physical ability, faith, regional or national origin, age, or any other marker of identity – the consequences are serious. Fairness and mutual respect corrode, the rule of law suffers, democracy if nominally present is weakened, and the interests of ordinary people are inevitably treated as disposable compared to those of a narrow elite – *even if the majority collude in the unfairness.*

There is said to be wisdom in numbers but at times the majority can head in very unwise directions, carried away by fear, heated political rhetoric, the distractions of political charisma, ignorance, and a host of other profoundly human reasons. The framework of law is often needed to protect us against ourselves.

The web of international agreements and laws that support human rights is steadily strengthening. There is increasing acceptance of international norms, and growing rejection of arguments that are made by this or that group or big power for exempting its actions from the law.

For rights to be real, the responsibility to respect them must also be embraced. In the best functioning communities, there is a balanced sense of rights and responsibilities. A society that respects human rights is one in which people not only have a clear sense of their rights but also of their duties to each other.

Political Systems

The global trend is democratic. Not without reverses, often at the cost of bloodshed and brutality, the number of democratic states has steadily increased since the end of the Cold War in 1990. That event itself set many states off on a democratic transition. At about the same time, democracy was consolidating in much of Latin America, and there was a wave of democratization in Africa.

In 2011 a democratic wave started to sweep through the Middle East and North Africa as people mobilized against corrupt and authoritarian rule. In 2011 and 2012 there were changes in government in Tunisia, Egypt, Morocco, Libya (after Western military intervention), and Yemen, and a bloody civil war began in Syria. Exactly what direction the changes would eventually take was unclear.

48% of people live in established democracies

Mali: Attempted coup 2012, widely interpreted as side-effect of transformation in Libya as expatriate Malian servants of the Gaddafi regime returned home.

Living politics
The share of the world's people living under different political systems *2012*

👤 = 5 million people

👥 dependent territory **6.3m**

👤 state of disorder **1.5m**

👤 military dictatorship **4.3m**

monarchy or theocracy **125m**

effective or formal one-party rule **1,728m**

weak, uncertain or transitional democracy **1,648m**

established democracy **3,287m**

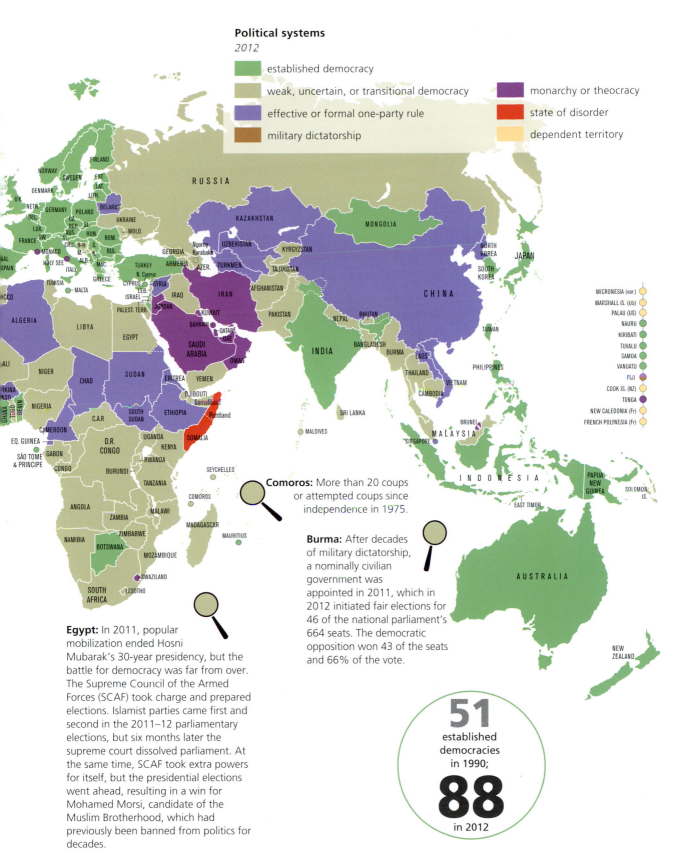

Political systems
2012

- **established democracy** (green)
- **weak, uncertain, or transitional democracy** (tan)
- **effective or formal one-party rule** (purple-blue)
- **military dictatorship** (brown)
- **monarchy or theocracy** (purple)
- **state of disorder** (red)
- **dependent territory** (light yellow)

MICRONESIA (var.)
MARSHALL IS. (US)
PALAU (US)
NAURU
KIRIBATI
TUVALU
SAMOA
VANUATU
FIJI
COOK IS. (NZ)
TONGA
NEW CALEDONIA (Fr)
FRENCH POLYNESIA (Fr)

Comoros: More than 20 coups or attempted coups since independence in 1975.

Burma: After decades of military dictatorship, a nominally civilian government was appointed in 2011, which in 2012 initiated fair elections for 46 of the national parliament's 664 seats. The democratic opposition won 43 of the seats and 66% of the vote.

Egypt: In 2011, popular mobilization ended Hosni Mubarak's 30-year presidency, but the battle for democracy was far from over. The Supreme Council of the Armed Forces (SCAF) took charge and prepared elections. Islamist parties came first and second in the 2011–12 parliamentary elections, but six months later the supreme court dissolved parliament. At the same time, SCAF took extra powers for itself, but the presidential elections went ahead, resulting in a win for Mohamed Morsi, candidate of the Muslim Brotherhood, which had previously been banned from politics for decades.

51 established democracies in 1990; **88** in 2012

77

Religious Rights

Faith is often a matter of government policy, and in some countries is the cornerstone of the state. Almost a quarter of the world's states have a formal link to a religion enshrined in their constitution or laws. What that means in practice varies widely. An official religion can mean intolerance, discrimination, or repression for other faiths – but a state-backed religion has also proved to be compatible with secularism in the state and tolerance in society. The greatest intolerance and violence can spring from religious groups that are, or were at one time, marginalized by the state.

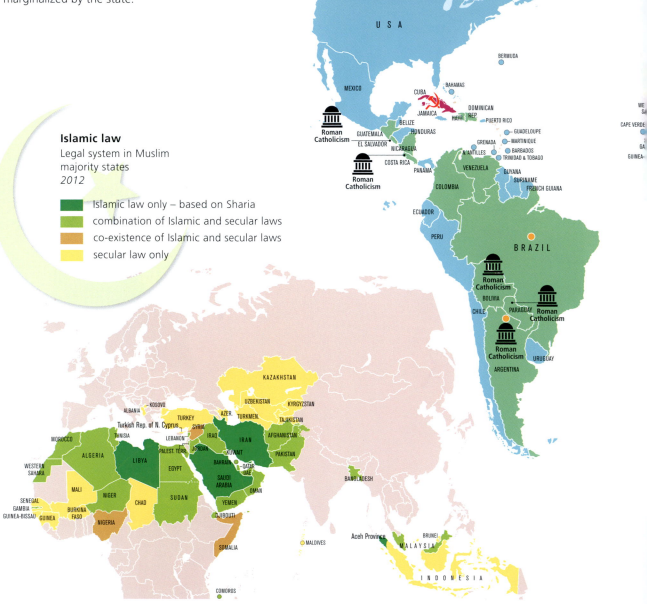

Islamic law
Legal system in Muslim majority states
2012

- Islamic law only – based on Sharia
- combination of Islamic and secular laws
- co-existence of Islamic and secular laws
- secular law only

◀ 26 Ethnicity & Diversity; 76 Political Systems

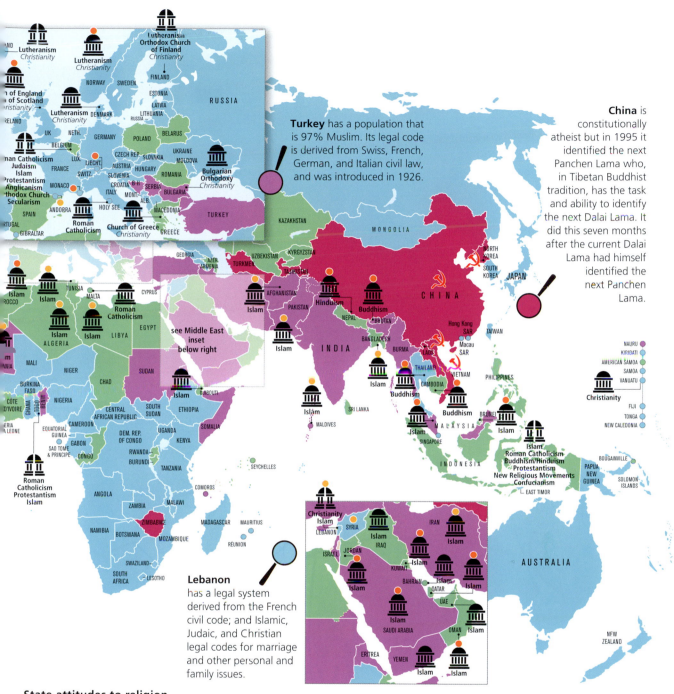

Turkey has a population that is 97% Muslim. Its legal code is derived from Swiss, French, German, and Italian civil law, and was introduced in 1926.

China is constitutionally atheist but in 1995 it identified the next Panchen Lama who, in Tibetan Buddhist tradition, has the task and ability to identify the next Dalai Lama. It did this seven months after the current Dalai Lama had himself identified the next Panchen Lama.

see Middle East inset below right

Lebanon has a legal system derived from the French civil code; and Islamic, Judaic, and Christian legal codes for marriage and other personal and family issues.

State attitudes to religion
2012 or latest available data

- discriminates against all religions and interferes with religious freedom
- favours religion of majority and interferes with or limits freedom of other religions
- favours religion of majority but tolerates other religions
- tolerates all religions

 state declared atheist in law

state religion established in law

state recognizes more than one religion or religious group

monarch must be of given religion

head of state or government must be of given religion

Copyright © Myriad Editions Limited

79

Human Rights Abuses

In some countries the contract of accountable authority between the state and the citizen is missing, and the greatest menace that citizens face comes from the state that should represent, empower, and guard them. In 34 countries, there are credible reports of extra-judicial execution. As with other abuses, the state has not always authorized the actions and may even be trying to stamp them out. Forces within the state often regard themselves as above the law they should staunchly uphold. And non-state groups – militias, gangs, private security guards – are also responsible for extreme abuses in many countries.

The foundational idea of human rights is that there is something special and deserving of respect about every person. Killing people, whether done according to that country's laws or illegally and arbitrarily, reveals an erosion of that respect. Reducing people to commodities, enslaving and trading them reveals something equally malign. Among trafficked women and girls, 95 per cent have been violently assaulted or threatened in order to force them to perform sexual acts.

Extreme abuse of human rights
2011

Worst form of abuse for which there are credible reports:

- extra-judicial executions & other lethal force
- torture
- arbitrary arrest and detention
- mistreatment by police and/or prison authorities
- violent and/or abusive treatment of refugees, asylum seekers, or immigrants
- no human rights abuses recorded
- no data available

Amita, Middle East to UK: Domestic servant, took new job, passport stolen, no pay, no liberty, 16–18 hour working day, raped. Escaped.

Josephine, eastern Congo: Kidnapped by the Lord's Resistance Army, her grandfather killed in front of her, forced labour and sexual services, saw further murders, escaped when sent out to find food and walked 40km to find safety.

Sabine, 23, France: Given by her parents in part payment for a car, used as domestic servant and hired out to men for sex, tortured and beaten, identification papers stolen. Dumped at a hospital when she fell ill. Parents were sentenced to 30 years in prison.

Mylee, Philippines to Saudi Arabia: Went to Saudi Arabia to work as maid, raped repeatedly, escaped after several months.

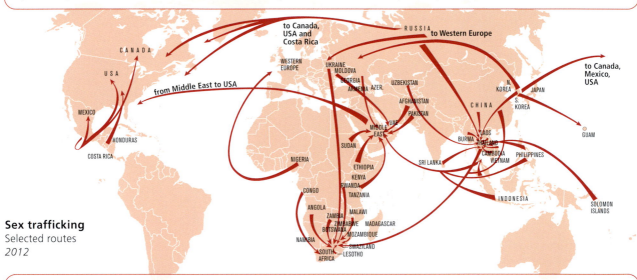

Sex trafficking
Selected routes
2012

Karina, 19, Lima, Peru: Moved to city to work as waitress and fell in love with a man who forced her into sex with men in nightclubs. Escaped after two years.

Maira, 15, Honduras: Recruited with two other girls with offer of work in Houston. Held captive, beaten, raped, and forced to work in cantinas that doubled as brothels. Escaped after six years. Her two friends remain missing.

Alissa, 16, Dallas, USA: Dated and moved in with an older man who persuaded her to work as escort. Tattooed her with his nicknames to brand her as his, and advertised her on internet. Assaulted and threatened her. She escaped.

Olga, 23, Moldova: Went to Dubai for a job. Met at airport by a couple who forced her into prostitution with beatings and threats. She escaped.

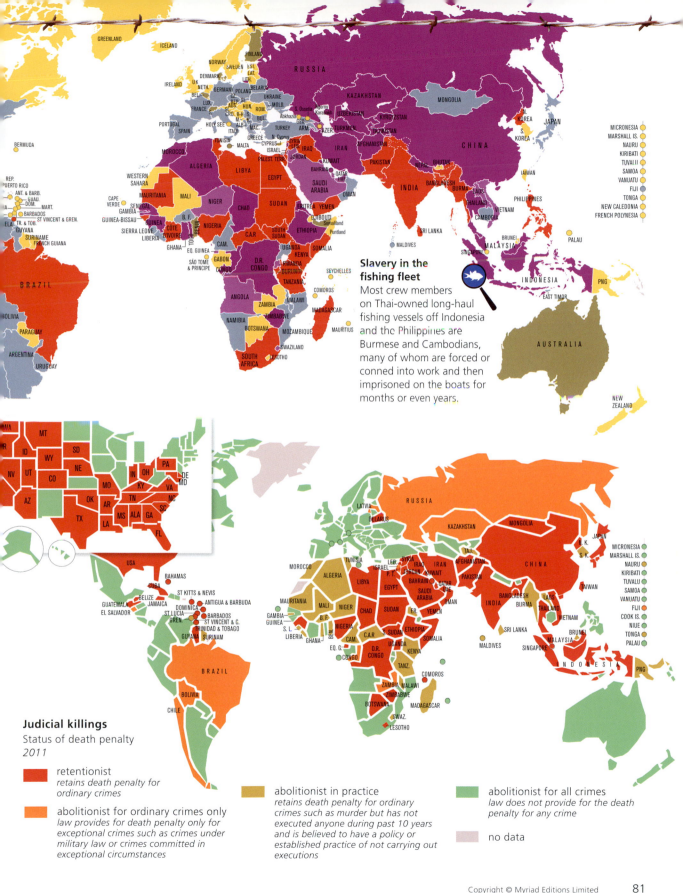

Slavery in the fishing fleet
Most crew members on Thai-owned long-haul fishing vessels off Indonesia and the Philippines are Burmese and Cambodians, many of whom are forced or conned into work and then imprisoned on the boats for months or even years.

Judicial killings
Status of death penalty
2011

retentionist
retains death penalty for ordinary crimes

abolitionist for ordinary crimes only
law provides for death penalty only for exceptional crimes such as crimes under military law or crimes committed in exceptional circumstances

abolitionist in practice
retains death penalty for ordinary crimes such as murder but has not executed anyone during past 10 years and is believed to have a policy or established practice of not carrying out executions

abolitionist for all crimes
law does not provide for the death penalty for any crime

no data

Children's Rights

As with other groups, respect for the rights of children is steadily improving – yet that only throws into starker relief the abuses that continue. Too many children are not registered at birth, which deprives them of the rights and recognition of citizenship before they even get started in life. In developing countries, one child in six between the ages of 5 and 14 is in work, often doing tasks that will cripple them in later years. One child in eight who should be attending primary school does not – a total of 67 million absentees between the ages of 5 and 11. And just over 40 per cent of them live in countries affected by violent conflicts.

USA and **Somalia**: the only countries *not* to have ratified the UN Convention on the Rights of the Child, which came into force in 1990.

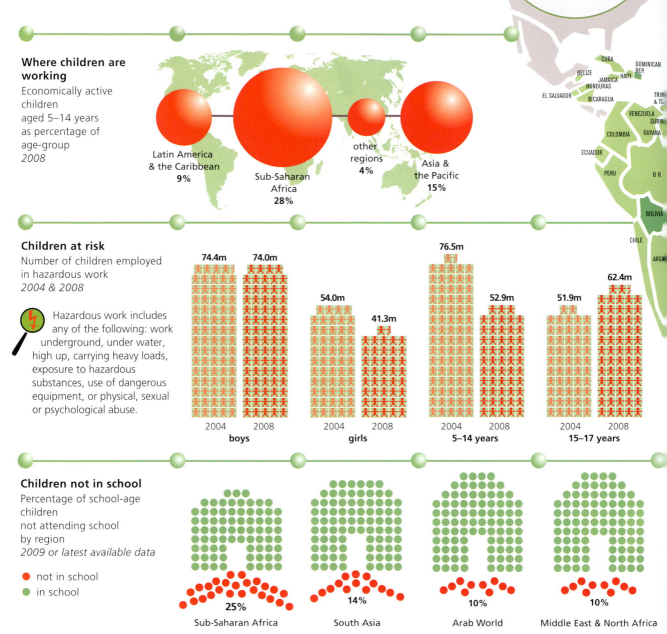

Where children are working

Economically active children aged 5–14 years as percentage of age-group
2008

Latin America & the Caribbean
9%

Sub-Saharan Africa
28%

other regions
4%

Asia & the Pacific
15%

Children at risk

Number of children employed in hazardous work
2004 & 2008

Hazardous work includes any of the following: work underground, under water, high up, carrying heavy loads, exposure to hazardous substances, use of dangerous equipment, or physical, sexual or psychological abuse.

74.4m 2004 — 74.0m 2008 — **boys**

54.0m 2004 — 41.3m 2008 — **girls**

76.5m 2004 — 52.9m 2008 — **5–14 years**

51.9m 2004 — 62.4m 2008 — **15–17 years**

Children not in school

Percentage of school-age children not attending school by region
2009 or latest available data

● not in school
● in school

25% Sub-Saharan Africa

14% South Asia

10% Arab World

10% Middle East & North Africa

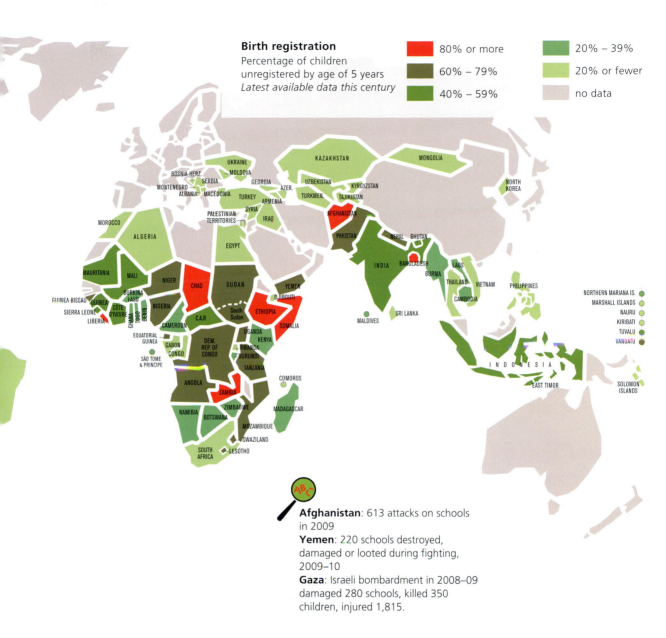

Birth registration
Percentage of children
unregistered by age of 5 years
Latest available data this century

80% or more	20% – 39%
60% – 79%	20% or fewer
40% – 59%	no data

Afghanistan: 613 attacks on schools
in 2009
Yemen: 220 schools destroyed,
damaged or looted during fighting,
2009–10
Gaza: Israeli bombardment in 2008–09
damaged 280 schools, killed 350
children, injured 1,815.

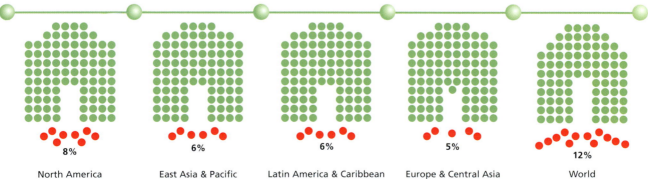

8%	6%	6%	5%	12%
North America	East Asia & Pacific	Latin America & Caribbean	Europe & Central Asia	World

Women's Rights

Everywhere, recognition of the equal rights of women is advancing, but the pace is highly uneven. In the 1950s, women as heads of democratic governments were unknown; in the 1960s and 1970s, they were a rarity; in the 1980s and 1990s they were uncommon but getting steadily less so. Yet today the question remains, why so few? Only 49 democratic countries have ever had a woman head of government, even counting appointed prime ministers in presidential systems.

In business it's even more unusual to find a woman in charge: only 12 of the 500 largest corporations in the world have a female CEO. In the UK, the Equal Pay Act entered force in 1972; 40 years later, full-time working women still earn 15 per cent less an hour than their male counterparts. And some 600 million women – more than half the world's working women – have insecure jobs, often outside the purview of labour law.

3%
of world's MPs were women in 1945

20%
in 2011

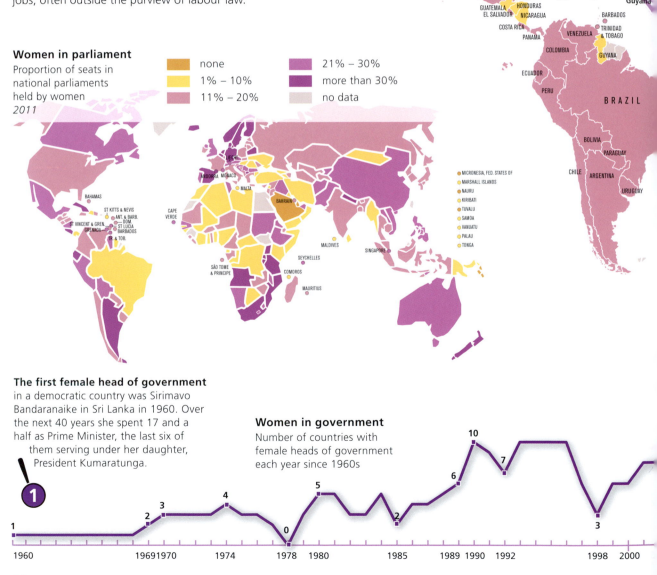

Women in parliament

Proportion of seats in national parliaments held by women
2011

- none
- 1% – 10%
- 11% – 20%
- 21% – 30%
- more than 30%
- no data

The first female head of government
in a democratic country was Sirimavo Bandaranaike in Sri Lanka in 1960. Over the next 40 years she spent 17 and a half as Prime Minister, the last six of them serving under her daughter, President Kumaratunga.

Women in government

Number of countries with female heads of government each year since 1960s

◀ 54 Goals for Development; 76 Political Systems

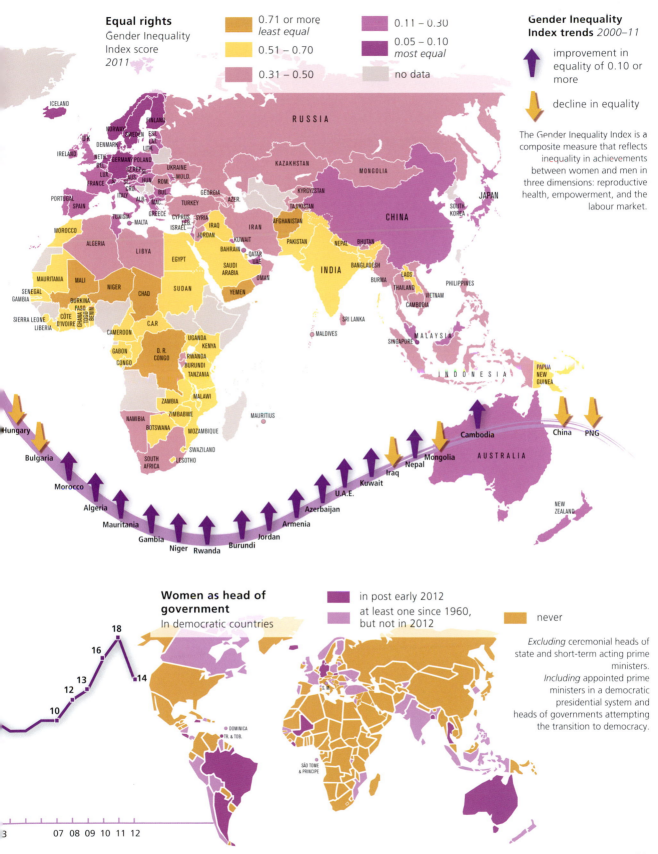

Equal rights
Gender Inequality Index score 2011

- 0.71 or more *least equal*
- 0.51 – 0.70
- 0.31 – 0.50
- 0.11 – 0.30
- 0.05 – 0.10 *most equal*
- no data

Gender Inequality Index trends 2000–11

- ↑ improvement in equality of 0.10 or more
- ↓ decline in equality

The Gender Inequality Index is a composite measure that reflects inequality in achievements between women and men in three dimensions: reproductive health, empowerment, and the labour market.

Women as head of government
In democratic countries

- in post early 2012
- at least one since 1960, but not in 2012
- never

Excluding ceremonial heads of state and short-term acting prime ministers.
Including appointed prime ministers in a democratic presidential system and heads of governments attempting the transition to democracy.

85

Gay Rights

There are 113 countries where sexual activity and relationships between people of the same sex are legally allowed, 76 where they are illegal. But the reality experienced by gay people is much more diverse than that implies. There remain many countries where same-sex relations are legal for women but not men, many countries where social reality is more oppressive than the law, and others where it is more liberal. The extent of legal rights varies considerably, even in countries where homosexuality is legal – just as the degree of punishment varies where it is illegal.

The acceptability or not of gays serving in the military is an interesting litmus test of the degree to which acceptance of homosexuality is normalized and people are treated as citizens – with the same rights, duties and choices – regardless of sexual preference.

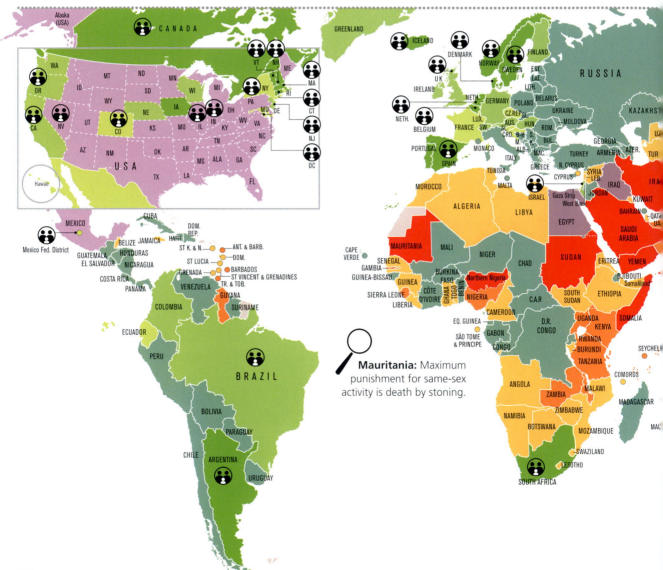

Mauritania: Maximum punishment for same-sex activity is death by stoning.

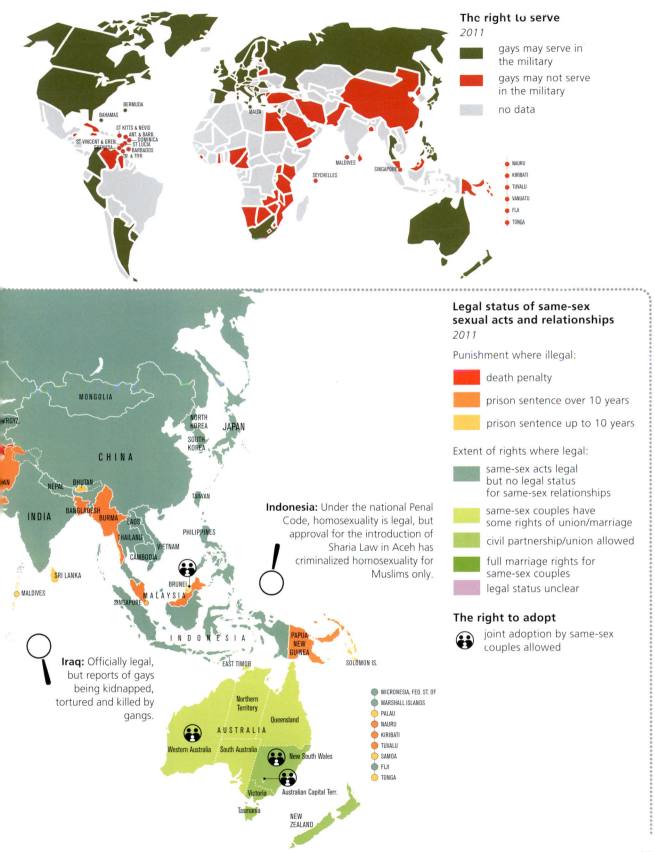

The right to serve
2011

- gays may serve in the military
- gays may not serve in the military
- no data

BERMUDA
BAHAMAS
ST KITTS & NEVIS
ANT. & BARB.
ST VINCENT & GREN.
DOMINICA
GRENADA
ST LUCIA
BARBADOS
TR. & TOB.
MALTA
MALDIVES
SEYCHELLES
SINGAPORE

NAURU
KIRIBATI
TUVALU
VANUATU
FIJI
TONGA

Legal status of same-sex sexual acts and relationships
2011

Punishment where illegal:

- death penalty
- prison sentence over 10 years
- prison sentence up to 10 years

Extent of rights where legal:

- same-sex acts legal but no legal status for same-sex relationships
- same-sex couples have some rights of union/marriage
- civil partnership/union allowed
- full marriage rights for same-sex couples
- legal status unclear

The right to adopt

joint adoption by same-sex couples allowed

Indonesia: Under the national Penal Code, homosexuality is legal, but approval for the introduction of Sharia Law in Aceh has criminalized homosexuality for Muslims only.

Iraq: Officially legal, but reports of gays being kidnapped, tortured and killed by gangs.

MONGOLIA
NORTH KOREA
SOUTH KOREA
JAPAN
KRGYZ
CHINA
NEPAL
BHUTAN
TAIWAN
INDIA
BANGLADESH
BURMA
LAOS
THAILAND
PHILIPPINES
VIETNAM
CAMBODIA
SRI LANKA
MALDIVES
BRUNEI
MALAYSIA
SINGAPORE
INDONESIA
PAPUA NEW GUINEA
EAST TIMOR
SOLOMON IS.
Northern Territory
Queensland
AUSTRALIA
Western Australia
South Australia
New South Wales
Victoria
Australian Capital Terr.
Tasmania
NEW ZEALAND

MICRONESIA, FED. ST. OF
MARSHALL ISLANDS
PALAU
NAURU
KIRIBATI
TUVALU
SAMOA
FIJI
TONGA

PART FIVE
HEALTH OF THE PEOPLE

The health of the people is in many ways a reflection of the health of a society. Good health is a basic need, and access to good health care is a basic right. It is acknowledged as a central part of the contract between state and citizen in many countries, even if in much of the world it has no traction and no reality. The ability to provide proper health care is a sign that at least part of the energy of the society is put towards caring for its members. So in many countries, the inability – or in some, the refusal – to provide proper health care is a sign of how far society has to go before it is really upholding ordinary citizens' well-being.

The other side of this coin is less about collective action and more about the individual. For good health is not only a result of the care that people receive from properly trained personnel in properly equipped clinics and hospitals, it is also a result of the care we take of ourselves. Care for ourselves and care for others, when balanced, are intimately bound together. Even where large-scale provision for health care is possible and achieved, people's health and longevity can still vary significantly. And countries that, if judged by wealth alone, have very different capacities for providing health care for their populations sometimes turn out to have very similar results, because of how resources are organized and how people take care of their own health.

Malnutrition persists, and the number of undernourished people in a world that steadily gets richer has remained stubbornly steady for two decades – albeit in a rising population so the proportion of undernourished is falling. But the opposite problem, obesity, is now a global epidemic. It is one of the life-style ailments of a changing world, contributing to serious diseases.

The deficiencies revealed by the persistence of undernourishment are largely about scarcity and inadequate resources to maintain a decent and healthy way of living. On the other side, part of the problem revealed by the obesity epidemic is the difficulty people have escaping the trap of their own appetites and patterns of consumption. These are often not just social habits but effective physiological dependence on the animal fats and sugars that cheap processed foods contain.

Even more is this the case with smoking. Tobacco is addictive and remains the only legal, mass-marketed consumable in which harm is inherent in the core function. It is not a side effect, nor a result of using it wrongly; use tobacco as advertised and harm ensues. It is one of the five main life-style causes of cancer.

But if a consideration of obesity and smoking leads us to think about human short-sightedness and capacity for self-harm, looking at health issues is also inspiring. Resources and knowledge have been mobilized that are capable of defeating diseases. There is no cure for HIV/AIDS but its spread has been stopped and numbers of deaths and new infections are declining. Likewise, many forms of cancer are treatable or preventable; the advance of medical science has opened the path towards eventually defeating it.

With health, however, as with almost everything, the distribution of resources and therefore of access to treatment and preventive education is unequal. Richer countries inevitably have better access to both. As a result, despite scientific advances, the estimated incidence of cancer is expected to double by 2030. For mental and behavioural disorders, the number of known sufferers is proportionately about the same in high-income and low-income countries, but the difference between *per capita* spending on medicines in high-and low-income countries respectively is over 1,500 to 1; for antipsychotic drugs, it is over 2,700 to 1.

Health is a development issue, not only because greater economic development tends to bring about better health care and better public health as clean water and sanitation facilities are provided, but also because a population weakened by illness is less economically productive. The relatively light disease burdens of the richer countries – and a few striking cases such as Libya (under Gaddafi, interestingly enough) and Cuba – are part of the benefits of their economic growth. And the heavy disease burdens of some other countries not only reflect but also contribute to their weaker economic performance.

Beyond a country's wealth, however, a considerable body of statistics shows that fairness and equality are good for public health. Among the richer countries, it is the more egalitarian that have the best health records – both in physical and mental health. The social fabric that contributes to even, friendly relations, eases health issues by encouraging people to help and take the pressure off each other. High levels of income inequality appear to inflict damage on that fabric by highlighting the divisions in society.

Overall, huge advances have been registered – and all other things being equal, will presumably continue to be registered – in the treatment of diseases including cancer. This brings enormous relief to millions of people. Meanwhile, alongside the ailments brought us by nature and by our natural physiology, the way we live and behave continues to generate the problems that medical science has to solve. The next step, surely, is to figure out how to live better.

Malnutrition

For the past two decades the number of undernourished people worldwide has remained stubbornly steady, although undernourished people now represent a smaller proportion of an increased global population. Deficiencies in diet are as serious a problem as insufficiencies of food. The absence of vitamins in daily intake can lead to crushing ailments.

Food prices soared in 2007 to 2008, leading to serious violence in at least 30 countries. The economic crunch of 2008 to 2009 (and longer in some countries) raised fears that, even in some rich countries, hunger would return and undernourishment rise again. In 2012, the combined impact of severe drought in the USA – a major food supplier to the world – and floods and drought elsewhere was predicted to raise global food prices once more.

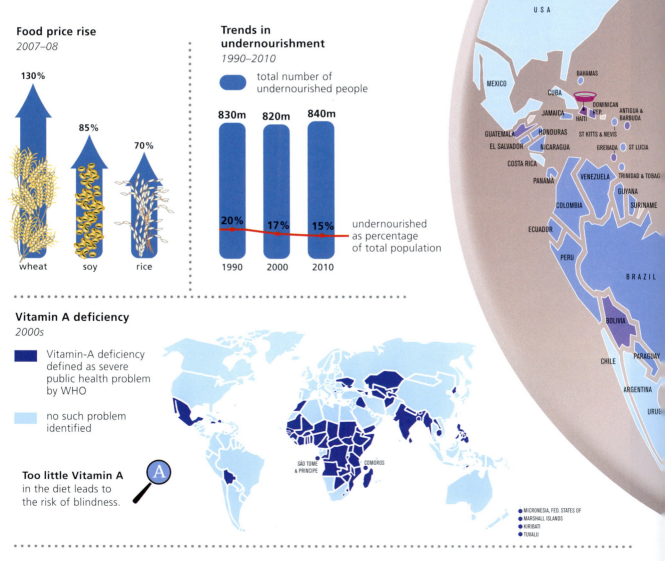

Food price rise
2007–08

- 130% wheat
- 85% soy
- 70% rice

Trends in undernourishment
1990–2010

total number of undernourished people

1990	2000	2010
830m	820m	840m
20%	17%	15%

undernourished as percentage of total population

Vitamin A deficiency
2000s

- Vitamin-A deficiency defined as severe public health problem by WHO
- no such problem identified

Too little Vitamin A in the diet leads to the risk of blindness.

- MICRONESIA, FED. STATES OF
- MARSHALL ISLANDS
- KIRIBATI
- TUVALU

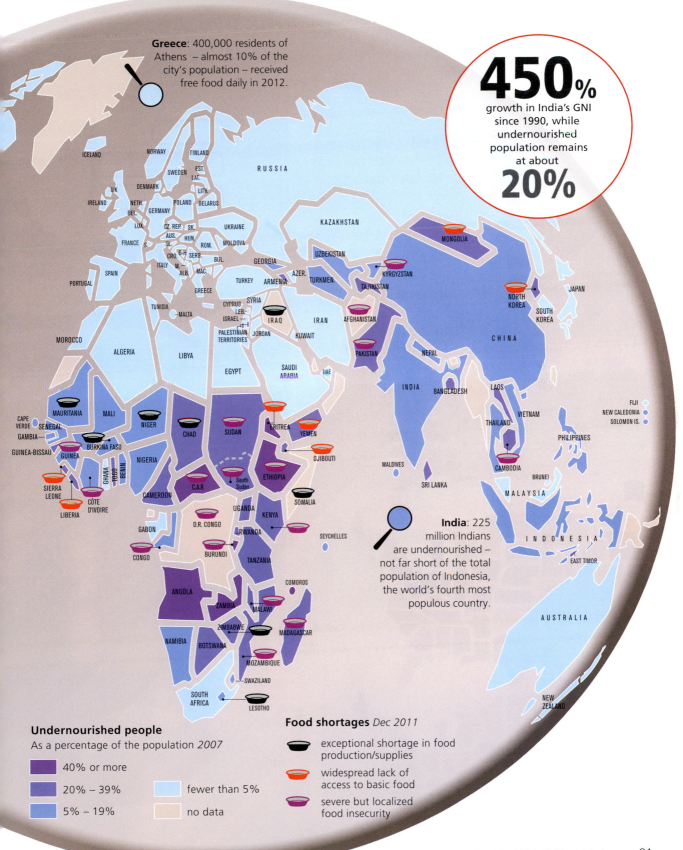

Greece: 400,000 residents of Athens – almost 10% of the city's population – received free food daily in 2012.

450% growth in India's GNI since 1990, while undernourished population remains at about **20%**

ICELAND
NORWAY   FINLAND
SWEDEN   EST.
          LAT.
DENMARK   LITH.
UK   POLAND BELARUS
IRELAND   NETH.
BEL.   GERMANY
LUX.   CZ. REP. SK.
AUS.   HUN.
FRANCE   SL.   ROM.   MOLDOVA
S.   CRO. B-H SERB.
ITALY   M.   BUL.
          ALB. MAC.

RUSSIA
KAZAKHSTAN

PORTUGAL SPAIN
TUNISIA   MALTA
                    GREECE   TURKEY   ARMENIA
                    CYPRUS   AZER. TURKMEN.
                    LEB.   GEORGIA
MOROCCO   ISRAEL   SYRIA   IRAQ   IRAN
          ALGERIA   PALESTINIAN JORDAN
                    TERRITORIES
          LIBYA   EGYPT   KUWAIT
                    SAUDI
                    ARABIA   UAE

UZBEKISTAN
KYRGYZSTAN
TAJIKISTAN
AFGHANISTAN
PAKISTAN   NEPAL
                    CHINA
MONGOLIA
NORTH KOREA   JAPAN
SOUTH KOREA

INDIA   BANGLADESH
          LAOS
VIETNAM
THAILAND

FIJI
NEW CALEDONIA
SOLOMON IS.

CAPE VERDE
SENEGAL   MAURITANIA MALI
GAMBIA   NIGER
GUINEA-BISSAU BURKINA FASO
GUINEA   GHANA TOGO BENIN
SIERRA LEONE CÔTE D'IVOIRE NIGERIA
LIBERIA

CHAD   SUDAN   ERITREA   YEMEN
                              DJIBOUTI
          South Sudan ETHIOPIA
C.A.R.   CAMEROON
                    SOMALIA
GABON   UGANDA   KENYA
D.R. CONGO RWANDA
          BURUNDI
CONGO   TANZANIA

SEYCHELLES

MALDIVES
SRI LANKA

PHILIPPINES
BRUNEI
MALAYSIA
INDONESIA
EAST TIMOR

CAMBODIA

India: 225 million Indians are undernourished – not far short of the total population of Indonesia, the world's fourth most populous country.

COMOROS
ANGOLA   ZAMBIA MALAWI
ZIMBABWE MADAGASCAR
NAMIBIA   BOTSWANA
          MOZAMBIQUE
          SWAZILAND
SOUTH AFRICA LESOTHO

AUSTRALIA

NEW ZEALAND

Undernourished people
As a percentage of the population *2007*

- 40% or more
- 20% – 39%
- 5% – 19%
- fewer than 5%
- no data

Food shortages *Dec 2011*

- exceptional shortage in food production/supplies
- widespread lack of access to basic food
- severe but localized food insecurity

Obesity

With 1.5 billion adults – more than a fifth of the global population – overweight or obese, and the incidence of obesity more than double that of 1980, the World Health Organization has declared obesity a global epidemic.

Two-thirds of the world's population live in countries where there are more deaths from excess weight than from undernourishment. Cheap processed foods are particularly high in animal fats and sugars. In rich countries, the unhealthy diet of those on low incomes and in poverty is fuelling the obesity epidemic, which is in turn contributing to serious diseases. Health services are struggling to cope with the strain.

Increased risk of disease
Percentage of cases attributable to being overweight or obese
2008

23%	ischaemic heart disease
7%–41%	cancer
44%	diabetes

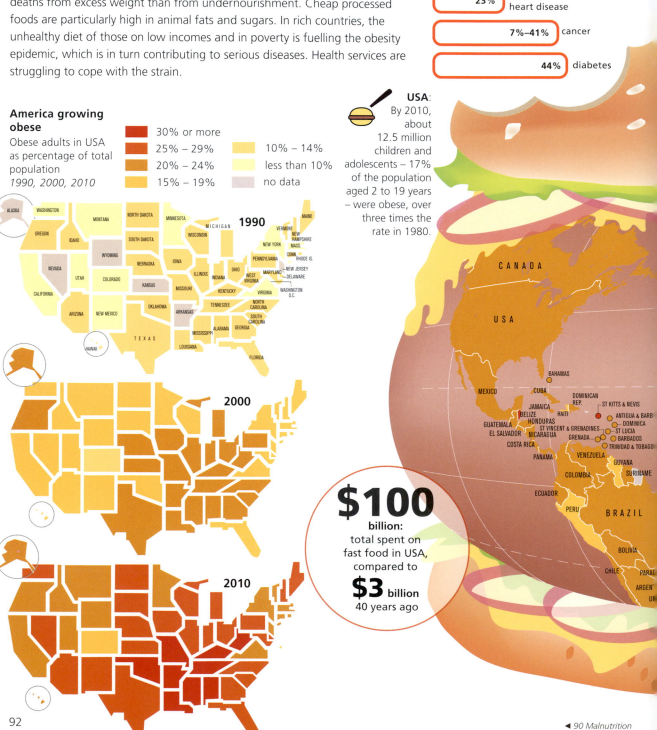

America growing obese
Obese adults in USA as percentage of total population
1990, 2000, 2010

- 30% or more
- 25% – 29%
- 20% – 24%
- 15% – 19%
- 10% – 14%
- less than 10%
- no data

USA: By 2010, about 12.5 million children and adolescents – 17% of the population aged 2 to 19 years – were obese, over three times the rate in 1980.

1990
2000
2010

$100 billion: total spent on fast food in USA, compared to **$3 billion** 40 years ago

92

◄ 90 Malnutrition

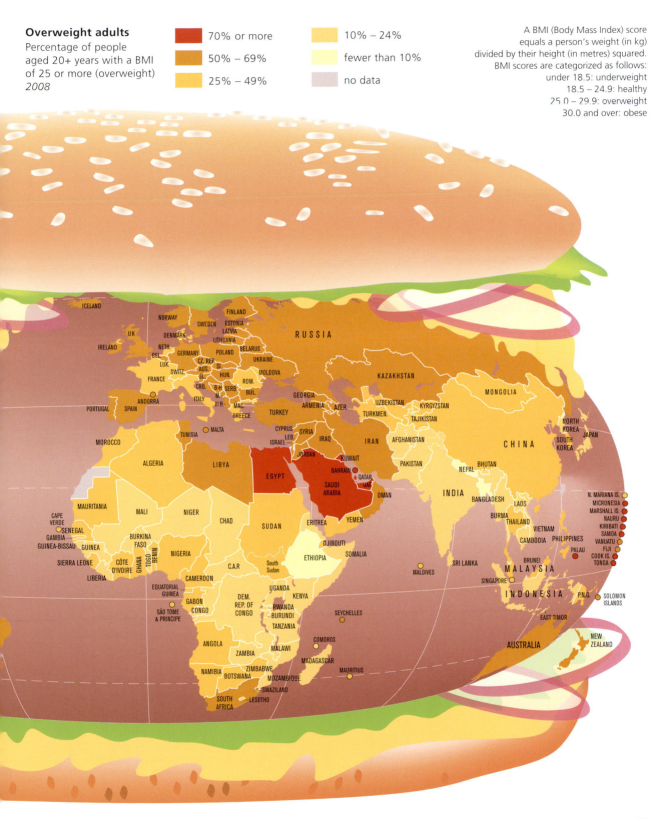

Overweight adults

Percentage of people aged 20+ years with a BMI of 25 or more (overweight) *2008*

- **70% or more**
- **50% – 69%**
- **25% – 49%**
- **10% – 24%**
- **fewer than 10%**
- **no data**

A BMI (Body Mass Index) score equals a person's weight (in kg) divided by their height (in metres) squared. BMI scores are categorized as follows:
under 18.5: underweight
18.5 – 24.9: healthy
25.0 – 29.9: overweight
30.0 and over: obese

93

Smoking

Tobacco smoke contains 4,000 known chemicals, of which at least 250 are harmful and 50 cause cancers. Between a third and a half of smokers die from tobacco-related diseases, losing on average 15 years compared to life expectancy. Of the 6 million currently dying each year from tobacco-related causes, 600,000 are non-smokers, dying because of other people's smoking.

Tobacco causes a death every six seconds. Compared to 100 million deaths from tobacco in the 20th century, current trends are for up to 1 billion tobacco-related deaths by the end of the 21st.

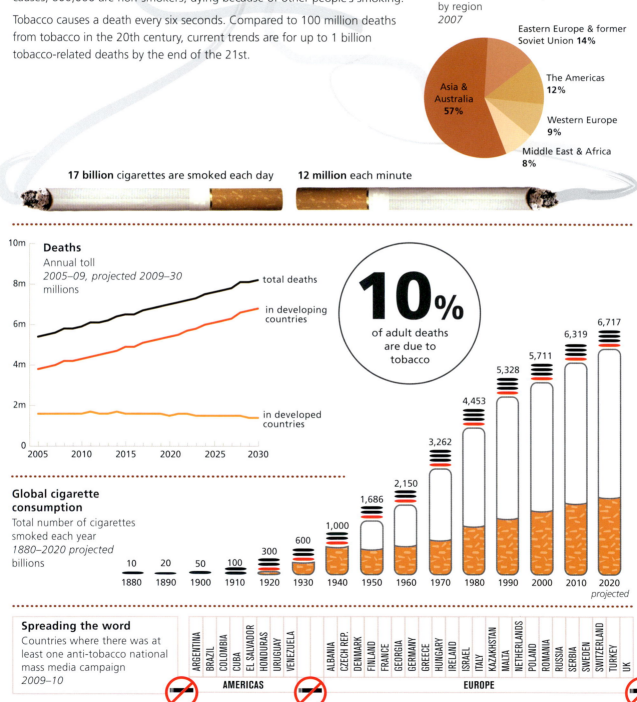

Where cigarettes are being smoked
Share of total consumption by region
2007

Eastern Europe & former Soviet Union **14%**

The Americas **12%**

Western Europe **9%**

Middle East & Africa **8%**

Asia & Australia **57%**

17 billion cigarettes are smoked each day

12 million each minute

Deaths
Annual toll
2005–09, projected 2009–30
millions

total deaths

in developing countries

in developed countries

10%
of adult deaths are due to tobacco

Global cigarette consumption
Total number of cigarettes smoked each year
1880–2020 projected
billions

| 10 | 20 | 50 | 100 | 300 | 600 | 1,000 | 1,686 | 2,150 | 3,262 | 4,453 | 5,328 | 5,711 | 6,319 | 6,717 |
| 1880 | 1890 | 1900 | 1910 | 1920 | 1930 | 1940 | 1950 | 1960 | 1970 | 1980 | 1990 | 2000 | 2010 | 2020 *projected* |

Spreading the word
Countries where there was at least one anti-tobacco national mass media campaign
2009–10

AMERICAS: ARGENTINA, BRAZIL, COLOMBIA, CUBA, EL SALVADOR, HONDURAS, URUGUAY, VENEZUELA

EUROPE: ALBANIA, CZECH REP., DENMARK, FINLAND, FRANCE, GEORGIA, GERMANY, GREECE, HUNGARY, IRELAND, ISRAEL, ITALY, KAZAKHSTAN, MALTA, NETHERLANDS, POLAND, ROMANIA, RUSSIA, SERBIA, SWEDEN, SWITZERLAND, TURKEY, UK

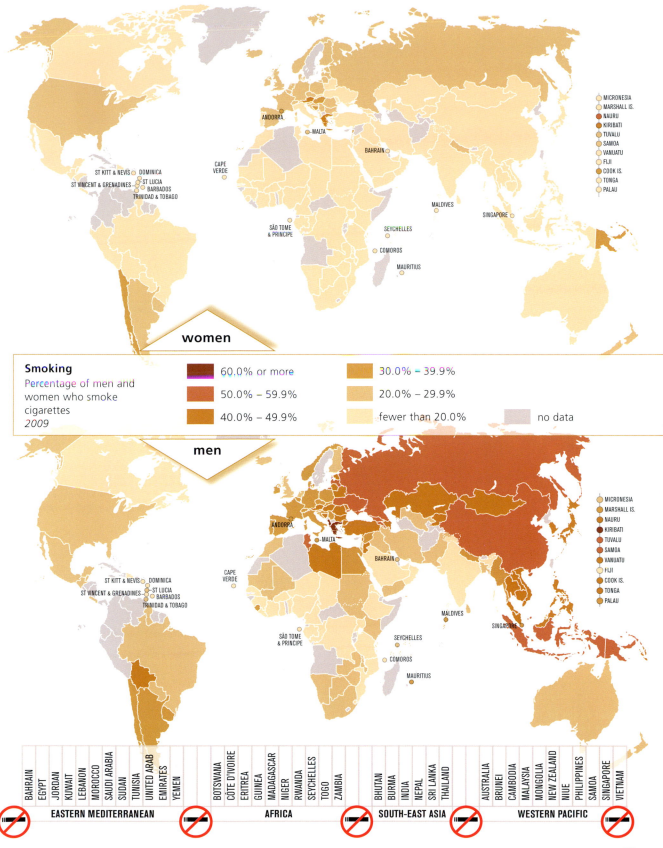

women

Smoking

Percentage of men and women who smoke cigarettes
2009

![60.0% or more] 60.0% or more	![30.0% – 39.9%] 30.0% – 39.9%
![50.0% – 59.9%] 50.0% – 59.9%	![20.0% – 29.9%] 20.0% – 29.9%
![40.0% – 49.9%] 40.0% – 49.9%	![fewer than 20.0%] fewer than 20.0% ![no data] no data

men

MICRONESIA
MARSHALL IS.
NAURU
KIRIBATI
TUVALU
SAMOA
VANUATU
FIJI
COOK IS.
TONGA
PALAU

EASTERN MEDITERRANEAN
BAHRAIN
EGYPT
JORDAN
KUWAIT
LEBANON
MOROCCO
SAUDI ARABIA
SUDAN
TUNISIA
UNITED ARAB EMIRATES
YEMEN

AFRICA
BOTSWANA
CÔTE D'IVOIRE
ERITREA
GUINEA
MADAGASCAR
NIGER
RWANDA
SEYCHELLES
TOGO
ZAMBIA

SOUTH-EAST ASIA
BHUTAN
BURMA
INDIA
NEPAL
SRI LANKA
THAILAND

WESTERN PACIFIC
AUSTRALIA
BRUNEI
CAMBODIA
MALAYSIA
MONGOLIA
NEW ZEALAND
NIUE
PHILIPPINES
SAMOA
SINGAPORE
VIETNAM

Cancer

Cancer is a generic name for diseases characterized by the growth and spread of abnormal cells. It is believed to be the commonest cause of death worldwide, responsible for 13 per cent of all deaths. Though treatments and preventive strategies are improving, the estimated incidence of cancer more than doubled from 1975 to 2008, and it is expected to double again by 2030.

As the world's population grows, and improvements in general health mean that people live longer on average, cancer looms ever larger. In countries where prosperity is advancing, bringing with it changes in lifestyle, diet, and tobacco use, the incidence of cancer is rising. Although the rate of cancer is currently four times greater in high-income countries than elsewhere, rates in poorer countries are increasing rapidly.

Cancer is most treatable when caught early. On a large scale, early diagnosis requires education and active screening programmes as part of comprehensive health care – more likely prospects in richer than in poorer countries.

> Beating cancer now is a realistic ambition because, at long last, we largely know its genetic and chemical characteristics.

James Watson, 2009
Molecular biologist and geneticist, co-discoverer of structure of DNA

Unequal death rates
Once cancer has been contracted, the rate of death is five times higher in poorer than in richer countries.

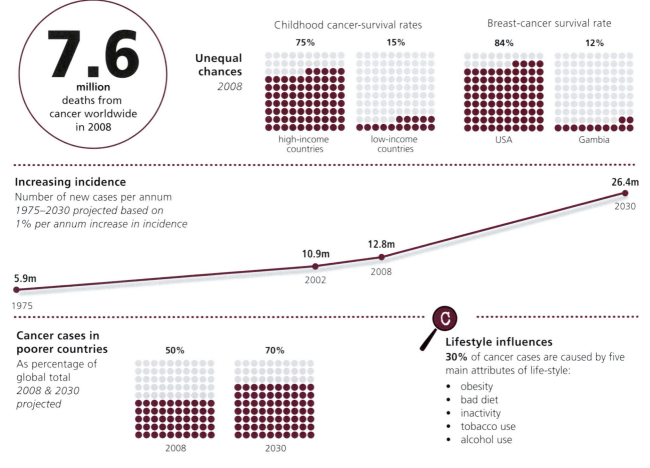

7.6 million deaths from cancer worldwide in 2008

Unequal chances *2008*

Childhood cancer-survival rates
75% — high-income countries
15% — low-income countries

Breast-cancer survival rate
84% — USA
12% — Gambia

Increasing incidence
Number of new cases per annum
1975–2030 projected based on 1% per annum increase in incidence

5.9m 1975
10.9m 2002
12.8m 2008
26.4m 2030

Cancer cases in poorer countries
As percentage of global total
2008 & 2030 projected

50% 2008
70% 2030

Lifestyle influences
30% of cancer cases are caused by five main attributes of life-style:

- obesity
- bad diet
- inactivity
- tobacco use
- alcohol use

◀ 94 Smoking

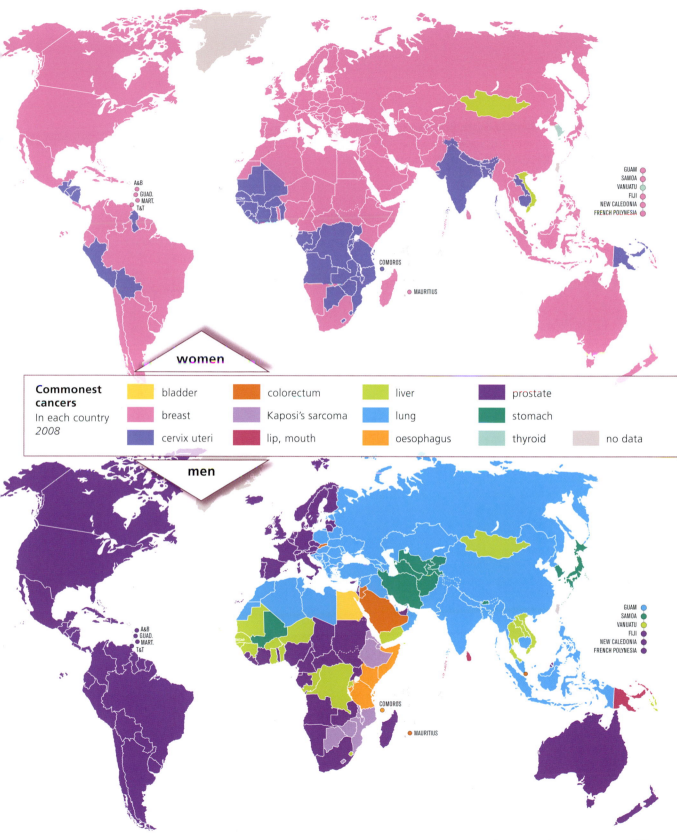

women

Commonest cancers

In each country *2008*

bladder		colorectum		liver		prostate	
breast		Kaposi's sarcoma		lung		stomach	
cervix uteri		lip, mouth		oesophagus		thyroid	no data

men

GUAM
SAMOA
VANUATU
FIJI
NEW CALEDONIA
FRENCH POLYNESIA

GUAM
SAMOA
VANUATU
FIJI
NEW CALEDONIA
FRENCH POLYNESIA

A&B
GUAD.
MART.
T&T

A&B
GUAD.
MART.
T&T

COMOROS

MAURITIUS

COMOROS

MAURITIUS

97

HIV/AIDS

HIV/AIDS has claimed more than 25 million lives over three decades. In 2010, there were approximately 34 million people living with HIV, 10 per cent of them children below the age of 15.

A cure for HIV infection has not been found, but effective treatment with anti-retroviral drugs allows patients to restrict the virus and enjoy healthy and productive lives. And with knowledge about how the virus is passed on through sexual contact and shared needles used for drugs, infection can be avoided.

Neither denying the problem nor trying to bar the door to people living with HIV/AIDS (as 49 countries still do) has worked as a preventive strategy. But, thanks to treatment and education, the numbers of new infections and deaths are declining. So, the epidemic can be stopped – but only if more resources are provided to fight it.

The impact of HIV/AIDS
Percentage of people aged 15–49 infected with HIV
2009
WHO regions

- 20.0% or more
- 10.0% – 19.9%
- 1.0% – 9.9%
- fewer than 1%
- no data

Number of children orphaned by AIDS

- 1 million or more
- 100,000 – 999,999

Living and dying with HIV/AIDS
Adults and children
1990–2010

- —— new HIV Infections
- —— AIDS-related deaths

Regional distribution
2010

- Africa
- Americas
- Eastern Mediterranean
- Europe
- South-East Asia
- Western Pacific

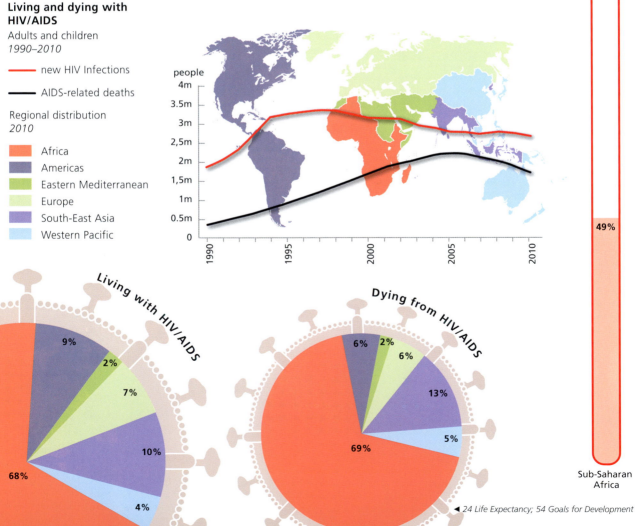

10.4m

49%

Sub-Saharan Africa

Living with HIV/AIDS

9%
2%
7%
10%
68%
4%

Dying from HIV/AIDS

6%
2%
6%
13%
5%
69%

◀ *24 Life Expectancy; 54 Goals for Development*

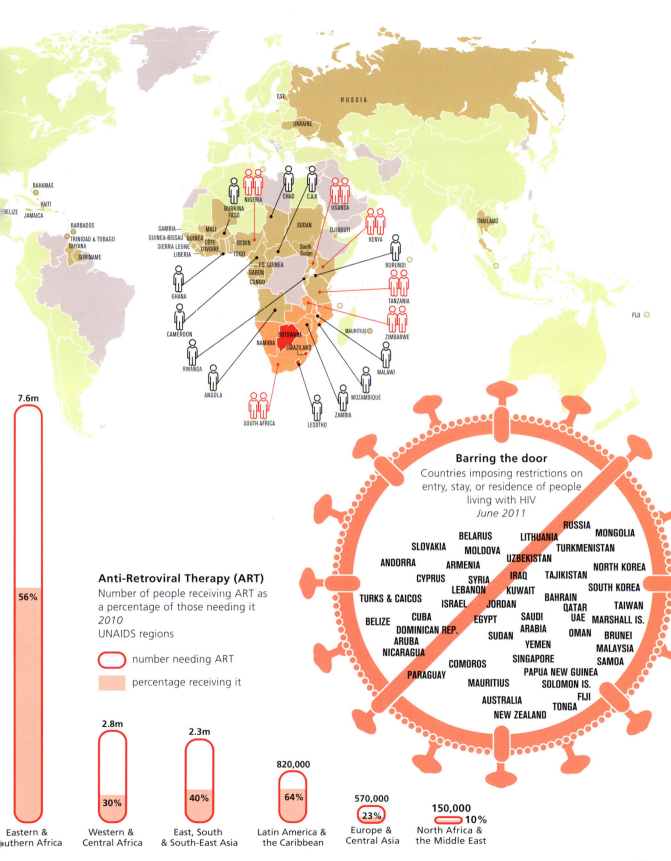

BAHAMAS

HAITI

BELIZE

JAMAICA

BARBADOS

TRINIDAD & TOBAGO

GUYANA

SURINAME

EST.

RUSSIA

UKRAINE

GAMBIA

GUINEA-BISSAU

SIERRA LEONE

LIBERIA

GUINEA

MALI

CÔTE
D'IVOIRE

BENIN

TOGO

BURKINA
FASO

NIGERIA

CHAD

C.A.R.

SUDAN

South Sudan

UGANDA

DJIBOUTI

KENYA

THAILAND

EQ. GUINEA

GABON

CONGO

GHANA

CAMEROON

RWANDA

ANGOLA

NAMIBIA

BOTSWANA

SWAZILAND

SOUTH AFRICA

LESOTHO

ZAMBIA

MOZAMBIQUE

MALAWI

MAURITIUS

ZIMBABWE

TANZANIA

BURUNDI

FIJI

7.6m

56%

Anti-Retroviral Therapy (ART)

Number of people receiving ART as
a percentage of those needing it
2010
UNAIDS regions

number needing ART

percentage receiving it

2.8m

30%

2.3m

40%

820,000

64%

570,000

23%

150,000

10%

Eastern &
Southern Africa

Western &
Central Africa

East, South
& South-East Asia

Latin America &
the Caribbean

Europe &
Central Asia

North Africa &
the Middle East

Barring the door

Countries imposing restrictions on
entry, stay, or residence of people
living with HIV
June 2011

RUSSIA

BELARUS   LITHUANIA   MONGOLIA

SLOVAKIA   MOLDOVA   TURKMENISTAN

ANDORRA   ARMENIA   UZBEKISTAN

CYPRUS   SYRIA   IRAQ   TAJIKISTAN   NORTH KOREA

LEBANON   KUWAIT   SOUTH KOREA

TURKS & CAICOS   BAHRAIN

ISRAEL   JORDAN   QATAR   TAIWAN

BELIZE   CUBA   EGYPT   SAUDI   UAE   MARSHALL IS.

DOMINICAN REP.   ARABIA   OMAN   BRUNEI

ARUBA   SUDAN   MALAYSIA

NICARAGUA   YEMEN   SAMOA

COMOROS   SINGAPORE

PARAGUAY   PAPUA NEW GUINEA

MAURITIUS   SOLOMON IS.

FIJI

AUSTRALIA   TONGA

NEW ZEALAND

Mental Health

Worldwide about 450 million people suffer mental and behavioural disorders. Hundreds of millions more have psychological problems. Around 20 per cent of the world's children and adolescents have mental problems of some degree; about half of mental disorders begin before the age of 14. People with mental disorders are at greater risk of catching and passing on communicable diseases, and of committing suicide. About 800,000 people take their own lives each year and this is the third leading cause of death among young people.

In many countries, mental disorder is a taboo subject, more shaming to a family than other diseases and any other behaviour. As a result, the human rights of psychiatric patients are routinely abused in most countries – physical restraint, isolation, and the denial both of basic needs and of privacy. Alongside this, the stigma attached to mental disorder leads to this large and highly visible health issue being under-resourced. Average global spending on mental health is less than $2 per person per year, and in low-income countries the average is less than 25 cents per person – about one fifteenth of what is needed.

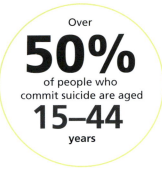

Over
50%
of people who commit suicide are aged
15–44
years

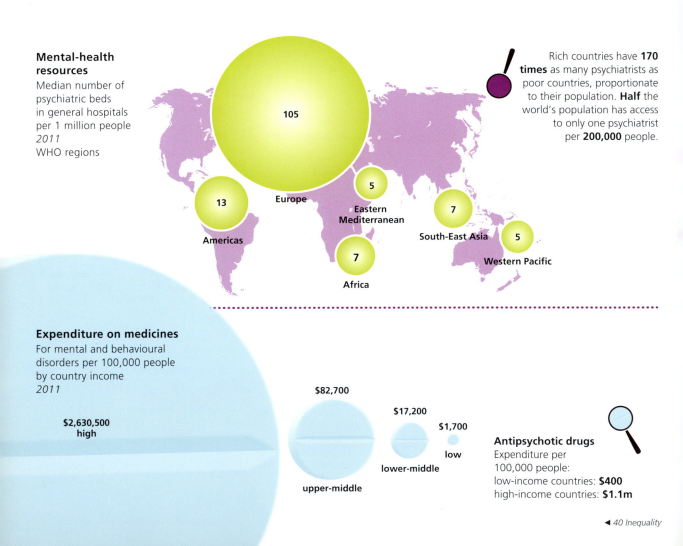

Mental-health resources
Median number of psychiatric beds in general hospitals per 1 million people
2011
WHO regions

105
Europe

13
Americas

5
Eastern Mediterranean

7
South-East Asia

7
Africa

5
Western Pacific

Rich countries have **170 times** as many psychiatrists as poor countries, proportionate to their population. **Half** the world's population has access to only one psychiatrist per **200,000** people.

Expenditure on medicines
For mental and behavioural disorders per 100,000 people by country income
2011

$2,630,500
high

$82,700
upper-middle

$17,200
lower-middle

$1,700
low

Antipsychotic drugs
Expenditure per 100,000 people:
low-income countries: **$400**
high-income countries: **$1.1m**

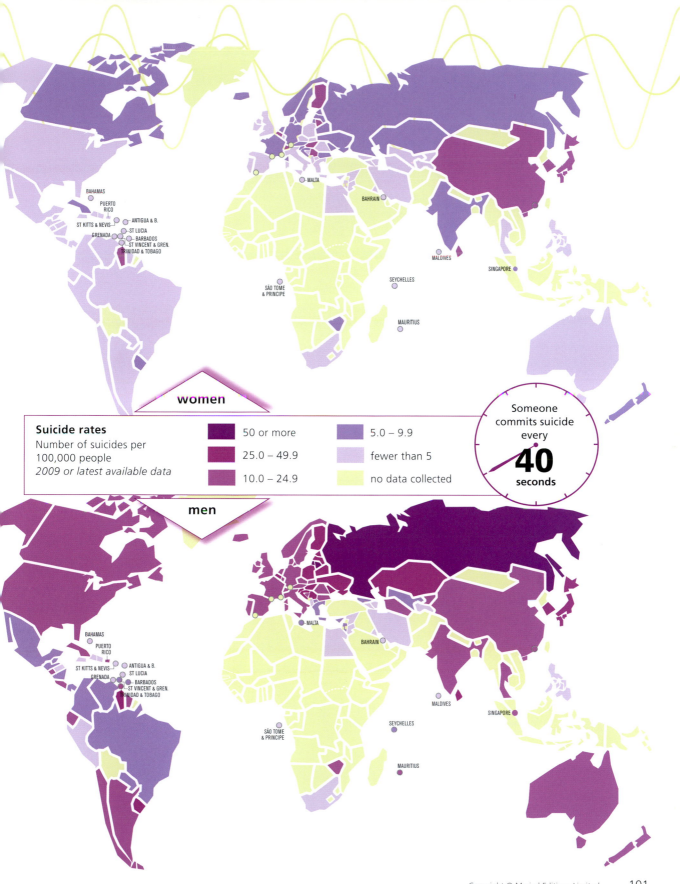

women

Suicide rates

Number of suicides per
100,000 people
2009 or latest available data

- 50 or more
- 25.0 – 49.9
- 10.0 – 24.9
- 5.0 – 9.9
- fewer than 5
- no data collected

Someone
commits suicide
every
40
seconds

men

BAHAMAS
PUERTO RICO
ST KITTS & NEVIS
ANTIGUA & B.
ST LUCIA
GRENADA
BARBADOS
ST VINCENT & GREN.
TRINIDAD & TOBAGO

MALTA
BAHRAIN
MALDIVES
SEYCHELLES
SINGAPORE
SÃO TOME & PRINCIPE
MAURITIUS

Living with Disease

The burden of ill health on countries' populations is normally expressed in terms of the number of years of life lost compared to average life expectancy. But the burden of disease is greater than that: years are lost not only to premature death but also to disability and ill health. This century, the World Health Organization has adopted a new measure – the Disability Adjusted Life Year (or DALY) – to reflect this fuller sense of the disease burden. The DALY is calculated as the combined total of years of potential life lost to premature death plus years lived with disability. It is possible to compare all the countries for which there are data by breaking the DALY total down to reflect the rate per 100,000 people.

As a way of measuring the burden imposed by disease, it is limited to measuring time (rather than, for example, intensity of suffering while ill). But it is a fuller measure than the alternatives and is increasingly used.

A fraction over 50 per cent of the world's population lives in countries with a DALY of between 10,000 and 20,000 per 100,000 people. That can be thought of as the global norm. Two small, rich countries (Iceland and Kuwait) do better than that, and 83 other countries – some big and richly blessed with natural resources – do worse.

Cuba and the **USA** have precisely the same disease burden

National disease burden

DALYs per 100,000 people
2004

A DALY (Disability Adjusted Life Year) measures the number of years lost due to ill-health, disability or early death.

	9,800 – 14,999	*the rich country norm*
	15,000 – 19,999	*the middle income norm*
	20,000 – 39,999	*heavy disease burden*
	40,000 – 59,999	*intense burden*
	60,000 – 82,500	*extreme burden*
	no data	

Iceland
has the lightest disease burden

Sierra Leone
has the heaviest disease burden

Denmark
has the heaviest
disease burden of the
Scandinavian countries

Russia
has the heaviest disease
burden of any country
of the former Soviet Union

ICELAND
NORWAY
SWEDEN
FINLAND
DENMARK
ESTONIA
LATVIA
UK
IRELAND
NETH.
BEL.
LUX.
FRANCE
SWITZ.
GERMANY
POLAND
LITHUANIA
BELARUS
CZ. REP.
SL.
AUS.
HUN.
UKRAINE
MOLDOVA
ROM.
RUSSIA
KAZAKHSTAN
MONGOLIA
ANDORRA
MONACO
S.M.
PORTUGAL
SPAIN
ITALY
CRO.
B-H
SERB.
ALB.
BUL.
MAC.
GREECE
TURKEY
GEORGIA
ARMENIA
AZER.
UZBEKISTAN
TURKMEN.
TAJIKISTAN
KYRGYZSTAN
NORTH
KOREA
JAPAN
SOUTH
KOREA
CYPRUS
LEB.
SYRIA
IRAQ
IRAN
AFGHANISTAN
CHINA
TUNISIA
MALTA
ISRAEL
JORDAN
KUWAIT
BAHRAIN
QATAR
UAE
PAKISTAN
NEPAL
BHUTAN
MOROCCO
ALGERIA
LIBYA
EGYPT
SAUDI
ARABIA
OMAN
INDIA
BANGLADESH
BURMA
LAOS
MICRONESIA, FED. STATES OF
MARSHALL ISLANDS
NAURU
KIRIBATI
TUVALU
SAMOA
VANUATU
FIJI
COOK ISLANDS
NIUE
TONGA
APE
RDE
MAURITANIA
MALI
NIGER
CHAD
SUDAN
ERITREA
YEMEN
THAILAND
VIETNAM
PHILIPPINES
MBIA
SENEGAL
BURKINA
FASO
NIGERIA
C.A.R.
South
Sudan
DJIBOUTI
ETHIOPIA
SOMALIA
CAMBODIA
BRUNEI
PALAU
-BISSAU
GUINEA
SRI LANKA
MALAYSIA
ERRA LEONE
COTE
D'IVOIRE
GHANA
TOGO
BENIN
LIBERIA
EQUATORIAL
GUINEA
CAMEROON
UGANDA
KENYA
MALDIVES
SINGAPORE
GABON
CONGO
DEM.
REP. OF
CONGO
RWANDA
BURUNDI
SEYCHELLES
INDONESIA
PAPUA
NEW
GUINEA
SOLOMON
ISLANDS
SÃO TOME
& PRINCIPE
TANZANIA
EAST TIMOR
ANGOLA
ZAMBIA
MALAWI
COMOROS
MADAGASCAR
NAMIBIA
ZIMBABWE
BOTSWANA
MOZAMBIQUE
MAURITIUS
AUSTRALIA
SWAZILAND
SOUTH
AFRICA
LESOTHO
NEW
ZEALAND

PART SIX
HEALTH OF THE PLANET

We know enough to understand the outlines of the deep global, environmental predicament we are in. We neither know nor understand all the details but we can see that the economic and industrial path we have been on for the last two centuries, along which we are not only still moving today but actually accelerating, is unsustainable in the long term.

Scientific knowledge may be imprecise on some of the key details but on the big issues there is no doubt. We are more people than ever before, using more water than ever before, and basic arithmetic shows that the majority of the world's population will face water scarcity before 2030. As our economic output has soared, we have pumped large amounts of carbon dioxide and other greenhouse gases into the atmosphere over the past 200 years and the laws of physics say the effect of that is to increase the global average temperature, which is happening. And at the same time, we have generated waste and thrown it away as garbage with abandon, and if we go to the right places we can see the consequences of that with our own eyes.

All these things we know. What we do not know is exactly how negative the consequences will be, how the different kinds of impact we have on the natural environment might interact with each other, and what the timescale is.

We can fill in some of the gaps in knowledge by taking note of the warning signs, and others by looking at projections whose assumptions are borne out by recent developments. It is not just in demography and resource use that this is a time of more and most and never before. There are increasing signs of human impact on the natural environment – on water supply, on plant and animal life, on land, and at sea.

Into the gaps in knowledge walk two contrary temptations: one is complacency – perhaps it will be all right; and the other is alarmism – we're doomed whatever we do. These two reactions are completely at odds with each other. Yet in another way they are mutually supportive because they both lead to inaction. If we are doomed and if we will probably be all right, the logic of both positions is to do nothing.

Not everybody is or should be a scientist and, while scientists could sometimes be of more help if they could only learn to express themselves in everyday language, nor does everybody even have to comprehend scientific arguments. People often come to intuitive understanding and that can be enough.

There is, fortunately, a growing awareness that action can and must be taken to slow the damage we are inflicting on the natural environment and steadily to change course. It is often said that this awareness has grown primarily in richer countries that can afford it but that is not really true. In India and in Kenya, among others, there are examples of important movements of environmental protection and care. Consciousness of the importance of the natural environment is by no means a rich-country luxury. There is at least one country in which the right of people to live in a supportive natural environment is inscribed in the constitution – the Philippines.

Action can be taken by individuals – in Europe and North America, for example, plenty of people sort their garbage so as much as possible can be recycled. Action can be taken by towns such as those that have introduced regulations including bans on the use of plastic bags. Action can be taken by property speculators, opting for carbon-neutral new buildings. By companies and government departments making their offices more energy efficient. By house owners putting solar panels on their roof for heating, and water butts in their back yards. By drivers opting for greener, smaller cars. Or for cycling or taking public transport whenever possible.

In the end, however, action has to be taken by governments, or little of any moment will move. They have the resources and the power to regulate and shape behaviour in ways that could at least slow the loss of biodiversity, limit waste, constrain energy use, and slow global warming. Some such actions have been taken; some forest cover is being regained, and many areas of land are protected from industrial use and urbanization.

Thus far, action has been limited. Many governments are aware that if they set out on that path, they will be committed to actions that are opposed by important lobby groups that carry economic weight and can exert political pressure. Equally, many citizens may find any consequent constraints on their behaviour to be an unreasonable imposition, which they too will oppose. A bold government might look at the example of smoking bans imposed by several countries in restaurants, cinemas, offices, pubs, and bars, and contemplate how angrily they were opposed at first, and how in most places where they have been implemented, they were accepted and tobacco consumption has fallen as a result.

But in general, political caution is at odds with caution on the environment. For on this decisive issue there is really no alternative in the end: to be cautious, we will have to be radical.

Warning Signs

The world faces a deep environmental crisis. Scientific precision about the risks is impossible, both because the study of this kind of risk is future-facing and because in some key respects (such as the number of species) the information we have is not complete. The frequency and scale of natural disasters seems to be increasing, but whether this is a limited fluctuation or a long-term trend is not yet clear.

The range of uncertainty in some projections and risk assessments is such that it is just possible, if in every case actuality turns out to be at the safer end, that overall, humanity will not be in too bad shape a century from now. But the mid-points in many of the projections combine to show a future that will not be like the past. We cannot assume the risks will be the same as we have previously faced.

Ordinary citizens find it even harder than scientists to get to grips with the scale of what may happen and the timescale on which it is unfolding. But there is evidence around us that things are changing in the natural world – and not many of the changes are to the good.

Shrinking Arctic ice: Sea-ice is shrinking in area and thickness. Mid-winter 2012, the volume of Arctic sea-ice was the lowest ever recorded for that time of year. Along the coast of Canada and Russia, a summer sea route has opened up, used by 32 cargo ships in 2011.

Polar bears threatened: As the ice shrinks this affects seals who breed on ice, and polar bears who hunt seals. The polar bear population is declining.

Losses from natural disasters in 2011:

$380 billion
– nearly double the previous record set in 2005

Melting permafrost in Alaska: A temperature increase of 3°–4°C since 1950 is causing roads and buildings to subside. The absence of summer sea-ice is leading to coastal erosion.

Glacial change in the Andes: The Quelccaya Glacier, Peru, is retreating 10 times more rapidly than it did in the 1970s and 1980s – by up to 60 metres a year.

Extinction: Current rates at which plant and animal species are becoming extinct are estimated to be 100 to 1,000 times faster than the average rate over the millennia of the planet's existence. Projections suggest up to 50% of known species are at risk of extinction by 2100.

Ocean dead zones: Industrial effluent has caused a surfeit of algae, which consume oxygen as they decay, producing 400 "dead zones" in the world's lakes and seas, covering a total of 245,000 square kilometres.

Human impact of natural disasters

Affected people

○ 1991–2000

○ 2001–2010

Number recorded as killed

1991–2000

2001–2010

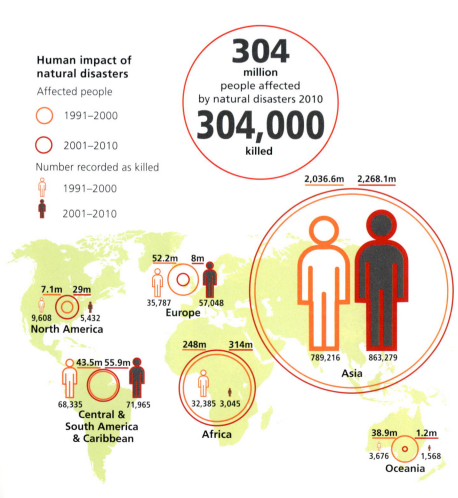

304 million people affected by natural disasters 2010
304,000 killed

2,036.6m   2,268.1m

789,216   863,279

Asia

52.2m   8m

35,787   57,048

Europe

7.1m   29m

9,608   5,432

North America

43.5m   55.9m

68,335   71,965

Central & South America & Caribbean

248m   314m

32,385   3,045

Africa

38.9m   1.2m

3,676   1,568

Oceania

Changing ranges: Studies of the distribution of bird and butterfly species in North America and northern Europe over the past 35 years or so have revealed marked expansion northwards, with no southward expansion.

North Atlantic hurricanes: With annual fluctuations, the frequency and power of hurricanes trended down in the half century before the 1990s and has trended upwards since 1990.

Fires in Russia: Russia experienced forest fires in 2010 that killed 62 people and caused widespread destruction of crops to such an extent that world food prices rose. Fires in 2011 were more widespread, but fewer occurred in densely populated areas and farmland.

Floods in Pakistan: Monsoon flooding in Pakistan affected 18 million people, killing about 1,800, destroying almost 2 million homes. Monsoon floods in 2011 killed at least 300 people.

These days the water evaporates faster and the grass dries very quickly. Last March it rained, but very little. So now I try to cultivate. We have greatly changed our life but so far not much is going better.

A Maasai herder, Kenya, December 2011

Water mining in China: Urbanization, industrialization, increasing use of irrigation, and river pollution in northeast China are using up water from underground aquifers at an unsustainable rate.

Coral bleaching: When coral dies, it goes white – a natural process accelerated by warmer seas, pollution, increased exposure to UV radiation and chemical pollution, among other things. In 1998, the Great Barrier Reef had its most extensive coral bleaching for 700 years, followed in 2002 by an even more extensive bleaching.

Lemurs in Madagascar: Lemurs are among animals producing their young at what is now the "wrong" time. Their breeding season is no longer synchronized with the growing season and the availability of food, putting their survival at risk.

Asian tiger mosquito: Carrying diseases including dengue and encephalitis varieties, this mosquito is spreading faster than almost any other animal species via the trade in tyres. These are ideal breeding grounds and have carried it into Africa, Australia, southern Europe, South America, and parts of the US states east of the Mississippi River.

Rapid rise in Antarctic: Temperatures in the Antarctic Peninsula have risen by 2.8°C over the last 50 years, leading to melting of ice shelves and increased glacier loss. Local flora and fauna are affected, including breeding colonies of Adélie penguins.

Vulture deaths in India: Three species of vulture have suffered a 97% decline in numbers. This has been traced to the widespread use of the drug diclofenac to prevent arthritis in cattle. The vultures' vital clean-up role has been taken over by feral dogs, leading to a rise in rabies.

Ocean acidification: An increasing concentration of carbon dioxide in the atmosphere has raised the acidity of the oceans by 27% over the past 200 years, which is affecting the shell growth of tiny organisms at the base of the food chain.

116 Climate Change; 118 Planetary Boundaries ▶

Biodiversity

The world is steadily losing species of plants and animals. In some species the rate of loss is accelerating. Efforts to stop or just slow the rate of loss have so far proven ineffectual, although among some of the states that are custodians of the world's forests, efforts to prevent further forest loss are starting to prove successful. While the world lost 3 per cent of forest cover from 1990 to 2010, among the ten biggest holders of forests, accounting for 65 per cent of the world total, the rate of loss was just 1 per cent. But the lost forest was largely rainforest, which has the richest biodiversity of any natural environment.

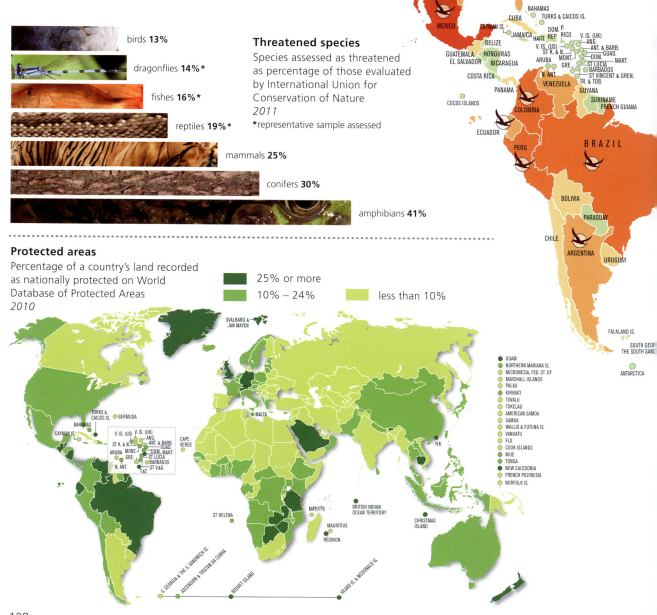

birds **13%**

dragonflies **14%*

fishes **16%*

reptiles **19%*

mammals **25%**

conifers **30%**

amphibians **41%**

Threatened species

Species assessed as threatened as percentage of those evaluated by International Union for Conservation of Nature
2011

*representative sample assessed

Protected areas

Percentage of a country's land recorded as nationally protected on World Database of Protected Areas
2010

25% or more

10% – 24%

less than 10%

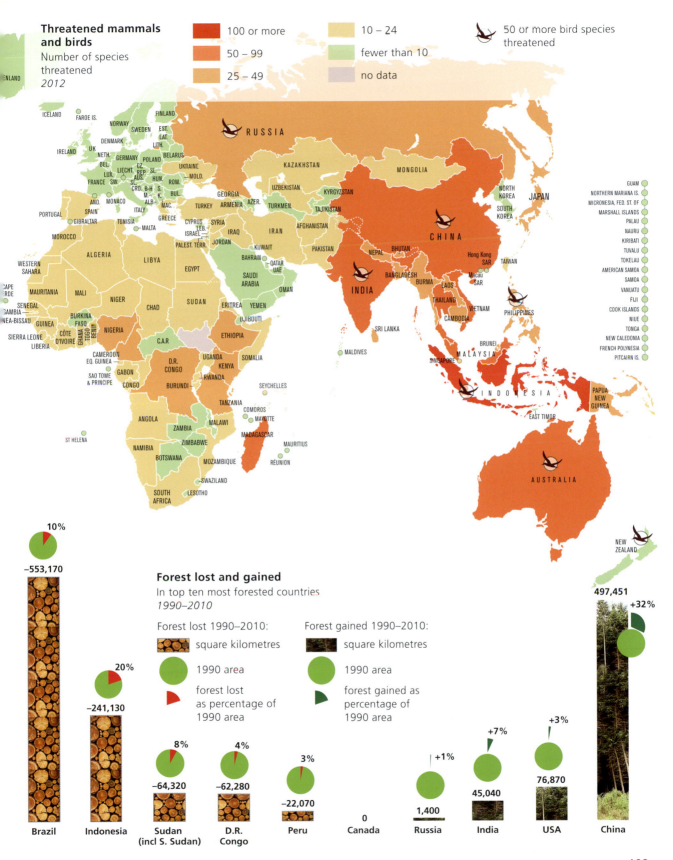

Threatened mammals and birds

Number of species threatened
2012

- 100 or more
- 50 – 99
- 25 – 49
- 10 – 24
- fewer than 10
- no data

50 or more bird species threatened

Forest lost and gained

In top ten most forested countries
1990–2010

Forest lost 1990–2010:
- square kilometres
- 1990 area
- forest lost as percentage of 1990 area

Forest gained 1990–2010:
- square kilometres
- 1990 area
- forest gained as percentage of 1990 area

Country	Value	Percentage
Brazil	–553,170	10%
Indonesia	–241,130	20%
Sudan (incl S. Sudan)	–64,320	8%
D.R. Congo	–62,280	4%
Peru	–22,070	3%
Canada	0	
Russia	1,400	+1%
India	45,040	+7%
USA	76,870	+3%
China	497,451	+32%

Water Resources

The world as a whole has plenty of water, but like every natural resource, nature distributes it unevenly and people's access to it is determined not only by nature but also by how the country is governed, its wealth, and how much of that wealth is devoted to meeting the needs of ordinary people.

There are two kinds of water scarcity. One results from over-withdrawal – taking more water out of the ground than is naturally restored by rainfall. The other is a social and economic issue – when there is no adequate infrastructure for delivering clean water to all. Unless these issues are addressed, estimates suggest that by 2025 two-thirds of the world's population will experience shortages of a clean water supply.

Large parts of both India and China face water problems. To hedge against the potential problems this could pose for their food supply, they and other governments have purchased large tracts of water-rich, arable land in Sub-Saharan Africa.

Total annual water withdrawal
1900–2000, 2025 projected
cubic metres

579 — 1900
1,382 — 1950
3,973 — 2000
5,235 — 2025

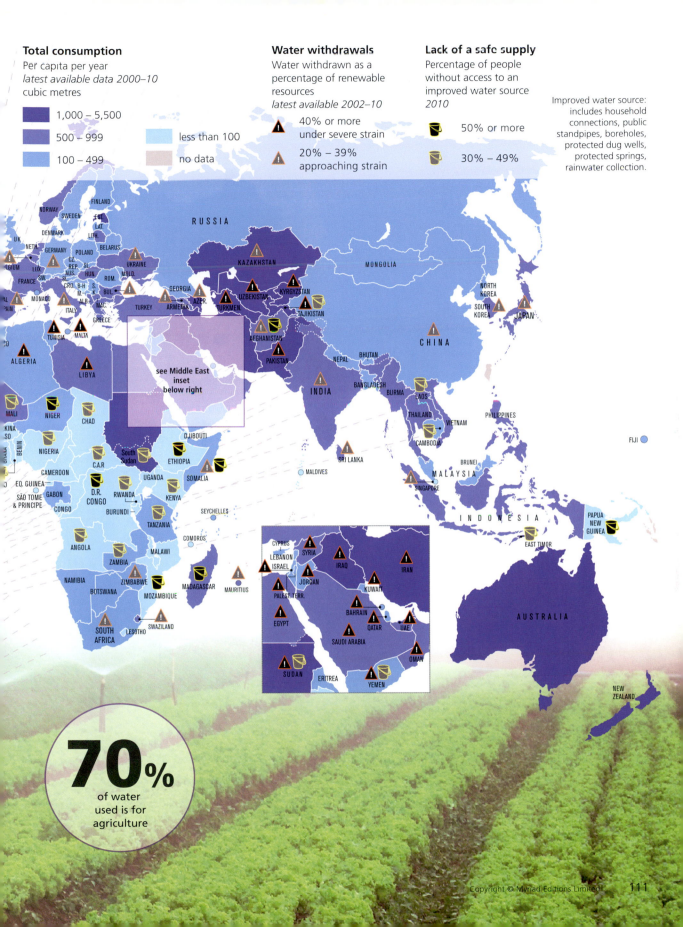

Total consumption
Per capita per year
latest available data 2000–10
cubic metres

- ■ 1,000 – 5,500
- ■ 500 – 999
- ■ 100 – 499
- ■ less than 100
- ■ no data

Water withdrawals
Water withdrawn as a percentage of renewable resources
latest available 2002–10

- ⚠ 40% or more under severe strain
- ⚠ 20% – 39% approaching strain

Lack of a safe supply
Percentage of people without access to an improved water source
2010

- 🪣 50% or more
- 🪣 30% – 49%

Improved water source: includes household connections, public standpipes, boreholes, protected dug wells, protected springs, rainwater collection.

70% of water used is for agriculture

NORWAY
SWEDEN
FINLAND
EST.
LAT.
LITH.
DENMARK
UK
NETH.
BELGIUM
GERMANY
POLAND
BELARUS
LUX.
CZ.
SW.
REP. SL.
FRANCE
AUS. HUN.
MONACO
SL. ROM.
CRO. B-H. S.
M. K. BUL.
ALB. MAC.
ITALY
GREECE
TUNISIA
MALTA
ALGERIA
LIBYA
MALI
NIGER
CHAD
DJIBOUTI
BURKINA FASO
BENIN
NIGERIA
South Sudan
C.A.R.
ETHIOPIA
SOMALIA
CAMEROON
UGANDA
EQ. GUINEA
GABON
D.R. CONGO
RWANDA
KENYA
SÃO TOME & PRINCIPE
CONGO
BURUNDI
TANZANIA
SEYCHELLES
ANGOLA
MALAWI
COMOROS
ZAMBIA
NAMIBIA
ZIMBABWE
MADAGASCAR
MAURITIUS
BOTSWANA
MOZAMBIQUE
SWAZILAND
SOUTH AFRICA
LESOTHO

RUSSIA
UKRAINE
KAZAKHSTAN
MONGOLIA
MOLD.
GEORGIA
ARMENIA AZER.
UZBEKISTAN
KYRGYZSTAN
TURKEY
TURKMEN.
TAJIKISTAN
NORTH KOREA
SOUTH KOREA
JAPAN
AFGHANISTAN
CHINA
PAKISTAN
NEPAL
BHUTAN
INDIA
BANGLADESH
BURMA
LAOS
THAILAND
VIETNAM
PHILIPPINES
CAMBODIA
SRI LANKA
BRUNEI
MALAYSIA
MALDIVES
SINGAPORE
FIJI
INDONESIA
EAST TIMOR
PAPUA NEW GUINEA
AUSTRALIA
NEW ZEALAND

see Middle East inset below right

Middle East inset
CYPRUS
LEBANON
SYRIA
IRAQ
IRAN
ISRAEL
JORDAN
PALEST. TERR.
KUWAIT
BAHRAIN
EGYPT
QATAR
UAE
SAUDI ARABIA
OMAN
SUDAN
ERITREA
YEMEN

111

Waste

There is slowly growing recognition in a handful of countries that waste is a serious global problem. Most of what we use, we throw away, much of it thoughtlessly and some of that becomes a hazard to life and to nature. There are countries and local authorities that have passed laws to regulate the use of plastic bags and these seem to be having an effect.

Access to improved sanitation facilities has increased in most countries since 1990 and this not only improves public health but is also a part of waste management; a few countries, however, have moved in the wrong direction.

China: Banned flimsy plastic bags in 2008, and after 3 years it was claimed to have reduced annual use by 24 billion plastic bags, and saved the equivalent of 3.6m tonnes of oil.

Mumbai: The municipal corporation banned bags thinner than 50 microns after they blocked drains and contributed to major flooding in 2005.

South Australia: Since a plastic bag ban was imposed in 2009, household rubbish has been reduced by half.

Sanitation

Percentage of population with access to improved sanitation facilities
2010

- less than 25%
- 25% – 49%
- 50% – 74%
- 75% – 99%
- 100%
- no data

⇧ access has increased by 25 percentage points or more *1990–2010*

⬇ access has declined *1990–2010*

Tonnes of disposable nappies
3,266,000
in USA
690,000
in UK

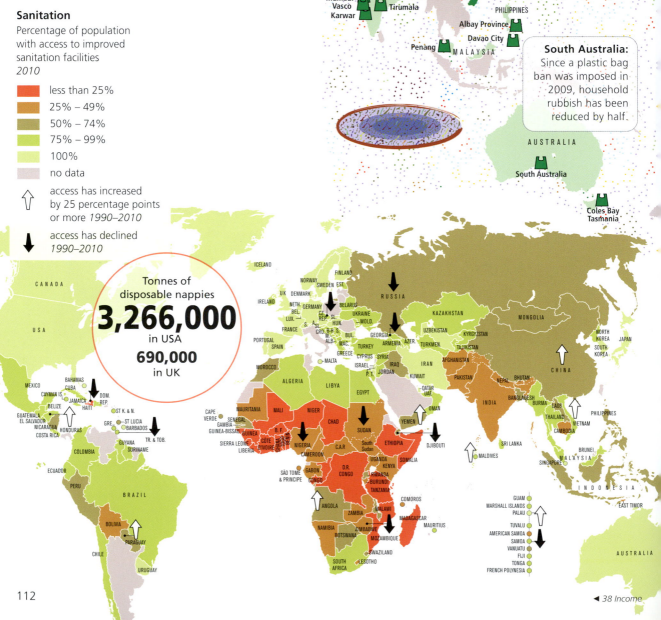

◄ 38 Income

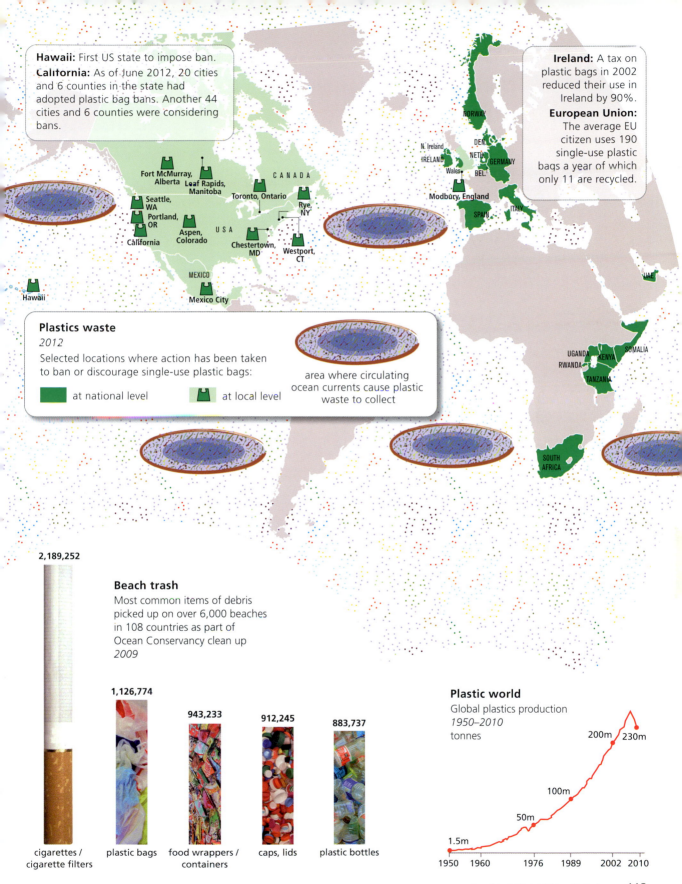

Hawaii: First US state to impose ban.
California: As of June 2012, 20 cities and 6 counties in the state had adopted plastic bag bans. Another 44 cities and 6 counties were considering bans.

Ireland: A tax on plastic bags in 2002 reduced their use in Ireland by 90%.
European Union: The average EU citizen uses 190 single-use plastic bags a year of which only 11 are recycled.

NORWAY
N. Ireland
IRELAND
Wales
DEN.
NETH.
GERMANY
BEL.
Modbury, England
SPAIN
ITALY
UAE

Fort McMurray, Alberta
Leaf Rapids, Manitoba
CANADA
Toronto, Ontario
Rye, NY
Seattle, WA
Portland, OR
USA
Aspen, Colorado
California
Chestertown, MD
Westport, CT

MEXICO
Hawaii
Mexico City

UGANDA
RWANDA
KENYA
SOMALIA
TANZANIA

SOUTH AFRICA

Plastics waste
2012
Selected locations where action has been taken to ban or discourage single-use plastic bags:

- ■ at national level
- ■ at local level

area where circulating ocean currents cause plastic waste to collect

Beach trash
Most common items of debris picked up on over 6,000 beaches in 108 countries as part of Ocean Conservancy clean up
2009

2,189,252
cigarettes / cigarette filters

1,126,774
plastic bags

943,233
food wrappers / containers

912,245
caps, lids

883,737
plastic bottles

Plastic world
Global plastics production
1950–2010
tonnes

1.5m
50m
100m
200m
230m

1950 1960 1976 1989 2002 2010

Energy Use

Everything that runs, runs on energy. As countries get richer they use more energy until a point comes when their economic base shifts from natural resources and industry to information and the service sectors. Most energy comes from oil, gas, coal, and uranium, whose extraction and use carry risks of pollution, sometimes with catastrophic effect.

The climate-change risks of continuing to emit so much carbon by using oil, gas, and coal have led to interest in alternatives. Because each has benefits and drawbacks, the lobbies for and against each one have cogent arguments. Nuclear power can look good from a climate perspective, less so when viewed through the lens of hazardous waste. Biofuels seem environmentally responsible, but producing them takes so much energy it is not clear how big the gain is, and they also take land out of food production. The wind, waves, tide, and sun are all sources of unending energy, but it has not so far been feasible to harness them on the necessary scale.

Whatever differences these energy sources make, the key alternative in the end may well turn out to be simply using less.

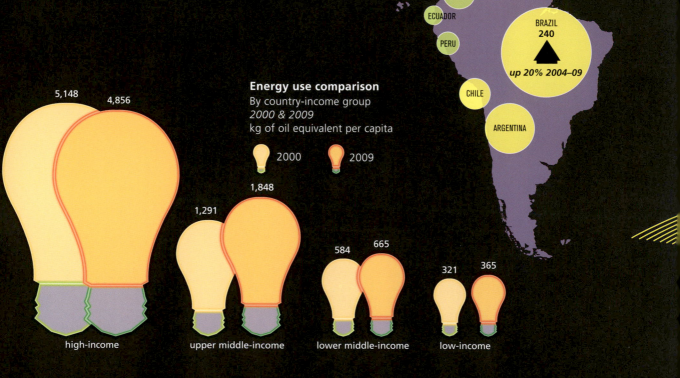

1970–2011 human population nearly **doubled** while number of cars grew **fivefold**

CANADA 254

USA 2,163

MEXICO 175

CUBA

REST OF THE AMERICAS

T. & T.

VENEZUELA

COLOMBIA

ECUADOR

PERU

BRAZIL 240
up 20% 2004–09

CHILE

ARGENTINA

Energy use comparison
By country-income group
2000 & 2009
kg of oil equivalent per capita

2000   2009

5,148   4,856
high-income

1,291   1,848
upper middle-income

584   665
lower middle-income

321   365
low-income

114

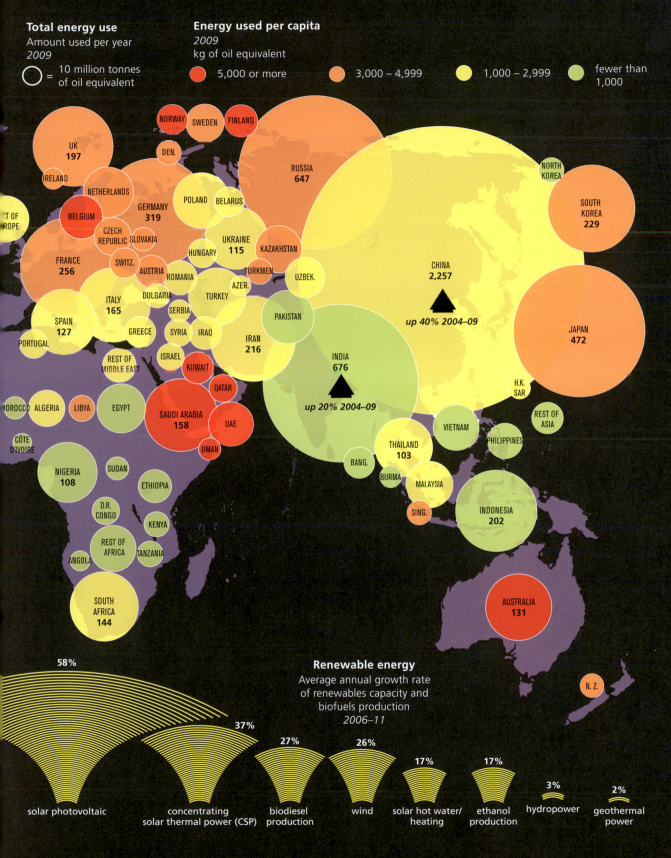

Total energy use
Amount used per year
2009

◯ = 10 million tonnes of oil equivalent

Energy used per capita
2009
kg of oil equivalent

● 5,000 or more
● 3,000 – 4,999
● 1,000 – 2,999
● fewer than 1,000

NORWAY SWEDEN FINLAND

UK **197**

IRELAND

DEN.

RUSSIA **647**

NORTH KOREA

SOUTH KOREA **229**

NETHERLANDS

GERMANY **319**

POLAND BELARUS

T OF ROPE

BELGIUM

CZECH REPUBLIC SLOVAKIA

UKRAINE **115**

KAZAKHSTAN

FRANCE **256**

SWITZ.

AUSTRIA

HUNGARY

ROMANIA

TURKMEN.

UZBEK.

CHINA **2,257**

▲ *up 40% 2004–09*

JAPAN **472**

ITALY **165**

BULGARIA

SERBIA

AZER.

TURKEY

PAKISTAN

SPAIN **127**

GREECE

SYRIA IRAQ

IRAN **216**

INDIA **676**

▲ *up 20% 2004–09*

H.K. SAR

PORTUGAL

ISRAEL KUWAIT

REST OF ASIA

REST OF MIDDLE EAST

QATAR

OROCCO ALGERIA LIBYA EGYPT

SAUDI ARABIA **158**

UAE

VIETNAM

PHILIPPINES

CÔTE D'IVOIRE

OMAN

BANG.

THAILAND **103**

NIGERIA **108**

SUDAN

ETHIOPIA

BURMA

MALAYSIA

INDONESIA **202**

D.R. CONGO

KENYA

SING.

ANGOLA

REST OF AFRICA

TANZANIA

SOUTH AFRICA **144**

AUSTRALIA **131**

N. Z.

Renewable energy
Average annual growth rate of renewables capacity and biofuels production
2006–11

58%
solar photovoltaic

37%
concentrating solar thermal power (CSP)

27%
biodiesel production

26%
wind

17%
solar hot water/ heating

17%
ethanol production

3%
hydropower

2%
geothermal power

115

Climate Change

The basic science of global warming and climate change is well established and is in doubt barely anywhere. The earth is habitable because of the effect of the so-called 'greenhouse gases' that prevent too much warmth escaping from the planet. Among the key greenhouse gases are carbon and methane. Any buildup of these gases intensifies the greenhouse effect and causes the planet to get warmer. This much has been understood since the mid-19th century.

In the past 200 years, about half a trillion tonnes of carbon dioxide (CO_2) have entered the atmosphere, mainly through use of coal and oil. Then there is methane, produced by raising livestock and a variety of industries as well as landfill sites. Less has been emitted but it is 20 times as effective a greenhouse gas as CO_2. Nitrous oxide (emitted mainly from agriculture) is 300 times as effective.

International climate change talks aim at controlling emissions to a maximum of 450 parts per million (ppm) of CO_2 equivalent in the atmosphere. This has been calculated as giving a 50:50 chance of restricting average global temperature increase to 2°C above pre-industrial era levels. This small-sounding increase will have a major impact on many regions' climate, and most of the expected effects are harmful – more floods, more droughts, shorter growing seasons.

While 450 ppm may give an even chance of staying within the 2° limit, there is also an even chance of further warming. Many scientists argue that to be sure of staying below 2°, the atmospheric concentration needed to be kept to 350 ppm – a level already exceeded.

Greenland ice sheet
As the ice melts, the height of surface ice decreases and is exposed to warmer temperatures at lower altitudes. This could accelerate melting and lead to the ice-sheets breaking up, with consequent sea-level rise over the coming three centuries.
1°C–2°C

CANADA
2%

USA
26%

CENTRAL AMERICA
& CARIBBEAN
2%

SOUTH
AMERICA
3%

Amazon rainforest
Rainforest is continually being cut down and there could come a critical point in the next 50 years at which the hydrological cycle in the remaining forest no longer functions. This could result in a serious reduction in rainfall, and the loss of much more forest.
3°C–4°C

West Antarctic ice sheet
The ice-sheets are frozen into submarine mountains, the structure of which could be weakened by a warming ocean. The subsequent melting of the ice now above sea level could lead to a sea-level rise over the next 300 years of as much as 5 metres.
3°C–5°C

◀ 106 Warning Signs; 114 Energy Use

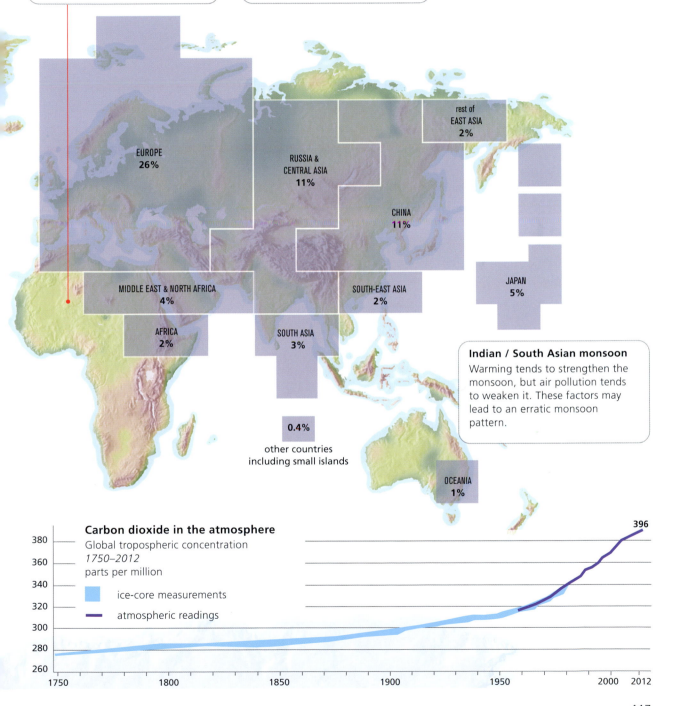

Saharan and West African monsoon

Small changes to the monsoon have triggered abrupt wetting and drying of the Sahara in the past. Drier conditions would produce additional dust across the Sahara, which affects distant rainfall too.

3°C–5°C

Sea-level rise

A widely accepted projection is for the sea level to rise by 18–59 cms by 2100. At present, actually observed sea-level rise is tracking the upper end of that range. Small island states and low-lying coastal cities face severe risks.

Past emissions and future consequences

share of total CO_2 emissions from fossil fuels and cement *1950–2007*

1% = 9,310 million tonnes CO_2

temperature increase at which transition could be triggered

EUROPE
26%

RUSSIA & CENTRAL ASIA
11%

rest of EAST ASIA
2%

CHINA
11%

JAPAN
5%

MIDDLE EAST & NORTH AFRICA
4%

SOUTH-EAST ASIA
2%

AFRICA
2%

SOUTH ASIA
3%

0.4%
other countries including small islands

Indian / South Asian monsoon

Warming tends to strengthen the monsoon, but air pollution tends to weaken it. These factors may lead to an erratic monsoon pattern.

OCEANIA
1%

Carbon dioxide in the atmosphere

Global tropospheric concentration
1750–2012
parts per million

ice-core measurements

atmospheric readings

396

Planetary Boundaries

Humanity's impact on the natural environment increases as population grows and industrial and agricultural production grow with it. We have never been here before – there has never been so much activity, never such a large population – so many of the consequences of our environmental impact are unknown. We don't really know how far we can go before the consequences get very serious. And compared to how much is already known about climate change, biodiversity loss and other issues, not much at all is known about the interaction between the impacts.

The concept of planetary boundaries, generated by a multinational group of 29 scientists brought together by the Stockholm Resilience Centre, is an attempt to deal with both these gaps in our knowledge. The idea looks likely to be an important part of the debate about environmental impact and policy in the coming decade.

Not every scientist agrees with the way in which the boundaries are defined and calculated. Some think they are too tight, some find them too loose. Some think a couple more boundaries should be brought into the picture.

Contested as it is, the concept of planetary boundaries brings the key issues into sharp relief. Inside the boundaries (wherever they precisely lie) we are operating more or less safely. If we transgress them, we don't know what will then unfold. According to one group of scientists, we have crossed three; there is time to ensure we do not cross more.

Planetary Boundaries
Assessment of the extent to which safe operating levels have been reached or transgressed
2012

████ boundary
(limit of safe operating level)

estimated current level

chemical pollution *not calculated*

aerosols *not calculated*

	Measured by:	Boundary calculated as:
Climate change	Carbon dioxide in atmosphere	Increase to not more than 350 parts per million
Ocean acidification	Aragonite depletion in ocean	Reduction to not less than 80% of pre-industrial level
Ozone depletion	Concentration of ozone in stratosphere	No more than 5% reduction from pre-industrial level
Phosphorus cycle	Phosphorus in oceans	11 million tonnes per year
Nitrogen cycle	Nitrogen removed from atmosphere	35 million tonnes per year
Fresh water	Human consumption	4,000 cubic kilometres per year
Land use	Land used for crops	15% of land surface
Aerosols	Particles in the atmosphere	Not calculated
Chemical pollution	Concentration of toxic substances in environment	Not calculated
Biodiversity	Loss of species	10 species extinct per million per year

◀ *106 Warning Signs; 116 Climate Change*

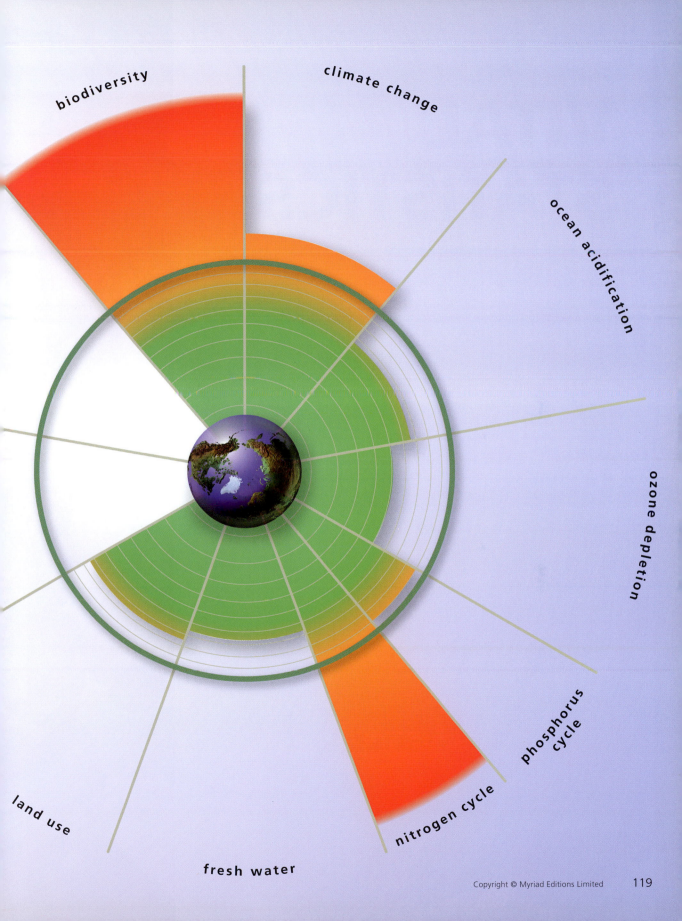

biodiversity

climate change

ocean acidification

ozone depletion

phosphorus cycle

nitrogen cycle

fresh water

land use

PART SEVEN

VITAL STATISTICS

Indicators of Wellbeing

	Official capital	Land area 1,000 hectares 2008	Population 1,000s 2010	Population rate of change 2005–10	Migrants (excluding refugees) as % of total 2000	Life expectancy at birth 2009	Literate adults as % of adult population 2010 or latest
Afghanistan	Kabul	65,209	31,412	2.6%	0.3%	48	–
Albania	Tirane	2,740	3,204	0.4%	2.8%	73	96%
Algeria	Algiers	238,174	35,468	1.5%	0.7%	72	73%
Angola	Luanda	124,670	19,082	2.9%	0.3%	52	70%
Antigua and Barbuda	Saint John's	44	89	1.1%	23.6%	74	99%
Argentina	Buenos Aires	273,669	40,412	0.9%	3.6%	75	98%
Armenia	Yerevan	2,820	3,092	0.2%	10.5%	70	100%
Australia	Canberra	768,230	22,268	1.7%	21.9%	82	–
Austria	Vienna	8,245	8,394	0.4%	15.6%	80	–
Azerbaijan	Baku	8,266	9,188	1.4%	3.0%	68	100%
Bahamas	Nassau	1,001	343	1.4%	9.7%	76	–
Bahrain	Al-Manámah	71	1,262	11.1%	39.1%	74	91%
Bangladesh	Dhaka	13,017	148,692	1.1%	0.7%	65	56%
Barbados	Bridgetown	43	273	0.2%	10.9%	76	–
Belarus	Mensk	20,748	9,595	-0.5%	11.4%	70	100%
Belgium	Brussels	3,023	10,712	0.6%	9.1%	80	–
Belize	Belmopan	2,281	312	2.1%	15.0%	73	–
Benin	Porto-Novo	11,062	8,850	3.0%	2.5%	57	42%
Bhutan	Thimphu	4,700	726	1.9%	5.7%	63	53%
Bolivia	La Paz	108,438	9,930	1.6%	1.5%	68	91%
Bosnia and Herzegovina	Sarajevo	5,120	3,760	-0.1%	0.7%	76	98%
Botswana	Gaborone	56,673	2,007	1.4%	5.8%	61	84%
Brazil	Brasilia	845,942	194,946	0.9%	0.4%	73	90%
Brunei	Bandar Seri Begawan	527	399	1.9%	36.4%	77	95%
Bulgaria	Sofia	10,864	7,494	-0.6%	1.4%	74	98%
Burkina Faso	Ouagadougou	27,360	16,469	3.0%	6.4%	52	29%
Burma	Nay Pyi Taw	65,755	47,963	0.7%	0.2%	64	92%
Burundi	Bujumbura	2,568	8,383	2.9%	0.7%	50	67%
Cambodia	Phnom Penh	17,652	14,138	1.1%	2.2%	61	78%
Cameroon	Yaoundé	46,540	19,599	2.2%	1.0%	51	71%
Canada	Ottawa	909,351	34,017	1.0%	21.3%	81	–
Cape Verde	Praia	403	496	1.0%	2.4%	71	85%
Central African Republic	Bangui	62,300	4,401	1.8%	1.8%	48	55%
Chad	N'Djamena	125,920	11,227	2.7%	3.4%	48	34%
Chile	Santiago	74,880	17,114	1.0%	1.9%	79	99%
China	Beijing	932,749	1,341,335	0.5%	0.1%	74	94%
Colombia	Santafé de Bogotá	110,950	46,295	1.5%	0.2%	76	93%
Comoros	Moroni	186	735	2.7%	2.0%	60	74%
Congo	Brazzaville	34,150	4,043	2.7%	3.8%	55	–
Congo, Dem. Rep.	Kinshasa	226,705	65,966	2.8%	0.7%	49	67%
Costa Rica	San José	5,106	4,659	1.6%	10.5%	79	96%
Côte d'Ivoire	Yamoussoukro	31,800	19,738	1.8%	11.2%	50	55%
Croatia	Zagreb	5,592	4,403	-0.2%	15.9%	76	99%
Cuba	Havana	10,982	11,258	0.0%	0.1%	78	100%
Cyprus	Lefkosia (Nicosia)	924	1,104	1.3%	17.5%	81	98%
Czech Republic	Prague	7,726	10,493	0.5%	4.4%	77	–
Denmark	Copenhagen	4,243	5,550	0.5%	8.8%	79	–

Education	Under-nourished	Over-weight	Improved facilities % with access to		DALYs	
primary enrolment 2010 or latest	as % of population 2007	adults as % of population 2008	water source 2010	sanitation 2010	years lost to ill-health, disability or early death per 100,000 people 2004	
–	–	12%	50%	37%	76,578	Afghanistan
85	–	54%	95%	94%	15,921	Albania
94	–	48%	83%	95%	16,114	Algeria
–	41%	26%	51%	58%	79,754	Angola
88	21%	59%	–	–	16,049	Antigua and Barbuda
99	–	64%	–	–	15,599	Argentina
84	21%	55%	98%	90%	18,841	Armenia
97	–	61%	100%	100%	11,070	Australia
–	–	50%	100%	100%	12,069	Austria
85	–	57%	80%	82%	18,945	Azerbaijan
91	6%	69%	–	100%	18,626	Bahamas
97	–	70%	–	–	12,015	Bahrain
86	26%	8%	81%	56%	26,569	Bangladesh
–	–	68%	100%	100%	16,401	Barbados
94	–	56%	100%	93%	22,076	Belarus
99	–	52%	100%	100%	12,948	Belgium
97	–	71%	98%	90%	20,042	Belize
92	12%	26%	75%	13%	42,929	Benin
87	–	24%	96%	44%	23,916	Bhutan
94	27%	50%	88%	27%	25,544	Bolivia
87	–	58%	99%	95%	16,079	Bosnia and Herzegovina
87	25%	36%	96%	62%	49,246	Botswana
95	6%	53%	98%	79%	19,475	Brazil
93	–	31%	–	–	11,351	Brunei
97	–	54%	100%	100%	18,296	Bulgaria
63	8%	13%	79%	17%	54,802	Burkina Faso
–	–	19%	83%	76%	28,825	Burma
99	62%	15%	72%	46%	60,637	Burundi
95	25%	13%	64%	31%	36,464	Cambodia
92	22%	38%	77%	49%	45,774	Cameroon
99	–	61%	100%	100%	11,531	Canada
83	11%	38%	88%	61%	17,197	Cape Verde
69	40%	17%	67%	34%	55,133	Central African Republic
61	39%	16%	51%	13%	60,031	Chad
95	–	65%	96%	96%	12,995	Chile
–	10%	25%	91%	64%	15,279	China
90	9%	50%	92%	77%	19,142	Colombia
87	47%	20%	95%	36%	24,949	Comoros
59	13%	22%	71%	18%	36,740	Congo
–	–	11%	45%	24%	65,555	Congo, Dem. Rep.
–	–	60%	97%	95%	12,519	Costa Rica
57	14%	27%	80%	24%	60,795	Côte d'Ivoire
89	–	53%	99%	99%	15,369	Croatia
99	–	53%	94%	91%	13,937	Cuba
99	–	56%	100%	100%	12,010	Cyprus
–	–	62%	100%	98%	14,326	Czech Republic
95	–	48%	100%	100%	13,447	Denmark

Indicators of Wellbeing

	Official capital	Land area 1,000 hectares 2008	Population 1,000s 2010	Population rate of change 2005–10	Migrants (excluding refugees) as % of total 2000	Life expectancy at birth 2009	Literate adults as % of adult population 2010 or latest
Djibouti	Djibouti	2,318	889	1.9%	13.0%	60	–
Dominica	Roseau	75	68	-0.3%	8.3%	74	–
Dominican Republic	Santo Domingo	4,838	9,927	1.4%	4.2%	71	88%
East Timor	Dili	1,487	1,124	2.1%	1.2%	67	51%
Ecuador	Quito	27,684	14,465	1.5%	2.9%	75	84%
Egypt	Cairo	99,545	81,121	1.8%	0.3%	71	66%
El Salvador	San Salvador	2,072	6,193	0.5%	0.7%	72	84%
Equatorial Guinea	Malabo	2,805	700	2.8%	1.1%	53	93%
Eritrea	Asmara	10,100	5,254	3.2%	0.3%	66	67%
Estonia	Tallinn	4,239	1,341	-0.1%	13.6%	75	100%
Ethiopia	Addis Ababa	100,000	82,950	2.2%	0.6%	54	30%
Fiji	Suva	1,827	861	0.9%	2.2%	69	–
Finland	Helsinki	30,459	5,365	0.5%	4.2%	80	–
France	Paris	55,010	62,787	0.6%	10.7%	81	–
Gabon	Libreville	25,767	1,505	1.9%	18.9%	62	88%
Gambia	Banjul	1,000	1,728	2.8%	16.6%	60	46%
Georgia	Tbilisi	6,949	4,352	-0.6%	4.0%	71	100%
Germany	Berlin	34,877	82,302	-0.1%	13.1%	80	–
Ghana	Accra	22,754	24,392	2.4%	7.6%	60	67%
Greece	Athens	12,890	11,359	0.3%	10.1%	80	97%
Grenada	St George's	34	104	0.3%	12.1%	73	96%
Guatemala	Guatemala City	10,843	14,389	2.5%	0.4%	69	74%
Guinea	Conakry	24,572	9,982	2.0%	3.8%	52	39%
Guinea-Bissau	Bissau	2,812	1,515	2.0%	1.2%	49	52%
Guyana	Georgetown	19,685	754	0.2%	1.5%	67	–
Haiti	Port-au-Prince	2,756	9,993	1.3%	0.3%	62	49%
Honduras	Tegucigalpa	11,189	7,601	2.0%	0.3%	69	84%
Hungary	Budapest	8,961	9,984	-0.2%	3.7%	74	99%
Iceland	Reykjavik	10,025	320	1.5%	11.3%	82	–
India	New Delhi	297,319	1,224,614	1.4%	0.4%	65	63%
Indonesia	Jakarta	181,157	239,871	1.1%	0.1%	68	92%
Iran	Tehran	162,855	73,974	1.2%	2.8%	73	85%
Iraq	Baghdad	43,737	31,672	2.9%	0.3%	66	78%
Ireland	Dublin	6,889	4,470	1.4%	19.6%	80	–
Israel	Jerusalem	2,164	7,418	2.3%	40.4%	82	–
Italy	Rome	29,411	60,551	0.6%	7.4%	82	99%
Jamaica	Kingston	1,083	2,741	0.4%	1.1%	71	86%
Japan	Tokyo	36,450	126,536	0.0%	1.7%	83	–
Jordan	Amman	8,824	6,187	2.9%	45.9%	71	92%
Kazakhstan	Astana	269,970	16,026	1.1%	19.5%	64	100%
Kenya	Nairobi	56,914	40,513	2.6%	2.0%	60	87%
Kiribati	Tarawa	81	100	1.6%	2.0%	68	–
Korea, North	Pyongyang	12,041	24,346	0.5%	0.2%	70	100%
Korea, South	Seoul	9,873	48,184	0.5%	1.1%	80	–
Kuwait	Kuwait City	1,782	2,737	3.8%	68.8%	78	94%
Kyrgyzstan	Bishkek	19,180	5,334	1.1%	4.0%	66	99%
Laos	Vientiane	23,080	6,201	1.5%	0.3%	63	73%

Education	Under-nourished	Over-weight	Improved facilities % with access to		DALYs	
primary enrolment 2010 or latest	as % of population 2007	adults as % of population 2008	water source 2010	sanitation 2010	years lost to ill-health, disability or early death per 100,000 people 2004	
44	26%	34%	88%	50%	35,428	Djibouti
93	–	57%	–	–	16,038	Dominica
80	24%	55%	86%	83%	21,303	Dominican Republic
82	31%	13%	69%	47%	28,090	East Timor
95	15%	56%	94%	92%	17,713	Ecuador
93	–	70%	99%	95%	18,613	Egypt
94	9%	63%	88%	87%	18,867	El Salvador
54	–	36%	–	–	56,480	Equatorial Guinea
36	65%	11%	–	–	27,457	Eritrea
94	–	51%	98%	95%	18,900	Estonia
83	41%	8%	44%	21%	47,529	Ethiopia
89	–	67%	98%	83%	17,753	Fiji
96	–	53%	100%	100%	13,205	Finland
98	–	46%	100%	100%	12,262	France
80	–	44%	87%	33%	31,510	Gabon
67	19%	28%	89%	68%	36,037	Gambia
100	6%	53%	98%	95%	15,715	Georgia
97	–	55%	100%	100%	12,536	Germany
76	–	30%	86%	14%	34,141	Ghana
99	–	49%	100%	98%	11,826	Greece
93	21%	56%	–	97%	18,911	Grenada
95	22%	54%	92%	78%	22,026	Guatemala
73	16%	22%	74%	18%	44,488	Guinea
52	22%	21%	64%	20%	59,745	Guinea-Bissau
95	8%	45%	94%	84%	27,666	Guyana
–	57%	32%	69%	17%	36,911	Haiti
97	12%	52%	87%	77%	20,009	Honduras
91	–	58%	100%	100%	17,941	Hungary
98	–	56%	100%	100%	9,803	Iceland
91	19%	11%	92%	34%	27,316	India
95	13%	21%	82%	54%	23,854	Indonesia
99	–	55%	96%	100%	17,517	Iran
88	–	65%	79%	73%	53,044	Iraq
96	–	61%	100%	99%	11,692	Ireland
97	–	60%	100%	100%	10,031	Israel
98	–	49%	100%	–	11,245	Italy
80	5%	56%	93%	80%	16,314	Jamaica
100	–	22%	100%	100%	10,170	Japan
89	–	69%	97%	98%	14,935	Jordan
89	–	57%	95%	97%	27,583	Kazakhstan
82	33%	21%	59%	32%	42,452	Kenya
97	–	81%	–	–	24,065	Kiribati
–	35%	17%	98%	80%	21,749	Korea, North
99	–	31%	98%	100%	12,928	Korea, South
88	–	79%	99%	100%	9,829	Kuwait
84	11%	47%	90%	93%	23,066	Kyrgyzstan
93	22%	15%	67%	63%	29,205	Laos

Indicators of Wellbeing

	Official capital	Land area 1,000 hectares 2008	Population		Migrants (excluding refugees) as % of total 2000	Life expectancy at birth 2009	Literate adults as % of adult population 2010 or latest
			1,000s 2010	rate of change 2005–10			
Latvia	Riga	6,229	2,252	-0.5%	15.0%	72	100%
Lebanon	Beirut	1,023	4,228	0.8%	17.8%	74	90%
Lesotho	Maseru	3,035	2,171	1.0%	0.3%	48	90%
Liberia	Monrovia	9,632	3,994	4.5%	2.3%	56	59%
Libya	Tripoli	175,954	6,355	1.9%	10.4%	72	89%
Lithuania	Vilnius	6,268	3,324	-0.5%	4.0%	73	100%
Luxembourg	Luxembourg	259	507	2.1%	35.2%	81	–
Macedonia	Skopje	2,543	2,061	0.2%	6.3%	74	97%
Madagascar	Antananarivo	58,154	20,714	2.9%	0.2%	65	64%
Malawi	Lilongwe	9,408	14,901	3.0%	1.8%	47	74%
Malaysia	Kuala Lumpur	32,855	28,401	1.7%	8.4%	73	92%
Maldives	Malé	30	316	1.4%	1.0%	75	98%
Mali	Bamako	122,019	15,370	3.1%	1.2%	53	26%
Malta	Valletta	32	417	0.4%	3.8%	80	92%
Marshall Islands	Majuro	18	54	0.8%	2.7%	59	–
Mauritania	Nouakchott	103,070	3,460	2.5%	2.9%	58	57%
Mauritius	Port Louis	203	1,299	0.7%	3.3%	73	88%
Mexico	Mexico City	194,395	113,423	1.3%	0.7%	76	93%
Micronesia, Fed. Sts.	Palikir	70	111	0.3%	2.4%	69	–
Moldova	Chisinau	3,287	3,573	-1.1%	11.4%	69	98%
Mongolia	Ulaan Baatar	156,650	2,756	1.6%	0.4%	69	97%
Montenegro	Podgorica	1,381	631	0.2%	6.8%	75	–
Morocco	Rabat	44,630	31,951	1.0%	0.2%	73	56%
Mozambique	Maputo	78,638	23,391	2.4%	1.9%	49	55%
Namibia	Windhoek	82,329	2,283	1.9%	6.3%	57	89%
Nepal	Kathmandu	14,300	29,959	1.9%	3.2%	67	59%
Netherlands	Amsterdam	3,388	16,613	0.4%	10.5%	81	–
New Zealand	Wellington	26,771	4,368	1.1%	22.4%	81	–
Nicaragua	Managua	12,140	5,788	1.3%	0.7%	74	78%
Niger	Niamey	126,670	15,512	3.5%	1.3%	57	29%
Nigeria	Abuja	91,077	158,423	2.5%	0.7%	54	61%
Norway	Oslo	30,428	4,883	1.1%	10.0%	81	–
Oman	Muscat	30,950	2,782	2.7%	28.4%	74	87%
Pakistan	Islamabad	77,088	173,593	1.8%	2.3%	63	56%
Palestinien Territories	–	602	4,039	2.6%	43.6%	–	95%
Panama	Panama City	7,443	3,517	1.7%	3.4%	77	94%
Papua New Guinea	Port Moresby	45,286	6,858	2.4%	0.4%	63	60%
Paraguay	Asunción	39,730	6,455	1.8%	2.5%	74	95%
Peru	Lima	128,000	29,077	1.1%	0.1%	76	90%
Philippines	Manila	29,817	93,261	1.7%	0.5%	70	95%
Poland	Warsaw	30,633	38,277	0.1%	2.2%	76	100%
Portugal	Lisbon	9,150	10,676	0.2%	8.6%	79	95%
Puerto Rico	San Juan	887	3,749	-0.2%	8.1%	–	90%
Qatar	Doha	1,100	1,759	15.2%	86.5%	78	95%
Romania	Bucharest	22,998	21,486	-0.3%	0.6%	73	98%
Russia	Moscow	1,638,139	142,958	-0.1%	8.7%	68	100%
Rwanda	Kigali	2,467	10,624	2.9%	4.5%	59	71%

Education	Under-nourished	Over-weight	Improved facilities % with access to		DALYs	
primary enrolment 2010 or latest	as % of population 2007	adults as % of population 2008	water source 2010	sanitation 2010	years lost to ill-health, disability or early death per 100,000 people 2004	
93	–	54%	99%	–	19,615	Latvia
90	–	63%	100%	–	18,161	Lebanon
73	14%	41%	78%	26%	41,163	Lesotho
75	32%	23%	73%	18%	70,241	Liberia
–	–	65%	–	97%	14,414	Libya
94	–	57%	–	–	18,401	Lithuania
96	–	57%	100%	100%	12,341	Luxembourg
87	–	53%	100%	88%	16,777	Macedonia
98	25%	11%	46%	15%	35,656	Madagascar
91	27%	21%	83%	51%	58,748	Malawi
94	–	45%	100%	96%	14,616	Malaysia
96	10%	41%	98%	97%	19,952	Maldives
75	12%	21%	64%	22%	62,726	Mali
91	–	62%	100%	100%	11,141	Malta
80	–	80%	94%	75%	24,578	Marshall Islands
76	8%	39%	50%	26%	35,732	Mauritania
94	–	49%	99%	89%	16,801	Mauritius
98	–	69%	96%	85%	14,702	Mexico
–	–	77%	–	–	15,051	Micronesia, Fed. Sts.
88	–	49%	96%	85%	20,892	Moldova
90	27%	47%	82%	51%	20,343	Mongolia
83	–	55%	98%	90%	16,802	Montenegro
90	–	49%	83%	70%	16,684	Morocco
92	38%	23%	47%	18%	48,090	Mozambique
89	18%	35%	93%	32%	30,131	Namibia
–	17%	9%	89%	31%	29,514	Nepal
99	–	48%	100%	100%	11,486	Netherlands
99	–	64%	100%	–	11,612	New Zealand
92	19%	58%	85%	52%	17,453	Nicaragua
57	16%	14%	49%	9%	78,040	Niger
61	6%	29%	58%	31%	56,297	Nigeria
99	–	55%	100%	100%	11,790	Norway
77	–	58%	89%	99%	11,892	Oman
66	25%	24%	92%	48%	26,112	Pakistan
75	21%	–	85%	92%	–	Palestinien Territories
97	15%	61%	–	–	14,694	Panama
–	–	48%	40%	45%	28,634	Papua New Guinea
85	10%	51%	86%	71%	16,826	Paraguay
94	16%	48%	85%	71%	17,672	Peru
92	13%	27%	92%	74%	19,525	Philippines
96	–	56%	–	–	14,911	Poland
99	–	55%	99%	100%	13,615	Portugal
–	–	–	–	–	–	Puerto Rico
93	–	72%	100%	100%	10,301	Qatar
90	–	49%	–	–	17,685	Romania
92	–	58%	97%	70%	27,885	Russia
96	32%	20%	65%	55%	59,702	Rwanda

Indicators of Wellbeing

	Official capital	Land area	Population		Migrants	Life expectancy	Literate adults
		1,000 hectares 2008	1,000s 2010	rate of change 2005–10	(excluding refugees) as % of total 2000	at birth 2009	as % of adult population 2010 or latest
Samoa	Apia	283	183	0.3%	5.0%	70	99%
São Tomé and Principe	São Tomé	96	165	1.6%	3.2%	68	89%
Saudi Arabia	Riyadh	214,969	27,448	2.7%	27.8%	72	86%
Senegal	Dakar	19,253	12,434	2.7%	1.6%	62	50%
Serbia	Belgrade	7,747	9,856	0.0%	5.3%	74	–
Seychelles	Victoria	46	87	0.7%	12.8%	73	92%
Sierra Leone	Freetown	7,162	5,868	2.6%	1.8%	49	41%
Singapore	Singapore	69	5,086	3.5%	40.7%	82	95%
Slovakia	Bratislava	4,810	5,462	0.2%	2.4%	75	–
Slovenia	Ljubljana	2,014	2,030	0.3%	8.1%	79	100%
Solomon Islands	Honiara	2,799	538	2.7%	1.3%	71	–
Somalia	Mogadishu	62,734	9,331	2.2%	0.2%	51	–
South Africa	Pretoria	121,447	50,133	1.0%	3.7%	54	89%
South Sudan	Juba	64,433	10 625	–	–	n/a	27%
Spain	Madrid	49,919	46,077	1.2%	14.1%	82	98%
Sri Lanka	Colombo	6,463	20,860	1.0%	1.7%	71	91%
St. Lucia	Castries	–	174	1.1%	5.9%	74	–
St. Vincent and Grenadines	Kingstown	–	109	0.1%	7.9%	73	–
Sudan	Khartoum	186,148	43,552	2.5%	1.7%	59	70%
Suriname	Paramaribo	15,600	525	1.0%	7.5%	72	95%
Swaziland	Mbabane	1,720	1,186	1.4%	3.4%	49	87%
Sweden	Stockholm	41,033	9,380	0.8%	14.1%	81	–
Switzerland	Bern	4,000	7,664	0.7%	23.2%	82	–
Syria	Damascus	18,378	20,411	2.0%	9.8%	74	84%
Taiwan	Taipei	3,226	23 113	1.3%	–	78	96%
Tajikistan	Dushanbe	13,996	6,879	2.9%	4.0%	68	100%
Tanzania	Dar es Salaam	88,580	44,841	0.7%	1.5%	55	73%
Thailand	Bangkok	51,089	69,122	2.2%	1.7%	70	94%
Togo	Lomé	5,439	6,028	-1.3%	2.7%	59	57%
Tonga	Nuku'alofa	72	104	0.6%	0.8%	71	99%
Trinidad and Tobago	Port-of-Spain	513	1,341	0.4%	2.6%	70	99%
Tunisia	Tunis	15,536	10,481	1.1%	0.3%	75	78%
Turkey	Ankara	76,963	72,752	1.3%	1.9%	75	91%
Turkmenistan	Ashgabat	46,993	5,042	1.2%	4.0%	63	100%
Uganda	Kampala	19,710	33,425	3.2%	1.9%	52	73%
Ukraine	Kyiv	57,938	45,448	-0.6%	11.6%	68	100%
United Arab Emirates	Abu Dhabi	8,360	7,512	12.3%	70.0%	78	90%
United Kingdom	London	24,193	62,036	0.6%	10.4%	80	–
United States	Washington D.C.	916,192	310,384	0.9%	13.5%	79	–
Uruguay	Montevideo	17,502	3,369	0.3%	2.4%	76	98%
Uzbekistan	Tashkent	42,540	27,445	1.1%	4.2%	69	99%
Vanuatu	Port-Vila	1,219	240	2.5%	0.3%	71	82%
Venezuela	Caracas	88,205	28,980	1.7%	3.5%	75	95%
Vietnam	Hanoi	31,007	87,848	1.1%	0.1%	72	93%
Yemen	Sanaá	52,797	24,053	3.1%	2.1%	65	62%
Zambia	Lusaka	74,339	13,089	2.7%	1.8%	48	71%
Zimbabwe	Harare	38,685	12,571	0.0%	2.9%	49	92%

Education	Under-nourished	Over-weight	Improved facilities % with access to		DALYs	
primary enrolment 2010 or latest	as % of population 2007	adults as % of population 2008	water source 2010	sanitation 2010	years lost to ill-health, disability or early death per 100,000 people 2004	
90	–	86%	96%	98%	16,836	Samoa
98	–	37%	89%	26%	33,751	São Tomé and Principe
86	–	71%	–	–	15,453	Saudi Arabia
73	19%	28%	72%	52%	39,066	Senegal
94	–	56%	99%	92%	16,802	Serbia
94	8%	58%	–	–	16,297	Seychelles
–	35%	28%	55%	13%	82,444	Sierra Leone
–	–	28%	100%	100%	10,542	Singapore
–	–	58%	100%	100%	15,340	Slovakia
97	–	61%	99%	100%	14,002	Slovenia
81	11%	68%	–	–	19,257	Solomon Islands
–	–	22%	29%	23%	68,800	Somalia
85	–	68%	91%	79%	44,148	South Africa
–	–	–	55%	–	–	South Sudan
100	–	58%	100%	100%	11,352	Spain
95	20%	22%	91%	92%	24,521	Sri Lanka
91	8%	54%	96%	65%	15,586	St. Lucia
95	–	58%	–	–	18,743	St. Vincent and Grenadines
39	22%	25%	58%	26%	38,779	Sudan
90	15%	58%	92%	83%	21,237	Suriname
83	19%	50%	71%	57%	50,860	Swaziland
96	–	50%	100%	100%	11,478	Sweden
94	–	44%	100%	100%	10,745	Switzerland
95	–	66%	90%	95%	13,660	Syria
–	–	–	–	–	–	Taiwan
97	26%	34%	64%	94%	25,000	Tajikistan
96	34%	24%	53%	10%	48,494	Tanzania
90	16%	31%	96%	96%	20,525	Thailand
93	30%	21%	61%	13%	41,837	Togo
99	–	88%	100%	96%	–	Tonga
93	11%	65%	94%	92%	19,721	Trinidad and Tobago
98	–	56%	–	–	14,653	Tunisia
95	–	64%	100%	90%	15,246	Turkey
–	7%	44%	–	98%	26,320	Turkmenistan
92	22%	21%	72%	34%	50,471	Uganda
89	–	52%	98%	94%	23,689	Ukraine
90	–	72%	100%	98%	10,036	United Arab Emirates
100	–	62%	100%	100%	12,871	United Kingdom
91	–	69%	99%	100%	13,937	United States
99	–	57%	100%	100%	16,245	Uruguay
87	11%	48%	87%	100%	19,669	Uzbekistan
97	–	65%	90%	57%	17,783	Vanuatu
92	7%	68%	–	–	16,061	Venezuela
94	11%	10%	95%	76%	15,327	Vietnam
73	30%	46%	55%	53%	35,531	Yemen
91	44%	18%	61%	48%	62,500	Zambia
–	30%	29%	80%	40%	67,959	Zimbabwe

Economy & Environment

	GNI PPP$		Human Development Index	Gini Index	Gender Inequality Index	Government gross debt	Corruption Perceptions Index
	total millions 2010 or latest	per capita 2010 or latest	2011	2009 or latest	score 2011	as % of GDP 2010	score 2010
Afghanistan	36,503	860	0.398	29.40	0.71	–	1.5
Albania	27,294	8,740	0.739	34.51	0.27	60%	3.1
Algeria	287,203	8,120	0.698	–	0.41	–	2.9
Angola	104,266	5,400	0.486	–	–	31%	2.0
Antigua and Barbuda	1,795	15,350	0.764	–	–	93%	–
Argentina	629,310	15,250	0.797	45.84	0.37	48%	3.0
Armenia	17,503	5,450	0.716	30.86	0.34	39%	2.6
Australia	823,018	38,380	0.929	–	0.14	18%	8.8
Austria	333,875	39,390	0.885	–	0.13	70%	7.8
Azerbaijan	83,936	9,050	0.700	33.71	0.31	11%	2.4
Bahamas	10,502	24,580	0.771	–	0.33	47%	7.3
Bahrain	–	24,710	0.806	–	0.29	32%	5.1
Bangladesh	269,657	1,800	0.500	31.02	0.55	–	2.7
Barbados	5,183	18,830	0.793	–	0.36	114%	7.8
Belarus	128,961	14,250	0.756	27.22	–	18%	2.4
Belgium	417,252	37,800	0.886	–	0.11	97%	7.5
Belize	2,139	5,970	0.699	–	0.49	82%	–
Benin	14,048	1,580	0.427	–	0.63	31%	3.0
Bhutan	3,622	4,950	0.522	–	0.49	–	5.7
Bolivia	46,041	4,610	0.663	57.26	0.48	37%	2.8
Bosnia and Herzegovina	33,520	8,970	0.733	36.21	–	37%	3.2
Botswana	27,492	13,710	0.633	–	0.51	13%	6.1
Brazil	2,144,886	10,920	0.718	53.90	0.45	66%	3.8
Brunei	19,661	49,730	0.838	–	–	0%	5.2
Bulgaria	101,238	13,250	0.771	45.32	0.25	18%	3.3
Burkina Faso	20,658	1,250	0.331	–	0.60	28%	3.0
Burma	93,539	–	0.483	–	0.49	43%	1.5
Burundi	3,379	400	0.316	33.27	0.48	48%	1.9
Cambodia	29,424	2,040	0.523	44.37	0.50	30%	2.1
Cameroon	44,507	2,230	0.482	38.91	0.64	13%	2.5
Canada	1,309,483	37,280	0.908	–	0.14	84%	8.7
Cape Verde	1,841	3,790	0.568	–	–	80%	5.5
Central African Republic	3,465	780	0.343	56.30	0.67	33%	2.2
Chad	13,653	1,210	0.328	–	0.74	36%	2.0
Chile	250,480	13,900	0.805	52.33	0.37	9%	7.2
China	10,221,684	7,570	0.687	41.53	0.21	18%	3.6
Colombia	419,515	9,000	0.710	58.49	0.48	37%	3.4
Comoros	802	1,080	0.433	–	–	52%	2.4
Congo	12,899	3,050	0.533	47.32	0.63	17%	2.2
Congo, Dem. Rep.	21,354	320	0.286	44.43	0.71	30%	2.0
Costa Rica	52,491	10,840	0.744	50.31	0.36	39%	4.8
Côte d'Ivoire	35,756	1,800	0.400	41.50	0.66	67%	2.2
Croatia	82,527	18,730	0.796	33.65	0.17	40%	4.0
Cuba	–	–	0.776	–	0.34	62%	4.2
Cyprus	24,831	30,180	0.840	–	0.14	–	6.3
Czech Republic	241,005	23,640	0.865	–	0.14	40%	4.4
Denmark	227,982	40,290	0.895	–	0.06	44%	9.4

Shadow economy	Military expenditure	Energy Use		CO$_2$ emissions	Water withdrawals		
as % of formal economy *1999–2007*	as % of GDP *2009*	million tonnes oil equiv. *2009*	kg oil equiv. per capita *2009*	tonnes per capita *2008*	cubic metres per capita *2010 or latest*	as % of total renewable resources *2008 or latest*	
–	1.8%	–	–	0	938	36%	Afghanistan
34%	2.0%	2	538	1.3	595	4%	Albania
33%	3.8%	40	1,138	3.2	196	53%	Algeria
47%	4.2%	12	641	1.4	43	0%	Angola
–	0.7%	–	–	5.1	78	3%	Antigua and Barbuda
25%	0.8%	74	1,853	4.8	865	4%	Argentina
44%	4.7%	3	843	1.8	920	36%	Armenia
14%	2.0%	131	5,971	18.6	1,152	5%	Australia
10%	0.7%	32	3,784	8.1	452	5%	Austria
58%	3.5%	12	1,338	5.4	1,384	35%	Azerbaijan
27%	1.4%	–	–	6.5	–	–	Bahamas
18%	3.6%	9	8,096	21.4	386	206%	Bahrain
35%	1.1%	30	201	0.3	241	3%	Bangladesh
–	1.0%	–	–	5.0	226	76%	Barbados
46%	1.8%	27	2,815	6.5	435	7%	Belarus
22%	1.3%	57	5,300	9.8	590	34%	Belgium
43%	1.0%	–	–	1.3	570	1%	Belize
50%	1.5%	3	404	0.5	19	0%	Benin
29%	–	–	–	1.0	466	0%	Bhutan
66%	1.7%	6	638	1.3	234	0%	Bolivia
34%	1.4%	6	1,580	8.3	90	1%	Bosnia and Herzegovina
33%	3.2%	2	1,034	2.5	107	2%	Botswana
39%	1.6%	240	1,243	2.1	306	1%	Brazil
31%	3.2%	3	7,971	27.5	302	1%	Brunei
35%	1.9%	17	2,305	6.6	817	29%	Bulgaria
41%	1.3%	–	–	0.1	76	8%	Burkina Faso
–	–	15	316	0.3	729	3%	Burma
40%	3.2%	–	–	0	43	2%	Burundi
49%	2.5%	5	371	0.3	160	0%	Cambodia
32%	1.6%	7	361	0.3	58	0%	Cameroon
16%	1.5%	254	7,534	16.3	1,470	2%	Canada
35%	0.6%	–	–	0.6	49	7%	Cape Verde
45%	1.8%	–	–	0.1	17	0%	Central African Republic
44%	6.4%	–	–	0	42	1%	Chad
19%	3.1%	29	1,698	4.4	718	1%	Chile
13%	1.5%	2,257	1,695	5.3	410	20%	China
37%	4.1%	32	697	1.5	308	1%	Colombia
39%	–	–	–	0.2	17	1%	Comoros
46%	1.4%	1	356	0.5	14	0%	Congo
47%	1.1%	23	357	0	12	0%	Congo, Dem. Rep.
26%	0.7%	5	1,067	1.8	656	2%	Costa Rica
45%	1.4%	10	535	0.4	82	2%	Côte d'Ivoire
32%	1.6%	9	1,965	5.3	143	1%	Croatia
–	3.1%	12	1,022	2.8	676	20%	Cuba
28%	2.0%	3	2,298	7.9	167	18%	Cyprus
18%	1.6%	42	4,004	11.2	165	13%	Czech Republic
18%	1.4%	19	3,369	8.4	119	11%	Denmark

131

Economy & Environment

	GNI PPP$		Human Development Index	Gini Index	Gender Inequality Index	Government gross debt	Corruption Perceptions Index
	total millions 2010 or latest	per capita 2010 or latest	2011	2009 or latest	score 2011	as % of GDP 2010	score 2010
Djibouti	2,149	2,440	0.430	–	–	58%	3.0
Dominica	812	9,370	0.724	–	–	86%	5.2
Dominican Republic	89,600	8,960	0.689	48.44	0.48	29%	2.6
East Timor	4,046	3,570	0.495	31.93	–	–	2.4
Ecuador	114,008	8,830	0.720	48.99	0.47	18%	2.7
Egypt	491,329	6,160	0.644	32.14	–	74%	2.9
El Salvador	40,552	6,390	0.674	46.57	0.49	51%	3.4
Equatorial Guinea	16,635	23,570	0.537	–	–	8%	1.9
Eritrea	2,841	540	0.349	–	–	145%	2.5
Estonia	26,541	19,510	0.835	–	0.19	7%	6.4
Ethiopia	86,087	1,030	0.363	29.76	–	37%	2.7
Fiji	3,880	4,450	0.688	–	–	56%	–
Finland	198,866	37,180	0.882	–	0.07	48%	9.4
France	2,254,888	34,440	0.884	–	0.11	84%	7.0
Gabon	19,655	13,150	0.674	41.45	0.51	18%	3.0
Gambia	2,246	1,290	0.420	–	0.61	57%	3.5
Georgia	22,235	4,960	0.733	41.34	0.42	39%	4.1
Germany	3,115,390	38,140	0.905	–	0.09	80%	8.0
Ghana	39,439	1,600	0.541	42.76	0.60	41%	3.9
Greece	312,704	27,380	0.861	–	0.16	142%	3.4
Grenada	1,033	7,550	0.748	–	–	115%	–
Guatemala	66,844	4,600	0.574	53.69	0.54	18%	2.7
Guinea	10,211	1,020	0.344	39.35	–	89%	2.1
Guinea-Bissau	1,795	1,180	0.353	–	–	48%	2.2
Guyana	2,606	3,560	0.633	–	0.51	61%	2.5
Haiti	11,619	1,110	0.454	–	0.60	16%	1.8
Honduras	28,648	3,740	0.625	57.70	0.51	26%	2.6
Hungary	195,457	19,270	0.816	31.18	0.24	80%	4.6
Iceland	8,991	28,720	0.898	–	0.10	97%	8.3
India	4,159,721	3,560	0.547	36.80	0.62	69%	3.1
Indonesia	1,008,241	4,170	0.617	36.76	0.50	27%	3.0
Iran	839,981	11,380	0.707	38.28	0.48	12%	2.7
Iraq	108,103	3,350	0.573	30.86	0.58	112%	1.8
Ireland	150,094	32,520	0.908	–	0.20	96%	7.5
Israel	210,846	27,630	0.888	–	0.14	78%	5.8
Italy	1,923,684	31,130	0.874	–	0.12	119%	3.9
Jamaica	19,747	7,450	0.727	–	0.45	140%	3.3
Japan	4,411,692	34,780	0.901	–	0.12	220%	8.0
Jordan	35,077	5,810	0.698	37.72	0.46	61%	4.5
Kazakhstan	175,727	10,610	0.745	30.88	0.33	11%	2.7
Kenya	66,568	1,630	0.509	47.68	0.63	51%	2.2
Kiribati	352	3,510	0.624	–	–	–	3.1
Korea, North	–	–	..	–	–	31%	1.0
Korea, South	1,422,703	29,010	0.897	–	0.11	–	5.4
Kuwait	–	58,350	0.760	–	0.23	11%	4.6
Kyrgyzstan	11,291	2,180	0.615	33.43	0.37	63%	2.1
Laos	15,129	2,390	0.524	36.74	0.51	61%	2.2

Shadow economy	Military expenditure	Energy Use		CO₂ emissions	Water withdrawals		
as % of formal economy 1999–2007	as % of GDP 2009	million tonnes oil equiv. 2009	kg oil equiv. per capita 2009	tonnes per capita 2008	cubic metres per capita 2010 or latest	as % of total renewable resources 2008 or latest	
–	3.5%	–	–	0.6	25	6%	Djibouti
–	–	–	–	1.9	244	–	Dominica
32%	0.6%	8	826	2.2	393	17%	Dominican Republic
–	–	–	–	0.2	1,105	14%	East Timor
32%	3.5%	11	796	1.9	1,194	4%	Ecuador
35%	2.2%	72	903	2.7	973	95%	Egypt
45%	0.6%	5	828	1.0	230	5%	El Salvador
31%	0.1%	–	–	7.3	31	0%	Equatorial Guinea
40%	4.2%	1	142	0.1	121	9%	Eritrea
31%	1.8%	5	3,543	13.6	1,337	14%	Estonia
39%	1.4%	33	402	0.1	81	5%	Ethiopia
32%	1.9%	–	–	1.5	100	0%	Fiji
18%	1.6%	33	6,213	10.6	309	1%	Finland
15%	2.1%	256	3,970	5.9	512	15%	France
48%	1.2%	2	1,214	1.7	101	0%	Gabon
44%	0.7%	–	–	0.3	52	1%	Gambia
66%	5.6%	3	723	1.2	411	3%	Georgia
16%	1.4%	319	3,889	9.6	391	21%	Germany
41%	0.7%	9	388	0.4	49	2%	Ghana
28%	3.0%	29	2,609	8.7	841	13%	Greece
–	–	–	–	2.4	97	–	Grenada
51%	0.4%	10	701	0.9	249	3%	Guatemala
39%	1.6%	–	–	0.1	188	1%	Guinea
41%	1.6%	–	–	0.2	136	1%	Guinea-Bissau
34%	1.0%	–	–	2.0	2,222	1%	Guyana
56%	0.2%	3	263	0.3	134	9%	Haiti
48%	0.8%	4	592	1.2	184	1%	Honduras
24%	1.1%	25	2,480	5.4	557	5%	Hungary
16%	–	5	16,405	7.0	539	0%	Iceland
22%	3.1%	676	560	1.5	621	34%	India
19%	0.9%	202	851	1.7	517	6%	Indonesia
18%	2.6%	216	2,951	7.4	1,306	68%	Iran
–	6.3%	32	1,035	3.4	2,616	87%	Iraq
16%	0.6%	14	3,216	9.9	227	2%	Ireland
22%	6.9%	22	2,878	5.2	282	102%	Israel
27%	1.4%	165	2,735	7.4	790	24%	Italy
35%	0.5%	3	1,208	4.5	223	6%	Jamaica
11%	1.0%	472	3,700	9.5	714	21%	Japan
19%	5.5%	7	1,260	3.7	166	90%	Jordan
41%	1.3%	66	4,091	15.1	2,218	29%	Kazakhstan
33%	1.8%	19	474	0.3	73	9%	Kenya
–	–	–	–	0.3	–	–	Kiribati
–	–	19	795	3.2	361	11%	Korea, North
27%	2.7%	229	4,701	10.4	549	37%	Korea, South
19%	4.3%	30	11,402	30.1	441	2075%	Kuwait
40%	0.8%	3	559	1.2	2,015	44%	Kyrgyzstan
30%	0.3%	–	–	0.3	718	1%	Laos

133

Economy & Environment

	GNI PPP$		Human Development Index	Gini Index	Gender Inequality Index	Government gross debt	Corruption Perceptions Index
	total millions 2010 or latest	per capita 2010 or latest	2011	2009 or latest	score 2011	as % of GDP 2010	score 2010
Latvia	36,538	16,350	0.805	–	0.22	40%	4.2
Lebanon	59,540	14,260	0.739	–	0.44	137%	2.5
Lesotho	4,275	1,840	0.450	–	0.53	38%	3.5
Liberia	1,365	340	0.329	38.16	0.67	119%	3.2
Libya	105,745	16,740	0.760	–	0.31	0%	2.0
Lithuania	58,634	17,870	0.810	37.57	0.19	39%	4.8
Luxembourg	31,050	63,950	0.867	–	0.17	17%	8.5
Macedonia	22,798	10,830	0.728	44.20	0.15	18%	3.9
Madagascar	19,851	950	0.480	47.24	–	35%	3.0
Malawi	12,816	850	0.400	–	0.59	43%	3.0
Malaysia	403,891	14,110	0.761	46.21	0.29	54%	4.3
Maldives	2,563	5,450	0.661	–	0.32	65%	2.5
Mali	15,758	1,020	0.359	38.99	0.71	28%	2.8
Malta	10,325	23,160	0.832	–	0.27	67%	5.6
Marshall Islands	–	–	..	–	–	–	–
Mauritania	8,338	1,950	0.453	–	0.61	86%	2.4
Mauritius	17,914	13,670	0.728	–	0.35	51%	5.1
Mexico	1,632,957	14,360	0.770	51.74	0.45	43%	3.0
Micronesia, Fed. Sts.	388	3,420	0.636	–	–	–	–
Moldova	11,976	3,340	0.649	38.03	0.30	30%	2.9
Mongolia	10,118	3,630	0.653	33.03	0.41	–	2.7
Montenegro	8,073	12,590	0.771	29.99	–	44%	4.0
Morocco	149,302	4,620	0.582	40.88	0.51	50%	3.4
Mozambique	21,654	920	0.322	45.66	0.60	32%	2.7
Namibia	14,668	6,380	0.625	–	0.47	18%	4.4
Nepal	36,196	1,200	0.458	–	0.56	36%	2.2
Netherlands	694,664	42,610	0.910	–	0.05	64%	8.9
New Zealand	121,277	28,050	0.908	–	0.20	32%	9.5
Nicaragua	16,148	2,630	0.589	52.33	0.51	82%	2.5
Niger	11,178	720	0.295	34.04	0.72	18%	2.5
Nigeria	354,946	2,160	0.459	–	–	16%	2.4
Norway	286,347	57,100	0.943	–	0.08	54%	9.0
Oman	68,305	24,960	0.705	–	0.31	6%	4.8
Pakistan	484,362	2,780	0.504	32.74	0.57	57%	2.5
Palestinien Territories	–	2,710	0.641	–	–	–	–
Panama	44,896	12,910	0.768	52.34	0.49	41%	3.3
Papua New Guinea	16,564	2,400	0.466	–	0.67	–	2.2
Paraguay	32,767	5,440	0.665	51.95	0.48	15%	2.2
Peru	259,567	9,070	0.725	47.96	0.42	18%	3.4
Philippines	370,748	3,950	0.644	44.04	0.43	47%	2.6
Poland	731,509	19,010	0.813	34.21	0.16	56%	5.5
Portugal	261,578	24,710	0.809	–	0.14	83%	6.1
Puerto Rico	–	–	–	–	–	–	5.6
Qatar	–	–	0.831	41.10	0.55	18%	7.2
Romania	306,370	14,060	0.781	31.15	0.33	35%	3.6
Russia	2,726,810	19,190	0.755	42.27	0.34	10%	2.4
Rwanda	12,259	1,150	0.429	53.08	0.45	18%	5.0

Shadow economy as % of formal economy 1999–2007	Military expenditure as % of GDP 2009	Energy Use		CO$_2$ emissions tonnes per capita 2008	Water withdrawals		
		million tonnes oil equiv. 2009	kg oil equiv. per capita 2009		cubic metres per capita 2010 or latest	as % of total renewable resources 2008 or latest	
29%	1.2%	4	1,871	3.3	176	1%	Latvia
33%	4.1%	7	1,580	4.1	317	19%	Lebanon
31%	3.3%	–	–	–	25	2%	Lesotho
44%	0.9%	–	–	0.2	60	0%	Liberia
34%	2.8%	20	3,258	9.5	796	711%	Libya
32%	1.1%	8	2,512	4.5	704	10%	Lithuania
10%	0.5%	4	7,934	21.5	136	2%	Luxembourg
38%	1.7%	3	1,352	5.8	502	16%	Macedonia
41%	1.1%	–	–	0.1	899	4%	Madagascar
42%	1.1%	–	–	0.1	82	6%	Malawi
31%	2.0%	67	2,391	7.6	488	2%	Malaysia
30%	4.0%	–	–	3.0	19	16%	Maldives
41%	2.0%	–	–	0	545	7%	Mali
27%	0.7%	1	1,931	6.2	134	71%	Malta
–	–	–	–	1.9	–	–	Marshall Islands
–	3.8%	–	–	0.6	572	14%	Mauritania
23%	0.2%	–	–	3.1	568	26%	Mauritius
30%	0.5%	175	1,559	4.3	704	17%	Mexico
–	–	–	–	0.6	–	–	Micronesia, Fed. Sts.
–	0.4%	2	687	1.3	483	16%	Moldova
18%	0.9%	3	1,194	4.1	195	1%	Mongolia
–	1.4%	–	–	3.1	255	–	Montenegro
35%	3.3%	15	477	1.5	428	43%	Morocco
–	0.9%	10	427	0.1	39	0%	Mozambique
30%	3.3%	2	764	1.8	152	2%	Namibia
37%	1.4%	10	338	0.1	345	5%	Nepal
13%	1.5%	78	4,729	10.6	639	12%	Netherlands
12%	1.2%	17	4,032	7.8	1,200	1%	New Zealand
45%	0.7%	3	540	0.8	247	1%	Nicaragua
–	1.0%	–	–	0.1	202	7%	Niger
–	0.9%	108	701	0.6	79	4%	Nigeria
19%	1.6%	28	5,849	10.5	622	1%	Norway
18%	8.7%	15	5,554	17.3	516	84%	Oman
36%	2.4%	86	502	1.0	1,057	74%	Pakistan
–	–	–	–	0.5	112	50%	Palestinien Territories
–	1.1%	3	896	2.0	147	0%	Panama
37%	0.5%	–	–	0.3	61	0%	Papua New Guinea
39%	0.9%	5	749	0.7	88	0%	Paraguay
58%	1.2%	16	550	1.4	728	1%	Peru
42%	0.9%	39	424	0.9	875	17%	Philippines
27%	1.7%	94	2,464	8.3	313	19%	Poland
23%	1.6%	24	2,266	5.3	812	12%	Portugal
–	–	–	–	–	264	14%	Puerto Rico
19%	2.5%	24	14,911	49.1	377	381%	Qatar
33%	1.4%	34	1,602	4.4	320	3%	Romania
44%	3.1%	647	4,561	12.0	455	1%	Russia
–	2.2%	–	–	0.1	17	2%	Rwanda

135

Economy & Environment

	GNI PPP$		Human Development Index	Gini Index	Gender Inequality Index	Government gross debt	Corruption Perceptions Index
	total millions 2010 or latest	per capita 2010 or latest	2011	2009 or latest	score 2011	as % of GDP 2010	score 2010
Samoa	782	4,200	0.688	–	–	–	3.9
São Tomé and Principe	318	1,910	0.509	–	–	78%	3.0
Saudi Arabia	609,782	22,540	0.770	–	0.65	11%	4.4
Senegal	23,810	1,910	0.459	39.19	0.57	38%	2.9
Serbia	80,826	11,230	0.766	28.16	–	44%	3.3
Seychelles	1,835	21,050	0.773	65.77	–	83%	4.8
Sierra Leone	4,851	820	0.336	–	0.66	57%	2.5
Singapore	283,254	55,380	0.866	–	0.09	97%	9.2
Slovakia	124,807	23,120	0.834	–	0.19	42%	4.0
Slovenia	54,356	27,140	0.884	–	0.18	37%	5.9
Solomon Islands	1,192	2,200	0.510	–	–	26%	2.7
Somalia	–	–	..	–	–	–	1.0
South Africa	517,673	10,280	0.619	67.40	0.49	36%	4.1
South Sudan	–	–	–	–	–	–	–
Spain	1,465,197	31,640	0.878	–	0.12	60%	6.2
Sri Lanka	104,568	4,980	0.691	40.26	0.42	–	3.3
St. Lucia	1,830	8,520	0.723	–	–	77%	7.0
St. Vincent and Grenadines	1,184	8,260	0.717	–	–	82%	5.8
Sudan	88,573	2,020	0.408	–	0.61	68%	1.6
Suriname	3,991	7,610	0.680	–	–	18%	3.0
Swaziland	5,910	4,950	0.522	–	0.55	18%	3.1
Sweden	372,623	39,660	0.904	–	0.05	40%	9.3
Switzerland	391,004	48,960	0.903	–	0.07	55%	8.8
Syria	104,626	5,150	0.632	–	0.47	27%	2.6
Taiwan	758,600	–	–	32.60	–	40%	6.1
Tajikistan	14,692	2,120	0.607	–	0.35	37%	2.3
Tanzania	62,999	1,420	0.466	37.58	0.59	44%	3.0
Thailand	565,806	8,120	0.682	–	0.38	44%	3.4
Togo	5,391	890	0.435	34.41	0.60	28%	2.4
Tonga	477	4,640	0.704	–	–	–	3.1
Trinidad and Tobago	32,255	24,040	0.760	–	0.33	40%	3.2
Tunisia	95,577	8,130	0.698	–	0.29	40%	3.8
Turkey	1,129,893	15,180	0.699	43.23	0.44	42%	4.2
Turkmenistan	37,765	7,350	0.686	–	–	7%	1.6
Uganda	41,804	1,240	0.446	44.30	0.58	18%	2.4
Ukraine	303,807	6,560	0.729	27.51	0.34	40%	2.3
United Arab Emirates	350,971	49,050	0.846	–	0.23	18%	6.8
United Kingdom	2,230,578	36,590	0.863	–	0.21	77%	7.8
United States	14,635,600	47,120	0.910	–	0.30	92%	7.1
Uruguay	45,719	13,890	0.783	42.42	0.35	55%	7.0
Uzbekistan	87,747	3,090	0.641	–	–	10%	1.6
Vanuatu	1,035	4,450	0.617	–	–	–	3.5
Venezuela	350,192	11,950	0.735	43.50	0.45	39%	1.9
Vietnam	267,048	2,960	0.593	37.57	0.31	53%	2.9
Yemen	60,117	2,350	0.462	37.69	0.77	41%	2.1
Zambia	17,831	1,370	0.430	–	0.63	27%	3.2
Zimbabwe	–	–	0.376	–	0.58	56%	2.2

136

Shadow economy as % of formal economy 1999–2007	Military expenditure as % of GDP 2009	Energy Use		CO$_2$ emissions tonnes per capita 2008	Water withdrawals		
		million tonnes oil equiv. 2009	kg oil equiv. per capita 2009		cubic metres per capita 2010 or latest	as % of total renewable resources 2008 or latest	
–	–	–	–	0.9	–	–	Samoa
–	–	–	–	0.8	53	0%	São Tomé and Principe
18%	11.0%	158	5,888	16.6	928	936%	Saudi Arabia
44%	1.7%	3	243	0.4	222	6%	Senegal
–	2.2%	14	1,974	6.8	418	3%	Serbia
–	0.8%	–	–	7.8	161	–	Seychelles
46%	0.6%	–	–	0.2	110	0%	Sierra Leone
13%	4.3%	18	3,704	6.7	82	32%	Singapore
18%	1.5%	17	3,086	6.9	127	1%	Slovakia
26%	1.6%	7	3,417	8.5	464	3%	Slovenia
34%	–	–	–	0.4	–	–	Solomon Islands
–	–	–	–	0.1	378	22%	Somalia
27%	1.5%	144	2,921	8.9	272	25%	South Africa
–	–	–	–	–	–	58%	South Sudan
23%	1.2%	127	2,756	7.2	705	29%	Spain
44%	3.5%	9	449	0.6	639	25%	Sri Lanka
–	–	–	–	2.3	98	–	St. Lucia
–	–	–	–	1.8	93	–	St. Vincent and Grenadines
–	1.3%	16	372	0.3	1,037	58%	Sudan
38%	1.1%	–	–	4.7	1,396	1%	Suriname
–	–	–	–	1.1	962	23%	Swaziland
19%	1.3%	45	4,883	5.3	286	2%	Sweden
9%	0.8%	27	3,480	5.3	360	5%	Switzerland
19%	4.2%	23	1,123	3.6	867	86%	Syria
25%	2.5%	–	–	–	–	–	Taiwan
42%	1.0%	2	342	0.5	1,903	75%	Tajikistan
56%	1.2%	20	451	0.2	145	5%	Tanzania
51%	1.8%	103	1,504	4.2	845	13%	Thailand
–	1.6%	3	445	0.2	33	1%	Togo
–	–	–	–	1.7	–	–	Tonga
33%	0.5%	20	15,158	37.4	178	6%	Trinidad and Tobago
37%	1.2%	9	881	2.4	296	61%	Tunisia
31%	1.8%	98	1,359	4.0	573	18%	Turkey
–	–	20	3,933	9.7	5,415	101%	Turkmenistan
42%	2.0%	–	–	0.1	12	0%	Uganda
50%	1.2%	115	2,507	7.0	801	28%	Ukraine
26%	3.6%	60	8,588	25.0	740	1867%	United Arab Emirates
13%	2.7%	197	3,183	8.5	213	9%	United Kingdom
9%	4.7%	2,163	7,051	18.0	1,583	16%	United States
51%	1.1%	4	1,224	2.5	1,101	3%	Uruguay
–	–	49	1,758	4.6	2,358	118%	Uzbekistan
–	–	–	–	0.4	–	–	Vanuatu
34%	1.0%	67	2,357	6.1	359	1%	Venezuela
15%	2.2%	64	745	1.5	965	9%	Vietnam
27%	3.5%	8	324	1.0	162	169%	Yemen
47%	1.7%	8	617	0.2	163	2%	Zambia
62%	–	10	763	0.7	334	21%	Zimbabwe

137

Notes & Sources

For sources available on the internet, in most cases only the root address has been given. To view the source, it is recommended that the reader types the title of the page or document into a search engine.

Part One: Who We Are

Evans NJ. Indirect passage from Europe: Transmigration via the UK, 1836–1914. *Journal for Maritime Research* 3(1) (2001): 70–84.

Seabright P. *The Company of Strangers*. Princeton, NJ: Princeton University Press, 2006, p. 205.

20 The States of the World
Sovereignty won; State formation
Turner B (editor). *The Statesman's Yearbook 2008: The politics, cultures and economies of the world*. Hampshire: Palgrave Macmillan, 2008.
The World Factbook. www.cia.gov [Accessed 13 April 2012].

22 Population
UNFPA. *State of World Population 2011. People and possibilities in a world of 7 billion*. www.unfpa.org
United Nations Department of Economic and Social Affairs: Population Division, Population Estimates and Projections Section, and World Fertility Policies 2011. esa.un.org
The World Bank. World Development Indicators online. data.worldbank.org
The World Factbook. www.cia.gov
People in the world
UN Population Division. World Population Prospects. The 2010 Revision. esa.un.org
Changing population
esa.un.org

24 Life Expectancy
UNAIDS www.unaids.org
Life expectancy; Gender difference
WHO. *World Health Statistics 2011*. Part II. Global health indicator tables and footnotes. www.who.int
The World Factbook. www.cia.gov
Growing older
Riley J. Estimates of regional and global life expectancy, 1800–2001. *Population and Development Review* 31(3) (2005); 537-43. Table 1. www.jstor.org
WHO 2011. op.cit.

26 Ethnicity & Diversity
Ethnic, national, and racial minorities; The language of government
The World Factbook. www.cia.gov
BBC News country profiles. news.bbc.co.uk
Ethnologue: Languages of the World. www.ethnologue.com
Minority Rights Group. *World Directory of Minorities and Indigenous Peoples*. www.minorityrights.org
Federal Research Division, US Library of Congress. Library of Congress Country Studies. lcweb2.loc.gov
Migrants
UN Population Division Dept. of Economic and Social Affairs. International Migration 2009. www.un.org/esa

28 Religious Beliefs
O'Brien J, Palmer M. *The Atlas of Religion*. London: Earthscan, 2007.
The World Factbook. www.cia.gov
Mapping the global Muslim population. The Pew Research Center / Pew Forum on Religious and Public Life, Washington, DC, Oct 2009. www.pewforum.org
A report on the size and distribution of the world's Christian population. Dec 2011. www.pewforum.org

30 Literacy & Education
Provost, C. Global teacher shortage threatens progress on education. 7 Oct 2011. www.guardian.co.uk
Adult illiteracy; Enrolment in education
The World Bank. World Development Indicators online. data.worldbank.org
The World Factbook. www.cia.gov
20% of adults...
UNESCO Institute for Statistics. Adult and youth literacy: Global trends in gender parity. UIS Factsheet, Sept 2010, no.3. www.uis.unesco.org

32 Urbanization
UN Habitat. *State of the World's Cities 2010/2011*. www.unhabitat.org
Pavgi K. The 7 fastest-growing cities in the world. 26 Oct 2011. www.foreignpolicy.com
Urban population; City scale
The World Bank. World Development Indicators online. data.worldbank.org
Ten largest cities; There were 1.2 billion...
UN Dept. of Economic and Social Affairs: Population Division, World Urbanization Prospects, 2009 Revision. File 11a. esa.un.org

34 Diversity of Cities
Cities around the world
The largest cities in the world by land area, population and density. Largest cities and their mayors in 2011. www.citymayors.com
10 biggest metro areas. www.dimensionsguide.com
Individual city entries on en.wikipedia.org
McFarlane, C. Sanitation in Mumbai's informal settlements: Governance, infrastructure and cost recovery, 2008. www.irmgard-coninx-stiftung.de
Iraq smog 'kills 3,600 in month'. BBC News, 9 Jan 2007. news.bbc.co.uk
Gatored Community. 12 July 2009. www.snopes.com
Emergy D. Alligators in the sewers. urbanlegends.about.com
Comparative wealth of city dwellers
The richest cities in the world. 22 Aug 2009. www.citymayors.com

Part Two: Wealth & Poverty

38 Income
Gross National Income; Growth spurt; Economic output increased...
The World Bank. World Development Indicators online. data.worldbank.org
The World Factbook. www.cia.gov
Who crashed in the 2008 crash?
Gallup. Chinese struggling less than Americans to afford basics. www.gallup.com

40 Inequality
Distribution of wealth; World poverty; 16% of global economic...
The World Bank. World Development Indicators online. data.worldbank.org
The hands of a few
The world's billionaires 2008, 2009, 2011. www.forbes.com

42 Quality of Life
Relative human development
UNDP. *Human Development Report 2011*. Table 1. hdr.undp.org
The happiness league; Daily experience of life
High wellbeing eludes the masses in most countries worldwide. 19 April 2011. www.gallup.com.
The alternative view
Colwell J. North Korean 'Global Happiness Index' ranks China no. 1, USA dead last. 31 May 2011. www.shanghaiist.com
North Korea: One of the happiest places on Earth? 1 June 2011. www.newsfeed.time.com
Quality carbon
The World Bank. World Development Indicators online. data.worldbank.org

44 Transnationals
UN Population Division. World Population Prospects. The 2010 Revision. esa.un.org
Corporate wealth
The World Bank. World Development Indicators online. data.worldbank.org
The World Factbook. www.cia.gov
Global 500 money.cnn.com
Business Pundit: Scary (but true) facts about Walmart. www.businesspundit.com
McDonalds. www.aboutmcdonalds.com
Kraft. en.wikipedia.org
Nestle. en.wikipedia.org
Wheel of Fortune; Profitability
Global 500. money.cnn.com
The World Bank op.cit.

46 Banks
Bank wealth; Weighed in the balance...
The World Bank. World Development Indicators online. data.worldbank.org
Fortune Global 500 2011. money.cnn.com

Comparative wealth; World annual output...
World's 50 biggest banks 2011. 7 Sept 2011. www.gfmag.com
The World Bank. World Development Indicators online. data.worldbank.org
Cap in hand; Peaks and troughs of the banking crisis
Iceland ex-PM Geir Haarde found guilty of banking crash failure. 23 April
  2012. www.worldfinancialpost.com
Bank bail-outs cost taxpayers £4,4/3bn. 28 Oct2008. www.telegraph.co.uk
The true cost of the bank bailout. Bloomberg analysts, quoted by PBS, 9
  March 2010. www.pbs.org
A national sex strike! 27 March 2012. www.dailymail.co.uk
From excessive levels...
Duncan H. Something went very wrong with UK banking and we need to
  put it right. 30 June 2012. www.dailymail.co.uk

48 Corruption
Level of corruption
Transparency International. Corruption Perceptions Index 2011.
  cpi.transparency.org
The shadow economy
Schneider F, Buehn A, Montenegro CE. Shadow economies all over the
  world. The World Bank, 2010. Table 3.6.6. www-wds.worldbank.org
Estimate of assets...
Revealed: global super-rich has at least $21tn hidden in secret tax havens.
  22 July 2012. www.taxjustice.net
Stewart H. £13tn hoard hidden from taxman by global elite. 21 July 2012.
  www.guardian.co.uk
The World Bank. World Development Indicators online. data.worldbank.org
Riley T. Time to tackle tax havens. 28 Nov 2011. www.newint.org

50 Debt
Government gross debt
General government gross debt. www.imf.org
Current account balance
The World Factbook. www.cia.gov
Net debt
The Global Debt Clock. www.economist.com
CIA World Factbook. www.cia.gov
UN Population Division. World Population Prospects. The 2010 Revision.
  esa.un.org

52 Tourism
Economic significance of tourism; Departures; Arrivals
The World Bank. World Development Indicators online. data.worldbank.org
Projected change tourist trips
International tourists to hit 1.8 billion by 2030. 11 Oct 2011. PR11079.
  www.media.unwto.org

54 Goals for Development
The Millennium Development Goals Report 2011. New York: United
  Nations, 2011. www.un.org
The World Development Report 2011. Washington DC: World Bank, 2011.
  wdr2011.worldbank.org
Millennium Development Goals
Millennium Development Goals: 2011 Progress Chart. www.un.org
Overseas aid
The World Bank. World Development Indicators. data.worldbank.org
OECD Development Co-operation Directorate (DCD-DAC). www.oecd.org
Zimmerman F, Smith K. More Actors, more money, more ideas for
  international development co-operation. *Journal for International
  Development*. (2011) 23: 722-738.

Part Three: War & Peace
Pinker S. *The Better Angels of our Nature*. London: Penguin, 2011.
Bell C. *On the Law of Peace*. Oxford: Oxford University Press, 2008.
World Development Report 2011: Conflict, security and development.
  Washington DC: World Bank, 2011.

58 War in the 21st Century
At war; Beyond national borders; Two decades of growing peace
Uppsala University. Uppsala Conflict Data Programme. www.pcr.uu.se.
  Updated from press reports up to May 2012.

60 Warlords, Ganglords, and Militias
Non-state armed forces
Uppsala University, Uppsala Conflict Data Programme. www.pcr.uu.se.

Updated from press reports up to May 2012.
Child soldiers
Child Soldiers Global Report 2008. London: Coalition to Stop the Use of
  Child Soldiers, 2008. www.childsoldiersglobalreport.org

62 Military Muscle
Military spending; Armed forces top ten
IISS *The Military Balance 2011*. Oxon: Routledge, 2011. pp. 471-477.
Top military spenders; Nuclear weapons; Nuclear warhead stockpiles
Stockholm International Peace Research Institute. SIPRI Yearbooks 1989,
  2001 & 2011. Oxford: Oxford University Press.

64 The New Front Line
Drones
Drones team. Obama 2012 Pakistan strikes. 11 Jan 2012.
  www.thebureauinvestigates.com
Meikle J. Jimmy Carter savages US foreign policy over drone strikes. 25 Jun
  2012 www.guardian.co.uk
Reprieve. Drone strikes. www.reprieve.org.uk
Woods C. Drones: Barack Obama's secret war. 13 Jun 2012.
  www.newstatesman.com
Special forces
Ansari U. Sino-Pakistani Special Forces exercise begins. 14 Nov 2011.
  www.defensenews.com
Graham-Harrison E. British and US special forces rescue kidnapped aid
  workers in Afghanistan. 2 Jun 2012. www.guardian.co.uk
Urban M. Inside story of the UK's secret mission to beat Gaddafi. BBC News
  Magazine. 19 Jan 2012. www.bbc.co.uk
US special forces 'parachuted into North Korea'. The Telegraph. 29 May
  2012. www.telegraph.co.uk
Zhe Z. China's new special forces marching into view. 08 Sep 2009.
  www.chinadaily.com.cn
Cyber
Arthur C. Cyber attacks widespread, says report. 28 Jan 2010.
  www.guardian.co.uk
Associated Press. China victim of 500,000 cyber-attacks in 2010, says
  security agency. 9 Aug 2011. www.guardian.co.uk
Beaumont P. US appoints first cyber warfare general. 23 May 2010.
  www.guardian.co.uk
Beaumont P. Stuxnet worm heralds new era of global cyberwar. 30 Sep
  2010. www.guardian.co.uk
Hopkins N. US and China engage in cyber war games. 16 April 2012.
  www.guardian.co.uk
Marching off to cyberwar. The internet. 4 Dec 2008. www.economist.com
Reuters. Biggest series of cyber-attacks in history uncovered. 3 Aug 2011.
  www.guardian.co.uk
Silverstein R, Sahimi M. Obama's virus wars: mutually assured cyber-
  destruction. 8 June 2012. www.guardian.co.uk
Whitehead T. Cyber crime a global threat, MI5 head warns. 26 Jun 2012.
  www.telegraph.co.uk
Terrorism
Carter S, Cox A. One 9/11 tally: $3.3 trillion. 8 Sept 2011.
  www.nytimes.com
New York & Washington DC, Bali, Madrid, Beslan, London, Karachi &
  Rawalpindi. BBC world news. news.bbc.co.uk
Pidd H. Mumbai terror attacks suspect arrested by Indian police. 26 June
  2012. www.guardian.co.uk
Ugandans jailed for Kampala World Cup bombing. 16 Sep 2011.
  www.bbc.co.uk
Wikipedia. Terrorism in the People's Republic of China. en.wikipedia.org
World Bank, 2011: *World Development Report 2011: Conflict security and
  Development*. p5. worldbank.org

66 Casualties of War
The 21st-century toll; Death toll
Uppsala University, Department of Peace and Conflict Research. www.pcr.uu.se
Iraq Body Count. Iraqi deaths from violence 2003-11.
  www.iraqbodycount.org
BBC. Iraq war in figures. www.bbc.co.uk
Cave D. Mexico updates death toll in drug war to 47,515, but critics
  dispute the data. 11 Jan 2012. www.nytimes.com
Ratnayake R et al. The many victims of war: Indirect conflict deaths.
  Complex Emergency Database. Sept 2008. www.cedat.be
*The World Bank World Development Report 2011: Conflict, security and
  development*. wdr2011.worldbank.org

68 Refugees
Flight; Displaced; Stateless
United Nations High Commissioner for Refugees. *UNHCR Statistical Yearbook 2010*. Tables 1&2. www.unhcr.org
Major refugee populations; Over 85% of refugees…
UNHCR 2010, Table 5.
United Nations Relief and Works Agency for Palestinian Refugees. Where UNRWA works. www.unrwa.org

70 Peacekeeping
The UN Secretary-General's High Level Panel on Threats, Challenges and Change. *A More Secure World: Our shared responsibility.* United Nations, 2004. www.un.org
Forces for peace; Locations of missions; South Asian contributions
As of 29 Feb 2012. www.un.org
2,997 UN peacekeepers died…; There have been 66…
Peacekeeping Fact Sheet as of 7 June 2012. www.un.org
Non-UN operations
Center of International Cooperation. *Annual Review of Global Peace Operations 2012*. Table 5.10. London: Lynne Rienner, 2011.

72 Global Peacefulness
Institute for Economics & Peace. Global Peace Index. www.visionofhumanity.org

Part Four: Rights & Respects
76 Political Systems
Political systems
The World Factbook. www.cia.gov
BBC News Country Profiles. news.bbc.co.uk
Ethnologue: Languages of the World. www.ethnologue.com
Minority Rights Group, World Directory of Minorities and Indigenous Peoples. www.minorityrights.org
Amnesty International Report 2012. www.amnesty.org
Freedom in the World 2012 and 2011. www.freedomhouse.org
Federal Research Division, US Library of Congress, Library of Congress Country Studies. lcweb2.loc.gov
Living politics
Turner B (editor). *The Statesman's Yearbook 2008*. Hampshire: Palgrave Macmillan, 2008.
The World Factbook. www.cia.gov [Accessed 13 April 2012].

78 Religious Rights
O'Brien J, Palmer M. *The Atlas of Religion*. London: Earthscan, 2007.
The World Factbook. www.cia.gov
US State Department reports on religious freedom by country. www.state.gov
International Coalition for Religious Freedom country reports. www.religiousfreedom.com

80 Human Rights
Extreme abuse of human rights; Slavery in the fishing fleet
Amnesty International. *Amnesty International Report 2012*. Amnesty International: London. 2012. files.amnesty.org
Judicial killings
Amnesty International. Death sentences and executions 2011. Amnesty International: London. 2012. www.amnesty.org
Death Penalty Information Center. www.deathpenaltyinfo.org
Sex trafficking
US State Department. *Trafficking in Persons Report, 2011*. www.state.gov

82 Children's Rights
UNICEF. Childinfo: Monitoring the situation of children and women. www.childinfo.org
USA and Somalia
United Nations Treaty Collection. Chapter IV Human Rights: 11. Convention on the Right of the Child. treaties.un.org
Where children are working; Children at risk
Diallo Y et al. *Global Child Labour Developments: Measuring trends from 2004–2008*.Table 2. ILO: 2010.
Children not in school
The World Bank. World Development Indicators online. data.worldbank.org
Birth registration
UNICEF Statistics. Birth Registration. www.childinfo.org

Children & schools in conflict
EFA Global Monitoring Report. The hidden crisis: Armed conflict and education. UNESCO, 2011. unesdoc.unesco.org

84 Women's Rights
Global 500: Our annual ranking of the world's largest corporations. Top companies: biggest employers. money.cnn.com
Allen, K. Women look away now: You are working for free. 4 Nov 2011. www.guardian.co.uk
Progress of the World's Women 2011-2012. progress.unwomen.org
Equal Rights; Women in parliament
Human Development Report 2011. Table 4. UNDP, 2011. hdr.undp.org
Seager J. *The Atlas of Women in the World*. London: Earthscan, 2009.
Inter-Parliamentary Union. Women in National parliaments, Situation as of 30 Nov 2011. www.ipu.org
Women as head of government
Based on list of elected or appointed female heads of government, Wikipedia [Accessed 20 Feb 2012]. en.wikipedia.org
Excludes: ceremonial heads of state, short-term acting prime ministers. Includes: appointed prime ministers in a democratic presidential system, heads of governments attempting the transition to democracy (Bolivia 1979–80, Lithuania 1990–91, Liberia 1996–97, Kyrgyzstan 2010–11).

86 Gay Rights
The right to serve
Countries that disallow homosexuals from serving in the military. en.wikipedia.org
Legal status of same-sex acts and relationships
Jones B, Itaborahy E & LP. *State-sponsored Homophobia: A world survey of laws criminalising same-sex sexual acts between consenting adults*. IGLA, 2011. old.ilga.org
Johnson R. Legal Gay Marriage: Gay marriage laws by state and country. gaylife.about.com

Part Five: Health of the People
Wilkinson R, Picket K. *The Spirit Level: Why equality is better for everyone.* London: Penguin, 2010.

90 Malnutrition
The simmering food crisis. International Institute of Strategic Studies (London) briefing. Nov 2008. www.iiss.org
Moulds J. Food price crisis feared as erratic weather wreaks havoc on crops. 22 July 2012. www.guardian.co.uk
Undernourished people; Trends in undernourishment
United Nations Statistics Division. Millennium Development Goals Indicators. mdgs.un.org
Food shortages
FAO. Crop prospects and food situation, No. 4, Dec 2011. www.fao.org
India
The World Bank. World Development Indicators online. data.worldbank.org
UN Population Division. World Population Prospects. The 2010 Revision. esa.un.org
Greece
Farr LD. Food aid takes off in Athens. 15 Feb 2012. www.huffingtonpost.com
Smith H. Greek homeless shelters take in casualties of debt crisis. 10 Feb 2012. www.guardian.co.uk
Food price rise
Center for International Policy (Tortuga, Mexico), Americas Program. The food crisis strikes again. 19 Oct 2011 www.cipamericas.org
Vitamin A deficiency
WHO Global Database on Vitamin A Deficiency. Global prevalence of vitamin A deficiency in populations at risk 1995-2005. whqlibdoc.who.int

92 Obesity
WHO. Media Centre. Fact sheet No. 311: Obesity and overweight. www.who.int
Overweight adults
WHO. Global Health Observatory Data Repository. Overweight (body mass index ≥25). apps.who.int
WHO. Global Strategy on Diet, Physical Activity and Health. www.who.int
Increased risk of disease
Global Health Risks: Mortality and burden of disease attributable to selected major risks. WHO, 2009. p.18. www.who.int

America growing obese

Centers for Disease Control and Prevention (CDC). Data and Statistics. Obesity rates among all children in the United States. www.cdc.gov

CDC. US Obesity Trends: Trends by State 1985-2010. www.cdc.gov

$100 billion...

Fast food facts from the Super Size Me website. www.vivavegie.org

94 Smoking

WHO Fact Sheet No. 339. Tobacco. July 2011. www.who.int

Where cigarettes are being smoked

The Tobacco Atlas. Cigarette consumption. Inset 2: World cigarette consumption, by region, 2007. www.tobaccoatlas.org

Deaths; Global cigarette consumption

Shafey O, Eriksen M, Ross H, Mackay J. *The Tobacco Atlas*, 3rd Edition. Atlanta, Georgia: American Cancer Society, 2009. www.tobaccoatlas.org

Spreading the word

WHO Report on the Global Tobacco Epidemic, 2011: Warning about the dangers of tobacco. Tables 2.3.1-2.3.6. whqlibdoc.who.int

Smoking

WHO, 2011. Appendix VII. www.who.int

96 Cancers

Quotation from James Watson

Mukherjee S. *The Emperor of All Maladies. A biography of cancer*. London: Harper Collins/Fourth Estate, 2011. p.393.

Unequal death rates; Increasing incidence; Cancer cases in poorer countries; Lifestyle influences

WHO World Cancer Report 2008, International Agency for Research on Cancer, 2008. www.iarc

Globocan Cancer Fact Sheets. www.globocan.iarc

Commonest cancers

Ferlay J et al. GLOBOCAN 2008 v1.2, Cancer incidence and mortality worldwide: IARC CancerBase No. 10 [Internet]. Lyon, France: International Agency for Research on Cancer, 2010. globocan.iarc.fr [Accessed 16 Mar 2012].

98 HIV/AIDS

WHO. HIV/AIDS. Fact sheet No.360. HIV/AIDS. Nov 2011. www.who.int

UNAIDS. World AIDS Day Report: 2011, p.7. www.unaids.org

The impact of HIV/AIDS

United Nations Statistics Division. Millennium Development Goals Indicators. mdgs.un.org

Number of children orphaned by AIDS

UNICEF. *Children and AIDS: Fifth stocktaking report, 2010*. Goal 4. Protecting and supporting children affected by HIV and AIDS. www.unicef.org

Living and dying with HIV/AIDS

WHO/UNAIDS/UNICEF. Global HIV/AIDS response: Epidemic update and health sector progress towards Universal Access. Progress Report 2011. Annex 8 HIV and AIDS statistics, by WHO and UNICEF regions, 2010, p.210. www.unaids.org

Anti-retroviral therapy (ART)

UNAIDS. Data tables 2011. p.5. www.unaids.org

Barring the door

Mapping of restrictions on the entry, stay and residence of people living with HIV. UNAIDS, May 2009. Updated for developments as of June 2011. www.unaids.org

100 Mental Health

Mental Health Atlas 2011. Geneva: World Health Organization, 2011. www.who.int

WHO Fact sheet No.220. Mental health: Strengthening our response. Sept 2010. www.who.int

Fact File: 10 facts on mental health. www.who.int

Over 50%...; Mental-health resources; Rich countries have...; Expenditure on medicines; Antipsychotic drugs...

WHO, 2011. op. cit.

Suicide rates; Someone commits suicide...

Suicide rates per 100,000 by country, year and sex (Table). www.who.int [Accessed 13 April 2012].

102 Living with Disease

WHO. Death and DALY estimates for 2004 by cause for WHO Member States: Persons, all ages. DALY rates. www.who.int [Accessed 13 April 2012].

Part Six: Health of the Planet
106 Warning Signs

Human impact of natural disasters

International Federation of Red Cross and Red Crescent Societies. *World Disasters Report, 2011*. Annex: Table 13 www.ifrc.org

Shrinking Arctic ice

Vidal J. Weird weather around the world sees in 2012. *The Guardian*. 12 Jan 2012. www.guardian.co.uk

Asian tiger mosquito

Global Invasive Species Database. Aedes albopictus. www.issg.org

Changing ranges

Brommer J. The range margins of northern birds shift polewards. *Ann. Zool. Fennici* 41 (2004): 391–397.

Hitch AT, Leberg PL. Breeding distributions of north American bird species moving north as a result of climate change. *Conserv. Biol.* 21 (2007): 534–539.

Climate change is driving poleward shifts in the distributions of species. Cited by BirdLife www.birdlife.org

La Sorte FA, Thompson FR. Poleward shifts in winter ranges of North American birds. *Ecology* 88 (2007): 1803–1812.

Parmesan C et al. Poleward shifts in geographical ranges of butterfly species associated with regional warming. *Nature*, 1999. 399: 579-83.

Thomas CD, Lennon JJ. Birds extend their ranges northwards. *Nature* 399 (1999): 213.

Coral bleaching

Brokaw, T. Global warming: Signs and sources. dsc.discovery.com

Extinction

Lawton JH, May RM. *Extinction rates*. Oxford: Oxford University Press. 2005.

Fires in Russia

Wildfires in Russia more rampant in 2011, spread over east. *RIA Novotsi*. 7 June 2011 en.rian.ru

Billette A. Russian forests burn for second successive year. *Guardian Weekly*. 9 Aug 2011. www.guardian.co.uk

Floods in Pakistan

Pakistan Floods progress report July 2010-July 2011. www.oxfam.org

Singapore Red Cross. Pakistan floods: The deluge of disaster. 15 Sept 2010. reliefweb.int

Guerin O. Pakistan floods. BBC News. www.bbc.co.uk

Glacial change in the Andes

Peru's Quelccaya glacier could disappear within 10 years, specialist says. Andean Air Mail & Peruvian Times. 6 Aug 2010, quoting Jose Machare, a climate change specialist at Peru's Geological Society. www.peruviantimes.com

Lemurs in Madagascar

Walker G, King D, *The Hot Topic* London: Bloomsbury, 2008.

Melting permafrost in Alaska

Romanovsky VE. How rapidly is permafrost changing and what are the impacts of these changes? www.arctic.noaa.gov

North Atlantic hurricanes

Geophysical Fluid Dynamics Laboratory/NOAA. Hurricane power dissipation index. www.gfdl.noaa.gov

Ocean acidification

Ocean acidification. www.antarctica.gov.au

Ocean dead zones

Faeth P, Methan T. Nutrient runoff creates dead zone. World Resources Institute, 2005 Jan. archive.wri.org

Diaz RJ, Rosenberg R. Spreading dead zones and consequences for marine ecosystems. *Science* 321 (2008): 926-929. www.sciencemag.org

Earth Observatory. Ocean dead zones. 17 July 2010. earthobservatory.nasa.gov

Rapid rise in Antarctic

Vaughan DG. Antarctic Peninsula: rapid warming. British Antarctic Survey, Natural Environment Research Council. www.antarctica.ac.uk

Ducklow HW et al. Marine pelagic ecosystems: The West Antarctic Peninsula. Philosophical Transactions of the Royal Society. *B-Biological Sciences* 362 (2007): 67-94.

Shrinking Arctic ice

Byers M, Canada can help Russia with northern sea route. *The Moscow Times*. 8 June 2012. www.themoscowtimes.com

These days the water evaporates...

Vidal J. From Cairo to the Cape, climate change begins to take hold of Africa. *The Guardian* 01 Dec 2011 www.guardian.co.uk

Vulture deaths in India
Vultures are under threat from the veterinary drug diclofenac.
www.birdlife.org
Water mining in China
Economy EC. The great leap backward? Council on Foreign Relations.
Foreign Affairs, 2007 Sept/Oct. www.foreignaffairs.org

108 Biodiversity
Threatened mammals and birds
The IUCN Red List of Threatened Species. Summary statistics version 2012.1.
www.iucnredlist.org
Threatened species
Summary Statistics. Figure 2: The proportion of extant species on the IUCN
Red List of Threatened Species version 2011.2. www.iucnredlist.org
Protected areas
World Database on Protected Areas (2011) National stats for 1990-2010
from the 2011 MDG analysis. www.wdpa.org/Statistics.aspx
Forest lost and gained
FAO (2010) Global Forest Resources Assessment 2010. Global Tables.
www.fao.org

110 Water Resources
Hot issues: water scarcity. www.fao.org [Accessed 16 June 2012].
Maplecroft index identifies Bahrain, Qatar, Kuwait and Saudi Arabia as
world's most water stressed countries**.** 26 May 2011. maplecroft.com
Diouf J. Agriculture, food security and water: Towards a blue revolution.
OECD Observer no. 236, March 2003. www.oecdobserver.org
Total consumption; Water withdrawals; 70% of…
FAO. 2012. AQUASTAT database, Food and Agriculture Organization of the
United Nations (FAO). www.fao.org. [Accessed 12 June 2012].
Lack of a safe supply
The World Bank. World Development Indicators online. data.worldbank.org
The World Factbook. www.cia.gov
Total annual water withdrawal
Shiklomanov I. World water resources at the beginning of the 21st century.
The dynamics. Table 7. webworld.unesco.org

112 Waste
Plastics waste; Oceans
UNEP Year Book: Emerging issues in our global environment. United Nations
Environment Programme 2011. www.unep.org
The next wave of plastic bag bans. 7 June 2012. oceana.org
Braiker B. Los Angeles votes to ban plastic bags. 24 May 2012. USNews
Blog. www.guardian.co.uk
Plastic Bag Ban. plasticbagbanreport.com [Accessed 20 June 2012] .
Toronto plastic bag ban surprises Mayor Rob Ford. 7 June 2012.
www.bbc.co.uk
Top 5 places with plastic bag bans. 7 June 2012.
www.globaltvedmonton.com
Summers C. What should be done about plastic bags? 19 March 2012.
www.bbc.co.uk
Fleury J. Mumbai aims at total ban of plastic bags. 16 June 2012. articles.
timesofindia.indiatimes.com
Plastic bags banned in Karwar city limits. 9 Aug 2010. articles.timesofindia.
indiatimes.com
Plastic bags banned in Tirumala. 11 Aug 2010. www.hindu.com
Plastic bags to be seized in Vasco from today. 19 Aug 2011. articles.
timesofindia.indiatimes.com
Young T. Rajasthan bans use of plastic bags. 28 July 2010.
www.businessgreen.com
Watts J. China plastic bag ban 'has saved 1.6m tonnes of oil'. 22 May 2009.
www.guardian.co.uk
Plastic bags ban. 26 May 2011. www.clearchinese.com
Geganto R. Plastic bag ban fuels packaging wars. 16 June 2012. Philippine
Daily Inquirer. opinion.inquirer.net
Plastic ban comes into effect. 2 Jan 2011. www.igeorgetownpenang.com
South Australia – feedback on result of 2009 ban. www.paperbagco.co.uk
Coles Bay, Tasmania. en.wikipedia.org
Phase-out of lightweight plastic bags. en.wikipedia.org
Beach trash
UNEP op. cit. p.31.
Plastic world
UNEP op. cit. p.22.
Sanitation
The World Bank. World Development Indicators online. data.worldbank.org

Tonnes of disposable nappies
Early Day Motion 1169, Disposable nappy waste. 9 Dec 2010.
www.parliament.uk
Butler K, Gilson D. A brief history of the disposable diaper. May/June 2008.
www.motherjones.com

114 Energy Use
Total energy use; Energy use per capita; Energy use comparison
IEA data downloaded from The World Bank. World Development Indicators
online. data.worldbank.org
Renewable energy
Eric Martinot and REN21 Renewable Energy Policy Network for the 21st
Century. Renewables 2012 Global Status Report. www.map.ren21.net
1970–2011 human population…
Number of cars. The Physics Factbook. hypertextbook.com citing: Stein, Jay.
New cars for better future: Driving us crazy. Earthgreen, 1990
Tencer D. 24 Oct 2011. Number of cars worldwide surpasses 1 billion: Can
the world handle this many wheels? www.huffingtonpost.ca

116 Climate Change
Past emissions
Climate Analysis Indicators Tool (CAIT) Version 7.0. Washington, DC: World
Resources Institute, 2010.
Future consequences
Lenton TM et al.Tipping elements in the Earth's climate system. PNAS 105(6)
(2008): 1786–1793.
Shellnhuber HJ. Tipping elements in the Earth system. PNAS 106 (49)
(2009): 20561–20563.
IOM. Compendium of IOM's activities in migration, climate change and the
environment. Geneva: International Organization for Migration. 2009.
Sea-level rise
Brokaw T. Global warming: Signs and sources. dsc.discovery.com
Carbon dioxide in the atmosphere
Earth System Research Laboratory. Global Monitoring Division. Recent
Mauna Loa CO2. www.esrl.noaa.gov [Accessed 18 June 2012].
UNEP Vital Graphics, quoting David J Hofmann of the Office of Atmospheric
Research at the National Oceanic and Atmospheric Administration, March
2006. www.grida.no/climate
Blasing TJ. Recent greenhouse gas concentrations. DOI: 10.3334/CDIAC/
atg.032. Updated Dec. 2009. Carbon Dioxide Information Analysis Center.
cdiac.ornl.gov [Accessed 2011 March 29].
Neftel A et al. Historical carbon dioxide record from the Siple Station ice
core. In Boden TA et al, editors. Trends'93: A compendium of data on
global change. ORNL/CDIAC-65. Carbon Dioxide Information Analysis
Center. Oak Ridge National Laboratory; 1994.
Keeling CD, Whorf TP. Carbon Dioxide Research Group, Scripps Institution
of Oceanography, University of California; 2001.

118 Planetary Boundaries
Rockström J et al. Planetary boundaries: Exploring the safe operating space
for humanity. *Ecology and Society* 14 (2009): 2.
www.ecologyandsociety.org
Pearce F. From ocean to ozone: Earth's nine life-support systems. *New
Scientist* (Feb 2010) 2749. www.newscientist.com

Part Seven: Vital Statistics
Indicators of Wellbeing
Official capital: geography.about.com; infoplease.com; www.cia.
gov. **Land area:** Source for p22. **Population:** See source for p22.
Migrants: Source for p26. **Life expectancy:** Source for p24. **Literate
adults, Education:** Source for p.30. **Undernourished:** Source for p90.
Overweight: Source for p92. **Access to improved water:** Source for
p110. **Sanitation:** Source for p112. **DALYs:** Source for p102.

Economy & Environment
GNI: See source for p38. **Human Development Index:** Source for p42.
Gini Index: Source for p40. **Government gross debt:** Source for p50.
Corruptions Perception Index, Shadow economy: Source for p48.
Military expenditure: Source for p62. **Energy Use:** Source for p114.
CO2 emissions: The World Development Indicators worldbank.org.
Water withdrawals: Source for p110.

Index